1987

German Imperialism in Africa

German Imperialism
in Africa

From the Beginnings until the Second World War

edited by
HELMUTH STOECKER

Translated from the German
by Bernd Zöllner

C. HURST & COMPANY, LONDON

HUMANITIES PRESS INTERNATIONAL, INC.
ATLANTIC HIGHLANDS, NEW JERSEY

First published in 1986 in the United Kingdom by
C. Hurst & Co. (Publishers) Ltd.,
38 King Street, London WC2E 8JT,
and in the United States of America by
Humanities Press International, Inc.,
Atlantic Highlands, New Jersey 07716
© Akademie-Verlag Berlin, 1986
Printed in the German Democratic Republic

ISBNs

Hurst: 0-905838-95-5
Humanities: 0-391-03383-2

Library of Congress Cataloging-in-Publication Data

Drang nach Africa. English
  German Imperialism in Africa.

  Translation and enl. ed. of: Drang nach Afrika. 1977.
  Bibliography: p. 419.
  Includes index.
  1. Germany — Colonies — Africa. 2. Africa — Relations —
Germany. 3. Germany — Relations — Africa. I. Stoecker,
Helmuth. II. Title.
DT34.5 D713   1986   960   86-280
ISBN 0-391-03383-2

Contents

Abbreviations

A. A.	*Auswärtiges Amt* (Foreign Office)
ADAP	*Akten zur deutschen auswärtigen Politik* 1918—1945, D series (1937—1945), Baden-Baden/Frankfurt a. M. 1949—1962
AEG	*Allgemeine Elektrizitäts-Gesellschaft* (General Electrical Company)
DKG	*Deutsche Kolonialgesellschaft* (German Colonial Association)
DKGSWA	*Deutsche Kolonialgesellschaft für Südwestafrika* (German South West Africa Company)
DOAG	*Deutsch-Ostafrikanische Gesellschaft* (German East African Company)
DTG	*Deutsche Togogesellschaft* (German Togo Company)
DWI	*Deutsches Wirtschaftsinstitut* (German Institute for Economics, GDR) — now incorporated in the Institute for International Politics and Economics
GdS	*Generalinspekteur für das deutsche Straßenwesen* (Inspector General for German Roadways)
GP	*Die Große Politik* der Europäischen Kabinette 1871—1914. Sammlung der diplomatischen Akten des Auswärtigen Amtes, Berlin 1922—1927
Korag	*Koloniale Reichsarbeitsgemeinschaft* (National Colonial Association)
KWK	*Kolonialwirtschaftliches Komitee* (Colonial Economic Committee)
MA	*Militärarchiv* der DDR (Military Archive of the German Democratic Republic)
NA	*National Archives*, Washington, D.C.
NSDAP	*Nationalsozialistische Deutsche Arbeiterpartei* (Nazi Party)
OKW	*Oberkommando der Wehrmacht* (Armed Forces High Command)
RDR	*Rechnungshof des Deutschen Reiches* (State Office of Accounts)

RKolA   *Reichskolonialamt* (Imperial Colonial Office)
RMdI   *Reichsministerium des Innern* (Reich Ministry of the Interior)
SPD   *Sozialdemokratische Partei Deutschlands* (Social Democratic
            Party of Germany)
StBVR   *Stenografische Berichte über die Verhandlungen des Reichs-*
            tages (Verbatim reports of Reichstag Proceedings)
ZStA   *Zentrales Staatsarchiv* der DDR (Central State Archive of
            the German Democratic Republic)

IG-Farben   Largest German chemical trust
— Interessengemeinschaft
  Farbenindustrie AG
Kolonialrat   founded to advise the Colonial Depart-
  (Colonial Council)   ment of the Foreign Office, 1891—1908
Reich   "Deutsches Reich" was the official term
  (Empire)   for the German state in its entirety, as
                                     distinct from the Länder (states) of which
                                     it was constituted, 1871—1938

Reichstag   Central German Parliament, 1867—1945
Schutzgebiet   Official term for German colonies, 1884 to
  (lit. "Protected Area")   1919
Schutztruppe(n)   Official term for German colonial military
  (lit. "Protective Force(s)"   units, consisting of African mercenaries
                                     commanded by German officers (except
                                     in South West Africa, where Africans
                                     were not recruited), 1891—1918
Wilhelmstrasse   Synonym for German Foreign Office
Zentrumspartei   Large political party representing the
  (Centre Party)   Roman Catholic clergy and landowners,
                                     supported by Catholic lower middle class,
                                     peasantry and parts of working class in
                                     Western and Southern Germany, 1870 to
                                     1933

Contributors

Jolanda Ballhaus Ph. D.   Senior Assistant in the Faculty of History of Humboldt University, Berlin

Eberhard Czaya D. Econ.   Staff member of the Institute of International Politics and Economics, Berlin

Horst Drechsler Ph. D.   Professor of Modern History in the Faculty of History of Wilhelm Pieck University, Rostock

Richard Lakowski Ph. D.   Staff member of the Institute of Military History, Potsdam

Wolfgang Mehnert Ph. D.   Professof of Education in the Faculty of Near Eastern and African Studies of Karl Marx University, Leipzig

Helmut Nimschowski Ph. D.   Professor of the History of North Africa and the Near East in the Faculty of Near Eastern and African Studies of Karl Marx University, Leipzig

Adolf Rüger Ph. D.   Professor of Modern History in the Faculty of History of Humboldt Univers·

Peter Sebald Ph. D.   Staff member of the Central Historical Institute of the Academy of Sciences of the GDR

Helmuth Stoecker Ph. D.   Professor of Modern History in the Faculty of Asiatic Studies of Humboldt University, Berlin

I. The Historical Background

Until the middle of the nineteenth century, the city burghers and the aristocracy of Germany were hardly involved at all in the pillaging and exploitation of non-European countries that was being carried on by some European powers. There were no German colonial traditions to leave traces in the people's consciousness: colonies for trade and plantations seemed a concern of the British or Dutch, and nearly all German emigrants sought a new home in the United States of America. When, from the 1880s onward, German historians and advocates of colonialism — Max von Koschitzky being one of the first[1] — attempted to write about an "illustrious colonial past", their aim was to encourage chauvinism towards colonial expansion in the face of the apathy and negative attitude shown by a very large section of the German people. But they were creating a myth. This past consisted merely of episodic and mostly short-lived and unsuccessful schemes and attempts to obtain in one way or another some small share in the large colonial trade (especially the slave-trade) of the West European powers. Only in a few cases had it been possible to go beyond the devising of unrealistic plans (sometimes deep in the realms of fantasy) and actually undertake substantial but risky enterprises, which generally brought their initiators bad losses and disappointments.

The general course of such efforts from the sixteenth to the nineteenth century underlines the fact that without strong national and naval power absolutist princes and the rising German bourgeoisie were not in a position to take part in the partition of large parts of the world into colonies. Neither the ventures of the Welsers (a South German family of merchants and financiers) in Latin America, nor the attempt of a Brandenburg Elector to participate in the export of slaves from West Africa by founding a trading company solely for this purpose, nor the efforts made by governments of Austrian emperors and Prussian kings in the

[1] *Deutsche Kolonialgeschichte*, 2 vols, Leipzig 1887—88.

eighteenth century to obtain additional revenue through gaining a small share in the trade with Asia, created a point of departure for the colonial expansion of the later capitalist Germany; they in no way influenced the adoption of a policy of colonial expansion in the late nineteenth century. As in the case of Italy, whose territory was similarly fragmented, the princes, aristocracy and burgher class of the German states not only remained without their own colonies but also without an appreciable part in the semi-colonial exploitation of non-European nations through unequal trade: the strictly mercantilist trading, maritime and colonial policy of the great naval powers constituted a barrier that until the end of the eighteenth century could only be surmounted in a few exceptional cases.

Germany obtained its "colonial merchandise" (mostly via Hamburg and Bremen) from London, Amsterdam, Bordeaux and other European ports, whilst the colonial powers exported many German products, especially linen, to their colonies. The additional profit, which in many cases was very great, flowed into the pockets of foreign businessmen. Thus the German states did not share in the primary accumulation of capital by robbery and conquest outside Europe, a circumstance which, mainly determined by political disunion and the lack of appreciable naval forces, had a lasting effect on the development of capitalism in Germany.

The prehistory of German colonial expansion did not begin until the nineteenth century, when free-trade capitalism started to develop. Since the relaxation in mercantilist trade practices and navigation laws of the seapowers that had begun at the end of the eighteenth century, and especially since Napoleon's blockade of the continent had been lifted in 1813, merchants and shipowners (often combined in one person: merchant shipowner) from Germany — principally from Hamburg and Bremen — were able to establish direct links with Latin America and the Near East, and subsequently with South-East and East Asia as well as West Africa, Australia, and Oceania. This gradual advance into non-European markets was greatly facilitated by the progressive introduction of free trade in spheres of British influence and power. Barriers to commerce were removed step by step by a British bourgeoisie still fully confident of its absolute predominance on world markets. The partial opening of British colonies to the ships of foreign states by the navigation acts of 1822—24, the repeal in 1833 of the British East India Company's trade monopoly for China, and the abolition of all remaining restrictions on shipping and trade with the colonies from 1849 to 1854 gave many Germans who owned sailing vessels the possibility of undertaking charter voyages on non-European routes for English, Dutch, and even Chinese merchants.

From the 1850s to the 1870s a large number of German ships were involved in coasting in South-East and East Asia. At the same time, the
transition to free trade offered opportunities to a number of medium and
large commercial firms in Hamburg and Bremen (with branches and
subsidiaries in Bombay, Calcutta, Singapore, Hong Kong, Zanzibar,
Lagos, and elsewhere) to share in British trade with non-European
countries to a limited degree.

Since Britain had an interest in maintaining free trade in the Hanseatic
towns, it could not easily prevent the merchants of Hamburg and Bremen — still quite harmless to her as competitors — from laying claim to
the same principles overseas. Britain's economic superiority however
obliged many of them at first to resort to transactions which were smaller
and less profitable than those of their British competitors and sometimes
extremely disreputable (including the slave-trade). Many of these firms
maintained only minimum trade relations with Germany until the 1880s
and 1890s; they concentrated on exporting British industrial products
to Asia and Africa. Accordingly they usually financed their transactions
with loans from British banks, insured their shipments with British
insurance companies, and used British ships for these shipments, if they
had no vessels of their own at their disposal.

From 1832 onwards, Hamburg merchants and shipowners began to
participate sporadically in the semi-colonial trade on the West African
coast. Their ships took industrial and craft products (hardware, linen,
cottons, glassware, tobacco, spirits, etc.) to the British colonies and areas
under British influence, especially to the Gold Coast and Lagos, as well
as the Republic of Liberia, and later in lesser quantities to the French
and Portuguese possessions. In West Africa the ships received precious
woods, skins, ivory, coconuts, and palm-oil as return cargo. Bremen
commercial firms followed Hamburg's example from 1841 onwards.
Some Hamburg firms immediately established permanent factories
(trading agencies) in coastal towns, whereas those of Bremen carried on
an itinerant barter-trade from their ships.

In the 1840s palm-oil began to be the most important commodity
exported to Europe from West Africa. It was used in the manufacture
of soap and stearin candles, and later to an increasing extent in lubricants
for machines and vehicles. From around 1840 it achieved general distribution in Central Europe in connection with the Industrial Revolution;
in and around Hamburg there arose a processing industry which was
supplied with the imported palm-oil.

During the following decades German trade with West Africa expanded
and gained in importance as a part of German overseas trade. Although

it remained speculative to a certain extent and was by no means without hazards, larger firms such as C. Woermann (Hamburg, est. 1849), Wm O'Swald & Co. (Hamburg, est. 1852) and Fried. M. Vietor Söhne (Bremen, est. 1857) were able to record considerable profits through the unequal exchange of goods, i.e. trading overpriced European products against underpriced African ones. These and other German firms in most towns on the West African coast had the second place behind the British, but in some places (Lagos, for example) they occupied the first place in the European semi-colonial trade for considerable periods of time.

The expansion of German trade was closely linked with increases in the export of a product made in Hamburg: poor quality liquors, whose main ingredient was Prussian potato spirit. Cheap spirits and "rum", i.e. Prussian potato spirit in a slightly altered form, became the decisive means by which the Hamburg firms were successful in West Africa in the face of British and other competition and maintained for decades their important position. Through the export of spirits C. Woermann, a shipping and trading company, grew into one of the strongest trading firms on the entire coast of West Africa; for a long time it occupied the predominant place in Liberia's foreign trade. On demand of the firm's owner in 1855 the Hamburg Senate (the city government) concluded a friendship, trade, and shipping treaty with the government of Liberia in the name of the three Hansa towns (Hamburg, Bremen, Lübeck). This was followed in 1859—61 by a similar treaty with the Sultan of Zanzibar. Both treaties guaranteed the rights of the most-favoured nation for the Hanseatic merchants and captains.

Through its trade with Africa and Asia the bourgeoisie of Hamburg and Bremen was able to gain an increasing, but in the 1870s still minimal, share in the colonial and semi-colonial exploitation of non-European peoples. In spite of some competition in the retail trade, the Hanseatic merchants were more or less tolerated by British commercial and government circles as poor relations of sorts, participating in a small way in Britain's monopoly of international trade, which rested not only on the pre-eminence of British industry, but also on the power of British colonial governors and gunboats. This strange position had the advantage that Hamburg and Bremen raked in profits from the colonies without having to pay the costs of conquest and rule.

Although from the 1850s to the 1880s, German merchants could as a rule count on the assistance of British consuls and British warships in the event of actions of protest in Asiatic or African countries or of conflicts with the local authorities, the still very small Prussian (later North

German, then German) navy was stretched to the limit "showing the flag" along the coast of foreign continents and, wherever "German interests" seemed to require it, firing on coastal villages and staging punitive expeditions.

From the late 1850s onwards, in order to strengthen its position in the struggle with Austria for leadership in Germany, the government of Prussia sought to appear as the protagonist of the non-European and especially Far Eastern trading interests of the entire German bourgeoisie. An expedition of four warships dispatched to the Far East at the end of 1859 succeeded by intimidation in forcing unequal treaties on China, Japan, and Siam. These treaties secured the same special rights and privileges for the Prussian-led German Zollverein the Hanseatic towns and the Mecklenburg grand-duchies that Great Britain, France and the United States had obtained only shortly before by the use of armed force. Under the terms of the Prusso-Chinese Treaty of 1861, German merchants in the seaports of China (by far the most important market in the Far East) could claim consular jurisdiction and the de facto exterritoriality that went with it, together with very low customs tariffs. All of these were important conditions for the semi-colonial exploitation of China, and were to serve as a wedge for the later penetration of China by German imperialism. The expedition did not succeed in fulfilling its instructions to found a Prussian colony in the Far East or South America (as a base for the navy); accordingly, the captains of German warships stationed in the waters of Eastern Asia from 1869 onwards were ordered to look for a suitable place for a naval station.

Thus even before the foundation of the Reich in 1871 the German states (with the exception of Austria) took part in the semi-colonial subjugation of China. In 1876 a concentration of six German warships on the Chinese coast contributed to the pressure put on the government of China by Britain to open the Yang-tze river for European and American trade, which Peking had to concede.

This expansion in semi-colonial trade was not connected with any aims of establishing Prussian or German rule over entire territories. Before 1848 the demand for colonies as a means of acquiring new markets was occasionally raised in bourgeois newspapers, and during the 1840s there was even a short boom in highly impractical schemes for the founding of colonies for emigrants, but Prussian cabinets did not pay any attention to these ideas, neither before nor after the revolution. As for the other governments in Germany, such schemes seemed even more remote.

Individual journalists, adventurers, senior officials, academics, naval officers, businessmen and speculators. however, impressed and envious of the colonial wealth of Britain, time and again put forward propositions for the founding of colonies, and from the 1860s onwards this idea never completely disappeared from the reflections of the German bourgeoisie. But this bourgeoisie was not yet prepared to offer serious support to colonial projects. Therefore all such plans remained castles in the air. Their only significance consisted in the fact that they demonstrated the acquisitive inventiveness and sometimes the nationalist megalomania of their originators. Between 1850 and 1878, no political organization advocated colonial expansion in the form of annexations; apart from the expansionist frenzy which seized the ruling classes during the war of 1870—71, the colonial issue did not play any part in German politics during these years. The numerous plans for founding colonies have therefore been aptly compared with "bright soap-bubbles, which quickly burst in the wind of realism coming from foreign and domestic policy".[2]

The primary reason for this attitude was the prevailing influence of free trade views on the liberal bourgeoisie in Germany. According to these views the founding of colonies by the state was basically inexpedient. It was considered to be the joint task of all trading nations to open up non-European markets with as little interference from the state as possible and to conduct business there unimpeded by customs barriers or any other hindrances on the basis of "free competition". The standpoint of Friedrich List, who thought that the development of a German naval power after the British model should culminate in the establishment of colonies for the purpose of trade, did not become generally accepted. For instance, we find the following in Meyer's encyclopaedia in the article "Colonies" (1877): "Patriotic wishes for the founding of German colonies must be emphatically rejected as anachronistic and illusory. Ever since the colonizing states have been forced to give their colonies more freedom, and since commerce with foreign colonies has been open to us under the same conditions that are enjoyed by their mother countries, those economic disadvantages from which we suffered when we were excluded from trade with the New World have been removed. On the

[2] *H. Mauter*, Die ökonomische Expansion und expansive und annexionistische Bestrebungen der Berliner Großbourgeoisie 1847—1873, Ph. D. Thesis, Humboldt University, Berlin 1974, p. 189.

other hand, the administration, guarding and defence of colonies requires an expenditure of energy which is not matched by a corresponding
advantage. Even the establishment of a naval base is to be rejected as
expensive. It is the duty of every state, and thus also of the German
Empire, to regulate its domestic affairs as satisfactorily as possible.
Beyond our borders we should not seek anything other than peace and
an intercourse which is as unrestricted as possible."[3]

A further reason for its inactivity was that since its retreat over the
Prussian constitution the bourgeoisie had become accustomed to following Bismarck meekly in matters of foreign policy, and until 1884 Bismarck
did not want to have anything to do with colonies in the form of overseas
territories over which Prussia or the Reich would exercise sovereignty or
establish a protectorate. The negative attitude to colonial projects which
Bismarck was known to hold had the effect that proposals for the creation
by private enterprises of German colonies for settlement, trade and plantations did not receive sufficient financial support.

How are we to explain Bismarck's attitude? On the one hand, in line
with free trade theories, he did not believe in the profitability of colonies
founded by the state, and on the other hand he clearly realized that
Prussia or the North German Confederation were unable, on their own,
to exercise political power outside Europe. As late as 1869, after the
victories over Denmark and Austria, he addressed a circular to Prussian
missions overseas which read as follows: "The situation of Prussia does
not permit its representatives in distant quarters of the globe to pursue
practices which deviate from those of the representatives of other great
powers. On the contrary, it is advisable always to go hand in hand with
these representatives as much as possible ..."[4] One year previously he
had justified his policy of abstention to the Minister of War, Albrecht
von Roon, thus: "On the one hand, the advantages which people expect
from colonies for the commerce and industry of the mother country are
mainly founded on illusions, for the expenditure occasioned by the
establishment, support, and especially the maintenance of colonies very
often exceeds the gain which the mother country derives from them, as
is proved by the experience of England and France in their colonial
policy . . .." Prussia did not have an effective navy at her disposal, and
compulsory military service could hardly include duty in the tropics,

---

[3] *Meyers Konversations-Lexikon*. Eine Enzyklopädie des allgemeinen Wissens, vol. 10,
   Leipzig 1877, p. 157.
[4] Quoted from *B. Siemers*, Japans Eingliederung in den Weltverkehr 1853—69,
   Berlin 1937, pp. 75—76.

if — as was quite possible — conflicts with other colonial powers were to occur. Private individuals should no doubt pursue their own advantage overseas, Bismarck concluded, but a government undertaking would be misguided.[5]

With the foundation of the Reich and the Franco-German peace negotiations of 1871 another weighty factor was added to these considerations: the necessity of avoiding conflicts with Great Britain, the dominant colonial power, so as not to provoke an Anglo-French *rapprochement* directed against Germany. With this in mind Bismarck disregarded proposals for the annexation of French colonial possessions (especially Saigon) put forward by various Hanseatic shipowners, merchants, and liberal politicians though they were repeatedly championed in the bourgeois and Junker press during 1870 and 1871. For the same reason he rejected all plans for founding colonies that were submitted to him in the following decade. Only after the turn in economic and domestic policy at the end of the 1870s did he gradually change his attitude.

Before this change in policy a number of connections had been developed in Africa and trading bases established which could serve as points of departure for colonial penetration. The commercial firm and shipping line of C. Woermann maintained an extensive network of trading agencies along the West African coast from Monrovia to the mouth of the Congo; since the early fifties it had grown into one of the largest European trading firms in West Africa. In addition, there were approximately a dozen more German firms engaged in the very lucrative barter trade in this region; for Gaiser & Witt, who operated from the British colony of Lagos, it brought a capital of 750,000 marks by 1876. In the following year, another three German commercial firms were active in this colony, and in 1881 there were 45 German trade representatives, clerks, and sailors among the 112 Europeans living there. Five German ships sailed between Lagos and the neighbouring Porto Novo. In the sultanate of Zanzibar, a dependency of Britain since 1845 and the centre of the East African trade, the Hamburg commercial firms of O'Swald & Co. and Hansing & Co. had a very strong position, due in part to their close relations to English interests.

Two German protestant missionary societies should also be mentioned here. In South West Africa (the present-day Namibia) the Rhenish Missionary Society had established several settlements since 1842 and conducted an extensive trade there. Before 1878 it repeatedly applied

---

[5] ZStA, RKolA, no. 7155, p. 11, Bismarck to Roon, 6 Jan. 1868.

for the annexation of this area by Prussia. From 1847 onwards the North German Missionary Society maintained some stations north of the Volta estuary, on the Gold Coast.

Finally, voyages of geographical exploration had a certain part in the "prehistory" of German colonial expansion. The travel reports of Heinrich Barth and Carl Claus von der Decken[6] directed the attention of numerous readers in Germany to tropical Africa. They were followed in the 1860s by other German explorers: Karl Mauch travelled along the Zambezi from 1863 to 1872; in 1865—1867, Gerhard Rohlfs was the first European who, starting from Tripoli, crossed the Sahara and reached Lagos; Georg Schweinfurth pushed forward from the Upper Nile to the upper course of the Congo in 1868. These and other journeys of exploration met with a wide response in the press and gave fresh impetus to desires and plans for colonies.

Of the explorers mentioned, Rohlfs especially was interested in the commercial and political opportunities offered for European capitalist expansion in the areas through which he travelled. After he returned from West Africa, he pleaded for an extension of German trade up the Niger and Benue into the Sudan[7], and succeeded in interesting some Berlin businessmen in such a project. He was authorized by the Prussian government to organize a further expedition to the Sultan of Bornu in the Sudan and to take gifts from the Prussian king to the African ruler.

This mission was however undertaken in 1869 by Gustav Nachtigal, who similarly dedicated himself to the geographical exploration of the Sudan mainly with an eye to trade.[8] Nachtigal's expedition did not result in any immediate gains for German commerce but contributed to increasing European knowledge of the Sudan.

The German Society for the Exploration of Equatorial Africa (African Society) was founded in 1873 on the initiative of the Berlin Geographical Society. Its aim was to support and direct geographical exploration. In a manifesto the founders emphasized that the geographical opening up of Africa would be "of benefit to science on the one hand, to trade

---

[6] *H. Barth*, Reisen und Entdeckungen in Nord- und Central-Afrika in den Jahren 1849—1855, 5 vols, Gotha 1857—1858 (English edition, Travels and Discoveries in North and Central Africa, 4 vols, reprint London 1965); *C. C. v. d. Decken*, Reisen in Ostafrika in den Jahren 1859—1865, ed. by O. Kersten, 2 vols, Leipzig/Heidelberg 1869—1871.

[7] Petermanns Mitteilungen, 1867, no. 10.

[8] *G. Nachtigal*, Sahara und Sudan, 3 vols, Berlin 1879—1889 (English edition, Sahara and Sudan, 4 vols, London 1971—).

and industry on the other . . ."[9] The Imperial Government supported this society, the five expeditions which it sent to Africa until 1877 being chiefly financed from a fund at the disposal of the Emperor. The society's membership included leading representatives of the upper aristocracy, capitalist entrepreneurs and university professors who wished to use the young science of geography to open the way to new markets. At the outset this commercial aspect was not clear to all those involved but, during the seventies, it gradually moved to the forefront, partly due to the expansion of the older colonial powers. Annexations were not yet being seriously considered, but the society undoubtedly helped prepare the ground for Germany's transition to a policy of colonial expansion in Africa.

[9] Quoted from *A. Bastian*, Europäische Colonien in Afrika und Deutschlands Interessen sonst und jetzt, Berlin 1884, p. 61.

II. The Annexations of 1884—1885

It was only with the transition to protectionism and the promulgation of Bismarck's anti-socialist law in 1878/79 that the colonial issue became a matter of interest to important sections of the German ruling classes. In connection with the economic and domestic policy disputes of those years, influential representatives of the bourgeoisie approached the government with colonial plans or identified themselves with the demand for colonies. With the foundation of the Central Association for Commercial Geography and the Promotion of German Interests Abroad (October 1878) together with the West German Association for Colonization and Export (summer 1881), and above all with the publication of the pamphlet "Does Germany Need Colonies?" (1879) by Friedrich Fabri, supervisor of the Rhenish Missionary Society at Barmen), a public discussion of the pros and cons of colonization set in. A colonial movement led by National Liberal and Free Conservative politicians began, which resulted in the foundation of the German Colonial Association on 6 December 1882.

The name of the second of these associations reflects the basic idea underlying this movement, i.e. that colonial expansion was ultimately only the logical complement to the tariffs on industrial goods. While the duties created more favourable conditions for increasing German exports, entirely new markets were to be secured by the acquisition of colonies overseas. These were markets in which German commodities would enjoy a privileged position, perhaps a monopoly. The resulting economic prosperity would destroy the basis for the socialist influence among the masses; moreover, discontented elements (young men with a university education who were in badly paid positions were often referred to in this connection) would be able to find a wide field of action in the colonies. These ideas, developed by the propagandists Fabri, Hübbe-Schleiden and Weber, were taken up by numerous journalists and university teachers; from 1880 onwards many liberal and conservative newspapers adopted them, not least because of the impact of the economic depression which lasted well into the 1880s. The liberal Augsburger Allgemeine Zeitung (18 January 1882) thought, for example, that "the struggle for existence" would become "more and more difficult" and "profound resentment and dissatisfaction are spreading among wide sections of the lower classes, and socialism flourishes nowhere better than on such ground". The acquisition of colonies offered a "safety valve for the state" against the danger of revolution, because colonies "would, so to speak, become monopolized outlets . . . for the German Empire with its industrial overproduction . . . In this way it would be possible to achieve an expansion of our economic sphere" — an expansion which was "so necessary" for Germany's domestic calm. "Only through colonies", agreed the conservative Deutsche Reichspost (10 October 1882), could Germany be "made safe against social revolution". The Prussian conservative Kreuz-Zeitung (11 November 1882) said that internal reform must not be neglected, but must go hand in hand with "the expansion of our economic terrain through seizure of new areas of cultivation . . . without which we run the danger of disintegrating".[1]

"New areas of cultivation" in the early phase of colonial agitation mostly meant colonies for settlement. German emigrants, leaving for the United States in numbers that increased every year, were to some extent to be diverted to these colonies for the benefit of German capitalism. This concept revived colonial ideas of earlier decades and appeared especially suited to arousing the interest of the petty bourgeoisie and the peasantry.

The most influential supporters of the demand for colonies belonged to those circles which inspired and upheld the demand for high tariffs on industrial goods. These were leading representatives of the coal and steel industry in the Rhineland and Upper Silesia, together with the largest German bank, the Disconto-Gesellschaft, which was partly seconded by S. Bleichröder. Both banks stood in close relations to Bismarck's régime. We are here dealing with those sections of the bourgeoisie that founded the first monopolist combinations and modern finance capital in Germany. This strong pressure group, encouraged by the government, joined forces with the South German textile manufacturers and others interested in export. These factions urgently wanted "monopolized outlets" in order to overcome the persistent slump and intensified competition on the world markets which had been brought about by an increase in the duties imposed by other states. In Germany the new

---

[1] Source: *H.-U. Wehler*, Bismarck und der Imperialismus, Cologne/(W.) Berlin 1969, p. 151.

striving for monopoly profits, which marked the transition to monopoly capitalism and imperialism, was directly connected with the endeavour to overcome the economic crisis and subsequent depression.

From the time of its foundation, the executive committee of the West German Association for Colonization and Export consisted predominantly of industrialists. Among these were Henry Axel Bueck, the general secretary of the Central Association of German Industrialists, the owner of the Friedrich Krupp firm, Friedrich Alfred Krupp, Carl Lueg of the Gutehoffnungshütte and (soon after) Emil Kirdorf of the Gelsenkirchener Bergwerksaktiengesellschaft. Among the signatories of the appeal for the establishment of the German Colonial Association were Bueck and some of the most important capitalists involved in heavy industry, such as Louis Baare of the Bochumer Verein and Friedrich Hammacher, president of the Association for Mining Interests in Rhineland and Westphalia. Reaffirming the alliance between the industrial bourgeoisie and the richest landowners — an alliance which had been sealed by protective tariffs and Bismarck's law against socialists — leading political representatives of the Prussian aristocracy also put their signatures to the appeal: Duke Viktor von Ratibor, Count Adolf von Arnim-Boitzenburg, and Count Otto von Stolberg-Wernigerode. The guiding spirit behind the foundation of the Association in 1882, however, was the National Liberal politician Johannes Miquel who was closely associated with the Disconto-Gesellschaft. Miquel indicated the course which the Association should take during the first few years after its foundation.

"The majority of its members", writes K. Klauss, "consisted of small entrepreneurs, merchants, intellectuals, senior clerks and officials. Big industrialists, bankers, and members of the upper aristocracy represented only a numerically small group in the Association, but nevertheless occupied the leading positions. The Association was to prepare the way for German colonial expansion by propaganda and organization. Its special task was to support the foundation of colonies by private companies. This was intended to produce *faits accomplis*, in order to make it easier for the government to engage in a colonial policy while excluding the Reichstag.

"Moreover, the German Colonial Association was intended to play a certain role in home affairs. It focussed its propaganda activities above all on the middle classes, whose chauvinist instincts were to be stirred up and who were in this way to be tied more firmly to the ruling classes."[2]

---

[2] *K. Klauss*, Die Deutsche Kolonialgesellschaft und die deutsche Kolonialpolitik von den Anfängen bis 1895. Humboldt University, Ph. D. thesis, Berlin 1966, p. 5.

All attempts by the Association to promote the establishment of colonies run as capitalist enterprises miscarried, chiefly because the more wealthy members were unwilling to risk larger sums of money. (This lack of confidence was to be a characteristic feature of German colonial expansion throughout the next quarter century: the representatives of the upper bourgeoisie, who were pressing for official colonial initiatives, behaved for the most part very cautiously when it came to investing larger amounts of their own money in colonial ventures under a German "protectorate" — at least when government guarantees of minimum dividends were lacking.) The Association's propaganda did not overstep modest bounds until autumn 1884, and it cannot be said that in terms of publicity it provided much significant preparation for the colonial annexations of that year.

The Association left it to the government — obviously there was an understanding on this with the Foreign Office — to decide when and where annexations were to be undertaken. The most influential advocates of colonial expansion were too closely aligned with Bismarck's régime to increase the government's parliamentary difficulties by demands which might have been inconvenient for the Chancellor. The creation of a colonial empire could not but influence relations with Britain and France, and the German bourgeoisie was not in the habit of disturbing Bismarck's diplomatic manoeuvring by making demands concerning foreign affairs.

Those merchants of Hamburg and Bremen who were engaged in overseas commerce mostly supported free trade and were in many cases linked with English interests and dependent on good relations with Britain. They preferred not to be publicly associated with colonialist agitation, which might be regarded with suspicion by their British partners. The firms active on the coasts of Africa enjoyed neither economic power nor political influence in Germany. It is therefore absurd to regard them as decisive initiators of German colonial expansion whose spirit of adventure so impressed Bismarck that he was finally unable to turn down their requests for "imperial protection" for their endangered companies. The merchants Lüderitz, Woermann, Thormälen and Colin played a role in so far as their petitions — for the declaration of German protectorates over the areas which they were exploiting or intended to exploit — offered a convenient argument for adopting a policy of annexations. These traders in spirits, old muskets and gunpowder could from a distance be made to appear as bold Hanseatic champions of national interests whom the fatherland should not abandon.

After the policy of industrial tariffs had been decided upon in July

1879, Bismarck introduced an expansionist policy of extensive government support for foreign trade and the export of capital to non-European
countries. In this he was backed by the protectionist wing of the bourgeoisie, which henceforth could rely on a secure home market. The aim
was a larger German share in colonial and semi-colonial exploitation.
However, Bismarck still fought shy of annexations.

During the sixties and seventies a significant German sphere of influence had developed in the South Pacific, with the Samoan Islands as
its centre. Of the total imports of this archipelago, which came to 1.596
million marks in 1878, the German share amounted to 1.396 million
marks; and from the total exports of 2.576 million marks the corresponding share was 2.427 million marks.[3] From 1875 onwards, German
warships regularly cruised in the South Seas and in the following year a
coaling station was acquired for them through a treaty with the ruler of
Tonga. A treaty with Samoa in 1879 secured the economic exploitation
of the islands for German firms and another base for the German Navy.

When the largest of these firms, J. C. Godeffroy & Sohn, fell into
financial difficulties because of speculations in Germany, and its extensive Pacific possessions were in danger of falling into British hands, it
asked the government for assistance. As a result in February 1880 Adolf
von Hansemann (head of the Disconto-Gesellschaft) founded the Deutsche Seehandels-Gesellschaft to take over the Godeffroy possessions.
The new company — set up with Bismarck's approval — was headed by
Hansemann, Bismarck's banker Gerson von Bleichröder, and Hermann Wallich of the Deutsche Bank. Hansemann and Bleichröder made
this operation conditional on a guarantee of dividends totalling up to
300,000 marks annually from the funds of the Reich, to which Bismarck
consented. However, in the Reichstag a majority composed of deputies
of the left liberal parties and of the Catholic Centre Party disagreed and
threw out the corresponding government bill on 27 April 1880. While
the defeat of the government did not deter Hansemann and Bleichröder
from taking over the Godeffroy possessions — which soon developed
into a first-rate source of profit — it did demonstrate that the government
could not count on the imperial parliament approving any payments for
overseas expansion.

For this reason, two more measures which the government began
considering soon afterwards were only pushed ahead from mid-1883
onwards. The founding of a German overseas bank was to end the
dependence of commerce on British credit institutions "Such a bank",

---

[3] *H.-U. Wehler*, op. cit., p. 213.

said Hammacher, could "become a vital instrument for promoting the German export trade".[4] But negotiations with the large banking houses in 1884 made it clear that they would only take part in the foundation of an overseas bank at the price of substantial legal and financial concessions. The banking interests maintained an attitude of cautious restraint until the economic recovery which began in autumn 1886. Between 1886 and 1889 three German overseas banks were established with the active participation of the government.

The second of the measures that the government had been preparing since 1881 was the establishment of state-subsidized shipping lines to East Asia, Australia and Africa. A bill presented to the Reichstag on 23 May 1884 provided for the creation of subsidized mailboat connections with East Asia and Australia, but in reality the very last aim of these ships was to carry postbags. Here, too, it was, to quote the German Minister in Peking, von Brandt, a question of "emancipating ourselves from the English money, freight and produce markets"[5]. The state subsidies were to total up to 4 million marks per annum. Since Bismarck could not prevent the parliamentary group of the Centre Party, assisted by the left Liberals, from referring the bill to the budget commission, he had it presented again in the new Reichstag on 13 March 1885 and attempted to push it through with much passionate rhetoric. He succeeded only in part: a main line to West and South Africa which had been added in December was cancelled and the subsidy fixed at 4.4 million marks. In this form the bill was finally passed by a majority in the Reichstag against the votes of the Socialists, the People's Party, the left Liberals, the Polish deputies and a part of the Centre Party.

The subsidy of shipping was a direct continuation of protectionist policy, of which Engels wrote that it was "nothing but preparations for the ultimate general industrial war, which shall decide who has supremacy on the world market".[6] For the establishment of the East Asia line, the aim of increasing the export of railway materials and heavy guns was all-important.

On 26 May 1884, three days after the submission of the first mailboat subsidies bill, Bismarck had a telegram published which had been sent to the German consul in Cape Town on 24 April. In it the chancellor instructed the consul to declare officially that the establishments of the

---

[4] Source: *H.-U. Wehler*, op. cit., p. 236.

[5] Report of 17 Dec. 1875. Source: *H. Stoecker*, Deutschland und China im 19. Jahrhundert. Das Eindringen des deutschen Kapitalismus, Berlin 1958, p. 136.

[6] *K. Marx*, Capital, vol. 3, Moscow 1971, p. 489, no. 8.

Bremen merchant Adolf Lüderitz on the coast of South West Africa were under the protection of the German Empire. The decision of the government of Cape Colony to begin with the annexation of this area prompted Bismarck to lodge a blunt protest with the British government on 4 June. There followed in August the hoisting of the flag by German warships along the entire coast from the Orange River to the Kunene, far beyond the territory claimed by Lüderitz.

In South West Africa, members of the Rhenish Missionary Society had been active since 1842. As early as 1868 the society had asked the Prussian government to protect its stations in South West Africa and since 1880 the head of the society, Friedrich Fabri, had called for a German intervention in the country. But it was not the society which brought about Bismarck's declaration of a protectorate, but a request for protection from Lüderitz. In 1883, in the hope of finding gold and diamonds, this merchant had bought the coast from the Orange River in the South up to 26 degrees latitude from the chief of the Bethanie people Joseph Fredericks. The purchase was made with the help of a Rhenish missionary. Not only had the price been ridiculously low but Lüderitz had also deceived the Africans about the width of the coastal strip he was acquiring.

The hoisting of the German flag north of the areas claimed by Lüderitz, along the coast from 26 degrees to the Kunene (a distance of just under a thousand kilometres) had its origin in more important interests than those of the merchant. It had been ordered without Bismarck's knowledge by the specialist for colonial affairs in the Foreign Office, Heinrich von Kusserow, after a consortium set up by Hansemann and Bleichröder bought up a number of mining and land "rights" on this coast in June. The sellers were a German interest group which had been operating there since 1882. Kusserow was Hansemann's brother-in-law and had for several years been the most energetic supporter of colonial expansion in the Foreign Office. At first Bismarck was not exactly delighted by the independent action of his subordinate, but later he gave his approval when Hansemann requested protection from the Empire for his so-called rights.

In March 1883, the Hamburg merchant and shipowner, Adolf Woermann, asked for the annexation of the Cameroon coast. The firm of C. Woermann, which had for decades taken part in the extremely lucrative plundering of the West African peoples by the unequal barter trade, feared that its trade would be harmed if Britain and Portugal seized areas in which its trading agencies were situated, as they clearly intended to do. Moreover, Woermann was hopeful that German rule would lead to the destruction of the African monopoly in trade with the inland tribes and would open up direct access to the interior. At some time before the end of 1883 he entered into close relations with Hansemann and the Disconto-Gesellschaft.

Bismarck agreed to this proposal as well. On 19 May 1884 the consul-general Dr. Gustav Nachtigal, who had been dispatched to West Africa on a warship, was instructed to hoist the German flag in the places designated by Woermann and in accordance with the guidelines worked out by him. Nachtigal was able to discharge this commission in July 1884 after the representatives of Woermann's and a second German firm had by means of bribery and fraudulent promises induced the chieftains on the Cameroon coast to relinquish their sovereign rights. German colonial rule in the coastal area was finally established after the landing of Navy units in December 1884, which set fire to four villages and staged a massacre of the inhabitants.

Immediately before the hoisting of the German flag in Cameroon, Nachtigal undertook an annexation not provided for by Bismarck. He proclaimed German sovereignty over a coastal strip roughly 35 kilometres long and situated between the British Gold Coast colony and the coast of the present-day People's Republic of Benin (at that time regarded by France as her sphere of influence). This territory — the starting point for the establishment of the German colony of Togo — had since 1873 been a site of operations for the Bremen firm F. M. Vietor & Söhne (a company closely associated with the North German Missionary Society). Other German firms subsequently traded there. The leading German firm, Wölber & Brohm, had requested "protection by the Empire" because it feared the establishment of a British protectorate with high duties on German imports (especially spirits).

A fourth German colony came into being in New Guinea. Soon after taking over the Godeffroy possessions in the South Seas, Hansemann had begun to take an interest in this large island. In a memorandum of September 1880, he recommended the annexation of the island to Bismarck; but the Chancellor, who at that time was still very sceptical about the foundation of colonies under the auspices of the Reich, wrote on its margin: "With Samoan majorities [in the Reichstag — H. S.] such a thing cannot be undertaken."[7] After Bismarck had gone ahead with the first annexations in Africa, Hansemann and Bleichröder took up the issue again. They informed Bismarck in June 1884 that a syndicate which they had set up intended to send an expedition to the South Pacific in order to "acquire land on the widest scale and in such a way

---

[7] Source: *H.-U. Wehler*, op. cit., p. 225.

that it will now be possible, by uniting existing possessions and the additional land to be acquired, to form a colony based on the existing settlements of the Deutsche Handels- und Plantagengesellschaft in der Südsee . . ." (Through this company the two bankers ruled the former Godeffroy possessions.) They requested Bismarck to give orders "to register the land acquired and place it in suitable forms under the protection of the Empire."[8] After Bismarck had promised to do this, Hansemann's agent Finsch, pretending to be an explorer, seized extensive areas of northeastern New Guinea on which, before the year was out, commanders of German warships proceeded to hoist the German flag.

German colonial expansion on the coast of East Africa took a different course from the colonial annexations mentioned so far, which had been the result of the combined efforts of the Imperial Government (or its representatives), large banking-houses and merchants. From August/ September 1884 Bismarck intended to support and extend German trade by the establishment of a consulate general in the Sultanate of Zanzibar and the conclusion of a new trade agreement with the Sultan. Zanzibar was the central place for the commercial exploitation of East Africa from the Somali coast to Mozambique, which, even here, was shared between strong German and British firms. However, when Consul-General Rohlfs arrived in Zanzibar in January 1885 to take up his office, circumstances had arisen which led Bismarck to begin a policy of colonial annexation in East Africa.

In November and December 1884, the adventurer and nationalist psychopath Dr Carl Peters — acting on behalf of the Society for German Colonization which he had founded — made chieftains and village elders on the mainland west of Zanzibar, behind the coast in the areas of Usegula, Ugura, Usagara and Ukami, relinquish extensive tracts of land. He employed fraudulent promises, bribery and alcohol for this purpose. During his long residence in England Peters had become convinced that the establishment of a colonial empire offered great possibilities for acquiring wealth at the expense of oppressed peoples. He wanted to take advantage of the partition of Africa in order, as he later put it, "to obtain for myself personally an empire that was to my taste"[9].

The society had been formed in Berlin in March 1884 with the aim of raising capital for the "founding of a first German farming colony and

---

[8] Source: *K. Herrfurth*, Fürst Bismarck und die Kolonialpolitik, Berlin 1909, p. 135.
[9] *C. Peters*, Wie Deutsch-Ostafrika entstand, Leipzig 1912, p. 7.

the diversion of emigration towards this colony"[10]. It consisted of some
conservative aristocrats and officers together with several dozen members
of the middle classes, all of whom were hoping to obtain rich and easy
plunder in overseas countries. Peters obtained the capital by a very
simple method: the society unhesitatingly issued share certificates in
amounts from 50 to 5,000 marks for landed property in colonies which
were yet to be conquered.

After the necessary funds had been raised in this way, Peters and some
of his cronies travelled to East Africa. The society had notified the
government of the venture before their departure, but Peters did not
receive any official support. Only after his "treaties" with various
chieftains (which did not differ from similar documents supporting
"legal claims" in negotiations with other colonial powers) were placed
before Bismarck did the Emperor, on 27 February 1885, issue an imperial
charter for the society's dominions. The society was authorized to take
possession of more areas, right up to the eastern border of what was soon
to be the "Congo Free State". Bismarck evidently determined on this
step in view of British attempts to prevent the expansion of the new
German colony of Cameroon into the African interior so that he could
be certain of ensuring access to the markets of Central Africa for German
commerce from the east.[11]

The areas placed under German "protection" were claimed by Sultan
Said Bargash of Zanzibar. When the Sultan refused to recognize the
German annexation of these areas and to grant the society the right of
free transit through the coastal region under his control, Bismarck ordered the dispatch of a squadron of the German Navy. Since Britain was
hoping to reach an agreement with Germany on East African affairs,
Said Bargash found himself at the beginning of August without British
support and exposed to the threat of a German bombardment of his
capital. He capitulated and declared that he was compelled to recognize
the annexation. Subsequent Anglo-German negotiations on the transit
of German goods through the coastal areas produced a settlement
favourable to Peters' society which was forced upon the Sultan.

Bismarck had supported economic expansion by subsidizing shipping;
he had attempted to found an overseas bank, enlarged and activated the
consular apparatus, employed the Navy in non-European waters, and

---

[10] Presseinformation der Gesellschaft, source: *F. F. Müller*, Deutschland—Zanzibar—Ostafrika, Berlin 1959, p. 102.
[11] See also *H. P. Meritt*, Bismarck and the German Interest in East Africa 1884—1885.
In The Historical Journal, Cambridge, XXI (1978), pp. 109—114.

had continued penetration of semi-colonial countries (Germany had been, inter alia, one of the signatories to the Madrid Treaty of 1880 on the privileges of foreigners in Morocco). Why then did he decide in March/ April 1884 to go one step further and embark on a policy of colonial annexations? His decision was based on four considerations.

(a) In view of the rapidly advancing partition of territories still "free" in Africa, Asia and Oceania, it was imperative to act quickly if the German Empire was still to seize any colonial possessions without conducting a war against one or more of the colonial powers. This consideration weighed heavily, as it was feared that Germany would be increasingly excluded from trade with colonial and semi-colonial countries by the capitalist powers if she did not have her own colonies. Time and again it was pointed out to Bismarck that the position of German firms in areas still "free" could not be maintained, let alone be improved, without the annexation of these areas or at least the establishment of protectorates. (Although in their dealings with the Chancellor Kusserow and some businessmen exaggerated the imminent dangers, the basic substance of their warnings was real enough).

Thus it was not only a matter of future prospects, but also of existing export interests. Of great importance in this connection was the export of a product furnished by the East Elbe estates — potato spirits in the form of brandy — which had come to a standstill because of a loss of European markets. This branch of production was of particular interest to Bismarck, as may be inferred from the government's general policy with regard to spirits, including the important spirits monopoly bill of March 1886. Liquor headed the list of exports in trade with Africa: in 1883 spirits constituted 48 per cent of German exports to Africa, and in 1884 64 per cent of the weight of Hamburg exports to West Africa.[12]

A memorandum prepared by Woermann and adopted by the Hamburg Chamber of Commerce on 6 July 1883 had emphatically called upon Bismarck to acquire the Cameroon coast. Insisting on haste, the memorandum stated: "If Germany is not to renounce colonial possessions in that place for ever, now, so to speak, is the last moment to acquire them"[13]. The document promised much for German industry — from 1882 onwards in the throes of yet another crisis — through the elimination of

---

[12] H. Müller, Bremen und Westafrika. Wirtschafts- und Handelsbeziehungen im Zeitalter des Früh- und Hochkolonialismus 1841—1914. Part 1, Jahrb. d. Wittheit zu Bremen 1971, vol. 15, pp. 76—77; H. Stoecker (ed.), Kamerun unter deutscher Kolonialherrschaft. Vol. 1, Berlin 1960, p. 23.

[13] Source: H. Stoecker, Kamerun . . ., p. 57.

the African middlemen. This was something which only the establishment of colonial rule could achieve: "With its dense population of con-
sumers and the large markets described by all travellers, the interior of
Central Africa offers a particularly favourable sales area for European
industrial products, especially since not only all domestic goods but also
all services are paid for not with cash or bills of exchange, but always
with foreign wares. The opening of this market for German industry,
which needs to increase its exports, is therefore of the greatest value; it is,
however, hindered by the independent Negro tribes inhabiting the coast
no less than by foreign colonies . . ." Direct trade with the interior
"can . . . only be developed if the coast is in the possession of a European
power, and whichever power holds the coastal strip will have the lion's
share of the trade."[14]

Bismarck, therefore, had to fear that if Germany did not have colonial
possessions she might, in the long run, be displaced altogether from direct
trade with Africa, whereas the seizure of a number of bases on the coast
appeared to open up prospects of dominating the markets of the African
interior.

(b) The unusually favourable international situation in 1884—5. Because
of the British occupation of Egypt in 1882 (supported by Bismarck) and
colonial expansion by France and Russia in Africa, Central Asia and
Indochina (similarly supported by Bismarck and made possible by his
policy), the antagonisms between Britain and these two powers had
become acute. For this reason, and because of the renewal of the League
of the Three Emperors, Germany's position was relatively secure. It
could be assumed that Britain — the only power whose interests were
directly affected by the German annexations — would give way in the
face of Bismarck's blackmail in order to avoid increasing still further the
difficulties with which British foreign policy had to contend. In particular, collaboration between Germany and France in colonial matters
could compel Britain to accept Germany's becoming entrenched in
Africa and Oceania.

(c) The internal situation — which was of great weight in the Chancellor's calculations. From the governmental practice of Napoleon III
and Disraeli, Bismarck had been able to learn what possibilities colonial
chauvinism offered as a support for the position of the ruling classes in
capitalist states in general and for a Bonapartist regime such as his
own in particular. Bismarck intended to meet the increasing threat to
his reactionary policy and his Bonapartist dictatorship by stirring up a

[14] Ibid.

wave of chauvinism. The working class, the middle classes and the petty bourgeoisie were to be diverted from the struggle for their own interests through a sham grand national policy offering bright prospects to the entire people.

The Chancellor gave his attention to this aspect both before and after the Reichstag elections of October 1884, at first mainly with a view to weakening the free-trade left liberals who sympathized with bourgeois parliamentarianism on the English model. This movement, looked at superficially, appeared to be strengthened by the unification of the Liberal Alliance with the Progress Party that took place on 5 March 1884. With more than one hundred deputies, the Left Liberal Party (Freisinnige Partei) — which thus came into being — was second only to the Centre Party in the Reichstag. In view of infirmity of the 87-year-old Emperor it seemed as if serious danger might arise for Bismarck's régime from the close association of the party leaders with the Crown Prince, especially as discontent with the Chancellor's policies had become widespread among the bourgeoisie and the working class. Reviewing the situation, the socialist leader August Bebel wrote to Frederick Engels on 3 October 1884: "Since all the bluffs that have been tried since 1878 — the antisocialist law, protectionist policy, regressive revision of trades regulations, agrarian policy, social reform — have not satisfied the masses, and since the promised benefits of all these measures have not been forthcoming and discontent is growing more and more and becoming louder, a new remedy must be applied."[15]

The striking pugnacity — quite unwarranted by the objects at stake — with which Bismarck pursued his dispute with the British government in the summer and autumn of 1884 over rival colonial claims was, first and foremost designed to secure an election victory in October for the right-wing parties supporting the government.[16]

(d) The direct economic interests of the Disconto-Gesellschaft. Many facts have been published by historians in the GDR on the role of Hansemann in the early history of German colonial policy, a role ignored or reduced to insignificance in most recent West German and American publications; but, on the whole, this very complicated problem has still not been adequately researched. In particular, not enough light has been

[15] *August Bebels Briefwechsel mit Friedrich Engels*, ed. by W. Blumenberg, The Hague 1965, p. 187.

[16] Cf. *Die Geheimen Papiere Friedrich von Holsteins*, vol. 2, Göttingen 1957, pp. 174, 176—177; vol. 3, Göttingen 1961, pp. 116—117, 122.

shed on the relationship between Hansemann, Kusserow and Bismarck for us to determine Hansemann's role in the years up to 1885.

The colonial question played no small part in the election campaign of October 1884; government propaganda succeeded in creating a mood of colonial enthusiasm among sections of the petty bourgeoisie. But although the Left Liberals suffered a serious defeat, a Reichstag majority submissive to Bismarck failed to materialize. The colonial propaganda was completely lost on the proletarian voters: the Socialists were able to gain c. 10 per cent of the votes cast and to double the number of their parliamentary seats. Shortly before the election, Engels had written to Bebel: "The fact that the colonial humbug has not proved a success pleases me no end. This was Bismarck's cleverest trick, calculated to appeal to the philistine and conjuring up a world of hopeful illusions . . ."[17]

After the elections, Bismarck continued to use colonial policy as a weapon against those parties he called "enemies of the Empire". The fomenting of nationalist emotions and colonial chauvinism among the middle classes and the petty bourgeoisie was to strengthen the position of the regime at a time when both the antisocialist law and social insurance measures had proved incapable of checking the growth of the socialist working-class movement. In this context the importance which Bismarck for a time attached to the colonial question may be deduced from an instruction which he sent to the German Ambassador in London on 25 January 1885. In it he said: "At present, public opinion in Germany sets such great store by colonial policy that the government's position in home affairs largely depends on its success . . . The smallest corner of New Guinea or West Africa, even if in actual fact completely worthless, is at present more important for our policy than the whole of Egypt and its future."[18]

Domestic considerations thus played a notable part in the transition to the policy of colonial annexations in 1884—5. Nevertheless, the view put forward in more recent West German literature that it was a case of "social imperialism" is mistaken. Firstly, the use of the term "imperialism" for German colonial policy under Bismarck and his successor Caprivi (and generally for the colonial policy of this period) should be rejected since this amounts to a separation of imperialism and monopoly capitalism. Both terms denote the new stage the world capitalist system in its economic, social and political entirety had reached at the turn of the

[17] *K. Marx/F. Engels*, Werke, Vol. 36, Berlin 1967, pp. 215—216.
[18] *GP*, IV, pp. 96 ff., see also pp. 80—83, 150—151.

century. This stage was, and is, very different from earlier capitalism, and to use the term "imperialism" exclusively for colonial expansion and rule is to limit its scope, deprive it of its organic relation with monopoly capitalism and to deny its relevance for more recent history and the present. Secondly, the policy of colonial annexation as a diversion in domestic policy was for Bismarck only a tactical method tried for a time and not a permanent system.

Bismarck's support for the Congo plan of the Belgian King, Leopold II, also formed part of the policy of state assistance for German exports (especially spirits). In order to turn the vast Congo basin into his personal colony, Leopold — whose colonial scheme was not supported by the Belgian government and who therefore had to proceed as a "private individual" — founded the Association Internationale Africaine in 1876. This association, together with the Association Internationale du Congo, similarly set up by Leopold in 1882, was ostensibly intended to serve the geographical exploration of the Congo region, its commercial development and, in particular, the rendering of humanitarian aid for its inhabitants, by all the European powers and the United States. The activities of the Belgian King's agents in the Congo (under the cover of the Association) and the advance of the French in the same direction troubled the British government, and by a treaty with Portugal in February 1884 Britain recognized Portugal's "historic claims" to the mouth of the Congo. In this way Britain hoped to keep the Congo basin open to British trade.

Leopold, who possessed neither troops nor very much money, saw his weak position seriously threatened by the British action. He therefore had recourse to a stratagem whose execution, had its subsequent effects not been so terrible for the population in large parts of Central Africa, might have been made the subject of a comic opera: he applied to the powers for the recognition of the areas claimed by the Association, in which it had established a number of trading stations, as a "sovereign state" with himself as its head.

After he had succeeded in obtaining diplomatic semi-recognition of the Association as a political entity from the United States and in concluding a treaty with France on her right of pre-emption in the areas claimed (although certainly not controlled) by the Association, he applied to Bismarck for formal recognition. He calculated that if Germany took this step, the other European powers would follow suit.

Bismarck's attitude in the matter was exclusively determined by German trade interests. Although no German trading posts existed at the mouth of the Congo, extensive imports of German spirits, gunpowder, and rifles from Hamburg entered via the Woermann shipping line and the Dutch Nieuwe Afrikaansche Handels-Gennootschap. Since the British-Portuguese treaty provided for duties on these goods which amounted to an import embargo, the Chancellor and the French government lodged a protest. The British government therefore withdrew the treaty, which was very controversial in Britain, before it could be ratified by parliament. Bismarck, however, wanted not only to protect the German brandy and gunpowder trade, which had increased considerably on the Congo in 1883—4, but also to open up to German industry the large markets presumed to exist in the interior of Central Africa. As the price of recognition for the projected "state", he therefore required from Leopold unrestricted freedom of trade and equal rights for Germans with the Association's employees in the Congo, even if the "claims" of the Association should be ceded to France. The Belgian King finally assented, whereupon recognition by the German Empire was accorded on 8 November 1884.

One week later the so-called Berlin Congo Conference began. This could more correctly be termed a conference on the colonial partition of Africa. With the support of Bismarck and the French Prime Minister Jules Ferry, Leopold succeeded in obtaining general recognition of the "sovereignty" of the "Congo Free State". The General Act of the conference, signed on 26 February 1885, limited this "sovereignty" in so far as an international guarantee of an "open door" for the trade and shipping of all states was laid down for the entire Congo basin. The agreed free-trade zone extended, with certain reservations, right to the Indian Ocean. In the same year, Bismarck was reproached by missionary circles on the grounds that through the General Act this part of Africa had been "mercilessly abandoned to the pernicious torrent [of spirits]".[19] (As Adolf Woermann had been appointed a member of the German delegation, this outcome was hardly surprising.) The Chancellor had achieved his end in that the enormous territories granted to the "Congo Free State" had not fallen to a colonial rival but to a neutral régime supposedly subject to international control, which appeared to offer great opportunities for exploitation to German firms.

Many pro-colonialist historians attach no great importance to the conference of all the colonial powers, the United States, Russia and Austria-Hungary, convened on the initiative of Bismarck and Ferry

---

[19] *F. M. Zahn*, Der überseeische Branntweinhandel. Seine verderblichen Wirkungen und Vorschläge zur Beschränkung desselben. In Allgemeine Missions-Zeitschrift, vol. 13 (1886), p. 32.

and held from 15 November 1884 to 26 February 1885 in Bismarck's chancellery in the Wilhelmstrasse in Berlin. In reality it was an event of great consequence for the colonial partition of sub-Saharan Africa. It declared the international "legitimacy" of the colonial conquest and subjugation of the peoples of the continent. The participating powers agreed to cover up their acts of aggression with hypocritical, and in practice meaningless, "pledges" to "support the native population and improve their moral and material situation" (Article 6 of the General Act) and to end the slave-trade (Article 9). In order to put an end to overlapping "claims" of the colonial powers and to avoid future disputes over territorial "rights", a procedure was agreed upon to be observed in the case of annexations (Articles 34 & 35). In direct connection with the conference or under its influence numerous bilateral agreements on the partition of territories and the drawing of boundaries were concluded. These agreements (with the exception of the German colonies and South Africa) determined the political map of sub-Saharan Africa until the collapse of the imperialist colonial system.

Although Germany had only just begun to participate in the scramble for colonies, Bismarck as chairman of the conference was able in large measure to influence its course, and even partly to direct it. Thus the Chancellor of the German Empire materially contributed to the preparations for imperialist colonial dominion over Africa, despite the fact that imperialist objectives such as control over entire continents were far from his thoughts.

The fall of the Ferry government in France on 30 March 1885 led to the end of the Franco-German colonial entente. In May of the same year the Anglo-Russian crisis had subsided and England's international situation was substantially improved. Bismarck was therefore compelled to improve relations with England and he refrained from further colonial annexations of any importance. Colonial expansion did not rank so high in his foreign policy that he was prepared to risk a further complication of Germany's diplomatic position on its account — a position which from 1885—6 was noticeably worsening through the Bulgarian crisis and the deterioration of relations with France. By barter agreements with Britain and France, in which Bismarck relinquished some insignificant German "claims" in areas near Dubreka(Guinea), in Mahinland (South Nigeria), and the St. Lucia Bay (Natal) in exchange for small concessions from the two powers, the demarcation of German colonial possessions in the coastal areas was achieved. The German negotiators also had to recognize a number of British "rights" which had been hastily contrived for the sole purpose of preventing the expansion of

German South West Africa in an easterly direction to the Boer republics
and the expansion of Cameroon in a northerly direction to the banks of
the Benue.

These partition agreements were the result of typical colonialist
haggling over territories. Little heed was paid to natural frontiers, and
virtually no regard was paid to ethnic boundaries, African political
units, or African states. These and subsequent demarcation treaties led
to the division of many peoples into two or even three parts. The same
ruthless and unrestrained arrogance which had been exercised with
regard to the peoples of the coast was shown in the partition of countries
and peoples in the interior, sometimes before a European had even seen
them.

The colonialist enthusiasm prevailing among sections of the bourgeoisie in autumn 1884 gave way in the following year to an increasing
disillusionment, even in those sections of the upper bourgeoisie that had
called for colonies, since the expectations of early profits remained
unfulfilled. Germany, being a latecomer, had only been able to snatch
some coastal areas at the last minute and these had neither natural
harbours — except in East Africa — nor navigable rivers of any importance. The stubborn resistance of the Africans and Melanese, assisted
by impassable tropical forests, parched savannahs or mountainous
country, made no small contribution to the fact that the high expectations of German capitalists were not as yet fulfilled. Frederick Engels'
comment of October 1884 on Bismarck's "colonial humbug . . . conjuring up a world of hopeful illusions and calling for outlays which would
be slow to bring returns or even prove a heavy burden"[20] had proved
true all too soon.

The "Iron Chancellor" also saw himself disappointed. His intention of
having the colonies administered by chartered companies of interested
entrepreneurs and thereby depriving the Reichstag of any say in colonial
affairs, foundered within a few years either on the refusal of the entrepreneurs to pay the administrative expenses or, as happened in East
Africa, on the crass incompetence and adventurism of Carl Peters and
his cronies.

In spite of these results, the foundation of colonies in the 1880s was
more than just an episode. Territorial bases and other conditions were
created which made possible the conquest of extensive territories of the
interior in the 1890s.

---

[20] K. Marx/F. Engels, op. cit.

III. The Conquest of Colonies: the Establishment and Extension of German Colonial Rule

1. South West Africa 1885—1907

South West Africa (now Namibia), whose boundaries were arbitrarily fixed by its colonial masters in the late 19th century, comprises — from north to south — Amboland, Hereroland (or Damaraland) and Namaland. As the names of these regions suggest, the principal population groups are the Ovambo, the Herero and the Nama. The Ovambo can be left out of consideration here because they remained outside the sphere of German rule.

The central region of Namibia is peopled by the Herero, who are a Bantu-speaking people like the Ovambo. No accurate data are available on their numerical strength in the late 19th century. However, most experts agree that approximately 80,000 Herero inhabited the area at the beginning of German colonial rule. They were nomadic herdsmen who, unlike other Bantu, did not engage in crop raising. Although the soil was common property, their social system was not a primeval communism: the classless order was fast breaking up, and an influential aristocracy assuming control. The process of social differentiation had progressed so far that the contours of a class society were beginning to take shape. Relationships of dependence were emerging based on ownership of cattle, the chief form of private ownership.[1] As a result of an extensive barter trade, the Herero had acquired a sizable number of modern rifles in exchange for cattle.

The region to the south of Hereroland is inhabited by the Nama[2] or, to give them their own name, the Khoikhoin. They comprise the Nama

---

[1] There is so far no definitive study on social differentiation among the Herero.

[2] In colonialist publications the Nama are almost invariably described as "Hottentots". This word has not been used here because of its derogatory tenor, its original meaning being "stammerer".

proper[3] and the Orlam tribes[4] who entered South West Africa from across the Orange River at the beginning of the 19th century to escape annihilation by the Boers. The Nama, too, were nomadic herdsmen rather than tillers. In terms of socio-economic development, what has been said about the Herero also applies to the Nama. The principal distinction between the Herero and the Nama at the close of the last century was that the latter's herds were much smaller and that, generally speaking, cattle did not dominate their thinking to the same extent as among the Herero. It was noticeable in more than one respect that they had long lived in close touch with the Boers. It is estimated that there were about 20,000 Nama towards the end of the 19th century.

There were also two ethnic units living at various early stages of social organization: the Damara and the San (or "Bushmen"). Dependent on the Herero and Nama, they were estimated to number 30,000 and 3,000, respectively.

South West Africa's history in the 19th century was one of constant struggle between the Nama and the Herero for supremacy, which would have paved the way for the establishment of an African state. These efforts were thwarted by the activities of Rhenish missionaries and by German colonial aggression.

Chancellor Bismarck, reversing the "Trade follows the flag" doctrine, proposed to extend the "protection" of the German Reich over land "acquisitions" of German businessmen in territories claimed by no other colonial power. The "royal merchants", as Bismarck inappropriately called these capitalists, were to receive letters-patent modelled on the British royal charters that would entitle them to administer "their" colonies independently. In South West Africa, just as elsewhere, this policy ended in failure in a matter of years.

As for Adolf Lüderitz, his ambitions were greater than his financial resources. Since his hopes of quickly discovering gold and diamonds were not fulfilled, his financial situation deteriorated rapidly, and his acquisitions passed into the hands of prominent representatives of mono-poly capital, then in its infancy. The founding of the German South West

---

[3] In the late 19th century the Nama proper comprised the following tribes: the Veld-schoendragers, the Franzmanns, the Zwartboois, the so-called Red Nation, the Topnaars, the Zeib people, and the Bondelzwarts.

[4] Towards the end of the 19th century there were also the following Orlam tribes: the Witboois, the Berseba community, the Khauas, the Bethanie people and what had remained of the Afrikaaners.

Africa Company (Deutsche Kolonialgesellschaft für Südwestafrika),
which proceeded to acquire Lüderitz's possessions, took place on
30 April 1885. Its members included some of the richest men in Germany
such as Hansemann, Bleichröder, the Duke of Ujest and Count Henckel
von Donnersmarck. Banking interests were particularly well represented,
examples being — apart from Bleichröder and the Disconto-Gesellschaft
— the Deutsche Bank, Delbrück, Leo & Co., the Dresdner Bank and the
Bankhaus Sal. Oppenheim jun. & Co. From its inception, the German
South West Africa Company stressed its "patriotic" motives, pointing
out that it had been established to prevent South West Africa from
falling into foreign hands.

But when no minerals or ores were discovered during the year that
followed, the company lapsed into inactivity. There followed a period of
lack of interest which lasted from 1886 to 1892.

South West Africa presented the following picture in 1885:
First, there was the territory acquired by Lüderitz which in 1885 passed
into the hands of the German South West Africa Company. It comprised the coastal strip from the Orange River to Cape Frio (Walvis
Bay excluded) and the hinterland of Walvis Bay. This strip was a sandy
waste without any economic value, the sole purpose of Lüderitz's acquisition having been to forestall similar efforts by other colonial powers.

Second, there was the more extensive territory placed under the
"protection" of the German Reich. "Protection treaties" had been concluded with the following tribes in 1884 and 1885: the Bethanie people,
the Topnaars, the Berseba, the so-called Red Nation, the Rehoboths
and the Herero. They were designed as a kind of supplement to Lüderitz's contracts of purchase, as a legalization of the German penetration
of South West Africa.

Third, there was the territory inhabited by those tribes which had rejected German offers of "protection". The majority of the Nama tribes
such as the Witboois, the Bondelzwarts, the Veldschoendragers, the
Franzmanns and the Khauas had refused categorically to sign a treaty
with the German Reich. This part of South West Africa was looked
upon as a German sphere of interest by the German authorities.

For the time being, no appreciable changes occurred for the people of
South West Africa. Their internal struggle for supremacy continued to
command their undivided attention. They could hardly appreciate that
the situation had completely changed and the German colonialists had
become their chief enemy because the German presence in 1885 was
limited to a mere three imperial officials. So they all but ignored the
"German protectorate". The Nama chief Hendrik Witbooi waged war

as usual without paying any attention to the Germans. When during one of his campaigns against the Herero the horse of the Imperial Commissioner Dr. Heinrich Göring fell into his hands, the Kaiser's representative found himself obliged to make a request to Witbooi for the restitution of his mount. Later, on conquering Hoachanas, Witbooi's forces captured a German flag which the chief then sent to Göring with an accompanying letter.

The Herero, who had signed a treaty in 1885 because they had hoped to obtain protection against the Nama, realized more and more that the Germans were neither willing nor able to afford them protection. They became increasingly disenchanted with the arrangement and revoked the German "protectorate" in 1888.

Faced with this situation, the Foreign Office in Berlin decided to dispatch a small military contingent of about 20 men, disguised as explorers, to South West Africa in order to salvage what they could. This was an official admission that the company alone was incapable of maintaining any authority over the "colony" and at the same time a first step towards conquest, as essential to effective control. In January 1890 this so-called protective force was brought up to 50 men. Although the contingent was too small for any operation against the Herero or Nama, its mere presence did not fail to make an impression on the South West Africans.

But the authorities in Berlin were still undecided at that time on whether to keep the colony or not. When by mid-1889 the assets of the German South West Africa Company had dwindled to a mere 110,000 marks, it was clear that within a year or two the company would be at the end of its tether. German financiers were in no mood to invest further capital in South West Africa as they had made abundantly plain on previous occasions. But what was to become of the colony once the company's resources were exhausted? Since the German Foreign Office remained unwilling, in this case, to depart from Bismarck's approach in colonial matters mentioned above, all the indications were that South West Africa would soon have to be abandoned.

Meanwhile the company, having found "patriotism" too costly an affair, entered without a moment's hesitation into a deal with British capitalists under the terms of which the bulk of the company's estates and its mining concessions were to be sold for three million marks. However, such a contract required the approval of the German Chancellor who, after a long period of procrastination, ultimately withheld his consent.

The lack of official interest became even more pronounced in the first two years of Count Leo von Caprivi's chancellorship. As we know today, even the Kaiser was prepared "to give up South West Africa if necessary so that all our energies may be focussed on East Africa."[5] Caprivi declared that before the protective force could be reinforced it would need somewhat more to protect, and as German capital for South West Africa was not forthcoming, the Colonial Department agreed at last to allow British capital into the country. It felt that this was better than no capital at all. The result was the granting of the Damaraland concession which in no time at all passed into the hands of Cecil Rhodes.

At this time influential German colonial interests were busy persuading the Chancellor that the so-called protective force would have to be strengthened before capital could be expected to be channelled to South West Africa. It was chiefly leading members of the German Colonial Society and the German South West Africa Company (DKGSWA) who were trying to influence Caprivi in this direction. It seems that from about mid-1892 he found it virtually impossible to stand up to the pressure from pro-colonial circles any longer. At any rate, he declared in an address to the Reichstag on 1 March 1893, referring to the colony: "Now it is ours, German territory, and it must remain so."[6] When news came in November 1892 that the Herero and the Nama had made peace, Caprivi ordered the protective force to be raised to a level of 250 men. Thus the die had been cast in Berlin: South West Africa was to be kept and German rule extended well beyond the handful of strongholds which were firmly in German hands at the time.

Cecil Rhodes had in the meantime not remained idle. He had, in fact, managed to expand his economic interests in the German colony quite considerably. The British empire-builder used the (British) South West Africa Company as a lever and brought a number of subsidiaries such as the Kaoko-Land- und Minengesellschaft and the Hanseatische Land- und Minengesellschaft under his control in the following years. Subsequently the South West Africa Company also succeeded in extending its influence to the South African Territories Company. The upshot was that in the mid-1890s British monopoly capital represented by Cecil Rhodes was dominant in the South West African economy.

The failure of the Jameson Raid in early 1896, an operation aimed at incorporating the Boer republics into the British Empire, forced Cecil Rhodes to abandon his plans regarding South West Africa. In the following years his chief interest was the idea of a British Cape-to-Cairo con-

[5] ZStA, RKolA, no. 1549, p. 30, note by Nordenflycht, 31 Aug. 1891.
[6] StBVR, VIII. Leg. Per. II. Sess. 1892/93, vol. 2, p. 1359.

nection, for which support from the German imperialists was essential. For this reason Rhodes turned about and sought an arrangement with Germany. This new Anglo-German understanding removed, for the time being, any political dangers to German rule in South West Africa that might have arisen from Britain's economic preponderance there. By 1898 German financiers were in any case beginning to replace British capital by German capital primarily from the Deutsche Bank and the Disconto-Gesellschaft.

For such a policy to succeed it was necessary to manoeuvre the South West Africans into gradually accepting German colonial rule. In view of the German military presence, the Herero had agreed in 1890 to recognize the German "protectorate" once again. As they were still at war with Hendrik Witbooi, they did not want to take on the Germans with their superior weapons as well. The Herero had still not realized that the situation had changed with the coming of the German officials and soldiers and that the Germans were now the principal adversaries of all South West Africans. But despite the renewed acceptance of German "protection", the mood among the Herero was clearly anti-German.

Hendrik Witbooi, who had consistently refused to sign a protection treaty with the Germans, had consolidated his power in Namaland in the late 1880s. In spite of the German military presence his war against the Herero was continuing unabated. From the German viewpoint this conflict had its advantages and disadvantages, the merits outweighing the demerits. As long as the Africans were fighting each other, the Germans found themselves in the role of an outsider biding his time and gradually strengthening his position. On the other hand, the war between the Nama and the Herero made it impossible for Germans to settle in South West Africa in greater numbers.

In 1890 this prompted the Imperial Commissioner to make his first attempt to intervene in this inter-African conflict. In a letter he called on Hendrik Witbooi to stop making war on the Herero, who were under German protection. This made it clear to Hendrik Witbooi for the first time that the coming of the Germans confronted the South West Africans with an entirely new situation. He addressed a lengthy letter to Samuel Maharero, the Supreme Chief of the Herero, which paved the way for a *rapprochement* between the Nama and the Herero. In this letter he pointed out the unnatural character of an alliance between the Herero and the Germans. He said that the only reason why the Herero had given up their independence was their hatred of the Witboois, but that this was extremely shortsighted as in the event of the Witboois' defeat the Herero would soon share their fate. The war between the Nama and the Herero, he stressed, was of an entirely different nature from a war between Africans and Germans. There was always the possibility of peace between the Nama and the Herero.

However, it took more than two years for the idea of peace to become reality. In November 1892, the Nama and the Herero, who had been at war throughout the 19th century, concluded peace in order to cope better with the new situation that had arisen with the German penetration of South West Africa.

The peace agreement of November 1892 was a landmark in the history of South West Africa, leading to a realignment of forces. Early in 1893 Germans and Africans were confronting each other. Although the German colonialists had always pretended to favour an end of the war between the Nama and the Herero, they were now highly alarmed. They realized that they could no longer profit from the dispute between the two warring camps.

With the decision to raise the so-called protective force to a level of 250 men the die had been cast in Berlin. If South West Africa was to be retained, it had to be conquered in earnest. Within days of the arrival of the reinforcements, the German unit began military action by mounting a premediated attack on Hornkranz, Hendrik Witbooi's headquarters, the object being "to destroy the tribe of the Witboois".[7] Seventy-eight Nama women and children were killed in the raid whereas Hendrik Witbooi and most of his warriors escaped.

Thereafter, the military initiative shifted to Witbooi. While Captain Curt von François, commander of the military unit (called "Schutztruppe", i.e. protective force) and Landeshauptmann (administrator), remained in Windhoek, waiting for the arrival of artillery and further reinforcements, Witbooi pulled off a great coup: he dismounted most of the German "cavalry" by taking possession of their horses. His successful conduct of the war brought him support from many sides. Warriors from many other Nama tribes joined him to avenge the treacherous attack on Hornkranz. At the time of the Hornkranz raid Witbooi had commanded about 250 men with 100 rifles and 120 horses, but six months later he had 600 men with 400 rifles and 300 horses at his disposal.

Since Captain François was unable to bring the war he had unleashed against the Witboois to a successful conclusion, Caprivi sent Major

---

[7] ZStA, RKolA, no. 1483, pp. 41—48, Capt. von François to the Colonial Department, 12 April 1893.

Theodor Leutwein to South West Africa in late 1893. Leutwein, the third of the Reich's chief officials in the colony (he was Landeshauptmann from 1895 to 1898 and Governor from 1898 to 1904), differed from his predecessors in the methods he employed towards the Africans. Heinrich Göring (1885—1889/90) had sought to maintain the fiction of a German colony by his mere presence and, for want of military strength, had used diplomatic means to reconcile Africans to the German presence, and Curt von François (1889/90—1894) had dispensed with diplomacy from the first, immediately taking up the sword. But Leutwein tried to combine the two methods. Without renouncing the use of force, he showed a preference for diplomatic dealings. He played the various African groups off against each other, thereby ensuring that the numerous risings against German colonial rule that were to take place between 1894 and 1903 remained sporadic and uncoordinated. His success seemed to confirm that this was the most promising approach for German imperialism, but only until the Africans began to see through his manoeuvres. In 1904, when the "Leutwein system" collapsed, it became clear that he, like his predecessors, had been unable to stifle the desire of the African population for independence.

As a first move Leutwein forced the Khauas and Franzmanns to conclude a treaty with the German Reich. Then he had South West Africa covered by a network of small military posts which were essential for the actual subjugation of the country. To man the newly established posts, he asked for 250 additional troopers.

After the arrival of these reinforcements Leutwein embarked on a decisive campaign against the Witboois who had entrenched themselves in the Noukloof Mountains. It was an unequal struggle because artillery was used by the German side and in the end, the German superiority in weaponry left the Witboois with no choice but to surrender. Hendrik Witbooi agreed to the signing of a "treaty of protection and friendship" which clearly amounted to a compromise, the only way for the Germans to bring their 18-month-old war against Witbooi to an end. Its relatively conciliatory terms were not dictated by humanitarian considerations on the part of Leutwein, let alone by sympathy for the Africans, but by the sheer impossibility of bringing Witbooi to heel by force of arms.

Moreover, in designing the treaty, Leutwein was taking the long view. He knew full well that the war against Hendrik Witbooi would only be the first in a long series of wars between German imperialism and the people of South West Africa. Conversant as he was with British colonial history, he considered it the best and simplest method to play the Africans off against each other. Leutwein had in mind for the Witboois the role of a German mercenary force because they were known for their military prowess.

Although the Herero and Nama had made peace in November 1892, hostility between them continued, preventing joint action against the Germans. Leutwein fomented these tensions and finally managed in November 1895 to persuade the Witboois to pledge military allegiance to the Governor. He thereby opened what was to be the decisive breach within the African population, with the result that right up to the great Herero uprising in 1904 the Witboois remained on the German side.

With the war against the Witboois over, Leutwein's next objective was — in German colonial phraseology — the "settlement of the Herero question". The gist of his plan was to deprive the Herero gradually of their land and cattle, in other words their means of subsistence. As a first step, he concluded a treaty with Samuel Maharero in December 1894, establishing a southern border for Hereroland. Another treaty was signed the following year in order to define the northern border. This treaty served to isolate the Herero still further, to separate them from the Ovambo and to establish Crown territory in the north, which would be of strategic significance in the event of war against the Herero. Leutwein's negotiating partner was Samuel Maharero, whose close collaboration with the Germans in the period from 1894 to 1903 did much harm to his people. Maharero was seeking to strengthen his position as Supreme Chief. Ten years were to elapse before he revised his policy, chiefly under pressure from the lesser chiefs, and led the Herero rebellion against German imperialism.

Governor Leutwein, who in late 1894 had still spoken of a peaceful settlement of the "Herero question", began to adopt an increasingly bellicose attitude in 1895. By late October 1895 he was determined to employ force. To put his plans into effect, he demanded reinforcements to bring his unit up to a strength of more than 600 men.

Leutwein's policy was aimed at provoking the Mbandjeru or eastern Herero, who were already at a disadvantage owing to the establishment of a southern border for Hereroland. He was successful: in late March 1896 the Mbandjeru and Khauas staged a joint rebellion against the German regime. The war against the Mbandjeru served two purposes. Leutwein's close cooperation with Samuel Maharero and Hendrik Witbooi and the resulting isolation of the insurgents was calculated to have an intimidating effect on all other South West Africans, dissuading them from putting up resistance to the Germans. Furthermore, the representative of the German Empire practised cattle theft on a large scale. All told, 12,000 head of cattle were seized from the Mbandjeru in 1896—7. At the end of hostilities Leutwein staged a "trial" of the chiefs Nikodemus and Kahimemua who were sentenced to death by firing squad. They were executed the day after the judgement had been passed.

The rising of the Khauas and Mbandjeru in 1896 was an important event in South West African history because this was the first time that Nama and Herero tribesmen fought together against their principal adversary, the German imperialists. Since Samuel Maharero and Hendrik Witbooi at this stage collaborated with the colonial power, the Khauas and Mbandjeru found themselves in complete isolation and their rapid defeat was a foregone conclusion.

The following years saw a series of further uprisings by smaller South West African tribes. All took place in isolation from other tribes and therefore could not even achieve limited successes. Another characteristic of these risings was that Africans were all too frequently fighting each other. But in October 1903 came the rising of the Bondelzwarts which led on to the great uprisings of the Herero and the Nama.

With the colonial zealots in Germany eager to see South West Africa become a colony for German settlers, a discussion began at the beginning of the 1890s on how to effect the gradual transfer of the land into the hands of settlers. According to Captain François, occupation and not "protection" was the only way to solve the problem. He once remarked that the Africans' claim to land ownership could not be disputed with words, but only with rifles. When he occupied Windhoek in October 1890, the Herero protested but were unable to do anything about it. Two years later in Berlin, 13,000 square kilometres of "no man's land", which in reality was part of the best land of the Herero, was awarded to an English land company with one stroke of the pen.

Under François's successor, Theodor Leutwein, African losses of territory soon began to take on very large proportions and he considered it his foremost task to engineer the transfer of land and cattle to German settlers. But unlike François he was aware that, as long as German rule rested on the so-called protection treaties, the only possible approach was the gradual expropriation of the African population. Any other method would at once have provoked a general uprising.

Since the Herero had the best grazing land and the largest cattle herds in South West Africa, Leutwein turned his undivided attention to this people. As mentioned before, in 1894—5 he concluded agreements with Samuel Maharero on the northern and southern borders of Hereroland, thereby reducing by half the area originally used by the Herero to graze their cattle. In many instances, Leutwein also took advantage of the local uprisings that occurred before the great insurrections of 1904—7 to take away the land and cattle of the tribes concerned.

Yet the "creation of Crown Land" was but one side of Leutwein's land policy. Another was to place settlers directly in Herero territory from about 1897 onward. Whereas initially the Herero had refused to sell even an inch of land — their laws did not allow even their chiefs to do so as land was held in common ownership — Samuel Maharero began in 1897 to dispose of Herero land on a great scale as a result of the outbreak of rinderpest that year, in order to improve his precarious financial situation. He would not budge on the matter despite protests from the lesser chiefs. As for the German immigrants, they were anxious to settle in Hereroland because the land there was the best and the cheapest. Beside the creation of Crown land and the sale of land to farmers there were also arbitrary seizures of land by the latter.

Disaster struck the Herero with elemental force in 1897 when an outbreak of rinderpest wiped out large parts of their huge cattle herds, most of the animals perishing within six months. For the German settlers the outbreak turned out to be a boon: by the time the plague subsided, the price of cattle had risen to three times the previous level. It was only now, with the Herero out of competition, that the rearing of cattle became a profitable business. On the other hand, the cattle losses marked the beginning of a process in which the Herero ceased to be herdsmen and became wage labourers, which had always been the declared aim of their colonial masters.

The second half of the 1890s saw an increased influx of German settlers. While there were a mere 310 Germans in South West Africa in 1891, their number was almost ten times as high twelve years later; on 1 January 1903 the Germans numbered 2,998 and the total white population 4,640. From 1899 to 1903 alone the number of white farmers trebled, largely because the construction of the Swakopmund-Windhoek narrow-gauge railway meant a marked improvement in transport. Before long, no more land suitable for farming was to be had anywhere along the railway line. At the same time, a telegraph link was established between Swakopmund and Windhoek, and a 375-metre pier built in Swakopmund to improve landing facilities.

The Government began to encourage settlement. In 1901 the administration in Windhoek, for example, set up a fund to provide loans for German settlers, and plans were made for a large-scale influx of German farmers to begin in 1903. For this purpose the German Government set aside 300,000 marks and named Paul Rohrbach, well-known advocate of settler colonialism, Commissioner for Settlement. It was clear that the Africans were to be expelled from all their lands in a matter of years.

Since the mid-1890s the Rhenish Missionary Society tried to forestall this by demanding that inviolable reserves be established for the African population. The missionaries were concerned about the future of their stations. They realized that if the Africans living in the proximity of a mission station lost all their land and were forced to settle elsewhere, this would spell the end of the station. Indeed, that was what happened, for example, in 1901 when the mission station of Otjikango (Neu-Barmen) had to be closed down because the local Herero had been expelled from their pastures by German settlers. Five more stations were in danger of sharing the same fate.

The missionaries' idea was that the chiefs should bestow tribal lands on them as a gift, which would then serve as reservations. This would have made the Rhenish Missionary Society one of the biggest landowners in South West Africa. The Government, which had from the start been unsympathetic to the Mission's plans for the establishment of reserves, rejected the idea. But Leutwein was anxious not to forgo the Mission's cooperation in holding down the Africans and, rather than reject the proposals out of hand, he took the sting out of them by assuming personal responsibility for the whole matter. As a result, the Mission found itself outmanoeuvred with the promulgation of the "Imperial Decree of 10 April 1898 Pertaining to the Establishment of Reserves for Natives in the Protected Territory of South West Africa".

The Government was now in a position to determine the pace of the establishment of reserves. It set up only two, one in Namaland for the Witboois and another in Hereroland (Otjimbingwe). Further projects for Hereroland were rejected because the Government did not wish to see the construction of railways hindered. Leutwein decreed in May 1903 that only out-of-the-way areas of comparatively modest size were eligible as sites for new reserves. The decree went on to stipulate that "all farms already purchased by whites must, of course, remain outside the reserve and so must, subsequently, any farms that settlers might be interested in buying."[8]

The two reserves hardly hampered the expropriation of the South West African people. They were abolished after the great uprisings had been crushed.

---

[8] Leutwein to the Colonial Department, Sept. 1904, in: *Denkschrift über Eingeborenen-Politik* und Hereroaufstand in Deutsch-Südwestafrika, p. 79, in: Beilage zu Deutsches Kolonialblatt, No. 25, 15 Dec. 1904.

Long before 1884 the huge cattle herds of the Herero had attracted the interest of European traders, who offered mainly weapons and ammunition as payment for livestock. This was to remain so after the arrival of the Germans who also engaged in a brisk barter trade. Under Leutwein's governorship the South West Africans soon began losing livestock in large numbers. A supplementary clause added on 1 July 1895 to the treaty defining the southern border of Hereroland provided the Governor with a legal basis for "impounding" cattle that had strayed across the border line, and in October 1895 Leutwein even declared that a war against the Herero would be a profitable undertaking because of the size of their herds. The uprising of the Mbandjeru in 1896—7 proved very lucrative indeed as he seized no less than 12,000 head of cattle. The capture of livestock invariably accompanied the suppression of the local rebellions that occurred in the following years.

When German settlers came to Hereroland in large numbers between 1898 and 1903, some of them devised a new method of dispossessing the Herero of their livestock. They bought goods on credit and then placed them at the disposal of the Herero on the same basis. This they did several times before asking them to pay their debts. Since the Herero did not, as a rule, possess any money, the settlers demanded cattle instead, at a very low price. Nor did they have any scruples about seizing the cattle by force. As a result, large quantities of livestock changed hands after 1898.

When these settlers lost all restraint, Leutwein tried to clip their wings somewhat by issuing an order which provided that all trade should be on a cash basis. This measure was fiercely opposed for several years by the interested parties in the Kolonialrat (Colonial Council). The issue was finally "resolved" when the Imperial Chancellor decreed on 23 July 1903 that there should be a one-year limitation for debts resulting from transactions between Africans and Europeans. The effect was that the settlers now set upon the Africans more than ever in order to recover outstanding debts before the year was up.

The avarice of the German settlers and the losses caused to the Herero by the rinderpest in 1897 left the Africans in the colony, who had owned several hundred thousand head of cattle, with barely 50,000 in the years preceding the great uprisings. An official census taken in 1902 showed that the Africans owned 45,910 head of cattle whereas a few hundred German settlers, who had come to the country with almost no property ten years before, now owned herds totalling 44,490 head.[9]

[9] Cf. *Th. Leutwein*, Elf Jahre Gouverneur in Deutsch-Südwestafrika, Berlin 1906, p. 367.

To the complete surprise of the Germans, a great uprising of the Herero broke out on 12 January 1904. The Herero rose under the leadership of their Paramount Chief Samuel Maharero, who now reversed the ill-conceived policy he had pursued so far. This was largely because pressure had been brought to bear by the lesser chiefs.

There can be no doubt about the reasons behind the insurrection. It was the systematic expropriation of the Herero and their total lack of rights that goaded them to their uprising against German imperialism. They neither could nor would live any longer under these conditions. They were prepared to die fighting rather than wait in resignation until their last possessions had been taken from them.

Paradoxically, measures such as the establishment of reserves and the limitation on loans, which were designed to relieve the Herero's plight a little, increased their desperation. The creation of reserves made it clear to the Herero that the amount of land still left to them was dwindling rapidly while the decree establishing a 12-month time limit for the enforcement of claims on Africans caused settlers and traders to press them even harder for repayment. These measures hastened the outbreak of the rebellion.

Another factor acting as a catalyst was the construction of the Otavi railway. The building of the railway line from Swakopmund to Windhoek, which affected only the southern part of Hereroland, had left no land suitable for farming anywhere along its length that was not taken by German settlers. The Herero therefore knew what to expect from the projected construction of the Otavi line, which was to cut right across Hereroland. The Otavigesellschaft, the company financing the undertaking, demanded that the Herero cede not only the land directly required for the railway free of charge, but also slices of territory on both sides of the line, 20 by 10 kilometres in size with intervals of 10 kilometres between them plus all water rights within these slices. In negotiations with Samuel Maharero, Governor Leutwein finally persuaded the Paramount Chief to give up free of charge the land needed for laying the track. But Maharero was not prepared to make any further concessions. It was not difficult for the Herero to foresee that the construction of the Otavi line would set off an unprecedented rush of German settlers to Hereroland.

The fact that the Germans did not recognize any African rights helped bring matters to a head. Blinded by racist doctrines, many Germans described the Africans as "baboons" or even as "vermin" and treated them accordingly. Arbitrary acts of retaliation or "punishment" inflicted on them ranged from doses of "paternal chastisement" to murder.

To excuse such criminal behaviour, they often pleaded diminished responsibility due to "Tropenkoller" (tropical madness), a mental illness specifically invented for this purpose. When Germans were put on trial for crimes against Africans — a rare occurrence — the judge would, as a rule, dismiss the charges or pass only light sentences. A European who had killed the daughter of the chief of Otjimbingue was given three years' imprisonment by a court of appeal in 1903. As a matter of principle, courts doubted the credibility of African witnesses. Indeed, in those days the German Colonial League demanded that the testimony of seven Africans should be deemed equivalent to that of one white man. Deprived of all their rights, the indigenous population had the feeling of being slaves in their own country.

Pro-colonialist writers have never openly admitted the real causes behind the insurrection. Instead, they have tended to push fictitious or secondary factors into the foreground. The alleged causes of the uprising range from the "thirst for blood" of the Herero to "racial strife". The latter argument is particularly absurd because the Herero spared Britons, Boers, missionaries, and the women and children of the German settlers. Even the "weakness of the German forces" in the colony has been cited as a reason for the Herero uprising. Most writers refer to the activities of the traders, the credit limitations and the reservation issue, but all these were only subsidiary causes. The colonialist writer Rohrbach was not far from the truth when he stated that "those who gave their views about the motives involved concentrated above all on listing and criticizing insignificant circumstances and outward appearances."[10]

There was method in this, however. Laying bare the deeper causes of the uprising would have brought discredit on German imperialism per se. But if ostensible causes or contributory factors were emphasized, part of the blame could be cast on the Herero themselves and the other part on groups of settlers who had compromised themselves. This line of approach was fiercely resisted by the traders and settlers. Fearing the loss of compensation if they were held responsible for the rebellion, they did not hesitate to point out the real causes. But most writers continued to cite peripheral issues as the reasons for the insurrection.

Although the outbreak of the Herero rising took the German Government by surprise, this turn of events in South West Africa suited their intentions quite well. The insurrection afforded a long-sought pretext for a military conquest of the territory and the transformation of the "protectorate" into a genuine colony. The German minister in Lisbon,

[10] *P. Rohrbach*, Dernburg und die Südwestafrikaner, Berlin 1911, p. 329.

von Tattenbach, openly said to a Portuguese cabinet minister what many German diplomats and government officials were thinking in private when he declared that "however regrettable the Herero uprising may be, it will lead to that vast territory being taken into possession and German South West Africa becoming a well-ordered and promising colony rather than a so-called sphere of interest."[11]

The uprising had doubtless been planned long in advance. Since time was not on the Herero's side, with their plight becoming worse from year to year and the construction of the Otavi railway raising the spectre of total expropriation, they decided that at the beginning of 1904 the moment to act had come. Circumstances were favourable at the time because three out of the four German companies making up the "protective force" were operating in the far south of the country or were on their way there to deal with the rebellion of the Bondelzwarts, leaving Hereroland practically devoid of German troops. The decision to move into action was taken at short notice; this can be deduced from the fact that the 600 or so Herero working on the Otavi railway were not notified in time. The internment of these Herero labourers at the outset of the insurrection deprived the insurgents of 600 fighting men.

Leading the uprising was Samuel Maharero, Paramount Chief of the Herero. Since it was the Supreme Chief who gave the order to take up arms, all the Herero responded. This was a significant initial success.

Yet from the first the insurrection was a struggle born of desperation. The Herero were keenly aware that the opposing sides were unevenly matched owing to the inadequacy of their own equipment and the superior weaponry of their colonial masters who were able to count on unlimited supplies from Germany. But the Herero were determined to die rather than live under the German yoke any longer.

Samuel Maharero displayed considerable political shrewdness by attempting before the outbreak of the rebellion to unite all South West Africans for the struggle against German imperialism. In early 1904, just as in 1896, Hendrik Witbooi tipped the scales. If he had set up the standard of revolt, all Nama chiefs would have followed his example. Therefore, in a letter dated 11 January 1904, Maharero informed Witbooi that he was planning an insurrection against the Germans and invited him to join it. The letter failed to reach its destination, but even if it had, Witbooi would probably not have responded to Maharero's call. It was nothing short of a tragedy that the Herero and the Nama took up arms successively rather than simultaneously to cast off the hated yoke.

[11] ZStA, RKolA, no. 2115, p. 119, Tattenbach to Bülow, 1 July 1904.

The Herero rose up in arms on 12 January 1904. At one stroke they seized all of Hereroland, except for the fortified places which came under siege. More than 100 German settlers and soldiers lost their lives.

The Herero uprising turned out to be Germany's bloodiest and most protracted colonial war. In the initial stages the Herero were superior to their opponents; amongst other things, they had captured most of the settlers' livestock. But since they failed to take advantage of their temporary superiority to storm the fortified German centres, the initiative gradually passed to the enemy. The intention of the Herero was to bring about a decision in open battle. The Germans, however, were in no mood to take such a risk before the arrival of reinforcements had given them clear superiority. They knew only too well that time was on their side. While the situation for the Herero remained unchanged, the Germans were able to strengthen their position step by step through the constant influx of manpower and materials. In the early stages of the uprising, therefore, the Germans confined themselves to relieving the localities besieged by the Herero.

The war comprised two stages. During the first stage, lasting from January to June 1904, the German forces were commanded by Governor Leutwein. That phase saw much fighting, with the Germans sometimes incurring considerable losses, but it was by no means decisive. During the second stage, beginning in June 1904, the German troops were led by Lieutenant-General von Trotha, a butcher in uniform, who embarked on a campaign of annihilation against the Herero.

Leutwein divided the troops at his disposal into three detachments: an eastern, a western and a main detachment. The eastern detachment was entrusted with the task of sealing off the border with Bechuanaland. In setting up this force, Leutwein acted on the mistaken assumption that the Herero would try to cross the border before a decisive engagement had been fought out. In fact, there could be no question of this.

An advance party of the eastern detachment, consisting of about 50 men, was engaged in combat at Owikokorero on 13 March 1904. Seven officers (out of eleven) and 19 men (out of 38) were killed and three officers and two men wounded in the fighting, more than half the unit thus being lost. According to a German military writer, this engagement "was the beginning of the collapse of the eastern detachment".[12] The

---

[12] *A. von Engelbrechten*, Der Krieg in Deutsch-Südwestafrika, in: Zeitschrift für Kolonialpolitik, Kolonialrecht und Kolonialwirtschaft, vol. 8 (1906), p. 57.

losses suffered in the subsequent fighting and an outbreak of typhoid reduced the detachment from 534 to 151 men so that it had to be dissolved on 6 May 1904. As for the western detachment, designed to operate between Omaruru and Outjo, it was merged with the main detachment late in March.

The main body of troops did not become ready for action until March 1904. On 9 April the force was engaged at Onganjira by about 3,000 Herero. Only their superiority in arms and equipment enabled the Germans to repel the persistent attacks mounted by the Herero. A few days later, on 13 April, there followed an encounter at Oviumbo where the German main detachment was surrounded by the Herero. In view of the almost hopeless situation Leutwein ordered his force to retreat at nightfall, thereby saving the detachment from annihilation. A German military author observed later that the Oviumbo engagement had been a near disaster.[13] Under the impact of this traumatic experience, Leutwein decided to suspend all major operations against the Herero and to wait for further reinforcements. Shortly afterwards, he was informed that Kaiser Wilhelm II had made Lieutenant-General von Trotha Commander-in-Chief of the German forces in South West Africa.

When the new Commander-in-Chief arrived in South West Africa in June 1904, the war against the Herero had been going on for five months. By that time, despite a constant inflow of reinforcements, the powerful German Reich had not yet scored any major success. Rather, the Herero, at first severely underrated by the Germans, had turned out to be a formidable adversary. Almost all accounts of the war are unanimous in their description of the Herero as very valiant fighters. The Germans were especially surprised by the frequency of the offensive operations which the Herero launched in spite of their inferiority in weapons. Indeed, the German military even had to concede, though grudgingly, that the Herero were not wholly devoid of understanding in tactical matters.

The Herero stoutly defended every inch of their land, for they knew what they were fighting for and that the war for their independence was a just one. Several German authors reported that the Herero women supported their men from behind the lines, chanting slogans to encourage them to fight on with unfaltering courage. They shouted: "Whose land is Hereroland? Hereroland is our land!" These words, incidentally, are

---

[13] Cf. ibid., p. 64.

yet additional proof of the close connection between the uprising and the issue of land ownership.

In mid-May the Herero withdrew northward, in the direction of the Waterberg. This was a shrewd tactical manoeuvre. Whereas all previous engagements had taken place at no great distance from the railway, the German supply lines now became longer and longer. Everything the soldiers needed had to be transported by ox-wagon and this was soon to pose serious problems for the Germans.

Leutwein and von Trotha pursued the same aims: to end the uprising forthwith, to force the Herero to surrender unconditionally, and to take away their last possessions. But they differed on the means of achieving them. Leutwein always showed concern for the future of the colony after the crushing of the rebellion whereas von Trotha did not. The Governor realized that after a campaign of extermination against the Herero the colony would have lost most of its value for German imperialism. Hence his demand to spare the country's most important productive force, the people — and the cattle as well. But his views did not prevail. Faced with the failure of his strategy, he was not unhappy to relinquish his post as military leader.

In marked contrast, General von Trotha was a soldier and nothing else. He had already taken part in brutally suppressing popular uprisings in East Africa and China. His one ambition was to be able to report to the Kaiser that the revolt had been quelled.

After further reinforcements had arrived, he began the decisive assault on the Herero south of the Waterberg. The general ordered his forces to surround the mountain. But there were not enough men to seal off the whole area effectively. The odds were that the Herero could not be prevented from breaking out at some point or another. In deploying his troops, General von Trotha deliberately ordered the smallest German contingent to take up its position southeast of the Waterberg so that a breakthrough would most likely be in the direction of the Omaheke desert.

The Herero were determined to seek a decisive battle rather than avoid such an encounter by crossing the border, as was assumed on the German side. The date fixed by von Trotha for the assault was 11 August 1904. After two days of fierce fighting, in which the Germans brought into action 30 pieces of artillery and 12 machine-guns, the Herero had to yield to the German superiority in arms. In their attempt to pierce the German lines they ultimately discovered the only weak point and broke through there as von Trotha had anticipated. Stretched out before them was the sandy waste of the Omaheke desert into which they withdrew.

As the official history of the General Staff noted laconically: "The arid Omaheke was to complete what the German army had begun: the annihilation of the Herero people."[14]

The German troops immediately set off in pursuit of the Herero, whose losses had been relatively slight. To bring about their total destruction it was quite sufficient to prevent them from changing the direction of their flight. By 20 August or so the German forces had driven the Herero to the western edge of the Omaheke sandveld, and then, through constant harassment, they forced them to flee deeper into the sandveld itself. German units and patrols pursued the Herero to the last water-hole and drove them away from there. Von Trotha finally ordered the Omaheke to be sealed off by a 250-kilometre cordon in the west and southwest, making it virtually impossible for anyone to escape from the desert. This cordon was maintained until about mid-1905. As a result, the great majority of the Herero met a slow, agonizing death. The official history of the General Staff noted that the Omaheke had inflicted a worse fate on the Herero than "German arms could ever have done, however bloody and costly the battle."[15]

Lieutenant Count Schweinitz gave this account of what had happened: "All the way from Ondawu the path which the Herero had apparently taken while fleeing in a northeastern direction was lined with human skulls and skeletons and thousands of animal carcasses, mostly cattle. Especially the dense shrubs growing along the footpath, where the animals had sought protection from the scorching sun, were littered with hundreds of carcasses lying beside or on top of each other. In many places there were holes 15 to 20 metres deep, evidence of futile attempts to find water . . . All this permits the conclusion that the withdrawal was a march into death."[16]

Towards the end of 1904 the situation in South West Africa changed radically with the outbreak of the Nama uprising. The German authorities were taken completely by surprise, as they had been at the beginning of the year when the Herero rose in revolt. Hendrik Witbooi, rather than throw in his lot with the insurgents, had actually sent a 100-strong contingent to fight on the German side as he had done in all conflicts between Germans and South West Africans over the past ten years. The Germans,

---

[14] *Die Kämpfe der deutschen Truppen in Südwestafrika,* auf Grund amtlichen Materials bearbeitet von der Kriegsgeschichtlichen Abteilung I des Grossen Generalstabes, vol. 1, Berlin 1906, p. 207.

[15] Ibid., p. 189.

[16] Ibid., p. 218.

having hurriedly made peace with the Bondelzwarts, had therefore been able to concentrate on the struggle against the Herero. As a result, the central part and the northern half of the country became embroiled in war whereas the south, for the time being, remained calm.

Yet the calm was soon disturbed. Even before the outbreak of the Nama rebellion, Jakob Morenga, one of the leaders of the Bondelzwart rising in 1903, resumed fighting in the south in July and August 1904. He opened hostilities at the head of eleven men. By September he led 150 men armed with rifles and a few months later nearly 400. Morenga represented a new type of leader, a contrast to the traditional chiefs who had for so long collaborated with their German colonial masters. He owed the fact that he was commanding an armed unit to his own efforts.

In the first days of October 1904 the great Nama uprising began and the situation in Namaland changed overnight. The Germans were compelled to leave Morenga alone, at least temporarily, in order to confront their new opponent, Hendrik Witbooi. But despite the difficulties which the Nama insurrection brought for the colonial regime, its leading exponents immediately realized that it afforded them a pretext for making a clean sweep in Namaland as well.

Basically, the causes of the Nama uprising were the same as those of the Herero revolt, although the Nama had much less land and cattle than their neighbours to the north and so they had not been plundered so much by German traders and settlers. Also there had been no railway building in their country. They had, however, suffered greatly from a total lack of rights under the colonial regime. This emerges forcefully from a letter addressed by Hendrik Witbooi to Governor Leutwein. Asked about the reasons for the rebellion, Witbooi said that he had been prompted to rise in revolt against German rule by the countless murders and other outrages committed by the Germans in peace time. The Nama took up arms because they were unable to endure the German colonial yoke any longer. As Leutwein's deputy, Tecklenburg, wrote in a report to the Colonial Department: "The one and only reason for the rebellion is the desire to end German colonial rule."[17]

It was the threat of the settlers to "clear up" with the Nama after the Herero had been crushed that finally provoked the uprising. The threats ranged from the disarming of the Nama to the elimination of their chiefs and the dismantling of their tribal system.

[17] ZStA, RKolA, no. 2135, pp. 14—15, Tecklenburg to the Colonial Department, 3 Jan. 1905.

After Hendrik Witbooi had decided to lead his people into battle, he urged the other chiefs in Namaland to join in the rebellion. The Franzmann community under Simon Kopper, the so-called Red Nation under Manasse Noreseb and the Veldschoendragers under Hans Hendrik all responded to the call. But, under the influence of the Mission, Christian Goliath, chief of the Berseba community, Paul Frederiks, chief of the Bethanie people, and the Keetmanshoop tribe all refused to take part. The greater part of the Bethanie people, however, in open defiance of their chief, participated in the uprising under Cornelius. The Rehobothers (the so-called Basters) preferred to stay on the German side, Witbooi's appeal notwithstanding. The Zwartboois and Topnaars, who lived in the district of Outjo outside Namaland, and the Bondelzwarts in Warmbad were taken prisoner by the Germans in a *coup de main* before they were able to join in the rebellion.

The Witboois were the most populous of the Nama tribes and at the outset of the insurrection they numbered between 800 and 900 warriors, about one-third of them armed with rifles. The Franzmann community provided another 120 men, the Veldschoendragers 150 to 200, and the so-called Red Nation approximately 190.

About 40 settlers were killed in the uprising but the majority of the Germans in Namaland took refuge in fortified places which, with the exception of Nomtsas, withstood the onslaught of the Nama. The aim of the rebellion was to expel the Germans, not to kill them.

When he received news of the uprising General von Trotha called for reinforcements of 4,000 men and demanded that a railway be built from Lüderitz Bay to Kubub to safeguard supplies in the south. In the first few months of military operations in Namaland, the German troops scored two limited successes. In a surprise raid on the Veldschoendragers near Koes they annihilated part of that tribe. They also managed to dislodge Hendrik Witbooi from his settlement at Rietmond, the Witboois losing virtually all their possessions, notably their cattle.

As it turned out, Witbooi's expulsion from Rietmond resembled a Pyrrhic victory since it led to the adoption of guerrilla methods by the Nama. As a result, a major European power, with about 15,000 soldiers in South West Africa, was involved for two years in a war of attrition against what were initially 1,000 to 2,000 and later no more than a few hundred African guerrillas, unable to find an answer to this method of warfare.

The Nama and the Herero differed radically in their style of combat. While the Herero, hoping that their numerical strength would make up for their inferior weapons, met the Germans for a decisive battle at the

Waterberg, the Nama, aware that they were badly outnumbered, had no intention of allowing the Germans to force a showdown whose outcome would be a foregone conclusion. Instead they opted for the guerrilla tactics in which they excelled. They would appear all of a sudden, snipe at German patrols or raid German supply convoys, and then vanish into thin air. German casualty figures soon increased rapidly. Apart from Hendrik Witbooi, Morenga and Cornelius were past masters at guerrilla warfare.

However, in late 1905 the Witboois suffered an irreparable loss. When they staged a raid on a German supply convoy near Fahlgras on 29 October 1905, Hendrik Witbooi sustained a wound which soon proved fatal because no medical aid was available. Witbooi had been one of the most notable personalities in South West Africa. His intellectual ability and his qualities as a leader had made him the undisputed head of the Nama people. He had reversed his misguided policy of collaboration with the Germans by leading his people into battle and atoned for it through his death. He lives on in the memory of the people of Namibia as a popular hero who laid down his life in the struggle against German imperialism.

The Paramount Chief's death had a demoralizing effect on the Witboois, and a few months later they surrendered to the Germans. Their withdrawal from the common front of the Nama meant that the German colonial regime had gained its first major success. While the ranks of their adversaries had thinned considerably, the German troops were, however, still facing Nama formations led by Simon Kopper, Cornelius, Morenga, Morris, and Johannes Christian.

It is impossible here to give a detailed account of the 200-odd engagements between Nama and German forces. After the Bondelzwarts ceased fighting in late 1906 the Germans faced only 100 to 150 men led by Simon Kopper, chief of the Franzmann community, as well as a number of tiny Nama units without any military significance.

In February 1907 the commander of the German forces told the General Staff that he had no objections to lifting the state of war in South West Africa at the end of March. The military wanted to have the war officially declared over, even before the end of the fighting with Simon Kopper's guerrillas, because the long-drawn-out conflict was increasingly eroding the prestige of the German armed forces and because the economy of the colony, virtually at a standstill since the outbreak of the Herero uprising, urgently needed the end of military restrictions. Therefore the state of war was lifted "by order of His Majesty" on 31 March 1907. This did not, however, signal the end of hostilities. Morenga and Simon Kopper continued the struggle against German imperialism.

Jakob Morenga was shot dead by British police on the Cape Colony border on 20 September 1907. As for Simon Kopper, it was not until February 1909 that he agreed to cease hostilities against the Germans in South West Africa. Under the terms of the deal, which was arranged by the British Bechuanaland police, Kopper was granted an annuity. Through this agreement the German Government at last accomplished what it had been seeking for five years: an end of the fighting in the colony. But it owed this fact not to military successes, but to the diplomatic skill of the British authorities.

The losses which the South West African population suffered between 1904 and 1907 under the German policy of annihilation are indicated by the official census taken in 1911. It shows that in 1911 there were a mere 15,130 Herero left out of an original 80,000 and 9,781 Nama out of an original 20,000.[18] More than 80 per cent of the Herero and c. 50 per cent of the Nama had thus fallen victim to German colonial rule. The figure includes approximately 7,700 Herero and Nama prisoners of war who perished (according to official sources) in the humid and chilly camps set up on an offshore island. In addition, one-third of the Damara, who had not joined in the uprising, were killed simply because the German soldiers were unable to tell them from the Herero. Such was the staggering human cost of a quarter century of German colonial rule in South West Africa.

The genocide was compounded by robbery. The uprisings had offered the German imperialists a welcome pretext for a military conquest of the territory that would settle the land issue once and for all in their favour. Under the "Imperial Decree of 26 December 1905 Pertaining to the Sequestration of Property of Natives in the Protectorate of South West Africa", all of Hereroland and, a little later, Namaland were declared Crown territory. The whole of Hereroland and Namaland, with the exception only of the territory of the Berseba community, had thus passed into the possession of the German colonial rulers.

2. Cameroon 1885—1906

For a decade after the Cameroon coast had been declared a German "protectorate", foreign rule remained confined to the coastal area. In accordance with their instructions, the first two governors, Julius von

---

[18] *Report on the Natives of South West Africa* and their Treatment by Germany, London 1918, p. 35. The results of the census, contained in captured files of the German colonial administration, have been published only in this study.

Soden (1885—91) and Eugen von Zimmerer (1891—5), contented themselves with safeguarding the interests of two Hamburg-based commercial
firms; C. Woermann and Jantzen & Thormählen, at whose request the
territory had been annexed.

From the outset, these two firms had succeeded in obtaining the kind
of administration which suited their own ains. Bismarck, it will be re-
called, had rejected the idea of the new colonies being directly administered by the German Empire. What he had in mind was a system of government which would place no burden on the national budget and would offer
the opposition in the Reichstag few targets for attack. He felt that the
administrative machinery should be run and financed by the businessmen who were active in the colonies. But at the urging of Adolf Woermann an Imperial Commissioner remained in the protectorate after the
annexation as the representative of the Reich Government, and a colonial
administration with a governor at its head was established the following
year. Like other German merchants, Woermann flatly refused to make
any contribution towards the costs involved. This did not mean, of
course, that these businessmen gave up influencing the policy of the
colonial authorities. On the contrary: Woermann in particular, as Reichstag deputy for the National Liberal Party, was highly successful in further-
ing his own ends as a member of the Colonial Counil set up in 1890. Up
to the end of the century the colonial administration, which sent out
armed contingents to open up the interior of the country, pursued policies
entirely in line with the interests of the German commercial firms operating there. Among these, Woermann's ever-expanding company retained
its dominant position.

Until the mid-1890s it remained the administration's principal aim
to do away with the Duala people's monopoly of the inland trade, which
barred direct access to the markets and raw materials in the interior for
European traders, although the Duala chiefs had been given written
assurances that this monopoly would be respected. For the time being,
however, the administration did not have the troops necessary to open up
routes into the country by force. In fact, the power of Governor von
Soden did not reach much further than the guns of the warships which he
called in whenever there were signs of resistance among the coastal population, notably in the Abo and Wuri areas. As a result, the activities of
the commercial firms were restricted to a narrow coastal strip until the
end of 1892.

Woermann and Thormählen, who where thoroughly dissatisfied with
this state of affairs, called on the Foreign Office as early as 1885 to send
expeditions inland to establish German "claims" and break up the net-

work of indigenous middlemen. During the following years the government tried to comply with their wishes. A first expedition into the interior of south west Cameroon, undertaken in 1887, proved abortive in the face of the resistance shown by the Bakoko people. The next effort led to the establishment in 1889 of a jungle station at Yaoundé (in German: Jaunde) some 200 kilometres east of Douala. But the interior of the country remained inaccessible to German traders because the coastal peoples kept up their stubborn resistance. Therefore, the German firms urged the creation of a regular mercenary force to enforce and safeguard access to inland markets. This demand was supported in 1891 by the Deputy Governor, Karl Theodor Heinrich Leist, who pointed out that "experiences here have shown that without a protective force it will not even be possible to maintain authority in the immediate vicinity of the Governor's residence."[19]

When an uprising broke out in the Abo area in June 1891, the Imperial Government decided to grant the merchants' request. Captain von Gravenreuth bought 370 slaves, male and female, in Dahomey and formed a "police force" for the Colonial Administration from among their number. With the aid of this force a colonial official named Wehlan managed in 1892—3 to subjugate the Bakoko and the Mabea through several military operations conducted with ferocious cruelty, thus making the first major inroads into the hinterland of south west Cameroon. Wehlan, who had the rank of a Gerichtsassessor or junior barrister, ordered many villages to be burnt down, women, children and old people to be killed, and captives to be tortured to death in the most appalling fashion. According to a German engineer, a number of men who had been taken prisoner were "cut up with knives, hacked to pieces and mutilated because Assessor Wehlan had given orders not to use rifles to kill."[20] His men chopped off the heads of their fallen opponents to keep them as "souvenirs". In this fashion they succeeded in throwing major parts of south west Cameroon open to German trade.

Leist, who acted as Governor for a prolonged period while Zimmerer was on leave, turned out to be even more sadistic than his subordinate. When a tense situation arose in the "police force" in late 1893 because

[19] Report by Leist to the Colonial Department, 1 May 1891. Quoted from *R. Kaeselitz*, Kolonialeroberung und Widerstandskampf in Südkamerun (1884—1907), in: Kamerun unter deutscher Kolonialherrschaft. Studien, ed. by H. Stoecker, vol. 2, Berlin 1968, p. 20.

[20] Quoted from *A. Rüger*, Der Aufstand der Polizeisoldaten (Dec. 1893), in: op. cit., vol. 1, Berlin 1960, p. 144.

most of the men went without pay and none of them received sufficient food, he turned a deaf ear to all their complaints. The soldiers' wives, for the most part former slaves or "war booty", were forced to perform unpaid labour for the colonial authorities and flogged if they tried to escape this obligation. Abusing his high office, Leist compelled at least six of these women to have sexual intercourse with him. When on 15 December 1893 he ordered between 20 and 25 women to be stripped and administered 10 to 15 lashes with a hippopotamus hide whip in front of their husbands, this was too much even for these long-suffering men-at-arms. Before the end of the day they made an attempt to kill Leist and expel the Germans from Cameroon. Although the Duala chiefs refused to support the uprising because of their economic dependence on German firms, the small contingent, reinforced by some 100 Duala, managed to drive out all colonial officials, compelling them to seek refuge on some ships lying at anchor off the capital, and kept the Governor's residence occupied for a week or so. It was not until the arrival of a company of marines, dispatched on the orders of Wilhelm II, that German rule was fully restored. With the exception of 15 insurgents, who remained at large until March 1894, all captured members of the police force were summarily executed.

In Germany, the news about the uprising provoked a wave of indignation at the ruthless methods employed in running the colonies. Although Chancellor Leo von Caprivi and the head of the Colonial Department in the Foreign Office, Dr Paul Kayser, sought to vindicate Leist's behaviour, the government had no choice in the end but to take disciplinary action against Leist and Wehlan. The Social Democratic Party under August Bebel was unrelenting in its denunciation of such practices and used this and other colonial scandals to pillory colonialism in every form. The outcome of the disciplinary proceedings was that Leist was dismissed from government service in 1895 and that Wehlan was transferred to another post and fined 500 marks (£ 25 at the current rate of exchange) in the following year.

During the 1890s the administration finally succeeded in wresting the monopoly of access to the inland trade from the Duala and in depriving this formerly influential people of its power. German traders and commercial agents began to replace the Duala, but bloody campaigns by the small German mercenary force were necessary before they could penetrate the interior of the country. Under Governor Jesco von Puttkamer (1895—1906), the son of an ultra-reactionary Prussian Minister of the Interior of the 1880s and a nephew of Bismarck's, the inland parts of the colony were conquered step by step by a new military unit called a "protective force", set up in 1894. Made up of mercenaries recruited elsewhere in Africa, it soon comprised 200 men. For four years this force waged a fierce struggle against the Bakoko, Yaoundé, Bane, Bulu and other tribes before it become reasonably safe for German caravans to travel from Kribi, a locality on the south coast, to Yaoundé.

Since the commander of the force, Captain von Kamptz, believed that the traders operating in south west Cameroon were now safe, he embarked in late 1898 on a campaign to conquer Adamawa. Taking advantage of the fact that the bulk of the "protective force" had moved northward, the Bulu then began to step up their resistance to the expeditions and raids of European commercial agents. In September 1899 they attacked Kribi, which had become the centre of German trade on the southern coast of Cameroon, and put the government officials posted there to flight. The colonial force sustained heavy losses before it managed to split the insurgent Bulu and force one chief after another to accept peace treaties obliging them to provide slave labour and deliver stated amounts of ivory and rubber. Not until the spring of 1901 was the last stronghold of Bulu resistance destroyed. The Bulu insurrection marked a culminating point of resistance in south west Cameroon, bringing together several tribes against the invader. Armed with bows and arrows, with spears and flintlocks, the Bulu skilfully exploited the advantages which the jungle afforded them, but in the end they succumbed to the mercenaries who were equipped with modern weapons.

Under the protection of the military posts established in south west Cameroon in the closing years of the 19th century, the Germans traders and their agents penetrated deeper and deeper inland. Caravans moved through the country in large numbers in order to foist inferior or vastly overvalued European products on the village population in exchange for rubber, or to secure the rubber by sheer force.

The trading firms operating from Kribi began in 1900 to push towards south east Cameroon, an area rich in rubber and ivory. The Imperial Government and some German financiers, however, preferred to have the area plundered by copying the Belgian and French policy of awarding concessions, and agreed that a single concession should be granted for the whole region. Since it was much easier to get there via the Congo than from the Cameroon coast, and Belgian firms were already active in the region, the founders of the Gesellschaft Südkamerun (the concession company established in late 1898) were compelled to concede a considerable share of the capital stock to Belgian colonial monopolists.

The government granted this large and highly speculative monopolistic enterprise extensive rights in the south east, and immediately afterwards the Colonial Administration set itself the task of conquering this remote part of the country and opening it up to exploitation by the company. In 1899 a small mercenary force set up the police station of Sangha-Ngoko from where the vast tropical forests of southeast Cameroon were explored by 1903 and partly brought under control through demonstrations of military strength or expeditions which destroyed "unruly" villages. More often than not the troops were accompanied by employees of the Gesellschaft Südkamerun. The expansion of German colonial power here was synonymous with the expansion of the company's trade. The very influential chief of Bertous, who insisted on selling his goods to French traders, was simply deposed by the commander of the German troops after bloody fighting.

Like the south east, the extensive territories of north and north east Cameroon were "awarded" to the German Empire under treaties with other colonial powers before they had been conquered or, in parts, even explored. The northermost part of these territories (which covered the bulk of the Emirate of Adamawa and a minor part of the Sultanate of Bornu), however, was among those inland areas of Africa which had been extensively described by European explorers before 1880. When the demand for colonies was raised in Germany, one of the arguments invoked to justify claims to these regions was the journeys of exploration undertaken by Heinrich Barth, Eduard Vogel, Gerhard Rohlfs and Gustav Nachtigal. In particular Nachtigal's accounts of Bornu were well known. The explorer Eduard Flegel, who had reached the sources of the Benue River in 1882—3 during an expedition sponsored by the Deutsche Afrikanische Gesellschaft, set out on a journey to Adamawa in 1885, this time under the auspices of the Deutscher Kolonialverein. His mission was to set up "scientific and commercial stations" as starting points for the penetration and ultimate conquest of the Emirate. On Bismarck's instructions Flegel was empowered to "conclude treaties between the Reich and independent rulers in western Sudan" with a view to "opening up the Benue region and the hinterland of Cameroon to German trade."[21] These treaties were intended to prevent the territories in question from falling into the hands of other powers. Flegel's expedition proved a failure, however, because of the resistance offered by the National African Company, a government-supported British firm which was dominant on the Niger and Benue. Compelled by a changed international situation to improve relations with Britain, in 1886 Bismarck

---

[21] German Foreign Office to Flegel, 15 Feb. 1885. Quoted from *H. Stoecker, E. and H. Mehls*, Die Eroberung des Nordostens, in: op. cit., vol. 2, p. 60.

recognized the British "claim" to the Benue area up to a point some 50 kilometres east of Yola.

Further attempts to gain a foothold in Adamawa in order to prevent the British and French from cutting off the coastal jungle area of Cameroon from the grassland region in the interior remained equally unsuccessful, at least for the time being. A 370-strong expedition headed by the explorer Eugen Zintgraff, an employee of the Colonial Administration, suffered a disastrous defeat in Bandeng territory in 1891 and was forced to beat a hasty retreat. Finally a government-backed expedition sponsored by the Deutsche Kolonialgesellschaft and led by Lieutenant Edgar von Uechtritz and the geographer Siegfried Passarge met with limited success in 1893—4. Faced with French attempts to establish a presence in Adamawa, the British company helped the expedition to reach Garoua via the Niger and Benue Rivers. From Garoua it pressed on towards Bubandjidda, where it inflicted a severe defeat on the force of the Lamido, the local ruler. After the towns of Djurum and Assali had been sacked and set on fire, Uechtritz induced several rulers to sign "friendship treaties" which were meant to substantiate German "rights" in negotiations with other colonial powers. The Lamido of Ngaoundéré even signed a protection agreement.

On 15 November 1893 the British and German governments had concluded an agreement under the terms of which the border between Nigeria and Cameroon was extended from the Yola area to Lake Chad.[22] By recognizing far-reaching German "claims" the British hoped to strike a blow against the French, their main adversaries in Africa. On 15 March 1894, however, Germany and France signed a treaty on the eastern boundary of Cameroon which dashed these hopes by surrendering the bulk of the territory in question to the French, thereby enabling them to approach the Nile from the west. The protests of the DKG and the Alldeutscher Verband against the treaty were of no avail.

In deciding on these boundaries the three powers paid no attention whatsoever to ethnic, political or geographical considerations. The sole

---

[22] The satirical Social Democratic weakly "Der wahre Jacob" (No. 194, 1894) published a "Chat between two Berlin workers" on this treaty:

"Duseke: You got to admit that the English are generous. It says here in the paper that they've given us the whole southern shore of Lake Chad.

Puseke: Did that belong to England?

Duseke: No, to Africa.

Puseke: Well, mate, to show you how generous I am I'll give you all the houses south of Dönhoff Square as a Christmas present."

factor of any consequence was the relation of the three powers to one another. So Adamawa was divided into three parts, the largest being allotted to Germany, which also received a small portion of Bornu, thereby gaining access to Lake Chad.

However, the German authorities were not able for the time being to occupy the territories thus "acquired". It was not until the resistance of the population in the rain forest zone had been crushed that the Fulbe states of Adamawa were subjugated, the smaller ethnic groups independent of the Fulbe subsequently sharing their fate one by one. The leaders of the Deutsche Kolonialgesellschaft, to whom Woermann belonged, had pressed for occupation because they feared that unless the north east was brought under effective control the British and French would question the German "claim" and take over the trade in the area. Since the society felt that the Colonial Department of the Foreign Office and the administration in Cameroon were proceeding too slowly, it began to mount a propaganda drive for the establishment of a military station at Garoua.

The cautious approach was not to the liking of the more aggressive imperialists. In 1900, and even more so in 1901 when the French and British had reached Lake Chad, the DKG attacked the Colonial Department. In order to secure the military occupation of Adamawa and Bornu, it used every possible means of influencing public opinion such as placing articles in the bourgeois press and addressing letters to government departments.

The organization's stand on this issue must be seen in the context of the colonialist chauvinistic euphoria which had seized the ruling classes in Germany after the occupation of Kiaochow in late 1897. In the years of the Samoa crisis and the intervention in China when the process of carving up the colonial world came to an end and the struggle for its redivision began, the chauvinistic procolonial lobby claimed that every pre-emptive move, however insignificant, to annex or secure colonial territories was nothing short of vital to Germany. It made the same claims in this case although there could be no question of "German interests" in the north east of Cameroon.

While the DKG was urging a military thrust towards Garoua, German mercenary units had already invaded southern Adamawa. The conquest of the important Fulbe state of Tibati was launched at the beginning of 1899. Since its ruler refused to recognize German suzerainty, he was seized and bundled off to the coast where he died a few months later. His pro-German cousin was named to succeed him by the Governor, but within a year the Fulbe in Tibati rose in rebellion against this tool of the colonial power. In the course of the fighting the principality was devastated and lost its economic and political importance. Hostilities did not cease until the spring of 1901 by which time the administration had reached agreement with the Emir of Yola, Tibati's overlord, on the installation of another successor who also accepted German suzerainty. In August 1901 Tibati was used as a base for the conquest of the neighbouring state of Ngaoundéré whose capital was taken by a mercenary force. Since the ruler had been shot dead by one of the mercenaries, the German commander was able, partly by bribing individual dignitaries, to engineer the election as Lamido of a prince who had already signed a protection treaty.

In southern Adamawa the unequal struggle was decided a few months later (on 19 November), by the battle near Garoua in which a well-equipped German mercenary force consisting of five Europeans and 117 African soldiers defeated several thousand armoured horsemen and spearmen of the Emir of Yola. The outcome of the engagement, which left 300 of the Emir's troops dead on the battlefield, prompted many lesser princes to submit to the Germans and sign protection treaties in order to retain their position. The Emir, however, kept up his resistance. Forced out of Yola by the British, he assembled a new force of warriors (mostly armoured horsemen with lances), supplied by the princes owing him allegiance, in the northern principality of Maroua, the most powerful in Adamawa Yet on 20 January 1902 this force, too, was defeated in battle, with the loss of over 500 lives, by a small and well-drilled contingent armed with modern weapons and commanded by Lieutenant Hans Dominik, who gave orders after the engagement to slaughter the wounded left behind by the other side and to sack the town of Maroua.

The defeat suffered by the Fulbe at Maroua settled the fate of northern Adamawa. There too most of the rulers surrendered whereas the non-Mohammedan tribes which had not been subjugated by the Fulbe continued to defend their freedom (some of them were to do so successfully until the very end of German rule). The area south of Lake Chad was brought into subjugation later that year by a major expedition which had previously devastated the lands of the Bangwa, Bandeng and Bafut north of Douala by fire and sword and had subdued the Fulbe state of Banyo. This expedition, led by Lt.-Col. von Pavel, the commander of the "protective force", was in the nature of a predatory campaign. Villages which refused to satisfy Pavel's demands for provisions and ivory were pillaged, and the ivory thus captured was distributed among German officers and NCOs.

In the conquered territories, insufficiently docile rulers were deposed,

and dignitaries loyal to the fugitive Emir were executed. They were replaced by tools of the colonial power, subject to the orders of officers
appointed as "residents". Dominik later gave an account of how these
petty princes were made. He had ordered Djagara of Gulfei to be put in
jail to give him a taste of German power. Because of French complaints
Djagara was then questioned closely in the presence of two French officers. "It was brought home to him that we wanted to live on good-neigh-
bourly terms with the French and that any infringement would be severely
punished by Bülow to whom he would have to report in Dikoa every
other month. Incidentally, it was as Sultan that Djagara proudly rode
out of Kusseri at noon whereas he had arrived there as Kalifa (deputy).
The German Government could well be pleased to have such a vigorous
and intelligent Sultan showing a marked antipathy against the French."[23]
The rulers installed in such a fashion were to remain pillars of the German
colonial regime until the First World War.

The exercise of authority through residents in the vast areas of north
east Cameroon was modelled on British practice in India and in neighbouring northern Nigeria. It presupposed the existence of relatively
stable states which could be governed indirectly without much open
interference in their internal affairs. Residencies were far less costly to
the colonial power than a system of direct administration. The Colonial
Department of the German Foreign Office hoped in this way to establish
political control over the raw materials and manpower resources in the
north east while keeping expenditure in terms of costs, soldiers and material at a minimum.

A commercial expedition carried out in 1902—3 showed that the
north eastern part of Cameroon contained no mineral or vegetable
resources and therefore offered no prospect of a lucrative trade. The
cultivation of export crops required investments which no one was
prepared to make. As a result, exploitation by German capitalists made
little headway in that vast section of the colony. At the same time, the
decline of inland African trade caused by the blocking of traditional
routes to northern and central Africa led to the impoverishment of large
parts of the population.

German direct trading, coming in the wake of the raids by the "protective force", had begun to reach the hinterland in 1895—6. The "protective force" and the administration acted as trail-blazers: military
and administrative stations set up by raiding expeditions served as bases
of operations for German firms. The local African middlemen, pre-

[23] H. Dominik, Vom Atlantik zum Tschadsee, Berlin 1908, p. 184.

viously tolerated as a necessary evil, were now eliminated step by step so that trading profits would accrue solely to German traders.

From the second half of the 1890s the expansion of direct trading resulted in German commercial enterprises establishing themselves on the south and north west coasts and rapidly embarking on the pillage of the forest resources. The largest among them was the Deutsch-West-afrikanische Handelsgesellschaft, a company closely associated with the Dresdner Bank and active in several West African colonies. Founded in 1896 with a capital stock of 750,000 marks, it netted 1,350,000 marks in profits during its first few years of participation in the Cameroon trade. This competition does not seem to have harmed Woermann's activities, for his company underwent a considerable boom as the colony grew in size. In 1905 his firm maintained over 30 trading posts in Cameroon, and the Woermann-Linie, which operated a regular service between Hamburg and South West Africa, owned 36 steamships totalling 75,000 gross tons. Woermann, who had close links with the Disconto-Gesell-schaft, also had a sizeable share in plantations and in the Gesellschaft Südkamerun. His strong economic position enabled him to continue exerting considerable influence on the policies of the Colonial Depart-ment and the Cameroon Administration.

At the turn of the century, when wide stretches of inland territory were conquered, Cameroon's foreign trade experienced a substantial increase. Between 1891 (the first year for which foreign trade statistics are available) and 1906, exports rose from 4,307,000 marks to 9,946,000 marks while imports went up from 4,547,000 marks to 13,305,000 marks. During most years between 1896 and 1905 Cameroon ranked first among the German colonies in terms of exports, which consisted almost exclusively of rubber, palm kernels, palm oil, cocoa and ivory. Rubber was the most important item as can be seen from the fact that in 1906 the value of rubber exports exceeded that of all other goods put together. Exports of palm kernels and palm oil, used in Germany to make soap, candles and lubricating oils, were worth 2,958,000 marks in 1906, while exports of cocoa, grown on plantations from the mid-1890s, were valued at 1,167,000 marks. The amount of ivory shipped abroad increased rapidly up to 1905 but then declined abruptly because elephants had been hunted to extinction in large parts of the country.

On the import side, spirits headed the list at first, whereas in later years it was usually fabrics, followed by textiles of all kinds, silver coins, ironmongery, rice (to feed the plantation workers) and tobacco. Up to the end of the 1890s German commercial firms obtained Cameroonian products mainly in exchange for low-quality spirits made from potatoes, with imports reaching 20,000 hectolitres or 1,235,000 marks in 1898. Woermann, who was mainly responsible for encouraging alcoholism among the Cameroonians, replied to repeated criticism from Protestant missionaries by telling the Reichstag in 1889 that his steamship service to West Africa would not pay without the transportation of liquor. From the turn of the century two-thirds or more of the goods imported were of German origin, the rest mostly came from Britain.

The expansion of colonial trade to one area after another within Cameroon and its increasing volume inevitably affected socio-economic conditions, especially in the more accessible, directly ruled areas. Indigenous craft production declined as a result of European competition and administrative measures. Subsistence farming suffered enormously because a very large proportion of able-bodied men and women were constantly being pressed into service as porters in forest areas. In places it came to a complete standstill, which forced the remaining population to move elsewhere in search of a living. This marked the beginning of a decline in population and of pauperization particularly in Cameroon's jungle zone under German rule prior to 1914.

The establishment of large plantations in the coastal region had begun just before the turn of the century. Initially, it had been the colonial officials in Cameroon and in Berlin who had suggested setting up such estates on a major scale, referring to the favourable natural conditions and the success of the smaller plantations already existing. However, it was the proposals and expert opinions submitted by the explorer Eugen Zintgraff and the agricultural expert Ferdinand Wohltmann that prompted the founding of three major plantation companies which in the following years became three of the largest in Africa.

In January 1897 the Westafrikanische Pflanzungsgesellschaft Victoria was founded, the largest such company in Cameroon, with a capital of 2.5 million marks. By 1904 it owned 20,000 hectares of plantations acquired from the colonial authorities at very low cost while about 16,000 hectares were in the hands of various subsidiary companies.

This example was soon followed by others attracted by the prospect of high profits resulting from the exploitation of very cheap labour and a favourable cost-benefit ratio as well as high founders' gains. The Westafrikanische Pflanzungsgesellschaft Bibundi was founded before the end of 1897. It had a share capital of 1.5 million marks and 6,000 hectares of plantations, but subsequently expanded its acreage very considerably. Finally, the Molive-Pflanzungsgesellschaft was set up in 1899 with the participation of leading shareholders of the Kamerun-Land-und-Plantagen-Gesellschaft (which Woermann had founded back in

1885) and of the two companies just mentioned. Initially, their share capital amounted to one million marks and their landed property to 14,000 hectares.

A certain nexus of interests existed from the first between the Kamerun-Land-und-Plantagengesellschaft, the Victoria and the Bibundi because some major shareholders were involved in two or all of these companies, but the founding of the Molive-Pflanzungsgesellschaft by leading shareholders of the other companies represented a kind of merger of plantation interests. The key figures of this monopolistic group were Woermann, Thormählen, the potash magnate Wilhelm Oechelhäuser, the mine owner and colonial speculator Sholto Douglas, the landowner Prince Alfred zu Löwenstein, the colonial speculators Julius Scharlach and Max Esser, and Hermann and Viktor Hoesch of a well-known family of industrialists. Roughly half the capital of the most important company, the Victoria, was in the hands of five Rhenish families of industrialists — Esser, Hoesch, Schoeller, Hiller and Peill — who were closely connected with the A. Schaaffhausenscher Bankverein, as was the company itself. The capital of the group, concentrated in a few hands, dominated plantation economy and represented a power factor of the first order in the colony. Governor von Puttkamer, an early advocate of the plantation system, gave these companies full support.

Since the best results were achieved on the slopes of Mount Cameroon in proximity to the coast, up to 1905 most plantations were started in this area. During the first decade the principal crop was cocoa and the colony became its main producer within the German colonial empire. In 1907, cocoa was grown on an area of 7,673 hectares in Cameroon whereas Samoa, New Guinea, Togo and German East Africa altogether only accounted for 1,937 hectares. The relatively undeveloped German colonies were not yet in a position to meet the demands of the metropolitan power, but a systematic effort was made to expand cocoa production so as to become less and less dependent on imports from other countries.

The introduction of large-scale agricultural production by German plantation companies had far-reaching consequences for the indigenous population, primarily in western Cameroon, for it required dispossessing the local inhabitants of their land and the employment of agricultural labour. From the outset, the plantation workers consisted largely of men who had been forcibly recruited in a variety of ways. There was a shortage of manpower because the meagre wages doomed the workers to a life below the individual subsistence level, resulting in a very high mortality rate. The Deputy Governor A. Köhler gave this account of the situation in 1900: "These people lead a wretched existence. They are poorly paid, and partly in the form of worthless goods at that. Their diet is unsuitable and they are ill-housed and treated in the most savage fashion. This is how matters are on average. So you will no longer find anyone who is willing to work on the plantations."[24]

As has already been mentioned, some speculators with ample means regarded the conquest of the southeast as an opportunity to make handsome founding and other profits. The government had long been out to channel more capital into the colonies in order to make them into more productive sources of raw materials. It was prepared, therefore, to hand over vast undeveloped areas to interested financiers while asking for almost nothing in return. In November 1898 the Colonial Department of the Foreign Office granted the well-known colonial speculators Scharlach and Douglas a concession under the terms of which the Gesellschaft Südkamerun acquired possession of the "Crown territory" to be established shortly throughout the southeast, in other words the land not currently cultivated by the local population, and was given an option on the "land of the natives". The company was thus awarded a title to one-fifth of Cameroon's territory (81,597 square kilometres) in exchange for an obligation to give the government a 10 per cent share in the profits. Its founders included, apart from Scharlach and Douglas who pocketed 2 million marks each in foundation profits, Woermann, the bankers Schinckel (Norddeutsche Bank) and Hinrichsen (Hardy & Hinrichsen), the banker and industrialist Esser (A. Schaaffhausenscher Bankverein) and four leading Belgian monopolists active in the Congo. Half of the capital stock, which totalled 2 million marks, came from the Belgians and 750,000 marks from the Disconto-Gesellschaft and its nominally independent subsidiary Norddeutsche Bank as well as Woermann and Schinckel personally. So the Disconto-Gesellschaft was the firm's mainstay on the German side.

Although the Gesellschaft Südkamerun had considerable resources at its command, its leading figures had no intention whatsoever of developing the 8 million hectares handed over to them on a major scale. In fact, the purpose of the venture, which was modelled on the Belgian Congo companies in terms of structure and methods, was quick enrichment by stock exchange speculation and ruthless exploitation. The same can be said of the Gesellschaft Nordwest-Kamerun, founded the following year, which was awarded a similar concession for an area of about 80,000 square kilometres between the Sanaga and Nigeria. The

---

[24] ZStA, RKolA, no. 3227, pp. 51ff, Report by Köhler to the Colonial Department, 1 June 1900.

initial capital amounted to 4 million marks, of which Prince Christian Kraft zu Hohenlohe-Öhringen contributed 2 million and his two business partners Schoeller and Hiller 1 million each.

In order to enable the newly formed companies to take possession of "their" territory, the colonial authorities sent out military expeditions to subdue the local population. Following the troops were company agents who embarked immediately on the plunder of the region's natural resources. Both companies, writes A. Rüger, refused to "recognize the people living there as the owners of the products obtained by their own labour. They said that the Cameroonians were not entitled to sell anything belonging to the companies. Consequently, they had no right to claim payment for the goods but should be satisfied with the small wages they received for the work they performed. Since the concessionnaires also declared that they were the only ones allowed to carry on 'trade' in those areas, the commercial firms inevitably took a stand against them, demanding that the concession system should be abolished or reformed. This competition grew in fierceness as a result of the rubber boom."[25]

The companies which had been granted concessions "confined themselves to appropriating whatever natural resources were within easy reach. As soon as the riches of one part of the country were depleted, they turned to another part. Therefore, the commission which had been charged with investigating the South West African and Cameroonian companies on the demand of the parliamentary opposition in Germany was unable to avoid the conclusion that the companies had feathered their nest but made no contribution to the development of Cameroon."[26] The rapacious practices of the companies were also a major factor in provoking the uprisings which occurred in the south and northwest of Cameroon in 1904—5.

Criticism from various quarters (Erzberger, Alldeutscher Verband, etc.) finally led the government to revise the concessions. As a result, the Gesellschaft Südkamerun in 1905—6 was granted full ownership of 1.55 million hectares of tropical forest, roughly one - fifth of the area originally allotted to it, in which it could maintain a monopoly. The population living in the company's territory was left nothing but some reservations. The Gesellschaft Nordwest-Kamerun, for its part, failed to secure possession of any territory, but retained the monopoly which Governor von Puttkamer had granted them concerning the exploitation

[25] *A. Rüger*, Die Entstehung und Lage der Arbeiterklasse unter dem deutschen Kolonialregime in Kamerun (1895—1905), in: Kamerun . . ., vol. 1, p. 172.

[26] Ibid., pp. 172—173.

of the "no man's land" in the westernmost part of the territory awarded to them in 1899 (over 1 million hectares).

The trading activities of the Gesellschaft Südkamerun began to increase rapidly in 1903, when the exploration of the southeastern district had been largely completed. At the same time, the coastal firms started penetrating into its area from the west. They all had but one desire: to squeeze rubber and other raw materials out of Cameroon as quickly and cheaply as possible so that it could be shipped to Germany and the rest of Europe. Old flintlock rifles and powder were the principal items given to the inhabitants of south Cameroon in exchange for rubber, ivory and further local products. Other articles traded were salt, sheath knives, matches, iron, brass and copper wire, small knives and scissors, glass beads, mirrors and coloured cloth. The German firms charged exorbitant prices for European goods. The Gesellschaft Südkamerun is known, for example, to have sold salt at a price ten times higher than usual in Germany. Such practices were the rule: goods worth 50 pfennigs (before 1914 equivalent to about 6 pence) were demanded in exchange for a box of matches. The profits made in such transactions amounted to between 500 and 1,000 per cent.

In 1906, when popular resistance in the southeast district had reached its climax, the district judge Lämmermann was sent into the area to investigate the "causes of the unrest". His report, which lays special emphasis on the trading methods used, reads in part: "Besides permanently engaged traders, Cameroonians and later also Europeans were hired to fit out caravans for commercial expeditions . . . The traders would display their merchandise in the villages of the rubber-growing area to put the local residents in a buying mood. But since the rubber had to be obtained first, the traders would move on to the next villages, always leaving articles behind, and recover their debts in the form of rubber on their way back . . .

"As a result, the porters, both men and women, were kept from tending their fields for too long . . . The provisions they carried and the articles to be bartered for food were hardly sufficient for the journey into the rubber country, much less for an excessively long stay there and the return journey. So the traders and porters had no choice but to secure food through robbery and theft or to obtain rubber very swiftly by felling trees and trading it for provisions. Most of the chiefs complained that the trade caravans were stealing food, leaving filth in their huts and raping the women. But the natives are helpless in the face of these unwelcome guests . . . White men, insisting on their master status, took the liberty of committing criminal offences. But in the eyes of many 'old colonials' such acts were not punishable."[27] The author of the report also noted that in this respect there was no difference between the representatives of the Gesellschaft Südkamerun and the agents of the coastal firms.

The practices of the traders were matched by those of the "Imperial Protective Force". Excesses were frequent, especially when troops were on patrol to ensure "security" in this or that area. Complaints about such episodes fill whole volumes in the records of the Imperial Colonial Office. Acts of brutality were committed not only by African soldiers or NCOs but also by German officers.

Not until the turn of the century was a well-ordered administrative apparatus brought into being. The administration of the colony, which in 1901 transferred its headquarters from the trading centre of Douala to Buea in the immediate vicinity of the large plantations, evolved into a strictly bureaucratic set-up which by 1904 was staffed by 29 German officials. While the local authorities in the coastal region were headed by civilian district commissioners, administrative functions in the interior were at first exercised by the heads of military stations and later by civilian station chiefs. District commissioners and station chiefs wielded absolute power in their respective areas. A fairly recent monograph on the administration has this to say on the role of the district commissioner: "He was free to issue administrative directives and impose duties on the population almost at his discretion. A generally valid regulation existed in Cameroon only with regard to the collection of taxes. The authoritarian nature of the district commissioner's rule over the coloured population was reinforced by the fact that all powers — legislative, executive and judicial — were concentrated in his hands." The administration of the colony demanded above all that the local authorities "ensure law and order within the district, augment the government's revenue and, in addition, meet the expectations of entrepreneurs."[28] All lower administrative bodies were concerned to enlist the support of the village elders and chiefs with a view to achieving their ends, e.g. the collection of taxes and the recruitment of manpower, etc.

[27] Report by district judge Lämmermann, 25 May 1906. Quoted from *R. Kaeselitz*, op. cit., pp. 37—38.

[28] *K. Hausen*, Deutsche Kolonialherrschaft in Afrika. Wirtschaftsinteressen und Kolonialverwaltung in Kamerun vor 1914, Zurich and Freiburg 1970, pp. 100 and 104.

Needless to say, military force remained a factor of decisive importance for the maintenance of German rule. The mercenary force, baptized "Imperial Protective Force" in 1895, comprised 40 German officers, 53 NCOs and 900 African mercenaries in 1900. Five years later the corresponding figures were 60, 70, and 1,150. Although the Governor was authorized to give instructions to the commander of the force, the senior officers were inclined to act independently. The repeated instances in which officers acted without authorization from the civilian authorities in the conquest of Cameroon's interior reflected the elevated status of the officers' corps within imperialist Germany, which was becoming the most aggressive and expansionist among the great powers. Dominik, Pavel and others counted on support in the highest echelons of the military hierarchy — with good reason as it turned out.

As the interior of the country was increasingly brought under German sway, several Protestant missionary societies and the Roman Catholic Pallottine Congregation redoubled their efforts to win adherents among the unconverted. The English Baptist Mission, active among the Duala from 1845, had been replaced in 1886 by the Protestant Basle Missionary Society, which was German in all but name, in the course of a "streamlining operation" of the German government. In the following two decades the Basle missionaries extended their influence among the Duala and neighbouring ethnic groups right into the grassland zone. In addition, German Baptists began to establish stations in 1891, and American Presbyterians did the same in the south from 1890. The Basle missionaries in particular often worked hand in hand with the administration, performing all manners of services as interpreters, go-betweens and informers. On the other hand, quarrels between the Basle missionaries and German traders and officials ensued whenever the latter's ruthless and inhuman practices (notably the confiscation of land in favour of the plantation companies) put specific interests of the mission at risk. The Pallottins, who had begun their activities at Edea southeast of Douala in 1890, were less inclined to friction with the authorities. On the whole, the work of the missions suited the intentions of the colonial regime. They all strove to turn the Cameroonians into docile servants willing to work. The government made a point of keeping the missionaries out of the Muslim areas because it did not want to complicate the situation of the local rulers collaborating with the German authorities.

As in East and South West Africa, major outbreaks of resistance and uprisings occurred in Cameroon between 1904 and 1907. Popular resistance against marauding traders and colonial troops reached its peak in the inland areas of the south and in the southeast. In the end, the

administration managed to crush all risings by sending out one punitive
expedition after another, burning down villages as a matter of routine
and massacring those resistance fighters taken prisoner, but the mercenary units suffered heavy losses, and several defeats were sustained. In
particular, the Ndsimu in the southeast offered bitter resistance; in
1904 the fact that the bulk of the "protective force" was temporarily
tied down in the northwestern part of the colony favoured their struggle.
Preparations for an uprising were at the same time under way in the district of Yaoundé. The mercenary forces operating in the southeast found
themselves in a difficult position in March 1905: part of their number
had been encircled by the Nyong-Maka and the rest was scattered and
too weak to conquer the main centres of the resistance. So the administration ordered a large-scale "southern expedition" to be undertaken,
whereby these centres, with the exception of the Maka territory, were
largely "pacified" though not completely subjugated in a savage campaign
which lasted until March 1907.

The absence of powerful tribal units and the frequently weak cohesion
between the tribes in southern Cameroon were to the advantage of the
colonial power in that a resistance movement operating on a major scale
and under a united leadership did not emerge. But at the same time, this
fragmentation represented a serious obstacle to the establishment of
a stable system of colonial rule. Once a tribe had been subjugated and the
"protective force" had moved on to wage war against another tribe,
the first, recently conquered tribe frequently managed to shake off the
control of the conquerors again. While the brave and costly resistance
offered by these tribes failed to avert defeat, which was historically inevitable, it delayed the extension of German rule within Cameroon quite
considerably.

An uprising in the northwest began in January 1904 with a successful
attack by the Anyang on a military expedition headed by the station chief
of Ossidinge and designed to open up new districts to the trading activities
of the Gesellschaft Nordwest-Kamerun. The death of the station chief
and the rout of the few surviving mercenaries set off a general uprising.
Within 18 days all trading posts of the company and the administrative
station in the Cross area had been destroyed, and all German and African
employees and troops killed or driven away. Tribes speaking different
languages (Anyang, Keaka, Banjang, Boki) united for a systematic
struggle with the aim of expelling the Germans once and for all and
ending years of colonial rule in the region. It took the greater part of the
"protective force" almost six months to "pacify" the Cross area although
the mercenaries were equipped with modern weapons and the insurgents

were armed only with muzzle-loaders. The campaign ended with the execution of the leaders of the uprising. Some of those who had taken part were hanged as late as 1910.

At the time of these uprisings trouble was also brewing among the Duala, who were becoming increasingly impoverished because the German authorities had forced them out of the trade with the inland peoples. In June 1905 the chiefs of the Akwa Duala addressed a petition to the Reichstag and the Imperial Government, demanding that "instructions be given to the German Administration here to end the harassment of our people and our King lest irregularities should occur." They emphatically called for the recall of Governor von Puttkamer and his judges and district commissioners and urged that "consuls be sent here instead of judicial officials", for these were turning "honest German government into an extortionate and deceitful form of government."[29] At the same time, they protested against the demolition of their houses, the obligation to perform unpaid forced labour, the iniquities of the judicial system with its harsh penalties and floggings, the violation of the rights guaranteed under the 1884 treaty, and other abuses. (As late as January 1905 60 chiefs and heads of families had been imprisoned for eight days because individual members of their clan or family had failed to pay taxes. It was routine practice to inflict whippings for trifling offences).

The signatories of the petition had to pay dearly for their courage. Puttkamer had the supreme chief of the Akwa and four others condemned to between 18 months and 9 years imprisonment with hard labour, while another 18 were given prison terms of 3 months with hard labour. After strong protests from the Social Democrats and some members of the Centre party in the Reichstag — the Social Democratic deputy Georg Ledebour described the sentence as a "travesty of justice, an outrage and abuse of authority" — the head of the Colonial Department, Prince Hohenlohe-Langenburg, could not but order a retrial. In October 1906 the more drastic penalties were reduced and the rest somewhat increased. In his summing up the judge, Rudolf Asmis, cited two political reasons for his decision: the "recognition of a master-servant relationship between the white race and the black race" and the fact that "the primary intention of the accused has been to change conditions in Douala". He said that the chiefs, in filing complaints about colonial officials, had

---

[29] Quoted from *A. Rüger*, Die Duala und die Kolonialmacht 1884—1914. Eine Studie über die historischen Ursprünge des afrikanischen Antikolonialismus, in: Kamerun . . ., vol. 2, p. 204.

committed a punishable offence because "the Negro, despite his inferior status, . . . thus sets himself up as a judge of their behaviour, thereby showing an utter lack of any feeling of subordination."[30] Hohenlohe's successor, Bernhard Dernburg, had the judgement upheld; the supreme chief and some other chiefs were deposed and all those who had lodged complaints thrown into jail. Amid bursts of applause from the Social Democratic members of the Reichstag, August Bebel described the whole episode as "outrageous and inhuman".[31]

The Social Democrats had supported the Duala on these and other matters both in parliament and in the press. In numerous articles and reports, their newspaper Vorwärts exposed the "colonial morass in Puttkamerun" and dispelled the myth of the civilizing mission of German colonialism while the Leipziger Volkszeitung, in its edition of 10 February 1906, published the full text of the petition signed by the Akwa chiefs. Scathing press reports and the stand taken by the Social Democrats and the bourgeois opposition against the methods of colonial rule in Cameroon were a major factor in bringing about Puttkamer's downfall. The government found itself compelled to dismiss and replace the Governor. But in a final statement to the Imperial Chancellor, Dernburg stressed that while certain aspects of the handling of administrative and judicial matters in Cameroon were objectionable, he saw no reason for bringing criminal charges or taking disciplinary action against any of the officials involved.

The political and economic changes which began around 1895 may be said to have come to a conclusion by 1905—6. The greater part of the colony had been occupied by military force; well-financed companies had come into being and were playing a major role in the colonial economy; the trading firms had greatly extended their sphere of operations and stepped up the exploitation of the colony; and the stage had been set for railway construction. The sole beneficiaries of this development were the German merchants, industrialists, big landowners and banking magnates with interests in Cameroon and the British and Belgian capitalists who were also making profits by taking part in its colonial enslavement.

[30] Quoted from *A. Rüger*, op. cit., pp. 213—214.
[31] Ibid., p. 214.

3. Togo 1884—1900

From the middle of the 19th century onwards the Slave Coast of West Africa had again been increasingly drawn into the orbit of European trade through the export of domestic products, primarily palm oil and kernels. Britain had occupied the Volta River estuary while the mouth of the Mono River, including Anecho (then also known as Little Popo), was considered a French sphere of interest. For the time being the two powers were content to exercise control over the river mouths, their chief trading centres. Their representatives did not bother to seek *de jure* possession of the 50-kilometre stretch of sandy beach between Anecho and Lomé (Be Beach), a village located further west, because they believed that the area would be divided among the two powers in the course of future delimitation.

Most of the inhabitants of the coastal strip were Ewe, but there existed no political ties above the village or local level. Although there were head chiefs who claimed a measure of allegiance, power was exercised by the village chiefs. The most important among the coastal settlements was Anecho, with 4,000 to 6,000 inhabitants; Porto Seguro had about 2,000 whereas the remainder had only a few hundred. Behind the coast was a large lagoon on which a number of settlements with several thousand residents each, including Gridji and Togo, were situated. The coastal settlements lay on territory which the lagoon villages regarded as their own, and many former inhabitants of these villages had made their homes on the coast. The chief of Gridji, for example, was the overlord of Anecho, appointing the chiefs there and charging them with the collection of duties. As the export trade grew in scope, the coastal centres assumed increasing importance as *entrepôts*, with goods being exchanged for money rather than other goods and Africans from other parts of West Africa settling down there. As a result, the coastal chiefs saw no reason why they should pay taxes to the village chiefs and do their bidding any longer.

Four German firms with relatively modest resources and with headquarters in Hamburg and Bremen were active in the area. The oldest among them, Friedrich M. Vietor, had been doing business there from 1856, and the others were mostly run by former agents of that firm. They were engaged in trade along the coast from Accra to Lagos. At the beginning of the 1880s their situation in Gold Coast colony deteriorated: the British government, eager to shift the financial burden of the Ashanti war onto other shoulders raised import duties on spirits, powder and tobacco, and worst hit by these duties were the German firms. In the event of British rule being extended eastward to Anecho, the virtual exemption of German firms there from customs duties would have ended. So when Chief G. A. Lawson, who had links with English traders, became head chief in Anecho, the German traders were greatly alarmed. In February 1884 at their instigation the captain of the German warship Sophie sent a party of sailors ashore with bayonets fixed and they proceeded to round up all local chiefs. The chiefs were forced to take part in "negotiations" on board the ship and two Africans were subsequently taken to Germany as hostages.

After these acts of violence the agent of the German firm of Wölber & Brohm, Randad, was able to induce the head chief and the chiefs of Anecho on 5 March 1884 to petition the German Emperor to declare a protectorate over the area. Yet Bismarck, mindful of his overall strategy, decided to respect the French "claims" and to put the request in abeyance. Consul-General Nachtigal received no other instructions on the area for his West African tour than to release the two hostages. So when the Möwe cast anchor off Anecho on 2 July, to the disappointment of the German agents, Nachtigal did not proclaim an annexation.

A mere 50 kilometres further west, however, there seemed to be a chance of annexing territory and hurting British colonial interests. So Nachtigal took up a proposal made by Randad and ordered the Möwe to turn back. On 5 July, a protection treaty was signed with the chiefs of the lagoon village of Togo and two small coastal villages, Lomé and Bagida. The most important settlement, Porto Seguro, remained outside the protectorate.

By entering into this treaty the chiefs of Togo were seeking to gain the ascendancy over Chief Mensa of Porto Seguro, for they laid claim to the export duties which the trading agencies had hitherto paid him. The Germans gave them assurances to this effect, only to break their pledge in 1885. Understandably enough, Mensa refused to accept the treaty and to hoist the German flag.

So German rule in Togo began with a treaty which was designed to play the Africans off against each other. But treaties of this kind were not meant to legitimize colonial pretensions in the eyes of the Africans, but to establish a "lawful claim" vis-à-vis the other colonial powers, and it was only because Britain respected the "claim" that it could be upheld. The result was the annexation of a coastal strip about 20 kilometres in length, including the villages of Lomé and Bagida, and a disputed claim to another 15-kilometres stretch of land containing Porto Seguro. This fell far short of what would have been needed as starting-point for a colony. There were only two options: to extend the coastal strip through negotiations in Europe or to abandon it.

Protracted negotiations with France ended on 24 December 1885 with the adoption of a joint protocol whereby the French "claims" to Anecho and Porto Seguro were ceded to the German Empire in return for German "claims" to a tract of land on the Dubreka River in Guinea.[32] This brought to an end the first stage of the colonial partition of the area with Germany's newly acquired territory being enlarged to cover a 50-kilometre coastal strip. The German strip did not, however, extend as far as the mouths of the Mono and Volta Rivers.

The reason why no enlargement took place on the west side was that "German" Matin territory in the Niger delta, available as a bargaining object for a deal with Britain, was used in favour of the much more influential German firms in Cameroon to extend that colony up to the Rio del Rey. For the African population annexation was synonymous with partition, the Ewe and other peoples finding themselves torn apart.

The first period in the history of the new colony, which lasted about ten years, witnessed an immediate rise in trading and the gradual establishment of a relatively small administrative machinery. The "peaceful development" of Togo was often described in Germany as exemplary. The Kölnische Zeitung wrote on 10 November 1894: "Our model colony, which has been built up almost from scratch and has prospered on the basis of its own customs revenue with almost no financial support from the Reich, has so far caused us no worries at all, unlike Cameroon, South West Africa and East Africa. German blood has never been shed there . . ."

The "self-supporting" colony was a pure myth given the fact that until 1899 it received a total of 1.7 million marks in subsidies from the Afrikafonds, a fund allegedly serving scientific purposes, and from other sources.[33] But the myth, created in the late 1880s, was carefully fostered by the advocates of colonial expansion, and before long Togo had been assigned a place within the German colonial system as a shop-window colony.

The territory failed to attract much interest among German big business circles or from the Colonial Society, because the Togo coast, unlike other German possessions, was very small, its outlook was quite uncertain

---

[32] For full text see *Handbuch der Verträge* 1871—1964, ed. by H. Stoecker with the collaboration of Adolf Rüger, Berlin 1968, p. 67.

and business opportunities were limited to trading. During the first decade there were no urgent reasons for rapidly enlarging the colony or setting up a costly apparatus of government. Togo remained the preserve of small German commercial firms and a handful of bureaucrats (two in 1885, seventeen in 1894).

The proclamation of German suzerainty led to changes in the commercial field. German traders were henceforth assured of a free trade zone in which the import duties imposed on spirits, powder and tobacco were very low (initially there were none at all), whereas in the neighbouring British Gold Coast colony they amounted to between 50 and 100 per cent. This gave rise to a flourishing period of smuggling. For the sake of convenience the contraband was landed in the immediate vicinity of the border between Togo and the Gold Coast and transported inland to British-ruled territory from there. The fishing village of Lomé, which

[33] The financial development of the colony of Togo 1885—1899:

Year	Revenue	Expenditure (in marks)	Additional expenditure	
	(according to the official budget)		from Afrikafonds	from special fund for civil servants
1885—86	—	48,300	—	21,500
1886—87	—	98,300	—	21,000
1887—88	46,300	93,400	43,855	29,100
1888—89	97,700	108,400	50,347	29,100
1889—90	94,400	123,300	28,848	29,100
1890—91	96,000	129,400	71,379	29,100
1891—92	150,900	167,400	59,412	29,500
1892—93	220,400	204,400	88,000	29,500
1893—94	221,700	245,700	96,500	29,500
1894—95	376,600	410,200	115,400	29,500
1895—96	382,000	388,700	36,670	29,500
1896—97	303,100	345,500	154,344	
1897—98	301,000	492,000	202,055	
1898	384,000	692,000	246,542	
1899	856,000	851,000	216,840	

Sources: Revenue and expenditure according to the colonial budget, customs and taxes according to *C. W. Newbury*, The Western Slave Coast and its Rulers, Oxford 1961, pp. 162, 166 and 213. Additional data from ZStA, RKolA, nos. 6503—6511, Jahresberichte allgemeinen Inhalts aus Togo and nos. 6587—6592, Manuskripte zu den Jahresberichten von Togo.

was situated directly on the border, as a result experienced an unprecece-
dented boom, which prompted the first German official at post there
to observe: "Strictly speaking, Lomé owes its rise to smuggling, for
initially Quitta (or Keta) imposed customs duties while the fishing spot
of Lomé did not."[34] Within a year Lomé's imports rose from a mere
trifle to over a million marks, with spirits accounting for 380,000 marks,
tobacco for 300,000 marks and powder for 120,000 marks.[35] In this way
the "protectorate" revealed its true function, which was to protect
German exports of liquor. Up to 1914 cheap spirits were always about
one quarter of Togo's overall imports.

The personnel needed to maintain authority were kept at a minimum
because the whole colony was within the range of naval artillery. The
first German official to arrive, in the summer of 1885, the Imperial Commissioner E. Falkenthal, had only half a dozen military police at his
disposal. He therefore found himself compelled to come to terms with
the chiefs of the coastal settlements and lagoon villages, to pay them
annuities and to allow them to retain most of their prerogatives. In particular, the ten head chiefs receiving annual payments were to serve as
"elements of law and order" within the structure of government. They
were exhorted to be "faithful in the discharge of their duties", which
included the promotion of trade, the settling of disputes, road building
and the maintenance of public order. It should be emphasized that
during the first decade of German rule the German authorities had no
choice but to adapt to the circumstances in that way. It was the local
chiefs who really ruled over the people, deriving their power less from
traditional rights than from their position in trade. They were either
merchants themselves or linked to influential merchants by family ties.
Through innumerable commercial or family connections the inhabitants
of the Togo coast were well informed about the situation in the neighbouring colonies. Since there were no border barriers, the adoption of
sharp measures by the German intruders could easily have led to a mass
exodus of people.

As it turned out, the dominant traders-cum-chiefs, once they had been
brought under colonial rule, exploited the new conditions that had arisen
for trading in palm oil and kernels, spirits or slaves — the kind of trade
favoured by German colonialism. Influential African merchant families
bolstered up their position as traders, landowners and in local social life,
especially in the fast-expanding town of Lomé. The head of one such

[34] *R. Küas*, Togo-Erinnerungen, Berlin 1939, p. 120.
[35] Deutsche Konsulatszeitung, 28 Oct. 1885, in ZStA, RKolA, no. 3829, p. 15.

family, Octavio Olympio, an uncle of Sylvanus Olympio, who was later to become the first president of the Republic of Togo, benefited from the town's growth as the proprietor of a brickworks. In Lomé and Anecho this development led to the employment of hundreds of wage-earners whereas in the immediate hinterland African farmers produced cash crops exclusively destined for export. Thus certain sections of the population tried to adjust to the conditions of alien rule.

But the course of development was increasingly determined by the German officials who sought to control every aspect of African life. They sought to force the African traders out of business through customs and market regulations and to prevent the emergence of an African intelligentsia. Their concepts of colonial rule were rooted in great power chauvinism and in a racist and militaristic outlook, which found its expression in the practice of flogging and in all manners of oppressive measures, of which there were many in thirty years of German rule, down to the days of the last governor, Duke Adolf Friedrich von Mecklenburg. These officials were mainly colonialists by conviction who saw their task in Africa as their mission in life without, of course, neglecting their personal interests.

The colonial bureaucrats considered it their primary task to "maintain law and order", to promote German trade and to enlarge the colony's territory step by step. Their narrow-minded and inflexible methods often enough brought them into sharp conflict with the German traders. Committed to the laissez faire doctrine and financially weak, these were bent on making the largest possible profits without any serious investments. They had no intention whatever of setting up trading agencies in the colony's interior because local products were available more cheaply at the river mouths in the neighbouring British and French colonies. While the traders wanted to enjoy the advantages of German rule, they were not necessarily dependent on trade in the German colony. They absolutely refused to finance measures of the German administration.

The first owner of a trading firm to spend most of his time in Togo and to show special interest in the development of the colony was J. K. Vietor, who arrived in 1887. It was not until after the turn of the century that larger companies entered the scene.

The German missionaries, especially the North German Mission, were often branded as unpatriotic by the colonial bureaucracy, too. The Mission, which had been active in the Volta region for decades, supported German colonialism in many ways, but it did not depend on the colonial power for its activities. It was only at a later stage that the "patriotic" type of missionary came to the fore.

Despite the upswing in coastal trading the Deutsche Kolonialgesell-schaft deemed it necessary to conquer an extensive stretch of inland territory, because a colony limited to a narrow coastal strip would have made little sense once the authorities in the adjacent colonies had put an end to the smuggling of liquor. The absence of a natural boundary on the coast and of a natural link with the interior was bad enough, but to make matters worse a mountain range in the interior running from the south-west to the north-east cut the hinterland of the coastal strip in two. And wherever German officers set foot, they found that there were already commercial ties linking the interior with the Mono River on one side of the mountain range and with the Volta River on the other. The trade in salt, cloth, farm produce, livestock and slaves passed through traditional channels, which were convenient and cheap but led into British or French colonial territory. For this reason the representatives of the colonial power were eager to secure access to the two rivers at least in the hinterland. They therefore strove

(i)   to claim territory in the interior politically with a view to negotia-tion with the British and French governments;
(ii) to conquer the claimed territory by armed force and thereby es-tablish effective authority over it;
(iii) to develop economic ties between the claimed territory and the German-ruled coastal strip.

In some inland areas the third task had to be tackled before the second because the establishment of colonial rule was a lengthy and costly affair for which no basis existed in Togo right into the latter half of the 1890s. By the time the powers agreed on the principle of "effective occu-pation", the German colonial authorities had hit upon a method — the establishment of "scientific stations" — which enabled them to raise annexationist claims even before the African population had been over-powered.

During the first decade, territorial claims were extended about 250 kilometres inland by way of "scientific" expeditions and the setting up of "scientific" stations. The use of this method made it possible to conceal the colonial objectives from the German people and to draw on the Afrikafonds, a fund set aside for scientific purposes, rather than on the colonial budget as a source of finance.

An expedition led by Dr. Ludwig Wolf, a captain in the medical corps, in March 1888 was the first to penetrate into the north (the eastern border with French-ruled Dahomey had already been fixed up to 9° Lat). establishing a station called Bismarckburg in the Adeli region. But to gain access to the Volta River in the west, the mountains had to be crossed. In 1888—9, Captain Curt von François, leading a "scientific expedition", reached the river and pressed on towards Salaga, an important trading centre. Salaga however, could not be annexed: since German and British forces were at that time ill-equipped for a race against each other, the authorities in both colonies simply declared the Salaga area to be "neutral zone". In order to underscore German claims, the Imperial Commissioner von Puttkamer in March 1890 set up a "scientific station" called Misahöhe in the mountains near the only pass leading in a westerly direction.

Since it was impossible to direct the trade caravans in the interior towards the German Togo coast by force, the German colonial authorities sought to attract the trading Hausa to that area. Unlike the British in the neighbouring Gold Coast colony they imposed no public ban on the slave trade so that slave dealers ran no risk of their merchandise being set free. This led to an increase in the slave trade as the colonial bureaucracy connived at the traditional institution of slavery until a new, colonial system of exploitation based on forced labour and work performed in lieu of taxes had been created. In newspaper articles and petitions to the Reichstag the German explorer Gottlob Adolf Krause repeatedly denounced the autöoritis' consent to the slave trade as a practical example of the "civilizing mission" of a colonial power. This attitude was absolutely inconsistent with the slogans used by the German government to justify its colonial conquests in East Africa.

The year 1894 marked the beginning of a new phase in the development of Togo. As the race of the colonial powers to secure control of the entire hinterland of West Africa gathered momentum, the Pan-German League (Alldeutscher Verband) and the DKG hoped to extend the colony beyond Togo's open northern borders right to the Niger, but found themselves confronted with far-reaching British and French interests. So they fitted out a large expedition which was chiefly designed to prepare the way for further annexations.

The Administrator (Landeshauptmann) of the colony, Jesko von Puttkamer, saw the chance offered by the biggest "private" German expedition ever undertaken in West Africa to assert German power over territories, notably in the Volta region, claimed by virtue of treaties with Britain. Therefore the expedition also pursued this aim, even to the extent of murdering the fetish priest of Krachi, Bosomfo, who was considered anti-German. In its bid to outstrip the French the expedition in late 1894 and early 1895 penetrated as far as Sai on the Niger, having passed through Salaga, Yendi and Pama on its way there. Its culminating achievement was later alleged to be the conclusion of a treaty with the Sultan of Gwandu. In actual fact the Sultan categorically rejected this "treaty" and refused to sign it.[36] But this did not prevent the German authorities from invoking it to back up territorial claims.

Since each of the three colonial powers involved was able to produce treaties with African chiefs and rulers secured by means of fraud and blackmail, effective occupation was needed in order to convert colonial "claims" into reality. In 1894, partly drawing on the military equipment of the expedition, Puttkamer transformed the small police unit into a 150-strong mercenary force with this end in mind. An occasion for demonstrating the strength of the new force arose in March 1895 when the head of Misahöhe station, Baumann, reported that the population of the Tove region had liberated an arrested chief. The villages between Lomé and Misahöhe were burnt down, and all signs of resistance suppressed. Following this, the mercenary force moved on to Kete-Krachi, a station set up on the upper Volta in December 1894. In an engagement at Tachi, which was also deliberately provoked, they gave another display of their military superiority. It was in this way that the German administration in southern Togo began to impose colonial rule in earnest.

In September 1895 a new German expedition advanced into the interior. When the Sultan of Yendi, ruler of the Dagomba, refused to grant them passage on account of the murder of the fetish priest in Krachi, the entire colonial soldiery available (4 Europeans, 91 soldiers and 46 porters armed with breech-loaders) were sent to attack him. But the Dagomba stoutly defended their country with several thousand men. While the colonial troops managed to break through towards Yendi and burn down that town, they did not succeed in destroying the Dagomba force. The troops battled their way to Sansanne-Mango where they founded a station in December 1896 and went on to expand the German sphere of influence northward by setting up further stations at Gurma and Pama. However, the direct route from Krachi to Sansanne-Mango remained under the control of the Sultan of Yendi. Concurrently, other German officers starting out from Krachi advanced in a northeastern direction to Sugu, Semere and Bafilo in 1896—7 and founded stations there. As in the north they found that the French had already established stations in the region.

---

[36] Cf. *W. Markov and P. Sebald*, The Treaty between Germany and the Sultan of Gwandu, in: Journal of the Historical Society of Nigeria, vol. IV, no. 1, Dec. 1967, pp. 141—153.

One aspect of the rivalry among the colonial powers was that each power incited the African population against the others. This turned out to be to their general disadvantage. They found it advisable, therefore, to delimit the boundaries of their "own" colonial sphere within which they would be free to put down rebellious African tribes without the interference of imperialist rivals. During the Franco-German negotiations of 1897 the German side had to abandon their dreams of a colonial empire on the Niger and give up the northern stations of Gurma and Pama and the northeastern station of Sugu. They were given the so-called Mono Triangle in return, which meant that just behind the coast the border was advanced eastward to the Mono River. This was, however, a worthless concession because all commercial transports continued to pass down the Mono to Grand Popo in Dahomey.

The nothwestern border was fixed in Article 5 of the so-called Samoa Agreement of November 1899. This deal was more favourable to German interests in the South Seas than to those in Togo as the latter received neither the important trading centre of Salaga nor the Volta Triangle, i.e. the coastal strip extending to the mouth of the Volta River. Similarly, the major portion of the Dagomba kingdom was assigned to the Gold Coast while the Germans were left with Yendi, which they had burnt down.

At the turn of the century the Togo colony had thus assumed a more or less definitive and rather curious shape. It consisted of a narrow coastal area with a 550-kilometre strip of hinterland attached to it, the two having no ties, economic or otherwise, with each other. The colony had an area of 87,200 square kilometres and a population of almost one million. The population of the coastal strip numbered only about 20,000, and that of the Misahöhe district, which was subjugated in 1895—6, about 80,000. This meant that 90 per cent of the population had not yet been conquered.

The commander of the police force, von Massow, observed after his contingent had been raised to a level of 500 men: "The time has come to move towards definitive control over the territory."[37] A coordinated programme for occupation was worked out, and measures were taken in 1896—7 to subdue the Konkomba, who had risen in revolt against brutal colonial officials. All the "campaigns" now waged followed the same pattern: settlements were set on fire, cattle were stolen and defenceless people were shot down to provoke African resistance. The "ringleaders" were "shot while attempting to escape". When von Massow

[37] ZStA, RKolA, no. 4395, p. 20, Report by Massow to the Governor, 6 Oct. 1897.

returned to the coast with a small part of the mercenary force during the spring of 1898, he wrote in his report: "A breakthrough has been achieved at last . . ." Not only the tribes involved, but also those in the neighbouring areas "have been given a taste of German power."[38] At the turn of the century the stations in the hinterland witnessed some major military operations and a large number of minor ones. What the chief of San-sanne-Mango station, G. Thierry, noted in a report was also true of the other districts: "All tribes in the district had to be subdued by force."[39]

It is impossible to say how many thousand people were killed during the military conquest of Togo. But it is a fact that the mercenary force used up more than a million cartridges between 1896 and 1900. The German public was largely kept in the dark about the reasons for the many small military campaigns and the methods employed. The linguist G. A. Krause, an eye-witness of developments in Togo, aptly observed in 1900: "Each time a war with the natives breaks out through the fault of some official, the people back home are told nothing but that a war has taken place, that it is over now and that they have to foot the bill. There is never any mention of the whys and the wherefores . . . According to the telegraphic message all is quiet in the protectorate. Everything is indeed quiet, the dead lie peacefully in their graves and the wounded on their sick-beds, and the rest have been put to rout."[40]

Until the end of German rule Germans not belonging to the colonial administration needed special permission to enter the northern districts. As in the other German colonies military force formed the backbone of German rule.

4. German East Africa 1885—1906

The territories conquered by bands of mercenaries between 1889 and the turn of the century which were later to form the colony of German East Africa are varied in character. Behind a humid coastal lowland belt lies a plateau 1000—1200 metres in altitude with extensive stretches of savannah, dry mountain areas and broad steppes, and in some parts tropical rain forest. These areas are bounded in the north by Mount Kilimanjaro and other peaks and by Lake Victoria, in the west by Lakes

[38] ZStA, RKolA, no. 4392, pp. 199 and 201, Report by Massow to the Governor, 11 Feb. 1898.
[39] ZStA, RKolA, no. 4393, p. 50, Report by Thierry to the Governor, 12 Aug. 1898.
[40] Berliner Tageblatt, 13 Jan. 1900.

Tanganyika and Nyasa (now Lake Malawi), and in the south by the Ruvuma. The peoples and tribes were as varied as the landscape. In the interior they were mostly Bantu-speaking, politically independent ethnic units living mainly by crop farming (the Nyamwesi, Hehe, Ngoni, Kimbu, Chagga, Makonde et al.), but there were also peoples such as the Sukuma, and the nomadic Masai (belonging to the Nilotes), in the northeast, who were cattle herders. Other Nilotes, such as the Haya east of Lake Victoria, were both crop farmers and herdsmen. The social and economic conditions of the peoples in the interior were in general those of a primeval society in a state of decline or dissolution and in some cases, as with the Nyamwesi and the Chagga, there were the first signs of the formation of a state.

Social conditions were considerably more developed in the coastal area from Tanga to Lindi, and in the densely populated kingdoms of Burundi and Rwanda in the extreme northwest, which were only conquered at the turn of the century. Economic, political and cultural development in the coastal area had been characterized for more than a thousand years by the mingling of Africans and Arabs. Arabs had settled on the islands off the coast and at strategic points on the mainland. They controlled the slave trade and the trade in ivory and other products in the African hinterland. From the mid-nineteenth century they had been establishing more and more plantations, which were worked by slaves, and produced sugar, cloves and coconuts for export to other countries. In general they were on friendly terms with the African chiefs and often married African women. Their descendants continued to call themselves Arabs and to practise Islam, although they merged more and more with the indigenous population, whom they called Swahili (Arabic for "coast dweller"). In time a highly-developed Afro-Arab Islamic culture evolved, into which many Africans were assimilated. The Swahili towns on the mainland, such as Bagamoyo, Pangani, Tanga and Kilwa, were important manufacturing and trading centres but not the focus of political power. Supreme power over the whole coastal area — a power that in practice did not amount to much — was claimed by the Arab Sultan of Zanzibar. The Sultanate was the centre of East African maritime trade. It had been the headquarters of the overseas slave trade in the first half of the century but, as a result of declining demand and of the 1873 agreement between Great Britain and Zanzibar banning this trade, had greatly decreased down to 1880 and became insignificant in the 1880s.[41]

---

[41] *J. M. Gray*, Zanzibar and the Coastal Belt, 1840—1884, in R. Oliver and G. Mathew (eds), History of East Africa, Vol. I, Oxford 1963, p. 241.

In the kingdoms of Rwanda and Burundi, which were virtually untouched by European influences, the structure of an early class-society
had emerged. For centuries cattlebreeding aristocrats, from whom the
royal dynasties had been drawn, had ruled the Hutu, a mainly crop farming people. The aristocracy, the Tutsi, made up about one-tenth of the
whole population and kept themselves strictly apart from the Hutu,
from whom they demanded taxes and services.

In November-December 1884 the psychopathic — and, as turned out
later, also criminal — adventurer Carl Peters by means of fraud and
bribery obtained the "rights of sovereignty" over 140,000 square kilometres of land (in Uzigua, Nguru, Usagara and Ukami) west of Dar es
Salaam and Pangani from local African chiefs, and on 27 February in
the following year Bismarck had the Emperor sign a document proclaiming a German protectorate over these territories. Peters' company
(Gesellschaft für deutsche Kolonisation) was also empowered to take
over further territories as far as the frontiers of the "Congo Free State",
which it promptly did in 1885 by a series of contracts similar to those
concluded by its founder.

Sultan Said Bargash was forced by Germany in August 1885 to recognize the annexation of these areas to which he had laid claim, which
included the Sultanate of Witu, and at the end of the year he signed a trade
treaty with the Reich. By an agreement with Great Britain of 1 November
1886 and a similar agreement with Portugal of 30 December 1886 the
frontiers of the new German protectorate were fixed in the north, east
and south. The southern border with Mozambique was to be the River
Ruvuma; the northern border with British Africa, later Kenya, ran in
a northwesterly direction from Jassin (on the coast north of Tanga)
along the northern slopes of Kilimanjaro to Lake Victoria. The islands
of Zanzibar, Pemba and Mafia together with a coastal strip on the mainland ten nautical miles wide were left to Britain's protégé, the Sultan of
Zanzibar. The two agreements were important steps towards the colonial partition of East Africa between the three powers and roughly
laid down the borders of what later became German East Africa, since
the Berlin Conference Act had virtually decided that Lake Tanganyika
was to be its western frontier. The only remaining doubts concerned the
extreme northwestern frontier on the far side of Lake Victoria.

In the Anglo-German agreement Great Britain had expressed her
willingness to persuade the Sultan to make a further concession to Peters' Company (known as "Deutsch-Ostafrikanische Gesellschaft Carl
Peters und Genossen" from April 1885 onwards — DOAG); namely,
the permission to use the ports of Pangani and Dar es Salaam, which it

needed in order to have access to its territories. This permission the Sultan now granted, at the same time leasing the levying of customs duties to the DOAG, which had already begun to set up trading posts without paying attention to Zanzibar's sovereignty on the coast. By April 1888 eighteen such posts had been established, and the Deutsch-Ostafrikanische Plantagengesellschaft, a subsidiary of the DOAG, even set up a tobacco plantation near Pangani.

Peters was regarded as a mere amateur by the big merchants of Hamburg and the Berlin bankers, and was thus unable to raise the capital the DOAG required to continue its activities. The government therefore intervened and induced Emperor Wilhelm I to make available 500,000 marks from his own purse for a reorganized company. Only after this state backing was assured were industrialists and bankers prepared to become involved — the Berlin banks of Mendelssohn, Warschauer and Delbrück, the Elberfeld banker von der Heydt (with 400,000 marks) and the industrialists Krupp, Haniel, Hoesch, Gruson and Oechelhäuser. The German firms of Hansing & Co and O'Swald & Co in Zanzibar also participated, and on 23 February 1887 the reconstituted DOAG was established with a capital of 3,480,000 marks, and Peters, of whom Bismarck was growing increasingly distrustful, was sent to East Africa as Director. The DOAG has been accurately described as "a joint enterprise of the monopolistic industrial and financial oligarchy and of the feudal-industrial land-owning aristocracy, a perfect example of a monopolistic colonial enterprise."[42]

Attempts by the DOAG to extend its power and begin exploiting the areas assigned to it quickly met with resistance from the Africans. At the beginning of 1887 two trading posts south of Dar es Salaam were attacked, and other posts were deserted by the workers employed there. In order to bring the coast and its ports completely under its control, the DOAG made a further agreement on 28 April 1888 with the new Sultan of Zanzibar, Said Khalifa, by which the Sultan assigned to the Company total control of the coast for 50 years, the company, for its part, undertaking to continue to pay a rent to the Sultan for the right to levy customs duties in the ports. This agreement was very similar to that concluded a year earlier with the previous Sultan Said Bargash by the British Imperial East African Company concerning its own adjacent coastal strip.

Up to this point there had been no German colonial rule in East Africa but only a "sphere of influence" of the financially weak DOAG,

---

[42] *F. F. Müller*, Deutschland—Zanzibar—Ostafrika. Geschichte einer deutschen Kolonialeroberung 1884—1890, Berlin 1959, p. 170.

which, since it had no means of asserting power, apart from a few dozen mercenaries from Zanzibar, was in no position to impose colonial conditions on the East Africans. Its representatives on the trading posts were tolerated but not seen as masters. The attempt by the DOAG to establish its rule in the coastal area on the basis of the new treaty and at the same time improve its financial situation by raising a poll tax and other levies from the population and by introducing a register of those owning land, as a prelude to expropriation, caused universal indignation among the Swahili and Africans and rapidly led to the complete collapse of the company's weak position on the mainland. By their arrogance, the way they offended the religious feelings of the Moslems, their disrespect for the Sultan's flag and their general brutality, the agents of the DOAG had made themselves detested everywhere.

The dream of an easily acquired colony which could quickly be turned into a source of profit thus came to an abrupt end. On 4 September 1888, under the leadership of the Arab Abushiri ben Salim al-Harthi, who owned a small sugar plantation near Pangani, armed attacks on the company's men began in the port. The movement rapidly spread to the other coastal towns, although a squadron of five German warships was cruising off the coast. With the general support of the population the DOAG representatives were driven out of most of the towns or taken prisoner. Bagamoyo (which was bombarded and partially destroyed by the cruiser Leipzig on 22 September) and the German base in Dar es Salaam were besieged by thousands of warriors, who embarked on their final attack at the end of December. By the turn of the year nothing remained of the DOAG's "protectorate" but the trading posts in these two places, which were held with the help of the German cruisers.

The population in the coastal area, from most of the Swahili trading and plantation aristocracy to fugitive slaves, had united against the colonial intruder. Tribes from the hinterland, such as the Yao in the south, also joined the movement and their warriors marched to the coast to help drive out the Germans. It is therefore totally false to describe the uprising of 1888—1890, as the apologists of colonialist policies did and still do, as a rebellion by Arab slave traders in defence of their barbaric activities.

The DOAG and the German Colonial Society soon made use of the myth of an "Arab rebellion", which was apparently first spread by Rohlfs, the explorer and former Consul General in Zanzibar, in order to set the scene in Germany for a military intervention in East Africa. Fabri, a propagandist for colonial expansion, and Langen, a sugar manufacturer from Cologne and Deputy Chairman of the DOAG since

1888, organized an "anti-slavery" campaign in order to whip up colonial chauvinism. As influential groups of the bourgeoisie took the view that Germany, as a new colonial power, could not afford the loss of prestige that would follow a retreat from East Africa — even Great Britain had had difficulty in coming to terms with its defeat at Khartoum in 1885 — the three parties supporting the government and Bismarck joined in the campaign for a colonial war. On 23 October 1888 the Chancellor ordered the government press to write about the East African question as though "it were ultimately a question of the slave trade."[43] Thereupon the Catholic Centre Party, also much influenced by the Pope's support of a colonialist anti-slavery campaign launched by the French Cardinal Lavigerie, decided to follow the government's line.

Only the Social Democrats, led by August Bebel, who were increasingly identifying themselves with Marxism, rejected colonialism on principle and opposed the policy of intervention in East Africa. On 26 January 1889 Bebel stated in the Reichstag:

"What is this East Africa Company? A small group of rich capitalists, bankers, merchants and industrialists, i.e. a small group of very wealthy people whose interests have nothing to do with those of the German people, whose colonial policies are determined solely by their own interests . . . and who are merely concerned to use their greater power to add to their wealth in every possible way at the expense of a weaker people. Never shall we support such a policy. All colonial policies are basically attempts to exploit a foreign people to the greatest possible extent. Wherever we look in colonial history in the last three hundred years, we find atrocities and the oppression of whole peoples, not infrequently ending with their total destruction. The driving force is wealth, wealth and nothing but wealth. And in order to render possible the fullest and undisturbed exploitation of the African peoples, millions of marks are to be provided from the taxpayers' pockets, from the national exchequer, for the benefit of the East African Company . . ."[44]

For reasons of European diplomacy Bismarck not only wanted at all costs to avoid a conflict with Great Britain in East Africa — "England is more important for us than Zanzibar and East Africa," he wrote on 11 December[45] — but hoped if possible to act together with Great Britain. Despite the rivalry between the colonial powers, they shared an interest in stamping out any anti-colonial movements. He reached an agreement

---

[43] Source *F. F. Müller*, op. cit., p. 401.

[44] StBVR, 7. Leg. Per. IV. Sess. 1888/89, Vol. 1, pp. 627—628.

[45] Source: *F. F. Müller*, op. cit., p. 393.

with the British government to impose a joint blockade on the East African coast which came into force on 2 December 1888 and was carried out by cruisers of the two powers. Portugal and Italy joined in the blockade, and the French blockaded the coast of Madagascar. Although the measure was intended to prevent weapons from reaching the East Africans by sea, they were able to smuggle in the arms and ammunition they needed via Zanzibar and neighbouring states.

It soon became evident that the forces led by Abushiri were not to be put down by means of a sea blockade. To start with Bismarck had hoped to avoid any direct military intervention that went beyond the blockade and occasional landings of naval detachments. But it proved impossible to put to use the authority of Sultan Said Khalifa on the mainland — it had collapsed — and the DOAG showed itself unable to provide the necessary funds for engaging a unit for mercenaries and waging war. So the Chancellor decided to give orders for military intervention and for the "protectorate" of the DOAG to be placed under the administration of the Reich. On 30 January 1889, against the votes of the Social Democrats and the left Liberals, the Reichstag empowered the Chancellor to spend up to two million marks "for measures to suppress the slave trade and protect the German interests in East Africa."[46] As this sum proved inadequate, a further two million marks was voted shortly afterwards. Captain Hermann Wissmann, an explorer, who had made two crossings of Central Africa, one for the DOAG and another for King Leopold II of Belgium, was appointed Reich Commissar for East Africa to lead operations.

Wissmann recruited 600 Sudanese mercenaries in Egypt, together with 350 Shangaans from Mozambique, 50 Somalis and some others. The so-called "Wissmann Unit" in Zanzibar, consisting of 80 German officers and NCOs together with the African mercenaries, which had 26 pieces of artillery and 7 naval vessels, launched an attack on the mainland at the beginning of May 1889. They landed at the bridgeheads of Bagamoyo and Dar es Salaam and raised the siege of the two ports, storming the camp of Abushiri and massacring and plundering as they went. In the following month they attacked the warriors of Bwana Heri, ruler of Uzigua, and put them to flight; his seat at Sadani was shelled and subsequently sacked. In July first Tanga, then the rich port of Pangani, hitherto untouched, were captured. Wissmann's men vied with the sailors from the German cruisers in the plundering of the latter place. The conquest of the northern coastal strip was completed by a series of mopping-

[46] Reichsgesetzblatt, 5 Feb. 1889.

up operations in the areas between the towns, in the course of which numerous villages were burned down.

The success of the mercenaries was not only due to their superior strength of arms. The huge masses of warriors that had joined forces in the autumn of 1888 to defend themselves against the German intruders had mostly returned home to their native villages before May. Above all, however, the spontaneous movement that had gripped all sections of the population had proved to be short-lived. The wealthy Arabs and Swahilis in the towns feared that the continuation of the war would result in the loss of their possessions, and were inclined, following the example of the Sultan of Zanzibar, to give way. Thus the aristocracy in Pangani negotiated with an envoy of Wissmann's on the surrender of the town but without success. There was neither a unified command nor a common ideology. Only a certain proportion of the fighters were Moslems, and these lacked the spirit of fanaticism necessary to the waging of a "holy war".

Abushiri and his supporters tried in vain to unite the chiefs of the interior in the fight against the Germans. In response to his call 8,000 Hehe and Ngoni made their way to the coast but instead of fighting the Germans, they plundered and ravaged African villages. Fleeing to the north with a few faithful followers, he was finally taken captive by a village chief and handed over to a group of mercenaries. On 15 December 1889 Wissmann had him executed with two of his lieutenants. With the subjugation of Simbodia of Usambara in February and Bwana Heri of Uzigua in April 1890 the northern coastal hinterland was also brought under control; in May Wissmann moved southwards with an army of 1,200 men and quickly brought about the subjugation of Kilwa, Lindi and Mikindani. The "peace party" of the wealthy merchants was strong in these places, and only in Kilwa was there any serious resistance.

In all these conquered areas the new masters ushered in their rule with a reign of terror. Many Africans suspected of having taken part in the uprising were killed out of hand, others executed after summary conviction by court martial. Chiefs who submitted without resistance were given a German flag and later employed by the colonial administration. Wissmann worked to bring the more powerful rulers and chiefs over to the side of the new colonial power, and a number of these, such as Paramount Chief Kingo of Morogoro, fought side by side with the mercenaries in the last stages of the war against Abushiri.

Negotiations between Germany and Great Britain on the definitive partition and demarcation of the powers' colonial possessions in East Africa led to the Heligoland-Zanzibar Treaty of 1 July 1890[47], which laid down the frontiers of "German East Africa" as they remained until 1919. Germany gave up her "claims" to Witu, Somaliland and Uganda and also left Zanzibar with Pemba to Great Britain. In return she was given Heligoland and Britain's consent to the proposal that the Sultan should cede to Germany against compensation the coastal area captured by Wissmann. Great Britain recognized the eastern border of the "Congo Free State" as the western border of the German colony, the administration of which passed officially from the DOAG to the German Reich on 1 January 1891.

No "German interests" were lost by the renunciation of all territories north of the frontier between German and British East Africa. The request of the Sultan of Witu, instigated by two German travellers, the brothers Denhardt, to put his country under a German protectorate had been vaguely acceded to in 1885 but an attempt by a "German Witu Company" at the end of 1887 to establish itself there quickly collapsed. Requests by the DOAG that a German protectorate be established on the Somali coast were rejected by Bismarck. He also strongly opposed attempts by the "Emin Pasha Committee" (founded in Berlin in 1888) to add Buganda and other territories north of Lake Victoria to the German colony, under the pretext of rescuing the German adventurer Eduard Schnitzer ("Emin Pasha"), cut off in what is now northern Uganda. Bismarck left these territories to England in 1889. He expressely disassociated himself from a marauding raid through Kenya to Uganda undertaken by Carl Peters (who had left the DOAG) on behalf of the Committee with a small party of mercenaries, and even called on the British government to prevent Peters' expedition from setting foot on territories claimed by Britain.

The Heligoland-Zanzibar Treaty had been prepared by Bismarck and the Treaty itself was concluded by his successor Caprivi. Since it did not add to German colonial possessions but pledged Germany not to expand its colony to the north and northwest, it aroused indignation in chauvinist circles of the German bourgeoisie. Drawing Great Britain closer to the Triple Alliance was far more important for Bismarck and Caprivi than colonies in Africa; the influential circles that had supported Peters' "Emin Pasha Expedition", on the other hand, thought that the treaty was neglecting national interests, and their rejection of it led to the foundation of the Pan-German League (Alldeutscher Verband) as the rallying-point for extreme expansionist elements.

---

[47] Published in *Das Staatsarchiv*, Sammlung der offiziellen Aktenstücke zur Geschichte der Gegenwart, Vol. 51 (1891), pp. 151ff.

In the autumn of 1890 Sultan Said Khalifa received 4 million marks from the DOAG in compensation for the cession of the coastal areas. The money was advanced to the DOAG by the German government, together with a further 6.25 million marks to "compensate" the company for surrendering the "sovereignty" it had claimed but never succeeded in establishing. If the cost of the military operations is added to these sums, one finds that, even before its official foundation, the new colony cost the German state some 20 million marks.

At the end of 1890 preparations began to extend German rule within the frontiers negotiated with Great Britain — to Mount Kilimanjaro in the north and Tabora and beyond in the west. Over a period of ten years or so the "protective force", as the mercenary army was renamed in 1891, with a strength of 2,000 men to start with, and later 3,000, succeeded in subjugating the population of the interior step by step. Trained to be totally obedient and paid relatively highly, the soldiers (askaris) now recruited in the colony proved to be dependable henchmen willing to massacre and pillage whenever there was a chance to do so.

Control of the subjugated peoples was based on a series of army posts set up from 1889 onwards, each commanded by an officer and generally the base of a military unit. 17 such posts had been set up by 1895 — six on the coast and the remainder at strategically important points in the interior, such as Tabora in the centre of the colony and Ujiji on Lake Tanganyika. With the relatively small forces initially at its disposal the administration set out both to make its rule in the coastal area secure — at the end of 1890 a revolt in Uzigua was put down by the usual method of burning villages to the ground, and a similar fate awaited an uprising in Nguru at the beginning of 1891 — and to subdue further areas in the interior. The fact that there were so many different tribes and peoples to deal with made the conquerors' task all the easier, and even where larger tribes were able to ward off the enemy for a few years, they were eventually overcome with quick-firing guns.

Of great importance for the control of the interior was the caravan trail from the coast via Tabora to Ujiji and to Karagwe, west of Lake Victoria, which had been used by Arab traders for a long while. The trading centre of Tabora was the largest settlement in the land of the Nyamwesi, which was divided into many chieftainships. It was ruled by Sikki (or Isike), paramount chief of the district of Unyanyembe, who had set up a fort near the caravan route, some five kilometers from the town, and had a well-armed and well-organized force at his command. He refused to have any dealings with the Europeans. In order to bring the route firmly under German control, the officer in charge of the army post that had been set up in Tabora decided in June 1892 to attack Sikki's fort but with his five German officers and 88 men only succeeded in penetrating the outer defences, after which the invaders were forced to withdraw with heavy losses. A second attempt in August, with bigger forces and two cannons, also failed. Sikki then counter-attacked, almost completely destroying a unit commanded by Lieutenant von Prince and blocking the caravan route.

In January 1893 Lieutenant von Prince embarked on a third attempt to take Sikki's fort with a force of almost 150 men. With the help of an old cannon Sikki held out for three days. Then the attackers stormed the interior of the fort. Sikki took refuge with his family in the powder room and blew it up, determined rather to die than be taken prisoner. When the attack was over, Prince had the dying paramount chief brought out and hanged. Yet the resistance of the Nyamwesi was still not broken. At the end of 1893 the Germans launched a campaign against Chief Kandi, who had tried to stir up the other Nyamwesi chiefs to join in a common war against the intruders. Not until 1894 were the Nyamwesi finally subjugated.

An attempt to occupy the lands of the warlike Hehe people resulted in extensive counter-attacks by their Chief Mkwawa, who in September 1891 succeeded in ambushing and destroying a large-scale "punitive expedition" led by Captain von Zelewski, the man who had ordered the devastation of Uzigua two years earlier. Governor von Soden telegraphed to Berlin as follows: "Zelewsky's expedition wiped out. Presumably 10 Europeans and 300 blacks killed. 300 Mausers all ammunition 2 cannons 2 Maxims in enemy hands. Remaining 4 Europeans and 60 natives fled to Mounda . . . Situation critical."[48] In the course of the following two years Mkwawa, who had fortified his headquarters at Iringa with high walls, repulsed further German attacks. The first defeat of the Hehe was inflicted by a corps of more than 600 men under the command of the next Governor, Colonel von Schele, who encircled Iringa on 30 October 1894, shelled it, and then sent in his men. Previously army posts had been set up to the north of the Hehe territories and two chiefs won over to the German side. Mkwawa escaped from his fort and for four years continued to fight for his people's independence. In 1897 Governor Liebert offered a reward of 5,000 rupees for Mkwawa, dead or alive, and ordered all captured Hehe warriors to be shot. The Hehe, whose lands had been ravaged time and again and whose cattle herds had been driven away by the detachment of mercenaries, now began to

[48] ZStA, RKolA, no. 279, p. 47.

lose hope, and they were gradually split up and set against each other. In July 1898, seeing himself in a hopeless situation, Mkwawa preferred suicide to capture.[49] The victors severed his head and sent it to Germany.

By their bitter resistance the Hehe had succeeded in delaying for years the establishment of German rule in the wide areas south of the Moro-goro-Tabora trading route. They had repeatedly stopped traffic along it. Not all tribes were able to record such successes against the far superior German troops but it was only after breaking desperate resistance by means of systematic terror that the Germans were able to establish their control. The "protective force" was thus continually occupied in the 1890s with campaigns of conquest and "punitive expeditions". Alfred Zimmermann, an official in the Colonial Office, described the years 1892—1894 in his Geschichte der deutschen Kolonialpolitik (1914) as follows:

"While these events were going on in the interior of the colony (the war against the Hehe, etc.), the struggles of the protective force in the coastal regions were continuing undiminished. At the end of February 1892 the Sultan of Ugogo, a friend of the Wahehe, was punished; in March an expeditionary force burned down the villages of the Mahenge-Mafiti, as a result of which fresh fighting broke out in the summer. At the beginning of June an expedition against Sultan Meli at Mount Kilimanjaro proved particularly unhappy. Misdemeanours by black soldiers had incensed his people, and they killed one of the soldiers. The officer in charge of the post peremptorily demanded satisfaction . . . Meli finally defended himself, and in the course of the fighting the officer in charge, von Bülow, and a second officer were killed, together with 32 soldiers . . . In January 1893 Chief Sikki's fort in Unyanyembe was stormed and Sikki killed. In March Chief Masenta's headquarters on the road to Tabora was captured, and in July the Marambos were subjugated. In August the force led by von Schele defeated Chief Meli and crushed all resistance in the Kilimanjaro area. In September the main seat of the Mahehe Chief Sinjangaro was captured, and in November Colonel von Schele . . . attacked the Wabena on the Upper Ulanga. Subsequently the Mafiti and the Mahenge were punished again. In March and April [1893] further fighting took place against Bwana Heri, who had recently become more powerful, and in September 1894 the force engaged the Mawudji in the south of the colony."[50]

[49] A. Redmayne, Mkwawa and the Hehe Wars, in Journal of African History, Vol. IX, 3 (1968), pp. 409—436; H. Loth, Griff nach Ostafrika, Berlin 1968, pp. 76—84.
[50] A. Zimmermann, Geschichte der Deutschen Kolonialpolitik, Berlin 1914, pp. 196f, 199. There is as yet no detailed historical account of the wars of the 1890s.

The campaigns of conquest came to an end, generally speaking, with the incorporation into the colony of the kingdoms of Rwanda and Burundi. In Burundi, which was torn apart by civil war between rival aristocratic factions, King Mwezi II Gisabo assented to recognize German rule following an invasion by a military unit which burned down the main centres of habitation and inflicted a serious defeat on the Barundi at Ndago on 5 June, by virtue of its quick-firing guns. Some 500 Barundi were killed.[51] However, the King and other leaders of the aristocracy continued to attack German expeditions which penetrated the country, and only a detachment of mercenaries led by Captain von Beringe, which advanced as far as Usumbura (now: Bujumbura) in 1903, succeeded in finally subjugating the King on 23 June, after 350 of his warriors had fallen. The colonial government then recognized him as ruler of the whole country and promised to support his central power against local rulers, yet right down to the end of German rule it did not prove possible to stabilize the authority of the King, and thus of the colonial government, in every part of the country.

Rwanda, similarly weakened by the infighting of the Tutsi aristocracy, proved an easier victim. An aristocratic faction led by one Kabare, which sought to collaborate with Germany in order to guarantee its leading position and continue its exploitation of the peasants and herdsmen, set Yuhi V. Musinga, a minor, on the throne as King at the beginning of 1897 and he acknowledged German supremacy on 20—23 March.[52] The aim of the annexation of the two densely populated countries was to use their considerable reserves of labour for the German plantations and to control their profitable ivory export trade.

In almost all their campaigns and "punitive expeditions" the German commanders deliberately played on the rivalries between tribal chiefs. and tribes frequently took part in warfare against their neighbours on the side of the Germans in the hope of reward or payment, even fighting against people of their ethnic unit. Captured chiefs who had fought against the Germans were executed, usually hanged; those who surrendered without a struggle were given a German flag, confirmed in office,

---

[51] *J.-P. Chrétien*, L'expédition du Capitaine Bethe contre Mwezi Gisabo (juin 1899), in Culture et Société. Revue de civilisation burundaise, Vol. III, 1980 (Bujumbura), pp. 205—212.

[52] *G. Launicke*, Zum antikolonialen Widerstand der Völker Burundis und Rwandas (1897—1916), in K. Büttner and H. Loth (eds), Philosophie der Eroberer und koloniale Wirklichkeit. Ostafrika 1884—1918, Berlin 1981, pp. 352—355.

and turned into servants of the colonial government — though in the first years they were often highly unreliable, it must be added.

The expansion of the colonial powers in East Africa during the 1890s brought about the spread of infectious diseases, which, made worse by natural disasters such as droughts and plagues of locusts, caused great loss of human life and decimated whole areas. Rinderpest, brought to Northeast Africa by Italian and British troops, spread eastwards from Lake Tanganyika from the end of 1890, and in a short time destroyed almost the entire cattle stocks in a number of areas, among them the country of the Nyamwesi.[53] Hunger and mass starvation followed; the explorer Oscar Baumann, for example, recorded in 1891 that some two-thirds of the Masai died after the loss of their herds.[54] The ability of the peoples in such areas to resist the Germans became perceptibly less. In the following years smallpox and dysentery caused the death of tens of thousands. Dr Becker, the government surgeon, calculated that in 1898 more than 150,000 fell victim to these diseases, which were spread by the trade caravans.[55] The situation was aggravated by the mercenaries' destruction of crops and theft of food supplies, and in Dr Becker's view three-quarters of a million people died of hunger in the colony between 1894 and 1898.[56]

After conquest, the representatives of the colonial power found it necessary to seek the support of the Arabs, whom they had earlier dubbed "slave traders", in establishing an administrative structure, especially in the areas adjoining the coast. The pattern of administration was as follows:

(1) in the coastal towns and their immediate vicinity government was directly in the hands of the German officials; (2) in the coastal districts and certain districts in the interior the administration was headed by a German district commissioner or station chief, assisted by a number of akidas (middle-rank officials, generally Arabs), to each of whom were assigned as subordinates a number of jumbes (village headmen, generally Africans); (3) in most interior districts the tribal, especially the paramount chiefs (some appointed by the Germans) were directly subordinate to the German officials, whose instructions they had to fulfil among their

---

[53] Cf. *H. Kjekshus*, Ecology Control and Economic Development in East African History. The Case of Tanganyika 1850—1950, London 1977, pp. 126—132.

[54] *O. Baumann*, Durch Massailand zur Nilquelle, Berlin 1894, p. 165.

[55] *M. Becker*, Über Bahnbau in Deutsch—Ostafrika, in Deutsches Kolonialblatt, vol. XV, no. 22 (15. 11. 1899).

[56] Ibid.

tribes; (4) in the high plateaux of the northwest, Burundi, Rwanda and Bukoba, so-called residentships were introduced, as in northeast Cameroon. Here the African states remained intact, or were restored, with German "residents" as advisers to the rulers, who retained control over administration, the police and the courts vis-à-vis their own subjects. The main task of the akidas, the jumbes and the chiefs was to collect the "hut tax", obtain workers for the German plantations and mobilize mass labour for local road construction or the cultivation of new crops, ordered by the governor.

The hut tax was introduced in 1898. It amounted to 6—12 rupees per year in urban areas, 3 rupees in villages, and could be paid in kind or by labour. It led to a decrease in the construction of huts and in particular to an added burden on the women, who were forced to do extra labour on the fields. Moreover, many men who were unable to pay in money or in kind were taken away to do forced labour on the plantations.

During the terms of office of four successive governors (1893—1906), all from the officer corps, the German colonial regime in East Africa acquired a reputation for the methods of the Prussian barrack-square and for bureaucratic arbitrariness. Of Schele's governorship Zimmermann writes: "The arbitrary rule of the officers created bad blood. With their sticks they made the natives stand to attention in front of every white man, tried in the coastal places to drive the dogs from the streets in one concerted action, and made no secret of the fact that they regarded the traders merely as a necessary evil."[57] In 1895, after Schele, who had refused to submit to the authority of the Colonial Department of the German Foreign Office — i.e. a non-military body — had been replaced by Wissmann (who had in the meantime become a morphine addict), and Wissmann in turn had had to be removed from office, Colonel Eduard Liebert (from 1897 Major-General) took over the post of Governor at the end of 1896. Liebert was a co-founder of the German Colonial Society and the Pan-German League. Later he became Chairman of the German Anti-Social-Democrat Association and finally joined the Nazi party in 1929. A fanatical racist, Liebert considered the Africans incapable of developing their own export production and wanted to turn the colony into a land of German farmers. Since government grants still considerably exceeded Germany's trade with the colony (1898: grants 7.66 million marks, trade 4.14 million; 1899: grants 9.39

---

[57] *A. Zimmermann*, op. cit., pp. 199—200.

million marks, trade 3.57 million),[58] Liebert gave orders that the hut tax was in future to be paid only in cash.

This measure, introduced in 1899 at a time when the population was on the brink of starvation, provoked a wave of protests and revolts, which were bloodily crushed. After one such revolt by the Chagga, near Kilimanjaro, had been suppressed, the commanding officer, one Johannes, had nineteen of their chiefs and village elders hanged. There was an uprising in the Matumbi mountains, and in the south the powerful Yao chief Machemba rebelled when called upon to pay additional taxes. When Liebert was relieved in 1901, it was not because of these rebellions — which were mostly kept secret in Germany — but because he repeatedly exceeded the bounds of his authority.

At this time a number of missionary societies had begun their activities in the colony. The Protestant Missionary Society for German East Africa, founded in Berlin in 1886 at the instigation of Carl Peters, was in its early years virtually a part of the DOAG. It saw its principal task as "teaching" the natives to work. The Catholic St Benedict Missionary Association played a similar role, and during the anti-colonial movement of 1888—9 missionaries of both these societies assisted the German forces in many ways, as did the predominantly French Congregation of Black Fathers. After the colony was taken over by the Reich, the Berlin Protestant Missionary Society and the Leipzig Evangelical-Lutheran Mission settled in the colony, and others followed. Despite differences of opinion on the purposes and methods of converting and "civilizing" the Africans, they accommodated themselves to the system of colonial rule and in no way adopted a politically neutral stance, as later historians have asserted. Many missionaries cooperated on principle with the administration and the military, some even with German firms; others were occasionally to be found taking the part of the Africans against officials and plantation owners but were careful not to indulge in "unpatriotic" critism of the colonial system as such.

In order to exploit the conquered territories more fully, the DOAG and other German firms once more penetrated into the areas adjacent to the coast after 1890. Between 1892 and 1898 many coffee plantations were founded in the Usambara mountains, and these were joined by a series of new roads and bridges to the road leading to the port of Tanga. To make the area more accessible in 1891 a subsidiary of the DOAG began to build a railway from Tanga via Korogwe to Mombo (129 kilometres), of which a mere 40 kilometres had been completed by 1897.

[58] Ibid., pp. 254—255.

In 1899 the company announced that it had no funds to continue the work and the Imperial Government took over the project. It was completed in 1905 at a total cost of 7.8 million marks. The delay in completing this railway line — work was again interrupted in 1902—3, as the Reichstag twice refused to vote further grants — was connected with the general failure of the coffee plantations. Although some 6 million marks was invested in them, until 1906 none of the companies registered a profit. The reasons were the collapse of the coffee price in Europe and insufficient attention to soil and climatic conditions. Attempts to plant tobacco, coconut palms and cotton also failed to start with. More success came with the introduction of the sisal agave from Florida. From 1902 onwards production rose so sharply that by 1907 it was the leading export crop. Rubber trees also began to be planted in larger numbers.

Thus while the plantations failed to come up to the expectations colonialists had put in them before 1906, the trade of the DOAG, Hansing & Co. and other firms with the Africans brought high profits. Intermediate and retail trade was, for the greatest part, in the hands of Indian small traders and peddlers, who were indispensable for the German wholesale firms, since they reached the furthest areas of the colony. But there were also Indian wholesale traders who offered competition to the Germans. The Indians bought up the Africans' produce (above all rubber and the products of their animal husbandry, such as skins and hides) and sold them cotton goods, clothes, small ironware, spirits, etc. This trade, in which the African peasants were often forced to take part because of the taxes demanded from them, amounted to depriving them of the fruits of their labour: they received extremely low prices for their products, and were charged high prices for the goods they bought. The German firms, with the DOAG at their head, and the Indian petty bourgeoisie, who were tolerated by the administration and the German firms as a "necessary evil", pocketed the profits.

Since the opening of the British Uganda Railway in 1902 from Mombasa via Nairobi to Kisumu on Lake Victoria, much of the trade in the areas between Tanga and Lake Victoria was drawn into the British sphere. This competition made the Colonial Department of the German Foreign Office return to the idea, first propounded in the 1890s, of a railway link between Dar es Salaam and Morogoro (209 km), which was built 1905—7. It was owned by the Ostafrikanische Eisenbahngesellschaft, founded in 1904 by the Deutsche Bank, the Disconto-Gesellschaft, Mendelssohn, Bleichröder and other banks, and by the DOAG; the first two of these had each taken a quarter of the shares.

The resistance of the peoples of "German East Africa" to foreign subjugation considerably delayed the establishment of a colonial export economy. The statistics show that the export of the traditional commodity of ivory declined more and more after 1890; between 1899 and 1906 rubber was the principal export. Exports of rubber, copra and coffee rose gradually between 1898 and 1906 but remained at a modest level; from 1903—4 sisal hemp, skins, hides and wax were also exported. The products of the Africans' gathering, arable and livestock farming exceeded those of the German plantations but exports down to 1902 did not amount to even 50 per cent of the imports, half of which consisted of cotton goods and rice, the other half largely of goods required by the administration and the European population, e.g. in 1900 for the construction of the railway. Imports of spirits, both for Africans and Europeans, were disproportionately large.

It must also be pointed out that up to and including 1904 the colony's main trading partner was not the German Reich but Zanzibar, and that there was a considerable trade with India. Some 90 per cent of the rice imported came from India, and cotton goods, though produced mainly in England and Belgium, reached East Africa via India and Zanzibar. Trade with Germany was in fact greater than the statistics reveal, since not a few shipments from and to Hamburg took the route via Zanzibar, but even allowing for this, it is clear that in 1906 the colony had no significance for Germany neither as a source of raw materials nor as a market. At the beginning of the twentieth century German East Africa was still an undeveloped colonial source of raw materials and needed considerable subsidies from the exchequer (1900: 6,035,000 marks; 1901: 6,700,000 marks; 1902: 5,259,000 marks) while providing appreciable profits for the DOAG (1900: 321,855 marks; 1901: 214,183 marks; 1902: 198,321 marks)[59].

The tighter colonial control became and the greater the extent of the exploitation, the more destructive the results were for the Africans. Until 1906 this was especially so in the coastal districts and in the district of Moshi, where the levy of taxes at the very time when the harvest had been destroyed by swarms of locusts (1897—8) contributed to great hunger and to many deaths by starvation. In Tanga, for instance, the population fell by half in a single year.[60] In the succeeding years, too, the collection of taxes resulted in a dramatic deterioration in the conditions of life for the rural population, because often more was demanded

---

[59] *R. Tetzlaff*, Koloniale Entwicklung und Ausbeutung. Wirtschafts- und Sozialgeschichte Deutsch—Afrikas 1885—1914, (West)Berlin 1970, p. 70.

[60] Ibid., p. 52.

from the villagers, whether in cash or in the form of labour, than they were able to pay without ruining their health or selling what little property they had, including their animals. One missionary wrote as follows concerning the Chagga: "The people had such a fear of government forced labour, especially in the fever-ridden steppes, that they would do anything to get hold of the three rupees necessary. Some sold their small stock for a ridiculous price to Indians and Baluchis from the British territories, who carried off large numbers of goats and sheep."[61] This labour in lieu of taxation often took the form of road construction or of work on German plantations far from where the villagers lived.

Since very few Africans were prepared to work voluntarily for the extremely low wages paid on the plantations, the planters usually made use of men pressed into service by the local administration or by corrupt chiefs. In Usambara in 1896, for instance, a worker on contract received the equivalent of 20 to 30 pfennigs per day, and his food (rice).[62] The pay and conditions of workers on the German plantations in the districts of Wilhelmsthal (now Lushoto) and Tanga were below the individual subsistence level. Unfortunately, information on the mortality rate of these workers, which was probably very high, is not available for the period in question.

Whereas the numerous uprisings and acts of resistance in the colony between 1890 and 1905 were confined to single tribes, sometimes merely to a few villages, the Maji-Maji uprising, begun by the Matumbi south of the mouth of the Rufiji in mid-1905, spread to a large part of the colony in the space of a few weeks. A German employee of the Disconto-Gesellschaft, who was working in one of the affected areas attributed it mainly to the collection of the hut-tax: "The negroes have practically no worthwhile market for their agricultural products; they have disposed of nearly all their cattle and goats in order to pay the tax, and only very few of them have any animals left. A man who cannot pay the tax is made to work for the post somewhere far away from his family and is at the mercy of the askaris, who use whips made of hippopotamus hide. Much as he hates this work, he has to comply, since otherwise his remaining animals will be taken away and his hut, with all the possessions in it, burned to the ground."[63]

---

[61] Source: *J. Franke*, Zur Herausbildung von Lohnarbeitsverhältnissen bei den Chagga unter den Bedingungen der deutschen Kolonialherrschaft, in K. Büttner and H. Loth, op. cit., p. 214.

[62] *J. Herzog*, Geschichte Tanzanias (ms), p. 51.

[63] ZStA, RKolA, np. 1055, pp. 132—134, W. Lieblinger to the Board of the Disconto-Gesellschaft, 3 Oct. 1905.

The Tanzanian historian A. J. Temu has shown that the revolt was directed not only against the German authorities but also against the unfair trade, which had been extended to the most remote areas in the south by numerous Indian and African traders.[64] But there is no doubt that the main aim of the movement, which lacked a leading centre, was the restoration of independence.

The uprising began at the end of July with a protest against the forced cultivation of cotton, introduced in the southern coastal areas by the Governor, Count von Götzen, on the model adopted in Togo. All men living in the villages where fields had been prepared for this purpose by order of the German authorities, had to work 28 days a year on these plantations without pay. The Matumbi destroyed the fields, and then attacked German plantations, after having rubbed the "miracle-water" (maji) of the prophet Kinjikitile on to their bodies and made themselves invulnerable, as they thought.

In the following weeks the Ngindo, Makonde and other tribes further south joined the revolt. The military post at Liwale was stormed and the garrison killed, while the post at Songea was besieged for several weeks. By the end of August the uprising had reached the southern half of the district of Dar es Salaam, then spread to the entire southeast of the colony, where the majority of the tribes south of a line from Dar es Salaam to the northern end of Lake Nyasa joined in, sometimes attacking military posts, towns and trading posts with a thousand men or more, but more often operating with small, mobile raiding parties which avoided direct confrontations with the enemy and attacked under cover.

In order to put down the uprising, which was one of the most powerful anticolonial movements in the history of East Africa, reinforcements were sent to the colony. The units marching into the affected areas had orders to starve the population into submission. Villages were therefore burned down, cattle and food stocks confiscated, and the harvest destroyed on the fields. Insurgents who were captured were either put do death or sentenced to years of forced labour in chains. In Songea alone 48 Ngoni warriors were publicly hanged on 27 February 1906, while tens of thousands were killed in the fighting or massacred by the askaris and the familiar "auxiliaries". The numbers of those who starved to death were even greater. Thus of the c. 30,000 Pangwa tribesmen living by Lake Nyasa, only 1,000—1,500 were left after the revolt. Other tribes suffered

[64]   A. J. Temu, Tanzanian Societies and Colonial Invasion 1875—1907, in H. Y. Kaniki (ed.), Tanzania under Colonial Rule. Historical Association of Tanzania 1980, pp. 117—118.

similar losses. The Tanzanian historian G.C.K. Gwassa has estimated that a total of between 250,000 and 300,000 people died. In the following years whole areas in the south were almost entirely depopulated, and the official annual report for 1906—7 states that in the districts of Rufiji, Lindi, Kilwa and especially Songea, agriculture "was in a pitiful state as a result of the great number of casualties."[65] Even extended tribal wars of the past had not had such disastrous consequences. According to an American correspondent who travelled in Tanganyika in 1952—3, the south had even then "not fully recovered from the German terror half a century ago. The economy of the region has never been successfully rebuilt."[66]

The administration succeeded in crushing the revolt in the several centres by April and May 1906, though it still flared up again from time to time, and not until July 1907 did the Governor declare the state of war to be over in the district of Songea. The Maji-Maji uprising, together with the parallel risings in South West Africa and Cameroon, played an important part in forcing the Reich government under Bülow to modify its entire colonial policy.

---

[65] *Jahresbericht* über die Entwicklung der Deutschen Schutzgebiete im Jahre 1906—07, p. 4. According to an official statement in the Reichstag African deaths through fighting, starvation and disease amounted to 75,000. StBVR, Sess. 1907—1909, vol. 622, Appendices p. 3693.

[66] *J. Gunther*, Inside Africa, London 1955, p. 404.

IV. Economic Expansion and Political Aims in South Africa 1884—1898

Since the late seventies German capitalists recognized South Africa's considerable economic potential, but colonial annexations by the German Reich were no longer possible, as the failure of an attempt by Lüderitz showed. In 1884 he tried to establish a territorial link between Angra Pequena on the coast of South West Africa and the Boer Republic of the Transvaal and acquire land along the Zulu coast, but his plans came to nothing owing to the resistance of the British and also Bismarck's disapproval. The German government and German business circles interested in South Africa had to reckon with two groups of forces who had managed to consolidate their exploitation of the African population before 1870: the Afrikaner farmers (Boers) and the British colonial power. The latter was using its dominant position to penetrate the economics of the Boer Republics and bring the Orange Free State and the Transvaal as well as Zululand and other independent African territories step by step under British rule.

International finance capital, still in its beginnings, witnessed its first South African boom during the seventies. With the introduction of deep level mining the newly founded Kimberley diamond mines required complex machinery and capital beyond the reach of the individual digger. A number of German firms taking part in the Kimberley boom, such as Eduard Lippert of Hamburg, profited mainly from trading with the mining companies. German immigrants such as Alfred Beit, Julius Wernher and Max Michaelis, who had emerged from the early days of turbulent, wild competition as notable South African diamond magnates, were drawn into the financial world of London and Paris, where they prospered; German banks had no part at all in the creation and growth of the diamond monopoly of De Beers, headed by Cecil Rhodes.

The second South African boom began with the discovery of the huge gold deposits on the Witwatersrand (Transvaal) in 1886. British South African groups which already ruled over the diamond mines dominated the most important gold-mining companies and syndicates that were founded between 1887 and 1892. Again, German immigrants played an important part in these enterprises, most of them associated with British finance. This time, however, German and French financiers also sought a share in the very high profits, and in late 1889 the Deutsche Bank started to show a serious interest in Transvaal gold.

Georg Siemens, the effective head of the Deutsche Bank, formed a banking consortium at that point to finance gold-mining enterprises in Transvaal with an amount of up to 2 million marks. The crisis of the following year presented the consortium, which was backed almost exclusively by the Deutsche Bank, with an opportunity, as Helfferich wrote, "to acquire valuable mining property or participate in such".[1] In early 1893, Siemens' plan to found his own company in South Africa, with his brother-in-law Görz at the helm, actually came to fruition. Adolf Görz & Co. GmbH of Berlin and Johannesburg opened business with a subscribed capital of 3,200,000 marks. "It acquired major interests in various parts of the Witwatersrand," wrote Helfferich, "and used these in part as a basis for setting up its own mining companies which remained under its control. The Rand Central Ore Reduction Works was founded as a metallurgical enterprise to process ore waste . . ."[2] The Deutsche Bank and Görz collaborated with Siemens & Halske in 1895 to build the Rand Central Electric Works, the first big plant of this kind to supply the Witwatersrand gold mines with power and light. Adolf Görz & Co. yielded very high dividends in its first two years of business (1894: 35 per cent, 1895: 50 per cent).

Siemens planned to break the monopoly which the Rhodes clique, and with them British high finance, held on the buying and selling of Transvaal gold. "It could prove important to a country with a gold currency such as Germany," he wrote several years afterwards, "that some of the gold also be shipped directly to Germany. The idea was to instruct the managers of some mines whose capital was German to ship the gold directly to Germany . . ."[3] This would have meant a direct attack on London's dominating role on the international gold market. "Had German capital succeeded in taking possessions of the gold fields in the Transvaal," says Jerussalimski, "this would have strengthened the financial and economic position of the young German imperialism sub-

---

[1] K. Helfferich, Georg von Siemens. Ein Lebensbild aus Deutschlands grosser Zeit, Vol. 2, Berlin 1923, p. 287.

[2] Ibid., pp. 287—288.

[3] Ibid., pp. 288—289.

stantially. That is the reason why Georg Siemens . . . was so keenly interested in the affairs of the Transvaal."[4]

Other big German banks also engaged themselves in the Transvaal gold fields. In 1895 the Dresdner Bank joined with G. & L. Albu to found the General Mining and Finance Corporation Ltd., which had a capital of £ 1.25 million; in 1894 it had participated with the Darmstädter Bank in founding the Süd-Afrikanische Metallurgische Vereinigung, GmbH, renamed African Metals Company a year later. These companies had considerable interests in a wide range of mining enterprises in the Boer Republic.

German banks were at the same time penetrating other sectors of the Transvaal economy by means of collaboration with the authorities of this republic of Boer farmers. The British government was supporting Rhodes' plans for a railway and customs union between the British Cape Colony and the Transvaal, and it was fear of British subjugation which prompted leading Boers to encourage close relations with the Reich and favour a broad penetration of German capital into their economy (or, more accurately, the economy which was being run on their territory).

German capital struck its strongest roots in sectors where the Boer state either held control or granted concessions of a monopoly character, i.e. communications (railways), the building materials industry (cement), flour mills and state finance. The political framework had been created by the visit which President Krüger of the Transvaal paid to the German Kaiser (8 July 1884) and the Treaty of Friendship and Trade between Germany and the Transvaal of 22 January 1885, under which the Reich was guaranteed most favoured nation rights; the economic starting point was Krüger's award of a monopoly concession for railway construction in the Republic to a Dutch syndicate in August 1884.

When the syndicate founded the Nederlandsche Zuid-Afrikaansche Spoorweg Maatschappij (Netherlands South African Railway Company) in Amsterdam in 1887, the Berlin banks Berliner Handelsgesellschaft and Robert Warschauer & Co. took part; along with the Dutch bank Labouchère Oyens & Co. they purchased substantial share packets and offered obligations on the German market. In about 1889 the Deutsche Bank joined this consortium, whose activities apparently led to several loans being signed primarily in Germany. (A British enquiry found that in 1897 almost half the shares in the Railway Company were held by

---

[4] *A. S. Jerussalimski*, Die Aussenpolitik und die Diplomatie des deutschen Imperialismus Ende des 19. Jahrhunderts, Berlin 1954, p. 127.

German or Austrian investors.) The Company's objective was to build a railway from Delagoa Bay in the Portuguese colony of Mozambique to Pretoria, capital of the Transvaal. The project had great political significance, since such a link would provide the Boer Republic, surrounded and threatened as it was, with its only route to the sea that was not dependent on Britain. It was an outstanding coup for the banks involved and a number of German industrial firms; apart from the interest and dividends on the money invested (with dividends averaging 11 per cent until 1899), it brought the suppliers high profits. The engineering side was entrusted to Lenz & Co., a railway building company which was part of the Berliner Handelsgesellschaft group; most of the orders for materials went to the Köln-Deutzer Waggonfabrik and the Verein für Bergbau und Gußstahlfabrikation in Bochum, keeping both of them going during the crisis of the early 1890s. Construction went on until 1895, whereas the rail routes from the Transvaal to the ports of Cape Town, Port Elizabeth and East London in Cape Colony had been completed by 1892.

In 1889 leading German bankers and industrialists, as well as the government of the Reich, had realized the value of the railway link between Delagoa Bay and Pretoria as a means of access to the Transvaal which would enable them to penetrate the Boer economy.[5] First steps were taken. The Deutsche Ostafrika-Linie was founded by a banking consortium under the Disconto-Gesellschaft and the Berliner Handelsgesellschaft with a capital of 6 million marks and was headed by the Hamburg shipping magnate Adolf Woermann. In July 1890 it opened its regular service from Hamburg to Delagoa Bay. The newly founded line received from the government the 900,000 mark annual subsidy which the Reichstag had approved in January 1890 for scheduled traffic to East Africa, with sailings every four weeks. The service broke the British monopoly on shipping to South Africa. Through freight traffic from inland German cities to Johannesburg facilitated the export of German goods to the region, which had become the subject of exceptionally high hopes, because gold exports from the Transvaal kept growing, and with it the Republic's economic importance.[6]

Penetration by the big German banks proceeded apace in the early 1890s. The Berliner Handelsgesellschaft managed to grab many key

[5] For details see *G. W. F. Hallgarten*, Imperialismus vor 1914, Vol. 1, Munich 1963, pp. 367ff.

[6] Cf. *K. Brackmann*, Fünfzig Jahre deutscher Afrikaschiffahrt. Berlin 1935, p. 35; also StBVR, 7. Legislaturperiode, V. Sess. 1889/90. vol. 3, Annex no. 106.

positions in the Transvaal. In 1891 it dispatched Wilhelm Knappe to Pretoria, where he helped set up a National Bank and Mint and was soon appointed a director of both, together with other representatives of German banking capital.[7] In 1890 Eduard Lippert had opened the first cement factory in Transvaal near Daspoort, Pretoria; in 1894 the Nobel Dynamite Explosives Co. (an Anglo-German firm controlled by the Hamburg-based Dynamit AG, which was close to the Deutsche Bank) was awarded monopoly rights, with Lippert's assistanc, for the supply of explosives to the mines and the armed forces. Systematic bribery of a number of influential people in the Republic resulted in exceptionally high profits for the firm, which represented mainly German capital interests, at the expense of the mainly British gold-mining companies.

The rest of the German armaments industry was also eager for some of the Boer market. Krupp and Ludwig Löwe, a weapons factory which had strong connections with the Disconto-Gesellschaft, captured most of the orders; Krupp artillery began to arrive in Pretoria. This development was reflected in a sudden rise of German exports to the Transvaal. Whereas Germany's statistics for 1892 did not list any exports to the Boer Republic, the figures for 1893 for the first time showed a noteworthy volume of sales which rose to about 6 million marks in 1894[8] and kept growing for a number of years. Although German trading with the Transvaal never came near the British level, the London newspapers started to sound the alarm.

In June 1895 the railway from Pretoria to Lourenço Marques, the port in Delagoa Bay, was officially opened amid spectacular celebrations, and President Krüger visited one of the German warships anchored in the Bay. Krüger and the Kaiser sent each other dispatches to mark a new era of "German-Boer friendship". According to information which Adolf Görz gave Ambassador von Hatzfeldt, and which was almost certainly exaggerated, German capital investments in the Transvaal by the end of the year exceeded 500 million marks.[9] (In 1895 a "Kaffir boom"

---

[7] For details see Carl Fürstenberg, Die Lebensgeschichte eines deutschen Bankiers. Niedergeschr. v. *H. Fürstenberg*, Wiesbaden 1961, pp. 198, 271 and 485—486; *Der deutsche Beitrag* zur Entwicklung Südafrikas (Pretoria 1962), p. 14.

[8] *R. J. S. Hoffman*, Great Britain and the German Trade Rivalry 1875—1914; Philadelphia 1933, p. 205.

[9] *GP*, vol. 11, no. 2613, p. 33. In a letter to Queen Victoria dated 8 Jan. 1896, Wilhelm II put German capital interests in the Transvaal at about 300 million marks. Cf. *F. Thimme*, Die Krüger-Depesche, in Europäische Gespräche, 1924, no. 3, p. 243.

had driven the price of Transvaal gold shares up, and until the collapse in September 1895 the shares of the major mining companies totalled £ 215 million, equivalent to 4,300 million marks.[10])

The sympathy shown by the Transvaal government, which regarded Germany as the lesser of two evils, was requited more and more frequently among the German bourgeoisie, particularly its colonialist and Pan-German elements, with an affection for their "Low German kinsmen" which was obviously related to expansionist ambitions. Already in 1884 the famous historian Heinrich von Treitschke had expressed the view that it would be "a natural turn of events if an ethnically related Germany . . . were to undertake the protection of South Africa's Teutonic population and enter upon the British legacy."[11] Since this question has never been examined systematically, it is impossible to say how far Treitschke's thinking took concrete shape in ruling circles or whether state promotion of economic expansion was ultimately intended to serve political ends going beyond preserving the Transvaal's independence as a state. Of course, defending the status quo against Britain was essential if any further aims were to be reached.

However that may be, economic penetration in the Transvaal drew the attention of the German Foreign Office and the Kaiser to the area, and in 1894—5 they began to see the Boer Republic as a kind of prospective German sphere of influence. In 1893—4, the German Foreign Office had already taken part in warding off energetic attempts by Rhodes to establish control over Delagoa Bay and the railway to Pretoria. German diplomats emphatically supported the efforts to this end of Krüger's Secretary of State Leyds, who received an assurance from the Portuguese government in August 1893 that the Bay would not be ceded to British interests. But the Portuguese government was financially weak, and in July 1894, when it began to waver, the German Ambassador in Lisbon delivered a note containing a powerful threat to the effect that any submission to British advances "would force Germany to break with Portugal in order to guarantee its national rights and ad-

---

According to a memo by von Mühlberg, legation counsellor in the German Foreign Office, dated 13 Feb. 1896, German mining investments amounted to approximately 100 million marks. ZStA, A.A., no. 11842, p. 175.

[10] *C. G. W. Schumann*, Structural changes and business cycles in South Africa 1806 to 1936, London 1938, p. 91.

[11] *H. v. Treitschke*, Deutsche Kämpfe, Leipzig 1896. pp. 48—49.

vantages in the future alone and by that method which circumstances would dictate".[12]

When 20 British marines went ashore in Lourenço Marques in September 1894 to help put down an uprising by local Africans, the German government protested and sent two warships to the port, a move which the Kölnische Zeitung described as "an unambiguous hands off to English aspirations".[13] Count Joachim Pfeil, Carl Peters' notorious associate, was named German consul in Lourenço Marques at the end of 1894, and at the same time the German government assured the Transvaal Republic of its support in protecting the status quo in the Delagoa Bay (including, if necessary, by financial means) and stressed its wish to strengthen the position of the Republic.[14]

In November 1894, Wilhelm II pressed the Chancellor to acquire Mozambique (i.e. Delagoa Bay) from Portugal, and the German Foreign Office grew increasingly disquieted as it observed the preparations of the Rhodes clique to incorporate the Transvaal and its gold deposits into the British Empire by means of a customs and economic union. When Rhodes openly declared his intentions in Britain in January 1895, the German press, from the Kreuzzeitung to the Vossische Zeitung, protested indignantly and announced that Germany would defend its significant interests in the Transvaal. The Boers could count on German support in resisting British blackmail.

At the same time, the German commitment in the Transvaal and involvement in railway construction were arousing the increasing suspicion of the British government. Even before the railway was completed, Colonial Secretary Lord Ripon decided to cut off the Transvaal's remaining chance of access to the sea south of Mozambique, and this was achieved when Britain annexed Tongaland in May 1895. In February 1895, Foreign Secretary Lord Kimberley informed Berlin that "the German government's attitude towards the South African Republic was creating a mood there which could not be reconciled with the latter's international status". In the Transvaal, he claimed, the conviction was spreading "that Germany's support could definitely be relied on . . . In

---

[12] Note of 10 July 1894. Source: *G. W. F. Hallgarten*, Imperialismus vor 1914, vol. 2, Munich 1963, pp. 533—534.

[13] Kölnische Zeitung, 17 Oct. 1894.

[14] Marschall to Herff, 3 Dec. 1894, in: *G. W. F. Hallgarten*, op. cit., pp. 536—537. Cf. also *P. R. Warhurst*, Anglo-Portuguese Relations in South-Central Africa 1890—1900, London 1962, p. 132: *British Documents* on the Origins of the War 1898—1914, Vol. I, London 1927, p. 323.

this respect Britain was most sensitive . . ." The German Foreign Secretary, von Marschall, replied that Germany's "material interests . . . demanded that the Transvaal be maintained as an economically independent state and that the status quo be made secure regarding the railways and Delagoa Bay".[15] In October the British Ambassador warned the German Foreign Secretary "that continuation of the German attitude to the Transvaal could lead to serious complications".[16] The rivalry between the two powers for predominant influence in the Boer Republic had acutely aggravated the colonial antagonism between them which had become apparent since late 1893. German domination would have wrecked the plans for a united South Africa under British control and, in the long term, might even have jeopardized British rule in Cape Colony.

When news reached Berlin in the last days of December 1895 that the conflict which Rhodes had been fanning between the Pretoria government and the British mining companies in Johannesburg had taken a serious turn, the German Foreign Office warned Great Britain not to intervene militarily; Marschall emphasized that Germany "would be unable to accept the change in the status quo Cecil Rhodes respectively the Cape government were striving for, since this would severely impair our commercial interests"[17], and he went so far as to threaten the British ambassador with a continental alliance against Britain.

As soon as the German Foreign Office learned about the armed attack on Johannesburg (Jameson Raid) which Rhodes' Chartered Company began on 29 December, the German Ambassador in London was instructed to request his passports if the British government declared its approval for the invasion. Accompanied by Kayser, head of the Colonial Department, Marschall went to see the Kaiser in Potsdam, and, in agreement with the High Naval Command, proposed that German troops should be landed on the pretext of protecting Germans in Pretoria. Orders were given for a detachment of marines to be sent to Pretoria from the cruiser Seeadler lying in Delagoa Bay and for a large unit of colonial troops to be transported to the Transvaal from German East Africa.

On 2 January Marschall instructed the German Ambassador in London to deliver a note protesting against the attack, stating explicitly that the German government "is not prepared to accept any change in the international status of the South African Republic as laid down in

---

[15] *GP*, vol. 11, no. 2577, pp. 3—4.

[16] Ibid., no. 2578, p. 6.

[17] Ibid., no. 2586, p. 16.

treaties".[18] But when in the same evening the news arrived that Rhodes' accomplice Jameson and his unit had been defeated and taken prisoner, he ordered the ambassador speedily to retrieve the note which had been delivered to the British Foreign Office but not yet opened. The failure of the British attack made the dispatch of German troops to the Transvaal superfluous, and Krüger, who seemed to distrust the intentions of the German government, had in any case already asked for a postponement of this move.

Although Marschall apparently did not think further steps necessary, the Kaiser, in a state of extreme chauvinistic excitement, wanted to use the crisis to gain huge grants from the Reichstag for building the German war fleet. On 3 January, he demanded the mobilization of the Marines and deployment of troops to the Transvaal, and insisted that Germany should declare the Boer Republic a protectorate. To restrain him from this hazardous step, which would inevitably have led to a war with Britain, Marschall immediately had a telegram from the Kaiser to President Krüger (the "Krüger Telegram") drafted and approved, which was an open challenge to the British rivals and was well understood as such across the Channel. In this telegram Wilhelm congratulated the President for having succeeded, "without appealing for assistance from friendly powers . . . in restoring peace and safeguarding the country's independence against attacks from without by your own actions against the armed hordes which disrupted the peace by breaking into your country".[19]

Marschall managed to distract Wilhelm from his dangerous plans by means of the dispatch, but its publication naturally contributed to the chauvinist war hysteria being fostered against Britain by the bourgeois German newspapers. This was the first time that the Anglo-German antagonism in international politics showed itself in all its gravity. Eulenburg, a close friend of Wilhelm and Ambassador in Vienna, told the Foreign Minister of Austria-Hungary that it must be "in Germany's interest to counter vigorously, if necessary, the infinite extension of Britain's sphere of power in Africa, where we should be keeping watch on the prestige and development of our colonies".[20]

The bourgeois German press was unanimously ecstatic about the Krüger Telegram. The German Colonial Society (Deutsche Kolonial-gesellschaft), which had demanded active support for the Transvaal's independence in June 1895, and the Pan-German League conveyed de-

[18] Ibid., no. 2600, p. 27.

[19] Ibid., no. 2610, pp. 31—32.

[20] Ibid., no. 2608 note, p. 30.

clarations of assent to the government, expressing their thanks for its "resolute" attitude.

However, Germany did not take any further political steps of any significance in support of the Transvaal, since France and Russia did not respond to German suggestions for a common approach, while Vienna and Rome displayed outright alarm at the conflict with Britain and clearly were not willing to support the policy of their German ally. On 7 January the Chancellor, Prince Hohenlohe, warned the Kaiser, presumably at the request of the Foreign Office, that Wilhelm's plans for a possible occupation of Lourenço Marques would result in an immediate alliance between Britain and France. "At the present time any initiative on our part is out of the question," he wrote to his Emperor, "if we are not to incur the danger of being pushed further and further against Britain by France and Russia and isolating ourselves."[21] Wilhelm reluctantly gave way to this urgent advice. Marschall, who had recommended to Krüger that the Transvaal should seek international guarantees for its neutrality, withdrew his suggestion several days later and advised the Boers to take a moderate line.

The Krüger Telegram was a spontaneous act, and Marschall did not fully foresee the effect it would have on the attitude of the British bourgeoisie. By shaking its fist at Britain the German government wanted to show that Germany would not accept the further expansion of Britain's African empire unless there were compensations, and that Britain would be well advised to seek good relations with the Triple Alliance.[22]

But Germany's statesmen were clearly sobered by the confrontation with Britain in January 1896. They realized that, given Germany's isolation and the lack of a powerful naval force, the most they could hope for was to preserve and perhaps expand the existing economic foothold in the Transvaal. While German diplomacy continued to support the status quo in Delagoa Bay and in the Transvaal in 1896—7, the idea of a German sphere of influence in the Transvaal had to be abandoned, even though certain colonialist circles and the Pan-German League clung to this ambition.

In the summer of 1898, Foreign Secretary Bernhard von Bülow wrote to the German Ambassador in St. Petersburg: "Once the feelers we put out to the Russians and French revealed that we were isolated vis-à-vis Britain in protecting German interests in South Africa, the only course left to us was to arrive at a direct understanding with the British on the

[21] Ibid., no. 2618, p. 38.
[22] Cf. *A. S. Jerussalimski*, op. cit., pp. 142ff.

South African question."[23] The initiative in this direction had been taken on the diplomatic level by the Ambassador in London, Hatzfeldt, who, in view of definite signs of imminent British aggression against the Transvaal and Delagoa Bay, at the suggestion of Holstein asked his government in April 1897 "whether it would not be worth while attempting to find out — as long as the crisis in South Africa has not become acute — if an understanding with Britain could not be arrived at which would at least enable us to win compensations for something which we will lose in any case". Wilhelm II and Hohenlohe had empowered him to approach Lord Salisbury, the British Prime Minister,[24] and in the following year an agreement was reached. The "understanding" took the form of the Angola Treaty of 30 August 1898 which provided for Portugal's colonies to be shared between the two powers if that financially extremely weak country should prove unable to repay its debts to one of the signatories. The agreement allocated southern Mozambique, including Delagoa Bay, to Britain, and this, of course, meant that Germany completely gave up its political relations with the Transvaal, leaving the Rhodes-Chamberlain group a free hand.

The political and military reasons for Germany's change of policy are obvious enough. The compensations for abandoning the Boers and giving up aims of political expansion in South Africa seemed to be substantial and attractive. Chamberlain, the British Colonial Secretary, was prepared to conciliate the Germans, not only for the sake of those aggressive plans for South Africa of which he was a leading proponent, but also because he strove for an alliance with Berlin. "Well!" he wrote to his fellow cabinet minister Balfour, "it is worth while to pay blackmail sometimes."[25] The German government was clearly expecting that the British desire to take over Delagoa Bay would soon bring about the partition of the Portuguese colonies. But there were other reasons, too, for renouncing political support to the Boer Republic, and these were seen in its economic conditions.

Eberhard Czaya describes economic development thus: "When A. Goerz and Company Ltd. was registered in Johannesburg late in 1897 as a company according to British law, South Africa was already accounting for 120,000 kg out of a total world gold output of 432,000 kg. The big, universal gold boom was just going through a crisis due to over-

---

[23] *GP*, vol. 14, no. 3877, p. 361, Telegram sent by Bülow to Radolin on 2 Sept. 1898.
[24] *GP*, vol. 13, no. 3404, pp. 20—21, Report by Hatzfeldt, dated 22 April 1898.
[25] Source: *J. L. Garvin*, The Life of Joseph Chamberlain, Vol. III, London 1934, p. 315.

speculation, and this again enabled the Deutsche Bank and other German contenders to take over control or at least purchase a stake in many weakened South African enterprises. It had become obvious, however, during 1896—7, that German finance capital had no long-term prospects, given the existing balance of forces, of holding its own against British resistance in the gold fields. The only approach which promised success was to cooperate with the established British monopoly groups.

"The Deutsche Bank now forged very close business links with British banks in order to make use of London for its South African transactions. The shares of most of the South African mining companies founded at the time by German financiers were put on sale in the City. Connections with the British bourgeoisie were made use of to expand the capital base and draw on British business experience. Moreover, funding in sterling was a great advantage, because it was the currency in general use in South Africa and the centres of the gold trade. London was accepted as the trading capital for gold, and the Cape route was preferred for shipments to the less convenient Delagoa Bay.

"If the Deutsche Bank, which had been so eager for independence from Britain, could not disengage its South African dealings from British capital, the other German banks which followed Görz's example in South Africa had even more difficulty.

"Certain British bankers, such as Sir Felix Schuster of the Union of London and Smiths Bank Ltd., who was close to Rothschild, played an extremely important part in setting up an Anglo-German financial partnership in South Africa; so, too, did banking families such as Lazard, Schröder, Speyer, Stern Brothers and others with ties of kinship to members of the German financial world.

"This Anglo-German partnership led to a controversy between the German owners of gold field shares led by Görz and those who benefited from the monopoly privileges granted by the Transvaal government. The big German banks turned against these privileges because they made mining more expensive. They were particularly scathing in their attacks on the dynamite monopoly held by the Nobel Trust, and the high freight charges demanded by the Netherlands South African Railway Company also came in for sharp criticism. The Berliner Handelsgesellschaft suffered a conflict of interests, since it was financing the railway line between Pretoria and Delagoa Bay and at the same time owned shares in the gold mines.

"The engagement of German finance capital in the gold mines and the ancillary power stations in the Transvaal, and the partnership with British finance, contributed not a little to the subsequent political reorientation, which was reflected in the Anglo-German agreement of 30 August 1898 on the partition of the Portuguese colonies and in Germany's withdrawal of support for the Boers."[26]

The state of research does not yet permit us to make precise assertions about the extent to which the German government was influenced in its decision to abandon the Boers to British imperialism by the Deutsche Bank's cooperation with British financial circles.[27] But in view of the bank's close connections with the German Foreign Office we can assume that economic interests and foreign policy conditioned each other in the decision-making process. Adolf Görz had complained to the Foreign Office several times about the attitude of the Krüger government towards the mining companies, and had gone so far as to comment in late 1897 that "German economic interests" would not be averse to the establishment of British rule in the Transvaal.[28]

German capital investments in the gold fields were far higher than in other sectors of the Transvaal economy, and the mining companies controlled by German banks were as keen as the British firms to see the destruction of a republic which was neither willing nor able to satisfy their demands for state recruitment of African labour, low charges for railway freight, an end to the state system of granting monopolies, and much more besides.

[26] *E. Czaya*, Die ökonomische Expansion nach Südafrika 1884—1898 (MS).

[27] Cf. also *G. W. F. Hallgarten*, op. cit., pp. 424—426.

[28] *J. J. Van-Helten*, German Capital, the Netherlands Railway Company and the Political Economy of the Transvaal 1886—1900, in: The Journal of African History, Vol. XIX, 1978, pp. 386—387; *J. J. Van-Helten*, Mining and Imperialism, in: Journal of Southern African Studies, Vol. 6, No. 2, 1980, p. 234.

V. Semi-Colonial Expansion into Morocco 1871—1898

In the last quarter of the 19th century there was a sharp surge in the struggle to carve up the globe. Even Morocco, which hitherto had not attracted much interest, became a target for the expansionist ambitions of some capitalist powers.

Morocco was a backward, feudal country. It was an absolute monarchy with the Sultan as its secular and spiritual leader. His power, however, was confined to the fertile, easily accessible plains, where his officials mercilessly exploited the peasants and nomads. Many of the Arab and Berber tribes in the Atlas and Rif Mountains, where some remnants of the old classless communal order had survived, refused to offer obedience or tribute to the central authority (makhzen). Feudal exploitation and oppression, the Sultan's frequent wars against rebellious tribes, countless tribal feuds and constant power struggles between rival contenders for the throne had created a situation which hindered economic development and weakened the country's ability to defend itself.

The struggle against Spanish and Portuguese invasions from the 15th to the 18th century had isolated Morocco from the economic and cultural developments taking place in Europe. Economic stagnation persisted into the 19th century. The towns had lost much of their former splendour. And yet there were many highly skilled crafts plied within their walls. The big merchants of Fez, Rabat and Tangier traded not only with the countries of northern and trans-Saharan Africa, but also with Europe.

Since the middle of the century, Britain, France, Spain and other powers forced the Sultanate to accept unequal treaties securing important privileges for their own diplomats and merchants. By extending the status of "protected persons" to subjects of the Sultan, the Europeans found supporters and agents for themselves within the country. At the same time, the country was repeatedly the victim of military aggression. Once France had established colonial rule in Algeria in 1830, defeated the Moroccan army at the River Isly in 1844 and forced Morocco to sign a treaty the following year amending its borders, the French army persisted with its incursions into Moroccan territory. France then began to annex areas under the Sultan's sovereignty. In 1859—60, 1884 and 1893, Spain also embarked on military campaigns against Morocco. In the contest for economic and political influence, Morocco became the object of a tug of war among capitalist powers.

When the German Empire started looking for a foothold it was immediately confronted by strong foreign competition, and by the protective measures which Sultan Moulay Hassan (1873—1894) took to defend his country against colonial subjugation. The Reich government responded to demands from industrial, mercantile and shipping quarters for broader relations with the Sharifian Empire by opening a German Consulate in Tangier in 1873 (whose head was two years later granted the status of a minister resident) and by beginning negotiations for a trade treaty.

Although the German bourgeoisie were primarily interested in the sub-Saharan regions of Africa, the increasingly bitter struggle between the colonial powers to divide up the rest of the earth prompted them to regard even Morocco, for all the difficulties it presented, as a desirable expansionist picking. As one of the signatories to the Madrid Treaty of 1880, Germany officially took its place among those states which enjoyed privileges in Morocco. The convention more or less sanctioned the rights which the capitalist countries had already acquired for themselves, including the institution of "protected persons". German traders in Morocco, too, made use of this by putting more and more local merchants, civil servants and landowners under the protection of their diplomatic representatives, thereby providing them with immunity from the overlordship of the Sultan. This was a specific method of economic and political infiltration. It encouraged the growth of a comprador sector and eventually threatened the sovereignty in the Moroccan state.

Bismarck, however, was not very interested in Morocco as an object for semi-colonial exploitation. Germany's Moroccan policy in the 1870s and 1880s was, rather, part of its European policy, and dictated by that policy's aims. Bismarck's diplomatic strategy was to encourage French and British expansion in North Africa in the hope of exacerbating the antagonism between Britain and France and preventing them from forming a coalition against Germany. At the same time, he calculated that France would not succeed in subjugating Morocco except at very great cost. The Chancellor assumed that colonial expansion in Morocco would make considerable demands on the French military forces and thus stifle any ideas of a war of revenge against Germany.

In 1875 Bismarck wrote: "In the ordinary course of events it is no disadvantage to us and nothing we would wish to oppose if French policy
seeks to establish a field for its activity in North Africa and the Turkish
Orient. The absorption of forces which France has deployed and committed there and the disputes which it becomes involved in divert it
from its aggressive sentiments towards Germany. All the other great
powers, including Italy and even Spain, have more cause than we do to
be jealous of France in the Mediterranean Sea."[1]

This encouragement for French colonial expansion did not mean
that the ruling circles in Germany wanted France to subjugate Morocco
sooner rather than later. Bismarck and military leaders considered that
in a war with France, Morocco would be an ideal base for a diversionary
attack against the French power in Algeria. In Bismarck's view, the mere
possibility of such a diversion provided him with an effective lever against
Paris even in times of peace. To avert this danger the government in
Paris would be compelled to transfer troops from the border between
Germany and France to the border between Algeria and Morocco. If
a war broke out, attacks could be launched from Morocco on the French
in Algeria, and France would be obliged to deploy substantial forces
in North Africa. Ten years later, Bismarck commented on the situation
in 1874: "Our relations with Morocco contained an important military
element in the eventuality of a war against France."[2]

Sometimes one aspect predominated and sometimes the other, according to the international situation. During periods of heightened tension
between France and Germany (1871—7 and 1885—9), military considerations were in the foreground, whereas Germany's Moroccan policy
in the years 1878 to 1884 was characterized by approval for French
colonial expansion in North Africa. Moreover, from the mid-1880s
Bismarck attempted, albeit in vain, to exploit the antagonisms between
the other powers in Morocco and draw Spain, Britain and Italy into a
coalition against France.

This policy, which was basically preserved into the 1890s, called
for a firm economic base for the German bourgeoisie in Morocco and
for an effective German political influence on the central Moroccan
authority. At the same time it required the maintenance of that authority,
because otherwise Morocco could not play the role ascribed to it in the
event of a war between Germany and France.

---

[1] *GP*, vol. 1, no. 194, Bismarck to the Ambassador in Paris, Prince von Hohenlohe,
10 Jan. 1875.

[2] Source: *P. Guillen*, L'Allemagne et le Maroc de 1870 à 1905, Paris 1967, p. 32.

It was therefore not simply the demands of foreign trade expansion, but also these considerations which caused the Imperial government cautiously to support attempts by German merchants, shipping companies and industrialists to gain a foothold in Morocco. The government helped to sponsor economic and geographical exploration and worked for a trade treaty which would contain a number of concessions from the Sultan (more open ports, repeal of bans on certain imports and exports, reductions in import duties) and for permission for German traders to purchase land without restriction. As in Turkey and China, the Foreign Office particularly supported efforts by the German armaments industry to win contracts for supplying weapons and military equipment.

Although the policy of maintaining the status quo in Morocco and strengthening the Sultan's power was primarily pursued so that the Reich government could achieve its aims in Europe, it did also suit the long-term colonial ambitions of the German upper bourgeoisie. If Morocco had lost its sovereignty at that time, Germany would probably have remained empty-handed. Thanks to the status quo, it had an opportunity to gain time and consolidate its economic and political positions sufficiently not to be excluded when the country was eventually divided up.

Systematic geographical and economic exploration paved the way and provided an impetus for the German bourgeoisie to penetrate Morocco in the 1880s and 1890s. Travels by geographers, traders, military officers and adventurers during those years investigated the country's potential as a target for colonial expansion, as previously information about the population, the climate, natural resources, etc., had been fragmentary. Amongst those who fulfilled this task were Adolph von Conring, Gerhard Rohlfs, Oskar Lenz, Jakob Schaudt, Max Quedenfeld, Johann Justus Rein, Otto Kersten, and Robert Jannasch. Their Moroccan expeditions were sponsored by various geographical and colonial societies.

The Central Association for Commercial Geography and the Promotion of German Interests Abroad, founded in 1879 with Jannasch and Kersten as its leaders, attempted to become the propaganda agency and organizational centre of German expansion in Morocco. By 1880 its better known members already included Werner Siemens, one of the founders of the Siemens electrical company, Adolf von Hansemann, head of the Disconto-Gesellschaft, Heinrich von Kusserow, Counsellor at the Foreign Office, and the explorer Gerhard Rohlfs. Although the association primarily represented the interests of companies in the Rhineland, Southern Germany, Saxony and Thuringia who manufactured or exported finished products, and the Hanseatic shipping lines, it came increasingly to serve heavy industry and high finance. When Krupp, Gruson, Siemens and the Berliner Maschinenbau AG (formerly L. Schwarzkopff) put out their feelers towards Morocco, this organization had already done much preparatory work for them.

In 1884, after some travels in Morocco, Otto Kersten produced a detailed report entitled "Germany's Interests in North-West Africa"[3] for the Foreign Office. He recommended developing substantial economic interests in Morocco so that Germany would be able to make claims of its own should the country be carved up by the European powers. He also suggested creating a German zone of influence south of Cape Nun, which in his opinion lay outside the dominions of the Moroccan Sultan. France's efforts to create a large colonial empire in North-West Africa could best be countered by "setting up an independent state of some kind in the south of Morocco"[4], which would at the same time give Germany access to the tribes in the Western Sahara and to the Western Sudan. The first step required was to set up trading stations on the Atlantic coast and to make a geographical survey of the region.

The Central Association acted on Kersten's advice and in 1886 sent a trade expedition led by Robert Jannasch to Morocco's most southerly coastal area. But the expedition failed, and over the next few years the association's leadership preferred to support a policy of "peaceful penetration", which they felt presented the best form of expansion under the prevailing conditions. Their priorities were to enable foreigners to purchase land without hindrance, to press for more ports to be opened to foreign trade, and a treaty with the Sultan's government on trade. The magazine Export, the organ of the Central Association, demanded "support and active promotion for all measures designed to open up Morocco economically. We must be ready to act wherever these economic interests are at stake; we and our representatives must spring without delay into any fresh gap in Morocco's crumbling political and economic defences . . . We shall work methodically, as Germans are accustomed to doing. Alongside the merchants, our scholars, engineers and others will investigate the country and its people, thereby helping to lighten some of the tasks confronting trade."[5]

---

[3] ZStA, A.A., no. 11877, pp. 145—152.
[4] Ibid.
[5] Export, no. 17/1889, p. 247.

In 1882 Germany accounted for little more than half a per cent of Morocco's foreign trade, with Britain taking 65 per cent and France 33 per cent. But in the course of the 1880s and 1890s German commerce with Morocco advanced considerably. A number of German merchants and the agents of major firms moved into the Moroccan coastal towns and established close links with local merchants and farmers, making "protected persons" of them and thus securing their dependence. They also started founding small factories to produce wax, soap, cigarettes and other items and acquiring land.

These German merchants often acted as agents for the big German firms during this "peaceful penetration" of Morocco. They and their employees knew the language and customs of the people and were acquainted with Moroccans who held important positions. They acted as hosts to travelling German traders and explorers, providing them with information about the country and the markets, and in some cases backed expeditions into the interior. The magazine Export regularly printed their reports about the state of the Moroccan market. The oldest and most influential of the German firms were Weiss and Maur in Mogador, Heinrich Ficke and Brandt & Toel in Casablanca, and above all Haessner & Joachimssohn in Tangier. The latter eventually became a shipping agency, bank, insurance company and commission house rolled into one. It played an important part as an intermediary in deals between the German arms industry and the Moroccan dynasty.

The Reich government and its diplomatic mission in Tangier, which achieved legation status in 1894, were particularly interested in deals of this kind, and gave especial support to the firm of Krupp. The arms makers from Essen had been quick to respond to the ruling dynasty's desire for a more up-to-date army and new coastal fortifications, which were intended to protect Moroccan sovereignty. In 1884 Sultan Moulay Hassan ordered a battery of field cannons from Krupp and two years later he commissioned a battery of mountain guns and had 12 of his artillerists trained on the firm's own ranges. In 1886, at the Sultan's request and with the support of the Imperial government, the company sent Lt.-Col. Wagner, a specialist in fortifications engineering, to Morocco to work out the plans for a coastal fort in Rabat-Sale. His designs for a project estimated to cost 30 million gold francs met with the Sultan's approval and Krupp thereupon sent the engineer Rottenburg to take charge of construction, which started in 1889. On his arrival the Sultan immediately appointed Rottenburg to be commissioner of fortifications, a post which he continued to hold until his death in 1906.

The appointment of Krupp's representative demonstrated the influence which the company enjoyed at the Moroccan court. This influence was not only lucrative for Krupp: other German companies manufacturing arms and munitions also gained from it. In 1887, for example, Krupp was able to pass on a large order for rifles, pistols and ammunition to Mauser of Oberdorf and Lorenz of Karlsruhe, with Haessner & Joachimssohn taking on the delivery. Imports of arms, gunpowder and ammunition were accounting at that time for more and more of Morocco's foreign trade. Nor did the German companies, including many Hamburg dealers, restrict their business to the Sultan's government; they also surreptitiously supplied the rebellious tribes in the Rif and Atlas Mountains.

Trading relations between the German Reich and Morocco received a twofold impetus when, in 1890, the Atlas-Linie and ·C. Woermann started a regular shipping connection between Hamburg and Morocco's Atlantic ports and the two countries signed a trade treaty. The treaty repealed a number of restrictions on exports and imports and limited import duties to 10 per cent ad valorem. These more favourable conditions enabled Count von Tattenbach, the German minister who had won Moulay Hassan's confidence, to win still more trading concessions. Thanks to his influence, German companies obtained further orders for war material. In 1893, for example, Simson & Co. of Suhl supplied a large quantity of rifles and ammunition. But Krupp remained the major arms supplier. An order for field guns and vehicles which it received in 1891 was worth almost 2 million gold francs.

From 1889 onwards German shipyards supplied Morocco with launches and tugs. The steamer Turki purchased by the Sultan was put into service as a coastal defence vessel with a German captain in command. After c. 1900, the other ships in the small Moroccan navy were also entrusted to German captains and naval officers.

As in the Bismarck era, one of the main motives of Germany's Moroccan policy in the 1890s was to drive a wedge between Britain and France, both of which were pursuing colonial ambitions in Morocco. For this reason, German diplomats supported British claims in Morocco, but without completely committing themselves to one side. They sought to preserve Germany's freedom of action and to maintain the status quo in Morocco for the time being.

In 1894—5, the German government took advantage of the murders of two Germans in Morocco to show the Sultan's government and the Moroccan people that the status quo included the country's semi-colonial position. In November 1894, after a German farmer had been killed near Casablanca, the cruiser Irene was ordered to Tangier and Casablanca.

When a German commercial traveller was robbed and murdered near Safi in April 1895, the government sent the cruiser Alexandrine to Tangier, and in early July a complete squadron, consisting of the frigate Stosch and the cruisers Hagen and Kaiserin Augusta, arrived to demonstrate its determination to protect "German interests" in Morocco effectively. In both cases the Reich compelled the Sultan's government to pay large sums in compensation and enforced the execution of the murderers. This violation of the dignity and sovereignty of an independent country, the demonstration of strength and the threat of intervention, caused disillusionment about the German Reich in the Moroccan government and destroyed faith in its policy of "friendship" towards Morocco. After the death of Sultan Moulay Hassan in 1894 relations between the two countries entered a state of crisis.

In 1898—9 the Reich again sent its warship to the Moroccan coast in order to enforce a settlement of other issues under dispute. Fears spread in French, British and Spanish government circles that Germany intended to occupy a part of Morocco. But at the time the Imperial government was not concerned with such objectives. Its intention was, rather, to maintain the positions it already had and to strengthen them by obtaining further concessions. It hoped that its strong economic and political footing in the country would enable it successfully to put forward territorial demands, or at least claim "adequate" compensation, if at some later date Morocco were to be divided among the colonial powers.

At the turn of the century German bourgeois writers could record the growth of German economic interests in Morocco. The German trading companies rose in number from 6 in 1889 to 22 in 1892 and 34 in 1900.[6] Not only did they carry on business with Germany: they also maintained links with the markets in Britain, Spain, Portugal and France. Germany's trade turnover with Morocco increased from 1,460,000 marks in 1889 to 10,400,000 marks in 1904. Its share of Moroccan foreign trade multiplied from 2.4 to 14.3 per cent.[7] This put Germany in third place behind Britain and France in Morocco's overseas trade. In fact, the activities of German companies in Morocco are not entirely reflected in the commercial statistics. German traders were also, as mentioned above, engaged in a great deal of trade with various European and non-European countries. A substantial proportion of freight traffic between the Moroccan ports had been taken over by German ships. The value of Moroccan

---

[6] *P. Guillen*, op. cit., p. 393.
[7] Ibid., p. 423.

business transacted by German companies around the turn of the century was approximately 15 million marks, hardly less than the corresponding sum for French firms. German firms were acquiring a great deal of land and founding their own capitalist agricultural enterprises.

At the beginning of the 20th century German imperialism therefore occupied an important position among the powers profiting from the semi-colonial status to which Morocco had been reduced.

VI. Colonial Rule after the Defeat of the Uprisings

1. South West Africa 1907—1914

The outcome of the great uprisings of 1904—07 was of fateful significance for the history of South West Africa. The German imperialists had broken the Herero's and the Nama's power to resist for years to come. The so-called Protectorate had become a German colony in the full sense of the term, and the Herero and Nama, previously cattle breeders and the masters of the country, were now penniless. On 18 August 1907 the Governor issued three ordinances permanently barring the African population from owning land and rearing cattle. From the age of seven all Africans were required to carry passes. Anyone unable to prove the source of his livelihood was liable to be punished for "vagrancy". These draconian measures were designed to keep the Africans indefinitely in the state of destitution and loss of rights in which they found themselves in 1907.

The expropriation of the Herero and Nama was essential for turning them into wage labourers. However, the Herero or Nama worker was not (in Marx's words) "free in the double sense, that as a free man he can dispose of his labour-power as his own commodity, and that on the other hand he has no other commodity for sale, is short of everything necessary for the realization of his labour-power."[1] Lacking individual freedom, the Herero and Nama were forced labourers, which meant that in some respects they were worse off than slaves. While slaves, being the property of their masters, were generally treated no worse than a valuable draught animal, no such considerations governed the treatment of forced labourers. During the remaining years of German colonial rule in South West Africa this remained the status of the Herero and Nama, which meant a far-reaching change in the country's social structure. But apart from these peoples, there were still the Rehoboth community,

---

[1] *K. Marx*, Capital, vol. 1, Moscow, n.d., p. 166.

the Bethanie people and the Ovambo, all of whom had not been expropriated. Consequently, one may speak only of the enforced proletarianization of part of the South West African population.

The German policy of annihilation had led to an acute shortage of labour. From 1907 to 1914 the managers of the land companies and the farmers were constantly complaining about a lack of manpower.

The nucleus of the workers consisted of the Herero and Nama, most of whom were employed as farm labourers. The journalist Oskar Bongard, who had accompanied Colonial Secretary Bernhard Dernburg on a fact-finding tour of South West Africa in 1908, had this to say about them: "The Herero as a member of a pastoral people is ideally suited to farming. Unfortunately, the Herero people have been largely wiped out by the war. A high percentage of those who survived are invalid due to the hardships they endured during the war, the terrible ordeal they went through in the sandveld where thousands died of hunger and thirst, and the venereal diseases they contracted in prison camps where infections spread with alarming speed. Furthermore, their cattle herds were destroyed by the war, and the Herero people, accustomed to a diet based on milk, developed scurvy in captivity where they were deprived of their staple food.

"Although it can be assumed that those who survived the war are the most robust of all, the health of the majority of them is impaired to such an extent that they cannot be expected to produce healthy offspring. This is especially true of the mothers who were young girls when they went through the terrible time in the sandveld. Also many woman are sterile because of venereal disease, and the Herero decided to cut down procreation through abortion lest children be born while they were held in bondage. Consequently, there is no hope in the foreseeable future of an increase in the number of workers, as required for the development of the country, from among the ranks of the Herero and the Hottentots (whose situation is much the same), the less so as there is a pronounced trend to emigrate territory."[2]

The German colonialists hoped to overcome the manpower shortage by recruiting Ovambo tribesmen. But since the Ovambo were only sporadically available as migrant labourers, usually for the duration of a few months, their employment could not solve the problem.

Hence the persistent call for foreign migrant labour. For example, the Otavigesellschaft wrote to Dernburg "that considering the con-

---

[2] *O. Bongard*, Dernburgs Studienreise nach Britisch- und Deutsch—Südafrika, in: Deutsche Kolonialzeitung, vol. 25 (1908), p. 704.

sistently unfavourable labour situation, notably the decline in the influx of manpower from Ovamboland and the reduced availability of Herero owing to work performed elsewhere in the Protectorate, business can be conducted in an orderly and profitable way only if the manpower deficit is made up by bringing in foreign workers."[3] The company was chiefly thinking of workers from Cape Colony, whose number exceeded 6,400 at the beginning of 1911.[4] After hopes of receiving migrant labourers from Angola had been dashed by the Portuguese colonial authorities, company managers on more than one occasion even demanded that Chinese coolies be imported instead, but this idea was rejected by the Reich Colonial Office.

Since it proved impossible to solve the manpower problem by engaging foreign migrant labour, the German colonial establishment began to concentrate on opening up what they described as "domestic reserves". What they had in mind was those thousands of Africans who, despite pass laws and compulsory registration, had evaded German control by withdrawing to the more inaccessible parts of the country. It was decided to hunt down without mercy Africans who were "roaming about", thereby escaping exploitation as forced labourers. At a farmers' annual meeting held at Grootfontein in August 1909 the demands raised almost unanimously were: "An increase in the police force, more sweeping powers to use firearms against natives, delegation of police duties to trustworthy farmers . . ."[5] The Deutsche Kolonial-Zeitung called for a merciless campaign against Africans trying to avoid the fate of becoming forced labourers: "Only draconian measures will help. Vagrancy must be punished with severity and the retreats of cattle thieves (i.e. the places to which these Africans had withdrawn — H.D.) must be destroyed by the police and the military continually staging raids. The Kaffirs in their hide-outs in the mountains, the Herero lurking in the bushveld and the Bushmen roving over the savannah — all of them must not feel safe for a single moment."[6]

For the indigenous population of South West Africa the years 1907 to 15 were a time of suffering and misery. Those among them who had

---

[3] ZStA, RKolA, no. 1229, p. 4, Otavigesellschaft to Dernburg, 9 Dec. 1907.

[4] Cf. *P. Überhorst*, Die Arbeiterfrage in den deutschen Kolonien, Thesis, University of Münster 1926, p. 261.

[5] ZStA, RKolA, no. 1500, pp. 74—75, Extract from a report by Conze, Director in the Colonial Office, 1909.

[6] *W. Külz*, Arbeiternot und Eingeborenenpflege in Südwestafrika, in: Deutsche Kolonialzeitung, vol. 28 (1911), p. 282.

managed to escape capture became the victim of virtual manhunts. Even Governor Bruno von Schuckmann found it necessary after some time to come out against the indiscriminate shooting of Africans. He declared: "There must be an end to the practice of opening fire on every Hottentot who is sighted, for otherwise there will never be quiet in the border areas."[7] And on the manhunts against the San ("Bushmen") he observed: "Our armed forces have made various commendable and remarkable forays into the Namib, driving the Bushmen there out of their hidingplaces and, it seems, shooting some of them. But I do not believe that the continuation of such hostile patrol operations against the Bushmen holds much promise. The only result will be that a few people are shot dead and that some others are captured, only to run away as soon as they have been handed over to a farmer."[8]

The Africans serving as farm labourers were completely at the mercy of their masters. When a farmer was dissatisfied with an African worker for some reason or other, he would often send him to the nearest police station with a written note saying the bearer had been lazy, disobedient or impudent. The police officer would then, as he thought fit, give the delinquent 10 to 15 lashes with the sjambok, a heavy hippopotamus hide whip, indicate the punisment on the written note, and send the worker back to his master who would put him to work again as if nothing had happened. While the statistics available about floggings recorded by the authorities are sketchy, these statistics do show clearly that floggings became much more frequent in the closing stages of German rule. Whereas flogging allegedly took place in only 187 cases in 1904—05, a much higher figure — 1,655 — is given for 1911—12.[9]

But most of the farmers and other employers did not take the trouble to send an African worker with whom they were dissatisfied to the nearest police station. Rather, they arrogated to themselves the right to manhandle their African labourers as they pleased, a practice euphemistically called "paternal chastisement". During the last years of German rule vicious beatings became so frequent that the Governor, Theodor Seitz, deemed it necessary to sound a note of warning. He wrote to a district commissioner in 1912: "Over the past few weeks I have received word from various quarters that in different parts of the country a mood of

---

[7] ZStA, RKolA, no. 2141, pp. 44—47, Schuckmann to the Colonial Office, 10 Aug. 1909.

[8] Ibid.

[9] Cf. *Kolonien unter der Peitsche*. Eine Dokumentation, ed. by F. F. Müller, Berlin 1962, p. 114.

despair is spreading among the natives. By all accounts, the reason is that acts of brutality commited by whites against natives have become alarmingly frequent, with police officers involved in some instances, and that the courts often fail to punish such wrongdoing as the natives' sense of justice demands. The reports say that the natives, who have lost all faith in the impartiality of our judges, become consumed with blind hatred of all that is white, and would ultimately be driven to self-help, i.e. rebellion. It is obvious that, unless vigorous remedial action is taken, the feelings of hatred among the natives will sooner or later erupt into a new uprising born of sheer desperation, an event that would spell economic ruin for the country."[10]

The Governor's call for a halt to the vicious floggings went unheeded. Indeed, the cases in which Africans were beaten to death by Germans or Boers on a flimsy pretext or without any reason at all became even more frequent. If those responsible were brought before a court of justice — which only happened in a few cases — they were usually acquitted or sentenced to small fines.

Even at this time of inhuman oppression of the South West Africans, there were still signs of resistance against German imperialism. The outrages committed provoked spontaneous acts of resistance, but these were isolated and limited to a few persons or small groups. The Herero and Nama in general were in no condition to strike any serious blows. Yet the occasional outbreaks of unrest were a constant reminder to the colonial masters that African resistance might flare up again at any time.

While official reports described the situation in Hereroland a few months after termination of the state of war as uneasy, the situation in Namaland — especially in the south — was in fact much more critical. There it was primarily the Bondelzwarts who gave the administration cause for disquiet. In December 1908 a Nama unit was set up under the command of Abraham Rolf, one of Morenga's lieutenants, to resume the struggle. It was almost entirely made up of Bondelzwarts who had escaped from the locations (reservations) or fled while on their way to new work sites. They raided numerous farms to provide themselves with the weapons and equipment they needed. The successful operations of the unit struck terror into the hearts of the German settlers in the southern part of Namaland.

---

[10] Governor Seitz to the District Commissioner, 31 May 1912 (confidential), in: *Report on the Natives of South West Africa* and their Treatment by Germany, London 1918, p. 203.

In early 1909, faced by superior German forces, ten men commanded by Abraham Rolf withdrew to British-ruled territory. When crossing the border they told a British police officer that "they would surrender to the Cape Government if they were given assurances that they would not be extradited. Otherwise they would fight to the last."[11]

The Cape authorities, however, did not feel bound by the assurances given by a British police officer and turned the group over to the Germans. Of the ten Nama, six were sentenced to death while four were condemned to life imprisonment and ordered to be kept in chains. (These four managed to escape from the jail in Karibib only a few months later.) The extradition and condemnation of the group must have given great delight to Oskar Hintrager, the Deputy Governor, for he wrote 46 years later in the Federal Republic of Germany: "The execution of the death sentences at Keetmanshoop made a deep impression on the natives. The extradition proceedings had brought home to them that there was no sanctuary any longer on the other side of the border."[12]

At the time, Hintrager warned against the Berseba people and the Bondelzwarts and set out resettlement plans. In a report dated 22 December 1908 he wrote: "As far as I know the natives here, it would be a great mistake to assume that the Bondels now confined to locations, or any other natives in the country for that matter, are satisfied with the turn their life has taken through the war. This cannot be otherwise because since the uprising the one-time masters of the country have been relegated to the status of people bound to respect the supremacy and laws of the white man and, above all, compelled to work if they want to live . . . We cannot change the present generation in a few years, and they will try again and again to cast off the yoke we must impose on them if German South West Africa is to be a German colony for whites . . . My view is that in the interests of the Reich and of the Protectorate we must not indulge in silly humanitarian sentiments, but practise a utilitarian policy, above all against the Bondelzwart locations, that perpetual source of danger in the south, before it is too late . . . Therefore, the Bondels now in locations must be deported to Grootfontein in the north where they will constitute no threat. This should be done by force, and the sooner the better. It may well turn out to be a difficult task involving bloodshed, but such an eventuality is preferable to the current state of constant insecurity. The experience gained during the last great rebellion

---

[11] ZStA, RKolA, no. 2147, p. 20, Humboldt to the German Foreign Office, 4 Jan. 1909.

[12] *O. Hintrager*, Südwestafrika in der deutschen Zeit, Munich 1955, p. 105.

has shown the usefulness of the transfer of the Khauas, Hottentots and Zwartboois to Windhoek in 1896 and 1898, respectively. Along with some others they were among the few who did not take part in the war. Once a native has been transplanted to some other area, he will no longer be a threat to peace, but learns to work and obey orders. What I have said of the natives near Warmbad is also true of the Stürmann people in Spitzkop, only that they may well be even more unreliable. After these, all Hottentots in the south must be removed to the north as soon as there are signs that they cannot be trusted, and Herero must be transplanted to the south instead . . ."[13]

In order to extinguish the last spark of resistance, Hintrager was thus proposing wholesale deportations within the colony. Since the administration considered the Bondelzwarts too numerous for such an experiment, they decided to deport comparatively small groups for a start: the so-called Stürmann Nama and the Veldschoendragers. The former numbered 80 and the latter 44. Both groups were accused of having tried to evade work they had been ordered to perform. Governor von Schuckmann gave the following account of the enforced resettlement of these Nama in February 1909: "The Stürmann location was surrounded by troops on 17 February of this year, and all natives found in the settlement were arrested and, after their ringleaders had been punished, transferred to the northern district of Grootfontein. Although they are kept under close surveillance there, they soon made an attempt to escape, which was thwarted only by pure chance. The primitive conditions obtaining in Grootfontein make it necessary for them to be tightly guarded all the time." He added that the Veldschoendragers, too, had "made a renewed attempt to escape in January of this year, having contrived to break the chains put on their feet."[14]

Having been constantly bombarded with Hintrager's demands, the Colonial Office in 1910 ordered these Nama to be transported to Cameroon. For 93 Nama (26 men, 40 women and 27 children) there now began a terrible ordeal. By August 1912 no more than 37 out of 93 deportees were still alive, and these were finally repatriated following the intervention of some Reichstag deputies.

A strike by workers engaged in railway building near Wilhelmsthal in September and October 1910 was probably the most important mani-

---

[13] ZStA, RKolA, no. 2147, pp. 55—67, Hintrager to the Colonial Office, 22 Dec. 1908.

[14] ZStA, RKolA, no. 2141, pp. 31—32, Schuckmann to the Colonial Office, 26 April 1909.

festation of resistance between 1907 and 1914. It was organized by Xhosa-speaking migrant workers from South Africa. When on 29 September 1910 a German construction firm paid its South African migrant workers less than the agreed wages, the workers either downed tools or went on a go-slow strike in protest. Thereupon, the firm called in German troops whose commanding officer, Captain Willecke, demanded that the strikers turn over three of their number who had acted as spokesmen. When this demand was refused, the soldiers staged a blood-bath, leaving 14 dead and 25 wounded. The construction firm found itself compelled to cease making unjustified wage deductions.[15]

The economy of the colony in 1907—14 underwent far-reaching changes, not least because of the further development of the territory's transport system. Before 1907 there were only two railway lines in South West Africa, one linking Swakopmund with Windhoek, and the other Swakopmund with Otavi.

The Swakopmund-Windhoek Central Railway, built from 1897 to 1902, was the first rail link in South West Africa. Because of faulty design and false economies the 382-kilometre track was in urgent need of re-construction within a few years of its completion. In 1910—11 the Karibib-Windhoek section was converted from narrow gauge (60 centimetres) to Cape standard gauge. Another narrow-gauge line, the 587-kilometre Otavi Railway linking Swakopmund with Tsumeb, was a private railway constructed between 1903 and 1906 on behalf of the Otavigesellschaft. It was chiefly intended for the exploitation of the copper deposits at Tsumeb. The Otavi Railway had a branch line leading from Otavi to Grootfontein (a distance of 90 kilometres) added to it in 1908, to help open up minor copper deposits. In 1910 the railway passed into the hands of the state on terms very favourable to the company.

In July 1908 the Southern Railway from Lüderitz Bay to Keetmans-hoop (366 kilometres) was opened. General von Trotha had called for such a connection in later 1904 in order to put down the Nama uprising. Construction got under way in late 1905. Running on Cape gauge, the railway provided access to the southern parts of the country. An 180-kilometre branch line from Seeheim to Kalkfontein was added in 1908 to 09, which traversed the far south-east, notably the territory of the Bon-delzwarts, and later enabled a link to be established with the railway network of the Union of South Africa. The next development was the

---

[15] Cf. *H. Loth*, Zu den Anfängen des Kampfes der Arbeiter Südwestafrikas gegen den deutschen Imperialismus. Unveröffentlichte Dokumente, in: Wissenschaftliche Zeitschrift der Karl-Marx-Universität Leipzig, vol. 10 (1961), pp. 351ff.

opening in April 1913 of the North-South Railway, a 506-kilometre Cape gauge line connecting Windhoek with Keetmanshoop.

Two further railway projects were under consideration from about 1912: a branch line from Windhoek to Gobabis and the Amboland Railway, which were to serve, respectively, the eastern part of the colony and the northern part, inhabited by the Ovambo. Since Amboland was still outside the area effectively controlled by the German authorities, the Amboland project was given priority: such a railway would make it much easier to subjugate the Ovambo and recruit them as labour for German mines and farms. Surveying the route was completed in late 1913, and building commenced in March 1914, but had to be discontinued the following year because of the war.

By the end of 1913 South West Africa was considered to have a well-developed transport system. The railway network, totalling 2,104 kilometres of track, was the most extensive in any German colony.

As a result, colonization of the territory by German farmers proceeded apace. While in over twenty years of German colonial rule land for 480 farms had been sold by early 1907, land for no less than 202 farms was sold in 1907 alone. By the year 1913 the number of European farms had risen to 1,331. The white population, totalling 3,701 people in 1903, reached a figure of 14,840 by 1913. However, the high-flown ambitions of colonial zealots who drew naive comparisons between South West Africa and the Union of South Africa, conjuring up the prospect of South West Africa attracting hundreds of thousands of German settlers, proved to be an illusion. Since an investment capital of 40,000 to 50,000 marks was required for a medium-sized farm, the number of newly established farms began to decline in 1909. The administration sold only 147 holdings that year, 100 less than the year before. This trend continued right to the end of German rule although large areas of government-owned territory were still available.[16]

A memorandum on the settlement issue drafted by the administration in 1913 contains a description of the land ownership structure. According to this source there were seven landowners holding more than 100,000 hectares (including the Rhenish Mission with 140,000 hectares and the Catholic Mission with 130,000 hectares) and eleven holding between 50,000 and 100,000 hectares. The remaining pattern was as follows: 88 farms between 20,000 and 50,000 hectares; 275 farms between 10,000 and 20,000 hectares; 481 farms between 5,000 and 10,000 hectares; and

---

[16] Cf. *F. Wege*, Zur Entstehung und Entwicklung der Arbeiterklasse in Südwestafrika während der deutschen Kolonialherrschaft (thesis), Halle 1966, pp. 60—61.

257 farms under 5,000 hectares. These figures show that while medium-sized holdings were predominant, large estates were gaining in significance.[17]

The year 1908 saw the introduction of the first karakul sheep whose "Persian lamb" skins were soon to become a much demanded export item. By 1914 there were 1,165 pure-bred and about 21,000 hybrid sheep, the starting-point for the large-scale raising of karakul sheep in South West Africa in later years. In addition, there were over 53,000 sheep raised for wool in 1913. The Deutsch-Südwestafrikanische Wollzüchterei GmbH, a company established in 1911 with the Prince of Schaumburg-Lippe providing most of its capital stock of 2.5 million marks, intended to profit from the great demand for wool in Germany. Acquiring 221,000 hectares, it became the second largest landowner in the colony.[18] The raising of ostriches was begun in 1912. By 1913 there were 205,643 head of cattle.

While farming and trade were the dominant features of the colonial economy before the great uprisings, the focus of interest shifted to mining during the last years of German rule. A search for diamonds had been going on unsuccessfully for more than twenty years when in May 1908 an African accidentally found some of these precious stones in the Namib, not far from Lüderitz Bay. This discovery set off a rush among settlers to the diamond-bearing region to stake out claims. Colonial Secretary Dernburg thereupon ordered a 100-kilometre strip south of 26° to the Orange River sealed off to the point where it had not yet been occupied by prospectors, the measure taking effect on 22 September 1908, and granted the Deutsche Kolonialgesellschaft für Südwestafrika (DKGSWA) the exclusive right to appropriate diamonds in the area. In addition, he issued a directive on 25 February 1909 establishing an official sales agency, Diamantenregie des südwestafrikanischen Schutzgebietes, directed by a consortium of big banks, which he invested with the right to market all diamonds mined in South West Africa. By selling large numbers of these precious stones on the Antwerp Diamond Exchange, the agency began in 1909 successfully to challenge the Anglo-South African De Beers Company, which enjoyed a near-absolute monopoly at the time. This was yet another German attack on an important position of British imperialism.

[17] Ibid., p. 63.
[18] Cf. *H. bei der Wieden*, Wollschafzucht in Deutsch—Südwestafrika, in: Vierteljahresschrift für Sozial- und Wirtschaftsgeschichte, vol. 58 (1971), No. 1, pp. 67 bis 87.

Dernburg's policy of favouring big business interests and virtually excluding the settlers from the bonanza caused much resentment among the latter. The Colonial Secretary's practices became the object of a fierce controversy which his conservative, pan-German and middle-class adversaries exploited to undermine his position.

While in 1908—09 the diamonds were simply picked up, sifted out or washed out by hand, it became necessary from 1910 onwards to mechanize operations, which presupposed larger investments and entailed the employment of an evergrowing number of African labourers. In 1913—14 there were between 4,500 and 6,000 of them, the majority being Ovambo and the rest migrant workers from South Africa.

Diamonds valued at 152 million marks (4.6 million carats) were recovered in South West Africa from 1908 to 1913. The rise in production is shown by the following figures:

1908	38,275 carats	51,180 marks from exports
1909	483,266 carats	15,435,522 marks from exports
1910	846,695 carats	26,869,014 marks from exports
1911	773,308 carats	23,034,146 marks from exports
1912	1,051,777 carats	30,414,078 marks from exports
1913	approx. 1,500,000 carats	58,910,000 marks from exports.[19]

The patience which the "patriots" of the DKGSWA had displayed for over twenty years at last paid dividends, for in 1909 the company paid its shareholders 64 per cent. In the same year its share prices went up by 2,000 per cent. Similarly, the shares of the (British) South West Africa Company, the Otavigesellschaft and the South African Territories Company rose enormously in value. So a number of monopolists managed to squeeze huge profits out of the colony in the final years of German colonial government.

Beside diamonds, copper was of considerable importance in the country's mining industry. The rich deposits of Tsumeb (the Otavi mines) were thoroughly examined in 1895 and in 1900—01, but it was only after the completion of the Otavi Railway in 1906 that mining operations could begin. Between 1906 and 1913 copper exports rose as follows:

1906	46,877 marks
1907	1,282,515 marks

[19] *O. Hintrager*, op. cit., pp. 115, 177.

1908	6,296,000 marks
1909	4,654,862 marks
1910	5,697,208 marks
1911	3,753,703 marks
1912	6,523,258 marks
1913	7,929,000 marks[20]

The bulk of the ore came from the Otavi mines which succeeded in quintupling their output between 1907 and 1913. In 1913 these mines produced about 70,000 metric tons, of which roughly 50,000 metric tons were shipped. The two other copper mines were of secondary importance.

In conclusion, let us take a look at South West Africa's exports, which chiefly consisted of diamonds, copper, cattle, hides, and ostrich feathers. In terms of value, they were as follows:

	Total	Diamonds and copper
1900	907,565 marks	—
1907	1,616,000 marks	1,282,515 marks
1908	7,795,000 marks	6,347,180 marks
1909	22,071,000 marks	20,090,384 marks
1910	34,692,000 marks	32,566,222 marks
1911	28,573,000 marks	26,787,849 marks
1912	39,035,000 marks	36,937,336 marks
1913	70,302,830 marks	66,839,000 marks[21]

These statistics furnish incontrovertible proof that the lion's share in the colonial exploitation of South West Africa under German rule went to the big banks participating in the diamond sales monopoly (Berliner Handelsgesellschaft, Darmstädter Bank, S. Bleichröder, Delbrück, Leo & Co., Deutsche Bank, Disconto-Gesellschaft, Dresdner Bank, Mendelssohn & Co., Nationalbank für Deutschland, Sal. Oppenheim jr. & Co., A. Schaaffhausenscher Bankverein, M. M. Warburg & Co., Jacob S. H. Stern and others), with the Berliner Handelsgesellschaft also deeply involved in diamond mining, and a smaller group of big banks led by the Disconto-Gesellschaft, of which the Otavi Minenund Eisenbahn-Gesellschaft was a subsidiary. The last-named company, founded by Adolf von Hansemann, paid dividends of up to 45 per cent

---

[20] Ibid., p. 177.
[21] Ibid., p. 178.

prior to 1914[22] while the Koloniale Bergbau Gesellschaft, which had close ties with the Berliner Handelsgesellschaft, was able to give dividends of between 2,400 and 3,800 per cent.[23] Another company also closely associated with the Berliner Handelsgesellschaft, the Pomona-Diamanten Gesellschaft, whose proceeds in 1913—14 far surpassed those of all other companies put together, paid dividends of 40 per cent in 1912, the year it was founded, and 175 per cent in the following one.[24]

2. German East Africa 1906—1914

After the Maji-Maji uprising had been crushed, the German colonial power sought to consolidate its rule in the colony. It strengthened its military and police forces there and increased administrative efficiency in order to prevent further rebellions or, should they break out, suppress them swiftly. With the same purpose in mind, the sons of a number of African chiefs were admitted to government schools so that they might fill posts in the middle and lower echelons of the administration. The main reason, however, why no further major insurrections occurred up to the end of German rule was not the preventive measures taken by the colonial power but the fact that the first great uprising going beyond tribal boundaries did not produce a political and ideological force capable of continuing the struggle against the colonial yoke. The road from a rebellion sanctified with animist rites to a stable and vigorous political liberation movement was too long to be covered in a couple of years.

The government, represented by Colonial Secretary Dernburg and Governor von Rechenberg, who served in that capacity from 1906 to 1912, managed to initiate a new stage in the exploitation of the colony. This gave rise to a certain increase in the output of tropical raw materials, but the amount was still far from significant given the requirements of imperialist Germany. To open up large parts of the interior, a central railway line was built which could handle vastly greater quantities of export products than the slow-moving and costly caravans. Railway construction and plantation development called for the investment of

---

[22] *M. Müller-Jabusch*, Franz Urbig zum 23. Januar 1939. Gedruckt im Auftrag der Deutschen Bank. Berlin (1939), p. 143.

[23] *R. Burkhardt*, Deutsche Kolonialunternehmungen. Ihr Schicksal in und nach dem Weltkrieg (thesis), Berlin 1940, p. 34.

[24] *Von der Heydts Kolonialhandbuch*, 1914, p. 280.

capital, which the big German banks were now willing to provide, especially if the risks involved were reduced by government guarantees. Between 1904 and 1914 the sums invested in the colony by German firms rose quite considerably.[25]

Until 1906 the only railway projects undertaken were two branch lines linking the coast with two nearby but not very important centres of production and communications. The Usambara Line, running from Tanga to the plantation area around Mombo, was completed in 1905 while the Dar es Salaam-Morogoro line was begun that year and put into service two and a half years later. In May 1908 the Reichstag, by endorsing a government loan, voted the funds necessary for continuing the latter, "Central" line to Tabora after Dernburg had stressed the economic significance of the project and its military importance (for the suppression of any further rebellions). After Tabora had been reached in 1912, the Central Line was extended to Kigoma on Lake Tanganyika, and from March 1914 the 1,252-kilometre Tanganyika Railway provided a direct link between Dar es Salaam and Kigoma.

As J. Iliffe has noted, the locomotives steaming into the interior brought the colonial economy in their wake.[26] In the areas served by the railway large numbers of African farmers began to produce crops for export. Plantation schemes were started in some of these areas to grow sisal, rubber and cotton.

The growing of sisal called for considerable investments because expensive machinery was needed to process the hemp, and light railway tracks were required to transport the bales. It took about half a million marks to establish a fairly large plantation.[27] Agave cultivation was undertaken only on large fields by German companies, notably the DOAG, which was making a handsome profit within a few years of starting production of this crop. Although trading and banking in the colony realized on the whole higher profits than the plantation owners, the Sisal-Agaven-Gesellschaft (capital: 1.5 million marks) managed to pay a dividend of 25 per cent in both 1912 and 1913.[28] The Deutsche Agavengesellschaft (capital: 1,156,400 marks) declared 20 per cent in 1913, and the Ostafrikanische Kompagnie (capital: 1.4 million marks), which also owned rubber and cotton plantations, 15 per cent in 1912.[29]

---

[25] Unfortunately, no statistics are available to underline this point, but the rapid increase was very much apparent.

[26] J. Iliffe, A Modern History of Tanganyika, Cambridge 1979, p. 135.

[27] W. Arning, Deutsch—Ostafrika gestern und heute. Berlin 1942, p. 262.

[28] J. Iliffe, op. cit., p. 147.

By contrast, some smaller companies had only just begun to pay their way by 1913—14.

The area under cultivation increased from 1,390 to 24,750 hectares between 1905 and 1913 while the value of the fibres harvested and exported during that period rose from 1.1 to 10.3 million marks.[30] Between 1909 and 1912 sisal was second only to rubber in the export statistics, and in 1913 it moved up to first place, accounting for 30 per cent of the colony's exports in terms of value, because rubber prices had fallen sharply that year.

Similarly, rubber trees were being increasingly grown on German plantations from 1900 onwards. Before that year virtually all rubber was extracted from trees growing wild in jungle areas by Africans who then sold it to traders. But wild rubber was from now on gradually superseded by plantation rubber both in East Africa and in the world at large. By 1907 between five and seven million trees had been planted in twelve districts of the colony, and two years later the output from plantations was higher than that derived from trees growing wild. In 1913, the plantations supplied 94 per cent of the colony's rubber exports, valued at 6.16 million marks.[31] Up to the outbreak of the international rubber crisis of 1913 the plantations (which included over 300 smaller estates because capital requirements were relatively low) raked in profits on such a scale that they became an international target for speculation and British financiers paid high prices to acquire some of the more important holdings. Then, however, the crisis forced the smaller planters to give up or to switch to other crops while the larger companies recorded losses.

From 1902 the cultivation of cotton was promoted by the colonial administration as a "national task" designed to reduce the dependence of German industry on the United States step by step. After the compulsory growing of this crop by African farmers had come to an end with the Maji-Maji uprising, Dernburg tried to persuade industrialists to establish cotton plantations in the colony. As a result, the Leipziger Baumwollspinnerei set up large plantations (30,000 hectares in size) near Sadani in 1907, investing 1.5 million marks in them during the next three years. Heinrich Otto, a Stuttgart industrialist, started a large plantation (4,000 to 5,000 hectares) near Kilosa in the same year, putting

[29] R. Tetzlaff, Koloniale Entwicklung und Ausbeutung. Wirtschafts- und Sozialgeschichte Deutsch—Ostafrikas 1885—1914, (West)Berlin, 1967, p. 122.

[30] Ibid., p. 118.

[31] Ibid., p. 124.

1.6 million marks into this undertaking up to the end of 1910. Other South German and Saxon textile manufacturers followed their example.[32] However, the results were disappointing for these German firms because the managers were unfamiliar with local conditions and pests destroyed the bulk of the crops. The losses incurred forced some of the plantation companies to close down in a matter of years. Others made few, if any, profits although all of them were subsidized directly or indirectly by the administration and by the Colonial Economic Committee.

The reason why from 1911 onwards cotton exports nevertheless exceeded two million marks annually was the increase in cotton grown as cash crops by African farmers on their own fields. In the aftermath of the Maji-Maji uprising the authorities began to develop African cash crop farming in the districts of Rufiji, Kilwa, Bagamoyo and Mwanza (Sukumaland). At the request of the administration, the Colonial Economic Committee (an institution financed by German industrialists and the government) founded experimental stations and instructed peasant farmers in cotton growing. It had seeds distributed and ginneries set up.

There ensued a considerable increase in cotton growing as thousands of African farmers were eager to earn some money that way. But from 1908 these farmers too, suffered setbacks owing to drought and pests. Even more harmful for them were the practices employed by the firms which bought the crops. The district commissioner at Rufiji reported in early 1909: "The DOAG has contrived to monopolize the purchase of raw cotton and to dictate farm prices. It has achieved this by establishing a ginnery and by engaging the leading Indian merchant here to buy up cotton. . . . Regrettably, the efforts undertaken by the Office and the Committee have only had the result of lining the pockets of the DOAG."[33] The DOAG induced the buyers to pay only 7 hellers per pound of raw cotton as against 14 to 15 hellers paid previously. Thus the firm introduced into German East Africa the merciless bleeding of indigenous producers which big companies were already practising in the British colonies of West Africa.

But the cultivation of cotton by African farmers continued to expand despite the ruthless methods of the DOAG (which had allied itself in the cotton business with Hansing & Co., Wm O'Swald & Co. and another German commercial firm). Estimates put the acreage farmed by Africans

[32] Ibid., pp. 139—140.
[33] District commissioner Grass to the Governor, 18 Jan. 1909. Source: *R. Tetzlaff.* op. cit., pp. 143—144 (ZStA, RKolA, no. 8181, pp. 215—222).

in 1912/13 at 15,600 hectares and the area farmed by Europeans at 12,900 hectares.[34] The total yield attained by African peasant farmers in Sukumaland south of Lake Victoria rose from 21,496 to 676,000 kilograms between 1908 and 1913, making Mwanza the most important of all cotton-growing districts.[35]

The development of coffee growing[36] followed a similar pattern. While most attempts to grow this crop on plantations in Usambara were not very successful or failed completely, the outcome was different on the slopes of Mt Kilimanjaro and Mt in Moshi district, where production increased by leaps and bounds from 1906 onwards. By 1914 there were about 100 plantations with 2.8 million coffee trees, but only 880,000 of these had borne fruit by that time. It was Bukoba district in the northwestern part of the colony, however, which became the principal coffee-growing area. The Haya inhabiting that region began to cultivate coffee on a major scale once the completion of a railway line in nearby Uganda had made it possible to sell the crops. In terms of value, coffee production by these African peasant farmers went up from 51,564 marks to 719,079 marks between 1905 and 1912 when they accounted for 39 per cent of the colony's coffee exports. The official statistics do not indicate how large (or rather small) their share in the proceeds of European commercial firms was.

African cash crop farmers and stock breeders — from 1909 to 1913 hides and skins occupied third place on the list of export goods — produced a considerable and increasing part of German East Africa's exports. The administration of the colony, intent on raising output under all circumstances, supported the Volkskulturen (or "people's farms") as the smallholdings of African peasant farmers were called, whereas the plantation interests, looking upon them as unwanted rivals, rejected and opposed them as an obstacle to the "solution of the manpower question" for the plantations. Especially during Rechenberg's tenure this conflict of interests was a constant source of friction between German plantation owners who ascribed their lack of success to inadequate government support and the Governor who took a dim view of the prospects of small and medium-sized German estates. Rechenberg, with the successful development of African cotton production in neighbour-

[34] R. Tetzlaff, op. cit., p. 147.

[35] R. A. Austen, Northwest Tanzania under German and British Rule. Colonial Policy and Tribal Politics 1889—1939, New Haven and London 1968, pp. 270 to 271.

[36] The paragraph on coffee growing is based on R. Tetzlaff, op. cit., p. 133.

ing British-ruled Uganda in mind, deemed it essential to encourage cash crop farming in the overall interest of German capitalism.

While the production of sisal, rubber, cotton and other tropical raw materials had made headway in the colony by the time the First World War broke out, a comparison with British practices in Uganda showed that the Germans were still beginners — not in the ruthless exploitation of natural resources, but certainly in the development of tropical agriculture under colonial conditions.

Although some major firms had a difficult time in the colony and a fair number of small planters came to grief, German East Africa was a lucrative source of profits for the DOAG, the two banks operating in the colony (Deutsch-Ostafrikanische Bank and Handelsbank für Ostafrika), the two shipping companies (Deutsche Ostafrika-Linie and Deutsche Nyanza-Schiffahrts-Gesellschaft), and the trading and sisal planting companies.

Right to the end of German rule the DOAG remained the dominant economic factor in the colony. With a subscribed capital of 8 million marks (10 million from 1913) this subsidiary of the Deutsche Bank and the Disconto-Gesellschaft (represented on the supervisory council by Karl Helfferich and Franz Urbig, respectively) was by far the best-financed of all enterprises active there. Operating either directly or through subsidiaries of its own, it held a virtual monopoly in key areas of German East Africa's colonial economy. Together with the trading firms closely linked with it, the company controlled the purchase of export products from both African smallholders and European plantations. Apart from owning important estates, the DOAG had secured the exclusive right to buy the products of numerous European plantation owners by granting them loans, mortgages, etc., and thus brought them into a state of dependence. In 1913 the newspaper published by the planters in Usambara complained that "the economic fortunes of the colony are dependent on and controlled by a single company. If the management of this financial group suddenly decided to revoke the payments and loans granted to plantations and to collect the money paid in anticipation of future deliveries, approximately 75 per cent of the capital invested (by the planters) so far would have to be written off."[37]

Through its retailers the DOAG sold farm implements and all manner of utensils. Moreover, the company enjoyed the prerogative of issuing banknotes for use in the colony, a privilege no longer commonly granted

---

[37] Usambara-Post, 25 Oct. 1913, Source: R. Tetzlaff, op. cit., p. 135.

to a private institution. Then, too, it controlled both banks and had shareholdings in the three (still insignificant) mining companies, the Deutsche Holzgesellschaft für Ostafrika, the Lindi-Handels- und Plantagengesellschaft and many other firms. Between 1905 and 1913 the DOAG netted 7,016,000 marks in profits, with its trading agencies accounting for almost half this sum.[38] By the outbreak of the war in 1914 it had 21 such agencies, operated nine plantations totalling 35,000 hectares with 150,000 coconut palms, seven million sisal agaves, 500,000 rubber trees and 400,000 coffee trees, and employed 120 Europeans and 4,400 Africans.[39]

The Imperial Colonial Office did nothing to promote industrial development. Apart from a brewery in Dar es Salaam employing over 100 Africans and Indians and a building firm, only several dozen small businesses processing local raw materials came into existence such as sawmills, sugarcane and oil mills, and soap and cigarette factories. As a mere supplier of raw materials the colony remained dependent on imported industrial goods both under German and British rule.

According to the statistics published by the administration the colony's total exports attained a value of 35.55 million marks in 1913, almost three times as much as in 1907. This compared with imports amounting to 53.36 million marks (as against 23.81 million in 1907). Exports included sisal hemp (10.3 million marks), rubber (6.6 million marks), hides and skins (5.5 million marks), cotton (2.4 million marks), copra (2.3 million marks), ground-nuts (1.9 million marks), way (1.4 million marks) and coffee (900,000 marks). Imports included cotton fabrics worth 13 million marks, rice (3.7 million marks), flour, fruit and other foodstuffs, rolling stock, various tools and implements, and ironmongery.[40]

While the colonial power managed to establish increasing control over this trade, its share in the colony's total trade was still only 53 per cent in 1912 (according to incomplete data). India and Britain remained very important trading partners, accounting for 80 per cent of cotton cloth imports. Rice was mainly imported from India, and one-third of rubber production went to Britain.[41] The German Reich, itself surrounded by a wall of high protective tariffs, could not afford to grant preferential customs treatment to East Africa or its other colonies be-

[38] R. Tetzlaff, op. cit., p. 164.
[39] M. Müller-Jabusch, op. cit., pp. 142—143.
[40] Statistisches Jahrbuch für das Deutsche Reich, 36th vol., 1915, pp. 464—465.
[41] Die deutschen Schutzgebiete . . ., 1911/12, Berlin 1913, pp. 101, 112—113 and 132.

cause this would have invited prompt retaliatory measures from other colonial powers and harmed Germany's much more extensive trade with British and French possessions. This state of affairs was yet another sign of the disparity between the economic strength of German imperialism and the very modest size of its colonial holdings, a circumstance which Lenin emphasized[42] and which did much to exacerbate the antagonisms between Germany and the western powers before 1914.

The increase in the production of export goods was partly achieved by carrying retail trade, as always conducted on an inequitable basis, into the remotest parts of the colony. Colourful cotton cloth and dresses, ironmongery, spirits and other overpriced import products were offered to the village population, thereby inducing them to grow and sell cash crops. The cattle-raising peoples were also increasingly selling their produce to traders, a development encouraged by the administration through measures against rinderpest and other cattle diseases.

The main reason for the increase in African agricultural output, however, was that during the last seven years of German rule the authorities made a great drive to collect taxes. The most important of these (until the end of 1912) was the "hut tax" payable by villagers and amounting to 3 rupees (4 marks) annually. In order to raise the money, a family had to sell either 30 pounds of unginned cotton, 50 pounds of rice or 40 pounds of ground-nuts. The revenue from the house and hut tax, which added up to 5.1 million marks in 1912, indicates what quantities had to be produced and sold in order to meet the tax requirements.[43] If the income from farming was insufficient, the men were as before forced to work on the plantations or on railway projects to earn the necessary money.

In the interior of the country, it became the principal task of tribal and village chiefs, who had been turned into auxiliaries of the administration, to see that export crops were grown. In some areas, e.g. in Bukoba and Mwanza districts, local rulers and German officials even resorted to force. The Mwanza district commissioner, Gunzert, made use of the local mercenary unit to enforce the cultivation of cotton.[44]

The economic and social consequences of the administration's relentless export drive were very far-reaching indeed. In important parts of the country manpower was diverted to European-owned plantations, or to production for export, and as a result subsistence farming declined

---

[42] Cf. *V. I. Lenin*, Selected Works, Moscow 1968, p. 227.
[43] *Die deutschen Schutzgebiete . . .*, 1912/13, Berlin 1914, p. 408.
[44] *R. A. Austen*, op. cit., p. 100.

steadily. The upshot was that more and more foodstuffs had to be imported (the 1913 figure was 5,049,000 marks according to official statistics), making the population increasingly dependent on foreign sources of supply — a legacy Tanzania still has to contend with today. At the same time, the importation of ironmongery and textiles from Europe and India destroyed the artisan sector in villages and coastal towns. As Governor von Rechenberg reported in 1907, the latter were anyway badly affected by the administration's decision to restrict maritime traffic to a few seaports furnished with customs posts. "Anyone travelling along the German coast from Pangani to the Rufiji," he wrote, "will find only one place which has gained in stature under German rule: Dar es Salaam, the seat of government. Major localities such as Pangani, Sadani and Bagamayo have declined, even though recently they have shown a few signs of improvement. A number of medium-sized places have virtually lost all significance . . . Ruined stone houses are frequent reminders of their erstwhile prosperity."[45]

One of the most important social consequences was a further increase in the number of migrant workers on German plantations, and of other workers. According to the official statistics African wage labourers in the colony totalled 172,000 in 1913, 91,892 of whom were employed "all the year round" on European-owned plantations and by settlers.[46] Even so the shortage of manpower on the plantations was not overcome right to the end of German rule, and many settlers kept on demanding that the "manpower problem" should be solved by officially introducing labour conscription for all male Africans. As most plantation owners paid extremely low wages and beat their workers on the slightest pretext, plantation work was generally very unpopular or even hated outright.

Although the administration did not officially sanction labour conscription, direct compulsion was employed in some areas. As the Koloniale Rundschau reported in 1912, a "system of work cards" was in force at Usambara "which requires every adult native male to work for a European business for a specified period [90 days]."[47] The journal

---

[45] ZStA, RKolA, no. 1056, pp. 48—56, Report by Rechenberg, 15 July 1907.

[46] *Die deutschen Schutzgebiete* . . . 1912/13, p. 20. The second is an average figure which includes neither the extra hands hired during the harvest season nor the labourers who were on their way to the plantations or back home, a journey often lasting several months. So in reality the number of contract and migrant workers was higher than stated in the source.

[47] Koloniale Rundschau, 1912, p. 657.

added that "in the Kilimanjaro area . . . children, aged nine and under, work for Europeans on a considerable scale."[48]

The effects of colonial rule were so dramatic that they led to a decline in the population which worried colonial circles in Germany from 1912. These effects, which varied from one part of the colony to another without being fundamentally different, included the loosening and break-up of family ties, the spread of previously unknown diseases resulting in premature death or sterility, a falling standard of nutrition caused by the decline of African farming, and a high mortality rate among porters and plantation workers. Some doctors and missionaries sounded the alarm. In 1913, for example, the missionary Van der Burgt (of the White Fathers), who had lived among the Nyamwesi from 1892, reported that since his arrival their numbers had been "cut by one third if not by half".[49] Wherever he went in the area of Ussumbwa there were "abandoned or half deserted, destroyed villages, and traces of fields which once used to be tilled . . . Most able-bodied men and youths are dragged or lured away by recruiters or they leave of their own accord to work on the coastal plantations or on the railway . . . If things go on like this the Wassumbwa (Nyamwesi) race will simply die out or be wiped out . . . Not even a third of them come back. Many die en route of smallpox and dysentery, and others are never heard of again by their families." The Protestant superintendent Löbner confirmed this description of the situation in the south of Nyamwesi territory[50] and similar accounts were given of the conditions prevailing in other parts of the colony, e.g. Ufipa on Lake Tanganyika.[51]

The death rate among plantation workers was at least 7 to 10 per cent annually. Indeed, on some estates it was much higher than that.[52] After 1907 these workers continued bringing worm disorders, syphilis and tuberculosis into areas previously free of these diseases. "Once their contract has expired, they can leave", wrote a government medical officer working in the colony, "without anyone caring in the least that these people take syphilis, gonorrhea and other infectious diseases back

---

[48] Ibid., p. 661.
[49] *J. M. M. Van der Burgt*, Zur Entvölkerungsfrage Unjamwesis und Ussumbwas, in Koloniale Rundschau, 1913, pp. 706 and 708—709.
[50] *M. H. Löbner*, Zur Entvölkerungsfrage Unyamwesis, in Koloniale Rundschau, 1914, p. 267.
[51] Cf. *H. Kjekshus*, Ecology Control and Economic Development in East African History. The Case of Tanganyika 1850—1950. London 1977, p. 160.
[52] *R. Tetzlaff*, op. cit., p. 253.

home with them."[53] A former high medical officer of the "protective force" summed up the situation as follows: "A young man left his home in the prime of life to return a broken man grown old before his time, to find his hut and fields gone to rack and ruin, and his family in distress. Worse still, he brings all his diseases with him, infecting his family and his people."[54]

Apart from taking measures against plague and leprosy and carrying out some major immunization campaigns against smallpox, the administration did almost nothing to halt the spread of infections. It was one of the most appalling consequences of German rule that in many parts of the colony the population was decimated by disease. As a result some areas even saw a further spread of the tsetse fly, which ruled out any livestock farming in the infested territory.[55]

The catastrophic conditions in the areas drained of their manpower gave rise to mounting criticism from various quarters in Germany. This prompted Governor Schnee, who had replaced Rechenberg in 1912, to issue a decree on 5 February 1913 requiring recruiters to obtain a licence from the authorities and all labour contracts to be approved by the district commissioners. The decree forbade the hiring of women, children and old people, fixed daily working hours at a maximum of ten and required the plantation managers to provide medical care for their workers. After the decree had taken effect on 1 October 1913 some of the worst practices in the "recruitment business", reminiscent of the slave trade, came to an end, but the situation on the plantations remained much the same. This was because the managers disregarded the new decree as they had disregarded an earlier one issued on 27 February 1909, which contained similar provisions. Six months before the new decree was issued, on 23 August 1912, Schnee had abolished the hut tax and replaced it by a poll tax of 3 to 5 rupees, which proved an even greater burden on the African taxpayers and necessarily increased "labour in lieu of taxes".

---

[53] C. Ittameier, in Wissenschaftliche Beiträge zur Frage der Erhaltung und Vermehrung der Eingeborenen-Bevölkerung. Ergebnisse der Eduard-Woermann-Preisaufgabe. Hamburgische Universität. Abhandlungen aus dem Gebiet der Auslandskunde, vol. 13, Hamburg 1923, p. 21.

[54] O. Peiper, Der Bevölkerungsrückgang in den tropischen Kolonien Afrikas und der Südsee — seine Ursachen und seine Bekämpfung. Veröffentlichungen aus dem Gebiet der Medizinalverwaltung, vol. XI, No. 7, Berlin 1920, p. 23.

[55] Report by the British East Africa Royal Commission of 1935. Source: J. Clagett Taylor, The Political Development of Tanganyika, Stanford and London 1963, p. 72.

There was a marked increase in German immigration into the colony during the years leading up to 1914. In 1913 the European population numbered 5,336, roughly four fifths of them being Germans.[56] The largest group was formed by plantation managers and farmers (882), who kept clamouring for more government support notwithstanding their privileged position and the assistance they were receiving already from the authorities. Governor Schnee did much to accommodate them. He established advisory bodies at the district and local level in which "non-official" Europeans were predominant, and he agreed to a reorganization of the Gouvernementsrat, a consultative council set up in 1903, to ensure a majority elected by the European population. At the same time, he ordered a reduction in land prices for German settlers seeking to enlarge their plantations. And he satisfied yet another demand of the racist settlers by restricting the immigration of Indians and their right to acquire real estate in urban areas. These concessions to the settlers did not diminish the Governor's power in the colony, but like simultaneous steps taken by the authorities in South West Africa and Cameroon they demonstrated the racist character of German colonial policy.

After the suppression of the Maji-Maji uprising the missionary societies were able to expand their influence on the indigenous population. In 1913 there were a total of 465 mission stations in the colony, with some 108,000 pupils (according to data provided by the societies) receiving instruction in mission schools[57], which were held to be the most important means of winning converts. But the massive influx recorded by the mission schools from 1911 onwards was not — as most missionaries realized — attributable to a sudden surge of interest in the Christian message. Rather it would appear that the main reason was the urge of young people to avoid the wretched life of migrant and seasonal labourers. Only a tiny minority, however, had any chance of securing a job in which they could put the knowledge acquired in school to practical use. The education they received was not least intended — as a result of the alliance between mission and administration — to turn them into obedient and disciplined subjects patiently enduring their fate.

As for the administration itself, it maintained 10 government schools and 89 subsidiary schools with a total roll of 6,100 pupils in that year to supply low-level officials and auxiliary staff for the administration, the "protective force" and German firms.

---

[56] *Statistisches Jahrbuch* für das Deutsche Reich, 36th vol., 1915, p. 457.

[57] *R. Tetzlaff*, op. cit., p. 276.

Judicial practice in the colony provided "striking" evidence that the "humane native policy" introduced by Dernburg was nothing but a myth. The cases in which corporal punishment was inflicted (this kind of treatment was reserved for Africans) kept rising from year to year, so that by 1912 the number of floggings had reached 8,057 or 48 per cent of all penalties imposed. (In neighbouring British East Africa the respective figures were 380 and 4.2 per cent).[58] The frequent use of this humiliating form of punishment was meant to intimidate the African population.

While no major uprisings occurred in the period 1907—1914, resistance continued in many areas. There were signs of unrest and rebellions in several districts. The Nyataru, the Nyiramba, the Nyisansu and some neighbouring tribes in Kilimatinde district staged the "Turu Rebellion" in 1908, which was, however, swiftly suppressed. Since the administration in Dar es Salaam feared that a new Maji-Maji movement might develop, it despatched further military contingents from Arusha, Tabora and Kilimatinde into the areas in question to cow the local population into submission through demonstrations of military strength.[59] Between 1907 and 1911 troops were called out five times to cope with rebellious tribes,[60] e.g. in 1909 when the Chagga were trying to stop settlers from stealing more and more of their land.[61] From 1908 onwards anti-colonial aspirations expressed in Islamic terms were propagated among the Moslem population in the coastal region. The district commissioner in Lindi in 1910 thereupon proposed that all individuals suspected of anti-government agitation should be deported to the South Seas.[62]

In the summer of 1911 southern Burundi witnessed a major uprising by peasant farmers and herdsmen which was provoked by trade caravans regularly traversing this area. It had its roots in the severe exploitation to which the people in that area were subjected. The German resident

---

[58] *C. C. Dundas*, Report on German Administration, pp. 102—104. Source: *L. H. Gann*, Heinrich Schnee (1871—1949), in L. H. Gann and P. Duignan (eds.), African Proconsuls. European Governors in Africa, New York 1978, p. 521.

[59] *G. C. K. Gwassa*, The German Intervention and African Resistance in Tanzania, in I. N. Kimambo and A. J. Temu (eds), A History of Tanzania. Nairobi 1969, p. 112.

[60] *C. C. F. Dundas*, A History of German East Africa, Dar es Salaam 1923, p. 44.

[61] *R. Tetzlaff*, op. cit., p. 108.

[62] ZStA, RKolA, no. 702, pp. 32ff, Report by district officer Lindi to the Governor, 16 Feb. 1910.

in the area proclaimed a state of war and had the insurrection put down.[63] In a parallel development (1910—12), peasants in northern Rwanda who had joined the Nyabingi movement and were led by a claimant to the throne, Bilegeya, and his brother Ndungutse staged a rebellion against King Yuhi V. Musinga, who had the backing of the colonial power. The northern provinces were wrested from the King and his aristocratic supporters driven away. During their advance towards the royal residence the insurgents were able to repulse the first attack of a German mercenary force, but they were ultimately defeated in May 1912.[64]

The effects of German rule on the peoples and tribes of the country which was later named Tanganyika (with Rwanda and Burundi no longer forming part of it) differed in degree from one part of the country to another, but their main features are clearly discernible although the sources left by the colonial authorities are biased and unreliable and many aspects require a closer examination than has so far been undertaken. The policy of reducing the colony to a politically oppressed and economically dependent supplier of tropical raw materials was not only based on military might but also on the constant use of other coercive methods of a non-economic nature (including the obligation to pay taxes). This policy led to the physical destruction of a considerable part of the population and the pauperization of even larger numbers, not only in material terms. Where Africans succeeded in producing for the market on a substantial scale, they were subjected to a typically colonial extreme defraudation. The "modern" school of colonialist apologetics, as represented by the US historians L. H. Gann and P. Duignan, seeks to minimize these main features of the development of German East Africa without being able to deny them altogether.

3. Cameroon 1906—1914*

Developments in Cameroon after 1906 were much influenced by changes in German colonial policy, which reflected the stage of imperialism

---

[63] *G. Launicke*, Zum antikolonialen Widerstand der Völker Burundis und Rwandas (1897—1916), in K. Büttner and H. Loth, Philosophie der Eroberer und koloniale Wirklichkeit. Ostafrika 1884—1918, Berlin 1981, p. 355.

[64] Ibid., pp. 357—363.

* This section is partly based on studies by *H. Kaselitz* née *Winkler* and *A. Rüger*, in: Kamerun unter deutscher Kolonialherrschaft. Studien, ed. by H. Stoecker, vol. 1, Berlin 1960; vol. 2, Berlin 1968.

reached at the turn of the century. The end of the partition of the world amongst the major imperialist powers prompted Germany to intensify the exploitation of her colonial possessions. Important financial circles began to play a more active role in the colonies as can be seen from the building of railway lines and the founding of new colonial firms.

In Cameroon existing plantations were enlarged and new ones established. Railway construction was begun and trade expanded. In the financial year 1909—10, for example, the Bibundi and Meanja plantation companies increased cocoa cultivation considerably, and the Deutsche Kautschuk-AG and the Gesellschaft Süd-Kamerun increased rubber cultivation. The number of plantations rose from 23 to 58 between 1906 and 1913, most of the new estates being rubber, tobacco and banana plantations. During the same period the area under cultivation increased from 7,296 to 28,225 hectares. In 1913, cocoa was grown on 13,161 hectares, oil palms on 5,044 hectares, rubber on 7,177 hectares (1911 figure), bananas on 2,164 hectares, and tobacco on 153 hectares. All told, the plantation companies owned 115,147 hectares of land in 1913. With the exception of a few reservations set aside for the local population they had appropriated virtually all the fertile land on the slopes of Mount Cameroon.

Soaring world market prices for rubber, a result of the rapid development of the automobile industry, were the main reason for the setting up of new rubber plantations and the depletion of Cameroon's natural rubber resources by trading and concession-holding companies. The rubber boom, which reached its climax in 1910, brought the rubber plantations in the British colonies gigantic profits. During that year, several British plantation companies were able to pay a dividend of between 200 and 300 per cent. Some German capitalists also hoped to profit from the boom, but the decline in rubber prices resulting from increased output and the loss of Cameroon in the First World War shattered these hopes.

Among the biggest rubber plantation companies were the Kamerun-Kautschuk-Co. AG, set up in 1906 with an initial capital of 3 million marks, and the Deutsche Kautschuk-AG, a subsidiary of the Westafrikanische Pflanzungsgesellschaft Victoria, founded in 1907 with an initial capital of 2.5 million marks. The principal shareholders of the Deutsche Kautschuk-AG were Max Esser and other capitalists already occupying leading positions in Cameroon's major plantation companies.

The reason why new tobacco plantations were set up in the years preceding World War I was the success of the experiments which a planter by the name of C. Räthke had achieved in the Bakossi region. The year 1910 saw the founding of the Deutsche Tabakbaugesellschaft

Kamerun mbH, which in 1913 was transformed into the Tabakbau- und Pflanzungsgesellschaft Kamerun AG, with a share capital of 2.6 million marks. In 1911 the Bremer Tabakbaugesellschaft Bakossi mbH was founded with a share capital of 400,000 marks (raised to 2 million marks in 1914). Behind these firms were German tobacco manufacturing interests. The most important of the banana plantation companies was the Afrikanische Frucht-Kompanie GmbH, a firm started in 1910 with a capital of 450,000 marks and closely associated with Laeisz, a Hamburg shipping company. It increased its capital twice before the First World War, bringing it up to 1.75 million marks.

The two large companies which had received concessions of land developed along different lines. Owing to the exceedingly rapacious practices of the Gesellschaft Nordwest-Kamerun, the population in the area under its control preferred to deliver their products to German firms outside the area or to powerful British competitors beyond the Nigerian border. Despite active support from the administration (the population of many villages was forcibly resettled to facilitate the recruitment of porters), the company failed to evolve from an unsound speculative undertaking into a "respectable" colonial firm of major standing. It was unable, owing to a chronic shortage of capital, to exploit fully the area assigned to it and to make the northern railway line into a paying venture through the transport of export products. So in 1910 Dernburg's successor, Friedrich von Lindequist, decided to revoke the concession. In taking this step, he acted in agreement with Dernburg's view that African farms in Cameroon's forest areas would offer the best chance of a rapid increase in the production of export goods, a view that was increasingly gaining acceptance in colonial circles at the time. The debt-ridden Gesellschaft Nordwest-Kamerun shared the fate of other firms set up by Prince Hohenlohe-Öhringen: it was soon practically bankrupt.

By contrast, the Gesellschaft Süd-Kamerun managed to increase its sales figures substantially after the rubber crisis of 1907—08 had forced the company to raise its capital to 3 million marks (whereby the Belgian share in the firm became even larger). With natural rubber resources dwindling because of the ruthless methods employed, the company decided to adopt a more cautious approach. It established plantations (in 1913 there were 19 with a work force of 1,500) and in 1909 ended its competition with the coastal firms by joining their syndicate, which was directed against African suppliers, and by fixing purchase prices prevented members from outbidding each other. As a result, the company was able to pay handsome dividends: 8 per cent annually from 1909 to 1911 and about 5 per cent in 1912.

It should also be mentioned that after 1906 the companies running plantations or holding concessions of land set up factories for the processing of palm oil. These small works were the earliest modest beginnings of industrial production in Cameroon. The first factory was established by the Gesellschaft Nordwest-Kamerun at Manfe on the Cross River in 1908, followed by others at Victoria, Maka and Mpundo.

From 1907 onwards, the Colonial Office and the administration of Cameroon leaned more and more towards the view that, as the example of the British colony Gold Coast had shown, "native farming" in the forest areas would make it possible for the output of export products to be raised more swiftly. Missionary circles in particular had expressed this opinion for years. Finally, the visible effects of ruthless overexploitation prompted the administration in 1912 to put forward a programme to encourage the growing of cocoa and oil palms among the African population. However, some of the measures initiated for this purpose such as the enforced establishment of plantations by chiefs in some places turned out to be rather ineffective because of the lack of manpower. Only the Duala, acting without support from the colonial authorities, cultivated cocoa as a cash crop with some success. Other coastal groups followed their example.

Compared to previous years the pattern of exports and imports remained largely the same but there were significant changes in volume. Exports (rubber, palm kernels, palm oil, cocoa and ivory) went up from 9,946,000 marks in 1906 to 26,151,000 marks in 1913 while imports (fabrics of many kinds, textiles, ironmongery, railway materials, silver coins and paper money, dried fish, canned fish and meat, rice, alcoholic liquor, beer, salt and tobacco) rose from 13,305,000 marks to 34,616,000 marks. These figures, compiled by the customs offices in the colony, are based on the prices then current in Cameroon. If they had been calculated on the basis of the prices current in Hamburg or London, imports would have been assessed lower and exports much higher.[65]

---

[65] Rudin errs in maintaining (p. 282) that the colony's adverse balance of trade (from 1894) was due to the importation of building and railway material. He ignores the fact that such material was not imported on a substantial scale until 1906 and that the "Statistics of the Protectorate", provide no accurate picture of the import-export ratio. Statistics compiled in Hamburg show the imports from Cameroon reaching Germany via Hamburg from 1910 to 1912 to be higher by 3 to 4.5 million marks than the total export figures given by the Protectorate for this period. Cf. Karl Rathgen's strongly critical remarks in Deutsches Koloniallexikon, vol. II, pp. 25—26 and pp. 185—7 of the present publication.

So although the "Statistics of the Protectorate" cannot be taken at face value, it is clear that exports rose at least threefold in terms of value between 1906 and 1914, with the prices of some of the main products actually declining.

The increase had to be paid for by Cameroon with the destruction of natural resources. During the period under consideration it ranked first among Germany's colonies as a supplier of tropical raw materials, primarily rubber, for the German market. Like most other export products, rubber was still predominantly obtained by gathering because the yields of plantations remained minimal for the time being. Nor did the planting of oil palms on a major scale produce substantial results prior to 1914. The only plantation crop to assume importance for the export trade was cocoa (5.7 million marks in 1913).

Apart from Germany, the only other purchaser of Cameroonian goods worth mentioning was Britain which bought 3.1 million marks' worth of products in 1912. As far as imports were concerned, the British lost ground but remained the only rivals, accounting for 16 per cent of total imports in 1912.

Whereas in 1898 the German government had rejected a British proposal for a joint ban on the sale of weapons and ammunition to Africans in West Africa, it reversed its position after the uprisings which took place between 1904 and 1907. It acceded to the Brussels Agreement concluded by the colonial powers on 22 July 1908 for this purpose, and in late 1908 Governor Theodor Seitz strictly prohibited any trade in weapons with Cameroonians. Measures taken in 1907 and 1910 in line with Dernburg's "native policy" to reduce the sale of alcoholic liquor to Africans remained ineffective: imports of spirits and beer kept on rising.

One factor enabling Cameroon's natural resources and people to be exploited on an increased scale was the construction of railways. This began later in Cameroon than in the other German colonies, mainly because the population offered such prolonged resistance to colonial subjection. After Adolf Woermann had first suggested building a railway line in the mid-1890s, some capitalists interested in Cameroon decided in 1900 to form a syndicate for the purpose of founding a company which would construct and operate a railway linking the coast with the interior of the country. The syndicate (Woermann, Scharlach, Schoeller, F. Lenz and others), having been granted a preliminary concession by the government, resolved to build a line from Bonaberi (Douala) to Bare (Manenguba Mountains). As it lacked the necessary funds it found itself compelled to cede its rights to a consortium headed by the Berliner Handelsgesellschaft, which agreed to finance the venture when the government offered highly favourable terms. The consortium consisted of the Bank für Handel und Industrie (Darmstädter Bank), the Disconto-Gesellschaft, the Nationalbank für Deutschland, the A. Schaaffhausen'sche Bankverein, S. Bleichröder, Von der Heydt & Co., the Norddeutsche Bank, M. M. Warburg, Friedrich Krupp and C. Woermann. In 1906 it founded the Kamerun-Eisenbahngesellschaft, with an initial capital of 16,640,000 marks, which was awarded the concession to build and operate the railway by a legislative act. The Reich guaranteed a 3 per cent interest on a capital share of 11 million marks and the gradual reimbursement of this share from 1911 onwards at 120 per cent of its nominal value. In addition, the newly founded company was granted land and mining rights on both sides of the track for a 90-year period.

The construction work, which began in 1907 after the population at the northern end of the line had been crushed into submission, was put into the hands of the Deutsche Kolonial-Eisenbahn- und Betriebsgesellschaft, a subsidiary of the Lenz group, which had direct links with the Berliner Handelsgesellschaft. The 160-kilometre Manenguba or Northern Railway began traffic on 1 April 1911. It was the only railway in the German colonies at the time which was financed and run on a private basis.

Colonial Secretary Dernburg, pursuing his railway programme, succeeded in 1908 in winning acceptance for the idea of building a second line in Cameroon, to be financed from the public purse. The project he had in mind was the so-called Midland Line, which would lead from Douala via Edea to Widimenge and require an outlay of 44 million marks. The annual report of the Imperial Colonial Office described its purpose as follows: "It will be of great military significance in that it will make it possible, in the event of a rebellion occurring in the south, to reinforce and relieve the military stations there without delay and, by swiftly crushing the rebellion, prevent a general uprising. Economically, the line will be of the utmost importance. Apart from the fact that it will not be a rival for a railway linking the Batanga coast with the south, say Ebolowa, the line will provide access to the densely populated Bakokoland and the river area of the Sanage and Nyong right to the southernmost and easternmost borders of the Protectorate."[66] The military considerations put forward here are revealing: Cameroon was officially declared to be "pacified" at the time. In reality, the German colonial regime never succeeded in subduing the entire population of Cameroon.

---

[66] Denkschrift über die Entwicklung der Schutzgebiete in Afrika und der Südsee im Jahre 1907/8, Part C, p. 18.

Originally, the line was to be 360 kilometres long, but by December 1913 only 150 kilometres (up to the Nyong River) had been completed. The administration had cleared the way for the construction of both railways by conquering and protecting the territory by armed force, by expropriating the African owners in summary proceedings and forcibly recruiting labourers in great numbers.

The extension of the plantation system, the construction of railways and, most important, the greatly expanded activities of commercial and concession-holding companies in the interior led to a steep increase in the demand for wage labourers. The companies needed ever larger numbers of porters to carry inland products to the coast and imported goods inland because pack-animals were unable to live under tropical forest conditions and the railways linked only a small part of the colony with Douala, the colony's principal seaport. Since it was still impossible to meet more than a fraction of the manpower requirements by hiring workers, coercive measures continued to be applied in the recruitment of labour. As a result of the ruthless use of such methods by the authorities the number of porters, plantation workers, railway building labourers, et al., rose from year to year. According to estimates by H. Winkler there were at least 150,000 of them in 1914, but probably the figure was much higher.

"The methods employed to produce manpower were manifold," she wrote after an investigation of the conditions facing workers in Cameroon before 1914. "The recruiters made people drunk or took advantage of their ignorance, bribed chiefs to provide the requested number of labourers, or simply resorted to brute force. After 1906 the demands for a law providing for compulsory labour by Africans grew more insistent among those groups of the German bourgeoisie which had a stake in the colonies,"[67] but the government refrained from such a step because it would have caused a public outcry in Germany.

Contrary to what is often alleged in colonialist literature, the working and living conditions of the labour force showed no signs of improvement after 1906. The much increased recruitment had dire consequences, especially for the worst affected areas (the coastal region and southern Cameroon). Mortality figures among the labourers were staggering, attaining 20 to 30 per cent annually on some plantations. R. R. Kuczynski arrived at an average yearly mortality rate of 13 per cent for 1913 and

---

[67] *H. Winkler*, Das Kameruner Proletariat 1906—1914, in: Kamerun unter deutscher Kolonialherrschaft. Studien, ed. by H. Stoecker, vol. 1, Berlin 1960, p. 248.

of 16 per cent for 1914 for railway labourers.[68] Many of the recruits (often chained together) did not even survive the hardship of the march from their native locality to their intended place of work. Those who did arrived in a state of complete exhaustion, and the conditions they met were in general not suited to help them back on their feet. Similarly, the porters, who were frequently ill-fed, were on their marches exposed to a variety of illnesses, especially infectious diseases and influenza. The traders often left sick porters lying by the wayside and secured replacements in the next village. Even Colonial Secretary Wilhelm Solf saw fit in 1913 to remonstrate with the German Chamber of Commerce in South Cameroon: "It is a sorry spectacle to see the villages drained of all menfolk, to watch women and children carry burdens, to find a whole people condemned to an itinerant way of life . . . Family ties are severed because parents, spouses and children are separated from each other. No more children are born because the women are separated from their husbands for most of the year . . ."[69]

As a rule, forced labourers were denied a wage sufficient to reproduce their labour power. "Starvation wages, excessively long hours, malnutrition, poor shelter, female and child labour, the breakdown of family life, an early death, floggings and chains — such was the fate of the workers in Cameroon," writes H. Winkler. "While the population sank deeper into misery as a result of growing impoverishment, the dividends paid by the big companies rose. The Westafrikanische Pflanzungsgesellschaft Victoria, for example, paid a dividend of 8 per cent in 1907, 1908 and 1909, of 15 per cent in 1910 and 1911, of 18 per cent in 1912, and of 20 per cent in 1913."[70]

So developments in Cameroon after 1906 clearly disprove the claim that the year 1906 marked the advent of a better and more humane colonial regime. By referring to "the new spirit governing the treatment of the natives" (Rudin), "a genuine contribution to the cause of culture and civilization" (G. Ritter) or the "understanding policy adopted towards the natives" (Townsend), pro-colonial historians have attempted to disguise the real nature of the policies which Dernburg and his successors pursued vis-à-vis the population in the colonies before the outbreak of the First World War.

---

[68] *R. R. Kuczynski*, The Cameroons and Togoland. A demographic study, London 1939, p. 61.

[69] ZStA, R KolA, no. 6286, Letter by the German Society for the Protection of Natives to Colonial Secretary Solf, 6 Feb. 1914.

[70] *H. Winkler*, op. cit., p. 280.

Such historians often cite the colonial school system as an important cultural achievement, but only a relatively small number of children and young people benefited from it. It was almost exclusively in the hands of the missionary societies. The two government schools in Douala and Victoria, where children and young people were taught reading, writing and arithmetic, and some basic skills so that they could be employed later as clerks, tax collectors, overseers, and auxiliary postal employees or railwaymen, were supplemented in 1906 and 1908 by similar establishments at Gatoua and Yaoundé. By 1913 these four schools put together had 833 pupils on their roll. By contrast, the missions were running 631 schools (by their own account) in 1913, most of these being village schools in which a teacher or auxiliary teacher mainly gave instruction in religion and German as well as imparting manual and domestic skills. The course lasted three or sometime four years, the Basle mission in particular providing some additional instruction for a few pupils. Apart from two teachers' training colleges there were no institutes of higher education.

"Despite government inaction", writes Karin Hausen, "the number of pupils virtually tripled between 1906—07 and 1912—13, rising from 15,472 to 43,419. These figures are all the more astounding as teaching remained confined to the forest zone with its low density of population. The main factor was the keen interest shown by individual villages, which did not even cease when the missions asked them to finance the building of schools and to pay the teachers a salary. There were frequent complaints by missionaries that they were unable to meet requests for school education because of a lack of personnel and funds ... In many instances the number of mission pupils exceeded the number of converts".[71] As in Togo, the question as to which language should be given preference in the classroom caused friction between the administration and the Protestant missionaries. Finally, a decree issued by the Governor in 1910 made the amount of state aid for the mission schools (which totalled 30,000 marks in 1913, i.e. 70 pfennigs per pupil) dependent on the children's demonstrable proficiency in German.

Between 1906 and 1914 the people of Cameroon continued to offer passive as well as active resistance to the policy of expelling them from their land, forcing them to work for German firms or the administra-

---

[71] *K. Hausen*, Deutsche Kolonialherrschaft in Afrika, Wirtschaftsinteressen und Kolonialverwaltung in Kamerun vor 1914, Zurich and Freiburg 1970, p. 179. The statistics on missionary schools should not be taken at face value because some missionary societies or their superiors tended to exaggerate the results of their work.

tion, recruiting them for unpaid labour on road and bridge projects and imposing taxes on them. As a rule all able-bodied men in a village ran away at the approach of a recruiting party. In many cases all residents would abandon their village to escape the payment of taxes or forced labour. They would settle elsewhere in the tropical forest or cross into neighbouring British or French territory. In 1909, for example, some 10,000 Njems from south-east Cameroon migrated into French territory to evade forcible recruitment as porters.

There was no end to local insurrections and cases of unrest. The Maka, for example, a long-suffering people forced to labour for government stations and continually exposed to crimes committed by itinerant traders, staged a rebellion in 1910, after a consultation between all the chiefs, in a desperate attempt to get rid of their tormentors. Colonial troops dispatched to the area crushed the uprising in two months of bloody fighting.

The Imperial Colonial Office had to admit even in its annual reports, which were intended for the German public, that considerable sections of the population had not accepted German rule. The report for 1911—12 noted: "Even though the Protectorate has not witnessed any serious uprisings, the situation is explosive enough, and the expeditions which were necessary here and there to suppress incipient rebellions are evidence that vigilance remains a constant necessity." There followed a list of local resistance operations.[72] Although all these risings were drowned in blood, they still hindered the extension of direct colonial exploitation to the whole of Cameroon.

In those parts of the colony in which the German authorities had established a relatively stable system of administration, they sought to cope with "insubordination" by inflicting severe punishment on "unruly subjects". According to official statistics the number of sentences passed rose from 3,150 in 1907—08 to 6,360 in 1910—11 and to 11,229 in 1912—13. The respective figures for prison terms were 1,907, 3,516 and 5,452, and those for corporal punishment 924, 1,909 and 4,800.

The real figures for the debasing practice of flogging were higher because only penalties imposed by district commissioners and station chiefs at their place of residence were entered into the registers. The arbitrary whippings inflicted on the orders of officials, army officers and employers went unrecorded although they were a common feature of life in Cameroon.

---

[72] Denkschrift . . . 1911/12, p. 59.

The closing years of German rule were marked by a sharp conflict between the colonial regime and the Duala, who had fallen into poverty since the loss of their monopoly on intermediate trade. Governor Theodor Seitz decided in 1910 that the Duala should be removed from their traditional settlement area in the town of that name, the colony's major communications and trading centre, and that they should be relocated outside the town's precincts. They were to receive 40 pfennigs per square metre as "compensation". Racist, "hygienic" and economic arguments were put forward in support of the plan to turn the town into a living and business area reserved for Europeans. The physical separation of Africans and Europeans was, in the wors of district commissioner Röhm, "absolutely necessary in order to escape or avert as long as possible the danger which the English are now facing on the African West Coast (cf. Lagos, Sierra Leone and Calabar) and which is looming over us in Douala, viz. a development leading to social and political equality with the natives."[73] A government medical officer recommended the removal of the Duala on the grounds that malaria, which was endemic among them, might spread to Europeans, and the Cameroon administration noted dispassionately: "The government, the municipality, the railways, the old-established so-called Duala firms, the recently established firms from the south, the building contractors and other private people all need building land in the European quarter to expand."[74]

Colonial Secretary von Lindequist approved the expropriation plans. "From the outset, the Duala looked upon the plans of the administration as a threat to their economic existence," writes Rüger. "So they registered a protest. Initially, they believed that well-founded objections would be sufficient to avert the impending danger and that the whole matter was a question of law and justice. It was only in the course of their struggle that they realized that the colonial power did not care about the law and that they were facing not just an economic or legal dispute but a political test of strength with an adversary . . . In a written petition to the Reichstag of 8 March 1912 the chiefs set out their objections in detail. They declared, inter alia, that they could not be expected

---

[73] Quoted in *A. Rüger*, Die Duala und die Kolonialmacht 1884—1914. Eine Studie über die historischen Ursprünge des afrikanischen Kolonialismus, in: Kamerun . . ., vol. 2, p. 291.

[74] Quoted in *A. Rüger*, op. cit.

'to abandon the treasured legacy of our ancestors . . . at a price which is nothing short of ludicrous'."[75]

Since these protests were of no avail (the Reichstag passed the petition on to the government), Paramount Chief Rudolf Manga Bell eventually invoked the provision of the treaty of 12 July 1884 which had expressly stipulated "that the land cultivated by us now and the places the towns are built on shall be the property of the present owners and their successors."[76] A violation of the treaty provisions, the chiefs warned in a written complaint of 20 February 1913, "may well prompt the natives to consider whether it might be wiser under the circumstances to revoke the treaty and enter into a treaty with another power."[77]

The Cameroon administration, however, went ahead with its plans, flouting the treaty with the express approval of Colonial Secretary Wilhelm Solf. The chiefs' refusal to accept compensation payments and to put up with the expropriation order delayed matters somewhat, but after Rudolf Manga Bell was deposed as paramount chief and three German warships had given a demonstration of military might off the Cameroon coast, the administration proceeded to expel the Duala from the town by force. This operation was interrupted only in March 1914, at the demand of the German parliament, when many of the Duala's houses and huts had already been demolished. Manga Bell had turned for help to a democratic journalist, Helmut von Gerlach, who by means of a renewed petition secured a suspension order from the Budget Commission of the Reichstag.

"Solf, however, supported by the entire right-wing press, the colonial entrepreneurs and powerful colonial interests, managed to persuade wavering members of the bourgeois parties, from the Centre to the Progressive People's Party, to change their mind, achieving this end by careful tactics, misleading information and pressure on individual deputies", writes Rüger.[78] So the bourgeois majority in the Budget Commission and in the Reichstag as a whole empowered him to conclude the expropriation by force, with the Social Democrats and the Polish deputies maintaining their opposition.

Manga Bell, who had begun to organize a resistance movement embracing the whole of Cameroon and cutting across tribal differences, was

---

[75] *A. Rüger*, Die Widerstandsbewegung des Rudolf Manga Bell in Kamerun, in: Etudes africaines, ed. by W. Markow, Karl Marx University, Leipzig 1967, p. 109.

[76] Quoted in *A. Rüger*, op. cit., p. 110.

[77] Ibid., pp. 114—115.

[78] Ibid., p. 120.

arrested with a number of his followers after a chief standing high in the Germans' favour had betrayed him to missionary, and the latter had passed the information on to the authorities. Although the missionary societies active in Cameroon repeatedly urged Governor Karl Ebermaier to adopt a moderate attitude, the administration on Solf's instructions charged Manga Bell and his secretary with high treason. When British warships approached the coast a few days after the outbreak of the First World War, the two men were sentenced to death and executed after a summary trial. Ebermaier rejected pleas for mercy from the bishop of the Catholic mission and from Protestant missionaries: the German colonial regime sought to cow its African subjects by terror up to the end.

As a result of the Franco-German agreement on Morocco of 4 November 1911, the colony was greatly increased in size on its eastern and southern borders, acquiring an area of 280,000 square kilometres from French Equatorial Africa. The "new" Cameroon consisted of barely accessible tropical forest. What made the exchange deal significant in the eyes of the German Foreign Office and others cherishing the dream of penetrating into the Belgian Congo was the fact that Cameroon now had two points of contact with that vast colony — a small step along the road to "German Central Africa". French companies holding concessions in the territory ceded to Germany were to retain their monopolistic rights. The transfer was scheduled to take place from 1912 to 1913, but in practical terms the incorporation into Germany's colonial system had not been completed when the war broke out in 1914.

What were the consequences of German rule for the peoples of Cameroon? The different parts of the country were affected by the colonial regime in varying degrees, depending on the duration of German control and the intensity of "economic development". Hardest hit was the population in the large forest region, including the coastal strip. In Adamawa and the northern territories the effects were similar but less incisive because the instruments of the colonial regime were few and far between there and because the lack of communication links with the coast (except for the Benue-Niger route leading via British-ruled Nigeria) greatly hampered German firms in their attempts to gain a foothold.

But what applied to all parts of Cameroon in equal measure was that they were subjected to the despotic and repressive rule of an alien power exclusively serving the interests of the ruling class of that power. The foreign rulers intervened sharply in the economic and political conditions which had emerged by the end of the 19th century. Their savage methods of repression, the deportation of hundreds of thousands compelled to perform forced labour under the most adverse conditions, and the spread of infectious diseases partly brought in from Europe caused great loss of human life and a decline in the population which invites comparison with the effects of the Atlantic slave trade in previous centuries. The rape of the country's natural resources and the ruthless exploitation of its people led to widespread misery and poverty. At the same time, the colonial power prevented the emergence of an African bourgeoisie which might have entered into competition with German firms. In the forest zone the existing African socio-economic and legal system showed signs of disintegrating. The colonial power began to replace it with a system fully geared to the economic needs of German monopoly capitalism. The role assigned to the oppressed people of Cameroon was that of helots deprived of all rights and doomed to slave labour for their foreign masters.

4. Togo 1900—1914

The period from 1900 to the end of German rule witnessed a considerable increase in colonial activity. The hinterland was connected to the coastal region as regards the administration and, to some degree, the economy. New joint-stock companies began to establish plantations and to gain a foothold in commerce. As this took place without any major military operations and resulted in clearly visible infrastructural development, Togo continued to be looked upon as a "model colony". But the fact remains that in every area of life the colonial regime gave rise to sharp conflicts with the population. If, in contrast to other German colonies, there were no great uprisings, the reason was that in the south the ease with which the population could leave the colony set certain limits to oppression by officialdom, while in the north large areas remained unconquered and colonial exploitation did not develop much.

Military conquest went hand in hand with the establishment of a well-functioning administration, which was essential to colonial exploitation. The system of government was simple in structure. Its head was the Governor, who in 1897 had transferred his official residence from Anecho to Lomé. Togo was divided into the coastal districts of Lomé and Anecho and the inland districts of Misahöhe, Atakpame, Kete-Krachi, Sokode and Sansanne-Mango. In each of the inland districts there was also a German-run subsidiary station. The district commissioners (or station chiefs) combined in their hands administrative, military and judicial powers, which were exercised autocratically. Many of these officials remained in Togo for several decades; all were imbued with pronounced racialist sentiments coupled with arrogance, often enough designed to conceal a lack of education and linguistic proficiency.

Their rule was based on support by mercenary troops and on a judicial system with a preference for corporal punishment. Since Togo, unlike the other German colonies in Africa, had no "protective force" but only a 500-strong "police contingent", all political and military powers were united in the hands of the colonial bureaucracy. Even major campaigns were described as police operations, which made it easier to conceal their true character from the German public. For colonial officialdom armed contingents were indispensable not only for punitive expeditions but also for the supervision of forced labourers, the transmission of orders to chiefs, and other duties.

The chieftaincy was useful for the functioning of the colonial system because it was economical and convenient to rely on men holding a position of authority within the African communities. Consequently, the administration retained chiefs who displayed "good behaviour", but removed those who revealed anticolonial sentiments, using the most drastic methods for this purpose, not even stopping short of murder. The installation or official endorsement of chiefs, which had become routine procedure in the closing stages of German rule, was used as a demonstration of colonial power to impress the population. To give the chiefs the necessary authority in dealing with their people, the administration allowed them to hire some village policemen and to share in the exercise of judicial powers and thus in the collection of court fees. The execution of certain orders, e.g. the provision of "tax workers", gave them some latitude to exercise power on a small scale.

One way in which the colonial administration sought to strengthen its grip was through the judiciary. The number of sentences inflicted rose from 1,072 in 1901—02 to 6,009 in 1911—12 while the number of cases in which corporal punishment was imposed by the authorities went up from 162 to 733 during the same decade. Many of the sentences inflicted were for so-called crimes against the state (953 in 1911—12).[79]

---

[79] ZStA, RKolA, no. 5090, Strafverzeichnis der Eingeborenen, pp. 30, 33, 34, 40, 41; No. 5378, Die Prügelstrafe. Allgemeines, p. 144.

Dernburg's attempts to restrict corporal punishment were to no avail nor were proposals to codify the rights of the Africans, which the colonial bureaucracy rejected as a matter of principle.

On the whole, although it was usual for officials to exact services from villagers, it proved only partly possible up to 1907 to use the vast labour force that was potentially available for colonial purposes. In many instances the administration ordered Africans to build or clean roads with the sole aim of demonstrating its power. It remained doubtful whether there was any economic sense in road-building because the tsetse fly made it impossible to use animal-drawn vehicles.

The general introduction in 1907 of compulsory labour for administrative purposes, or alternatively payment of a tax, afforded the administration a new possibility of raising its revenue. At the same time, the lack of employment opportunities in Togo prompted thousands to migrate temporarily to the Gold Coast in search of work.

The political and administrative measures initiated led to what were in part considerable changes in tribal patterns. Even more important were the changes brought about by the development of the infrastructure which gave the southern part of the arbitrarily created territory a measure of inner cohesion. As a result, a new economic and political entity emerged in this part of the Slave Coast.

Lomé, which had fast developed into a commercial centre (its population rising from 2,300 to 7,400 between 1897 and 1913), eclipsing Anecho, was turned into an efficient port for the colony. The first steps were the construction of a pier (completed in 1904) and of the 45-kilometre Lomé-Anecho coastal railway (completed in 1905), which made it possible for all imports to be unloaded at Lomé. Railways leading inland were built: the 119-kilometre Lomé-Palime line (completed in 1907) running in a northwestern direction to the Togo Mountains and the 168-kilometre Lomé-Atakpame line (completed in 1911—12), which was meant to be extended to Sokode and Sansanne-Mango, running due north. The last two lines were built and all three were run by the Deutsche Kolonial-Eisenbahn-Bau- und Betriebs-Gesellschaft, a subsidiary of the bank Berliner Handelsgesellschaft.

As it turned out, the railways were able to complete with the cheap river transport in the neighbouring colonies so that by 1914, according to official estimates, roughly one-third of the colony could be considered part of the German-controlled coastal economic zone. The transport links with the interior were established in the interests of the financially stronger companies which had begun to penetrate Togo. The insistent demands of the older trading firms for a branch line leading into the

palm-growing area behind Anecho were, on the other hand, not fulfilled.

The conquest of a large inland area with fertile soils and a relatively
high population density appeared to open up new vistas for colonial
exploitation. German companies with the necessary capital soon appeared on the scene, and a debate over economic policy began. The
question was whether the state should primarily encourage large plantations or peasant farms ("Volkskulturen"). Plantations were run by
Europeans and mostly financed by joint-stock or other companies for
the purpose of growing export crops on large areas while the
term "Volkskulturen" was used to describe smallholdings on which
cash crops were grown by African peasants. The dispute was largely
over the most profitable methods of exploitation and the share of the
different capitalist groups in the economy of the colony.

Characteristically, leading German colonial officials considered
plantations run by Europeans to be the principal objective of the colonial
economy in tropical Africa. This view resulted largely from racist pre-
judice, which the agricultural expert of the Colonial Department, Goldberg, expressed in these words in 1892: "I am now totally convinced
that natives, unless they have attended school or find themselves under
the constant influence of Europeans, are unable to grow cotton, coffee,
cacao or any other crop unknown to them at a profit."[80]

Such opinions had no basis in fact. On the coast, the cultivation of
export crops by African farmers had a tradition going back to before
the beginning of German rule. Between 1865 and 1870 cotton was grown
because the American Civil War had sent prices soaring. Similarly,
during the period of German rule prominent Africans set up large plantations in the areas surrounding Anecho and Lomé. By 1894 Olympio
had planted 11,000 coffee trees in Lomé, Madeiros had planted 6,500
in Bagida, d'Almeida had planted 1,500 in Anecho, Aite Ajavon had
planted 500, etc.[81] They were however exposed to the ups and downs
of the world market as the "protectorate" did not protect indigenous
producers. After a prolonged period of depressed prices the African
farmers cut down their coffee trees again.

Another example was the cultivation of maize, aided by very good
natural conditions, especially in the southern part of the country. There
were indications of a big increase in marketing possibilities abroad as

---

[80] ZStA, RKolA, no. 7815, p. 36, Report by Goldberg to the Foreign Office, 1 Jan.
1892.

[81] ZStA, RKolA, no. 6503, Jahresberichte allgemeinen Inhalts aus Togo, p. 183.

early as 1892, but the administration imposed a ban on all exports.
After the ban was lifted at the beginning of the twentieth century, exports
soon reached a record figure of 30,000 metric tons valued at 3.5 million
marks (1908).[82] African production of two other traditional export
items — palm kernels and palm oil — also demonstrated the efficiency
of indigenous farming.

Under the impression of rapidly increasing cocoa production by
African farmers in the neighbouring British-ruled Gold Coast, the growing of cash crops by Africans was officially recognized in Togo after the
turn of the century, partly because the quality of the soil in the coastal
region had little attraction for European plantation companies and
because the inhabitants of the Togo Mountains fiercely resisted any
attempts to rob them of their land.

About this time a newly formed business group appeared in the colony. In 1896 the mine-owner Sholto Douglas, who already took part
in the exploitation of Cameroon, fitted out an expedition to explore
the colony geologically. The conquest of the unexplored hinterland
appeared to promise the possibility of high profits, which explains why
the expedition, headed by a mining engineer named Friedrich Hupfeld, first took part in the military subjugation of the tribes in the country's interior. While Hupfeld did not discover any mineral deposits
worth exploiting, he "acquired" an area of about 300 square kilometres
on the orders of Douglas at a price of 2,485 marks with the support of
the administration. This he did by resorting to fraud, blackmail and
violence, most of the sum being paid in the form of cheap spirits, so
that even the future Governor, Count von Zech, had to admit: "Legally
speaking, these contracts are in my opinion null and void or may at
least be contested by the natives because (i) they believed they were
negotiating with the government; (ii) they were unaware of the scope
of the contracts; (iii) the barter objects were absolutely disproportionate
to the value of the land."[83]

In the following years Hupfeld became the leading capitalist in Togo.
In 1902 he founded the German Togo Company (DTG), which initially
had a capital of 750,000 marks, this sum being increased to one million
in 1906 and to 1.3 million in 1911. Most of the shareholders were civil
servants, officers, merchants and industrialists, the largest number of
shares being held by the Königlich-Württembergische Hofbank and

---

[82] *O. F. Metzger*, Unsere alte Kolonie Togo, pp. 22, 233.

[83] ZStA, RKolA, no. 3653, Pflanzungsunternehmen des Sholto Douglas, p. 29,
Marginal note to a draft letter by the Colonial Department of Feb. 1898.

by Sholto Douglas. The company, set up with the intention of running plantations as well as engaging in trading activities, purchased Douglas's landed property at a price of 220,000 marks. The company hoped to derive profits from land speculation and the exploitation of cheap labour, and it also realized that the establishment of a wide network of trading agencies in the hinterland would give it a clear advantage over smaller firms with less capital at their disposal.

Faced with this threat, the smaller German firms suddenly discovered their affectionate feelings for the African population. In a joint petition addressed to the Colonial Department on 22 December 1902, they protested against the land claims of the DTG, describing them as a "great danger to our legitimate trading interests and to the rights of our hard-working natives."[84] This marked the beginning of the public dispute as to whether plantations or peasant farms should form the backbone of colonial development, which led to mutual recriminations in the press and in the Reichstag. The true reason for the protest was expressed in a letter addressed to the Colonial Department on 11 February 1903 by the Association of West African Traders: "The older-established firms in Togo find it strange that such advantages should be granted to companies which have not rendered any comparable services to the colony."[85] So what was at issue was not the wellbeing of the Africans, but the question as to who would exploit them and how they could best be kept quiet.

Well-founded fears of an angry response from the Africans ("Such speculation will only result in rebellion, murder and mayhem," said the traders[86], and of an exodus to the adjoining colonies of other powers ultimately led to the revision of the land purchase agreements made by the DTG. Under pressure from revolutionary Social Democrats and colonial circles opposed to a policy of granting land concessions, a commission was set up to examine the claims of the society. But the membership of the commission, which consisted of a company representative, a district commissioner and a missionary, made it clear that the interests of the society and not the rights of the Africans would be upheld. As a result of its findings, the company, although it had to give back a major portion of the land it had "acquired", was able, under the terms of a new agreement concluded in 1910, to retain an area of approximately 13,000 hectares. This area was sold to three subsidiary

---

[84] ZStA, RKolA, no. 3642, p. 22.
[85] Ibid., p. 95.
[86] Ibid.

companies in what proved a very lucrative transaction. The three subsidiaries were the Agu-Pflanzungsgesellschaft, founded in 1907; the Togo-Pflanzungs-A.G., established in 1911; and the Gadja-Pflanzungs-A.G., founded in 1914. As early as 1904 the Deutsche Togo-Gesellschaft had acquired the only European-run plantation on the coast so that all major plantations in Togo were in its hands. Hupfeld was chairman of all these companies, the shareholders consisting partly of the owners of the Gesellschaft and partly of a multitude of middle-class investors.

By the end of 1913 the plantation companies Kpeme, Agu, Gadja and Togo, whose capital totalled about 2.5 million marks, had 1,830 hectares under cultivation, with sisal being grown on 634 hectares, coconut trees on 565 hectares, cacao on 83 hectares, rubber on 80 hectares, oil palms on 90 hectares, and rubber plus cacao and oil palms on 158 hectares. The plantations employed a permanent African workforce of 620 as well as eight Europeans.[87] It had, however, become apparent that the European-run plantation system was not the most promising approach for colonial profiteers, although the administration did much to assist the plantations by providing labour and building a railway line to Palime.

The aim was now to force the African farmers to grow those export crops which suited the interests of German imperialism and which it would have been uneconomical to grow on plantations. Cotton was a case in point. The Colonial Economy Committee (KWK) had initiated the cultivation of cotton in 1900 to enable Germany to become steadily less dependent on imports from North America. A reasonable price would have prompted the African farmers to grow cotton of their own free will. Yet with German firms unwilling to pay such a price, the crop was "introduced" by military force, German officials even prescribing the farming methods to be employed. The harvest was then bought up by soldiers from the nearest military station at a price fixed by the authorities. When the Togo-Gesellschaft took charge of the marketing and processing, no substantial changes occurred: administrative coercion remained the basis of peasant farming in Togo. Ten years later there were still warnings that this allegedly flourishing sector of the economy would collapse if the state abandoned its coercive policies. Most of the export, which began in 1902, was handled by the DTG.

By contrast, the colonial power did almost nothing to encourage the growing of oil palms and maize by peasants. In fact, wherever these

---

[87] ZStA, RKolA, no. 3417, p. 111, Plantation Statistics.

came to compete with the plantations, they were not supported by the administration. African farmers in the Togo Mountains, for example, began to grow cacao after the turn of the century on the advice of migrant Togolese workers from the Gold Coast, and not because of German encouragement. In 1913 there were 45,000 fruit-bearing cacao trees and 201,000 others, with exports adding up to 334 metric tons.[88]

The development of African peasant farming has often been represented as an achievement of the German merchant capitalists, but though the commercial firms doubtlessly profited from the growing of export crops by Africans, they were its beneficiaries rather than its originators.

During this period major companies gained a foothold in Togo's trade, notably the DTG and the Deutsch-Westafrikanische Handelsgesellschaft, the latter with a subscribed capital of 2,225,000 marks. This made it necessary for old-established firms to adapt themselves to the new conditions. The merchant F. Oloff, for example, who had been active in Togo from 1889, set up the Bremer Kolonial-Handelsgesellschaft A.G. in 1905. The company, founded with an initial capital of 1.23 million marks, made a net profit of 300,000 marks per annum between 1909 and 1912 and was able to pay a dividend of 17.5 per cent from 1908 to 1911.[89] But competition remained considerable (in 1913 the Association of West African Traders had 12 firms affiliated to it) so that no firm was able to gain a monopoly. Precise data are not available concerning the profits which German trading firms extracted from Togo. The palm oil products exported between 1899 and 1913 were valued at 37.5 million marks, and the rubber exported between 1903 and 1913 at 9.5 million marks. The value of exports and imports combined rose from 3.54 million marks in 1896 to 19.77 million marks in 1913.[90] When a profit margin of 30 per cent, as given by the firms themselves, is taken as a basis of calculation, it becomes clear that these firms raked in several million marks in profits each year.

Almost nothing was done to develop industries. Since initial geological prospecting revealed that neither the country's bauxite resources nor the iron ore deposits near Banjeli were worth exploiting, no mining industry was set up. In 1914, there existed only 10 cotton ginneries, three refineries for palm oil products and one for sisal, a soap factory, and a lime kiln.

[88] ZStA, RKolA, no. 8023, p. 50.
[89] ZStA, RKolA, no. 3660, Die Bremer Kolonial-Handelsgesellschaft Mercator-Oloff, pp. 7—46.
[90] *O. F. Metzger*, op. cit., p. 22.

The apologists of German colonialism have all praised Togo's health and education facilities. But the facts show that these fitted logically into the overall pattern of imperialist colonial policy.

While not all colonial officials shared the racist view that Africans could not be educated at all, there was agreement on the advisability of leaving them uneducated. The first government school was established at Anecho in 1890 only because the local chiefs had demanded it, referring to the situation in the neighbouring colonies, and had donated 1,000 marks for this purpose, a handsome sum at the time. A second school was built at Lomé in 1902 because a number of employees with primary education were needed for the administrative machinery. Later on — again at the insistence of the Africans — Dernburg agreed to the opening of an intermediate school. The contribution of the German authorities to education was minimal: in 1912 the two government schools had 181 pupils on their roll, the teaching staff consisting of two Germans and eight Africans. The agricultural school at Nuatja, which was to impart some basic farming skills, proved a failure because its pupils were forcibly recruited. More important were the 342 mission schools, which in 1912 were attended by a total of 13,098 pupils (i.e. about three per cent of the school age population). A mere 15,000 marks was earmarked for these schools in the colony's budget, this sum remaining unchanged from 1906.[91] There was no access to higher education in Togo, which explains why many Togolese sent their children to the adjoining British colonies for education and training.

Any assessment of the mission schools must take into account that they often built upon the African population's thirst for knowledge. Especially in those areas where trade was an important factor, such as the coastal strip and the Volta region, the Africans recognized the advantages of a European-style education. The main reason why they sent their children to mission schools was to enable them to learn English. The Protestant missionary societies, which offered English lessons in order to expand and consolidate their influence among the population, thus found themselves at odds with the administration which disapproved of lessons conducted in a European language other than German. The dispute between the administration and the missionary societies over this issue lasted twenty years. But despite these tactical differences, there was agreement on all matters of principle.

Two Protestant missionary societies had been operating in Togo since precolonial days: the North German Mission, based in Bremen,

---

[91] ZStA, RKolA, no. 4081, Die Schulen in Togo, p. 3.

and the Basle Mission. The Steyl Mission, a Roman Catholic society, was active in the colony from 1892. Both in Togo and in Germany, these societies supported the Reich's colonial policy, but in order to maintain their influence among the Africans they occasionally spoke out against excesses or misdemeanours committed by colonial officials or assumed the role of mediator. In those rare cases in which a missionary caused the colonial authorities serious trouble, his society was requested to recall him, as in the case of Father Rochus Schmidt at Atakpame in 1905.

The health system also bore the stamp of a colonialist policy. The few available government medical officers looked chiefly after the European community; health care for Africans was confined to medical attention for the handful who were able to pay for treatment and medicines and to the containment of epidemics in order to prevent depletion of the labour force. Even so, at a time when thousands of Africans were dying of smallpox in the colony, only one doctor was made available for vaccination whereas up to four doctors were working on a commission for the study of sleeping sickness, which was not widespread in Togo.

In the field of health care, too, the Africans displayed a good deal of initiative. For example, they presented the bricks for the Anecho hospital in 1893. (When the building was completed, it was decided that only Germans would be treated there). According to the government medical officer the African orderlies working at the Anecho hospital showed great skill, but they were unable to gain further qualifications.

The history of Togo under German rule reveals that the colonial power reluctantly had to take into account the relatively advanced state of the indigenous population in the south of the country and its links with the neighbouring colonies. There was active resistance to German rule right from the start as well as passive resistance: individuals or whole village populations migrated to the adjoining territories under British or French rule. The turn of the century then saw the emergence of a national liberation movement which was to gain independence for Togo sixty years later. Leaders of the movement were Africans with a relatively assured economic position in the coastal towns of Lomé and Anecho, i.e. early representatives of an African bourgeoisie. The chiefs of Anecho were among them on account of their position in commerce.

The files of the Imperial Colonial Office contain several petitions from these Togolese, indicating a gradual increase in their demands, from minor reforms within the framework of the colonial regime to the termination of German colonial rule. Initially, the demands were put

before the Governor, and then before Colonial Secretary Wilhelm Solf
while he was in the colony on a tour of inspection. Finally, in May 1914,
the representatives of Lomé and Anecho simultaneously addressed petitions[92] to the Reichstag. They list all the outrages perpetrated by the
colonizers, from the first Administrator to the Governor then in office,
Duke Adolf Friedrich zu Mecklenburg, including the latter's alleged
sexual intercourse with teenage African girls. But not only the crimes of
individuals were enumerated there. The general lack of rights, the practice of corporal punishment, the economic reprisals — indeed the whole
of German colonial policy — led the Togolese to conclude after 30 years
of German rule that they wanted to get rid of the colonial power. The
documents make nonsense of all subsequent attempts to glorify conditions in the "model colony".

A few months later the Togolese people showed their feelings very
clearly. As soon as word came of the outbreak of the Great War, the
inhabitants of the Volta region cast off the German yoke even before
British soldiers appeared on the scene. The German mercenary unit,
having withdrawn into the interior and blown up the newly installed
transcontinental radio station at Kamina near Atakpamé, surrendered
after a few engagements on 25 August 1914. This marked the end of
German rule notwithstanding the strenuous efforts of interested parties
in Germany to secure a larger colony in the region in the event of a German victory.[93]

---

[92] Petitions in: ZStA. RKolA, no. 4235, pp. 154—202. The petitions were referred
to the Imperial Chancellor in 1915.

[93] Cf. *P. Sebald*, Die Kriegsziele der deutschen Togo-Interessenten im Ersten Weltkrieg. Wiss. Zeitschrift der Humboldt-Universität Berlin. Gesellschafts- und sprach-
wiss. Reihe, vol. 13, 1964, pp. 872—875.

VII. The German Empire in Africa before 1914: General Questions

1. Analysis of Official Statistics

One of the basic sources of information for an investigation into the social and economic development of the German colonies is official data on population, administration budgets, trade etc. contained mainly in the annual reports and used by writers and journalists to support their own particular theories. That these official statistics are often unreliable and sometimes totally useless — except in the case of certain small areas — was recognized and repeatedly stated by specialists in the early years of the twentieth century.[1] Thus data on the population figures for the larger colonies during the final decade of German rule are full of blatant contradictions (e.g. Cameroon: 1908, 3,500,000; 1909, 3,000,000; 1912, 2,717,000; 1913, 2,537,000; German East Africa: 1908, 7,000,000; 1909, 10,000,000; 1913, 7,496,000[2]), which are the result of repeated corrections of inevitably rough calculations.

With an eye on the criticism to be expected from deputies and among the public at large, the colonial budget submitted to the Reichstag deliberately concealed vital items of expenditure and thereby conveyed a consciously false picture of the cost of German colonial policy to the

---

[1] Cf. *R. Hermann*, "Kolonialstatistik", in: F. Zahn, Die Statistik in Deutschland nach ihrem heutigen Stand, Munich—Berlin 1911, Vol. II, p. 955; *K. Rathgen*, Article on "Handel", in: Deutsches Koloniallexikon, Vol. II, p. 25f.; *A. Meyer-Gerhard*, Article on "Entvölkerung", op. cit. Vol. I, p. 565f; *R. R. Kuczynski*, The Cameroons and Togoland, A Demographic Study. Oxford 1939, pp. 23—39, 376f.

[2] The German Colonial Office could not help admitting the limited value of some of the population statistics. Cf. *Reichskolonialamt*, Die deutschen Schutzgebiete in Afrika und der Südsee 1911—1912, Berlin 1913, p. 63: "Precise information is still lacking on so many districts that the total figure of 2,537,423 natives for the known parts of Cameroon can hardly be regarded as even roughly accurate; at the most one can take it as a minimum."

state, i.e. to the German taxpayer. These costs were in reality far higher than the budget revealed.

Nor is the official information on the foreign trade of German colonies repeatedly quoted in the literature, whether of the old, apologetical school or by more recent critical writers, of much greater value. It is taken in the main from the so-called "protectorate statistics" and is based on the customs returns of the individual colonies, calculated by different methods down to 1902. Nor was any uniform practice adopted later, except for the fact that, with the exception of South West Africa, duties were based on value. The basis of calculation for imports and exports was local market prices,[3] which as a rule varied a great deal from European prices, especially for colonial produce. European industrial goods cost more in the colonies than in Europe, colonial raw materials cost less, and the difference often far exceeded the transport costs. Thus even if one ignores other omissions and errors, it cannot come as a surprise that the "protectorate statistics" derived from the price levels of colonial non-equivalent commodity exchange give a quite different picture of the trade between Germany and her colonies than do the national statistics based on prices in Germany. For example, according to the "protectorate statistics" in 1912 German exports to all overseas territories, excluding Kiaochow, amounted to 88.7 million marks. This sum included gold and silver coins and other coinage to the value of 5.5 million marks, leaving 83.2 million marks for all other exports. According to German statistics, on the other hand, these exports amounted to 49.135 million marks, and precious metals to the value of 3.234 million marks. Discrepancies arising from delays by transport cannot possibly account for such differences. In interpreting the Reich figures on German exports one must note that the origin of the goods exported is not taken into account, but certain of these goods — petroleum and rice are obvious examples — came from other countries and were only shipped to the colonies through German ports.

One can conclude that the "protectorate statistics" on the trade of the German colonies considerably exaggerate imports from Germany (calculated according to world prices) and give a false picture of trade relations between the colonies and Germany, their most important

---

[3] Cf. the "Neuordnung der kolonialen Handelsstatistik", § 2, in: Deutsches Kolonialblatt published on 1 Sept. 1902, p. 391, and K. Kucklentz, Das Zollwesen der deutschen Schutzgebiete in Afrika und der Südsee, Berlin 1914, p. 120f; also Kolonial-lexikon, Vol. II, p. 33.

trading partner.[4] With exports, too, there are glaring discrepancies with the statistics on German foreign trade,[5] which are far from accurate and must be used with care. This also applies to figures on German trade with semi-colonial countries such as Morocco (down to 1912), for these figures generally ignore the export of the most expensive armaments and military equipment — guns, armoured turrets and armour plating, artillery ammunition etc. — "in deference to the receiving countries". Such goods, on which of course no duties were levied, do not figure in the statistics of the importing countries either.[6]

2. The Economic Significance of the German Colonies

In such circumstances conclusions as to the economic importance of the colonies for the German Empire cannot be based on completely reliable statistical information. Nevertheless the main lines of development are clear, and the published figures do offer a number of points of reference in certain areas.

Down to the end of the 1890s trade between the colonies as a whole and Germany was totally insignificant. They played no part in Germany's capitalist economy, either as producers of raw materials, or as markets, or as spheres for capital investment. The German Empire imported tropical raw materials — largely via London, Rotterdam, Antwerp, Trieste and other non-German ports — from the colonies and spheres of influence of other powers, as well as from Latin America. In 1896, for example, imports from the Dutch East Indies (1.7 per cent of total German imports) exceeded those from all the German colonies put together (0.09 per cent) by almost eighteen times. (The corresponding figures for German exports are 0.4 per cent and 0.195 per cent).[7]

Although exports from the colonies to Germany rose considerably between 1900 and 1914, they were still far from able to meet German

---

[4] The figures given in *M. E. Townsend*, The Rise and Fall of Germany's Colonial Empire 1884—1918. New York 1930, Chap. IX, on the economic development of the colonies, are useless in view of the quality of these statistics.

[5] Examples in *O. Mayer*, Die Entwicklung der Handelsbeziehungen Deutschlands zu seinen Kolonien, thesis, Tübingen 1913, p. 87f, 98f, 101.

[6] Cf. Liebknecht's Reichstag speech of 11 May 1914, in: Reden und Schriften, vol. 7, p. 260.

[7] *Statistisches Jahrbuch* für das Deutsche Reich, vol. 18, Berlin 1897.

requirements in respect of tropical raw materials and foodstuffs. They
were an extremely small factor in the balance of trade. In 1906, for
instance, Bebel stated that the loss of German trade with Denmark
(300 million marks in 1905) would matter far more than the loss of the
entire trade with the colonies (64 million marks in 1904).[8] According
to Reich statistics German trade with the colonies in 1904 amounted
to less than 0.5 per cent of the entire German foreign trade,[9] a proportion that did not change until 1914. In 1912 and 1913 the four German
colonies in Africa together still exported to Germany less than a tenth
in value of what Germany imported from the whole of Africa, and when
one compares the total exports from these colonies to Germany with the
total German imports from colonies and semi-colonial countries outside Europe, the position becomes even worse.[10]

Of the products of the German colonies only two supplied all or a
considerable proportion of Germany's needs, viz. diamond production
in South West Africa, which in 1913 exported a quarter of total world
production (in value terms),[11] and sisal cultivation in German East
Africa. Cameroon, German East Africa and Togo supplied a modest
percentage of rubber (12.33 per cent in 1910), cocoa and vegetable fats
and oils.

The cultivation of tobacco in Cameroon was unimportant for the
colony's export trade, while coffee-planting in German East Africa was
still in its infancy in 1914. The same applies to cotton in East Africa
and Togo. Although exports of cotton from German East Africa increased more than tenfold between 1906 and 1913, exports from German East Africa and Togo combined amounted in 1913 to only 3 million
marks, against total German cotton imports of c. 600 million marks for
that year.[12] The copper ores mined in South West Africa went mostly
to the USA; copra and phosphate, the main products of the Pacific
colonies, to Australia and Japan.

In 1913 imports of the most important overseas raw materials to
Germany amounted to 3,248.4 million marks, only 1.6 per cent of which
(52.8 million marks) came from the German colonies (excluding Kiao-

[8] StBVR, 1905—6, vol. 5, col. 4065ff.

[9] *Statistisches Jahrbuch* für das Deutsche Reich, vol. 26, Berlin 1905, p. 321.

[10] Ibid., vol. 35 (1914), Berlin 1914, p. 253.

[11] *R. Scheibe*, Article "Diamanten" in: Deutsches Koloniallexikon, vol. I, p. 451.

[12] Cf. *Unsere Kolonialwirtschaft* in ihrer Bedeutung für Industrie, Handel und Land-
     wirtschaft, ed. Dr Warnack, publ. Kolonial-Wirtschaftliches Komitee e.V. Berlin
     (1914), pp. 14, 21. The figures are taken from official statistics.

chow)[13]. At the same time, there had been a rapid rise in imports from the colonies since the turn of the century, as the following table shows:

	Imports from the Colonies (in millions of marks)	Exports to the Colonies (in millions of marks)
1900	6.4	17.6
1905	17.6	35.7
1910	49.4	45.1
1912	52.5	49.1
1913	52.8	54.6[14]

Imports thus trebled between 1905 and 1913. Included in the exports during this period are building materials and equipment for railway - construction in a number of colonies, which account for a considerable part of this increase, particularly in South West Africa.

According to the official annual report for the German colonies for 1912—13, 399 of the total of 421 German firms working there had a nominal capital amounting to 506.1 million marks.[15] The capital of the foreign firms, mainly British, involved in exploiting the German colonies, was put at 88.9 million marks in 1913.[16] In neither of these cases do the figures give an accurate picture of the extent of the capital investment, since a considerable number of the larger firms were not exclusively, or even predominantly, active in the German colonies (this is particularly true of West Africa), and since in many German firms the nominal capital was higher than that actually invested and "put to work". There are evidently no estimates available of capital investment in the German colonies which are based on a precise examination of the numerous sources and which avoid such errors and pitfalls as those mentioned.[17]

---

[13] Ibid., p. 91—92.

[14] Ibid., p. 92. In 1913 the imports to Germany from the individual colonies were as follows (in millions of marks): East Africa 14.6; Cameroon 13.1; Togo 7.3; South West Africa 7.5; New Guinea 7.0; Samoa 3.3. (On these official figures cf. the remarks above, however.)

[15] Die deutschen Schutzgebiete in Afrika und der Südsee 1912—1913, Berlin 1914, Statistischer Teil p. 77.

[16] F. Hupfeld in: Koloniale Rundschau, vol. 1913/10. The French firms in New Cameroon, handed over Germany in 1911, are not included.

[17] The memorandum of the Colonial Department "Die deutschen Kapitalinteressen in den deutschen Schutzgebieten (ohne Kiautschou)", Reichstag document No. 564, 1906, puts private investment for 1906 at 229, 131, 559 marks. H. Feis, Europe, the World's Banker 1870—1914, New Haven 1930, pp. 74, 77, puts German capital

The sum quoted in the annual report for 1912—1913, compared with the total German overseas investment, put by Lenin at approximately 35,000 million marks in 1910[18] (by the outbreak of the war it had slightly decreased), would produce a figure of 1.4 per cent, but in fact the percentage was obviously still smaller, and not to be compared with investment in semi-colonial territories, let alone in European countries.

Although capital investment and the export of raw materials rose considerably, and in some cases enormously, during the last ten years of German rule, it was obvious that even given a longer space of time imperialist Germany would only be able to satisfy her craving for sources of tropical raw materials, spheres of investment and markets, to a very limited extent in these colonies. The sober statistics on the significance of the colonies for the German economy make it abundantly clear why she was attempting to penetrate the colonies of other powers and persistently pursued the aim of "German Central Africa". It would, however, be a mistake to conclude, in view of the insignificance of the German colonies for the economy of the German Empire as a whole, that the colonies were of no account at all as a source of profit for German finance capital. They were never of primary interest in this respect, but the big banks in particular, with their connections with the large-scale German firms engaged in shipping, trade, plantation development and mining, can be shown to have made substantial profits on their investments. Until the turn of the century a large part of these profits consisted of founders' profits, official "compensation", subsidies etc. Even after 1900 many of the profits made by large-scale colonial enterprises came from the German treasury — a fact often mentioned but never analysed, any more than the whole relationship between big business and the state within the context of Germany's imperialist policy of expansion down to 1914 has ever been thoroughly and systematically investigated.

A striking contrast with the insignificant economic importance of the German colonies, except for diamond production in South West Africa, is provided by the amount of government money spent from the end of the 1890s onwards for conquering, consolidating and developing the colonial territories, money taken chiefly from German tax revenues. The following subsidies were paid by the Reich between the beginning

---

investment in the whole of Africa in 1914 at around 2,000 million marks and observes that investment outside the German colonies was higher than in the colonies themselves.

[18] *V. I. Lenin*, Selected Works, Moscow 1968, p. 214.

of German rule and 1914: German South West Africa 278 million marks; Kiaochow 174 million marks; German East Africa 122 million marks; Cameroon 48 million marks; German New Guinea 19 million marks; Togo 3.5 million marks; Samoa 1.5 million marks.[19] This gives a total of 646 million marks, exclusive of loans.

Subsidies in the immediate pre-war years, chiefly for "protective forces" and other military units, were as follows:

	1912 (1,000 marks)	1913 (1,000 marks)
South West Africa	13,828	14,627
Cameroon	4,344	2,804
German East Africa	3,618	3,604
New Guinea	1,208	1,327
Kiaochow	8,298	9,508[20]

The total amount of state expenditures was, in fact, far higher. The suppression of the uprisings in South West Africa between 1904 and 1907, for example, cost some 400 million marks. Then there were shipping subsidies, part of the costs of the Navy and many other outlays. As P. Sebald shows in his essay on Togo, even the true costs of conquest and administration were occasionally concealed, so as to present German colonial policy as less of a burden on the exchequer than it really was. The English economic historian W. O. Henderson calculated that the total cost to the German taxpayer of German colonial policy between 1884 and 1914 can have hardly been less than 2,000 million marks.[21] It should be noted, as Karl Liebknecht pointed out in 1907,[22] that colonial expenditure by the German Empire was "predominantly military in nature."

This contradiction between the extent of state expenditure and the actual economic significance of the colonies can be explained as follows. On the one hand the colonies conquered up to 1914 were seen as merely the first step on the road towards a vast and territorially contiguous colonial empire of far greater economic importance. A central Africa

---

[19] E. *Volkmann*, "Reichszuschüsse", in: Deutsches Koloniallexikon Vol. III, p. 153.
[20] Taken from E. *Volkmann*, "Finanzen", in: Deutsches Koloniallexikon Vol. I, p. 618—623, and *Brüningshaus*, "Kiautschou", ibid. Vol. III, p. 282.
[21] W. O. *Henderson*, Studies in German Colonial History, London 1962, p. 34.
[22] K. *Liebknecht*, Reden und Schriften, Vol. I, Berlin 1958, p. 272, note 2.

ruled by Germany was envisaged as the main supplier of tropical raw materials, which were being imported from the colonies and spheres of influence of other powers. The existing colonies provided an excellent training ground for such a purpose, where soldiers, administrators and capitalist entrepreneurs could gather experience and learn eventually to outdo their British rivals. Also the Colonial Economic Committee (KWK) — a joint institution of government bodies and private firms — could carry out an extensive research programme in the field of colonial agriculture.

Therefore the view expressed by the West German historian R. Tetzlaff, for instance, that the colonies had no real economic importance for the German Empire but that their significance was basically that of a political status symbol, an attribute regarded as essential for a world power, does not go to the heart of the economic aspect of the question. Nor can the political role of the colonies be adequately assessed by giving it merely symbolic significance.

This leads to the other side of the question, namely the importance of a colonial empire for nationalistic and racist propaganda, directed at all parts of the people, but above all at the middle classes and the petite bourgeoisie and aimed at instilling ideas of a "master race." As the class struggle intensified in Germany, the ruling classes made increasing use of imperialist ideology in general, and colonial ideology in particular, in order to counter the influence of socialist and democratic views. A good example is the "Hottentot Elections" of 1907, which D. Fricke has accurately described as a "general attack with the ideology of imperialism on the thinking of large sectors of the German people."[23] The colonies were thus not a symbol of the nation's demand for world power status, passing over class distinctions, but a powerful weapon in the ideological battle against the working class, the standard-bearer of historical progress.

Finally, the colonies had a certain propaganda value for the policy of naval armament. The very existence of overseas possessions was used to justify all the Navy Bills, both in the Reichstag and before the public in general. In the case of war, however, the colonies could not have been effectively defended by the Navy, as the naval chiefs well knew, and no naval bases were set up on colonial territory.

---

[23] *D. Fricke*, Der deutsche Imperialismus und die Reichstagswahlen von 1907, in: Zeitschrift für Geschichtswissenschaft, 1961, no. 3, p. 538.

3. Big Banking and the German Colonies 1884—1906

In the final stage of the territorial partition of the world in the last quarter of the nineteenth century, i.e. during the conquest and annexation or semi-colonial penetration of hitherto uncolonized areas of Africa, Asia and Oceania, the German Empire as late-comer, had few spoils to record. In 1897 her colonial possessions consisted only of a few relatively poor and scattered colonies in sub-Saharan Africa and the South Pacific, whose economic development, geared to the raw material and market needs of German imperialism, was still in its infancy, especially as in most of these colonies it was little more than the coastal areas that were under German control.

The only important finance house to show serious interest in this colonial empire was the Disconto-Gesellschaft under Adolf von Hansemann, who was until the mid-1890s the most powerful German banker. Together with Bleichröder he took over German interests in the South Pacific in 1880 in the form of the Godeffroy Empire and founded the colony of New Guinea in 1885, which became virtually his own private domain. He invested considerable sums in it down to its absorption into the Reich in 1899, without, however, deriving any significant income from it. Certain interests of Hansemann's played an important part in the annexation of the larger part of the coast of South West Africa. At the time of this annexation he acquired an interest in the large trading and shipping company of Adolf Woermann, who had instigated the annexation of Cameroon, where his firm occupied a leading position. The Disconto-Gesellschaft had a dominant interest in the German East Africa Line, founded in 1890, of which Woermann became head.

Hansemann and Bleichröder, who seconded most of the former's colonial ventures, had close connections with the Bismarck regime. The Disconto-Gesellschaft and Bleichröder worked hand in glove with the German Foreign Office, and some of their activities, such as the foundation of the DKGSWA in 1885, were in the nature of favours to Bismarck, who could not afford to allow areas annexed on his orders to be revealed in public as economically uninteresting, or to let colonial charter companies such as the DOAG, collapse after having received considerable subsidies from the government.

Until the end of the nineteenth century the representatives of big business generally regarded participation in ventures in the German colonies as a sacrifice in the general interest of their own class. There was therefore little willingness to invest large sums there. Even Hansemann proved reluctant to do so in the African colonies, for the basic prerequisites for establishing plantations and mining companies were missing. These were stable political control of the areas concerned, an adequate supply of workers, and a transport system (in 1895 there was just one single stretch of railway in the entire German colonial empire, 14 kilometres long).

Apart, therefore, from Hansemann's hobby-horse New Guinea, the involvement of big banking in the German colonies down to the turn of the century was confined to acquiring free "rights" which could later be put to speculative use or sold to the exchequer, and to securing control of certain trading and shipping companies. The banks were only prepared to invest seriously when the basic conditions for safe profits were assured: real "pacification" to ensure a stable administration ("government by junior official and lieutenant", typical of the 1890s, and the associated scandals inspired little confidence in the capitalists), the construction of a modern communications network and the settlement of the labour problem. They refused, however, to bear the costs of these measures, leaving them instead to the government.

A typical example of the relationship between big banking and the exchequer was the government's support for the DOAG, an important joint venture of the financial and industrial oligarchy, which had virtually collapsed by 1888. Its so-called "rights" were saved in 1888—89 at a cost of 9 million marks, which were used to put down the resistance movement and send a squadron of warships to the area. In 1890 a further 4 million marks was paid to the Sultan of Zanzibar for ceding the coastal area in which the Company was working to Germany, and in the same year the DOAG received 6.25 million marks to compensate it for giving up its "rights of sovereignty" to the German state — which virtually amounted to a present of this sum. As a result, the Company was able to pay an annual dividend on preferential shares of 5 per cent after 1891, while holders of ordinary shares got nothing until 1900.[24] A number of other colonial firms controlled by the banks also received appreciable sums of money from the government at various times, albeit not of the same magnitude.

The only change in this situation that had occurred by 1906 was that after 1897 serious attempts were made in Cameroon, Togo and German East Africa to set up plantations in order to increase production of tropical raw materials. The centre of these activities was Cameroon. At the beginning of 1897 a consortium closely associated with the A.

---

[24] *F. F. Müller*, Deutschland—Zanzibar—Ostafrika, Berlin 1959, pp. 507—511; *von der Heydt's Kolonialhandbuch* 1912, p. 103.

Schaaffhausensche Bankverein founded the West African plantation company called Victoria with a capital of 2.5 million marks; the Bibundi Company was founded the same year (initial capital 1.5 million marks), and in 1899 the Molive Company (initial capital 1 million marks). A number of the larger shareholders had an interest in two or even all three companies. Thus capital concentrated in a few hands controlled an entire branch of production and enjoyed a virtual monopoly of capitalist land cultivation in Cameroon, becoming a first-rate economic and political power in the colony.[25]

The leading role of the Disconto-Gesellschaft in this complex is unmistakable. In another case Hansemann and his associates directly backed an attempt to organize systematic large-scale spoliation of natural resources (and men) in the interior of south Cameroon by means of a chartered land company endowed by the government with wide monopolistic rights. The model for this was the terroristic plundering of the riches of the "Congo Free State" by Leopold II of Belgium and his monopolist group, which yielded huge profits. The Gesellschaft Süd-Kamerun founded at the end of 1898 as a joint German-Belgian company produced a very large founders' profit. Almost half the initial capital of 2 million marks was provided by the Disconto-Gesellschaft and persons close to it, the remainder by leading Belgian capitalists engaged in the Congo.

4. Big Banking and the German Colonies 1906—1914: The "Dernburg Era"

The foundation of the plantation companies indicated that past methods of colonial trading had not been adequate to guarantee the function of the colonies as suppliers of raw materials for German industry. Shortly after the turn of the century a clear divergence arose between the need to make better economic use of the colonies and certain aspects of German colonial rule, and within a few years this conflict became a crisis for German colonialism itself.

The move towards better economic use of the colonies was an im-

---

[25] Cf. *A. Rüger*, Die Entstehung und Lage der Arbeiterklasse unter dem deutschen Kolonialregime in Kamerun (1895—1905), in: H. Stoecker (ed.), Kamerun unter deutscher Kolonialherrschaft. Studien, vol. I, Berlin 1960, pp. 164—165.

mediate result of the development of German capitalism into its imperialist stage at the turn of the century. Characteristic of this stage on the international level, as Lenin wrote in 1916, was "a colonial policy of monopolist possession of the territory of the world, which has been completely divided up."[26] Lenin added: "Colonial possession alone gives the monopolies complete guarantee against all contingencies in the struggle against competitors . . . The more capitalism is developed, the more strongly the shortage of raw materials is felt, the more intense the competition and the hunt for sources of raw materials throughout the whole world, the more desperate the struggle for the acquisition of colonies."[27] By increasing the production of raw materials in its own colonies, Lenin further pointed out, the bourgeoisie can the more easily monopolize the sources of these materials, make itself economically more efficient, increase its profits and defeat its competitors.[28]

Under these new world economic conditions, the German colonies became somewhat more interesting for the German banks, though by no means really significant. They were still reluctant to make large capital investments there — Austria-Hungary, Russia and Latin America were more profitable — but they aimed at a situation in which raw material production in the colonies would be increased in the long term and the dependence of German industry on foreign cartels reduced, at least in certain fields. They also had an eye on the stock exchange profits to be made from railway building and economic development — loan commissions, issue profits and so on. Differences of opinion now began to arise within the ruling classes. Representatives of the monopolies expressed their dissatisfaction with the sluggish pace of the development of the "protectorates" and with the methods being employed there (the barbaric decimation and even wiping-out of the African population, i.e. of the basis of future exploitation, the destruction of natural resources and a one-sided policy of concessions). In the course of 1906 these differences came to a head with the demand for the "modernization" of the methods of government and exploitation employed, following the Herero and Nama uprisings in South West Africa, the Maji-Maji uprising in East Africa and further revolts in northwest and southeast Cameroon, which had revealed the utter bankruptcy of government policies. The spectacular intervention of Erzberger, of the Catholic

[26] *V. I. Lenin*, Selected Works, p. 232.
[27] Ibid., p. 228.
[28] Ibid., p. 229.

Centre Party, on grounds of party tactics further increased the pressure on the government.

On 5 September 1906 Bernhard Dernburg, one of the directors of the Darmstädter Bank and a specialist in re-organizing bankrupt enterprises, was appointed as Deputy Director (and virtual head) of the Colonial Department of the German Foreign Office. By this appointment Bülow, the Imperial Chancellor, hoped to overcome the crisis (and at the same time to pave the way for the entry into the government coalition of the liberal Freisinnige Vereinigung — to which Dernburg belonged — and to seek a rapprochment between financial circles in this party and the National Liberals). The appointment of a prominent banker to this post was intended to initiate a marked change in German colonial policy and persuade the banks and other big corporations to invest. Dernburg, who was on the board of 38 companies, was the first important banker to be given a leading position in the government — on 17 May 1907 he became State Secretary of the newly-founded German Colonial Office — where he represented banking interests, above all those of his friend Carl Fürstenberg, head of the Berliner Handelsgesellschaft. The raising of the Colonial Department of the Foreign Office to the status of a separate government office headed by a State Secretary bore public witness to the increased significance of Germany's colonial empire.

Dernburg's appointment signalled a second phase in the development of German colonial policy, namely the transition from an extensive pattern of development — as seen in the ruthless exploitation of human beings and of natural resources — to a more rationalized and intensive form of development. Shortly after assuming office, Dernburg informed the governors of all the colonies of the principles which he considered should govern development over the coming decade. These were:

1. Expansion of transport, especially railways;
2. Promotion and intensification of production of raw materials;
3. Investigation and exploitation of mineral resources;
4. Solution of the so-called "labour problem".[29]

These points made the essence of Dernburg's policy clear. His basic intention was to turn the German colonies into long-term sources of

---

[29] Directive of 17. 11. 1906 quoted in *D. Schulte*, Die Monopolpolitik des Reichskolonialamts in der "Ära Dernburg" 1906—1910. Zu frühen Formen des Funktionsmechanismus zwischen Monopolkapital und Staat, in: Jahrbuch für Geschichte, vol. 24, Berlin 1981, p. 12.

raw materials, areas of financial investment and sales markets, thus confirming the characteristic evolution of colonialism into its imperialist stage, as outlined above. It amounted to making the colonies economically totally subservient to, and dependent on, the requirements of the metropolitan power.

Under Dernburg the opening-up of inland territories by railway building, which had been repeatedly demanded in colonial circles, especially by the Pan-Germans, was put in hand, made possible by the higher sums of money voted by the Reichstag. A growing tendency in this direction had already been apparent between 1904 and 1906, and with the victory of the Bülow coalition in the Reichstag election of January 1907, there was a substantial majority prepared to vote larger sums for the development of the colonies. The Centre Party also soon supported the government line.[30] With the construction of railways substantial investment in the colonies began for the first time, with the iron and steel industry also deriving profits. A considerable part of the money invested came from an issue of 3.5 per cent Colonial Loan Stock launched at the end of 1908 by a consortium of eleven banks, led by the Deutsche Bank. By the beginning of the war in 1914 it had attracted a total of 245 million marks.[31]

As D. Schulte has shown, Dernburg's connection with the Berliner Handelsgesellschaft and the Allgemeine Elektrizitäts-Gesellschaft (AEG) became even closer after his appointment as Colonial Secretary. "The basic traits of German colonial rule during the Dernburg era only become clear when, in an analysis of the development of railways, mining, diamond production and concession policies, one investigates not only the banks' general desire for profits but also this cooperation with the Berliner Handelsgesellschaft banking group. The Secretary was a skilful defender of the interests of the Handelsgesellschaft and its subsidiaries, such as the Lenz Group, and also the AEG . . . His concern was to achieve a complete monopoly of the available markets and colonial sources of raw materials for the benefit of this group."[32]

It was therefore logical that, when he visited British and German East Africa in 1907, and South and South West Africa in 1908, Dern-

---

[30] Cf. *J. Ballhaus*, Die Landkonzessionsgesellschaften, in: H. Stoecker (ed.), op. cit., vol. 2, Berlin 1968.

[31] *D. Schulte*, op. cit., p. 16.

[32] *D. Schulte*, Die "Ära Dernburg" (1906—1910). Zum Charakter der Herrschaft des Finanzkapitals in den deutschen Kolonien. Thesis, Humboldt-University, Berlin 1976.

burg should have taken with him Walther Rathenau, who at the time of the former visit was on the point of resigning from his position as proprietor of the Berliner Handelsgesellschaft in order to concentrate on his work as Director of the AEG.

Rathenau played a part in formulating the Colonial Secretary's conclusions on what he had observed during these visits. The most important of these was the decision to press ahead with the construction of further railways in all four African colonies, responsibility for the greater part of which Dernburg handed over to the Deutsche Kolonial-Eisenbahn-Bau- und Betriebsgesellschaft (Lenz & Co.), a subsidiary of the Berliner Handelsgesellschaft. The founders of this subsidiary included Fürstenberg, Rathenau and Schwabach (representing S. Bleichröder), while von Bodenhausen, a director of Krupp's, was taken on to the board. The construction of the main railway line in German East Africa, from Dar es Salaam to Tabora, was entrusted to a subsidiary of the Deutsche Bank, the Disconto-Gesellschaft and a few other banking houses.

The total capital invested in railway construction in the German African colonies, excluding harbour installations, has been put at over 430 million marks,[33] a large part of which came from the Colonial Loan of 1908 but at least half from the state treasury. On 7 May 1908 the government gained the approval of the Reichstag for a sum of 175 million marks to be spent on the construction of five railway lines with a total length of 1,450 kilometres.[34] Two years later a majority of the Reichstag voted in favour of a further 76 million marks for railways in South West Africa; 25 million of this went to the Otavi Minen- und Eisenbahngesellschaft for the sale of its railway to the exchequer, which immediately leased it back to the company.[35] There can be no doubt that the big banks, led by the Berliner Handelsgesellschaft, the Deutsche Bank and the Disconto-Gesellschaft, earned millions of marks as a result of the government's policy towards the railways.

Dernburg also justified the confidence of the big banks by approving railway tariffs favourable for their interests and by his mining policies. While acting against the numerous small bogus companies in the colonies, he cleared the way for the shares of the large-scale colonial companies on the stock market.

If any further proof were needed that Dernburg as State Secretary was in fact a creature of big banking, in particular of Fürstenberg's

---

[33] *D. Schulte*, Die Monopolpolitik . . ., p. 23.

[34] StBVR, 12. Leg. Per., 1. Sess. 1908, vol. 232, column 5221.

[35] *D. Schulte*, op. cit., p. 21.

Berliner Handelsgesellschaft, it is afforded by his policy towards the diamond industry.[36] When by chance diamonds were discovered near Lüderitz Bay in 1908, he issued a decree in favour of the German South West Africa Company (DKGSWA) which guaranteed it monopoly rights and thus ensured millions of marks profit for the Company and the big banks — the Disconto-Gesellschaft, the Dresdner Bank, the Deutsche Bank, Bleichröder and the Berliner Handelsgesellschaft — behind it. (The DKGSWA paid its shareholders a dividend of 64 per cent in 1909; in the course of the same year the shares rose by 2,000 per cent, and the banks sold a large proportion of their holdings at this price)[37]. In May 1910, during his last days in office, he succeeded in arranging agreements which guaranteed that the entire trade in diamonds should be handed over to a group of 18 big and medium-sized German banks led by the Berliner Handelsgesellschaft.[38] This monopoly immediately became a source of remarkably high profits, by far the largest such source for the banks in the German colonies.

The most important consideration behind Dernburg's frequently lauded "native policy" was his view that the "natives" constituted the most important factor in the development of the colonies as suppliers of raw materials. He emphasized in a speech to the Reichstag that only together with the "natives" could Europeans make use of the land and carry on trade; without the "natives" there could be no colonization. D. Schulte describes Dernburg's policies in this regard as follows:

"The fact that Dernburg saw the colonial labour force as the *conditio sine qua non* for the creation of surplus value is one of the sources of the legend that colonial rule during the Dernburg era was more humane than before — a hypothesis still put out, with little or no modification, by West German historians. Dernburg's policy of 'protection for the African population', which is generally overrated both in its extent and in its practical effects, was nothing more than an attempt to find a solution to the labour question which would serve the interests of monopoly capital more satisfactorily. Dernburg's so-called cultural and ethical programme rejected a destructive exploitation of the indigenous African and Asian peoples, since if the source of labour were destroyed, the real object of the exploitation process and the main source of profit would

---

[36] Cf. also pp. 145—8.
[37] *H. Drechsler*, Südwestafrika unter deutscher Kolonialherrschaft, Berlin 1966, pp. 278, 367.
[38] Cf. *M. Erzberger*, Millionengeschenke. Die Privilegienwirtschaft in Südwestafrika, Berlin 1910.

also be destroyed. The State Secretary was not interested in short-term action but aimed at the long-term, intensive exploitation of the colonies, which was only possible with a colonial labour force. The sole function of the colonially oppressed, in his eyes, was to guarantee the profit of the German capitalists.

"But the policies of non-economic coercion, land seizure and expropriation consistently supported by Dernburg, who was one of those responsible for the notorious South West Africa Native Decrees of 1907 and for the introduction of the poll and hut tax in all the colonies, led to the merciless exploitation of the most vital element. Financial bleeding-out in the form of taxes, levies and duties reached its zenith in 1910. The bias in the legal system emerges clearly from the penal records of the colonial administration. Dernburg failed either to reduce the number of sentences passed on members of the oppressed population or appreciably to alleviate their brutality and savagery. The shocking figures speak for themselves and prove the failure of the much-vaunted legal reforms . . . In short, the more flexible form of exploitation introduced by Dernburg between 1906 and 1910, albeit with scant success, was in essence anything but humane. He had no desire to rule with the whip, as the planters, the settlers, the Pan-Germans and others wanted him to, but there is a mass of examples to prove that in practice the high profits made by colonial companies, especially in railway construction, were paid for with the health and welfare of the local population."[39]

At the same time the "Dernburg Era", seen as a whole, was a reaction by the German colonial power to the Herero and Nama uprisings in South West Africa, the Maji-Maji uprising in East Africa and the insurrections in Cameroon. This wave of rebellions between 1904 and 1906 made it abundantly clear that rule by arbitrary terror and brute force needed to be supplemented by "constructive" measures if the peaceful situation desired was not to become a graveyard peace. Any substantial military campaigns, or the slaughter of the peoples of whole areas (as happened in the south of German East Africa), ran counter to Dernburg's policies of development and the interests of the banks. Furthermore, an increase in the production of raw materials for export required the encouragement and support of African farms. After 1906 we therefore find here and there a greater flexibility in the style of colonial rule, a better knowledge of African customs and institutions, and a greater readiness to seem friendly towards the indigenous population.

[39] *D. Schulte*, op. cit., pp. 36—37.

There was also an increase in the proportion of civilians in the administration.

But in general the methods of rule did not change. The military element remained decisive, with an autocratic bureaucracy at its side. Whenever there was a conflict with German settler-farmers, whose enslavement of African workers seemed inexpedient to Dernburg, he soon beat a retreat. As far as the brutal penal system was concerned, the only change was that the number of convictions rose sharply.

With the break-up of the Bülow coalition Dernburg was forced to resign on 9 June 1910. The blatantly preferential treatment that he accorded the banks had antagonized the conservative parties and the big landowners, and also many middle-class colonials, particularly the settler-farmers in South West Africa and German East Africa. Recalling the scandal that had been caused by Dernburg's unconditional transfer of millions of marks to the bank of his friend Fürstenberg, Friedrich von Lindequist, Dernburg's successor, a colonial civil servant of nationalist, pan-German sympathies, curtailed the privileges of the Berliner Handelsgesellschaft and thus deprived it of its powerful direct influence on colonial economic policy.

Yet the substantial involvement of the big banks in the colonies, which Dernburg had deliberately and consistently promoted, remained unchanged and continued to bear fruits. The German East Africa Company (DOAG), which had a monopoly in the colony — it controlled the biggest trading network, the only land concessions, the big plantations and the two banks — paid a 5 per cent dividend between 1906 and 1908, 6 per cent in 1909, 8 per cent in 1910 and 1911, and 9 per cent in 1912. The South Cameroon Company also prospered after adapting to the changes in colonial policy: it paid 8 per cent in 1910 and 1911, and 5 per cent in 1912. The biggest plantation in the German colonies, the West African Victoria Company, paid 15 per cent in 1910 and 1911, 18 per cent in 1912 and 20 per cent in 1913, and its shares rose from 75 per cent in 1907 to 450 per cent in 1914.[40]

Although the German colonies continued to have very little importance for German foreign trade, in the years immediately preceding the First World War the three largest of them were a source of profit for the financial institutions that largely controlled their economy. At the same time the colonies were a source of often considerable profits

[40] *von der Heydt's Kolonialhandbuch*, vol. 7, 1913, pp. 103, 342; *J. Ballhaus*, op. cit., p. 177; *K. Hausen*, Deutsche Kolonialherrschaft in Afrika. Wirtschaftsinteressen und Kolonialverwaltung in Kamerun vor 1914, Zurich and Freiburg 1970, p. 315.

for the colonial companies mentioned above, which, if they had not been founded by the banks, came under their influence or control between the 1880s and the turn of the century. Such were the Hamburg and Bremen wholesale firms of C. Woermann (Disconto-Gesellschaft), Deutsch-Westafrikanische Handelsgesellschaft (Dresdner Bank), Hansing & Co and Wm. O'Swald & Co (Deutsche Bank). These firms made large profits out of their trade in Africa because the values they exchanged were not equivalent. A work published in 1909 stated that the profits of Hamburg firms engaged in overseas trade "derived from three factors: the high value put on the goods sold, the low value put on the goods bought or bartered, and the high prices that could be achieved in European markets for overseas products."[41]

In addition to these there was a fairly small number of medium- and small-sized trading and plantation companies, some of which made similarly large profits; others, however, had to struggle for existence in the shadow of their giant rivals. As a rule these firms also became dependent on the banks as a result of the system of bank credits, which meant that the banks exerted almost one-hundred-per cent control over the economy of the colonies. Not a few of the smaller firms were financially weak, speculative enterprises which did not survive for long. There were also firms established after 1900 whose main purpose was to separate colonial enthusiasts from their money by offering shares in colonial companies. Thus in general one can say that immediately before the First World War the German colonies were the domain of German high finance and a small group of dependent trading, shipping and plantation companies, leaving medium- and small-sized firms with little chance of running profitable businesses independently.

5. Military Policy

Although the German General Staff, on the basis of experiences in the South West African War, had demanded the establishment of a regular colonial army in 1905, comparable to the British and French models, this never came about. For military, political and financial reasons the Reich government did not give its assent. It was obvious that any decision on a repartition of the colonies and spheres of influence would be reach-

---

[41] *Harry A. Simon*, Die Banken und der Hamburger Überseehandel, Stuttgart/Berlin 1909, p. 14.

ed on the battlefields of Europe, not in Africa or Asia, even though
there was an intention to deal a blow to the British position on the Suez
Canal. The German colonies were scattered and largely unsuitable for
land-based operations against a potential enemy, and without control
of marine communications with Germany, they could hardly be held
on to in the event of an extended war with Britain or France. Nor did
the colonies offer a source of African recruits in large numbers. Active
or passive resistance on the part of large sections of the population in
the colonies, or at least their "unreliable" attitude, made it hazardous,
if not totally unrealistic, to think in terms of deploying large units of
African troops in a possible war in tropical countries against one or the
other European power.

Therefore only the relatively small units of mercenaries, know as
"protective forces" (Schutztruppen) were set up in German East Africa
(1891) and in Cameroon and German South West Africa (1895). The
last-named consisted entirely of white men, whereas in German East
Africa and Cameroon the common soldiers and, to an increasing degree,
the non-commissioned officers were recruited from among Africans,
as was the Togo police force. In comparison with other Africans these
soldiers were well paid; this, together with the obedience drilled into
them, made them faithful instruments of the colonial power. Karl Liebknecht described their role in 1907 as being solely that of "suppressing
or containing the 'inner enemy' in the colonies, driving the unfortunate
natives to perform forced labour in the bagnios and, when they tried
to protect their country against the marauding invaders, to mow them
down and starve them into submission. This colonial army . . . is the
most bestial and revolting of all the instruments used by the capitalist
countries. There is hardly a crime in the calendar that the colonial
forces, whipped into a 'tropical frenzy', have not perpetrated."[42]

The records of the Reich colonial office show that Liebknecht was
not exaggerating. The "protective forces", under the command of German officers, razed villages to the ground, massacred the population,
murdered prisoners, raped and pillaged as a matter of course, and behaved just like the French or any other mercenary force in the colonies.
Among the officers there were many scapegraces. Some, like the later
murderer Prince Prosper von Arenberg, had broken the code of military
discipline in Germany or otherwise made themselves unacceptable
to their own circles but were still considered fit for service overseas.
In 1909, for instance, six out of fifty officers and sixteen medical officers

---

[42] *Liebknecht*, op. cit., p. 272.

in the Cameroon unit were subject to disciplinary proceedings.[43] Many saw colonial service as a means of "rehabilitating" themselves, while others hoped to promote their own careers through the ceaseless minor military actions that took place. Service in the colonies led almost automatically to more rapid promotion than was possible at home in peacetime.

Like the colonial armies of other powers, the "protective forces" were a breeding-ground for nationalist, chauvinist agitators like Eduard von Liebert, Paul von Lettow-Vorbeck, Georg Maercker and Franz Xaver von Epp. These units were directly subject to the Chancellor and had a common High Command in Berlin, in which officers of the German General Staff also served. The importance of the army for the establishment and maintenance of power in the colonies, and the military nature of German imperialism in general, were reflected in the correspondingly important position of the military in the apparatus of colonial rule. The regional administrations created after conquest were everywhere headed by officers of the "protective forces". Virtually beyond the control of the government, which was far away, they ruled numerous districts of inner German East Africa and Cameroon down to 1906, while in Togo and South West Africa they were the predominant group in the administration. From 1906 to 1914 their direct administrative role remained important, and until 1914 officers also accounted for most resident agents in the indirectly ruled territories of Cameroon and East Africa. Many governors came from the ranks of the officers. In East Africa Colonel von Schele (1893—5), who combined the post of Governor with that of Commander, was succeeded by Major von Wissmann (1895—6), who was a relative of General von Kameke, the Prussian War Minister, and who had commanded the troops in the colony a few years before. Wissmann was in turn followed by Colonel (from 1897 Major-General) Liebert (1896—1901; ennobled in 1900), a protégé of Count Waldersee, Chief of the Imperial General Staff, and Liebert by Captain (from 1901 Major) Count von Götzen, from the General Staff.

The importance of the military was increased by the structure of the colonial administration. The commanders of the colonial forces were answerable to the governors only in a very general sense; militarily they were subject to the High Command in Berlin (Section M of the Colonial

---

[43] *W. Petter*, Militärische Einwirkungen auf die deutsche Kolonialverwaltung in Afrika 1884—1918, in: Commission internationale d'histoire militaire. Actes du 4e Colloque internationale d'histoire militaire, Ottawa 1979, p. 230.

Department of the German Foreign Office, later the German Colonial Office), and could use this dual relationship to ignore or oppose the instructions of "their" governors and thus get their own way.

6. The Judicial System

Penalties played an important part in the establishment and maintenance of colonial rule. Punishments and repressive measures of many different kinds were inflicted on the subject peoples, frequently as the result of purely arbitrary decisions on the part of German officers and civil servants. All thorough studies show that the summary execution of prisoners was a routine procedure in the subjugation of "insubordinate", independent peoples and in the suppression of uprisings. But also in areas long regarded as "peaceful" it remained the rule for a long while that local officials could mete out punishment to individuals or whole villages solely at their own discretion, without trial, by virtue of their almost unrestricted powers.

These powers were formally limited by a "Decree of the Imperial Chancellor concering the Application of the Criminal Law etc. to the Native Populations in the Protectorates of German East Africa, Cameroon and Togo", issued on 22 April 1896[44] and by a similar decree issued by the chief administrative officer of German South West Africa on 8 November 1896, which laid down the following punishments: corporal punishment (flogging or birching), fines, imprisonment with hard labour, imprisonment in irons and death. Corporal punishment was not permitted for women, Arabs or Indians.

Rules of procedure were never legally formulated. It was only prescribed that fines in excess of 300 marks or 900 rupees, prison sentences of more than six months and the execution of death sentences required the confirmation of the Governor (in the case of fines and imprisonment in German East Africa, that of the senior judge). The decree of 22 April 1896 was the result of indignation over the crimes of Leist and Wehlan, two colonial officials in Cameroon, and more especially of Bebel's exposure of the murders committed by the Imperial Commissioner Carl Peters in East Africa. In the word of K. Hausen: "On the basis of 'If it's not allowed, then it doesn't happen', these decrees may have served to

---

[44] Published in *F. F. Müller* (ed.), Kolonien unter der Peitsche. Eine Dokumentation, Berlin 1962, pp. 132ff.

set people's minds at rest but in practice each administrative post continued to act completely without control."[45]

It was accepted on principle that Africans, Papuans and other indigenous peoples of the South Pacific had a status juridically inferior to the status of Europeans. This was the basis of the frequent, degrading corporal punishment meted out to servants, workers, porters etc., although corporal punishment had already been abolished in the German states before 1871 (in Prussia since 1848). The above-mentioned Decree of 22 April 1896, which remained in force until the end of German rule, allowed the corporal punishment or imprisonment in irons of "native workers" (up to 14 days) to be carried out on the application of their employers, for offences such as "persistent dereliction of duty," "indolence," "insubordination" and "leaving their place of duty without good reason." In practice plantation overseers, merchants etc. usually had their workers flogged without an official being present, as the Decree prescribed. The flogging of chiefs frequently ordered by junior officials was, however, strongly disapproved of by senior authorities, since in many areas colonial rule depended on the collaboration of the chiefs, whose willingness to cooperate and reputation among their own peoples was on no account to be destroyed.

Flogging and Birching in the German African Colonies

Year	German East Africa	Cameroon	German South West Africa	Togo
1901—2	3467	315	257	162
1902—3	4735	407	473	181
1903—4	4783	293	340	194
1904—5	5655	367	187	161
1905—6	6322	665	294	290
1906—7	5981	906	336	363
1907—8	4654	924	534	434
1908—9	3746	1334	703	620
1909—10	5799	1513	928	566
1910—11	5509	1909	1262	735
1911—12	5944	2851	1655	733
1912—13	8057	4800		832[46]

[45] *K. Hausen*, op. cit., pp. 169—170.
[46] Source: *F. F. Müller*, op. cit., p. 114.

The critical observations at the beginning of this chapter on the statistical information provided by official annual reports fully apply to the statistics relating to corporal punishment. The official figures, presented in the following table, can be shown to be considerably lower than the actual figures.

In East and South West Africa flogging was carried out with the kiboko or sjambok (whip made of hippopotamus hide), in Cameroon and Togo with a rope. The German Colonial Dictionary edited by Schnee, a former Governor of German East Africa, states: "The administration of punishment by flogging or birching may be carried out in one or two parts. In the case of flogging the number of blows may not exceed 25; in the case of birching it may not exceed 20. The second part of the punishment may not take place in less than two weeks after the first."[47]

Small wonder that before the First World War Cameroon was called "the twenty-five country" — though in the Union of 'South Africa (Republic of South Africa since 1961) since about 1950 the incidence of this barbaric practice has grown ever higher. There was in principle no difference between the administration of "justice" in the German colonies and that in the colonies of other powers (excluding Belgium and Portugal) but although flogging was no rarity in the French and British colonies, both at this time and later, it was far more frequently used as a form of punishment in the German colonies.

Dernburg attempted to reduce the practice of flogging to some extent, because it was a hindrance to the recruitment of workers and caused them to migrate to neighbouring colonies. In a decree issued on 12 July 1907[48] he demanded for the first time that the grounds for punishment be investigated before each case of flogging and drew attention to earlier regulations requiring that a doctor or medical orderly be present on each such occasion and that a report be submitted to the Governor's office in question. This decree met with immediate rejection on the part of German settlers and firms, and the settler newspaper Deutsch-Ostafrikanische Zeitung even called on its readers to ignore it.[49] Against this opposition Dernburg was powerless to put through even these modest demands.

---

[47] *J. Gerstmeyer*, Körperliche Züchtigung, in: Deutsches Koloniallexikon, vol. II, p. 367.

[48] Deutsches Kolonialblatt 1907, pp. 790 ff.

[49] Deutsch-Ostafrikanische Zeitung, 21. Sept. 1907 and 2. Nov. 1907, from *F. F. Müller*, op. cit., pp. 56 ff.

At the same time proceedings were instituted during Dernburg's term and that of his successors von Lindequist and Solf against a number of Europeans accused of sadistic treatment of Africans, but these nearly always ended in the acquittal of the accused or with the imposition of a light fine. On 31 May 1913 Hintrager, Deputy Governor of South West Africa, reported: "One can now generally observe that offences committed against the natives seldom meet with appropriate punishment. The natives are deprived of nearly all rights from the outset by the fact that most courts are only prepared to believe the statements of natives about white men if these statements are confirmed by other evidence. On account of the paternal right of corporal punishment that legal practice grants to every white employer, and pleading self-defence, the accused very frequently secure their acquittal . . . It is to the leniency of the courts that I attribute the marked increase in the number of cases of ill-treatment of the natives, of which missionaries and native affairs commissioners complain."[50]

7. Racism

Typical of the attitude of the vast majority of German officials in Africa and the apologists of German colonialism was, from the beginning, a denigration and contempt for the indigenous peoples as "culturally inferior", "morally depraved," "lazy and hopeless" etc. This became the basis of a moral and even historical justification of German colonial policy, often coupled with a rejection of what were claimed to be the "soft" policies of the British.[51] German colonialist propaganda lacked — a handful of exceptions among Christian missionaries only serve to confirm the rule — the cloak of liberal, progressive, often religious argument in which British colonialists of the 19th century dressed up their expansionist policies for the benefit of their own people. The German refusal to admit that the interests, let alone the right of the African peoples were of any relevance for the theory or practice of colonial rule found support from the mid-1890s onwards in the ideas of social Darwinism and in the pseudo-scientific doctrine of the biological, virtually

[50] Source: *Müller*, op. cit., pp. 141—142.
[51] First by Ernst von Weber in 1879; cf. *H. U. Wehler*, Bismarck und der Imperialismus, Cologne/Berlin (West) 1969, p. 292.

immutable inferiority of all "coloured" peoples, particularly "Negroes", compared with white men, i.e. Europeans.

There was no necessity to evolve new ideas in this field. All that the German bourgeoisie needed to do was to take over the racialist ideas that had been current in Britain (Hamilton Smith, Knox, Hunt), the USA (Morton, Nott, Gliddon) and France (Gobineau) since the 1840s and 1850s and been used to defend the practice of slavery and colonial subjugation of Africans and people of African descent. These ideas had a particularly wide currency in the USA. Alongside the pseudo-historical, irrational racialism of Gobineau, whose "Essai sur l'inégalité des races humaines" was re-edited in German in 1898—1900 by Ludwig Schemann, and of H. S. Chamberlain, whose "Die Grundlagen des 19. Jahrhunderts" (2 vols, 1899—1901) quickly became popular among the educated middle classes in Germany, we find the pseudo-biological doctrines of social Darwinism propagated by Gumplowicz and Ratzenhofer. All these racialist writers maintained that the "Negroes" were the lowest of all peoples. Gobineau and Ratzenhofer even saw them as "born slaves". It was asserted that black Africans are genetically incapable of engaging in higher intellectual activity.

Such racialist ideologies served to justify inhumane oppression and barbarism in the colonial affairs of Germany, other European countries and in the USA. Whereas there were certain limits to the capitalist exploitation of workers in Europe, the colonial entrepreneur readily saw the blacks, as Bebel said in 1889, as "an inferior race against whom anything is allowed, the only limit being that of one's own personal interest . . . They are thus required to work inhuman hours and are treated without the slightest regard for their physical or material well-being."[52]

These racist ideas about "coloured" peoples, propagated by an increasingly nationalistic press and taken up in many middle-class circles, soon acquired the status of official doctrine. This showed itself in Wilhelm II's rabble-rousing speeches and adoption of the slogan of the "yellow peril", in publications issued by the General Staff[53] and in the fact that the indigenous inhabitants of the colonies were not accorded the legal status of German citizens. In 1913 a government spokesman in the Reichstag stated that the theoretical possibility of allowing a "native" to take German nationality had only been adopted in the case of a few half-castes, since "pure natives" did not possess "the necessary

[52] StBVR, vol. 105, col. 628.
[53] Cf. *H. Otto*, Schlieffen und der Generalstab. Militärhistorische Studien 8 (N. F.), Berlin 1966, pp. 212, 214.

educational, economic and moral standard" to justify an equalization with Germans.[54] In contrast to the British and French practice, black Africans who had been domiciled in Germany for many years were on principle refused German citizenship by Prussia and other German states before 1918.

Legislation and administrative practice in the colonies tended more and more towards a strict racial separation. In 1905 the Governor of South West Africa published a decree banning marriages between whites and Africans, and in 1912 a special order required the birth of all "semi-white" children to be registered. The decree added: "If the cohabitation of a non-native man with a native woman becomes a source of public annoyance, the police may require the parties to separate and, if this does not happen within a specified time, may compel such a separation."[55]

In order to prevent a "colony of half-castes" from developing, the German Colonial Society (DKG) recruited single young women in Germany from 1898 onwards and sent them to South West Africa to work as servants for the settlers. 953 such women were taken to South West Africa until 1914, nearly three quarters of whom married there. The administration of the colony supported the programme since 1908, and Dernburg gave it his approval, declaring in 1909 that more white women were needed "in order to preserve the white race and white morality in South West Africa."[56] In Samoa, where for generations Europeans had married Polynesian women, and where in consequence a large "mixed" population had developed, State Secretary Solf issued a decree in 1912 banning any further such mixed marriages. In the German colonies "Nuremberg Laws" thus existed already before the First World War.

As early as 1895 Siegfried Passarge, a nationalist propagandist and in later years professor of geography at the Colonial Institute in Hamburg, proposed the "deliberate erection of a social barrier between the two races" in order to ensure the continued supremacy of the Europeans[57],

---

[54] StBVR, vol. 290, col. 5334 (Dr Lewald, German Ministry of the Interior, on 30 May 1913).

[55] Decree of the Governor of German South West Africa on the Half-Caste Population, 23 May 1912. Deutsches Kolonialblatt 1912, p. 752.

[56] R. V. Pierard, The Transportation of White Women to German South-West Africa, 1898—1914, in: Race. A Journal of Race and Group Relations, vol. XII, 1971, pp. 317—322, esp. p. 321.

[57] S. Passarge, Adamaua, Berlin 1895, p. 533.

and the German bureaucracy adopted just this approach. The principle of strict racial separation was put into practice by the expulsion of the Duala in Cameroon from their home town, and in later years this principle was one of the main elements of the colonial plans the Nazis worked out for a fascist empire in Africa. (During the Second World War this principle was also applied by the German fascist authorities in their policy of colonial oppression of the conquered peoples in Eastern Europe.) It was intended to secure the permanent degradation of the Africans to helotry; they were to be prevented by their ignorance and illiteracy from realizing their miserable situation and seeking their liberation. Rigid racial separation (partly inspired by German fascist sources) is also one of the mainstays of the present-day policy of apartheid in South Africa. It left little room for manoeuvre in dealings with the Africans and was bound to arouse their bitter opposition.

Many colonial officials and military officers went so far as to state that African tribes or groups which refused to submit unconditionally to the colonial regime were not entitled to exist at all but were a "barrier to progress", which had to make way for a superior culture. This diabolical argument was intended to justify any and every crime committed against the Africans, including genocide.

8. Public Health and the Decline in Population

A number of writers have pointed to the introduction of hygiene and public health measures as a positive achievement on the part of the German colonial administration. However, one must distinguish strictly between measures introduced for the benefit of Germans and other Europeans and those taken for the Africans. For the former group much was done, and conditions after the turn of the century corresponded to the high German standards in medicine; for the Africans, on the other hand, the situation was very different.

Apart from vaccination programmes undertaken in economically important areas, medical care was available to only a tiny percentage of the African population and was completely unable to check the decline in the population due to the infectious diseases brought in by the Europeans. In the coastal area of Cameroon, for instance, there were only 7 doctors and medical orderlies and 5 nurses in 1900, and one doctor and 8 nurses in 1905.[58] In 1911—12 there were a mere 29 German doctors in Cameroon, 15 of them army doctors, 9 belonging to the administration and the remaining 5 employed in treating sleeping sickness — in a total population of around 2.5 million.[59] There were no serious attempts to reduce the very high death rates among porters and plantation workers. With the exception of the successful vaccination campaign against smallpox, until 1911 hygiene measures were confined to places in which Europeans were living. In the years immediately preceding 1914 the authorities were forced to take extensive measures to combat the rapid spread of sleeping sickness, which had been brought into the colony since 1906, but the outbreak of the war put an end to these efforts.

Nor was the situation in the other colonies any different. In 1911, with a total colonial population of ca. 12 million, there were 138 doctors, primarily concerned with the needs of the 24,000 Europeans. For the African population, which suffered severely from malaria and infectious diseases imported by the Europeans, medical treatment was available only in a few centres — and in large areas such as central and north Togo there was none at all. Growing medical knowledge, especially of tropical diseases, greatly reduced the mortality rate among Europeans from the early 1890s onwards but many facts point to the conclusion that among the indigenous population the rate rose dramatically during the thirty years of German colonial rule. Only after 1912, when the alarming economic consequences of this became clear in colonial circles, were some measures taken to improve the state of public health.

The situation in the French and British colonies was much the same. Suret-Canale described the position of the doctors in French West Africa thus: "They were almost entirely occupied, right to the beginning of the First World War, with caring for members of the army and the colonial administration — occasionally also for the *colons*, firstly the Europeans, then their African employees . . . As far as the population at large was concerned, medical services were but a drop in the ocean and were only brought into action when epidemics threatened the lives of the Europeans as well."[60] The British Governor of the Gold Coast

---

[58] A. Rüger, Die Entstehung und Lage der Arbeiterklasse unter dem deutschen Kolonialregime in Kamerun (1895—1905), in: Kamerun . . . vol. 1, p. 232.

[59] H. R. Rudin, Germans in the Cameroons. A Case Study in Modern Imperialism, New Haven 1938, p. 351.

[60] J. Suret-Canale, French Colonialism in Tropical Africa 1900—1945, London 1971, p. 414.

stated in 1915 that medical services in the colony were available "almost exclusively for the European population."[61]

Although there are no reliable population figures for the larger German colonies,[62] and thus there is no possibility of drawing precise conclusions about population movements, reports and communications from officials, missionaries, doctors and scientists indicated a decline in numbers. These reports had become so numerous and alarming by about 1910 that between 1912 and 1914 there were public discussions of the causes of the decline, which in the long run would threaten opportunities to squeeze profits out of the colonies.[63] Figures published during these years for a number of areas indicated both a disastrous child mortality rate — 40 to 55 per cent was no rarity — which was not compensated for by a high birth rate, and the ravages of disease — endemic diseases such as malaria, smallpox and worm disorders, and infectious ones imported by the Europeans, such as tuberculosis, syphilis, measles, German measles, chicken-pox, scarlet fever and influenza. The areas last affected were in general those conquered last, and thus least exposed to colonial rule and exploitation. There were also the massacres of the inhabitants of entire areas during the process of conquest, and the countless subsequent punitive expeditions. In the south of German East Africa, for instance, between 200,000 and 300,000 inhabitants died as a result of the suppression of the Maji-Maji uprising of 1906.

Reports on German East Africa, Cameroon and Togo make it clear that the general decline in living standards had prepared the ground for the rising disease and mortality. Diseases were spread by caravans and by migrant workers travelling over long distances in increasing numbers. Among peoples who were generally undernourished, living in unhygienic conditions and with no resistance to imported infectious diseases, disastrous consequences were inevitable. During the final ten years of German colonial rule syphilis spread from the coastal areas to large parts of the interior and is evidently directly responsible to a large extent for the high rate of female infertility and infant mortality recorded in medical and other reports. A rapid rise in, and high frequency of, abortions is also recorded in many areas in the years leading up to 1914. The following reports, referring to the years 1911—12, give an

---

[61] From *M. Crowder*, West Africa under Colonial Rule, London 1968, p. 326.

[62] See pp. 185—7.

[63] Cf. Koloniale Rundschau, 1912—1914, esp. L. Külz in 1913, pp. 321 ff; also D. Westermann in Berliner Tageblatt, 24 and 25 Feb. 1914.

account of conditions in German East Africa, the German colony with
the largest population:

A report by Dr Wolff, an army doctor, on the district of Lindi, in the
south of the colony, referring to 1912: "The coastal population is increasing only very slightly . . . there are many cases of divorce; syphilis
and gonorrhoea are very common on the coast though rare in the interior, which is still somewhat isolated. The inhabitants of the interior
know this and therefore leave their wives at home if they themselves
have to journey to the coast."[64]

From the annual report of the district of Tabora for 1911:

"The present population is 405,500, previously it was put at half a million . . . The cause of this alarming decline is most probably recruitment,
which is nowhere more extensively practised than here. In the month
of March alone 1,105 people were recruited here. Though most of them
return, in many cases it is only after a period of years. If the losses were
confined to those who did not return, it would not be serious, for the
men would be giving their services to other parts of the protectorate,
but the losses are in fact far greater. The fact that the majority of the
men stay away for at least two thirds of the year means that their family
life greatly suffers. In addition, many return from the coast with diseases
which prevent their having healthy children. As a result the number of
children is small, especially children under the age of four."[65]

From the report of Dr Grothusen, an army surgeon, on the district
of Bukoba, in the north-west (1912):

"The most densely populated part of the district is inhabited by the
Wahaya, who are physically conspicuously weak and generally poorly
nourished. The morbidity and mortality rate among them, especially
among the children, is very high, and their numbers are slowly but surely
declining, due on the one hand to infectious diseases and on the other
to insufficient nutrition. Their staple food is bananas . . . The chief
source of infection appears to by syphilis, which is responsible for the
many abortions and the child mortality."[66]

[64] Source: *O. Peiper*, Geburtenhäufigkeit, Säuglings- und Kindersterblichkeit und
    Säuglingsernährung im früheren Deutschostafrika. Auf Grund amtl. Materials
    unter Beifügung von Statistiken. Veröffentlichungen aus dem Gebiet der Medizinal-
    verwaltung vol. XI, part 6, Berlin 1920, p. 18—19.

[65] Source: Ibid., p. 21—22.

[66] Ibid., p. 14f. Similar reports from Cameroon are quoted by *P. Mandeng*, Auswir-
    kungen der deutschen Kolonialherrschaft in Kamerun. Die Arbeitskräftebeschaf-
    fung in den Südbezirken Kameruns während der deutschen Kolonialherrschaft
    1884—1914, Hamburg 1973, pp. 174ff.

Dr Otto Peiper, a staff surgeon with the "protective force" in German East Africa from 1908 to 1913, reported as follows on the results of plantation labour:

"The workers are exposed to all manner of threats to their health on their often long journey to their work-place. Hundreds of thousands are to be found on the roadside every year; supplies of food and water are generally inadequate, their camps are contaminated, prostitutes set upon them and the villages through which the men pass are also inevitably infected. The advantages of using trains and boats are often outweighed by the disadvantages that arise when masses of men are transported in this way who have become infected with malaria, smallpox, dysentery and other diseases and who, in consequence of the exertions of the marches, with inadequate and unfamiliar nutrition, become weak and die.

"The survivors arrive exhausted at the plantations but their tribulations are not yet over. Conditions, particularly in the newer plantations, are absolutely unhygienic. Once one has seen how the Europeans live, surrounded by their servants, one is no longer surprised at the way the workers are accommodated and fed. The mortality rate reaches unbelievable heights — often 50 per cent and more, in Africa and the Pacific . . . After their contract has expired, those who survive, riddled with venereal and other diseases, make their way back home without supervision, infecting others as they go. But only a part of them reach their disrupted homes . . ."[67]

9. Education Policy

German bourgeois authors have described the schools set up for Africans by colonial administrations and Christian missionary societies as a great achievement of German rule. It has even been suggested that the education received here by the oppressed "compensated them fully for their loss of freedom".[68] Apologetics of this kind conceal the nature of

---

[67] *O. Peiper*, Der Bevölkerungsrückgang in den tropischen Kolonien Afrikas und der Südsee — seine Ursachen und seine Bekämpfung. Veröffentlichungen aus dem Gebiete der Medizinalverwaltung, vol. XI, part 7, Berlin 1920, p. 22—23.

[68] *C. Bachem*, in: Verhandlungen des deutschen Kolonialkongresses 1910 zu Berlin, Berlin 1910, p. 665.

educational policy at the time, which unambiguously served colonial oppression and exploitation.

There was a sharp racial barrier between schools for Africans and schools for Germans and other Europeans. A parliamentary representative of the Centre Party represented the aim of schooling for the 800 white pupils in German South West Africa and German East Africa in 1913 as "providing education which enables our young people to appear later before the rest as the truly dominant race in the country . . . in the sense of an intellectual rule over the other, subject race in the country . . ."[69]

Measures which would give sections of the oppressed population an elementary education (by the standards of Germany at the turn of the century) were recognized increasingly as necessary for economic exploitation in the colonies and the setting up of a stable, yet cheap apparatus of oppression. Therefore the education offered by the Christian missionaries was, as a rule, adapted to these objectives — although not without contradictions. In most cases, the "conversion of the heathen", which was the missionaries' official aim, was regarded as inseparable from education "in a Christian-patriotic spirit". The latter was important for the ideological indoctrination of the African population, an aim which even elementary instruction in reading and writing was made to serve.

At the same time, however, both the administration and the missionary societies saw a serious danger to colonial rule in offering fragments of advanced education to Africans. Disputes on educational policy were invariably dominated by the fear that European schooling could prove injurious to "white man's rule". As early as 1895, the geographer Siegfried Passarge warned of the consequences of educating West Africans: "Firstly, one would have gone to great pains to educate dangerous rivals, and secondly, the blacks would seek to throw the whites out as fast as possible." "Strict rearing" was necessary to ensure that the Africans were "well aware of their inferiority to the white man".[70]

Several years later Martin Schlunk, an eminent missionary teacher, echoed warnings about the dangers of "intellectual education" for Africans. Schlunk endorsed the view of the French colonial politician J. Harmand ("Domination et Colonisation", Paris 1910) that "the

---

[69] Deputy Kuckhoff (Centre) in: StBVR, XIII. Legislaturperiode (1912/14), vol. 285, p. 1634.

[70] S. *Passarge*, op. cit., pp. 532 and 529.

political effects of such education . . . are disastrous" since they fostered the "spirit of revolt" in the colonies.[71]

The views of a high-ranking official of the German Foreign Office illustrate how strong this view still was in official circles in 1928. Referring to British rule in former German East Africa, Dr. Theodor Gunzert wrote: "The present English education system is undoubtedly more intensive and concentrated than the German one used to be . . . This system . . . has met considerable distrust among the European population because it aims to rear 'cultivated Negroes' who could eventually give rise to a black intellectualism and with it the kind of racial struggles which are familiar in South Africa. In this respect, the German school system — which was limited to spreading . . . practical knowledge for use in the low grades of the administration — . . . was more practical for all its primitiveness, since it did not raise the intellectual level of the natives who went through it . . . to the degree mentioned."[72]

The basic aims of British educational policy in the colonies were not different from those of the Germans. But in view of the international recognition which advanced education in Germany enjoyed at this time, the extremely restrictive policies carried out in the colonies must be seen as symptomatic of German colonialism. Even the handful of "upper schools" could not match the eight-year elementary schools in Germany, which provided rudimentary education for the children of the working class and large sections of the lower middle class. Not one African from a German colony was permitted, until 1918, to enter a university in the "mother country". After the turn of the century, the gradual transition to intensive forms of colonial exploitation created a demand for Africans with some measure of European education, but even though the need was still relatively small it could not be met because of the low standards of schooling. This provoked repeated complaints from both the colonial authorities and German businessmen.

Even within the narrow confines of German colonial education, there were thus the seeds of long-term contradictions. This is an aspect of colonial rule which Karl Marx had observed back in the 1850s when predicting the future results of British rule in India: "From the Indian natives, reluctantly and sparingly educated . . . under English super-

[71] *M. Schlunk*, Das Schulwesen in den deutschen Schutzgebieten, Hamburg 1914, p. 112.
[72] ZStA, RKolA, no. 992, pp. 94ff, Dr Gunzert, Department IIIa of the German Foreign Office to Privy Councillor Dr Kastl, Managing Director of the Reich Confederation of German Industry, 8 May 1928.

intendence, a fresh class is springing up, endowed with the requirements for government and imbued with European science."[73] His words
sum up the basic contradiction of colonial education, the contradiction
between the aims — designed to assist colonial exploitation and oppression — and the potentially anti-colonial long-term effects.

This contradiction was reflected to a greater or lesser extent in the
attitude adopted by the Africans themselves towards the government
schools (run by the colonial authorities) and the Christian missionary
schools. In the early years of colonial rule the Africans had largely rejected these establishments, regarding them primarily as a part of the
colonial apparatus of oppression, but from the turn of the century
enrolment grew. More and more Africans recognized the importance
of the education provided there which, even in its most rudimentary
form, contained elements of an historically more advanced culture.

Yet the government and missionary schools were never completely
accepted by the whole population. This was mainly due to the attitude
of parts of the African aristocracy, who regarded the schools as a threat
to their social status and influence on members of their ethnic community.
Their attitude towards the colonial schools was supported by many of
the Africans, who, living under pre-capitalist social conditions, did not
see the practical advantages of "modern" education. Missionaries often
had to resort to giving children and parents little gifts in order to recruit
pupils.

The Moslem population often rejected the schools because of the
Christian religious instruction given. In the coastal regions of German
East Africa the colonial authorities slowly overcame the Moslems'
refusal to attend school by opening government schools with no Christian
religion on the curriculum. This was the major reason for the relatively
large number of government schools in this colony. Official statistics
for 1914 state that there were 105 government schools with about 6,000
pupils in German East Africa, compared with 4 government schools
with over 300 pupils in Togo.[74] The task of the government schools was
to develop "an intermediate class, equipped with better knowledge, to
function as subordinate officials . . ."[75] The majority were elementary
schools where attendance did not exceed 4 years. It was only the hand-

---

[73] *K. Marx*, The Future Results of British Rule in India. in: K. Marx and F. Engels,
   Collected Works, vol. 12, Moscow 1979, p. 218.

[74] *Statistisches Jahrbuch* für das Deutsche Reich, 35th vol., Berlin 1914, p. 449.

[75] For example the clergyman D. Paul in: *Verhandlungen* des deutschen Kolonialkongresses 1910, op. cit., p. 760.

ful of upper schools ("station schools") which offered 5 to 6 years of schooling.

The government schools occupied a special position in terms of importance and basic education standards. The upper schools at least were run by fully qualified German elementary school teachers, who imposed the pedagogical approach they had acquired in the Reich, usually without paying the slightest attention to the completely different social and cultural background of the African children and youths. Enforced in most cases by a draconian school discipline, the education here imparted to the young Africans had the effect of severing them from African cultural traditions, although the ideological effects varied considerably, depending on specific local conditions and the character of the pupil.

The authorities in the "settler colony" of German South West Africa saw to open a government school for Africans. An intermediate African stratum to maintain German rule was not deemed necessary. "The natives, blacks and Hottentots can, under such conditions . . ., be nothing but a particular social class within the population as a whole. They are workers and servants . . .," commented the colonial expert Paul Rohrbach in 1910.[76] In this spirit the ardently "patriotic" Rhenish Missionary Society assumed responsibility for education, to the satisfaction of the colonial authorities.

In all the German colonies, missionary societies ran the overwhelming majority of schools. They saw this as the best means of winning over African animists to the Christian faith. But in pursuing their religious and educational aims, the missionary societies were by no means united. In places where Catholic and Protestant societies were working side by side, vehement disputes often arose over the allocation of territory. Schools were frequently opened in a hurry so as to establish some kind of missionary base and forestall rival societies. The colonial authorities did not object to the resulting patchwork of creeds, for it suited their power interests to see the African population divided by the strife between different denominations. At no time were the various missions interested in working together closely to fulfil the educational needs of the Africans.

The rivalry between the missionary societies led, especially in the last decade of German colonial rule, to a notable increase in the number of missionary schools. The available statistics, however, present a highly

---

[76] *P. Rohrbach*, Die Kolonie. In: Die Gesellschaft — Sammlung sozialpsychologischer Monographien, vol. XIX, Frankfurt am Main, n. d., p. 10.

exaggerated picture. It was not unusual for the societies to count "a class which took place twice a week for an hour and a half under a shady tree as an independently constituted school."[77] Since these three hours a week were primarily devoted to Christian conversion, with the "instruction" mostly only of a sporadic nature and usually delivered by poorly trained African assistant teachers or assistant catechists, the use of the term "school" for such classes amounted to a deception of the German public. Besides, many missionaries were inclined to overestimate their educational activities for the sake of paltry state subsidies. The statistics compiled by the missionary societies must be analysed in this light. They claimed the following totals for 1911:

in Togo   150 Protestant schools with about 6,000 pupils and
               179 Catholic schools with some 7,000 pupils;
in Cameroon   413 Protestant schools with about 22,000 pupils and
               112 Catholic schools with about 10,000 pupils;
in German East Africa
               539 Protestant schools with about 30,000 pupils and
               479 Catholic schools with about 32,000 pupils;
in German South West Africa
               30 Protestant schools with about 3,500 pupils and
               24 Catholic schools with about 600 pupils.[78]

It should be borne in mind that only 55 of all the missionary schools were designated "upper schools", which provided more than the maximum 4 years of instruction offered by the "elementary schools" and were mostly intended to train assistant teachers and catechists. In German South West Africa there was just one "upper school" with a total of 12 pupils!

Religious instruction was the main subject in the curriculum of all missionary schools, and Christian dogma also had a strong influence on the teaching of secular subjects. The colonial rulers expected the missionary societies, above all, to produce humble and obedient subjects by means of this extended form of religious education which most

[77] *M. Schlunk*, Die Schulen für Eingeborene in den deutschen Schutzgebieten, Abhandlungen des Hamburgischen Kolonialinstituts, vol. XVIII, Hamburg 1914, p. 141.
[78] Figures quoted from *M. Schlunk*, Die Schulen für Eingeborene in den deutschen Schutzgebieten, pp. 54—55, 112—113, 134—135, 244 ff.

missionaries practised from personal conviction. They did their best
to explain to the young Africans that the Apostle Paul's command that
one "must be subject, not only to avoid God's wrath but also for the sake
of conscience" (Romans, 13, 5) meant unconditional submission to
colonial slavery. In this context, it was necessary to reconcile the Christian principle that all men are equal "before God" with the false doctrine
of the "inferiority of the black race". And yet that "equality before
God", although it was unambiguously applied only to the Hereafter,
must have prompted many a missionary to adopt an attitude of Christian
humanism towards the young Africans in practical schoolwork.

Here was an opportunity for African pupils which could be used to
provoke or promote a growth of consciousness in opposition to colonialism. This opportunity arose, not least, because the education they
received (particularly at the "upper schools") inevitably broadened
the horizons of the young Africans in spite of all the narrow limitations
of the system and its reactionary content. By acquiring the previously
unknown skills of reading and writing, they won greater self-confidence.

Besides religious instruction, a subject called "work education"
played an important part in the timetable of most elementary schools
in accordance with the missionary motto "ora et labora". In most cases
"work education" was nothing but child labour on the farms and plantations belonging to the societies. Even amongst the missionaries there
were some who protested that the time spent on "work" often bore
no acceptable relationship to the time spent on "prayer" and the modest
instruction which accompanied the latter. Moreover, "work education"
was designed to "discipline" the young Africans and turn them into
useful labour to be exploited by German firms in the colonies, and this,
too, was warmly welcomed by the colonial authorities. New skills unknown to the Africans were however rarely taught in the elementary
schools. The pupils therefore tended to regard the physical labour
demanded of them as an oppressive but unavoidable price to be paid
for the intellectual education they wanted. This kind of "work education"
discredited physical labour in the eyes of many Africans, particularly
since the upper missionary schools and the government schools usually
confined their instruction to "book learning".

The "schools for practical work" were of a different character. According to M. Schlunk there were 37 of these schools in 1911 (30 set up by
the missions, 7 by the administration), attended by about 800 pupils,
where small numbers of boys were trained for various trades and skills
— a policy which was undoubtedly of significance for the long-range economic development of the regions concerned.

The colonial authorities sought to exclude European languages, apart from German, from the curriculum of all schools for Africans. To start with, foreign missionary societies — and sometimes even German ones — had taught English (in a few cases French), but the administrations regarded this as a dangerous challenge to their position because of the strong British influence in many areas, especially Togo, even after the German annexation. The teaching of English, which was at first widespread, seemed to them to favour their imperialist rivals. The introduction of German as the only non-African language was the least that was expected of the missionary schools in order to "educate growing young natives in the German manner and according to German values", as Chief Commissioner (Landeshauptmann) Köhler of Togo wrote.[79]

There was a long-drawn-out argument within the colonial administration and also between the missionary societies about the status of German in relation to teaching in African languages, an argument which reflected the basic dilemma of colonial education policy. The disputes on the "language question" reveal important motives which also played a part in determining the "assimilative" method of French colonial education and the "associative" or "adaptive" British method.

Originally, Germany's colonial politicians agreed that using German as the sole language of instruction would bring the oppressed peoples closer to Germany and make it easier to maintain power. With the exception of Swahili, already widespread in German East Africa, African languages were to be banned from the classroom or, at most, used as "auxiliary makeshifts". This is clear from comments made in 1906 by the colonial governors.[80] The assimilation policy they advocated was aimed at reducing the use of and, if possible, eradicating the African languages. For example: Puttkamer, the Governor of Cameroon, repeatedly attacked all attempts "to promote forcibly a crude and nasty Bantu Negro dialect such as Duala, or even Bakwiri, to the status of a civilized language, thereby ignoring the true nature of these dialects". On the contrary, "their rapid disappearance from the face of the earth could only signify a step forward for culture".[81] Zech, the Governor of Togo, expressed a similar view.[82]

---

[79] ZStA, RKolA, no. 7306, p. 187, Report by Köhler, 12 Dec. 1897.

[80] ZStA, RKolA, no. 7309, pp. 38 ff, Inhaltsangabe der Eingabe der deutschen evangelischen Mission und der hierauf bezüglichen Berichte der Gouvernements, September 1906.

[81] ZStA, RKolA, no. 7307, pp. 129—130, Letter by Puttkamer, 15 June 1899.

[82] ZStA, RKolA, no. 4080, pp. 129—130, Letter by Zech, 25 May 1906.

The Protestant missionary societies strongly opposed educational assimilation because they knew that elementary instruction in the African languages was essential if they were to attain their missionary objectives. German lessons should be reserved for a small minority of African pupils who had been earmarked for missionary or administrative service. This attitude prompted some missionaries to study African languages thoroughly. They undertook valuable linguistic researches and translated texts, mostly Biblical, into languages which were now written down for the first time. This deeper knowledge of African languages taught a number of missionaries to appreciate their beauty and expressiveness and to defend them against the incompetent judgements of colonial officials. One missionary inspector wrote to the German Foreign Office expressly rejecting senseless condemnations of West African languages and arguing, with reference to Ewe: "It is a most beautiful language. There is certainly not one textbook in use in German elementary schools which one could not translate into Ewe."[83]

Doubtless, the Protestant missions rendered valuable services in promoting the use and study of African languages, but they increasingly resorted to the argument that instruction in these languages should be preferred to extensive teaching of German because the latter was potentially dangerous for colonial rule. The Council of German Protestant Missionary Societies warned in 1897 of the "danger" which now loomed, because of the spread of European languages in Africa, of an "educated proletariat emerging . . . which is presumptuous and also easily rebellious".[84] In 1904 this Council delivered a petition to the Colonial Department in which this argument was taken a stage further. The propagation of the German language, they wrote, could "become a threat to the colony . . . as in this manner one rears a conceited, presumptuous and easily dissatisfied breed; for the natives learn from the Europeans much that is damaging and are tempted, when they speak the language of the Europeans, to place themselves on an equal footing. For example those who are familiar with conditions in German South West Africa report that unconsidered, arrogant speeches by whites were taken seriously by natives and passed on to others, and that sentiments hostile to the natives expressed in the press were read, understood and believed."[85] Elsewhere, we find a warning that Africans with a knowledge of German

---

[83] ZStA, RKolA, no. 4078, p. 156, Letter by Mission Inspector Zahn, 25 July 1894.

[84] ZStA, RKolA, no. 7307, p. 105, Denkschrift des Ausschusses der deutschen evangelischen Missionsgesellschaft, 11 Nov. 1897.

[85] ZStA, RKolA, no. 7308, p. 86, Eingabe des Ausschusses, Dec. 1904.

would be able to read "Social Democratic newspapers, indeed, even publications such as 'Simplicissimus'".[86] (The latter was a liberal satirical weekly critical of the imperial establishment.)

The linguist Carl Meinhof also warned against widespread teaching of German in the colonies. In 1905 he described the propagation of European languages in the colonies as a "success with very dubious consequences". And then he put forward a new argument: "Until now we have not had to reckon with the possibility of a major uprising in Cameroon and East Africa because the tribes are too divided to undertake any united action. By introducing a European language, not only do we provide the people with the means to reach an understanding . . ., but we furthermore offer them the best tool for revolutionary propaganda . . ."[87]

In the latter years of Germany's colonial rule, opinions such as this — concerning the advantages of "associative" language and education policies in the colonies — met with growing approval. In 1908, the Central Council of the DKG, which had previously campaigned vociferously for German teaching in the missionary schools, passed a recommendation, by 5 votes to 3, that, "in view of the situation it is not, generally speaking, wise to provide instruction in the German language in the public native schools after all". This decision was taken after discussion of a motion passed by the Allenstein branch of the Society demanding, for the sake of "unconditional maintenance of our dominant position . . . that in the public and private native schools . . . the German language only be taught in exceptional cases which require special dispensation".[88] Missionary circles also registered the change that was taking place. In 1913, for example, Professor Schmidlin, who held the Chair in Missionary Studies at Münster University, commented with regard to the introduction of German in the Catholic missionary schools: "First they impetuously demanded that the missions introduce it, and after the missions had consented, they levelled bitter accusations against them".[89]

---

[86] K. Axenfeld, Der Aethiopismus in Süd-Afrika, Verlagsbuchhandlung Wilhelm Süsserott, Berlin, n. d., p. 12.

[87] Verhandlungen des deutschen Kolonialkongresses 1905 zu Berlin, Berlin 1906, pp. 345—346.

[88] ZStA, DKG, no. 948, p. 68, 71, Antrag der Abteilung Allenstein und Entschliessung, 29 May 1908.

[89] J. Schmidlin, Die katholischen Missionen in den deutschen Schutzgebieten, Münster 1913, p. 283.

Only in the settler colony of German South West Africa was the propagation of *spoken* German still considered useful. Moritz, a senior teacher from Berlin who made a detailed study of education policy in that colony, records the official view thus: "Reading and writing is . . . in the interests of his masters . . . not desired. This knowledge only nourishes the vanity of the coloured man and tempts him to abuse it."[90]

This dispute over two possible colonial language policies shows that the opposing camps were in no sense divided by antagonistic principles. Both were concerned to find the best method of maintaining colonial rule. When the German imperialists accepted the theory that teaching Africans German would enable them to unite against Germany, they were simply accepting the approach of all those "who believe that by limiting native education to native lines they may 'keep the nigger in his place'", to quote W. B. Mumford, a British expert in the field of colonial education.[91]

The new method had gained favour after the uprisings of 1904 to 1906, when the authorities demanded a stronger emphasis, in all mission schooling, on the cultivation of a submissive attitude towards the colonial rulers. The following passage from a syllabus adopted by all the missionary societies in Togo in 1906 illustrates the efforts made in this direction: "The German Kaiser is the guardian of the Togo protectorate. He has appointed a government in Togo whose head is the Governor . . . All natives are subjects of the German Kaiser. They must also be loyal and obedient to the government which the German Kaiser has appointed in Togo, that is to say: the Governor, the district commissioners and district chief and the civil servants working on their behalf".[92] "Obedience" and "loyalty" were the essential objectives underlying education in all missionary and government schools.

Although even a fragmentary secular education for Africans was regarded as a potential threat to colonial rule, it could not be dispensed with, for it was vital for economic exploitation in the colonies. Therefore the colonial authorities found themselves obliged to press for an extension of secular instruction (especially in reading, writing and arithmetic), at least in the "upper" mission schools. Agreements or school regulations to this end, which included a provision for modest state sub-

---

[90] *E. Moritz*, Das Schulwesen in Deutsch—Südwestafrika, Berlin 1914, p. 211.

[91] *W. B. Mumford*, Comparative Studies of Native Education in Various Dependencies, in The Yearbook of Education 1935, London 1935, p. 820.

[92] ZStA, RKolA, no. 4080, pp. 146—147, Niederschrift über Beratung betr. Schulordnung und Lehrplan der Missionsschulen, 31 Jan. 1906.

sidies, were notified in Togo and Cameroon in 1910 and in German South West Africa in 1913. A decision taken at the Bishop's Conference of the colony in 1912 prepared the ground for a similar measure in German East Africa. The curriculum was to follow the elementary school model in Germany, with rudimentary instruction in history, geography and nature study. There was almost no treatment of the Africans' own natural and social environment.

The colonial administration also felt the time had come to do something about the wildly fluctuating attendance of pupils at many missionary schools. The school board now had to give its pemission before a pupil could leave prematurely. The "Regulations for Missionary Schools in Receipt of State Grants" drawn up in 1913 laid down that in South West Africa adult Africans "to whom the pupil has a personal relationship of dependence" could be sentenced to a fine for keeping a child away from school, and if this occurred repeatedly, to a "flogging in accordance with the Imperial Chancellor's Decree of 22 April 1896".[93] This document must be the only educational ordinance of modern times providing for corporal punishment to be inflicted on parents and guardians. The clause demonstrates that the whole field of education remained firmly embedded in the overall system of colonialist rule by terror.

Under these circumstances, it is hardly surprising that the Africans were in two minds about the colonial schools. At first most Africans rejected such schooling, but this conflicted with the desire to use any opportunity, however small, to acquire a "modern" education. This was true even during the early years of German rule. An example can be found in the attitude of the Duala, who lived at the mouth of the Cameroon River. They had long acted as trading intermediaries, maintaining continual contact with Europeans. One of the most important demands which the Duala chiefs had always made of the German "protectors" was that they should open schools. The conflicts with the administration in which the chiefs were later embroiled can be attributed partially to their disappointments over education. When a Duala representative visited Germany in August 1906, he handed in a petition to the Chancellor requesting an extension of schooling (which had constantly been turned down) from 3 to 6 years and the establishment

---

[93] ZStA, RKolA, no. 1952, pp. 90ff, Schulordnung für Missionsschulen, die staatliche Beihilfen erhalten, 3 Sept. 1913.

of a trades' school for which the Duala would themselves pay.[94] The response was to extend instruction at the government schools to 5 years.

The Duala also tried to enable individual youngsters to attend an advanced school or a vocational college in Germany. The results of some brief "experiments" with a handful of young Africans from Cameroon and Togo, however, received a negative assessment from the administration. In July 1903 an academic institution in the United States asked the German government what experiences it had had of educating "natives" in Germany. The answer was that "the influence of civilization was often injurious to their character and their future existence in the protectorate".[95] This revealing opinion was shared by the missionary societies.

Adolf Woermann pointed to the motive behind the Africans' quest for education when he wrote as early as 1886: "The natives believe that the main reason for the great superiority of the Europeans is that they can read and write — 'you know book' is the expression they use to convey this view."[96] It was, indeed, this belief which strengthened many Africans' thirst for education, and enabled them to put up with floggings, child labour and discrimination against their own culture. And it was this belief which, since the turn of the century, led to attempts to set up independent schools and to overcome the educational barriers built by the colonial rulers. In 1902, for example, the Governor of Cameroon reported that the "education-hungry Bakweri" were beginning to emancipate themselves from the mission by opening their own schools.[97] It was noted that in German East Africa "some sultans in the northern areas of Tabora District have set up their own schools and are employing coloured teachers".[98] Moshi District also recorded the opening in 1904 of the first school designed to free the population from the influence and control of the missionaries.[99]

[94] ZStA, RKolA, no. 4300, pp. 38—39, Petition sent by Mpundo Akwa to the Imperial Chancellor, 29 Aug. 1906.

[95] ZStA, RKolA, no. 7308, p. 73, Draft of the reply given on 9 Aug. 1903 to an inquiry from the American Academy of Political and Social Science, Philadelphia, 2 July 1903.

[96] ZStA, RKolA, no. 4070, pp. 9ff, Adolf Woermann to Bismarck, 3 Mar. 1886.

[97] ZStA, RKolA, no. 4074, p. 40, Report by the Governor, 13 Dec. 1902.

[98] StBVR, XII. Legislaturperiode (1907/11), vol. 271, p. 403.

[99] Z. E. Lawuo, Education and Change in a Rural Community — A Study of Colonial Education and Local Response among the Chagga of Kilimanjaro between 1920 and 1945. Ph. D. Thesis, University of Dar es Salaam 1977, p. 63.

This movement, which the colonial authorities regarded with considerable suspicion, had become widespread by the time German rule came to an end. Certainly, independent ventures in the field of schooling were still aimed at improving the Africans' own positions under the colonial regime. But they contained, objectively, seeds of opposition to colonialism.

In claiming their right to education the Africans received support from the revolutionary working-class movement in Germany. Left-wing Social Democrats exposed the nature of colonial education policy and demanded that schools with high educational standards be built for the African population. "We want model schools, we want far more schools than are being built today, and on this point we would like to see much faster progress," declared Alfred Henke, a left-wing Social Democrat deputy in 1914, when the Reichstag was discussing the budget for the Imperial Colonial Office.[100] This attitude resulted from the already traditional solidarity of German revolutionary socialists with the anticolonial liberation struggle. Referring to the movement "whose ultimate aim is freedom from white rule", the same deputy had already told the Reichstag: "We . . . have great sympathy for this movement. It is clear to us that the Negroes are absolutely capable of education, and it is quite clear that in time they become much better educated than their white oppressors wish . . . Of course we . . . who are ourselves oppressed and exploited in Germany cannot lend our hands to oppressing and exploiting others."[101]

[100] A. Henke in StBVR, XIII. Legislaturperiode (1912/14), vol. 294, p. 7959 (9 Mar. 1914).
[101] Ibid., vol. 284, pp. 1524—1525.

VIII. Pre-1914 Efforts to Secure a Larger Share

1. Morocco 1898—1914

The world-wide struggle for the repartition of the colonial world, which began at the turn of the century, found its expression not only in the Spanish-American War and the Russo-Japanese War, but also in Germany's intense efforts to expand her economic and political positions in China, Turkey, Persia and Morocco. These semi-colonies were particularly vulnerable to *pénétration pacifique* by this far from pacific claimant to world power because they were not protected by the colonial administrations of other powers or by customs barriers or serious trade restrictions. Ironically, it was Morocco, a secondary rather than major target of German expansion, which gave rise to two of the three most dangerous international crises in the decade that preceded the First World War. This was partly because of the great significance which Morocco had assumed for France as a cornerstone of her colonial empire. No less important were two aspects which did not apply to the other semi-colonies mentioned here. For one thing, the iron and steel industry of the Rhine and Ruhr evinced a marked interest in Morocco's (overestimated) ore resources. For another, there was the fact that at the beginning of the century Morocco had been a semi-colony in which Germany as one of several powers enjoyed "treaty rights" and possessed economic interests, but that now it was being openly transformed step by step into a protectorate of one of her main imperialist rivals. That this was being done without granting Germany adequate "compensation" was considered to be absolutely unbearable by large parts of the German ruling class.

With the advent of the 20th century, the struggle between France, Britain and Germany over Morocco had mounted in intensity. The country's feudalistic socio-economic and state structure, the unequal treaties the capitalist powers had imposed on it during the 19th century and the despotic regime of Sultan 'Abd al-'Aziz, who was always ready to make concessions to the imperialist powers, facilitated the influx of European capital and the transformation of Morocco into a dependent state.

In the early 20th century, France was the most successful of the powers interested in Morocco, all of which relied more or less on the method of *pénétration pacifique*. It was these intense efforts to turn the Sultanate into a French protectorate (in recompense for the defeat of Fashoda, so to speak), which brought the "Moroccan issue", unresolved for more than twenty years, to a head. The French imperialists made no secret of their intention of "Tunisifying" Morocco, and in December 1900 the government in Paris secured recognition of Morocco as a French sphere of interest by Italy, which was given a free hand in Tripoli in return.

In the course of the 1880s and 1890s, a number of German firms had installed themselves in Morocco's seaports, making a handsome profit out of a semi-colonial trade. Krupp had gained a dominant position as a supplier of arms (see pp. 130—132), and Germany's diplomatic representatives had won political influence among the country's ruling circles by posing as the "guardians" of Moroccan independence. Yet Germany had failed to catch up with its British and French rivals in the economic and political spheres.

Having seen their hopes in South Africa disappointed, the German bourgeoisie began to cast covetous eyes on other territories not yet exclusively dominated by another power. Some Pan-German advocates of territorial expansion went so far as to call for a German sphere of influence on the soil of the Moroccan sultanate. Referring to increasing French penetration, they argued that Germany was entitled to play a prominent part in the partition of Morocco among the powers due to begin soon.

Count Joachim von Pfeil, a former member of the Peters clique who had fallen out with the founder of German East Africa and was now a leading member of the Pan-German League and (since 1887) of the German Colonial Society, undertook journeys of exploration in Morocco from 1897 to 1901. From early 1898 onwards, in contributions to journals and lectures, he drew attention to the country's riches. Owing to his access to governing and colonial circles, Pfeil was able to bring to the fore a man who was subsequently to become an even more influential advocate of imperialist expansion: Theobald Fischer, professor of geography at Marburg University. Fischer, founding member of the DKG and long-time chairman of the Marburg branch of the Colonial Society, had become a member of the executive of the Pan-German League in 1891.

In 1899 and 1901 Fischer also travelled in Morocco, his journeys being organized and paid for by the geographical societies in Berlin and Hamburg. The main purpose of these travels was to study economic possibilities and to draw public attention to "German interests" in that country. Fischer's numerous publications and lectures attracted much interest, and before long he was widely regarded as the foremost German authority on Morocco. Fischer praised western Morocco as ideal territory for settling German farmers and also drew attention to the country's rich and undeveloped mineral resources. Germany should insist on getting this excellent object for colonization. It was a matter of vital interest, he told the German Foreign Office in 1899, to take part in the imminent carve-up of Morocco. The same demand was raised by Pfeil, who in a memorandum published that year described the partition of the country as "the only possible and at the same time German solution to the Moroccan question". Southwestern Morocco would have to be placed "under German supervision".[1]

Since there seemed to be no forward movement on the matter, these advocates of colonial expansion and some capitalist interest groups decided to join forces in organizational terms. In October 1902 the Moroccan Society was created, to be reconstituted as the German Mediterranean Society in 1904. This was a centre for the systematic preparation of colonial aggression in Morocco, which tried to stimulate the government to act. The society's programme said the main objective was to "strengthen German interests in a suitable way should Morocco be partitioned."[2] Fischer was made honorary chairman. In late 1903 the society had 120 members, including leading representatives of the Pan-German League, the German Colonial Society and the Central Association for Commercial Geography, 30 shipowners and merchants (Woermann being one of them), two bankers (Wallich, of the Deutsche Bank, and Erlanger), 23 industrialists (including Wilmowski, a director of Krupp's; Wirth, president of the Industrialists' Federation; Lauters, representing mining interests and a building firm; and Burgers, general manager of the Schalker Gruben- und Hüttenverein), and twelve senior civil servants.

While the society was not markedly successful in its efforts "to strengthen German interests in Morocco" (its attempts to grow cotton there came to nothing), Fischer, Pfeil and their supporters met with

---

[1] ZStA, Papers of Count Joachim von Pfeil, no. 120, pp. 23—24, "Deutsche politische Gedanken über Marokko".

[2] ZStA, DKG, no. 286, pp. 18—19.

some response among the ruling class, and influential newspapers and journals took up their ideas. On the face of it, the government was exercising restraint, the official position being that German interests merely called for the maintenance of the "open door" principle by which all signatory powers of the Madrid Agreement of 1880 enjoyed equal rights in the field of trade. In actual fact, however, Chancellor Bülow had confidentially indicated as early as 1899 that he inclined towards the idea of a German presence in southern Morocco; the government let it be known that in the event of a carve-up it would insist on a share of the "Moroccan cake". In June of that year the German Ambassador to the Court of St James informed the British Prime Minister, Lord Salisbury, of a plan to divide Morocco among Britain, Germany, France and Spain, with Germany receiving the southern part of the Atlantic Coast and Britain the northern one. Salisbury professed no interest in the proposal, but Colonial Secretary Joseph Chamberlain returned to the idea several times in the following years during exploratory talks about an Anglo-German alliance. He suggested that the two powers should reach an agreement on the partition of Morocco to pave the way for a comprehensive "understanding". But this time the British offer went unheeded because Bülow regarded it as a threat to the German policy of a "free hand" and as an attempt to involve Germany in conflicts with France. On 9 August 1901 he instructed the Wilhelmstrasse that "for the time being we must not take sides in the Moroccan imbroglio but adopt a wait-and-see attitude and allow matters to run their course."[3]

But this did not mean that the plan had been abandoned. The wishes of governing circles in 1903 centred on Sous province in southern Morocco, including the port of Agadir, which the pan-German writers had long urged should be annexed. In September of that year, the Foreign Secretary, von Richthofen, instructed the German Ambassador in Madrid to raise the subject of Morocco's partition, which France was seeking to bring about, with the following objective in view: "Given our political standing in the world and, more specifically, our extensive economic interests in Morocco, we must be at pains to ensure that we will receive our share when the country is partitioned, say in the Sous region, or alternatively, that we will be given some other colonial territory by way of compensation, say Fernando Po."[4] The Spanish government, however, flatly rejected the idea of Germany gaining a territorial

---

[3] *GP*, vol. 17, no. 5185, pp. 341—342.

[4] Ibid., no. 5200, p. 355.

foothold in southern Morocco because of its own designs on the south Moroccan seaboard. Kaiser Wilhelm II, who cared little for Morocco, and the *éminence grise* of German foreign policy, Friedrich von Holstein, saw to it that the plan was not pursued any further, at least for the time being.

In 1899—1903 (and later as well) opinions among the ruling class varied as far as Morocco was concerned. The dominant feeling was not in favour of speedy partition, but there was a lurking fear that Germany might be left out in the cold in a carve-up brought about by France or Britain. The government hoped to consolidate its position by continuing its policy of *pénétration pacifique*, thereby gaining more influence in Morocco, which would later enable it to play a decisive part in determining the date and mode of partition.

The extension of commercial relations was a major factor in this respect. At the beginning of the 20th century, German trade with Morocco, much of which consisted in the sale of arms and ammunition to the Sultan's government, continued to expand, but without overtaking the trade of Britain and France. According to imprecise consular reports, it grew from 6.4 million marks in 1898 to 10.2 million marks in 1905.[5] Apart from war material, German exports consisted of ironmongery and other hardware, dyes, porcelain, earthenware, beer and spirits while German imports included almonds, wax, olive oil, hides and wool, i.e. raw materials for German industry. (The oil extracted from almonds was used in the chemical industry). The German commercial firms operating in Morocco increased the number of their branches there and acquired additional landed property. The value of the latter was estimated at one million marks in 1905 while German capital investment in the country totalled approximately 13 million marks, most of it at the disposal of the trading companies. The actually existing "German interests" were confined to the arms trade, other trading activities, commission business and shipping. It was not until late in 1905 that Morocco received a loan from Germany.

It goes without saying that these "German interests", especially those of the armaments industry, enjoyed the protection of the Imperial Go-

---

[5] According to *F. T. Williamson*, Germany and Morocco before 1905, Baltimore, 1937, p. 166. The German foreign trade statistics, based on returns from the German seaports, give somewhat lower figures. The real value of German exports was much higher because war material was for the most part not included. On the unreliability of these statistics cf. *Williamson*, op. cit., pp. 125 and 164—165; Th. Fischer in Deutsche Rundschau, Sept. 1905, p. 454.

vernment and of its diplomatic mission in Tangier which was run by people who in the opinion of British observers "failed often enough as diplomats but rarely as businessmen."[6] At the beginning of this century German commercial activities were vigorously promoted not only by the legation but also by nine consulates and vice-consulates. The postal service set up by the German Imperial Post Office in Morocco in 1899 served the same purpose.

Although the government was concerned to advance "German interests", the country was, before the first severe diplomatic crisis over Morocco, on the whole unimportant as a source of raw materials for Germany and significant as a market only for the arms industry. (The relatively modest size of Germany's economic stake did not prevent the representatives of the Imperial Government from exaggerating its importance in order to substantiate German pretensions). However, compared with the position of the French and British, "German interests" in Morocco were not small, because those powers, too, had not succeeded in bringing the country under their economic control to any appreciable extent.[7]

German policy towards Morocco was therefore dictated not so much by the interests already existing but rather by those hoped for. Many travellers and propagandists, notably Theobald Fischer, who had close links with Burgers and Thyssen, had emphasized Morocco's mineral wealth. Since Lorraine's iron ore deposits were insufficient to meet the demand, and Swedish ore supplies were coming to an end in 1912, the question of opening up new sources was exercising the minds of iron and steel industrialists of the Rhine and Ruhr[8] who increasingly looked upon the Sultanate as a potentially important new supplier. In 1902 firms such as the Schalker Gruben- und Hüttenverein AG and the Gewerkschaft Deutscher Kaiser, which belonged to the Thyssen group, with the backing of the German Minister began attempts to secure mining concessions at the Sultan's court, but to no avail. The following year, the Disconto-Gesellschaft, Krupp and the two companies mentioned set up a consortium to prospect for, and exploit, Moroccan ores. This consortium dispatched an expedition into the Sous region in early

---

[6] *W. B. Harris* and *W. Cozens-Hardy*, Modern Morocco, London 1919, p. 157.

[7] Th. Fischer estimated the volume of Moroccan foreign trade in 1905 at approx. 80 million marks. Britain accounted for c. 48 per cent, France for 21 per cent and Germany for 15 per cent. Deutsche Rundschau, Sept. 1905, p. 454.

[8] Rheinisch-Westfälische Zeitung, 8 May 1904, Quoted from: *G. W. F. Hallgarten*, Imperialismus vor 1914, vol. 1, Munich, 1963, p. 618.

1904 while simultaneously conducting negotiations with a group of French firms led by Schneider with a view to forming a Franco-German syndicate that would operate in Morocco.

After the signing of the treaty of 8 April 1904 (the *Entente Cordiale*) whereby Britain gave France a free hand in Morocco in return for recognition of her own "claim" to Egypt, the French redoubled their efforts to subjugate the Sultanate. In the shape of the Comité du Maroc founded on 17 February 1904, the representatives of the major French banks and of the country's heavy industry as well as the parliamentary advocates of expansion in Morocco had created an effective instrument for *pénétration pacifique* at an accelerated pace. A new situation had thus arisen. It was the antagonism between German and French imperialism which now set the pace in the struggle for hegemony over Morocco.

The Anglo-French treaty was seen as a serious danger by Chancellor Bülow. In instructions issued to the German Ambassador in Paris on 21 July 1904 he said, "The position of pre-eminence in Morocco which has been conceded to France in the Declaration of 8 April of this year affects German interests in two ways. Before the Anglo-French understanding was reached, no definite course had been laid down for Morocco's political future. The country was absolutely open to all powers with maritime or colonial aspirations. As a result of the Declaration of 8 April of this year, Great Britain has quitted the ranks of these powers unilaterally in France's favour, thereby giving France a near-monopoly in the bid for that valuable possession. The fact that as a result of the Declaration Germany's opportunities to gain a political foothold in Morocco are now limited, possibly even illusory, is in itself a severe disadvantage for us. To make matters worse, the settlement regarding Morocco has been reached without our being consulted, and France has ignored us completely, even after coming to an understanding with England. Moreover, France has paid a handsome price to England in return for a free hand in Morocco, but without having the slightest intention of granting an equivalent to Germany. If we were to recognize France's political privilege now without raising objections, we would inflict damage on ourselves without getting anything in return. We will, therefore, have to avoid such recognition as long as possible. For the time being it would be useful for us if the status quo were maintained in the Sharifian Empire and if the states which have not signed the Declaration of 8 April did not draw any conclusions for the benefit of France from the agreements on Morocco reached only between England and France . . . Even more severe and urgent than the political disadvantages are the dangers which arise from the Declaration of 8 April for our economic and commercial interests in Morocco. German trade with the Sharifian Empire has followed a continuous upward trend during the last decade . . .

"The German coal and steel industry has also directed its attention to Morocco in the hope that the country's rich mineral resources will provide an alternative to the industry's present sources of iron ore supplies, upon which its competitors are drawing to an increasing extent. Considering the steadily declining number of countries in which free trade and unhindered economic activity are still possible, Morocco's importance for us should not be underestimated. But precisely in this area the provisions of the Declaration have a damaging and restrictive effect . . . Transactions for the Sultan's government, in particular arms contracts, have hitherto in large measure passed through German hands. The restrictions planned by France would force German trade out of this promising market and, as far as concessions are concerned, deprive German industry of a field of activity with great prospects. Consequently, the German circles involved have already lodged complaints and expressed their misgivings, urgently requesting support against the French efforts to gain a monopoly . . . German industry has a vital interest in seeing full freedom of trade maintained in Morocco, including the granting of concessions and government contracts."[9]

Bülow's instructions leave no doubt as to the immediate motives of German diplomacy after 1904. Of special interest is his remark that "the steadily declining number of countries in which free trade and unhindered economic activity are still possible" was the reason why Morocco's importance as an object of German expansionism "should not be underestimated", for the Chancellor thus indirectly confirmed the correlation between the partition of the world, then virtually complete, and the increasing rivalries among the imperialist powers. It was a correlation which Lenin was the first to perceive clearly in its full dimensions and which played a prominent part in his theory of imperialism.

The demand that "adequate" compensation should be insisted on if the surrender of Morocco to France were to prove inevitable had been submitted to the government by the DKG in early May, and it subsequently appeared again and again in the deliberations of the ruling circles.

The international and the domestic situation prevented the Imperial Government from reacting to the Anglo-French treaty with an attempt to annex western Morocco as the Pan-German League was urging.

[9] *GP*, vol. 20/1, no. 6523, pp. 210—214.

In 1904—5 such an attempt would have overtaxed the strength of German imperialism and undoubtedly brought Britain and France still closer together. Furthermore, it would have placed a severe strain on German policy towards Turkey and reduced to nonsense the fraudulent claim that the Kaiser was a friend of the Mohammedans. The German Foreign Office deemed it wiser for the time being, both in the promotion of German capital interests in Morocco and in the struggle for colonies generally, to rely on non-annexationist methods of colonial expansion. In view of the crisis of German colonialism, brought to a head by the uprisings in the African colonies, they had virtually no alternative since new annexations would have endangered the parliamentary majority of the Bülow government. By taking advantage of Morocco's semicolonial status, especially the provisions of the Madrid Treaty of 1880 and the "open door", the Wilhelmstrasse hoped to thwart the ambitions of French imperialism, and ultimately to reach a position equal to that of France. In this way undesirable decisions were to be prevented and options kept open until the moment came to play a part in deciding Morocco's future or even to embark on a policy of annexation.

German diplomacy therefore strove in 1904—5 to strengthen the Sultan's hand in the face of increased French attempts at infiltration. Since the government in Paris was not prepared to pay any attention to the interests of the German rival and increased its efforts to establish a French protectorate in Morocco, Bülow determined to exploit the fact that Russia, France's ally, was preoccupied with the Russo-Japanese War and to force France to respect German "rights" and interests by means of a spectacular political demonstration. His decision had been partly due to the representations of German industrialists, notably Krupp, who sent his representative at the Sultan's court, Rottenburg, to Berlin in February 1905 to sound the alarm. Wilhelm II granted an audience to Krupp's envoy. His reception was described by the French historian Pierre Guillen: "His plea had made a deep impression and contributed much to the decision to take action against French policy."[10]

On 31 March 1905 the Emperor landed at Tangier in order to demonstrate to the world Germany's "rights" in Morocco and her intention to play a major role in all decisions on the repartition of the world. Wilhelm II told the French chargé d'affaires that Germany was insisting on free trade in Morocco and on full equality of rights with other powers. He said that he would deal directly with the Sultan as the free sovereign of an independent country, and added that he had the means "to assert

---

[10] P. Guillen, L'Allemagne et le Maroc de 1870 à 1905, Paris 1967, p. 866.

his legitimate claims and expected France to treat them with due respect."[11]

In an article "from an industrial source" the Kölnische Zeitung, a mouthpiece of the National Liberals, commented: "As soon as Morocco's various administrative branches are exclusively subject to French control and domination, concessions for foreign entrepreneurs in the field of railway construction and mining will be out of the question as they will be the preserve of the French. But that such concessions must be granted to open up Morocco to civilization in earnest is just as indisputable as the fact that these concessions give a boost to the trade of the power concerned and provide it with a solid backbone." (1 April 1905)

The Kaiser's spectacular gesture at Tangier made it abundantly plain that there was more at stake than Germany's interest in Morocco as a target of expansion, which the Wilhelmstrasse had systematically promoted and sometimes exaggerated. The central issue was the role of German imperialism in the world arena. Italy, Britain and Spain had received something substantial in return for surrendering Morocco to France. (In a secret treaty of 3 October 1904 Spain had given France a free hand, except in a part of the Mediterranean coast assigned to Spain). By contrast, the most aggressive of the great powers — and the strongest on the continent in military terms — had been treated as a negligible quantity by its rivals in the distribution of a colonial territory of great economic and military interest. It was felt that such a procedure could not be tolerated as it would entail a loss of prestige in the worldwide rivalry among the imperialist powers. "Retreat would invite comparison with Olmütz and eclipse Fashoda", the incensed Holstein wrote[12]. France was to be taught a lesson she would not easily forget and a resounding defeat inflicted on her Foreign Minister, Théophile Delcassé, the architect of the *Entente Cordiale*.

The government felt that the most promising way of thwarting France's ambitions would be to convene an international conference which would guarantee the maintenance of the status quo. Different sections of the ruling class interpreted this policy in different ways. The Pan-German League, which was fast becoming an instrument of the most aggressive elements of the German bourgeoisie, especially of leading figures of the çoal and steel industry of Rhineland and Westphalia, saw it as paving the way for the annexation of Moroccan territory and urged the govern-

---

[11] *GP*, vol. 20/1, no. 6589, p. 286, Minister von Schoen to the German Foreign Office 31 March 1905.

[12] *GP*, vol. 20/2, no. 6601, p. 304. Note by Holstein, 4 April 1905.

ment to stand firm and adopt a more aggressive and adventurist line. It demanded that the entire Atlantic coast with its hinterland should be seized. Important sections of the monopolist bourgeoisie (the Deutsche Bank, most other major banks, the electrical corporations, the big shipping companies in Hamburg and Bremen, and the export industry), however, remained committed to the idea of "peaceful penetration". The Deutsche Bank, in particular, which had close links with the German Foreign Office, felt that the policy towards Morocco should be subordinated to the requirements of the Baghdad Railway project. There was a clearly discernible tendency in these quarters to come to terms with French finance groups so that Morocco might be exploited jointly. The Imperial Naval Office also rejected the more extremist demands, for reasons of naval tactics.

The government tried to steer between both sections. It declined all offers for a direct understanding submitted by the French government, and forced France under threat of war to agree in July 1905 to attend the forthcoming international conference. But at the same time the men directing German foreign policy were worried by the increasingly unfavourable international situation, the self-confidence displayed by the French with British backing, and their efforts to turn the impending conference into a success of French policy. A French triumph at the conference would endanger the German imperialists' hopes for the maintenance of the status quo in Morocco and, moreover, impair the international standing of the German Empire. This prospect prompted senior diplomats and military leaders in late 1905 to turn to the idea of swiftly resolving the Moroccan question — as well as other issues — in Germany's favour by a war with France. But the determination of the British government to give France military support and the mass movement of the German working class for democratic freedoms and against war led the German government, which was not yet sufficiently prepared for a world war, not to pursue this idea.

Before and during the conference, held at Algeciras, Spain, from 16 January to 7 April 1906, the efforts of German diplomacy were aimed at scotching French plans to establish hegemony over Morocco, securing the full, unhindered participation of the German bourgeoisie in the plunder of Morocco and obtaining wide-ranging powers within the framework of the "reforms" to be prescribed for Morocco at the conference. But there was hardly any support for these aims at the conference. Great Britain was not alone in supporting the French claims; Russia, Spain, Italy and the other participating powers, except for Austria-Hungary, also aligned themselves with France. Faced with growing isolation, the

German delegation ultimately had no choice but to yield on the main issues and to recognize France's specially privileged position in Morocco. Although they managed to prevent Morocco's immediate transformation into a French protectorate and to secure terms allowing a measure of participation in the imperialist plundering of Morocco, the outcome still amounted to a resounding defeat considering the aims set by Bülow and Holstein.

Whereas the "Act of Algeciras"[13] signed by the participants on 7 April 1906 verbally acknowledged the sovereignty, independence and integrity of the Sultanate, its real effect was to restrict the country's sovereignty and independence quite considerably. The police force, the financial system and customs administration were placed under foreign control. France's "special interests" were recognized. The management of the Moroccan State Bank, which the conference decided to found, was virtually handed over to the Banque de Paris et des Pays Bas. Furthermore, France was given control over the police force in the Algerian-Moroccan border region and over the customs. With French and Spanish officers acting as instructors for Moroccan police units, the French gained decisive influence over the country's domestic affairs. All these rights and functions assigned to France greatly facilitated her policy of penetrating and subjugating Morocco.

The First Moroccan Crisis contributed to the formation of rival imperialist blocs and marked an important step along the road which led to the First World War.

Even after the severe political setback they had suffered at Algeciras, leading circles in Germany were in no mood to for go their share in Morocco's riches. The fanatical Pan-German advocates of expansion never lost sight of their aim of bringing western and southern Morocco under German rule in the event of the country losing its independence altogether.

At first, there were efforts to strengthen the German interests through increased "peaceful penetration", taking advantage of the "open door" guarantees contained in the "Act of Algeciras". With active support from the Imperial Government, German firms tried to secure investment projects such as port installations, telegraph lines, submarine cables, coastal shipping facilities, etc. But French monopolies, whose position was very strong, frustrated most of these plans, with the effect that the Berlin Foreign Office made special efforts to expand trade with

---

[13] Cf. *Handbuch der Verträge* 1871—1964, Verträge und andere Dokumente aus der Geschichte der internationalen Beziehungen, ed. by H. Stoecker with the collaboration of A. Rüger, Berlin 1968, pp. 100ff.

Morocco. As a result, trade increased from 7.3 million marks to 14 million marks between 1906 and 1910.[14] (Sugar now headed the list of German exports).

Influential representatives of the Ruhr coal and steel industry now sought to gain a broader foothold by cooperating with their French rivals. In 1907, Krupp obtained a 21 per cent participation in the Union des Mines Marocaines. This was a large international corporation which had just been founded by the Schneider-Creusot group and which Thyssen, Kirdorf of the Gelsenkirchner Bergwerks-A.G., the Metallurgische Gesellschaft and the Nationalbank soon also joined. The industrialists in question were thus following the line of the German Foreign Office, which was giving priority to Middle East expansion and was prepared to allow the French to dominate Morocco provided they made concessions in the Middle East. At the same time, Krupp and Kirdorf continued to use the Pan-German League as their mouthpiece, for direct German control over western Morocco would have suited them most.

The demands of the Pan-German League at this time found the support of another, not so powerful interest group, because the ambitions and especially the enormous claims of that group were incompatible with French dominance. The Mannesmann brothers from Remscheid, one-time joint owners of important rolling mills, had begun geological prospecting in Morocco in 1906. Before the end of that year they had managed, by way of gifts, large-scale bribery and promises, and with the support of the German Minister Rosen, to obtain from Sultan Moulay 'Abd al-'Aziz the permission to exploit numerous iron, copper and lead ore deposits which they estimated to be worth between two and three million marks. Their attempts to gain a dominant position in the exploitation of Morocco's mineral wealth, at first actively encouraged by German diplomacy, were bitterly opposed by the exponents of French imperialism which tried to invalidate the Mannesmanns' "claims" by means of a new mining law they proposed to the Sultan.

The Mannesmann brothers also founded a number of mining, industrial and commercial enterprises in Morocco, acquired huge estates (approx. 35,000 hectares between 1908 and 1914) and established farms. Through the Marokko Mannesmann-Compagnie, established in 1909, they attempted to monopolize German-Moroccan trade and to bring a major portion of Moroccan foreign trade into their hands. The Pan-German League, which the brothers were only too willing to support, immediately took up the cudgels for the "mining rights" of the Mannes-

[14] *Statistisches Jahrbuch* für das Deutsche Reich, vol. 32, 1911, pp. 272, 274.

manns, initiating a high-pitched campaign in the press. In the Alldeutsche Blätter, in pamphlets and in lectures, Class, Wirth, Pfeil and other leading lights of the League called for the partition of the Sultanate between France and Germany, claiming western and south-western Morocco (the site of Mannesmann's "rights") for German imperialism. They demanded that the Imperial Government should not even shrink from waging war against France in order to enforce "justice" for the Mannesmanns.

Even after 1906 the government remained anxious to sustain both variants of imperialist policy towards Morocco. But as it turned out, its main concern was to safeguard the main line of expansion — Asia Minor and the Middle East — which was financed by the Deutsche Bank and upheld by the Imperial General Staff. The government sponsored expansion in Morocco as long as it could serve as a complement to its Baghdad Railway strategy or at least did not interfere with that strategy. It felt that with Morocco still nominally independent it would remain possible, despite the French privileges, to expand German positions there by way of *pénétration pacifique* so that in the event of partition there would still be a chance of asserting colonial claims. But the government did not pursue this policy consistently between 1906 and 1911. One the one hand, it encouraged collaboration between German and French companies while acknowledging French primacy; on the other, it vehemently opposed French claims on various occasions.

Relying on the special status acquired at Algeciras, the French imperialists did their utmost to bring Morocco completely under their influence. The methods employed were manifold: economic, political, cultural and military. The French authorities skilfully exploited the country's inner conflicts, which mounted in intensity when a rival claimant to the Sultan's throne, Moulay Hafidh, who thought to be a champion of national independence, rose in rebellion (1907) and when the Moroccan population began to show increasing signs of resentment at the results of the Algeciras conference. They used uprisings by tribes in the Moroccan-Algerian border area as a pretext for systematically occupying Moroccan territory, and they reacted to the assassination of a French doctor by occupying the east Moroccan town of Oujda in April 1907. When local tribes showed resistance to the erection of European buildings near Casablanca, French troops occupied the town and its surroundings in August 1908.

In order to hamper the French advance, the German government backed Sultan 'Abd al-'Aziz against France in 1906/07, seeking to turn him into a pliant tool of German policy. But when his rival gained the upper hand, they dropped him and pinned their hopes on Moulay Hafidh, who was given arms and diplomatic support. Moulay Hafidh accepted this aid, but avoided any one-sided alignment with Germany although the Berlin government asked the other powers to recognize him as the legitimate ruler. An incident in September 1908, in which members of the French Foreign Legion escaped with support from the German consul in Casablanca, put an additional severe strain on Franco-German relations.

At the same time, until 1911 the Imperial Government shunned any political or military intervention against further French expansion in Morocco. There were several reasons for its inaction: (i) the general political situation (the Bosnian crisis, British support for French moves in Morocco, growing Anglo-German antagonism on account of naval rivalry); (ii) the negative attitude of its ally Austria-Hungary; and (iii) the unwillingness of powerful capitalist interests, notably the Deutsche Bank, to come out openly against France in Morocco. Finally, the efforts to win Moulay Hafidh, who had definitely become the country's ruler in September 1908, as an ally had ended in failure. (He had aligned himself with the French.) Mainly because of the situation created by the Bosnian crisis the Imperial Government decided to adopt a more conciliatory attitude towards the French and, politically speaking, to sound the retreat from Morocco. This led to the conclusion of the Franco-German agreement of 9 February 1909.[15]

The agreement strengthened France's position in that Germany expressly acknowledged "France's special political interests" and pledged "not to hinder these interests". France, for its part, promised not to hinder the economic activities of German subjects. The two parties declared that they would "seek to involve their nationals jointly in such business ventures as these are able to enter into". At the same time, the German government ceased to give overt support to the "claims" of the Mannesmann brothers and began encouraging collaboration between German and French companies in Morocco. This partial abandonment of earlier plans evoked an increasingly hostile response from politicians and newspapers in the Pan-German and nationalist camp. More and more insistently, the government was urged not to put up with France's unilateral demolition of Moroccan independence, but to secure acceptance of the Mannesmanns' dubious mining concessions and to safeguard Germany's "equal economic status" in Morocco. Its persistent

---

[15] *Handbuch der Verträge*, op. cit., p. 118.

efforts to arrange an agreement between the Mannesmanns and the Union des Mines Marocaines came to nothing in 1910, owing to the intransigence of the brothers who rejected any compromise formula which did not guarantee them a dominant position in Morocco's mines.

The further advance of French imperialism provided ample ammunition for attacks on the government of Chancellor Theobald von Bethmann Hollweg. French firms were gaining a decisive share in the international companies which had been formed after the Algeciras conference to "open up" Morocco (building railways, roads, ports and mines), and were pushing German companies out of their way. Whenever contracts for public works were awarded, the French invariably made the most lucrative deals. In 1910 France took control of the bulk of Morocco's revenue as a guarantee for a 90 million francs loan, while Spain extended its sphere of influence on Morocco's Mediterranean coast. The general course of developments in Morocco provoked resentment even among those sections of the German bourgeoisie who were directly interested in cooperating with France, and therefore the government found it increasingly difficult to withstand the pressure which the most aggressive elements of the ruling classes were exerting on it. In the spring of 1911, the Pan-German League, plying on the growing ill-feeling and unrest in the business world, began a strident campaign in which it once again demanded the partition of the Sultanate between Germany and France. The thirst for profits and power was clearly driving both powers into a conflict.

This was the situation confronting the German Foreign Secretary, Alfred von Kiderlen-Wächter, when the French Ambassador in Berlin officially notified him on 4 April 1911 that France would have to send troops into Morocco's interior to subdue rebellious tribes there. The Wilhelmstrasse now began to observe the changing Moroccan scene carefully, and the "Swabian Bismarck", as Kiderlen was derisively called by his detractors, worked out a plan of measures to be put into effect in the event of French reinforcements being moved up to Fez, the Sultan's residence. Chancellor Bethmann Hollweg and the Emperor agreed to his idea of securing a "pawn" on the south Moroccan coast. Kiderlen's answer to the French occupation of Fez was to dispatch the gunboat Panther to Agadir on 1 July 1911 in a provocative display of strength which resulted in the Second Moroccan Crisis and brought the world to the brink of war.

The published sources and the results of historical research, notably Fritz Fischer's "Krieg der Illusionen. Die deutsche Politik von 1911 bis 1914" (published in 1969), show that Kiderlen had the following objectives in mind as the instigator of the Panther incident and during the subsequent negotiations with France:

1. The dispatch of the gunboat, explained to the public as necessary because of (alleged) threats to (non-existent) German settlements in southern Morocco, was a very risky gamble which inevitably brought the danger of a European war very close. It was a risk deliberately taken[16] in order to extract colonial concessions from France. Kiderlen appears to have seriously believed that he would be able to intimidate the French and obtain substantial compensation from them without having to reckon with Britain's massive resistance and readiness to go to war.

2. The decision to send the Panther to Agadir had been much influenced by domestic developments. It was feared that the Social Democrats might score a great victory at the forthcoming general elections. Bethmann Hollweg, who was constantly criticized by the now very influential Pan-German League for his supposed moderation, needed a resounding foreign policy success so that the elections would take place in an atmosphere of triumphant chauvinism. The aim was to defeat the Social Democrats and, at the same time, to improve the government's relations with those parts of the ruling class which were vehemently demanding more active expansionism.

3. As regards the specific demands to be made to the French rival, the picture emerging from the sources is somewhat contradictory. Whereas Kiderlen, in a memorandum of 3 May 1911 intended for the Kaiser, said the aim of dispatching warships was to secure a "pawn" and then wait and see "whether France will offer us adequate compensation from her colonial possessions, in return for which we could then withdraw from the two ports"[17], Kiderlen and Undersecretary Arthur Zimmermann both repeatedly told representatives of the Pan-German League in confidential talks that the aim was to secure a permanent German foothold in southern Morocco. (Agadir was the maritime outlet of the Sous region, which the Association had urged should be occupied in a memorandum addressed to Kiderlen on 11 March.) The demand for the annexation of that part of Morocco was, in fact, the theme of the unrestrained propaganda campaign staged by the Pan-German lobby with the connivance of the Foreign Secretary. Within days of the Panther incident the League's chairman, Heinrich Class, published a pamphlet

---

[16] Cf. *K. Riezler*, Tagebücher, Aufsätze, Dokumente, prefaced and ed. by K. D. Erdmann, Göttingen, 1972 (Deutsche Geschichtsquellen des 19. und 20. Jahrhunderts, vol. 48), pp. 178—179.

[17] *GP*, vol. 29, no. 10549, p. 107.

entitled "Westmarokko deutsch!", but the prospect of a German-ruled western Morocco remained as remote as ever.

Some of Kiderlen's statements and his conduct at the Franco-German talks following the gunboat episode strongly suggest that he had set his sights primarily on the French Congo. At any rate he adopted a flexible approach on the "compensation" issue in order to extract as high a price as possible.

4. The incorporation of the French Congo into the German colonial empire was meant to be a step towards a great "German Central Africa", a desideratum of Pan-German policians since the late 1890s which had become the principal target of German colonial expansion in sub-Saharan Africa. On this score the views of the Pan-Germans tallied with those of the government and the big banks.

The exercise in gunboat diplomacy was welcomed by the coal and steel magnates, partly with the forthcoming elections in mind, partly in the hope of gaining control over the ores of southern Morocco. But when it became clear that the government would probably fail to gain a foothold in Morocco, they protested. Fritz Thyssen, Hugo Stinnes, Louis Röchling, Emil Kirdorf, and Krupp's manager, Frielinghaus, demanded on 27 July that Kiderlen should guarantee raw materials supplies from Morocco even if this "should give rise to serious consequences".[18]

Predictably, the Panther episode, which reflected a total disregard for political realities, proved a dismal failure. The decision in favour of a more or less veiled Fashoda, as Tirpitz put it, was taken in the first half of September. Germany's naval strength was thought to be insufficient for a major war, and international developments had followed a different course from what Kiderlen-Wächter had expected. Despite the hopes cherished by the German side, the British had made it abundantly plain that in the event of war they would come to the aid of the French. The Royal Navy was put on the alert, and the Director of Military Operations went to France to prepare joint military measures. Austria-Hungary indicated that she would not come to Germany's aid in the event of a war over Morocco. At the same time, the campaign of protest organized throughout Germany by the Social Democratic Party reached a climax owing to the efforts of the party's revolutionary wing, although the executive was temporizing. In those weeks the socialist labour movement defended world peace and proved that they were ready, in the words of

---

[18] Quoted from: *F. Fischer*, Krieg der Illusionen. Die deutsche Politik von 1911 bis 1914. Düsseldorf 1969, p. 128.

Karl Liebknecht, to "undo the designs hatched in the diplomatic thieves' kitchen of capitalism's colonial buccaneers."[19]

Protacted diplomatic negotiations between Germany and France ultimately led to the signing, on 4 November 1911, of conventions on Morocco and Equatorial Africa.[20] In these documents the German government conceded to France "full freedom of action" in Morocco and acquiesced in further military occupation and the establishment of a French protectorate. The French government promised to uphold the principles of the "open door" and equal economic opportunities for other powers. In Articles 5 and 7 of the convention on Morocco it undertook to show regard for the ore interests of the Mannesmann brothers by exempting ores from export duties, levying equal taxes on all mining enterprises and permitting the establishment of rail links between mines and ports. In return for the German concessions France ceded 295,000 square kilometres of territory in the French Congo adjoining Cameroon while at the same time receiving the so-called Duck's Bill, a strip of land at the northeastern tip of Cameroon 12,000 square kilometres in area.

Not only the most adventurist elements of the ruling class, as represented by the Pan-German League, but also very large sections of the bourgeoisie generally as well as the Junkers (East Elbe landowners) came out strongly against the treaty and passed strictures on the Imperial Government. Notwithstanding the government's attempts to justify its decision, it was obvious that German imperialism's policy of colonial expansion had suffered a severe setback. But since this policy resulted from the disparity between Germany's economic and military might and her very modest share in the exploitation of overseas colonies, it would have been inconceivable for Bethmann Hollweg to abandon it. On the contrary: he was put under even greater pressure to achieve some success in this area at long last. A memorandum of 2 December 1911 entitled "On Germany's Military Situation" and signed by the Chief of the General Staff, von Moltke, said that in the field of overseas policy Germany should "pursue an offensive strategy. Her fast-growing population points imperatively to the need for colonial expansion, even though such a course of action is bound to lead to a clash with England's notions of world domination sooner or later."[21]

---

[19] *K. Liebknecht*, Marokko-Hundstagspolitik, in: Gesammelte Reden und Schriften, vol. IV, Berlin 1961, pp. 451—452.

[20] *Handbuch der Verträge*, op. cit., pp. 123ff.

[21] Quoted from: *F. Fischer*, op. cit., p. 176.

The Second Moroccan Crisis put an end to all efforts to soften the Franco-German rivalry through an economic and financial rapprochement, which influenced relations between Berlin and Paris from 1906 and 1910, especially in the colonial sphere. It was now more manifest than ever before that the deep contradictions between the imperialist powers could not be resolved by peaceful means. Exacerbated by the waves of chauvinism let loose by aggressive interest groups, these contradictions drove the ruling classes of both countries on towards a military solution in keeping with the inner logic of the imperialist system.

Having been given a free hand in Morocco, on 30 March 1912 France forced the Sultan to sign a "protection treaty", thereby bringing the greater part of Morocco completely under their sway. Spain also took part in the outright subjugation of the country. Under the terms of the Franco-Spanish treaty of 27 November 1912 she received a 50-kilometre-wide strip along Morocco's Mediterranean coast.

Up to the outbreak of the First World War German imperialists continued to participate in the exploitation of Morocco. The Mannesmann brothers, although their prospects for ore mining were now gloomier than ever, managed to increase their enormous landed properties and to expand their trading network as well as establishing many plantations. Still hoping to create a German sphere of influence in the south, they supplied arms to the tribal leaders in the Sous region who were fighting the French.

Trade between Germany and Morocco attained 27 million marks in 1912, but dropped to 22.9 million in 1913.[22] In the field of Morocco's financial exploitation, in the mining sector and in the area of public works, German firms had very few chances after 1911. In 1913, therefore, the Berliner Handelsgesellschaft, the A. Schaaffhausensche Bankverein and the Deutsche Orientbank (founded in 1906 by the Dresdner Bank, the A. Schaaffhausensche Bankverein and the Nationalbank für Deutschland) sold their agencies and the landed property they had acquired for speculative purposes to French companies.

2. The Quest for "German Central Africa"

The idea of a powerful colony in Central Africa, "a German India in Africa" (W. Hübbe-Schleiden 1882) which would be the cornerstone of the German colonial empire, began to appear in German colonial

---

[22] *Statistisches Jahrbuch* für das Deutsche Reich, vol. 35, 1914, p. 253.

propaganda in the first half of the 1880s[23] and it influenced early attempts to expand the German "protectorates" along the coast toward the inland regions of the continent. Vast colonies, uniting large stretches of land into a single territory, would offer access to the markets of the African interior. These attempts only met with very limited success because the partition of Africa was already well advanced and other colonial powers promptly took preventive action (for example in 1885 Britain in Bechuanaland to forestall Germany), and because the Africans themselves put up an intense resistance. Thus for instance, the attempt in the early 1890s by the adventurer Eduard Schnitzer (known as Emin Pasha) to establish a territorial link between German East Africa and Cameroon was doomed to failure from its very inception.

It was no longer possible to create a large, undivided German empire in Africa without provoking serious conflicts with other great powers. When Bismarck and his successor, Caprivi, refused to risk confrontations with these powers for the sake of colonial issues, they could count on the relative lack of interest in tropical colonies among large sections of the German bourgeoisie until the mid-1890s. Germany did not until c. 1894 seek to add to the four scattered colonies of Togo, Cameroon, German South West Africa and German East Africa.

Although Germany's African colonies had great economic potential that was far from being fully exploited in the years before 1914, the ruling classes expressed increasing dissatisfaction from the mid-1890s onwards with the "crumbs" which their tardy country had collected from the colonial cake. Their discontent prompted intensive efforts to penetrate other powers' colonies by economic means[24] and later an attempt was made at further territorial expansion at the expense of the weakest rival (and, of course, at the expense of the Africans).[25]

When the administration of German East Africa sought to use the army rebellions on the Upper Congo which began in 1895 as an excuse to intervene in the Congo Free State, they were evidently responding

---

[23] One example is *B. Schwarz*, Ein deutsches Indien und die Teilung der Erde, Leipzig 1884.

[24] *L. Rathmann*, Zur Ägyptenpolitik des deutschen Imperialismus vor dem ersten Weltkrieg. In: Geschichte und Geschichtsbild Afrikas, Berlin 1960, pp. 73ff.; *M. Ashiwaju*, German economic and political penetration of Nigeria 1840—1900. Thesis, University of Leipzig 1968; *H. Müller*, Bremen und Westafrika. Wirtschafts- und Handelsbeziehungen . . . 1841—1914, part II. In: Jahrbuch der Wittheit zu Bremen XVII (1973), pp. 75—148.

[25] For the attempts of 1894—96 to turn the Boer republic of Transvaal into a German sphere of influence cf. chap. IV.

to the desires of chauvinist colonial circles for a redistribution of Central Africa. This was formulated in a petition to the Reich government from the Pan-German League on 25 March 1895: "In our opinion the most advantageous outcome of liquidating the Congo State would be for the northern part to be ceded to France and the southern part to an 'Africa British from the Cape to the Nile' and, should the Portuguese possessions in Africa then also be liquidated, an eleventh-hour opportunity would arise to make good the unfortunate earlier failure to establish a link between the German possessions in East Africa and in West or South West Africa and thereby to assure Germany of her rightful place in South Africa."[26]

Thus the concept of "German Central Africa", which was to become such an important objective, began to take shape.

In 1890 and 1894 the German government had thwarted British attempts to establish a territorial link between Northern Rhodesia and Uganda as part of the British connection from Cairo to the Cape which would have severed German East Africa from the "Congo Free State". They remained hesitant, however, about the proposal to divide up the enormous Congo colony, clearly expecting that this would create more foreign policy problems than benefits. But after Bülow had been appointed Foreign Secretary in 1897 he took up the suggestion to partition the Portuguese possessions. As the twentieth century drew nearer, German imperialism found that a redistribution of the colonies in its favour was very much on the agenda. Experience would show, however, that this redistribution could not be achieved by peaceful means.

Britain's diplomatic isolation and its plans for aggression against the Boer Republics prompted the British government in 1898 to take up Germany's proposals and agree to share Angola, Mozambique and Portuguese Timor between them if Portugal did not pay interest punctually on a loan that the two powers might grant it jointly. (Customs and other revenues from these colonies were to serve as security and in this event would be put under the control of British and German authorities.) Germany was to receive southern and northern Angola, northern Mozambique and Timor, while southern Mozambique and central Angola

---

[26] Source: *H. Loth*, Kolonialismus und "Humanitätsintervention". Kritische Untersuchung der Politik Deutschlands gegenüber dem Kongostaat (1884—1908), Berlin 1966, p. 82. The League's Chairman, Hasse, had already made a demand in the Reichstag in February 1894 that the government should work to achieve a large African empire that should stretch from Cameroon to East Africa. StBVR, II. Sess. 1893/94, vol. 2, pp. 1327—1328, 1330ff.

would fall to Britain. In return, the German government undertook to cease all support for the Boers.[27]

The Angola Agreement laying down these terms, which was signed by Germany and Britain in August 1898, was the first document stipulating far-reaching plans to enlarge Germany's colonial possessions in Africa by taking over a large part of the Portuguese colonial empire. The German government then sought to prepare the transfer with a policy of *pénétration pacifique* in southern Angola and by putting pressure on Britain and Portugal. But these intentions came to naught: the British government made sure that the Portuguese loan provided for in the treaty was never granted, and so there was no basis for dividing the Portuguese possessions.

It is significant how many annexationist hopes were voiced by the German side in the 1898 negotiations with Britain[28] and how Bülow, as Foreign Secretary, assessed the Agreement for Wilhelm II as a "great success", which would "secure for us the sole reversion of an area twice as large as the German Empire, enabling us to extend the borders of our two most important colonies in the best possible manner — with access to the Zambezi for East Africa and to Tiger Bay for South West Africa — and finally offering the desired prospects of two new, valuable bases on the Congo."[29] Was the German government already considering a land bridge between German South West Africa, Cameroon and German East Africa as a long-term aim? The present state of research does not permit a definite answer. It is a fact, however, that projects for building railways right across Africa from West to East began to be pursued seriously in Germany the following year.[30] After the turn of the century, when the hopes for a partition of Angola and Mozambique remained unfulfilled, the view taken in government circles was that Britain had cheated Germany of its price for neutrality in the Boer War.

---

[27] The text of the Angola Treaty of 30 Aug. 1898 is printed in: *British Documents* on the Origin of the War, 1898—1914, vol. I. London 1927, pp. 71—73. After the treaty was signed, Governor Liebert of German East Africa began preparations on his own initiative for a military occupation of the northern half of Mozambique. *E. v. Liebert*, Aus einem bewegten Leben. Erinnerungen, Munich 1925, p. 162.

[28] Cf. *GP*, vol. 14, no. 3806, Annex, Bülow to Hatzfeld, 8 June 1898.

[29] *GP*, vol. 14, no. 3867, Bülow to Wilhelm II, 24 Aug. 1898. Here, too, 1898 proved to be a significant date marking the start of colonial redistribution. Germany failed to do to Portugal what the USA succeeded in doing to Spain.

[30] *A. S. Jerussalimski*, Die Aussenpolitik und die Diplomatie des deutschen Imperialismus Ende des 19. Jahrhunderts, Berlin 1954, pp. 706ff.

"German Central Africa" finally became a direct aim of German imperialist expansion with the Morocco Agreement signed by Germany and France in 1909.[31] The craving for as big a share as possible of the natural resources in the primeval forests of the Congo Basin resulted in the demand that France hand over its Congolese colony, whose acquisition had originally been mooted during the first Moroccan Crisis; Wilhelm II attached particular importance to it.[32] The first efforts to penetrate into this colony took as their starting-point the agreement in the Morocco treaty of 1909 on joint colonial business ventures by citizens of the two countries. German diplomats actively promoted a project for a Franco-German financial consortium to exploit an enormous territory by the N'Goko-Sangha near the border with Cameroon. In 1911 after the parliament in Paris had put an end to this plan, which was bound up with fraudulent "claims to compensation" by French financiers, the Foreign Office under its new State Secretary, von Kiderlen-Wächter, tried to impose a scheme on the unwilling French government for a Franco-German railway to run from Cameroon through the French and Belgian Congo to German East Africa.[33] But this scheme came to nothing.

It was also in 1911 that Kiderlen-Wächter presented a formal demand for the entire French Congo as compensation for Germany's recognition of the French protectorate over Morocco. The sources show that the Panther incident at Agadir was primarily staged to further Germany's designs on the Congo. The day before the Panther anchored, Kiderlen-Wächter told Admiral von Müller, Chief of the Imperial Naval Cabinet, that "one must set oneself great aims in politics, not everyday ones . . . The extra piece of Central Africa that we would acquire was a link in the plan for crossing Africa as a counterplan to a British Africa from

[31] On the "Reorientation of German colonial policy" towards Belgium cf. *B. v. Bülow*, Denkwürdigkeiten, vol. 3, Berlin 1931, pp. 78ff.; *J. Willequet*, Le Congo belge et la Weltpolitik (1894—1914), Brussels 1962, pp. 227ff.

[32] A Colonial Office memorandum of 19 Sept. 1907 specified as maximum demand to France for compensation in return for relinquishing Morocco that Cameroon be enlarged by parts of the French Congo colony as far as the Ubangi and Congo Rivers in the south and east and the 5° latitude in the north, i.e. "Gabon and almost all of Middle Congo" and Dahomey. At some future time this combination of territories could perhaps be further enlarged by the Belgian Congo. *J.-C. Allain*, Agadir 1911. Une crise impérialiste en Europe pour la conquête du Maroc, Paris 1976, p. 398.

[33] *GP*, vol. 29, nos. 10573, 10574, Schoen to the Foreign Office, 15 June 1911, and Zimmermann to Kiderlen, 15 June 1911.

the Nile to the Cape."[34] On 17 July the Foreign Secretary wrote to the Imperial Chancellor von Bethmann Hollweg: "We must have the entire French Congo — it is the last opportunity, without fighting — to obtain something of use in Africa. Attractive pieces of the [French] Congo with rubber and ivory are of no use to us, however good they look; we must reach right up to the Belgian Congo so that we can take part if it should be divided up and so that we, for as long as this set-up still exists, obtain the connection across it to our own East Africa. Any other solution would mean defeat for us, and we can only avoid that by showing firm determination."[35] On the following day, Bethmann Hollweg explicitly approved these sentiments. Kiderlen tried to make it easier for the French government to hand over their Congo colony by offering them a part of northern Cameroon together with Togo in return.

After the First World War, Kiderlen's assistant in the newspaper world, Ernst Jäckh, wrote that his Morocco policy "not only aimed to find the way to a settlement between Germany and France, but also a way to [establish] a German Central Africa that would link together Cameroon, the Congo and German East Africa and connect them with German South West Africa by an agreement on the Belgian Congo and Portuguese Angola."[36]

In late 1911 imperialist Germany, internationally isolated as it was, had to accept a limited Congo compensation in one form or another. Given Kiderlen-Wächter's objectives, he opted for the formula which seemed to offer the best chances for setting up an unbroken link from Cameroon towards the south-east, in spite of vehement opposition from the Imperial Colonial Office under von Lindequist. (The latter regarded the territories to be ceded by France as worthless.) He also wanted Germany to be granted the right of pre-emption to parts of the Belgian

---

[34] W. Görlitz (ed.), Der Kaiser. Aufzeichnungen des Chefs des Marinekabinetts Admiral Georg Alexander von Müller über die Ära Wilhelms II, Göttingen 1965, pp. 87—88.

[35] Source: E. Jäckh (ed.), Kiderlen-Wächter der Staatsmann und Mensch. Vol. 2, Stuttgart 1924, p. 129. The German Naval Attaché in London described an interview with Kiderlen at that time as follows: "With the aid of a totally inadequate map from Stieler's Atlas, printed in 1868, Kiderlen allocated us large parts of French Central Africa with the hinterland and the northern bank of the Congo Estuary, counting, furthermore, upon the cession of the French claims to the Belgian Congo." W. Widenmann, Marine-Attaché an der Kaiserlich-deutschen Botschaft in London 1907—1912, Göttingen 1952, p. 183.

[36] E. Jäckh, op. cit., p. 224.

Congo, which was then enjoyed by France.[37] The Agreement finally signed by Germany and France on 4 November provided, among other things, for a part of the French Congo to the east of Cameroon, which touched the Belgian Congo in two places, to be transferred to Germany. Although the Morocco Treaty of 4 November 1911 was a severe defeat for German diplomacy, a number of important monopoly capitalists showed their approval of what Kiderlen-Wächter had achieved. Karl Helfferich, Director of the Deutsche Bank, drafted a declaration of support which was signed immediately by twenty leading bankers, industrialists and colonial entrepreneurs.[38] Most of the coal and steel magnates of the Rhine and Ruhr, however, rejected the treaty, complaining that government policy had not been sufficiently aggressive and that the result of the Panther demonstration was far too meagre.

Throughout 1912 and 1913, discussions took place in the press and in the Reichstag concerning various plans to build a railway from Cameroon to German East Africa; when the DKG held its annual meeting in June 1912, it set up a committee to look into the question.

No sooner had the Treaty between Germany and France been signed, in which Germany recognized the French protectorate in Morocco in return for parts of the French Congo, than German official circles turned their attention once more to sharing out the Portuguese colonies between Britain and Germany. (It is only a matter of secondary interest here that both the Morocco-Congo deal and the intended carve-up of Angola and Mozambique were also designed to weaken the Triple Entente.) Since the British government had declared a willingness to make some concessions to Germany's colonial ambitions (at the cost of third parties, of course), the German ambassador in London, Metternich, responded to a suggestion from the Reich Chancellor and proposed in late 1911 that Britain might take Mozambique and Germany Angola, while the British would pledge to support Germany in its intentions regarding the Belgian Congo.[39] "The second stipulation showed which way the

---

[37] Although Hallgarten has provided an outline of the background and motivations of this policy, which almost plunged Europe into war in 1911 (*G. W. F. Hallgarten*, Imperialismus vor 1914, vol. 2, 2nd ed., Munich 1963, pp. 219ff.), there is still no satisfactory comprehensive and detailed study based on the unpublished files.

[38] Among the signatories were Albert Ballin, Konrad von Borsig, Carl Duisberg, Friedrich Lenz, Max Schinckel, Alexander Schoeller, August Thyssen, Hermann Wallich, and Eduard Woermann. Vossische Zeitung of 10 Nov. 1911.

[39] *GP*, vol. 31, nos. 11338, 11339, Bethmann Hollweg to Metternich, 6 Dec. 1911 and Metternich to Bethmann Hollweg, 9 Dec. 1911. "Then", added Metternich, "we

wind was blowing," wrote Hallgarten. "It also demonstrated that this
was hardly a home-grown plan of the Ambassador's. The rather drily
formulated proposal — for acquiring the Belgian Congo and building
a railway from Cameroon to East Africa (*GP*, Vol. 31, No. 11 345) — was
no more nor less than the logical continuation of the policy on Morocco
and the Congo which Germany had been pursuing in the summer, which
Director Helfferich and the Deutsche Bank were busy turning to account from the practical angle at precisely the same moment . . ."[40]
Meanwhile, eminent ideologues such as Theodor Schiemann and Hans
Delbrück put forward suggestions aimed at a substantial expansion of
Germany's footholds in Central Africa in the newspapers.

A "German Central Africa" was — strange as it may seem — seen
as a step which might help to decrease antagonism between Germany
and Britain, and it was strongly supported for this reason especially by
a small but not insignificant group of the ruling class which took a more
objective view of the international balance of forces than was customary
amongst the overwhelming majority of that class, and particularly
amongst high-ranking army and naval officers and the more powerful
magnates of heavy industry. This group, which included Rathenau,
Ballin, Solf, Kühlmann and Metternich, was anxious to avoid, or at
least postpone, a war with Britain. It saw a large African colony as
an attractive alternative to the boundless ambitions which the Pan-
Germans harboured for annexing pieces of Europe, ambitions increasingly supported by the German bourgeoisie during the years 1911 to 1914.

Even Chancellor Bethmann Hollweg repeatedly showed sympathies
for this group, which was particularly opposed to further increases in
naval armaments. In January 1912, before some additions to the fleet

---

shall have laid the foundations of a colonial empire greater than any German government has ever dreamed about."

[40] *G. W. F. Hallgarten*, op. cit., vol. 2, p. 278. A French historian has written: ". . .
ces pourparlers donnent la mesure des convoitises allemandes en Afrique centrale;
l'accord franco-allemand de 1911 avait permis aux Allemands d'inaugurer l'ère
des réalisations territoriales, de devenir à l'ouest, comme ils l'étaient déjà à l'est, les
voisins du Congo belge et de couper en deux notre Afrique Equatoriale Française;
l'acquisition de l'Angola aurait constitué une nouvelle étape dans l'encerclement des
possessions de la Belgique et de la France et aurait incité les Allemands à revendiquer
la part du lion lors du dépeçage escompté de ces deux colonies. Ainsi se laissent
constamment entrevoir, à travers ces pourparlers, les projets germaniques de Mittelafrika." *P. Dubois*, Les négociations anglo-allemandes relatives aux colonies portu-
gaises de 1912 à 1914, Revue d'histoire de la guerre mondiale, 1939, p. 367.

were to be put before the Reichstag, he stressed to Valentini, head of the Imperial Civilian Cabinet, and Müller, head of the Imperial Naval Cabinet (both Cabinets were advisory bodies serving the Emperor), "our peaceful chances with England, if we refrained now from building new Dreadnoughts. We would be able to form a great colonial empire (Portuguese colonies, Belgian Congo, Dutch colonies) and drive a wedge into the Triple Entente . . ."

Observations like this were designed to influence Wilhelm II. Indeed, Müller reported that several weeks later, the Kaiser could already see "himself as the political leader of the United States of Europe with a colonial empire for Germany right across Central Africa".[41] Negotiations with the British government on the Portuguese colonies continued throughout 1912 and 1913. Even after the failure of Haldane's mission, the British Foreign Office tended to take an accomodating stance, in order to strengthen the opponents of rapid increases in naval armament within German government circles and to sidetrack Britain's impetuous and dangerous German rival into areas where no vital interests of British imperialism were at stake.

The attitude of the British Foreign Office gave the German negotiators certain possibilities, with the result that the Convention initialled in October 1913 by the British Foreign Secretary Grey and Germany's *chargé d'affaires* in London, von Kühlmann, granted the German side considerably more advantages than the Angola Treaty of 1898. The Convention provided for almost all of Angola (notably the entire coastline and the regions along the border with the Belgian Congo) as well as northern Mozambique (slightly reduced) to be allocated to Germany. Implementation could begin even "if in any part of the provinces of Mozambique or Angola the lives or property of British or German subjects, or the vital interests of the adjoining British or German dominions or protectorates, are endangered by local disturbances or by the action of the local authorities, and the Portuguese Government are not in a position to afford the necessary protection, or otherwise fail to do so . . ." (Art. 8).[42] The history of German imperialism and its expansionist

---

[41] *W. Görlitz* (ed.), Der Kaiser . . . Aufzeichnungen des Chefs des Marinekabinetts Admiral Georg Alexander von Müller . . ., pp. 107, 112.

[42] *British Documents* . . . vol. X, 2, no. 341, p. 539. The text of the Preamble also offered numerous opportunities to intervene in the Portuguese colonies. "The opportunities for constructing a large, compact German colonial empire were to be firmly underpinned in every direction," wrote the Embassy Councillor *Richard von Kühlmann*, who had participated in the negotiations, in his: Erinnerungen, Heidelberg 1948, p. 344.

policy suggests that not much time would have passed until those "vital interests" were considered to be "endangered", had the Convention actually been signed. There was so much at stake: the territories allocated to Germany amounted to about 1,600,000 square kilometres, whereas Germany's entire colonial possessions in Africa at that time totalled 2,660,000 square kilometres. Besides, these territories offered excellent natural harbours and a wide range of valuable natural resources.[43]

The British negotiators had managed to evade any clear stipulations on the subject of the Belgian Congo. Nonetheless, when the Germans claimed towards the end of 1913 that a virtual agreement had been reached informally on sharing the Belgian colony between the two powers, they did not voice any objections.[44] On the other hand there was no agreement on the German request for Britain's protectorate, Zanzibar, since the price the British demanded, Urundi, seemed too high.

The German Foreign Office and the Colonial Secretary, Wilhelm Solf, who had taken a look around Mozambique in August 1912,[45] prepared a takeover of the regions laid down in the Anglo-German Convention by promoting various forms of *pénétration pacifique* from 1912 onwards in collaboration with the Deutsche Bank and the Hamburg banking company M. M. Warburg & Co. The Deutsche Bank played the leading role in this, with Warburg assuming a kind of managerial function, but the guiding force behind the scenes was the Reich government, as the sources demonstrate clearly.

---

[43] The German minister in Lisbon, Friedrich Rosen, who played an important part in pursuing these plans, was later to write in his memoirs: "The ultimate aim of our colonial policy had to be a large, central African empire from the Atlantic to the Indian Ocean, an empire whose vast territory would have to be joined together and developed by railways and navigable rivers. There was nothing Utopian about this aim. Its realization was, in spite of the French option to purchase, simply the natural course of events, as they were bound to develop, so to speak, of their own accord once the Anglo-German agreement on the Portuguese colonial empire had come into force." *F. Rosen*, Aus einem diplomatischen Wanderleben, vol. 2, Berlin 1932, p. 84.

[44] *P. H. S. Hatton*, Harcourt and Solf: The Search for an Anglo-German Understanding through Africa, 1912—1914. In: European Studies Review I, No. 2, 1971, p. 128.

[45] *E. von Vietsch*, Wilhelm Solf. Botschafter zwischen den Seiten, Tübingen 1961, p. 111. In Mozambique Solf made a note that the Portuguese were "now fossilized and must make way for stronger and fresher nations. One positively feels that England or Germany must sometime lay her hands on these colonies." Op. cit., p. 124.

In mid-1913 an opportunity presented itself to purchase the majority of shares in the Benguela Railway, which was being built in Angola from Benguela to Katanga, through a German-Belgian consortium. At that time there was little capital available for projects outside Europe, and the necessary 30 million marks could not be raised through the banks. Therefore Bethmann Hollweg insisted that the money be funded by the state, and carried his point. Solf had already made sure in the negotiations with the British government that all the territory through which the railway was to run would fall to Germany under the Convention between Germany and Britain. However, the plan finally came to nothing, not least because of a French intervention in London.

In late 1913 an "Overseas Studies Syndicate" was formed by the Deutsche Bank, the Disconto-Gesellschaft, the Berliner Handelsgesellschaft (large Berlin banks), and the Hamburg companies Hamburg-Amerika-Linie (Hapag), Woermann-Linie, Norddeutsche Bank and M. M. Warburg & Co. The Friedrich Krupp A. G., Essen, also joined the Syndicate, which, in April 1914, sent a group of experts to Moçamedes in Angola to decide on the best route for a railway from the coast eastwards. Shortly before this, with the assistance of the German Minister in Lisbon, Rosen, and Ambassador von Schön in Paris, representatives of the Syndicate had drafted a concession from the Portuguese government to build a railway from Moçamedes to Humbe, near the border with German South West Africa, which Rosen was to submit to the Lisbon government.[46]

The Minister was able to link this proposal to a project presented to the Portuguese parliament in May for developing the colonial economy in Angola. £8 million was to be borrowed abroad for the purpose.[47] In July the Portuguese Foreign Minister Freire d'Andrade complained to the British Minister in Lisbon "that the Germans were becoming very pressing in their demands for the Angola loan of £ 8,000,000, which if obtained by them would include other concessions such as the port and railway in South Angola." German policy in Angola, he commented, "resembled that of a skilful general who before making a final attack occupied positions of advantage in various parts of the country. If the' Portuguese government made no attempt now to hinder those manoeuvres they would wake up one day and find that Angola had to all intents

---

[46] F. W. Pick, Searchlight on German Africa. The Diaries and Papers of Dr. W. Ch. Regendanz, London 1939, pp. 108 ff.

[47] Cf. S. E. Katzenellenbogen, Railways and the Copper Mines of Katanga, Oxford 1973, pp. 81—82.

and purposes become a German possession."[48] But this German scheme of infiltration also proved fruitless, as the Parliament in Lisbon did not give its approval to the project.

The idea behind the railway plan was both to link up with the railways in German South West Africa and to connect the coast with the ore mining region of Katanga, for the Imperial Colonial Office was, after the end of 1913, convinced that the Congo could be taken without much resistance if pressure were put on Belgium.[49] Since the East African Central Railway from Dar es Salaam to Lake Tanganyika was nearing completion, control over a route from the Atlantic to Katanga would enable the Germans to establish a communication link right across the continent without much difficulty, just as Kiderlen had attempted to achieve from Cameroon. This transcontinental connection would permit further *pénétration pacifique* in southern Angola und Katanga before an official German takeover, and "German Central Africa" would thus almost be attained. Moreover, there was a project afoot to purchase the big plantation company Cazengo in northern Angola. "Majority to be had for 6 mill. marks and thereby virtually control over Loanda, Ambaca Railway and all northern Angola", wrote Rosen, who was working to promote schemes of this kind, to Solf on 7 November 1913.[50]

A scheme pursued with regard to Mozambique came considerably nearer to reaching practical results. In May 1914, Helfferich persuaded the Syndicate to acquire a majority of shares in the Companhia do Nyassa, a charter company of monopoly character which enjoyed almost sovereign rights and nominally controlled about half of the area in northern Mozambique which had been earmarked for Germany, a territory almost as large as Britain. The outbreak of the First World War prevented the "rights" thus purchased for 3 million marks from being exploited (including the "right" to extract taxes from the people of the territory). It was intended virtually to unite the province of Niassaland, over which the company held claims, with the adjoining German East Africa. The Warburg representative responsible even headed his files "Provincial Administration of Niassaland".[51]

On the whole, *pénétration pacifique* made fairly substantial progress. Whereas there had not been much German capital involved in the Belgian

---

[48] *British Documents* . . ., vol. X, 2, no. 377, p. 577, Carnegie to Grey, 2 July 1914.

[49] *Documents diplomatiques français*, 3. S., vol. 8, no. 41.

[50] *F. Rosen*, op. cit., pp. 259—60.

[51] Ibid., pp. 165ff., 246—247, 249ff.; *F. W. Pick*, op. cit., pp. 115ff. Cf. *W. Regendanz*, Nyassaland, 2 vols., Magdeburg 1918.

Congo prior to 1908, by 1913 German firms had invested 20,578,000 gold francs there.[52] When the signing of the German-British Convention was delayed, Rosen pleaded in a memorandum of 30 May 1914 to the Foreign Office in favour of signature on the grounds that "such considerable German capital has already been committed to various colonial enterprises that there would inevitably be major losses and not entirely unjustified ill-feeling among our financiers should all their expenditure and work one day prove to have been in vain".[53]

As a West German historian who had himself been associated with imperial colonial policy wrote in 1955, there now seemed to be "immediate prospects that the programme of Central African concentration pursued by Germany under its Weltpolitik at that time would actually be implemented".[54] But the Convention was not signed, let alone implemented, for the British negotiators were not at all convinced of the urgency of dividing up the Portuguese colonies. In the summer of 1913 Metternich's successor Lichnowsky had already reproached Grey for regarding himself as a kind of medical adviser to the Portuguese colonies, while Germany wanted to inherit them.[55] Tactical doubts and diplomatic considerations on both sides led to the act of signature being postponed again and again until the July Crisis of 1914 rendered the document null and void. Such large sections of the ruling class in both countries (including the Pan-German League in Germany) had found fault with the Convention from the beginning that there were hardly any real prospects of its being put into force.

---

[52] *J. Willequet*, op. cit., p. 384. Germany's capital interests in the Belgian Congo before 1914 have not yet been looked into in detail. The Disconto-Gesellschaft seems to have led the field as one of the founders of the Compagnie du Chemin de fer du Congo. In 1909 the bank's proprietor, Franz Urbig, became a member of the railway's administrative board, and in the following year he joined the board of the copper company Union Minière du Haut Katanga, which had been founded in 1906 with a capital of 10 million Belgian francs. *M. Müller-Jabusch, Franz Urbig. Zum 23. Januar 1939.* Printed on behalf of the Deutsche Bank, n.d., pp. 140—141. The Deutsche Bank (represented on the board of directors by Helfferich), C. Woermann and the Deutsch—Ostafrikanische Gesellschaft all held shares in the Societé Commerciale Belgo-Allemande du Congo, which was founded in Brussels in 1912 and had a capital of 2 million francs. *Von der Heydt's Kolonial-Handbuch* 1913, pp. 307f.

[53] *GP*, vol. 37 (1), no. 14710.

[54] *M. von Hagen*, "Deutsche Weltpolitik und kein Krieg", Historische Zeitschrift, vol. 179, 1955, p. 303.

[55] *British Documents . . .*, vol. X, 2, no. 337, Grey to Goschen, 13 June 1913.

In February 1914 the German East African Central Railway reached Lake Tanganyika, and in April Solf approached Kiderlen's successor, von Jagow, once again with the suggestion of dividing up the Belgian Congo between Germany, France and Britain. Germany's aim should be "a broad link from German East Africa to those parts of Angola which fall within our sphere of interest".[56] Jagow was quick to act, but his move was thwarted immediately by an adamant refusal from France. Once more it became evident that any further hope of expansion of Germany's colonial possessions in Africa without a European war was an illusion.

It should be emphasized that Bethmann Hollweg, the German Foreign Office and the banks were not the only proponents of the Central African plans from 1911 onwards. For every major grouping within the German upper bourgeoisie, from the Pan-Germans to the Left Liberals around Friedrich Naumann, "German Central Africa" had become the decisive objective of colonial expansion beside Turkey. The differences of opinion about the best way of achieving this objective and the place it should be given in the list of main expansionist aims cannot obscure the fact of a general consensus in the ruling class on the subject of Central Africa, which was to continue until the defeat of German imperialism in 1918.

3. The German Share in the Exploitation of South Africa 1898—1914

South Africa, by which we mean the territory of today's Republic of South Africa without Namibia, was not among the countries attracting the biggest share of European capital at the turn of the century. Nevertheless, it was in South Africa that economic development determined by finance capital first began on the African continent. It was encouraged by the first-rate strategic situation, the many European settlers and the considerable mineral resources, and until today the activity of finance capital has been at its highest in South Africa. If we compare the size of the population with some major economic indicators, we can see how concentrated this economic involvement was. With 5,800,000 inhabitants (1910 = 4,600,000 Africans "Coloureds" and Asians; 1,200,000 people of European descent), South Africa had one of the largest populations in Africa, although this amounted to no more than 9 per cent

[56] J. Willequet, op. cit., pp. 444—447.

of the entire population of the continent. And yet, out of the £ 1,200 million which, according to Frankel, was invested in Africa from abroad between 1870 and 1936, 43 per cent flowed into South Africa, and before the First World War the proportion was even higher. In 1913, South Africa's share of African external trade was 57 per cent.

Another chapter deals with the Boer Republic of Transvaal and the way in which it entered the sphere of expansion of the big German banks and became the object of political conflict between German and British imperialism, (cf. p. 115). German diplomacy changed its course with the Anglo-German agreement on the Portuguese colonies of 30 August 1898, when Germany sacrificed the Boer nationalists and the Delagoa Bay territory, previously so hotly disputed between German and British imperialism, in favour of an Anglo-German understanding with regard to other aims of colonial expansion. When Britain's policies led to the South African War in 1899, the Kaiser's government refrained from making any gestures in support of the Boers, in contrast to their reaction at the time of the first and second Krüger Telegrams; Germany's neutral position gave the British a free hand to annex Transvaal and the Orange Free State.

This political retreat did not entail the surrender of economic influence. On the contrary, Germany's financial oligarchy remained committed to extracting as large a share as it could of the colonial profits which British financiers were making by plundering South Africa's natural resources and exploiting subjugated Africans (and later also Chinese coolies). The two monopolies controlled by German finance which enjoyed a privileged status under the Transvaal government, the Netherlands South African Railway Company and the German British Explosives Trust, clung tenaciously to their position. The Railway Company supported the Krüger government by granting it a loan of £ 2 million in March 1899;[57] during the war itself, the railway provided some valuable assistance to the Boer army.

When the Boers were defeated, the privileges that had been accorded to German capitalists by the Krüger government were lost. Prominent German businessmen, such as Wilhelm Knappe of the Berliner Handelsgesellschaft, were obliged to leave the country. In 1901 the British authorities expropriated the Netherlands South African Railway Com-

---

[57] *P. J. van Winter*, Onder Krugers Hollanders, vol. II, Amsterdam 1938, pp. 322 to 324; *J. J. Van Helten*, German Capital, the Netherlands Railway Company and the Political Economy of the Transvaal 1886—1900, in: Journal of African History, vol. XIX, 1978, pp. 384—385.

pany, offering the shareholders compensation in 1908. The South African branch of the Explosives Trust lost its monopoly without compensation, but escaped expropriation, although a British committee of investigation found that it had engaged in a considerable amount of bribery, from which, amongst others, Krüger's right-hand man, State Secretary Leyds, had benefitted, and that it had supplied the Boers with 20,000 dumdum bullets in May 1900. It was transformed to all appearances into a purely British company, but in fact this façade carefully concealed its primarily German ownership. But the British South African Explosives Company, as it had become, gradually lost its leading position, as the mining companies gave most of their orders to two new explosives companies of genuine British origin.

On the other hand, the change in German policy towards the Boers brought rewards for those German financial groups which had invested large sums in gold mining in the Transvaal. Their cooperation with British capital in the goldmining and power industries experienced a fresh upswing. The Deutsche Bank was keen to make money out of the collapse of the Boer Republics: in opening its South African branch it attempted to take the place of the Dutch banks which had been intimately linked with Boer government circles. But the plan failed owing to the strong position of the British banks and of the pound as leading currency.

Generally speaking, Germany's external trade with South Africa increased until 1914; but the shift from an active trade balance to a passive one, which became particularly clear after 1907, reflected a gradual change in the balance of forces between Germany and Britain in the latter's favour. Germany's position as a supplier to South Africa weakened as many of the Boer farmers became reconciled to British imperialism as a result of the concessions made to them to the detriment of the conquered Africans. (The Union of South Africa, a fruit of this compromise, was founded as a Dominion in 1910.) German exports to South Africa reached a record level in 1910, only to stagnate at a rather lower level from 1911 to 1913, while German imports from that country grew. From 1910 to 1914, Germany maintained an average 8.4 per cent of the South African import market, although it was becoming harder to keep up sales by this time.

There is no reliable information about the size of German capital investment in South Africa and its percentage of overall capital for the years before the war, although it is clear that a number of authors have overestimated the participation of European mainland capital in the exploitation of South Africa. The German Imperial Naval Office, for

example, stated that some 900 million marks had been invested by
Germany in 1900 in the Transvaal alone, 730 million marks of this in
mining. These statistics were presumably designed to support the case
for a larger war fleet.[58] Kubicek writes that most mining shares were
in continental hands from 1906 to 1914.[59] Such statements are probably
based on the fact that a number of major mining companies and houses
of finance in Johannesburg were founded by immigrants of German
extraction, ignoring the British or South African naturalization of most
of these businessmen and their very close links with British capital which
make it impossible to count them as members of the German bourgeoisie.
We must also remember that British interests held a considerable share
in the mining companies controlled by German banks (for example,
30 per cent in 1900 of the Goerz company and of the General Mining
and Finance Corporation).[60]

Paish[61], Gilbert[62] and others have warned against overestimating the
non-British participation. Frankel writes: "It is true that there was considerable German enterprise associated with the foundation of the Witwatersrand Gold Mining Industry, and an important German and French
holding of South African mining shares, but to regard the capital supplied
by continental investors as more than 8 % of all appears unwarranted".[63]

The accounts kept during the First World War by the South African
custodian of enemy property, published in the 1920s, give some indication as to the pre-war amount of German capital in the Union of South
Africa. The custodian calculated the total value of property held on
behalf of enemy aliens as about £14 million.[64] If the distortions and
redistributions resulting from the accounting procedures are taken into

[58] *Die deutschen Kapitalanlagen* in überseeischen Ländern. Zusammengestellt im
Reichs-Marine-Amte (Berlin 1900), pp. 10—11.

[59] *R. Kubicek*, Finance Capital and South African Goldmining 1886—1914, in: The
Journal of Imperial and Commonwealth History, vol. III, 1975, p. 387.

[60] Ibid., p. 393.

[61] *G. Paish*, Journal of the Royal Statistical Society, vol. 74, 1910/11, p. 197.

[62] *D. W. Gilbert*, The Economic Effects of the Gold Discoveries upon South Africa:
1886—1910, in: The Quarterly Journal of Economics, Cambridge, Mass., August
1933, p. 561.

[63] *S. H. Frankel*, Capital Investment in Africa, London 1938, p. 204. This estimate
relates to the whole of the Union of South Africa and Rhodesia.

[64] *Union of South Africa.* Report of the Custodian of Enemy Property (as at December
31st, 1925), Pretoria 1926. Cf. also *R. Kubicek*, Economic Imperialism in Theory
and Practice. The Case of South African Gold Mining Finance 1886—1914, Durham
1979, pp. 142—143.

consideration, the market value of pre-war investments owned by German Reich citizens amounted to about £ 13 to £ 16 million. A comparison with Frankel's figures for investments in the Union of South Africa in 1913[65] suggests that the German share of foreign capital in the private economy may have reached between 4 and 5 per cent.

Although the proportion of German capital investment was thus relatively low, it was concentrated in a small number of key areas of the economy. Mining properties alone accounted for £ 6.8 million of the proceeds from the sale of German assets.

Germany's most important asset in the gold fields of Transvaal was the holding company A. Goerz & Co. Ltd. in Johannesburg, with a registered capital of £ 1.5 million (or 30 million marks) in 1913. It was one of the leading financiers in South African gold mining alongside the Central Mining and Investment Corporation, Consolidated Gold Fields of South Africa and the General Mining and Finance Corporation. In 1906 Goerz decided to invest outside South Africa and purchased shares in Mexican and West African gold mines. Its main emphasis, however, continued to be mining rights and participation in gold mines in South Africa; it also owned shares in a diamond mine, in the Otavi-Minen- und Eisenbahn-Gesellschaft (South West Africa), and in the important British concession firm South West Africa Company Ltd. There were handsome profits. Dividends paid out in the first years ranged from 35 to 50 per cent, and later, from 1898 to 1904, for the most part from 10 to 15 per cent. The Goerz company was dominated by the Deutsche Bank, operating with the bankers Jacob S. H. Stern and, initially, the Berliner Handelsgesellschaft, for all of whom Goerz was the source of considerable surplus profits, including substantial foundation gains and commissions on the issue of new shares. The company's close links with the London capital market were a major factor in its success: a special share register was kept in London. Lord Battersea, a son-in-law of Sir Anthony de Rothschild, was chairman at one time. The Union of London and Smiths Bank Ltd., whose director was Sir Felix Schuster, was Goerz's banking partner in the City of London for many years.

The Deutsche Bank had also heavily penetrated the London-based Central Mining and Investment Corporation Ltd. (called "Corner House Group"), which in 1911 became a centre for capital concentration in South Africa and led the field in South African mining finance before the First World War with a registered capital of £ 5.1 million.

[65] *S. H. Frankel*, op. cit., pp. 89 and 150—151.

Apart from its gold-mining interests, it was a member of the diamond syndicate which controlled most of the diamond production in South Africa. German capital was represented on the board of directors primarily by Max J. E. Francke, the managing director of A. Goerz & Co. Ltd. in Johannesburg. The Corporation was dominated by mining magnates of German extraction such as Wernher, Beit, Michaelis, Eckstein and Reyersbach, who were closely connected with the City and eased the way for German capital.

German participation in the General Mining and Finance Corporation Ltd., founded in 1895 and based in Johannesburg, with an ordinary share capital of £ 1.9 million, increased when new shares were issued in 1902—3. A syndicate was formed by G. and L. Albu, the Dresdner Bank, the Disconto-Gesellschaft and S. Bleichröder, which purchased shares of a nominal value of £ 750,000. The same syndicate, joined by the A. Schaaffhausen'sche Bankverein of Cologne, in 1906 financed a further capital increase of almost £ 700,000, and in 1911 made an advance of £ 400,000 to the corporation. This combination of the Dresdner Bank, Disconto-Gesellschaft and S. Bleichröder was based on the example of A. Goerz & Co. with the Deutsche Bank, Jacob S. H. Stern and the Berliner Handelsgesellschaft. The corporation stressed the strong position of its German shareholders by setting up local boards in both London and Berlin (the latter managed by the Dresdner Bank) as well as the main board in Johannesburg. The core of its properties were nine mines with a paid-up capital in 1909 of over £ 5 million[66], but it also held shares in many other firms and possessed a large amount of land.

The Consolidated Mines Selection Company Ltd., London, with a registered capital of £ 600,000, had close links with the Bank für Handel und Industrie (Darmstädter Bank). This bank, managed at the time by Bernhard Dernburg, conducted the issue of shares to increase the company's capital in 1903 and the sale of mortgage bonds in 1905. The company had considerable investments in a number of South African gold and coal mines, ore interests in Brazil and other interests in West Africa and Australasia.

German capital also had a major stake in the South African energy sector. Siemens & Halske, in collaboration with the Deutsche Bank and Adolf Görz & Co. (the predecessor to A. Goerz & Co. Ltd.), built the Rand Central Electric Works, the first large electricity plant supplying the Witwatersrand mines.

---

[66] *R. Kubicek*, Economic Imperialism, p. 145.

But leading in the field of energy was the Victoria Falls and Transvaal Power Company Ltd., London, founded in 1906, which built four steam power stations in the Transvaal. This company and its subsidiaries, such as the Rand Mines Power Supply Co. Ltd., signed contracts to supply all the larger towns and major mining groups in the region with electricity and compressed air. The company's registered capital of £ 3 million came mainly from British sources. Of the more than £ 3 million first debenture bonds issued, the Dresdner Bank subscribed £ 625,000 in 1907, and then jointly with the Deutsche Bank £ 900,000 in 1909 and £ 1.3 million in 1911. As a result, the Victoria Falls and Transvaal Power Co. Ltd. fell within the sphere of interest of the Allgemeine Elektrizitäts-Gesellschaft (AEG), which played a decisive role in the construction of the power plants. Several plants were designed by Professor Georg Klingenberg, an AEG director. The Germans were represented on the board of directors by Emil Rathenau, Director-General of the AEG and Chairman of the Board of Directors of the Berliner Handelsgesellschaft, and Hans Schuster, who was on the board of the Dresdner Bank.

When alien property was liquidated after the First World War, it became apparent that there was also a large German stake in the diamond monopoly De Beers Consolidated Mines which had never been reflected on the board.[67]

The German financiers after c. 1900 probably did not extract the same rates of profit from their share in the colonial exploitation of South Africa as they obtained from the diamond mines in South West Africa. In the years before the war the gold mines did not pay such high dividends as they had done in the 1890s, and share prices fell. But the capital investments and the volume of trade were certainly considerably higher than in South West Africa. As a result the German monopolies' South African commitments, seen as a whole, proved more profitable than those in any German colony. Moreover, the profits from South Africa, unlike those obtained from the German colonies, did not require the government to pre-invest to any noticeable extent, nor to spend money on securing military and political control.

After Germany's blustering attempts to establish hegemony in the Transvaal had been abandoned, German finance capital thus took part in plundering South Africa in the framework of a fully developed colonial economy. German imperialism here had to accept the role of a junior

---

[67] *Union of South Afrika.* Report . . . Südafrikanische Wochenschrift, Berlin, no. 1401, 18 July 1922, p. 66.

partner, limited to the economic sphere, but the conditions were so favourable that, from the turn of the century onwards, German monopolies chose South Africa as the main area of their activities on the African continent. Within a very different international context, a situation not dissimilar was to develop after the Second World War, when West German finance capital built up substantial interests in the apartheid economy.

IX. The First World War

1. The War in Africa

The German ruling class embarked on the First World War determined
to gain world domination, which implied, inter alia, a redivision of
colonial possessions in Africa in Germany's favour. This aim was pursued
right to the bitter end in 1918. Although most belligerent great powers
attached considerable importance to objectives outside Europe, it was
clear from the start that the war, and thus the redivision of Africa, would
be decided in Europe. Consequently, the campaigns in Africa remained
a "side-show" of little importance in military terms. The attempts of
the Allies to occupy all German colonies after the beginning of the war
were motivated not by the economic value of these territories, but by
the strategic value to the German Navy of radio stations which might
transmit instructions to German warships, and of ports in overseas waters
which could serve as bases for attacks on Britain's and France's sea
communications. In the case of South West Africa, there was also a fear
of German ground attacks on the Union of South Africa. These might
be coupled with a Boer revolt instigated or supported by Germany.
Seen in the long term, the German colonies were regarded as welcome
war booty for the Allied powers which would enable them to "round
off" their own huge colonial possessions and exclude an extremely dangerous rival from the exploitation of Africa.

The General Act adopted by the Berlin Conference in 1885 had
stipulated in Articles 10 and 11 that in the event of war between powers
with colonial possessions in the Congo Basin there might be an understanding to neutralize this region, which included large sections of German East Africa and Cameroon. But after the Agadir crisis of 1911 the
prevalent opinion in the general staffs of the major powers was that
the impending war would spread to central Africa. And indeed, when
the war began, the antagonisms between the two camps immediately
proved so intense that the idea of maintaining a common front towards

the peoples of Africa as expressed in the third chapter of the General Act was abandoned very soon. The governments of Belgium, France and Germany gave some thought to the possibility of neutralization at first, and there were some diplomatic steps, but with no result.

The military operations in Africa, while ending in the complete occupation of the German colonies by the Allies, did not decide the fate of the colonies. These operations will, therefore, be described here only in brief outline.

At the outbreak of the war, the German colonies were only provided with mercenary units set up and equipped solely for the purpose of holding down the African population. (These were known as "protective forces" except in Togo where the unit was called "police troop".) Even after police units had been incorporated and German officials, farmers, employees, sailors and traders called up for military service, the German forces were still heavily outnumbered by the British, French, South African and Belgian forces confronting them. Moreover, the British maritime blockade imposed immediately after the outbreak of war cut off almost all their supply lines. So the German commanding officers were in no position to conquer the colonies of other powers but could only try to hold at least some of the German positions against the advancing Allied troops until the war in Europe had been decided. This corresponded to the instructions given by the central headquarters of the "protective forces" in Berlin, but after the failure of the blitzkrieg strategy in the Battle of the Marne and given the active or latent hostility of the African population such attempts had little chance of success. They did however claim numerous African and European lives on both sides.

Togo was the first among the German colonies to fall into the hands of the Allied powers, which thus won their first victory in the Great War. British and French colonial troops, who entered the territory on 6 August 1914 and encountered almost no resistance, were quick to occupy all major positions except for the Kamina radio station near Atakpamé. (This long-distance transmitter kept up wireless communications between Germany and the colonies in Africa.) After two brief engagements on the Lomé-Atakpamé railway line the Acting Governor Major H. G. von Doering blew up the radio station and surrendered on 26 August together with his officers, civil servants and a remnant of African mercenaries who had not yet deserted.

By contrast, the occupation of Cameroon by French and British forces was not completed until early 1916. On 28 September 1914 military contingents of these two powers were landed from warships and took Douala and Bonaberi without a fight. The five companies of the German "protective force" stationed there had retreated into the country's interior. By fighting only small delaying engagements in the Yaoundé region and in other areas (and because of poor coordination between the British and French commanders), the German troops managed to hold out until the end of 1915. Then they had to move southward and seek refuge in neutral Spanish Guinea (6—15 February 1916). In the northeastern part of Cameroon, Maroua was occupied by French forces as early as 14 September 1914; Garoua and Ngaounderé were taken by troops of both powers in June 1915, whereas a German company which had retreated into the Mora mountain fort did not surrender until February 1916.

In South West Africa, the occupation by South African forces also began in September 1914. Units put ashore in Lüderitz Bay advanced towards Windhoek in the succeeding months while other South African detachments, after the suppression of an anti-British rebellion by some Boer officers, moved into the German colony from Cape province across the Orange River. They occupied Windhoek in May 1915, driving the German forces to the northeast where the remainder of the "protective force" (some 3,400 men) under Governor Theodor Seitz surrendered at Khorab near Otavi on 9 July 1915.

The terms of surrender negotiated by Seitz and the South African Prime Minister and Commander-in-Chief Louis Botha were exceptionally generous. All German reservists were allowed to return to their homes in the colony. German private property was to remain untouched. (This meant that for the time being German economic positions were maintained at least de jure, and to some extent de facto). Botha treated his vanquished adversaries with leniency because he did not want to "impair the standing of the white race" in the eyes of the Africans in South West Africa and in the Union. He was thus following the example the British had given by their policy towards the Boers some years previously. At the same time, Botha wanted to secure documents valid in international law from which the South African government would be able to derive a claim to South West Africa in its dealings with the British.

What distinguished the war in East Africa from the hostilities in the other three colonies was the duration and extent of the fighting. In early November 1914, the German "protective force" commanded by Colonel Paul von Lettow-Vorbeck succeeded in preventing the landing of a British expeditionary corps which was seeking to gain a foothold near Tanga. On account of this victory and because the colony presented no danger to the Allied war effort, German rule could be maintained in large parts of the country until early 1916. Only when a large body of British, Indian and South African troops led by General Jan Christiaan Smuts began to mount an offensive, in April 1916, with Belgian and Rhodesian units simultaneously advancing from the west, the much reduced "protective force" had no choice but to retreat towards the south-east. On 4 September 1916 the Allies occupied Dar es Salaam. The German troops, constantly pursued by enemy forces, were able to hold out in the southeastern part of the colony up to November 1917 by undertaking long forced marches, attacking smaller enemy contingents, requisitioning food in the villages and forcibly recruiting soldiers and carriers from among the population of the areas they traversed. Seeing his forces steadily diminish, Lettow-Vorbeck then had to withdraw to Mozambique and, just before war's end, to Northern Rhodesia, where he surrendered on 14 November 1918. It had not been his primary aim to defend German East Africa, but to tie down Allied forces in a region far removed from the European theatre of war.

The military operations in East Africa were later seized upon by pro-imperialist German historians and publicists to create the myth of "our loyal native soldiers", the askaris, and "our faithful Africans". Carefully fostered by Lettow-Vorbeck and the former Governor, Heinrich Schnee, from 1919 onwards, this legend soon became a standard argument of German colonial propaganda between the two world wars. The alleged "loyalty of the natives" to Germany during the First World War was cited time and again as proof of the Reich's "achievements as a colonizing nation" and in support of its claim to colonies in Africa. The myth had, in fact, not been invented by Lettow-Vorbeck. During the peace negotiations at Brest-Litovsk in December 1917 the German delegation had rejected the Bolshevik demand that the colonial peoples should be granted the right to self-determination by arguing, inter alia, that the alleged faithfulness displayed by the "natives towards their German friends [had been] evidence of their attachment and their resolve to stay with Germany under all circumstances".[1]

"The loyalty of our Africans" soon became one of those catch-phrases which its originators hoped would acquire the status of unquestioned truth by being repeated over and over again. They had no scruples about ascribing the attitude of the small, privileged mercenary units, whose

---

[1] *Deutsch-sowjetische Beziehungen* von den Verhandlungen in Brest—Litowsk bis zum Abschluss des Rapallovertrages. Dokumentensammlung, vol. 1, 1917—1918, Berlin 1967, p. 197.

pre-war task it had been to uphold the colonial oppression of the African peoples by methods of terror, to the people at large whose attitude, as we shall see, was a completely different one. This is also true of the one-time leading figure of West German historiography, Gerhard Ritter, who deemed it necessary, forty years after the (hypocritical) condemnation of German colonial policy by the victorious powers at Versailles, to refute their "propaganda lies" about Germany's incapacity to "colonize other continents". He wrote: "Our colonial administration was no misrule to the detriment of the natives but (for all the mistakes made on points of detail which can nowhere be entirely avoided) a genuine instrument of culture and civilization as can best be gauged from the faithful devotion of the native black population, which during the world war manifested itself, especially in the southeast, in the heavy sacrifices made in terms of human lives."[2]

But what are the facts? In South West Africa the colonial administration had never risked including Africans in the "protective force", and the three small bodies of African auxiliary troops formed after the outbreak of the war were exclusively charged with police and guard duties. One of them, known as the Kamerunerkompagnie[3], was disbanded in March 1915 because it was considered unreliable. Another contingent, consisting of Rehoboths, a hitherto privileged group of mixed race, refused one month later to continue serving the Germans and took up arms against the colonial power. The "protective force" thereupon began a military campaign against the whole community, which suffered a severe defeat near Tsamkubis on 8 May. The Rehoboths escaped annihilation only because the approach of South African troops forced the German units involved to beat a hasty retreat. During the war the "protective force" conducted several operations against "Bushmen" (San) and other Africans. The long-planned deportation of the Bondelzwart to the north was carried out immediately after the beginning of the war, which did not prevent this Nama tribe from helping the advancing South Africans when they reached the north of the country. None of the indigenous ethnic groups living in South West Africa supported the German side during the war.

---

[2] G. Ritter, Geschichtliche Erfahrungen deutscher Kolonialpolitik, in G. Ritter, Lebendige Vergangenheit. Beiträge zur historisch-politischen Selbstbesinnung, Munich 1958, p. 147.

[3] The unit was largely made up of former mercenaries of the "protective force" in Cameroon who had been banished to South West Africa following a mutiny at Banyo.

Nor could there be any question of African support for the German forces or authorities in Togo; otherwise the Allied troops would hardly have managed to occupy the whole colony in three weeks, meeting very little resistance.[4] After they had learned of the state of war the local chiefs in Kpandu region on the border with the Gold Coast refused to obey the German officials, declaring the region to be British long before British troops arrived. The residents of Kpandu town put obstacles in the way of a motorized German reconnaissance patrol and took control of the telephone link with the district administrative centre Misahöhe.

Only very few of the Africans who had been recruited and armed by German officers and officials in the districts of Misahöhe and Atakpamé and in the north of the country actually turned up for duty when Allied forces were approaching. Many of those recruited went over to the other side. Even the greater part of the "police force", made up of about 500 mercenaries, offered no serious resistance. The majority of them either deserted before the few engagements occurred or refused to attack the enemy and ran away during the retreat to Kamina.

The situation in Cameroon differed from that in Togo in that the German authorities had armed forces at their command which were able to offer resistance until early 1916, but the population was either hostile at best indifferent, or assisted the Allied forces in many ways. The coastal peoples, notably the Duala and the Malimba, immediately sided with the British and French after the outbreak of hostilities and, by serving them as pilots, guides and scouts, enabled them to penetrate into the river mouths and occupy the coastal settlements. As the district commissioner Wieneke reported later, the German authorities realized after the arrival of the first British warships that "this is like a war in enemy territory". And he added: "A large part of our military measures, out of all proportion to our modest resources, had to be directed towards controlling and neutralizing the Duala population."[5] Before the Germans withdrew into the interior of the country a great number of Duala were shot or hanged.

The Islamic rulers and dignitaries of north Cameroon, who had been sent written requests to embark on a "holy war" against Britain and

---

[4] The following is drawn from M. *Nussbaum*, Togo — eine Musterkolonie?, Berlin 1962, pp. 116—119, whose account based on later reports by German officials is confirmed in the works of the British generals Gorges and Moberly.

[5] Source: A. *Rüger*, Die Duala und die Kolonialmacht 1884—1914. Eine Studie über die historischen Ursprünge des afrikanischen Antikolonialismus, in Kamerun unter deutscher Kolonialherrschaft, ed. by H. Stoecker, vol. 2, Berlin 1968, p. 254.

France alongside the Turkish Sultan and the German Emperor, preferred in all but a few cases to align themselves with the stronger Entente powers as soon as possible. Some of these rulers, who had been loyal servants of the German administration before the war, now made hundreds of warriors armed with rifles available to the Allies. In the southern grassland most of the chiefs complied with the orders they received as long as German troops were within reach and supplied these troops with porters and provisions because a refusal to do so would have entailed harsh penalties and requisitions. But among hundreds of chiefs only a handful proved to be really reliable tools. The most important of them was Atangana, the German-installed paramount chief of the Ewondo in Yaoundé district, who was totally subservient to the German authorities. For fear of Allied reprisals, he and his warriors followed the German troops into Spanish territory.

A Nazi military expert charged with analysing the experiences of the "protective force" in Cameroon noted later: "In the areas where the fighting took place the natives often served the enemy as spies, porters or auxiliary troops who would ambush German patrols or at least report their presence to the enemy forces . . . The protective force was left without native support in nearly all operations directed against the enemy's rearward communications. In most cases the inhabitants of territory occupied by the enemy supported the latter, reporting all attempts by German detachments to come closer."[6]

The fact that the small German mercenary force, composed mainly of Yaoundés (also known as Ewondo-Yaoundés), held out until the end of 1915, aided by the impassable jungle, the remoteness of Allied bases and also the lack of coordination between British and French commanding officers, pales into insignificance compared with this state of affairs. All the more so since there were acts of disobedience in the force from mid-1915 onwards. Some 170 men of the southeastern contingent mutinied in June and tried to make their way to the coast. They were pursued and scattered by other detachments.

As regards the war in German East Africa, pro-imperialist writers on colonial history have always emphasized the "brilliant leadership" of Lettow-Vorbeck and the "loyalty and bravery" of his askaris. Some historians, for example Gerhard Ritter, have also asserted that there was support for the German troops from the local population. There is no denying the fact that Lettow-Vorbeck was an astute soldier who skil-

---

[6] *H. Pürschel*, Die kaiserliche Schutztruppe für Kamerun. Gefüge und Aufgabe, Berlin 1936, pp. 67, 114.

fully took advantage of East Africa's natural conditions and, for the most part, made the right tactical decisions. But his conduct of the war was based on a policy of holding out to the last at any cost and he enforced this with absolute ruthlessness towards his own soldiers and the African population, with no regard whatever for the enormous casualties incurred.

Recent investigations have shown that compared with, say, Cameroon the "protective force" in East Africa enjoyed substantial advantages. As of March 1916 the German forces there, which had been greatly reinforced after the beginning of the war, consisted of 3,007 Europeans and 12,100 Africans, a much larger body of troops than had defended any other German colony. Moreover, the ratio between German officers and NCOs and African soldiers and NCOs was more favourable than in Cameroon. The Germans controlled railway lines and other routes of military importance until mid-1916. Also it was possible to a certain extent to circumvent the British blockade via neighbouring Mozambique which remained neutral until March 1916 (and whose governor had been bribed by German agents). The problem of supplying the troops with food was solved at the expense of the African population. Up to the spring of 1916 the economic prerequisites for defending the colony were, on the whole, adequate notwithstanding various difficulties.

The attitude of the Africans was similar to that in Cameroon. In the weeks that followed the outbreak of the war the population in many districts, notably in the border region, began to display clear signs of hostility, culminating in attempted rebellions and attacks on smaller German contingents. The Makonde highlands in the far south were the scene of an uprising which continued off and on into 1917 and was never fully suppressed by German troops. After the German victory at Tanga resistance died down in most places only to flare up again with the 1916 Allied offensive and spread to all areas in which military operations were taking place. During the fighting there were many attacks by the African population, both in the north and south, on German patrols and advance parties, and local uprisings never ceased.

The continual commandeering of food and the forcible recruitment of porters on a large scale provoked resistance among the Africans, especially in the south where they often left their villages at the approach of German troops to hide nearby. Forcibly conscripted carriers would try continually to get away although they knew that they were risking their lives. As the war dragged on it became increasingly difficult for the German forces and authorities to find any porters at all. "Because the German authorities relied on the chiefs to provide carriers and made them responsible for this task," writes Klaus Helbig, "there were even cases of chiefs going over to the British. In several areas it was not only individuals but whole tribes who went over to the enemy."[7] Summing up, Helbig says: "By their active resistance the Africans have hastened the collapse of German civil administration and also made the military defence of the German colony more difficult."[8]

So there can really be no question of large sections of the population having assisted the German regime. The only support came from part of the chiefs and Islamic rulers, most of whom had been installed in their office by the German authorities. Many of these chiefs were deposed by their own tribe before hostilities had ended, and in the northwest there were uprisings against rulers subservient to the Germans.

As in Cameroon, the mercenary troops (askari) were the mainstay of German rule and the defence of the colony. Recruited primarily among certain tribes (the Ngoni, Hehe, Nyamwesi and Sukuma), they enjoyed a privileged position owing to their relatively high pay. The composition of the "protective force" changed in the course of the war: initially an all-volunteer force, it later consisted to a considerable degree of askari who had been conscripted. The "old guard" mercenaries generally continued to fight for their masters as long as they believed in a German victory, especially as they were to receive the pay due to them from 1915 onwards at the end of the war. The others, however, deserted *en masse* after the Allied offensive began in April 1916. In some companies the desertions assumed such proportions that it became impossible to continue fighting. As the "protective force" retreated southward, there was no engagement in which askari did not flee in great numbers in order to return home or join the Allied troops.

Of the 14,600 askari who served in Lettow-Vorbeck's colonial army during the war, no more than 1,168 were left at the war's end. When the British General Edwards, on whose orders they were discharged after the German surrender, asked them about their intentions they replied that they would take a few months' rest and then join the (British) King's African Rifles.[9]

The illusion that the Allied troops would come as "liberators" was widespread in Togo, Cameroon and German East Africa (though not in South West Africa where the enslavement and brutal oppression of

[7] K. *Helbig*, Legende und Wahrheit. Der erste Weltkrieg in Ostafrika und die Rolle des Generals Lettow-Vorbeck. Thesis, University of Leipzig 1968, p. 167.

[8] Ibid., p. 180.

[9] F. S. *Joelson*, Germany's Claim to Colonies, London 1939, p. 100.

the Africans in the Union of South Africa was only too well known).
It resulted from isolation and lack of experience and a failure to under-
stand the nature of the imperialist system and the world war. Although
this illusion soon came to an end once the German colonies had passed
into the hands of the Entente powers, it was of considerable military
benefit to the Allies as long as the fighting continued. That the British
and French imperialists unscrupulously exploited this naive belief in
their "liberating mission" was, from their point of view, a matter of
course as were the attempts of the German imperialists to make use of
anticolonial movements in the British and French colonies and semi-
colonies to weaken the Allies.

The effects of the war on the population of the German colonies were
described by a Nazi military expert (1936) and a French colonial historian
as follows (1969):

Herbert Pürschel on Cameroon: "The result of Cameroon being turned into a battlefield was that the native population lapsed into a state
of extreme wretchedness and rot as reflected in a staggering infant
mortality rate, the spread of tuberculosis and venereal disease, and a
growing incidence of sleeping sickness — a state of affairs against which
very little could be done."[10]

Robert Cornevin on German East Africa: "The war left indelible
memories, especially in the southern half of the colony. But what the
blacks remembered were not the achievements of the whites but the
suffering and misery the war had brought in its wake: the forcible recruitment of thousands of porters, the neglect of European plantations
and indigenous crops, the flight of the villagers at the approach of the
askari with their requisition orders . . ."[11]

A senior German official in 1919 put the overall losses among porters
in East Africa at 100,000 to 120,000 on the German side and at 250,000 on
the Allied side. He estimated that in addition approximately 300,000
people in that part of the continent died from hunger, privation and
disease in the course of the First World War.[12] In other words: more than
half a million Africans paid for Lettow-Vorbeck's strategy of holding out
at all costs with their lives.

[10] *H. Pürschel*, op. cit., p. 84.
[11] *R. Cornevin*, The Germans in Africa before 1918, in Colonialism in Africa 1870 to
1960, vol. 1: The History and Politics of Colonialism 1870—1914, ed. by L. H. Gann
and P. Duignan, Cambridge 1969, p. 415.
[12] *W. Arning*, Deutsch—Ostafrika gestern und heute, Berlin 1942, p. 31. In Kenya
and Uganda the British authorities and military units recruited approx. 350,000

The attitude of the colonial powers towards the East African population during the war contrasted sharply with the way the belligerent Europeans treated each other. Theirs was a "gentlemen's war" — not the kind of slaughter taking place on the western front in Europe. Both sides knew full well that they were facing the African population as conquerors and that major uprisings were a distinct possibility. Hence the initial attempts to avoid hostilities in East Africa. Governor Schnee tried to abandon Dar es Salaam and other coastal towns to the British without a fight, and British settlers in Kenya demanded in public that East Africa should be kept out of the war.[13] During the hostilities the tendency towards "European solidarity" found its expression primarily in the mutual respect and consideration shown by officers on both sides. In neighbouring Northern Rhodesia British settlers in 1917 even temporarily entrusted an interned German officer with the command of a volunteer force they had set up to quell a local rebellion.

2. The War Aims

Contrary to what apologetic historians have asserted, the war aims of German imperialism were not formulated after the First World War had begun. Just as the war itself had been the logical result of the general development of the global economic and political system in the proceding decades, so too the objectives pursued by the warring powers had their roots in these developments. The First World War was, as Willibald Gutsche remarked, the continuation by other means of the Weltpolitik the ruling class had been practising since Bülow's day.

The continuity of German policy before and during the war can be seen very clearly in the aims pursued in Africa. From the outbreak of the conflict until defeat there was far-reaching agreement among Germany's ruling class that the Entente powers must be forced to concede demands which had been the focus of pre-war efforts at colonial expansion and

---

porters of whom 46,168 were officially reported to have "died while on duty" and 40,645 were reported missing. It is estimated that in Kenya alone 144,000 people perished during the war or as a result of the famine which followed in its wake. Cf. *R. M. A. van Zwanenberg*, An Economic History of Kenya and Uganda 1800 to 1970, London 1975, p. 10, who considers this figure to be much too low.

[13] *K. Forster*, The quest for East African neutrality in 1914, in: The African Studies Review, Waltham, Mass., vol. XXII, 1, 1979, pp. 74—76.

which the Imperial Government had pressed on the diplomatic level and by means of *pénétration pacifique*. The records of the very first top-level discussions show that the idea of building up a vast colonial empire and creating a "German Central Africa" was upheld as a matter of course.

Within two weeks of the war beginning, the director of the Deutsche Bank, A. von Gwinner, told the US Ambassador in Berlin that the price of peace would be "three thousand million dollars and the French colonies."[14] The head of the Hapag, Albert Ballin, a friend of Wilhelm II, demanded "substantial reparation payments and substantial colonial possessions" in a letter of 30 August to the Kaiser's chief naval adviser, Admiral Georg Alexander von Müller.[15] August Thyssen, a leading Ruhr industrialist, said in a memorandum dated 28 August that "when a peace treaty is signed . . . [Germany will have to] insist on being given not only the French and Belgian Congo but also Morocco as colonies"[16] In the following months the other leaders of the iron and steel industry also demanded extensive annexations in Africa.

Especially important in this context is the programme prepared by Heinrich Class, chairman of the powerful Pan-German League (Alldeutscher Verband), on the suggestion of Alfred Hugenberg, Chairman of the Krupp AG. Class, acting on behalf of the Association's executive committee, set it out in detail in a "Memorandum Concerning the Objectives of National, Economic and Social Policy of the German People in the Current War". Printed after its endorsement by Gustav Krupp von Bohlen und Halbach and Hugo Stinnes, the memorandum called for considerable territorial aggrandizement in Europe as well as far-reaching annexations of colonial territory at the expense of France, Britain and Belgium, inter alia the Belgian Congo, the French Congo, Senegambia, parts of the Portuguese colonial empire and French Morocco. It served as a guideline for the influential propaganda carried on by the Pan-German lobby during the war. The memorandum and deliberations of leading industrialists and some representatives of the East Elbe landowning interests gave rise to the petition of 20 May 1915 in which six large business associations set out their war aims, the first being the establishment of "a colonial empire which will meet Germany's wide-ranging economic interests to the full."[17]

[14] Source: *A. von Tirpitz*, Politische Dokumente, vol. 2, Hamburg and Berlin 1926, p. 67.

[15] Source: Ibid., p. 68.

[16] Source: *W. Basler*, Deutschlands Annexionspolitik in Polen und im Baltikum 1914—1918, Berlin 1962, p. 361.

[17] Source: *Dokumentation der Zeit*, Berlin 1952, no. 26, pp. 1203—1204.

Leading politicians of the bourgeois parties identified themselves with these objectives at an early stage. On 2 September the leader of the left wing of the Catholic Centre party, Matthias Erzberger, who maintained close links with Thyssen in those years, addressed a memorandum to high government officials, which reads in part: "In accordance with the plans of the late Foreign Secretary, von Kiderlen-Wächter, a large German Central Africa should be established. It would stretch from Dar es Salaam via Douala right to Senegambia with the following new acquisitions: the Belgian and the French Congo, Nigeria (from England), Dahomey and the French West Coast (from France). If our colonial possessions were rounded off in this way, we would avoid fragmentation and give fresh scope to the activities of German interests."[18] Leading right-wing opportunists in the Social Democratic Party such as Eduard David were quick to support such ideas.

In the first months of the war when the advance of the German armies in the West raised the prospect of a speedy victory over France and a compromise peace with Britain, there was little mention of British colonial territories among the targets of annexation. After all, "German Central Africa" could be created without including British colonies. But while most Hamburg-based overseas trading firms recommended restraint vis-à-vis the foremost colonial and naval power, such considerations played no part in the programme of the leading unofficial exponent of German colonial policy, Duke Johann Albrecht zu Mecklenburg, president of the German Colonial Society. He not only repeated Erzberger's demands more precisely but went much further. In a memorandum of 18 September[19] intended for Colonial Secretary Wilhelm Solf he wrote:

"The best policy would be to take advantage of the big cleaning-up now taking place to set up a great interconnected colonial empire in Central Africa and to get rid of unprofitable outposts in the South Seas instead, and to do so without showing any sentimentality towards our enemies, who have vowed to destroy us, or towards ourselves and the work we have done so far in various places . . .

My opinion is that as far as the eastern hemisphere is concerned, we should only retain or take some major naval and commercial bases of importance for us which we would be capable of defending. A coherent

---

[18] Source: *Tirpitz* op. cit., p. 71.

[19] ZStA, RKolA, no. 3985, pp. 35—6. Throughout the war the president of the society adhered to this programme, which he recapitulated in a letter to Solf of 25 March 1918. Ibid., pp. 117—118.

colonial empire in Africa will make up tenfold for the assets we will give up there by way of 'compensation' . . .

Considering that any fragmentation must be avoided and that France and Britain must if possible be weakened, I propose the following:

1. The British withdraw from Egypt. The latter's relationship with Turkey is to be settled from there as an internal affair. Germany and Turkey share equally in the control of and the revenue from the Suez Canal. We receive a first-class naval base in the Mediterranean.

2. Algiers and Tunis are ceded to Italy.

3. Morocco to Spain.
These two countries would thus be rewarded for their neutrality and be given much scope for their activities.

4. The northern boundary of our African colonial empire would begin south of 20° latitude in the West, at a point favourable for us, and then run eastward (the Cape Verde Islands being included), north of the bends made by the Senegal and Niger rivers and Lake Chad. The areas north of our border would be handed over as spheres of interest to the two states just mentioned. The Spanish enclaves and islands within the bounds of our colonial empire would be exchanged for the above territories in the negotiations with Spain.

Our northern boundary would continue along the border of Sudan to about 6° latitude, then turn eastward and finally reach the Indian Ocean at Kismayu so that all of Uganda and British East Africa (Kenya) would become German.

5. The southern boundary should run eastward from a suitable point in S.W. [German South West Africa] to reach the Indian Ocean in the vicinity of Beira.

6. All Belgian, French and British territories within these boundaries pass to Germany.

7. The Portuguese territories located within our colonial empire are ceded to Germany in return for a compensation payable by Britain.

8. All offshore islands pass to Germany.

9. Rivers should not form borders wherever possible. Where this is unavoidable as in the case of the Orange and Juba Rivers, the channel of the river has to serve as the border.

10. The Senegal, Niger, Congo and Zambezi Rivers must flow within German territory for the whole of their length.

11. Liberia comes under German administration.

12. A well-rounded, unitary colonial empire such as this can be developed on a large scale and kept in order more easily and cheaply than the fragments of territory we now have . . .

13. Madagascar must not remain French. But it is doubtful whether it would be practicable to annex the island. I would suggest restoring the old kingdom under native princes but under German protectorate and control. This would provide ample opportunities for our trade, and it would create a favourable impression . . ."

Duke Johann Albrecht thus demanded that all of France's and Belgium's colonial holdings in sub-Saharan Africa should pass into German hands along with Portugal's possessions (with the exception of southern Mozambique) and Britain's coloniғs (but not the Union of South Africa and the economically unimportant protectorates of Bechuanaland, Swaziland and Basutoland).

By the time the Colonial Secretary received this not exactly modest programme, he had already given an official opinion on the colonial war aims. Having been invited by Foreign Secretary Gottlieb von Jagow to make proposals for the colonial terms of a peace treaty with France and Belgium, he had submitted a detailed memorandum on 28 August including Portuguese colonies in a list of annexation demands. Solf advised that Portugal should cede Angola and northern Mozambique to Germany, while Belgium was to give up the Congo, and France her own Congo colony and her possessions in Equatorial Africa up to Lake Chad as well as Dahomey and the lands north of Togo up to the Niger (the territory of what is now Upper Volta and much of what is now Mali).[20]

The establishment of "German Central Africa" had thus been officially formulated as a war aim. The reason for demanding Angola was to bring the railway link between the key mining area of Katanga and the Atlantic seaports of Moçamedes, Benguela and Luanda under German control. Solf did not include any British colonies in his list because he did not believe that Britain could be defeated and therefore wanted to retain the option of a compromise peace with her. But from 1916 onwards, if not earlier, he joined in the demand for the annexation of British overseas possessions, e.g. Nigeria. Both the Colomal Secretary and the President of the DKG continued to hold these views throughout the war.

---

[20] *F. Fischer*, Griff nach der Weltmacht. Die Kriegszielpolitik des kaiserlichen Deutschland 1914/18, Düsseldorf 1964, pp. 115—116.

Both had included major portions of Portugal's colonial holdings in their annexation programme although Portugal was not involved in the war. The German government was still pursuing the aim of appropriating large sections of Mozambique and Angola (as it had in pre-war negotiations with London). In a directive dated 21 August 1914 Foreign Secretary von Jagow instructed his Undersecretary Zimmermann to make arrangements "that will enable us, in due course, to compel Portugal to abandon her neutrality . . ." It "should not be difficult to create a dispute on the German-Portuguese borders (i.e. the borders between the African colonies of the two powers) which we could use as a pretext for breaking with Portugal." He added that a break should not be provoked until the outcome of the war was certain, but "if the fortunes of war are on our side it would be of great importance for us to count Portugal among our adversaries when peace is concluded."[21] Portugal was no factor to be reckoned with in military terms but might be forced by a victorious Germany to part with her colonies.

The Imperial Government did not hesitate to adopt the idea of a German Central Africa as a war aim following Solf's memorandum of 28 August, apparently considering its justification to be self-evident. After all, Chancellor von Bethmann Hollweg had in July 1912 approved the substance of a programme in which Walther Rathenau described Central Africa and Asia Minor as the chief foreign policy objectives. The "Provisional Memoir on Guidelines for our Policy concerning a Peace Settlement", which Bethmann Hollweg had drawn up in close touch with Jagow and the director of the Deutsche Bank, Karl Helfferich, and forwarded to his deputy, Clemens von Delbrück, on 9 September, contained the clear statement that as far as colonies were concerned the primary objective must be the "establishment of a coherent colonial empire in Central Africa". It added that the question of colonial acquisitions required closer examination.[22]

This objective, which the Bethmann Hollweg cabinet continued to pursue after the failure of the blitzkrieg strategy in the Battle of the Marne, was held to be decisive whenever government ministers and officials, liberal and conservative politicians and business leaders met behind closed doors during the following four years to discuss Germany's

---

[21] Source: *W. Gutsche*, Der Einfluss des Monopolkapitals auf die Entstehung der aussenpolitischen Konzeption der Regierung Bethmann Hollweg zu Beginn des Ersten Weltkrieges, in: Jahrbuch für Geschichte, vol. 5, Berlin 1970, pp. 141. Cf. also *F. Rosen*, Aus einem diplomatischen Wanderleben, vol. 2, Berlin 1932, p. 228.

[22] Source: *W. Basler*, op. cit., p. 383.

war aims in Africa. Many proposals from these quarters for a peace settlement (whether assuming a British defeat or not) overtly or implicitly stressed the importance of creating a "German Central Africa".

In a memorandum of 29 October 1914 the Prussian Minister of the Interior Friedrich Wilhelm von Loebell had this to say about the colonial objectives of the war: "We need absolute freedom of the seas, we need colonies with defensible sea-ports, [colonies] which will supply raw materials and possibly serve as markets, [colonies] which can perhaps be self-sufficient economically and will display cohesion and freedom of manoeuvre vis-à-vis the British colonial empire. No untenable outposts in some distant corner of the world. As part of an adequate peace agreement with England the Belgian Congo would of course have to pass into German hands."[23] The last-named demand found its way into a fundamental statement of policy towards Belgium "in the event of a decisive German victory" which the Reich Secretary of the Interior, Delbrück, and the Undersecretary at the Foreign Office, Zimmermann, drew up on 31 December at the request of the Imperial Chancellor.[24]

The former chief of the General Staff and commander-in-chief, General Helmuth von Moltke, wrote in a message to the Emperor on 15 January 1915: "In recompense for the heavy toll exacted from Germany in this war we are not only entitled to economic advantages on the continent, but also to the creation of a German colonial empire in Central Africa, a demand which can only be addressed to England."[25]

The chairman of the firm of Krupp, Gustav Krupp von Bohlen und Halbach, wrote in a memorandum of 31 July 1915 intended for Wilhelm II: "It would appear premature to raise specific demands regarding overseas expansion as long as there is no way of saying where and how we can get the better of England. But one evident goal can be formulated right now apart from the fact that we must regain our colonies and protect the Dutch from being deprived of theirs, we need a vast but coherent colonial empire in Africa so that we can really pursue grand designs within its boundaries."[26]

[23] *Das Werk des Untersuchungsausschusses* der Verfassungsgebenden Deutschen Nationalversammlung und des Deutschen Reichstages 1919—1928. Fourth series: Die Ursachen des Deutschen Zusammenbruches im Jahre 1918, part 2, vol. 12, 1, pp. 187 and 192—193.

[24] Ibid., p. 197.

[25] *H. von Moltke*, Erinnerungen—Briefe—Dokumente 1887—1916, Stuttgart 1922, p. 412.

[26] *Krupp und die Hohenzollern*. Aus der Korrespondenz der Familie Krupp 1850—1916, Berlin 1956, pp. 152—153.

More statements like these could be quoted for the years 1916, 1917 and 1918.[27] This demand was supported not only by representatives of the big banks and heavy industry, but also by spokesmen for the textile industry and other manufacturing branches. Leading industrialists in the kingdom of Saxony, for example, demanded a large German colonial empire in Africa at a conference held by the Saxon government on 20 December 1915 to discuss the aims of the war.

Solf, anxious to be well-equipped for peace negotiations, ordered two commissions to be set up at the Colonial Office on 14 December 1915 to prepare the drafting of a definitive memorandum on colonial annexations. He charged the commissions with making lists of "enemy possessions according to a scale of values" as the basis for "minimum and maximum demands" and added more specifically: "The question of acquiring foreign protectorates should be examined in the light of (a) considerations of economic, transport and financial policy, and (b) considerations of power politics generally . . ."[28] The memorandum, which had not been fully completed by the end of 1917 (partly due to certain disagreements within the Colonial Office) was drafted by senior officials. While it was being prepared, Solf asked for comments from the chiefs of the Army and Navy Commands, the other ministries and the business associations.

The colonial business interests did not have to be asked twice. In a "strictly confidential" memorandum of January 1916, the Colonial Economic Committee (KWK) formulated both maximum and minimum demands. It said that, as a maximum, Germany should annex the Belgian Congo, French Equatorial Africa (and with it the Portuguese enclave Cabinda to secure full control over the Congo estuary), Senegal, the upper Niger region, the Gold Coast, Dahomey with its hinterland, and Nigeria as well as Madagascar, Northern Rhodesia, Niassaland, Kenya, Uganda, Zanzibar and Pemba. Should this prove impossible on political or military grounds, the paper said, Germany should regain her former colonies or acquire other territories of at least equal value, and in either case additional colonies in adjoining areas.[29]

Demands raised by the DKG on 16 June 1916 were identical with the maximum demands of the Economic Committee (KWK).

---

[27] Cf. *H. W. Gatzke*, Germany's Drive to the West . . . A Study of Germany's Western War Aims during the First World War, Baltimore 1950, and *F. Fischer*, op. cit., as well as *Das Werk des Untersuchungsausschusses* . . ., pp. 92 and 209—210.

[28] Source: *L. Rathmann*, Stossrichtung Nahost 1914—1918, Berlin 1963, pp. 102—103.

[29] *K. Helbig*, op. cit., pp. 32—33.

The organization was outspoken in setting out its reasons: "The large requirements of Germany and her allies for colonial raw materials, and the need to secure safe markets for her industry, especially to make up for the markets lost to our adversaries who intend to drive us out of more markets yet, make it all the more imperative to seek a substantial expansion of our colonial possessions without timidity as an equally favourable opportunity is not likely to present itself again soon."[30]

In confidential documents adopted in May, November and December 1916, in September 1917 and in April 1918, the government committed itself to the Central African scheme, in some cases extending it to include huge areas of Western Africa up to Cape Verde.[31] These plans were expressly endorsed by the Emperor and Quartermaster-General Erich Ludendorff.[32] From the end of 1916 onwards Solf, with increasing support from the Naval Command, subscribed to the view that large parts of West Africa would have to be annexed to finance the development of the colony in Central Africa without grants-in-aid from the Reich.

Colonialist writers such as Emil Zimmermann and Paul Leutwein, taking up Solf's public statements in 1917, presented "German Central Africa" as a natural and necessary complement to a German-dominated "Central Europe" as propaged by Friedrich Naumann.[33] In support of their argument they cited "economic necessities". Zimmermann, who had repeatedly made "information tours" in the Belgian Congo before the war, listed the raw materials of which Central Africa could become the major supplier: cotton, vegetable oils, timber, rubber and copper. And quite a few university professors of repute, such as the historians Hans Delbrück and Erich Brandenburg and the geographers Alfred Hettner and Karl Dove, supported this opinion in public. Delbrück, who tended to support Solf and his political friends during the war, fostered the idea of a "German Central Africa" from 1915 as an alternative to the annexation of Belgium. Writing in the Preussische Jahrbücher in 1917, he said that the countries of Central Africa offered

[30] Source: ibid., p. 33.

[31] *F. Fischer*, op. cit., pp. 292, 415—418, 792—796; *M. N. Mashkin*, Zur Geschichte der Kolonialziele des kaiserlichen Deutschland im Jahre 1918, in: Jahrbuch für Wirtschaftsgeschichte 1965/III, pp. 45 ff.; *L. Rathmann*, Berlin—Bagdad. Die imperialistische Nahostpolitik des kaiserlichen Deutschland, Berlin 1962, pp. 102 bis 103. Cf. also *A. von Tirpitz*, op. cit., p. 639; *H. W. Gatzke*, op. cit., p. 143.

[32] *Das Werk des Untersuchungsausschusses . . .*, p. 109.

[33] Cf. *E. Zimmermann*, Das deutsche Kaiserreich Mittelafrika als Grundlage einer neuen deutschen Weltpolitik, Berlin 1917; *P. Leutwein*, Mitteleuropa—Mittelafrika, Dresden 1917.

immense prospects: "They abound in natural resources, provide ample opportunity for settlement and many sources of income, and are well endowed with able-bodied men to serve as labourers or soldiers."[34]

The annexation programmes and memoranda of 1916—17 laid special emphasis on the Belgian Congo as the core of "German Central Africa". Taking issue with the Governor-General of occupied Belgium, General Moritz Ferdinand von Bissing, who had described the Congo as being of no value, Solf said emphatically "that in any event the conquest of the Congo is indispensable for Germany if she wants to retain her standing as a colonial power." He added that the territory was needed not only because otherwise "German Central Africa" would be impossible to achieve, but also because it contained rich deposits of coal, copper and tin.[35] The importance of Katanga's mineral wealth was stressed over and over again. As late as July 1918 government officials and a consortium of leading banks (Deutsche Bank, Disconto-Gesellschaft, Dresdner Bank and others) reached an understanding that British and Belgian shareholdings in the Union Minière du Haut Katanga, the company which controlled most mining operations in the province, should under all circumstances be expropriated in German-occupied Brussels before peace negotiations began.

The demand for "German Central Africa" was motivated not only by economic (sources of raw materials, markets, manpower) but also by military considerations. In the event of a European war — so the argument ran — so huge a colony could be defended much more easily than the smaller territories situated far from each other which Germany had ruled up to 1914. There would thus be no danger of Germany losing all her colonial possessions soon after the outbreak of war as had been the case in 1914—15.

When it became apparent in 1916—17 that Germany was suffering from growing lack of raw materials whereas the colonies of the Entente powers were making a considerable economic contribution to the Allied war effort, the military importance of the projected colonial empire received more attention from the Army Command. In an address to the Crown Council on 11 September 1917, later written down as a memorandum, Ludendorff pointed out that the maintenance of German foreign trade "in the next war" required "apart from Russia, overseas

---

[34] H. Delbrück, Versöhnungs-Friede. Macht-Friede. Deutscher Friede, Preussische Jahrbücher, vol. 168 (1917), p. 492. Cf. by the same author, Bismarcks Erbe, Berlin 1915, p. 202.

[35] Source: K. Helbig, op. cit., p. 36.

markets in South America, a colonial empire in Africa and naval bases within or outside the colonial empire."[36] A few months later, on 23 December, he stated the colonial demands of the Army High Command in more precise terms. He told the government that what was needed was "a great African colonial empire right across Africa with naval bases on the shores of the Indian and Atlantic Oceans."[37]

The Naval Command, also with the experiences of the war in mind, attached special importance to the establishment of a system of bases on Africa's coastline. The chief of the Admiralty Staff, Admiral Henning von Holtzendorff, called for a Central African colonial empire on 18 May 1917, describing as necessary "the acquisition of the bases needed to retain control over the colonial empire in a future war and to fight a trade war and protect our trading interests." He mentioned, "in addition to the seaports of the contemplated African colonial empire", the Azores and Dakar with Senegambia, which he said would also be in the interests of the Army because France would thus lose her traditional areas of recruitment in Black Africa.[38]

The departments responsible (the Colonial Office, the Naval Office, the Admiralty Staff, etc.) were busy in the spring and summer of 1918 selecting future naval bases and coaling stations. A commission formed at Solf's suggestion produced numerous memoranda on this subject. In collaboration with Admiral (ret.) von Grapow, the Woermann Linie and the Hapag, they carefully examined the merits and demerits of all major ports between Cape Verde and the Congo estuary — Dakar, Bathurst, Bissau, Bolama, Conakry, Freetown, Libreville and Pointe Noire — with a view to their climatic, nautical and economic suitability. In the end they opted for Dakar and Bathurst.

The demand for a large and territorially coherent colony in tropical Africa is to be found, stated clearly or vaguely (sometimes obliquely)

---

[36] *E. Ludendorff* (ed.), Urkunden der Obersten Heeresleitung über ihre Tätigkeit 1916/18, Berlin 1920, p. 433.

[37] Source: *F. Fischer*, op., cit., p. 792.

[38] Report by Holtzendorff to Wilhelm II on 18 May 1917. Source: *Das Werk des Untersuchungsausschusses*, pp. 209—210. Cf. also Holtzendorff's memoranda of 26 Nov. and 19 Dec. 1916. The former has been published in *B. Kaulisch*, Zur überseeischen Stützpunktpolitik der kaiserlichen deutschen Marineführung ..., Militärgeschichte, vol. 19, 1980, pp. 595—598; the latter in *A. Scherer* and *J. Grunewald* (eds.), L'Allemagne et les problèmes de la paix pendant la première guerre mondiale. Documents extraits des archives de l'Office allemand des Affaires étrangères, vol. 1, Paris 1966.

in virtually all programmatic statements made on colonial war aims by senior spokesmen for the ruling class within and outside the government between the outbreak of the war and the summer of 1918. There was a widely held belief that, much like India in the British Empire, "German Central Africa" would become the cornerstone of a future German world empire. Specific demands or proposals for the annexation of this or that colony in tropical Africa were complementary in character unless those who submitted them were advocating local interests, as in the case of the German traders and plantation owners from Togo who called for the annexation of Dahomey.

In a speech to the German Colonial Society in June 1917, however, Solf was much less extreme. In fact, he reduced his demands to the return of the German colonies, to part of the Belgian Congo (meaning Katanga), as well as Angola and Mozambique, and he even agreed — "provided the whole plan succeeds" — to cede South West Africa to the Union of South Africa because that colony would have no economic value after the exhaustion of the diamond fields. The reason for his restraint was that this was the first public announcement of the Central Africa scheme by a government representative, and his speech was also intended as a tentative peace feeler towards Britain.

Concerning the demand for "German Central Africa" there was little difference of opinion among the ruling class. While the debate on war aims was often very heated, it never centred on objectives outside Europe. It was taken for granted that a victory over France or both France and Britain would result in a substantial enlargement of colonial possessions. Only a small section of the Pan-Germans, led by Count Ernst zu Reventlow, and some conservative newspapers argued that it was impossible to pursue a successful colonial policy overseas as long as Britain enjoyed naval supremacy and that therefore annexations should remain confined to Europe.

Some differences arose as to whether West European territories conquered or claimed by Germany should be exchanged for colonial possessions, and if so to what extent. Exponents of the liberal imperialism represented by the "Popular Union for Freedom and the Fatherland" (Volksbund für Freiheit und Vaterland) rejected far-reaching overt annexations in Europe, especially the establishment of direct political control over Belgium, for domestic and foreign policy reasons. They cautiously suggested the priority of colonial expansion over annexation plans in Western Europe. The West German iron and steel magnates, on the other hand, insisted on the incorporation of Belgium and northern France. As early as May 1915 Hugenberg, speaking on behalf of the

Central Association of German Industrialists, told General E. F. K. von Gayl, commander of the VII Army Corps, that the members of the Association were "anxious not to see the opinion prevail in the ruling circles that we should look upon Belgium only as a 'bargaining counter' for obtaining colonies and suchlike."[39] In other words, the demand for annexations in Western Europe was put before the demand for possessions overseas without the latter being abandoned.

Divergences of opinion about the relative importance of different colonial territories occurred mainly among overseas trading firms which favoured the area of their business interests. A case in point was an early dispute among Hamburg merchants on the restoration and extension of positions in Eastern Asia and the Pacific. Was it of less importance than the Central Africa scheme? Since these merchants had little political influence their opinion did not carry much weight.

In addition to the general aim of "German Central Africa", the demand for Morocco was also raised frequently, although the coal and steel barons of the Ruhr were the only people to do so with undiminished emphasis. It became obvious soon after the beginning of the war that they had not accepted the results of the 1911 Agadir crisis but were still pressing for moves to establish dominance over the Sultanate. August Thyssen's memorandum of 28 August 1914, which urged that Morocco should be turned into a German colony, has already been mentioned. The seemingly more moderate demand for France's renunciation of all rights in Morocco, as put before the Chancellor with other demands on 8 December by the Chairman of the Central Association of German Industrialists, Max Roetger, and the vice-chairman of the Industrialists' Federation, Gustav Stresemann, served the same aim: to bring Morocco's mineral wealth under German control. And a memorandum by the economist Professor Hermann Schumacher listing the wishes of the iron and steel magnates also called for the seizure of Morocco. One of them, Hugo Stinnes, passed it on to the Imperial Chancellery.

Not surprisingly, the Pan-German League, which as late as January 1917 depicted Bethmann Hollweg as having been "politically responsible for our ill-fated policy towards Morocco, and thus having encouraged French sentiments of revanche"[40], remained wedded to Class's favourite project of a "German West Morocco". In his memorandum of autumn

[39] Source: *Handbuch der Verträge* 1871—1964, ed. by H. Stoecker in collaboration with A. Rüger, Berlin 1968, p. 151.

[40] Beschluss des geschäftsführenden Ausschusses des Alldeutschen Verbandes. Berlin, 21 Jan. 1917. In: *Deutsch-sowjetische Beziehungen* . . ., p. 855.

1914 the latter had put the seizure of French Morocco at the top of the list of colonial demands. General Eduard von Liebert in particular agitated for the annexation of Morocco's west coast at many meetings of the League and the German Fatherland Party. Writing in the columns of the Alldeutsche Blätter on 2 March 1918, he reiterated pre-war claims that Morocco was well-suited to become a German settler colony, adding only that the country's inhabitants could be used for military purposes. The general concluded that West Marocco would have to be "one of Germany's principal demands when negotiating a peace settlement" and that "as the experience of 1911 shows, this valuable territory can only be acquired by force under the law of conquest. The last opportunity to grasp it has now arrived."

Two years previously the Mannesmann brothers, who identified themselves with the organization's aims, had addressed a petition to the government in which they offered, "in the event of Morocco coming under German influence through a peace settlement", to make half of the net profits from their dubious "mining concessions" and half of their landed property in Morocco available free of charge "for the settlement of war-disabled ex-servicemen or for some other purpose to be stated by the Imperial Government."[41] Given the enormous extent of their "claims" and their holdings in Morocco, which had been confiscated by the French authorities, this was a rather crude example of the pursuit of business interests under a pretence of patriotism, which was typical of the Mannesmanns' style.

Commercial and shipping interests also wanted to be heard. The three Hamburg firms directly involved in Morocco (two trading firms and a shipping company) demanded in 1915 that German rule should be established over the country, or that at least the French protectorate imposed on the Sultan in 1912 should be revoked. An organization set up by these firms approached the Colonial Office in June 1918 to submit a "memorandum on the Economic Importance of Morocco and its Value as Settlement Territory". The authors gave a detailed account of the country's agricultural potential and mineral wealth, and painted the prospects for exploitation by German capitalists in glowing terms.

What prompted the Wilhelmstrasse to keep an eye on the Moroccan question was not so much the wishes of the Hamburg merchants but the demand of the coal and steel barons for long-term sources of raw materials. A programme for the peace settlement transmitted by the Foreign

---

[41] Source: *C. H. Mannesmann*, Die Unternehmungen der Brüder Mannesmann in Marokko, Leipzig 1931, p. 59.

Office to the Army High Command on 6 April 1918 said under the heading "Economic Demands for the Peace Treaty with France" that priority should be given to "straightening out the situation in Morocco". This would entail the demand for Morocco's "independence" — somewhat diminished by the granting of special prerogatives to German capital, especially in the mining sector. The programme described current Moroccan export duties (three per cent) *ad valorem* as "far too high to run German mining operations economically" (sic). The final demand was that "German concessions be recognized unconditionally without recourse to arbitration."[42] In other words, a German victory was to bring automatic endorsement, without further examination, of the Mannesmanns' fictitious rights to the exploitation of vast ore deposits in Morocco.

The preparations for a larger colonial empire after the war were not limited to the selection of African countries which imperialist rivals were supposed to relinquish in peace negotiations. In the economic field measures were taken to ensure that colonial exploitation could be begun immediately after the expected victory. In line with long-standing practice, extensive funds from the public purse were set aside for the support of colonial business undertakings.

As their property in most parts of Africa had been seized by the Allies and trade and communications links between Germany and Africa had been interrupted, many German colonial firms were doomed to inactivity. In order to keep these firms alive and provide them with capital for future operations their owners asked the government to give them compensation for the expected losses. Solf received numerous applications, promised to give them sympathetic consideration at the appropriate time, and made sure the firms in question benefited from tax relief and other financial assistance. Finally, in May 1917, the Budget Committee of the Reichstag sanctioned a loan of 20 million marks "for purposes of colonial reconstruction". After consultation with the DKG, Solf's Undersecretary Otto Gleim laid down the guidelines for the use of these funds. They were designed to serve a dual purpose:

"(a) To provide business enterprises based in the German protectorates since before the war with the cash required to resume their operations immediately after connections with the protectorates have been restored, either in the form of advance payments . . . or as loans . . .

---

[42] Source: *M. N. Mashkin*, op. cit., pp. 47—48.

(b) To enable the aforementioned business enterprises to maintain themselves along the lines envisaged for the duration of the war, especially by retaining the personnel needed for swift reconstruction, keeping their head offices open, and similar measures . . ."[43]

Not even the rapid deterioration of Germany's military situation after the Allied breakthrough at Amiens on 8 August 1918 (the "Black Day") led to the abandonment of the programme for colonial expansion. While Solf declared in a speech on 20 August that "we wish a settlement of colonial issues on the principle that colonial possessions should correspond to the relative economic strength of the European nations"[44], Erzberger — shortly before he entered the government on 3 October — reproached the old colonial powers for having far too large overseas possessions and demanded for Germany a Central African empire comprising the German, Belgian and Portuguese colonies[45]. As late as 28 September, Solf, in a speech delivered at Munich University, advocated a redistribution of African colonial territory at the expense of France, Belgium and Portugal.[46] His appointment as Foreign Secretary in the cabinet of Prince Max von Baden on 4 October, while retaining his previous portfolio, was meant to underline Germany's colonial demands in view of the coming peace negotiations.

It was only the final military defeat which forced a tactical retreat. The plan now was to have the "Central African Empire" placed under the joint control of the major powers, including Germany, of course — an idea which Solf had rejected as "utopian" as recently as 27 February 1918. During the following years the governments of the Weimar Republic repeatedly demanded that Germany should be allowed to take part in the exploitation of tropical Africa. The Nazi government, for its part, reverted to the war aims which Germany had pursued in tropical Africa during the First World War. All in all, colonial expansion in

---

[43] Source: *A. Rüger*, Die kolonialen Bestrebungen des deutschen Imperialismus in Afrika. Vom Ende des ersten Weltkrieges bis zur Locarno-Konferenz. Thesis, Humboldt University Berlin 1968, p. 84.

[44] Sources: *Schulthess' Europäischer Geschichtskalender*, 1918, I, p. 258.

[45] *M. Erzberger*, Der Völkerbund. Der Weg zum Weltfrieden, Berlin 1918, p. 150. For Erzberger's views cf. *A. Rüger*, Die kolonialen Bestrebungen des deutschen Imperialismus vom Waffenstillstand von Compiègne bis zur Unterzeichnung des Versailler Vertrages. Wissenschaftliche Zeitschrift der Humboldt-Universität zu Berlin, Gesellschaftliche und sprachwissenschaftliche Reihe, vol. XIII (1964), no. 7, p. 883.

[46] *H. W. Gatzke*, op. cit., p. 286.

Africa (and elsewhere) was an integral part of the overall policy of the ruling monopolist bourgeoisie, a policy which was deeply rooted in the socioeconomic and political structure of imperialist Germany.

It goes without saying that imperialist Germany's war aims regarding Africa were incompatible with the demands of the Bolsheviks for a peace without annexations based on every nation's right to self-determination. At the peace negotiations at Brest-Litovsk in December 1917 the Soviet delegation proposed, in accordance with Lenin's Decree on Peace, that colonial issues should be resolved by recognizing that those peoples who had enjoyed no political independence before the war should be able to exercise their right to self-determination freely and without outside interference. The German delegation replied that Germany insisted on the restitution of her colonies and that the exercise of the right to self-determination by the German colonies was "an impracticable proposition at the present time". A few days later Solf stressed that "the Russian demand regarding the right of the colonies to self-determination is totally unacceptable for us."[47]

The only people in Germany who rejected all colonial annexations and colonial policy in general were the representatives of the revolutionary labour movement, in particular the Spartacus Group.

[47] *Deutsch-sowjetische Beziehungen* . . ., pp. 168—9, 196—7 and 104.

X. The Colonial Aims of the Weimar Republic

1. 1918—1919

The failure of the summer offensive in 1918 and the subsequent rapid collapse of Germany's military might raised the spectre of a devastating defeat and put an end to all plans for colonial annexations. Faced with this situation, the political and military leadership resorted to a manoeuvre which it hoped would enable German imperialism to continue its policies by other means. On 20 August 1918, a few days after the crushing defeat of the German forces on the western front, Colonial Secretary Wilhelm Solf made a speech in which he declared, as authorized spokesman for the Hertling government and with Ludendorff's knowledge, that Germany would be prepared to seek a "peace settlement" with the Allies, whereby, inter alia, a joint colonial policy would be pursued after the war and Germany would retain the colonies she had acquired in the 1880s and 1890s.[1] Taking up Solf's proposals, Matthias Erzberger laid claim not only to Togo, Cameroon and German East Africa, but also to the Portuguese and Belgian colonies, while Friedrich Naumann suggested transforming Africa into a "joint colony of the European states" and establishing an "International League of Colonizing Powers" with Germany as a member and beneficiary.[2]

It was, of course, an illusion to believe that with victory so close at hand the Western Powers might be persuaded to relinquish their plan of carving up the German colonies among themselves. The keynote of Solf's speech, however, was remarkable in that it centred on the tactical concept of an understanding among the imperialist powers. This line of approach was consistently pursued under the Weimar Republic, and

---

[1] W. Solf, Gewaltpolitik oder Versöhnungspolitik? Berlin 1918.

[2] Cf. M. Erzberger, Der Völkerbund. Der Weg zum Weltfrieden, Berlin 1918; F. Naumann, Das Schicksal der Naturvölker im Zivilisationskrieg, in: Koloniale Rundschau, nos 9—10 (1918), p. 327.

as German imperialism gathered fresh strength, its economic and political objects were expressed in a new programme for overseas and colonial expansion. It is certainly no coincidence that Solf, a leading advocate of a flexible imperialist policy reflecting and exploiting the constant changes in the international power struggle, was rediscovered by pro-imperialist West German historians in the 1850s and, in a manner of speaking, held up as an example to the Foreign Office in Bonn.[3]

The political manoeuvre of August 1918 misfired. The Allies pressed ahead with their counter-offensive until the German surrender at Compiègne. But in the eventful months leading up to the signing of the Treaty of Versailles the interested sections of the German ruling class continued to pursue the colonial aims formulated by Solf, stressing the ideas of "collective colonialism". They were able to do so because although the November Revolution had overthrown the monarchy, it had ended in the victory of the bourgeoisie over the working class. Contrary to the assertions of propagandists of neocolonialism on more than one occasion, the transfer of ministerial responsibility to new men and the adoption of a republican form of government did not entail an abandonment of traditional colonial policy, but led to increased efforts to regain as large a share as possible of the exploitation of African and other non-European peoples, resources and territories.

The right-wing Social Democratic leaders brought to power by the November Revolution had not hesitated for a moment to ally themselves with the monopolist bourgeoisie and the generals. Before the war they had misused their position in the Social Democratic Party to try and dissuade the German labour movement from rejecting German colonial imperialism on principle and to plead for a "positive" role in administering and "civilizing" the German colonies. After the outbreak of the war they had, in one way or another, supported plans to annex the colonies of the enemy powers. As late as June 1918 the rightwing deputy Eduard David wrote in the columns of Vorwärts, the mouthpiece of this group, that "we would have no objections . . . if our colonial possessions were rounded off and enlarged by way of compensation and agreement"[4] under the terms of a peace treaty. Ebert, Scheidemann and Noske adhered to this line after November 1918 because it suited their own intentions and those of powerful financial and monopolistic interests.

[3] Cf. for example E. v. Vietsch, Wilhelm Solf. Botschafter zwischen den Zeiten, Tübingen 1961.

[4] Vorwärts, 20 June 1918.

The most important pressure group and propaganda agency of these forces was the Deutsche Kolonialgesellschaft (DKG). In mid-November 1918 and in mid-December of that year the governing body of this influential association called on the counter-revolutionary Council of People's Representatives (the new German government) to raise the demand for colonial territories "with all due emphasis" during the peace negotiations and to "insist on the restitution of the colonies occupied by our enemies."[5] When it became clear a few weeks later that the counter-revolutionary troops commanded by Noske would prevail over the revolutionary workers, the Council of People's Representatives replied that it had made the demand its own. At the same time, it requested an intensive propaganda drive to strengthen the government's negotiating position in colonial matters.[6] The peace negotiators were given instructions to this effect.[7]

The preparations for a propaganda campaign had been started by the DKG in December 1918 together with some newly founded colonial organizations, notably the Rat der Kolonialdeutschen (Council of Germans from the Colonies), later renamed Reichsverband der Kolonialdeutschen und Kolonialinteressenten (Reich Association of Germans from and with Interests in the Colonies). As soon as the government gave the starting signal the campaign got under way. Rallies, meetings, newspaper articles, pamphlets, posters, marches by former colonial soldiers, shop-window displays and other means were used to prepare the ground for the collection of millions of signatures in support of an appeal to the victor powers for the return of the occupied colonies. The operation was directed and financed by the group of bankers, industrialists and landowners engaged in the extraordinarily profitable exploitation of South West Africa's diamond deposits. Chief among them were the Berliner Handels-Gesellschaft and the industrial firms associated with it, the Deutsche Bank, the Disconto-Gesellschaft, S. Bleichröder, the Dresdner Bank and Jacob S. H. Stern. Not mentioned in the campaign, of course, was the real motive behind the propaganda offensive: the profit-making interests of the group. Its instigators wanted to make believe that without colonies the economic existence of the people would be at risk, their living space would become too constricted and "German honour" would be tarnished. At the same time the most prominent

---

[5] ZStA, RKolA, no. 5217, pp. 186—187, Strauch, Vice-President of the DKG to the Reich Government, 16 Nov. 1918.

[6] ZStA, DKG, no. 148, p. 250, Bernstorff to Strauch, 10 Jan. 1919.

[7] ZStA, RKolA, no. 7057, p. 29, Directives for the peace negotiators.

right-wing Social Democrat politicians attempted to dissuade the working class from its negative attitude towards colonialism. They argued that the colonies would become the nationalized property of a republic governed by Social Democrats, which would therefore assure all citizens of an "increase in production and wealth", full employment and "human happiness". Similarly, at the international Socialists' conference held in Berne in February 1919, the right-wing Social Democrats called for the restitution of Germany's colonies and not for recognition of the right of colonial peoples to national freedom and self-determination.

As the counter-revolution gained momentum, the campaign for colonies was stepped up as part of the domestic and ideological offensive launched by its leaders. Moreover, the government and interested parties hoped that strident propaganda would not fail to impress the victors and would make them more amenable to concessions. This proved an illusion, however, like earlier speculations that a peace could still be negotiated. Germany had not been alone in pursuing annexationist designs. Britain, France, Italy, Japan and the United States had also been out for spoils of war and they all shared the view that Germany would have to surrender her colonies to them.

Equally unsuccessful were the overtures made by the German government at the request of one of the directors of the Deutsche Bank, Kurt Weigelt, the chairman of the Darmstädter und Nationalbank, Hjalmar Schacht, the Association of West African Traders, the DTG, and various chambers of commerce. These parties hoped to secure a promise that German capital would be allowed to take part in the exploitation of and rule over the colonies by a "World Colonial Office" or some other "joint colonial organization" of the European imperialist powers and the United States. Proposals to this effect figured prominently in the German drafts for a peace treaty and for the League of Nations. The main argument put forward was that if German capitalists were denied any opportunity for colonial profits, this would inevitably jeopardize the capitalist system in Germany. On the other hand, if concessions on the colonial issue were made, the new republic would be prepared to serve as an anticommunist bulwark in Europe.

The victors, however, having demonstrated their strength and their military superiority, were in no mood for concessions. On 7 May 1919 they presented the German delegation in Versailles with the peace terms which they had drawn up amongst themselves. The draft peace treaty stipulated that Germany would have to relinquish all rights and claims to her overseas possessions, including all movable and immovable property in the colonies, in favour of the major Allied and associated powers. All economic and other colonial interest groups affected, all colonial associations and their local branches, all German parties representing imperialist interest (from the Social Democratic Party — SPD — to the German National People's Party — DNVP) and the coalition government headed by Scheidemann immediately showed great indignation. (Their repeated protests were later interpreted by some German and American historians as "protests of the German people".) The main argument they put forward was that Germany's colonial policy had earned her the right to participate in the possession of colonies in accordance with her strength and importance, economic and otherwise.

However, the Allied powers refused to make any concessions on the colonial issue, forcing the German government to sign unconditionally all articles of the peace treaty put before it. Concerning the colonial question they declared in a note of 16 June 1919 that Germany had resorted to "savage oppression, arbitrary and forcible deportation, and various forms of forced labour." They added that the Allies could not accept the responsibility for delivering the population of the German colonies to a fate from which the war had released them.[8]

So it was not Germany but these powers who were redistributing conquered colonial territories. Britain took possession of the greater part of German East Africa as well as smaller parts of Cameroon and Togo, most of the territory of these two colonies being allotted to France. South West Africa was handed over to the Union of South Africa while Rwanda and Burundi were given to Belgium and a small territory adjoining Mozambique to Portugal. As for Germany's former possessions in the Pacific, these were distributed among Australia, New Zealand and Japan. The allied powers sought to disguise the real nature of this carve-up by having the newly acquired territories subsequently entrusted to them by the League of Nations as "mandates".

2. 1919—1923

The outcome of the war was the result of its nature as an imperialist war of conquest. As the authors of a Marxist study of the history of the German working-class movement state, the system established under the

[8] Source: *Kommentar zum Friedensvertrag*, ed. by W. Schücking, suppl.: Urkunden zum Friedensvertrag von Versailles vom 28. 6. 1919, part 1, Berlin 1920, pp. 567—568, 604 ff.

Treaty of Versailles "added to the contradictions between the imperialist states, above all between the victors and the vanquished. Since
the law of the uneven development of imperialist states continued to
operate, the system contained the seeds of grave new conflicts and new
imperialist wars."[9] One of the main contradictions which remained and
even grew more acute in the following period resulted from the fact
that the First World War had not put an end to rivalry over colonies,
and to opportunities to profit from colonialism.

The Treaty of Versailles had put the seal of international law on the
loss of all German colonies. The Allied Powers except the Union of
South Africa had barred German capital from direct access to the sources
of colonial profit, the measures taken ranging from the confiscation of
all German capital interests to a ban on immigration, settlement, acquisition of land and the establishment of German firms or subsidiaries.
In response, the ruling class in Germany, seconded by parts of the middle
class, began to clamour for a revision of the colonial clauses of the peace
treaty. It became one of the principal goals of German imperialism's
revisionist and expansionist policies to regain sources of raw materials,
markets, capital outlets and spheres of influence, preferably colonial
territories in Africa and specifically the former German colonies, which
were, if necessary, to be administered as mandated territories. This
goal was pursued with remarkable intensity and perseverance.

The defeat suffered in the First World War and the ensuing loss of
power and extreme deterioration of Germany's international position
on the one hand, and the changed pattern of class struggle within Germany on the other, compelled pro-colonial interest groups, politicians
and propagandists to adapt their tactics to the new realities. They realized that the October Revolution had shaken the world imperialist system
to its roots, that the international labour movement was becoming increasingly revolutionized and that the colonial peoples' urge for freedom
was making itself felt more and more, but they underrated the impact
of these changes in the world arena and continued to overestimate their
own prospects. However, within the limits of their vision they sought
to take into account the altered conditions that had arisen and observed
all further changes with a view to making the most of them, if possible,
for the attainment of their goals.

Within weeks of the severe political defeat suffered at Versailles,
Solf's Successor as Colonial Minister, Johannes Bell, informed the
colonial associations about the government's long-term strategy in

[9] *Geschichte der deutschen Arbeiterbewegung*, vol. 3, Berlin 1966, p. 232.

colonial matters. He wrote: "The demand that Germany be readmitted into the ranks of the colonial powers must be raised incessantly and in an ever louder voice . . . Rather than sit back with arms folded we must now work unflinchingly to ensure that when the inevitable revision of the Versailles treaty occurs Germany will have her colonial rights restored to her. The German Colonial Society (DKG) should regard as its principal mission to help ever larger sections of the German people to become aware of the need for colonial possessions of our own and to spread the message that Germany has an inalienable right to her own colonies throughout the world."[10]

This was entirely in line with the demands of financial and industrial interests pressing for renewed overseas and colonial expansion. The words of the managing director of Norddeutscher Lloyd, C. Kettler, were typical of many similar statements made in those years. He wrote: "We demand the return of the colonies that have been stolen from us," and added that this claim would never become superannuated, was "inalienable" and would "exist in perpetuity".[11] So even before the peace treaty came into effect, every effort was being made to secure a revision of its terms. The primary object of Germany's African policies was and remained to regain the status of a colonial power, an aim subsequently reaffirmed in one way or another in all relevant programmes put forward by successive governments, the colonial organizations and the exponents of big business groups with colonial interests.

As for the tactics to be employed, opinions differed somewhat. One group of financiers and politicians associated with them favoured co-operation with the West European powers and the United States in order to secure better positions and, ultimately, take part in colonial exploitation and domination. Other interest groups inclined towards the view that the redistribution of colonial possessions in Africa should be obtained from the West European powers by playing on their desire to see the Weimar Republic turned into an anti-Soviet and anti-revolutionary bulwark. In practice, these two tactical approaches were often pursued concurrently, giving rise to political, economic and propaganda activities and manoeuvres in which the authorities, interested business groups and colonial associations went hand in hand.

[10] ZStA, DKG, no. 89, p. 228, Bell to the DKG, 20 July 1919. Also quoted in Deutsche Kolonialzeitung, 20 Aug. 1919.

[11] *C. Kettler*, Wir verlangen unsere geraubten Kolonien zurück, in: Deutsche Kolonialzeitung, 14 Aug. 1920, p. 74.

During consultations with DKG leaders in the late summer and autumn of 1919 Colonial Minister Bell described the prospects of a revision
of the colonial system as "not very good" and said that attention should
focus "less on the present period than on the more distant future" when
there might be a chance of a "more favourable colonial outlook". He
stressed that for the time being all that could be done was to try on every
occasion to make a little headway on the colonial issue during negotiations with the Western Powers. There was agreement that propaganda
should pave the way for such attempts by unceasingly stressing "the
need for Germany to have colonial possessions and the injustice she
had suffered in being robbed of her former colonies".[12]

The strategy conceived in broad outline in 1919 whereby the government and the propagandists would follow a two-track approach was
subsequently adhered to. After consultations with Bell and officials
from the Ministry for Reconstruction, the DKG resolved at its first
post-war general meeting in May 1920 to agitate for revision in every
conceivable manner.[13] All those who felt called upon "to influence and
lead others", Solf explained, should work to ensure "that the colonial
idea, the awareness of the need for colonial activities . . . take root among
the broadest possible sections of the people and bring forth a firm resolve
to regain for the Reich the overseas possessions it so sorely needs."[14]

Accordingly, substantial funds were made available for colonial
propaganda and for the publicizing of pseudoscientific theories extolling
colonial policy on cultural, social, national or racial grounds. Spurious
arguments that the Germans were a people without "Lebensraum"
(space to live), that colonies were a "vital national requirement" and
a symbol of "national honour" and "Germany's standing in the world",
that the Germans had a "right to colonies" and that it was their mission
as part of the white race to help "civilize undeveloped races" were taught
in schools, defended in academic studies, proclaimed from speakers'
platforms and bandied about in newspapers, periodicals, pamphlets and
books. Not infrequently, these speeches and writings also gave voice
to anticommunist and antipacifist sentiments. Those addressed to the

---

[12] ZStA, DKG, no. 146, pp. 72—73, Bell to the DKG, 4 Oct. 1919. In this letter Bell
summed up the results of the deliberations. In a speech to the National Assembly on
11 October 1919 he glorified the colonial past and called for a "revision of the peace
treaty, including the terms relating to our colonies".

[13] ZStA, DKG, no. 141, p. 103, Seitz to Chancellor Müller, 17 May 1920.

[14] W. H. Solf, Afrika für Europa. Der koloniale Gedanke des 20. Jahrhunderts, Neu-
münster in Holstein 1920, pp. 5—6.

working and the lower middle class sought to drive home the message that the restitution of Germany's colonies would put an end to hunger, misery and unemployment and satisfy the peasants' hunger for land. All Germans would then enjoy the blessings due to members of the higher race whose noble mission it would be to spread European culture and civilization whereas, in the words of a guide for emigrants and colonial settlers, the Africans were doomed on account of their "slave mentality" to "serve the master race".[15]

The aims pursued with this propaganda were twofold. As Diedrich Westermann, professor of African languages at Berlin University, wrote in the journal Koloniale Rundschau, the objectives were to "create a popular will to acquire colonies" and at the same time to make it "unmistakably clear to other nations that Germany neither does nor ever will consider herself absolved from her international mission and from her responsibility for taking part in the education of the undeveloped members of the human race."[16] In practice, this meant support for diplomatic initiatives of the government, chiefly in connection with the Locarno Conference.

On the domestic front, the advocates of colonial revisionism did their utmost to give their ideas the widest possible publicity and to halt the spread of democratic, socialist and communist views inconsistent with the demand for colonies. They employed a wide range of media for their propaganda, including films and radio broadcasts, both then in their infancy. Numerous cheap novels appeared on the market idealizing the "colonial hero" struggling in exotic African surroundings. A specific aim was to win the youth and the working class for the colonial cause. A publishing house, the Safari-Verlag, was founded and various organizations set up to foster colonial sentiments among various sections of the population. There were special associations for young people, boy scouts, students and workers. Right-wing Social Democratic leaders such as Noske, Cohen-Reuss, Quessel and Löbe and A. Stegerwald of the Christian trade unions played an active part in this propaganda. Only Communists and others dedicated to democracy and humanistic values did their utmost to show what was really behind the clamouring for colonies and a revision of the colonial system.

"Germany's right to colonies" was stressed during history and geography lessons in schools unless — and this was exceptional — teachers

---

[15] *H. Zache*, Deutsch—Ostafrika (Tanganyika Territory), Taschenbücher des Auswanderers, ed. by P. Rohrbach and H. Zache, Berlin, 1926, pp. 31—32.
[16] Koloniale Rundschau, Vol. 1/1925, pp. 1—2.

refused to do so. To some extent religious instruction was also employed. In addition, there were wall maps, visits to exhibitions, slide shows, lectures, etc., to drive home the intended message. Guidelines for the treatment of this subject in school lessons were provided by the state authorities while extracurricular activities were strongly supported by the colonial associations. In Prussia, Education Minister Konrad Haenisch, a right-wing Social Democrat, recommended in October 1919 that the provincial school boards take suitable measures to further the "Colonial Idea". This he hoped would "keep the Colonial Idea alive in Germany until times are more propitious for it to assume concrete shape again."[17] In other *Länder* of the Reich, where the Education Ministries were headed by bourgeois politicians, a decree had been issued in the summer of 1919, making it obligatory for schools to "cultivate the Colonial Idea". In Prussia, Education Minister Boelitz of the German People's Party promulgated a similar decree on 26 February 1923.

Those sections of the ruling class which were specially interested in a colonial role for Germany left no stone unturned to win the German people over to their demands, to divert them from their genuine social and national interests, to stir up nationalistic sentiments and to prepare them for international conflicts over colonies and spheres of influence. Since colonialist and racialist propaganda did not remain without influence on its originators, it increased their urge for renewed colonial expansion, with profit considerations remaining the prime motivating force. All the bourgeois parties in the Weimar Republic contributed: none forgot to include demands for colonial territories in its programme or to delegate leading politicians into the governing bodies of colonial associations.

The attitude of the SPD was much the same. The party's right-wing leaders more or less shared the bourgeois centre parties' views in matters of colonial policy. Yet there were certain points of disagreement within the party. The far right grouped around the Sozialistische Monatshefte (Noske, Quessel, Cohen-Reuss, Kranold, Schippel, Löbe, Kampffmeyer and others) openly demanded that Germany should have colonies.[18] But the decisive moderate right which formed the majority in both the party executive and the parliamentary group preferred to

[17] ZStA, Papers of K. Haenisch, no. 459, p. 449, Haenisch to Heinrich Schnee, 29 June 1920.

[18] *R. Sonter* (i.e. Richard Sorge), Der neue deutsche Imperialismus, Hamburg/Berlin, 1928, p. 175. Cf. also pp. 172—173. See also the detailed information given in *Klaus*

put their case in more ambiguous terms. Richard Sorge, a Communist writer on political affairs, described the situation as follows: "The real 'heavyweights' in the Social Democratic Party are trying to take the sting out of their pro-colonial attitude somewhat by referring to the most recent achievement, the League of Nations system of mandates. They are not calling for colonies, but for mandates to be awarded by the League of Nations."[19] A small left faction in the SPD rejected these colonial demands, but lacked any influence on party policy.[20]

In the Socialist International, the representatives of the SPD Executive pursued two objectives: (i) an open disavowal of earlier anticolonial resolutions, the last having been adopted at Stuttgart in 1907, and (ii) support for the colonial ambitions of German imperialism. At the Lucerne Conference in August 1919 they pushed through a resolution which described the seizure of the German colonies as "an injustice and a mistake" because, after all, the "colonial system continues to exist". Rather than call for the elimination of the colonial system, they proposed some changes to defuse the antagonisms among rival imperialist powers:

1. The League of Nations should guarantee for all states "equal economic opportunities in all colonies".
2. All non-self-governing colonies should be administered under the system of mandates.
3. Only the League of Nations should be empowered to award mandates.
4. Germany should be given the opportunity to become a mandatory power.[21]

On the basis of this resolution, the SPD leaders laid down the colonial aims of their party in the programme adopted by the Görlitz Party Congress in 1921: free access to all non-self-governing territories dominated by other powers and recognition of alleged vital German rights, including the right to colonial mandates.[22]

Mammach's study „Zur Unterstützung des Kolonialismus durch die rechten Sozialdemokraten in Weimar und heute", in Beiträge zur Geschichte der deutschen Arbeiterbewegung, 1961, no. 2, pp. 408ff.

[19] *R. Sonter (i.e. Richard Sorge),* op. cit., p. 173.

[20] Ibid., p. 176.

[21] In *Die Kolonialfrage im Frieden zu Versailles*! Dokumente zu ihrer Behandlung, ed. by Hans Poeschel, Berlin, 1920, pp. 236—237.

[22] Cf. Programme of the SPD, adopted at the Görlitz Party Congress on 23 Sept. 1921, in: *Geschichte der deutschen Arbeiterbewegung,* vol. 3, p. 626.

Except for propaganda, there was little the government and the various interest groups could do during the years of post-war crisis. The weakened position of German imperialism, the intractable differences with the Western Powers and the fierce class struggle in Germany left them little scope for pressing colonial demands internationally. On the diplomatic level, the government had to confine itself to formal refusals to accept the results of the war and to the announcement of "colonial claims". Every opportunity afforded by international negotiations, notably the conference at Spa in 1920, the League of Nations meeting at Geneva in 1921 and the economic conference at Genoa in 1922, was used to give maximum publicity to the colonial issue at home and abroad. The government notified the League of Nations in November 1920 that it would reserve all its "rights" in colonial matters indefinitely.[23]

In 1922, the government began to consider initiating negotiations on the matter. It hoped that the Genoa Conference would offer a first opportunity to link the colonial issue with the economic questions to be discussed there. According to joint proposals put forward by experts of the Ministry for Reconstruction, the Foreign Office and the Ministry for Economic Affairs, the following demands were, if possible, to be raised at the conference: readmission of German firms to the colonial territories, restitution of German capital confiscated in the former German colonies and the transfer of colonial mandates to the German Reich[24]. But, as it turned out, the conference provided no opening for broaching the subject. The year 1923 proved even less auspicious because the Ruhr conflict overshadowed all other foreign policy issues. But this year also saw the defeat of the revolutionary socialist movement in Germany, whose further advance would have put a stop to all colonial ambitions and whose repulse was a necessary condition for new imperialist expansion.

In 1920 a new authority responsible for colonial affairs had been established: the Central Colonial Administration in the Ministry for Reconstruction. Superseding the Colonial Ministry, it was entrusted with the task of "observing the development of the colonies ceded to other nations, the development of the colonial question in general and the possibilities of regaining colonial possessions", to quote from a ministerial

---

[23] For statement of 12 Nov. 1920 see E. G. *Jacob*, Kolonialpolitisches Quellenheft, Bamberg 1935, p. 49.

[24] ZStA, Reichswirtschaftsministerium, no. 14848, pp. 3ff.

communication.[25] It also supported the colonial associations and companies with colonial interests both politically and financially.

The government was concerned to keep the existing colonial firms going so that they could resume their activities in the colonies at the first opportunity. During the war they had first been exempted from taxes and duties to a large extent and then received millions of marks in aid. After the signing of the peace treaty it was primarily the Reichsverband der Kolonialdeutschen und Kolonialinteressenten which urged the state to hand out ever larger sums to the expropriated companies. These wanted to recoup their losses, suffered in a war they had helped to bring about, at the expense of the taxpayer. The government was sympathetic to their demands, even going to the length of putting draft legislation before the Reichsverband and other interest groups for consideration long before the Bills were submitted to Parliament. As a result, the major colonial enterprises received advance payments and other financial assistance from 1920 onwards, and were then indemnified in stages for the losses they had incurred as well as provided with reconstruction loans. This was enough to keep the major businesses afloat and, after several increases, it even sufficed to finance renewed German economic expansion in the colonial territories. As a result of this policy the colonial interests and institutions of the state and those of private groups and individuals became increasingly intertwined in a fashion typical of state monopoly capitalism.

The government of the German Reich was required, under the terms of the Treaty of Versailles, to indemnify Germans affected by the expropriation of assets in the former German colonies. Whereas the big companies were, as a rule, given adequate compensation in a matter of years, the "legitimate claims" of small farmers and other less-well-off colonials were treated quite differently. They were, as Friedrich Karl Kaul pointed out, "caught in the wheels of a relentless bureaucracy which after years of haggling left them with nothing but a few meagre crumbs ... For reasons of political expediency the bulk of these 'refugees', virtually all of them middle-class or lower middle-class people and hence 'patriotically minded', were kept discontented. This was the best way to ensure that the calls for the recovery of the 'lost territories' ... never ceased. So the issue of compensation for the war victims was ex-

---

[25] ZStA, DKG, no. 146, p. 60, Münch, on behalf of the Minister for Reconstruction, to Seitz, 11 June 1920.

ploited early on for the Reich's policy of seeking a revision of the Versailles Treaty."[26]

During the year in which the first payments were made the Committee on Colonial Economic Affairs (KWK) called upon all firms and companies concerned to prepare for a resumption of their overseas activities.[27] The appeal had been preceded by consultations with the Economic Policy Department of the Foreign Office. Summing up the results at a Committee meeting in November 1920, the representative of the Wilhelmstrasse said that after the unsuccessful attempt to win new "economically valuable colonies" during the war it had now become necessary for the German economy to seek a "complementary" role in foreign-ruled areas with an eye to "future interdependence".[28]

The Committee's appeal marked the beginning of a systematic effort to penetrate the colonies of other states economically. The German ambassadors accredited to the governments of the colonial powers were instructed to press for the repeal of regulations barring Germans from settlement and business activities in the colonies of these powers, and succeeded: the Portuguese were the first to make some concessions on this matter; next came the British and, much later, the French. This relaxation of restrictions enabled commercial and shipping interests, followed by settlers and plantation companies, to regain a foothold in tropical Africa. At the same time, some firms dislodged from the former German colonies sought to switch their operations to the Dutch East Indies where German capital had emerged from the war largely unscathed.

In South West Africa, only a small part of the German community — mostly civil servants and professional military men — had been expelled whereas the bulk of the settlers had remained. Traders and major enterprises had been allowed to carry on their business activities. It had been the view of the South African government that a harsher treatment of resident Germans might undermine the dominant position of the "white race". After the war, business groups of the Union of South Africa and large German companies operating in South West Africa as well as the governments of the two countries signed a number of agree-

---

[26] *F. K. Kaul*, Es knistert im Gebälk. Der Pitaval der Weimarer Republik, vol. 3, Berlin 1961, p. 112.

[27] *Verhandlungen des Vorstandes* des Kolonial-Wirtschaftlichen Komitees E. V. 1920, no. 1, Berlin, 25 Nov. 1920, pp. 33 and 58—9. Cf. also *G. A. Schmidt*, Das Kolonial-Wirtschaftliche Komitee, Berlin 1934, p. 11.

[28] *Verhandlungen des Vorstandes* des Kolonial-Wirtschaftlichen Komitees, pp. 10ff.

ments and treaties to harmonize their interests and to define the terms of a modus vivendi between Germans and Boers in the colony. Of most importance were the agreements on the merger of the big German South West African diamond companies and the corresponding South African corporations and the treaty between the two governments of 23 October 1923 defining the status and the rights of the Germans in South West Africa and their cooperation with white South Africans. It was the first time that a former enemy state concluded a treaty on colonial matters with the new German Reich. Advocates of colonial revision saw this as a partial success.

The large Berlin-based banks which were the dominant influence behind Germany's policies regarding South West Africa, and some of the industrialists associated with them, as well as Theodor Seitz, the last German Governor, had been seeking a compromise rather than a confrontation with the Union of South Africa. They had been at pains to exploit the South African attitude towards Britain and the close similarity between policies of open racist oppression pursued by the Union government within South Africa and the policies formerly pursued by the German government in South West Africa.

3. 1924—1929

The major Berlin banks, with Schacht and Weigelt as their chief spokesmen, had suggested as early as 1919 that, rather than emphasize the differences with the West European powers and the United States, the German Reich should stress the imperialist interests it had in common with the ruling class in these countries. The bankers were in favour of cooperating with Western states on an anticommunist and anti-Soviet basis which they hoped would enable Germany to come to terms with the Western Powers and achieve equal status (extending, inter alia, to colonial matters). In the mid-1920s these financial interests were able to increase their influence on colonial revisionist policy (Weigelt becoming a member of the DKG executive in November 1923), which gradually moved towards the line preferred by the bankers.

A certain degree of reconciliation with the Western Powers was the real objective underlying the foreign policy of German imperialism in the era of the relative stabilization of capitalism (1924—29). "What made Germany's international position so extraordinarily complicated," writes Wolfgang Ruge, "was the fact that powerful hindrances were obstructing such a rapprochement, primarily the antagonism between the victors and the vanquished of the last war. In order to overcome that antagonism, which had left Germany in a highly unfavourable position compared with her rivals, the German rulers sought (thereby adding to the complexity of the international situation) to use their relations with the Soviet Union as a trump card in their dealings with the leading powers of world imperialism, to heighten the contradictions within the victors' camp and to create favourable conditions for challenging the Western Powers (to begin with) on selected issues."[29] The chief bone of contention was the issue of reparations to which both sides accorded the highest priority.

When in mid-1923 the head of the Central Colonial Administration, A. Meyer-Gerhard, concluded that the end of the revolutionary post-war crisis was in sight, he conferred with other government departments to secure approval of a long-term plan for a propaganda drive preparing an official move on the colonial issue. The main aim was to rebut the charges which the allied powers had levelled at imperial Germany concerning the barbaric methods it had practised in its colonies. While these accusations were meant to justify the seizure and retention of the German colonies on moral grounds, they were nonetheless fairly close to the truth.[30] It was obvious that the governments of the Western Powers would not be able to make any major concessions in colonial matters as long as they publicly condemned German colonial methods. Before such concessions could be made, it was necessary to refurbish the tarnished image of German imperialism. The executive committee of the Koloniale Reichsarbeitsgemeinschaft (Korag), the umbrella organization of all colonial associations whose co-chairman was Theodor Seitz, now President of the DKG, endorsed the plan of the Central Colonial Administration and suggested that the propaganda campaign should get under way after the domestic situation had become stable, probably in 1924—25.

At this time, the German financial and industrial magnates set out to prove in the eyes of the world, as Ruge aptly observed, that they were "masters in their own house".[31] By crushing the Hamburg uprising, overthrowing the workers' governments in Saxony and Thuringia and

---

[29] W. Ruge, Deutschland von 1917 bis 1933, Lehrbuch der deutschen Geschichte (Beiträge), Berlin,1967, p. 258.

[30] ZStA, Reichsministerium für Wiederaufbau, no. 1833, pp. 17ff., Meyer-Gerhard to the Minister of Finance, 31 Aug. 1923.

[31] W. Ruge, op. cit., p. 245.

taking measures to check inflation and stabilize the monetary and economic system, they managed to consolidate their power, thereby gaining
more elbow room internationally for a more vigorous pursuit of their
revisionist and expansionist ambitions. When a Labour government
took office in Britain and Edouard Herriot became French premier
somewhat later, they viewed these events as encouraging because they
expected — not without reason — that the new governments would
adopt a more conciliatory attitude.

The German government came under mounting pressure to tackle
the colonial issue as rapidly as possible. But the prevalent opinion at
the Chancellery and the Foreign Office (where a Colonial Department
under the direct responsibility of Deputy Foreign Minister von Schubert
was re-established on 1 April 1924) was that it was necessary "to move
very carefully in this delicate issue" so as not to complicate the negotiations on reparations with the Western Powers.[32] And Foreign Minister
Stresemann stated early in July: "Germany's colonial claims will be
maintained at all times and asserted when the opportunity arises."[33]

But after the Dawes Plan had come into effect on 1 September 1924,
the government felt that the time had come to press its "colonial claims".
The agreements reached on reparations marked the beginning of closer
economic ties with the United States and Britain and made it possible
to formulate revisionist demands independently of the reparations issue.
To avoid the risk of its demands being rejected, the government decided
not to call for colonial mandates right away, but first to prepare the
ground for negotiations.[34] For this purpose it addressed a memorandum
to the member states of the League of Nations on 20 September 1924,
stating that it expected to be admitted "to an active part in the League
of Nations system of mandates in due course."[35]

Meanwhile the propaganda campaign financed primarily by the
Foreign Office had picked up momentum. January 1924 saw the publication of a pamphlet against the "myth of Germany's colonial guilt"
written by Heinrich Schnee, the last Governor of German East Africa,

---

[32] NA, F. C., Auswärtiges Amt, Büro des Staatssekretärs: Kolonialfragen, vol. 1
(hereafter referred to as *Kolonialfragen*), pp. E 187073—E 187074, telegram by
Maltzan to the German Embassy in London, 6 April 1924 (secret).

[33] ZStA, Reichstag, no. 1037, p. 456, Stresemann to the President of the Reichstag,
4 July 1924.

[34] NA, *Kolonialfragen*, p. E 187027—E 187028, Notes on Seitz's reception by Stresemann, 10 Dec. 1924.

[35] Ibid.

at the request of the Central Colonial Administration. In April of that year there were celebrations to mark the 40th anniversary of the annexation of South West Africa, the first of Germany's colonial acquisitions. A congress held on 17—18 September under the auspices of the Korag and financed by the Colonial Department of the Foreign Office gave various well-known figures another opportunity to call in unison for the readmission of the Reich to the colonial fold. The government expressed its thanks and declared that the objectives of the congress were in line with its own "concern to create the necessary conditions for an active German colonial policy in the future."[36]

In practical terms, this meant, on the one hand, sounding out the attitude of the Western Powers and making German colonial wishes better known in official quarters, either through diplomatic channels or via influential people. On the other hand, it involved detailed planning for a long-term strategy and for tactical moves by both the government and private bodies. Until the early years of Nazi rule this took place according to the "Colonial Policy Guidelines" submitted by the Colonial Department of the Foreign Office on 10 November 1924 after consultation with interested business circles, politicians, ideologists and propagandists and subsequently endorsed by Stresemann. The central idea was to achieve equal status with third parties in all colonies. Economically, the main emphasis was on the former German colonies and on Portugal's possessions in Africa, with South West Africa, Angola and Tanganyika being singled out for settlement and "Germanization". The Guidelines provided for continued determined efforts to acquire colonies in Africa, but specific territorial demands were to be raised only if circumstances permitted. The territories mentioned would be infiltrated to such an extent "that the possibility of their being mandated to Germany at a later date cannot be ruled out." Tanganyika, Cameroon and Togo were the first targets. The following "means to achieve these ends" were envisaged:

(1) Observing and influencing the policy of mandates by joining the League of Nations and its Permanent Mandates Commission.
(2) "Maintaining the German people's will to have colonies by every form of propaganda suitable for this purpose."
(3) Colonial propaganda abroad to win the backing of the United States and the West European powers for German colonial ambitions.

---

[36] ZStA, DKG, no. 147, p. 47, Colonial Department to Seitz, 9 Oct. 1924.

(4) "Promoting the German economic penetration of Cameroon, Togo and German East Africa as far as possible and participating in non-German enterprises in Portugal's African possessions."

(5) Channeling German emigration towards South West Africa and South Africa and consolidating economic positions there to strengthen German influence.[37]

In putting these plans into effect the Colonial Department made sure that all interested groups and institutions were cooperating in an organized fashion, and underwrote much of the cost involved in colonial propaganda, settlement and "Germanization" efforts, and the new big business drive for colonial expansion. Increasingly, the state and the financial and industrial corporations were combining their activities in this area.

The favourable international climate prompted bankers, businessmen, industrial and colonial associations, and bourgeois as well as Social Democratic politicians and cabinet members, during the first nine months of 1925, to join in public expressions of their wishes and demands. A case in point was the Berlin Colonial Week and Exhibition, held from 30 March to 8 April 1925 and addressed by Chancellor Luther and Foreign Minister Stresemann.[38] On that occasion Stresemann launched the expansionist "Volk ohne Raum" (people without space) slogan, which the writer Hans Grimm, who had worked for the Imperial Colonial Office during the First World War, sought to popularize soon afterwards (in 1926) by using it as the title of a propagandist novel dealing with South West Africa which went through many editions in the following years. Other activities included the founding in the Reichstag of a parliamentary colonial group by deputies of the Centre Party, the Bavarian People's Party, the German Democratic Party, the German National Party and the Social Democratic Party on 8 May 1925, a mass rally staged by the Korag in Munich early in June, and a meeting of the Bund der Auslands-

---

[37] NA, *Kolonialfragen*, p. E. 187034ff., Directives for our Colonial Policy, submitted by Brückner, head of the Colonial Department in the Foreign Office, 10 Nov. 1924.

[38] Cf. *Deutschland braucht Kolonien!* Werbebuch und Katalog der Kolonialausstellung im Berliner Rathaus 30. März bis 8. April anläßlich der Kolonialwoche Berlin 1925, ed. by Kolonialkriegerdank e. V., p. 18. Stresemann's contribution to this publication contained the following passage: "For our nation, cramped as it is for space and without access to the raw materials needed for food and industrial use, the colonial question is of the utmost importance. In the long run, the firm, inflexible resolve of our united people to engage in colonial activities is bound to prevail."

deutschen, an organization of Germans living abroad, in Berlin on 29 August. Addressing that meeting, Stresemann made it absolutely plain that "the recovery of the German colonies is an aim of German policy, and an immediate aim at that."[39] While colonies were not Stresemann's main objective, they played a certain part in his policies, a fact that has been ignored in most of the literature dealing with the Weimar Republic's foreign policy and international relations.

Stresemann made his remarks with an eye to the impending Locarno Conference. In an unsigned article published by the Hamburger Fremdenblatt on 14 September 1925 he defined the immediate tasks of German foreign policy as being to "oppose France's aggressive policy", to make Germany the "great mother country of the German cultural community", to seek a "revision of the eastern border" and to "assert Germany's claim to colonial activities and regain colonial possessions." Forward movement, he said, required "cooperation and understanding with the powers whose approval is at present crucial to the attainment of these ends." This, he added, presupposed above all recognition of the western border and the conclusion of a security pact with these powers, which had been associated with the idea of Germany's joining the League of Nations.[40]

Regarding the colonial question, Stresemann had put out diplomatic feelers during the preparation of the conference. Although London, Paris and Brussels avoided any specific territorial promises, they let it be known that they would be prepared to discuss the transfer of mandates as soon as Germany had loosened her relations with the Soviet Union, signed the treaties with the Western Powers and subsequently become a member of the League of Nations.[41] Luther, Stresemann and Schubert took this into account in formulating their tactics for the Locarno Conference. Their plan was to reiterate the demands contained in the memorandum of September 1924 and to secure at least their recognition in principle. Beginning with Germany's entry to the League of Nations, there would follow a series of further legal and territorial concessions so that Germany would ultimately be included in the "front of the civiliz-

[39] G. Stresemann, Vermächtnis. Der Nachlaß in drei Bänden, ed. by Henry Bernhard, vol. II, Berlin 1932, pp. 334—335.

[40] Ibid., p. 172.

[41] Cf. A. Rüger, Die kolonialen Bestrebungen des deutschen Imperialismus in Afrika (Vom Ende des ersten Weltkrieges bis zur Locarno-Konferenz). Thesis, Humboldt University Berlin 1969, pp. 237 ff.

ing powers active in Africa" confronted by the "ever-growing and partly obscure political aspirations of the black race."[42]

Pursuing these aims, at the conference on 8 October 1925 Stresemann demanded that Germany, in return for the conclusion of the "security pact" and her joining the League of Nations, should be recognized as a nation "entitled in principle to colonial mandates" and the German state acquitted of "colonial guilt".[43] The French Foreign Minister Briand observed that he considered the demand "regarding colonial mandates . . . to be fully justified in principle" and his Belgian counterpart Vandervelde added that "the practical side of the matter would depend, however, on Germany's political influence in the League of Nations."[44] The others remained silent. Briand's and Vandervelde's statements did not signify any tangible concessions — neither a withdrawal of the charges against German colonial methods nor a pledge concerning a specific colonial territory. At home, Stresemann and Luther interpreted the reactions of their treaty partners as acquiescence in their demands even though none of the powers had any intention of ceding colonies of their own to the German imperialists.[45] According to the account given later by the British Colonial Secretary L. S. Amery, the statements made at the conference only meant that Germany would be free to assume the obligations of a mandatory power if she managed somehow to acquire colonial territory.[46] So this subsidiary result of Locarno was hardly substantial.

The Western Powers hoped that in the long run the treaty would have the effect of diverting German imperialism's expansionist avidity in an eastward direction, notably against the Soviet Union. The German government, for its part, regarded the concessions made in return for the signing of the pact as no more than a first step. It was determined to press not only for the recognition of its claims, but for their implemen-

---

[42] *Locarno-Konferenz 1925*, Eine Dokumentensammlung, ed. by the Ministry of Foreign Affairs of the GDR, Berlin 1962, p. 143, Doc. no. 24; NA, *Kolonialfragen*, pp. E. 186932ff., Kurze Aufzeichnung der Kolonialfrage, falls sie auf der Konferenz in Locarno berührt werden sollte. Vorgelegt dem Staatssekretär von Brückner am 2. Oktober 1925.

[43] *Locarno-Konferenz 1925*, Doc. no. 25, p. 167.

[44] Ibid., pp. 166—167.

[45] Stresemann on 31 Oct. 1925 at a meeting in Dresden with local journalists (Vermächtnis, Vol. II, p. 213) and Luther on 23 Nov. 1925 in the Reichstag (*Schulthess' Europäischer Geschichtskalender* 1925, p. 171).

[46] *L. S. Amery*, The German Colonial Claim, London and Edinburgh 1929, pp. 122 to 123.

tation. On 23 October 1925 the Berlin branch of the DKG launched the slogan "We Demand Our Colonies Back", which was then publicized in all parts of Germany.[47] And Chancellor Luther, before leaving for London to sign the pact, vowed to achieve definite progress "towards the recovery of our colonies"[48]. He discussed the matter with British Foreign Secretary Austen Chamberlain, but his words fell on "deaf ears".[49] The Western Powers, which before the Locarno Conference had raised hopes of a colonial arrangement, were not prepared to share their possessions or their rule with the Germans and from now on flatly rejected all demands to this effect.

They thought it advisable, however, to make some concessions. Following her entry into the League of Nations Germany was admitted to the Permanent Mandates Commission in 1927, which implied equal legal status with the other Commission members and a voice in nego-tiations on the mandates. All European colonial powers (France being the last) agreed step by step, during the latter half of the 1920s, to lift specific bans and restrictions on the activities of German nationals and enterprises in the mandated territories and colonies. Finally, they agreed to put Germany on an equal footing with third parties in their colonies by applying the most-favoured-nation clause to her. None the less, Germany was denied the principal advantages which Britain, France, Belgium and the Netherlands were gaining from the control of their colonial holdings. This remained so even when her delegates to the League of Nations, looking for a suitable means of exerting pressure, were cynical enough to come out against slavery and forced labour in the colonies of the other powers. Germany's exclusion from the ranks of the colonial rulers was and remained the main point of inter-imperia-list friction over the colonial question.

While membership of the Mandates Commission afforded little more than a gain in prestige and fresh opportunities for verbal broadsides against the much-envied mandatory powers, the lifting of restrictions offered wide scope for a policy of economic penetration and "Germani-zation". With access to the colonies and mandated territories re-opened, trade and shipping[50] with Africa soon exceeded the pre-war figures.

---

[47] Der Kolonialdeutsche, vol. 5, No. 12, 1 Dec. 1925, pp. 250ff.

[48] *H. Luther*, Politiker ohne Partei. Erinnerungen, Stuttgart 1960, p. 400.

[49] Ibid., p. 401.

[50] By 1929 the Deutscher Afrikadienst again operated 38 ships totalling 244,540 gross tons (*F. Rode*, Die Entwicklung der deutschen Seeschiffahrt nach Afrika. Thesis, University of Marburg 1930, p. 22), not quite 20,000 tons below the pre-war level,

In 1929 imports from tropical Africa attained a value of 335.23 million marks as against 245.89 million in 1913 and 103.06 million in 1925. They chiefly consisted of primary products such as oilseeds, peanuts, rubber, cocoa, coffee, copper, vegetable fibres, hides and skins.[51]

The old companies, which in many cases pooled their resources by way of mergers, were concentrating on the main areas of interest laid down in the Colonial Policy Guidelines of the Foreign Office in 1924. They were able to achieve some success thanks to grants-in-aid or financial participation by the state. Important footholds were established in British Cameroon, in Tanganyika and in the Portuguese colonies while existing positions in South West Africa were consolidated. Some 95,000 hectares of plantation land were reacquired in British West Cameroon in 1924—5 and some 185,000 hectares bought in Tanganyika between 1925 and 1931. In South West Africa, approximately 170,000 hectares were purchased in 1926 as part of a government effort to promote German settlement there. The government made available some 34 million marks in compensation, reconstruction loans and financial participation to finance the acquisition of these estates and the operation of plantation companies and settlement schemes.

The settlement and "Germanization" policies pursued under government auspices in South West Africa, Tanganyika and Angola were coupled with measures to maintain the "racial purity" of the settlers by encouraging unmarried girls and women to join them. Organized settlement prepared the way for the subsequent recruitment of "fifth columns" from among the ranks of the German colonists.

On the eve of the Great Depression the German advocates of colonial expansion were thus able to register a number of successes. The German bourgeoisie was profiting from the exploitation of African and other

---

but the ships used were faster, more modern and capable of handling more cargo. Other vessels not covered here were to be found on the routes between Antwerp and the Belgian Congo and between Lisbon and the Portuguese colonies.

[51] W. Bast, Die Einfuhr des Deutschen Reiches aus den Tropen 1897—1932. Thesis, University of Bonn, 1936, pp. 113—114. While the value of imports fell to 139.87 million marks in 1932 as a result of the fall in prices caused by the crisis, imports of raw materials continued to increase in quantitative terms. German imports from tropical Africa were showing an upward trend, but the value of total German imports from Togo, Cameroon and Tanganyika in 1929 represented only 24.6 per cent of the 1913 figure. Ibid., p. 102. Even so Germany accounted for a larger proportion of trade with the former German colonies than of trade with other colonies. Cf. Koloniale Rundschau, no. 9—12/1932, p. 411.

peoples again, albeit not to the same extent as the capitalists in the states which had colonies of their own. Inevitably, the struggle for direct control over sources of colonial profits engendered political rivalry over colonial possessions.

Industrial and banking interests in the Rhineland began to re-enter the scene after the Locarno Conference. As Seitz observed during a series of speeches to the local branches of the Deutsche Kolonialgesell-schaft in Rhineland-Westphalia in 1926, "the colonial movement . . . was long hamstrung by the occupation of the Rhine and Ruhr region . . . But hardly had the French disappeared when our branches began to resume their activities everywhere."[52] At the opening event of the Colonial Week staged in Cologne, Mayor Konrad Adenauer impressed on his audience "the importance of our colonial policy".[53] Seitz was given assurances by industrial leaders that they would provide the Korag with continuous financial aid.[54] The dominant figure in the Cologne branch of the DKG (the most important in the region), Albert Ahn, a leading light of the "Cologne Coterie", was backed by other major capitalists such as Arnold Langen, general manager of Motorenfabrik Deutz and chairman of the local industrialists' association; Baron von Lüninck, chairman of the Rhenish Chamber of Agriculture, and Robert Pferdmenges, chairman of the bankers' association in Rhineland and Westphalia.

In a systematic effort, this group rapidly expanded its influence well beyond a purely local framework. One way of achieving this was the founding of the Missions-Verkehrsgemeinschaft (Mission Traffic Union) in 1927 under the chairmanship of Adenauer and the patronage of Joseph Cardinal Schulte, the Archbishop of Cologne, whose support prompted Catholic associations with over six million members to take out corporate membership. Among the business companies which joined the organization were Junkers Flugzeugwerke, Daimler-Benz-Mercedeswerke, Norddeutscher Lloyd, the Agrippina insurance group and other major firms. As the former Colonial Minister Bell disclosed in the press, they had joined "for what are primarily economic considerations — the long-term prospect of a substantial enlargement of the market." It was with this in mind that German missionaries and German personnel were sent overseas and Germans cars, motor cycles, boats and aircraft delivered, initially for missionary purposes. Bell was full

[52] Der Kolonialdeutsche, 1927, no. 1, pp. 3—4.
[53] Ibid.
[54] ZStA, DKG, no. 584/1, pp. 33—34, Minutes of Korag-Session, 4 Nov. 1927.

of admiration of the way "service to the fatherland was effectively combined with service to our Lord to further the twin causes of evangelization and colonization."[55] Later that year the Cologne branch of the DKG suggested staging a Special Colonial Show at the International Press Exhibition scheduled to take place in Cologne in mid-1928. The proposal was taken up by Kolonialkriegerdank, a welfare organization for former colonial soldiers, and endorsed by the Korag and the Foreign Office, which pledged full support and decided to use the show for effective pro-colonial propaganda.[56]

The preparations were thorough. At an extraordinary general meeting held in late January 1928 the Korag resolved on directives from which the following general objectives were derived: (i) "Attainment of Germany's full equality as a colonizing power in practical terms" and (ii) "Resumption of Germany's active colonial role." The tactical line of approach was set out in a "Colonial Action Programme" which stressed the need "to gain the widest possible backing for the colonial principles enunciated here . . . among the German people", then as a next step "to bring about the unanimity of all circles interested in colonies as to the colonial aims", and finally "to induce the government of the German Reich to embark on an active colonial policy along the lines of the tenets and objectives formulated by the Koloniale Reichsarbeitsgemeinschaft and to consult an expert nominated by the latter during all negotiations on colonial policy and prior to final decisions."[57]

The directive and the programme were to some extent a reaction to the stirring appeal for freedom launched by the League against Imperialism and Colonialism, which had been founded in Brussels in 1927 as the first anti-colonial organization ever to be established on an international level. The League's German section, supported by the KPD, did much to expose the colonial designs of German imperialism and the barbaric colonial practices of other powers, and to advance the cause of international understanding and solidarity with the peoples fighting for their freedom. It was little wonder, therefore, that the League's activities brought an angry response and counter-attacks from pro-colonial reactionary forces, and that the Ministry of the Interior immediately ordered the police to keep a sharp eye on it. In German politics, the battle lines on the colonial question were clearly drawn, with the imperialists ranged against the socialists and democrats.

[55] Der Kolonialdeutsche, 1 Sept. 1927, pp. 273—274.
[56] ZStA, RKolA, no. 6390; ZStA, DKG, no. 570.
[57] ZStA, DKG, no. 564, pp. 320—321.

On the other hand, in redefining its position the Korag, which was moving to the right, clearly dissociated itself from other imperialist formulas recommending a new outlook in colonial matters. Domestic opposition to the new German colonial policy, the continuing preponderance of the West European powers and, most important of all, the growing trend towards national liberation in Asia gave fresh substance to previously expressed doubts about the ability of imperialism in general and German imperialism in particular to retain or revive the traditional forms of colonial domination. The question was whether the old-style methods would not have to be replaced in the none too distant future by new instruments of control and exploitation. If so, why not make allowance for such an eventuality in good time?[58]

Solf, who as German Ambassador in Tokyo had gained first-hand impressions of the liberation movement in Asia, probably went further than anybody else in his reasoning. He wrote in July 1927: "The coloured peoples of the whole world have been seized by a powerful impulse for independence. The most striking expression of this striving can be found in China. Yet the idea for which the Chinese are fighting has also taken root among the inhabitants of India and South East Asia and among the Malays as well. Indeed, signs of such a movement are discernible even among the Negroes. We are talking today about 'Asia's Awakening', but 'Africa's Awakening' will not be long in coming ... movements of such elemental force are irresistible. Past history has shown that any attempt to stem the tide is a mere waste of effort. The only sensible policy is not only to adapt oneself to such currents but to try to guide or at least utilize them. Our situation offers the advantage that no coloured tribe today looks upon us as an oppressor and slave-driver." Solf concluded that Germany would have to "seek to adjust to the realities" and to cooperate with the West European powers and the United States, if only because "under the present circumstances ... her own colonial possessions would always be small and modest" and fall short of economic requirements. "Without abandoning our legitimate claims, it must be our immediate goal to win access to all countries producing raw materials."[59] Guided by similar considerations, Hermann Müller, the right-wing Social Democrat who was later to become Chancellor,

[58] See the answers published in the December 1927 issue of the Hamburg journal Europäische Gespräche to an inquiry about whether Germany should pursue a colonial policy.

[59] NA, FC. Auswärtiges Amt, Büro des Reichsministers: Kolonien, vol. I, pp. 392839ff, Solf to publishing executive Schmidt, Tokyo, 5 July 1927.

remarked in December 1927 that although "the German Reich has an undeniable right to colonial activities", it should "on practical grounds desist from striving for colonies." Vorwärts, taking issue with critical comments from the right, later described this statement as "the voice of economic and political common sense" exhorting the German republic to fight shy of "imperialist adventures along the lines of Kaiser Wilhelm."[60]

While none of the monopolistic financial and industrial groups rejected the policy of economic penetration, they continued to believe that this was not enough and that despite unfavourable circumstances it would be necessary to reimpose German political rule just as in the Kaiser's day. Rather than accepting the given conditions they were determined to bring the international situation into line with their own wishes and objectives. Furthermore, they were — as before — out to increase their influence on the bulk of the working population, which was in no mood for colonial adventures, and to rekindle flagging middle-class interest in colonial restitution. The Korag therefore placed less emphasis on legal matters and the guilt issue and more on promises that everyone would get a fair share of the profits derived from new German colonies. Increasingly, their arguments culminated in the "people without space" doctrine, which was bound to inflame chauvinism.

For all these reasons the forthcoming Special Colonial Show was seen as an event of the first order. The DKG prepared a "General German Colonial Programme" based on the Korag directives and calculated to create an impact. The document was meant to serve the threefold purpose of "publicizing the unity of the colonial movement in its methods and goals, paving the way for an understanding with those sections of the population and political parties which are still keeping aloof from the movement, and establishing a negotiating basis for solving the colonial problem in conjunction with other countries."[61] The programme was proclaimed at a rally in Cologne to mark the opening of the Colonial Show on 22 June 1928 and then disseminated in the form of 80,000 leaflets and reports in the bourgeois press.[62] But it was Mayor Adenauer who supplied the motto for the show: "Space without People and People without Space". This slogan, displayed in huge letters, was underscored

[60] Vorwärts, 4 Aug. 1928.

[61] ZStA, DKG, no. 585, p. 150, DKG General Secretary Duems at a general meeting of the Korag in Cologne, 22 June 1928.

[62] ZStA, DKG, no. 570, p. 111. The Tägliche Rundschau, a newspaper close to Stresemann, carried the full text on 23 June 1928.

by large maps showing Africa to be largely uninhabited and Germany to be overpopulated.[63]

The show was a faithful reflection of the Colonial Programme, which stated: "More than any other industrial nation Germany urgently needs a wider basis for its existence: new living space, sources of raw materials and export outlets. The African continent constitutes the vast reserve space for overpopulated Europe, and Germany asks for no more than her fair share of that reserve space under the same political and economic conditions as those under which the other major European powers are administering and utilizing it."[64] As noted in a Korag report intended for public consumption, the programme was hailed "by industrial and business leaders, by the professional corporations and by the entire press as an important event in the history of the colonial movement. Significantly, there were no signs of outright disapproval, except from communist quarters."[65]

The unanimity displayed by the representatives of the ruling class in the pursuit of new raw materials sources, markets and investment outlets did not enhance the prospects of success in any way. Those responsible for German foreign policy were unable, as they had been ten years before, to bridge the gulf between the expansionist aims and imperialist Germany's economic and political capacity to attain them (to say nothing of her military potential). How wide the gulf was could be seen from the reaction of the rival powers. Indicative of their sentiments was a meeting of the Union Coloniale Française, which was held after the Cologne event and attended by the Belgian Premier and Colonial Minister Jaspar, the Dutch Colonial Minister Koningsberger and the British Undersecretary of State for the Colonies Sir John Shockburgh. The declared aim of the Union was to "establish a ring of colonial powers opposing all forces and powers plotting subversion or revanche".[66] There was only one power plotting revanche: Germany.

This notwithstanding, German diplomatic efforts to achieve some progress on the colonial issues continued. But all further attempts were nipped in the bud. As far as France was concerned, Stresemann had

[63] ZStA, RKolA, no. 6390, pp. 80—81, Report of the Korag on the Colonial Show at the press exhibition in Cologne, 1928.

[64] ZStA, DKG, no. 585, p. 200, Summary of the programme given by Duems, General Secretary of the DKG.

[65] ZStA, DKG, no. 570, p. 60, Report of the working committee of the Korag, 28 Jan. 1929.

[66] ZStA, DKG, no. 138, p. 382, Eltester (Colonial Department) to Seitz, 7 July 1928.

informed the German Embassy in Paris in February 1927 that "Franco-German cooperation in the French colonies and mandated territories" would be welcomed "within the overall context of an understanding between Germany and France."[67] The results, however, were almost nil. Only a single joint venture was launched after a good deal of pre-varication: Les Cafés du Cameroun. Taking part in the project were the Crédit Lyonnais (a major bank), the Union Minière et Financière Coloniale and the German businessman H. Ruete. On Stresemann's suggestion the Foreign Office granted Ruete a loan of 500,000 marks despite certain doubts about the soundness of the enterprise. As later turned out, Ruete had secretly sold his shares to the Union Minière at the time the venture was launched in October 1928. By the time the fraud was discovered by the Wilhelmstrasse, the co-founder of Les Cafés had vanished into thin air together with his ill-gotten gains. So the test case of Franco-German cooperation ended in a loss of 500,000 marks for the Foreign Office.[68]

As far as Britain was concerned, the dominant feeling between 1928 and 1931 was one of apprehension that Tanganyika might be merged for administrative purposes with the neighbouring British colonies of Kenya and Uganda. This would have spelled the end or a diminution of Tanganyika's status as a mandated territory, which formed the legal basis of German hopes of securing the mandate. British discussions to this effect provided the bourgeois press and vested interests in Germany with plenty of material for protests and unfavourable comments over a period of years.[69] The German Foreign Office instructed its representative on the Permanent Mandates Commission of the League of Nations to oppose possible British moves in this direction and summoned the British Ambassador for clarification. The latter said reassuringly that "there seem to be no intentions to change the existing state of affairs."[70] That was the end of the matter.

---

[67] ZStA, RKolA, no. 3570, pp. 141ff, Brückner's memo for official use within the Foreign Office, 24 Feb. 1928.

[68] ZStA, RKolA, nos 3608—3613, Correspondence between the Foreign Office and the German Embassy in Paris.

[69] ZStA, Deutsche Reichsbank, Economic and Statistical Department (from 1926: Press Office), no. 1, 5, vol. 3ff. Cf. also Entschließungen der Deutschen Wirtschaftsverbände an die Reichsregierung betr. die englischen Annexionspläne in Ostafrika, no. 1, Nov. 1930; no. 2, Dec. 1930.

[70] ZStA, 07.01, FC. Reichskanzlei, no. 744, p. D 779375, Secretary of State Schubert at a cabinet meeting, 11 Feb. 1929.

Despite the attitude of the Western Powers an influential section of the pro-colonial interest groups and politicians believed, unlike the Foreign Office, that the negotiations on a revision of the Dawes Plan were a good opportunity to restate the case for colonies. This conclusion was reached at a meeting on 22 November 1928, which was attended by the directors of the Deutsche Bank and the Dresdner Bank, Brunswig and Wiethans, the general manager of the Woermann-Linie and the Deutsche Ostafrika-Linie, Amsinck, the Hamburg overseas merchant O. Riedel, the former Governors Hahl, von Lindequist, von Rechenberg, Schnee and Schultz-Ewerth, the former Minister for the Colonies, Bell, Secretary of State Kempner, and the two Reichstag deputies Sachs (German National People's Party — DNVP) and Cohen-Reuss (SPD). They charged Schnee, who was deputizing for the ailing Seitz, with making their views known to the government. They suggested a new argument for the negotiations: "In order to be able to pay reparations, despite her modest economic and financial resources, Germany must again lay claim to extensive colonial territories which lend themselves to the production of raw materials."[71]

Since the reparations issue was of prime importance, Stresemann did not find it politically expedient to follow this advice, but the Reichsbank President Schacht, the iron and steel magnate Vögler, the acting head of the Association of German Industry, Kastl, and the banker Melchior, whom the government had nominated as experts for the reparations talks, thought otherwise and decided to act independently. In a memorandum submitted to the Paris Conference they raised the demand for a colonial raw materials base as an absolute necessity for fulfilling any payments programme[72], but then dropped this condition so as not to endanger the reparations agreement, which offered other advantages. When the memorandum became the subject of a Reichstag debate, Stresemann on 24 June 1929 reiterated his fundamental position that Germany should be allowed to participate in the system of mandates to give her economy control over raw materials sources overseas. Explaining his tactical approach to Korag leaders, he said that the government would bring up the colonial question "as soon as agreement on the

[71] ZStA, DKG, no. 863a, pp. 453—454, Colonial Policy Directives, adopted at the meeting on 22 Nov. 1928.

[72] ZStA, Berliner Handels-Gesellschaft, no. 10081, pp. 50ff., Annual report of the DKG for 1929, Berlin 1930.

reparations issue has been reached with the other side and the Rhineland has been liberated."[73]

Although the government shared the objectives of the Korag, the latter was increasingly unhappy with the government's temporizing attitude. Seitz, who had long been used to taking his cues from the Foreign Office, aired his frustration in a letter to General von Epp, Reichstag deputy of the Nazi party and president of the Deutscher Kolonialkriegerbund, the colonial ex-servicemen's association: "I no longer believe that it is possible to achieve the least progress in concert with the government. So we are faced with the question whether it might not be appropriate to deliver strong public attacks on the government's current policy on mandates . . ."[74] This was something Epp did not have to be told twice. The Nazi general replied promptly that he had "long entertained the gravest doubts as to whether the government means business concerning the advocacy of colonial interests as we see them. It is my belief, therefore, that strong opposition to the government's current policy is the only way . . ."[75] The attitude of the shipping magnate Kettler of the Norddeutscher Lloyd was likewise grist to the mill of the Nazi ultras. "There is a danger", he wrote in a letter to the Korag, "that the apparent inability of the Foreign Office to move on the colonial question will entail severe political and hence economic disadvantages for our rights. In former German East Africa, in South West Africa and in Cameroon, English, South African and French traders are increasingly gaining ground against their German competitors . . . and the longer the current state of affairs lasts, the dimmer will be our prospects of ever again becoming masters of land that is ours as of right."[76]

4. 1929—1933

The banking and business interests in question continued to press for a more active pursuit of colonial revisionism, but without calling in question, at least for the time being, the cautious line taken by the Foreign

---

[73] This is how Seitz, President of the Korag, in a letter to the members of the Reichstag, dated 12 Feb. 1930, summed up Stresemann's comment, in Übersee- und Kolonialzeitung, no. 4/1930, p. 75.

[74] ZStA, DKG, no. 564, p. 98, Seitz to Epp. 7 Aug. 1929.

[75] Ibid., p. 89, Epp to Seitz, 20 Aug. 1929.

[76] Ibid., p. 69, C. Kettler to the Koloniale Reichsarbeitsgemeinschaft, 28 Aug. 1929.

Office in Berlin. Consequently, even their sharpest exponents kept their "opposition" within the limits of what was declared to be diplomatically desirable and even welcomed the fact that due to Schacht's and Kastl's initiative not only the country's "legitimate claim" to colonies but also the "economic need for colonial activity" had been officially acknowledged in Germany.[77]

The last-named aspect was given special prominence at a general meeting of the Confederation of German Industry on 20—21 September 1929. Kastl and the director of the Deutsche Bank, Kehl, emphasized in their programmatic speeches that colonial territories were assuming growing significance as suppliers of raw materials, markets for industry and areas for large-scale, long-term investments designed to open up new sources of raw materials for export and to increase the capacity of the colonial buyers. They said it was necessary for the German economy to turn its attention sufficiently early to this potentially lucrative field of activity to secure a fair share in it. Therefore, they argued, business and the state should not abandon their claim to an active part in colonial development and the extraction of overseas raw materials, and should make every effort to secure markets in the colonial territories of Africa and Asia.[78] Schacht expressed himself in a like vein in an address to the Chamber of Industry and Commerce in Munich.

These statements by prominent figures of German monopoly capitalism carried much weight, even more after the great economic crisis had spread to Germany. This was not only because colonial markets offered those who were able to exploit them advantages in terms of profits and security, but also because the chauvinistic clamour for colonies was a useful instrument in the ideological class struggle. This consideration prompted the Confederation of German Industry to give maximum publicity to the statements of its spokesmen.

One of the methods used for this purpose was the granting of financial means to colonial organizations and institutions, the funds coming either from the Confederation or industrialists' associations. The Confederation's Committee for Grants and Financial Support had twenty colonial associations on its list, with the Korag and the DKG taking the first two places.[79] The Committee met on 6 February 1930 to discuss

[77] ZStA, Berliner Handels-Gesellschaft, no. 10081, pp. 50ff, Annual report of the Deutsche Kolonialgesellschaft for 1929, Berlin 1930, p. 3.

[78] Übersee- und Kolonialzeitung, No. 19/1929, pp. 396—397.

[79] ZStA, RKolA, no. 6682, pp. 5—6, List and supplementary list of "Colonial associations known to the Confederation of German Industry".

the question of further aid to colonial associations with Privy Councillor Eltester of the Colonial Department of the Foreign Office. While the Committee remained "committed in principle to support for the Colonial Idea", it decided, as Eltester recorded, "to bring about a closer union of the associations and, consequently, a more effective use of the funds made available to them."[80] The merger of the associations, initiated by Kastl on instructions from the Confederation, took several years to accomplish. It began in 1931 when the Bund für Koloniale Erneuerung (League for Colonial Rejuvenation) joined the DKG and ended when all colonial associations were combined into the fascist Reich Colonial League in 1935—36.[81]

Leading representatives of German monopoly capital[82] made a point of demonstrating their growing interest in colonial markets and, hence, in the administration of the colonial movement. In early February 1930, Kastl along with Eduard Hamm, former Minister of Economic Affairs and now Acting Chairman of the Chamber of Industry and Commerce, and Herr Brauweiler, Chairman of the Federation of German Employers' Associations, joined the executive board of the DKG.[83] In the middle of that year, the chairmanship of the DKG's Colonial Economic Committee (KWK) passed from Friedrich Lenz, a businessman associated with the Berliner Handelsgesellschaft who had been in office since 1920, to August Diehn, general manager of the Deutsches Kalisyndikat. In May 1931, Konrad Adenauer was elected Vice-President of the DKG, a move engineered by banker Robert Pferdmenges, Chairman of the Cologne branch of the DKG.

The DKG leaders were of course eager to support the demands of the Confederation of German Industry. Leading the way was the Korag, which called on the Reichstag deputies on 12 February 1930 "to give due

---

[80] Ibid., p. 22, Eltester's memo of 6 Feb. 1930.

[81] The specific aim of this organization was "to penetrate the free trade unions" (ZStA, RKolA, no. 6759, pp. 4ff, Brückner to Külz, 31 Dec. 1930). Its Vice-President was Max Cohen-Reuss, Social Democratic member of the Reichstag and the Reich Economic Council. When the merger took place, Cohen-Reuss and Bernhard Otte, Chairman of the General Confederation of Christian Trade Unions, were given seats on the Executive Committee of the Deutsche Kolonialgesellschaft. From the outset the Bund had been supported by the Confederation of German Industry and the Colonial Department.

[82] Cf. note 69. The signatories included virtually all prominent financial and industrial figures.

[83] Übersee- und Kolonialzeitung, No. 3/1930, p. 47.

consideration, in connection with the current negotiations on the new reparations plan, to the enlargement of Germany's economic potential through the acquisition of overseas sources of raw materials as deemed necessary by the German experts in Paris and to ask the Reich Government to explain in what way it intends to take into account the proposals of the German experts and the statement of the late Foreign Minister Dr. Stresemann."[84] Following this, Schnee invited leading businessmen and colonial politicians to a meeting on 26 May 1930 in order to clarify "how the colonial issue should be treated now [with the agreement on the Young Plan ratified and the Rhineland occupation ended — A. R.] while ensuring that all interested circles act as much in unison as possible."[85] The following took part in the meeting: Kastl, Amsinck, Cohen-Reuss, Riedel, Ruppel (a senior government official and colonial expert), Schultz-Ewerth, Seitz and Solf.[86] They agreed that it had been correct for German foreign policy to focus on reparations and the evacuation of the Rhineland in the preceding years, but felt that the time had come "to push the German colonial question, which has so far been given a lower priority, more into the foreground." Finally they adopted the following "Directives for the Treatment of the German Colonial Question".[87]

(1) The mandated territories and colonies must be penetrated economically (and settlers placed where possible) with emphasis on the "vigorous pursuit of full economic equality".
(2) Germans in the mandated territories must be protected and "Germans must be permitted to carry out scientific and practical civilizing activities among the indigenous peoples" everywhere.
(3) Continued efforts are needed to dispel "the myth about our colonial guilt" once and for all.
(4) "Any annexationist designs of the mandatory powers" must be opposed (as in the case of Tanganyika).
(5) "Germany must strive for the possibility to engage in colonial activities of her own." In support of this demand, the authors invoked the charter of the League of Nations and a resolution adopted by the Socialist

---

[84] Übersee- und Kolonialzeitung, No. 4/1930, p. 75.
[85] ZStA, DKG, no. 553, p. 62, Schnee to Seitz, 7 May 1930.
[86] Ibid., p. 54, List of the participants in the meeting on 26 May 1930. Another representative of the Dresdner Bank as well as the banker Max Warburg, the Christian trade union leader Baltrusch, Bell and Lindequist were unable to attend, but gave their approval later on. Cf. Ibid., p. 44.
[87] Ibid., pp. 55—56.

International in August 1928, which had declared in typically imperialist fashion that "the backward peoples of Africa and some other areas are not yet capable of self-government and will depend on the European nations for guidance and support for a long time to come". They also reiterated the alleged "right to colonial activities of our own", resorting to the hackneyed "people without space" argument. And they added that the purpose of "colonial territories directly utilized" by the German economy was to provide a plentiful supply of foodstuffs and raw materials and to serve as settlement areas and markets for industrial goods.[88]

(6) "German foreign policy will have to make increased efforts to enable Germany to engage in colonial activities of her own . . . This is the logical way of continuing the policies initiated by Foreign Minister Dr. Stresemann in 1924 and later reaffirmed on several occasions, the last being his address to the Reichstag on 24 June 1929."

(7) "Colonial propaganda must be continued to this end. It should be designed, on the one hand, to strengthen and spread the Colonial Idea within the country, notably among working-class circles, and on the other hand, to back the German government in its official démarches aimed at the resumption of Germany's colonial labours."

Once again, a smooth transition to a new phase of colonial revisionism had taken place. It must be stressed that, contrary to what some historians maintain to this day, this development was not the result of popular pressure. Rather it was certain sections of the ruling class which harboured such ambitions and sought to foist them on the mass of the people as "German ideals".

On 28 June 1930 the Directives of 26 May were adopted by the Korag which, however, in view of the party affiliations of its member organizations, omitted from its resolution all passages which might have been construed as support for the foreign policy of Brüning's first cabinet. Speaking in the Reichstag on 26 June, Foreign Minister Curtius reaffirmed that the government was, basically, in agreement with the advocates of colonial revanche, and he promised to stand firm on the demand for colonies until this goal was attained. But since the colonial associations wanted to see their demand not only maintained but fulfilled as soon as possible, they urged Curtius and his successor von Neurath and the various governments from Brüning to Papen to abandon their

---

[88] The investment projects referred to by Kehl were not mentioned, presumably because the government, in its dealings with the Western Powers, was pleading insolvency and a lack of resource to cope with domestic economic problems.

tactically motivated restraint in favour of a tougher line whenever new
international negotiations were imminent, especially in 1932 on the eve
of the Lausanne Conference. As usual, they relied on propaganda material and resolutions and their chief spokesmen, Schnee and von Lindequist (deputy president of the DKG), made representations to Curtius,
Neurath and Chancellor von Papen.

But the outcome was always the same: the government gave assurances
that they would continue to seek a revision of the colonial system while
pointing out the impossibility of tackling the issue immediately with
any chance of success, and stressing their resolve to take the initiative
at the first opportunity.[89] But such an opportunity did not arise: European issues (reparations, rearmament, occupied territories) had to be
given priority. The diplomatic successes won in these areas during the
late 1920s and early 1930s no longer produced any colonial "by-
products". With the end of the Stresemann era, which had brought a
silver lining on the political horizon, the diplomatic offensive on the
colonial question had come to a standstill.

The policy of economic penetration fared no better, the Reich being
greatly hampered by the soaring budget deficit, which had reached
1,700 million marks in late 1929. Grants were drastically reduced even
while Stresemann was still in office. "The development programme of
the Foreign Office is currently limited to the promotion of German settlement in East and South West Africa," he wrote in a letter to Curtius,
then Minister of Economic Affairs, in April 1929.[90] This weighed all
the more heavily since many of the firms which had regained a foothold
in the mandated territories had at the beginning of the great economic
crisis not yet completed the reconstruction stage or become self-supporting. The difficulties which they as well as overseas and colonial traders
in general encountered in preserving old sales outlets and securing new
ones reached "monumental"[91] proportions. While these firms proceeded
to cut down their costs the Colonial Department tried to employ the
modest resources still available in such a way as to prevent newly estab-

---

[89] Curtius made such a statement to a delegation of the DKG on 18 Dec. 1930 (ZStA,
   DKG, no. 555, pp. 1—2), Neurath to Lindequist on 15 July 1932 (ZStA, RKolA,
   no. 7013, p. 51) and on 28 July 1932 (ZStA, DKG, no. 1114, pp. 7ff.), and Papen to
   Lindequist on 15 Aug. 1932 (ibid., pp. 5—6).

[90] ZStA, RKolA, no. 6716, p. 72, Stresemann to Curtius, 6 April 1929. Private Letter.

[91] This is how the situation was described by A. Hübbe, Director of the Hamburg
   Chamber of Commerce, at a meeting in Hamburg on 30 June 1930, in: Übersee- und
   Kolonialzeitung, 14/1930, p. 289.

lished businesses from falling into foreign hands, and preclude the collapse of the policy of "Germanization" and settlement and of the colonial associations. This end was largely achieved. But the prospect of an economic base overseas was as remote in 1933 as it had been in 1928—29.

The limited diplomatic and economic successes contrasted sharply with the strident propaganda of extremist circles. In the closing years of the Weimar Republic they borrowed their arguments from the Directives of 1930. They derived a multitude of sometimes mutually contradictory formulas from these and, by emphasizing specific aspects, adapted them to the requirements of every single colonial group.

In order to ensure coherence of purpose despite the multiplicity of activities and in order to exert a greater influence on the public, the Korag introduced two novel features. Firstly, the organization appointed prominent members of its Standing Committee to act as liaison officers with the press, their task being to "establish closer personal ties with the editors-in-chief of newspapers and to bring their influence to bear on them whenever required."[92] The local Korag committees were told that they were free to establish similar links with provincial newspapers. Moreover, it was decided to continue publishing press releases for newspapers at home and abroad.[93] Secondly, in a move indicating a realignment of the reactionary forces in the spring and summer of 1931, the Korag, the Arbeitsausschuss deutscher Verbände (Working Committee of German Associations) and the Bund der Auslandsdeutschen (League of Germans Abroad) formed the Deutsche Arbeitsgemeinschaft 1931, an organization designed to "conduct propaganda in the field of foreign policy and create a powerful domestic front in the closely related areas of colonial policy, revisionist policy [regarding the Treaty of Versailles — A.R.] and German minorities abroad."[94]

It was only natural that at a time of mounting class struggle the right-wing exponents of the bourgeoisie should be the most active champions of colonial revisionism. This did not, of course, rule out differences of opinion. As an example, a discussion on long-term strategy began among the leaders of the DKG in late 1930. Kurt Woermann, second son of Adolf Woermann (a well-known colonial capitalist before the

---

[92] ZStA, DKG, no. 571, p. 621, Report on the session of the Standing Committee of the Korag, 2 Feb. 1931.

[93] Ibid.

[94] Ibid., p. 253, Report on the session of the Standing Committee of the Korag, 2 March 1931. Schnee was made chairman of the Deutsche Arbeitsgemeinschaft and Epp chosen as Korag's representative on its Presidium. Cf. Ibid., p. 166.

First World War) and heir to the commercial firm C. Woermann, put forward the Nazi standpoint that the establishment of a dictatorship in Germany and eastward expansion should be given priority. By contrast, Seitz and Schnee (who succeeded Seitz as President of the DKG in late 1930 while remaining President of the Arbeitsausschuss) adhered to the formula set out above. But they shared the view that the standard-bearers of expansionism of whatever hue should work for the recovery of Germany's colonies. Woermann argued that the programme would have to point out "the way leading us to both our colonial and our national goal." This way, he said, "will take us via settlement in the East and labour . . . , as our grand national design . . . behind which our African colonial policy will have to take second place for a brief period . . ."[95]

At a meeting of the DKG executive board on 6 December 1930, Seitz and Schnee agreed that "the demand for colonies is only a specific task within the framework of a great policy of national liberation." They refused to put back their colonial aims even temporarily (so that their associations might help prepare a Nazi takeover, which they did not reject in principle by any means).[96] This attitude reflected the intentions of the industrial and banking interests, which did not want to see the drive for colonies postponed. Woermann, on the other hand, insisted that the situation first required an all-out effort "to strengthen and liberate Germany".[97] The other members of the executive board regretted this and subsequently set out (much like Schacht in the field of economic policy) to persuade Hitler's party to adopt a position more in line with their own views. For this purpose the DKG made use of Epp, who had close links with the Nazi newspapers Völkischer Beobachter and Der Angriff, and of its own propaganda experts. In 1931 the organization increased "cooperation with the NSDAP through a special lecture service" and "continued to meet the party's increased activities in the realm of colonial policy not only with inward approval, but with practical support and a readiness for closer cooperation"[98], according to a brochure published the following year to mark the organization's 50th anniversary.

The National Executive of the NSDAP, for its part, in 1931 issued a statement by Hitler in which he reassured the colonial interest groups

---

[95] ZStA, DKG, no. 749, pp. 171ff., K. Woermann to Seitz, 28 Nov. 1930.

[96] Ibid., p. 160, Schnee to Woermann, 28 Jan. 1931.

[97] Ibid., p. 161, K. Woermann to the Presidium of the Deutsche Kolonialgesellschaft, 22 Jan. 1931.

[98] Fünfzig Jahre Deutsche Kolonialgesellschaft 1882—1932, Berlin 1932, p. 112.

that he was not disregarding their wishes by any means. He referred to item three of the Party Programme which said: "We demand land (colonies) to feed our people and to settle our excess population on." Hitler then added: "We are committed to the return of the most important German colonies" and "we certainly do not reject the possibility of acquiring new colonies in future." But he added that the "acquisition of central European territory adjoining the existing Reich" was more urgent than securing territory overseas and that, furthermore, it was necessary to regain full sovereignty of the state before colonial endeavours could be given prominence.[99] The DKG diplomatically interpreted this statement as endorsement of the idea of "expanding German space . . . in the east of the Reich and overseas."[100] The statement gave rise to a "lively debate" within the Nazi party[101] in which the leaders of the DKG joined from outside. In the press, the radio and at public meetings, they emphasized time and again that it was not a matter of choosing between eastward expansion and overseas expansion, but that both goals were equally important and should be pursued more or less simultaneously.

An article from the pen of Duke Friedrich Adolf zu Mecklenburg entitled "The Colonial Movement 50 Years On" was characteristic of the tenor of this propaganda barrage. This ex-Governor and standard-bearer of colonialism, who was associated with the IG Farben company, described the reacquisition of colonies as a "major German objective". "Even if we manage to expand living space in central Europe," he wrote, "it will be impossible to meet all vital needs under the conditions of a temperate or even harsh climate. Industrialization has reached such an advanced stage in these latitudes that the tropical regions form a necessary complement . . ."[102] And Lindequist, acting President of the DKG, remarked in conversations with Chancellor von Papen and Foreign Minister von Neurath and in public: "Half-hearted measures will be to no avail."[103] The propaganda campaign reached its climax on 14 October 1932, the 50th anniversary of the founding of the DKG, when the colonialists celebrated with an assembly in the Reichstag building, followed by a rally of the colonial associations the following day. Spokesmen

---

[99] Quoted ibid., p. 111.
[100] Ibid., p. 112.
[101] Ibid.
[102] Berliner Börsen-Zeitung, 1 Jan. 1932.
[103] Ibid., 4 Sept. 1932.

for all organizations voiced their support for the twin goals of eastward and colonial expansion. One of them was General von Epp, who declared: "We want space and justice for our people, nothing else!" Goebbels had the speech published in the newspaper Der Angriff, calling it a colonial strategy for German fascism.[104] The pacemakers of imperialist policy, old and new, were drawing closer and closer together.

[104] Der Angriff, 17 Oct. 1932.

XI. The Colonial Aims and Preparations of the Hitler Regime 1933—1939

1. Tactical Restraint

The Nazi takeover on 30 January 1933 marked a critical juncture in German history. This also applied to the Africa-directed colonial ambitions of the German monopolist bourgeoisie because preparations to repartition the world by force now entered a new stage. Having been appointed Reich Chancellor, Hitler told the leaders of the army on 3 February that it would be the aim of future government policy, after a period of internal consolidation, rearmament and strengthening of Germany's international position, to seek territorial expansion.

Hitler outlined a programme along similar lines on 20 February to a selected circle of business magnates. But although the new Chancellor conformed to the profit and power interests of the leading financial and industrial corporations that were set on an expansionist course, the Nazi takeover did not result in immediate changes of any consequence in the treatment of questions of colonial policy. During its first few years the Hitler government adopted a very cautious stance in this matter.

Historians, especially in the Federal Republic of Germany, have sometimes doubted if the German fascists pursued any colonial aims outside Europe in earnest, citing their cautious approach and the seemingly contradictory statements made by Hitler before coming to power and in the years immediately afterwards. West German and British historians have denied the seriousness and continuity of Nazi Germany's colonial aspirations.[1]

---

[1] See for example *P. Kluke*, Nationalsozialistische Europaideologie, in: Vierteljahreshefte für Zeitgeschichte, no. 3, 1955, pp. 247—8; *H. R. Trevor-Roper*, Hitlers Kriegsziele, in: ibid., no. 2, 1960, pp. 125ff.; *D. Aigner*, Das Ringen um England, Munich-Esslingen 1969, p. 43, and *A. Kuhn*, Hitlers außenpolitisches Programm, Stuttgarter Beiträge zur Geschichte und Politik, vol. 5, Stuttgart 1970, pp. 112 and 215.

Admittedly, many of Hitler's pronouncements suggest that he was opposed to an overseas colonial policy. Thus he wrote in "Mein Kampf": "We shall at last abandon the colonial and trade policies of the pre-war period and embark on the territorial policy of the future."[2] On more than one occasion, Hitler said the overriding task was to make Germany a great continental power by way of conquests, especially in Eastern Europe.[3] He contended that the so-called problem of Lebensraum (living space) could only be solved "by gaining an area for settlement which will increase the territory of the mother country itself".[4] "Colonies cannot serve this purpose as long as they do not appear suited to European settlement on a major scale."[5]

Hitler's rejection of an overseas colonial policy, which he once described as "foolish", and his opposition to a naval build-up[6] were, however, of a tactical nature. The experiences of the 1914—18 war on two fronts led him to conclude that it was necessary, first of all, to establish the continental supremacy of German imperialism in agreement with Britain or at least without the latter intervening. He felt that "no sacrifice should be spared" to achieve this end.[7] France, on the other hand, was to be isolated internationally, and a "final reckoning" with her was to be prepared.[8] In Hitler's view, German hegemony on the European continent was absolutely essential if, later, complementary colonial territories overseas were to be won.[9] On the subject of the First World War, he wrote that by renouncing a colonial policy and a navy, Germany would have imposed "temporary limitations" on herself but would have opened the road to a "great and heroic future".[10] In 1932, amid a circle of close supporters, he summed up the Nazi programme for expansion in the words: "We need Europe and her colonies."[11] This was a clear indication that he had no intention of confining himself to the former German colonies.

The achievement of world dominion, therefore, included colonial expansion outside Europe on a major scale, but according to Hitler's

[2] *A. Hitler*, Mein Kampf, vol. 2. Munich 1933, p. 742.

[3] Ibid., pp. 753—754 and 741.

[4] Ibid.

[5] Ibid., vol. 1, p. 153.

[6] Ibid., vol. 2, p. 753.

[7] Ibid., vol. 1, p. 154; cf. also vol. 2, pp. 696—706.

[8] Ibid., vol. 2, p. 755.

[9] Ibid., pp. 689—690.

[10] Ibid., vol. 1, p. 154.

[11] *H. Rauschning*, Gespräche mit Hitler, Zurich and New York 1940, p. 30.

plan it was to take place at a later stage.[12] This was in line with his strategy of a step-by-step expansion of fascist German imperialism which is shown later in his diplomatic and military moves.

Obviously, Hitler cherished the illusory hope that German imperialism would be able, as a first step, to establish its hegemony over continental Europe in agreement with Britain. In early 1934 he declared: "If I succeed in drawing England and Italy over to our side, the first part of our struggle for power will be that much easier."[13] Even before, in his "Second Book" written in 1928, Hitler had rejected the idea "that England would immediately counter any bid for European supremacy" and advanced the following argument: "If Germany arrives at a fundamental political reorientation which no longer conflicts with England's maritime and trading interests but remains limited to continental objectives, any logical grounds for English hostility . . . will have ceased to exist."[14]

Having concluded that the biggest threat to the British Empire emanated from North America, Hitler initially believed in the possibility of dividing the world into spheres of interest, with Germany as the dominant continental power and Britain as the strongest maritime and colonial power. He opposed a German policy of colonial and overseas expansion for the time being because he gave priority to territorial aggrandizement on the continent and, especially, because he did not wish to antagonize Britain at too early a stage. Yet from the outset he considered the acquisition of colonies outside Europe to be a target of Nazi expansionism.[15]

This strategy explains why, as far as their official policy was concerned, the German fascists did not emphasize the colonial issue. However, the Nazi party had always identified itself with the demand for a return of the one-time German colonies as part of the "struggle against the Treaty of Versailles", which was at the centre of its foreign policy propaganda.

---

[12] Cf. also *K. Hildebrand*, Vom Reich zum Weltreich, Hitler, NSDAP und koloniale Frage, 1919—1945, Munich 1969 pp. 80—81.

[13] *H. Rauschning*, op. cit., p. 114.

[14] *Hitlers Zweites Buch*. Ein Dokument aus dem Jahr 1928, eingeleitet und kommentiert von Gerhard L. Weinberg, Stuttgart 1961, pp. 173—174.
Hitler had expressed similar views before, viz. his treatise "Warum mußte ein 8. November kommen" (Munich 1924). Cf. *K. Hildebrandt*, op. cit., pp. 456—457.

[15] The demand for colonies was also included in the February 1920 programme of the Nazi party See *Der Nationalsozialismus*, Dokumente 1933—1945, ed. by Walter Hofer, Frankfurt am Main 1957, pp. 28—29. .

Nazi deputies to the Reichstag and the daily Völkischer Beobachter, the official organ of the Nazi party, called for a revision of the treaty's colonial provisions.[16]

Hitler endorsed his party's demand for a redrawing of the colonial map in a statement before the general elections of 1930, but stressed again that the acquisition of Lebensraum adjoining the Reich must have priority.[17] Another sign of Nazi interest in the colonial question was the establishment of a Colonial Policy Sector (Kolonialpolitisches Referat) within the Military Policy Department (Wehrpolitisches Amt) of the executive of the Nazi party in 1932. With the exception of the German National Party no other political party had such an institution.

The restraint exercised by the German fascists after assuming power in 1933 with regard to the demand for the return of the German colonies must be seen against the background of the international situation in 1933—34. Especially in its dealings with Britain, Hitler's government was at pains to disguise its aggressive designs and to create the impression that the foreign policy of the Weimar Republic would on the whole be upheld. The immediate goal of the Nazi regime was to consolidate its power within the country and to gain friends among reactionary parties abroad. During a cabinet meeting on 7 April 1933,[18] at which Foreign Minister Konstantin von Neurath outlined his programme, emphasis was laid on the need to avoid any international conflicts until Germany had regained her full strength. Neurath said that it was necessary to refrain from any provocative show of strength and to seek close collaboration with Britain[19] and Italy. The cabinet decided to confine the treatment of the colonial question to the realm of propaganda with the aim of preventing the annexation of the one-time German colonies by the mandatory powers. This meant that, by and large, the policy of the Weimar Republic in this matter was to be continued.

Until 1935—36, therefore, colonial propaganda remained cautious, and no colonial demands were raised on the diplomatic level. The speech made by the Nationalist Leader Alfred Hugenberg, then Minister of

[16] W. W. Schmokel, Dream of Empire: German Colonialism 1919—1945, New Haven/London 1964, p. 14.

[17] W. Stuemer/E. Duems, Fünfzig Jahre Deutsche Kolonialgesellschaft 1882, 1932, Berlin 1932, p. 112.

[18] Documents on German Foreign Policy 1918—1945, Series C, vol. 1, Washington 1958, p. 606, Conference of Ministers and Cabinet Session on April 7, 1933.

[19] Cf. also the note by State Secretary von Bülow of 13 March 1933 on the international situation. ZStA, A. A., no. 60966, p. 13.

Economics, at the World Economic Conference in London in June 1933, where he demanded an African colonial empire for Germany as well as Lebensraum at the expense of the Soviet Union, remained an exception. His rashness was typical of the attitude of Nationalist circles eager to press home their demands at once without regard for the international situation. Hugenberg's speech led to a controversy with Neurath and contributed to his enforced resignation from the cabinet.[20]

With some justification, Wolfe W. Schmokel described the policy which the Hitler government pursued on the colonial issue in its first years as a "diplomacy by press interviews".[21] Its activities were confined to occasional remarks Hitler made to British journalists which cautiously reiterated Germany's "claim" to her former colonial possessions. At the same time, he underlined on several occasions that this issue would not be solved by military means and that Germany was not pursuing any strategic designs in the colonies. Hence the tactically motivated renunciation of a colonial and overseas policy, as first proclaimed in "Mein Kampf", did still not imply a renunciation of the one-time German colonies.[22]

The Nazi leaders' policy of treading warily on the colonial issue was also discernible in their attitude to the colonial associations. When the Gleichschaltung (enforced coordination with the fascist regime) of the organizations affiliated to the Korag took place in June 1933, they neither set up a centralized body nor subordinated them directly to the Nazi party. The executive of the DKG, the most important of the associations united in the Korag, was reorganized by vesting the President with greater powers and forming a committee consisting largely of Nazi party members to assist him. Then the Korag was transformed into the Reichskolonialbund (Reich Colonial League) to serve as an umbrella organization for the various colonial associations which continued to exist.[23] Only the Deutscher Kolonialverein (German Colonial Associa-

---

[20] *Documents on German Foreign Policy* 1918—1945, op. cit., pp. 256ff., Conference of Ministers on June 27, 1933.

[21] *W. W. Schmokel*, op. cit., p. 88.

[22] Despite his statements to this effect *K. Hildebrand* (op. cit., especially pp. 259 and 622—633) is unable to furnish any conclusive proof that the Nazi regime intended at one stage or another to renounce a revision of the colonial provisions of the Versailles Treaty in order to bring about a delimitation of interests between Germany and Britain.

[23] Besides nine associations, the Reichskolonialbund included the Hapag, the Norddeutscher Lloyd, the Deutsche Ostafrikalinie, the C. Woermann KG and the

tion), with its close ties to the German National Party, was dissolved. As before, the Colonial Society and the Korag, now rechristened Reichskolonialbund, were headed by the same person, the former Governor Heinrich Schnee, who had joined the Nazi party shortly before. His second-in-command in both organizations was Franz Xaver von Epp, a former colonial officer and general in the Reichswehr, who personified the link between the "colonial movement" and the Nazi party. Epp had been chairman of the Kolonialkriegerbund, an association of former colonial soldiers, from 1925 and a member of the Reichstag for the Nazi party from 1928. As head of the Military Policy Department in the party's national executive, he also became chief of the Colonial Sector set up in 1932. He thus occupied a key position. Technically, the newly formed Reichskolonialbund remained an independent organization, but in actual fact it became Nazified through reorganization and changes in personnel.

Points of contact between the "colonial movement" and German fascism had existed long before. The modern colonial ideology and the fascist ideology are both rooted in the profoundly reactionary imperialism of our century. In many respects the Nazi creed drew on the chauvinist thinking of the Pan-Germans who had championed colonial expansion before and during the First World War. The followers of the Nazi party and the colonial associations, although not identical in social composition, were largely middle-class people and petty bourgeois convinced that expansionism and the exploitation of foreign nations would offer them a way out of a life marked by insecurity.

If they had not already done so before the Nazi takeover, numerous one-time colonial officials and officers followed Schnee's example after January 1933 and hurriedly joined the Nazi party and its affiliated organizations. The former Governor of German East Africa, General Eduard von Liebert, a leading member of the Pan-German lobby, had done so as early as 1929. Well-known colonial figures such as Friedrich von Lindequist and Duke Adolf Friedrich zu Mecklenburg continued to occupy leading positions in the Reichskolonialbund and other bodies concerned with colonial matters.[24] Not surprisingly, therefore, the

---

Vereinigung Kameruner Pflanzer. Cf. *R. Lakowski*, Die Kriegsziele des faschistischen Deutschland im transsaharischen Afrika. Thesis, Humboldt University Berlin 1969, p. 29.

[24] Duke Adolf Friedrich zu Mecklenburg occupied a leading position in the DKG and was a member of the Publicity Council for German Economy, a department of Goebbels' ministry, in which capacity he undertook journeys to Africa and Latin America.

Gleichschaltung was carried out with alacrity in the summer of 1933 by the followers of the colonial associations with Schnee at the head.[25]

The cautious attitude of the Nazi government found scant favour with many adherents of the colonial organizations at first. They had hoped that the colonial demands would be pressed vigorously after the establishment of the fascist dictatorship. Taking up this theme, Epp declared at a congress of the naval and colonial ex-servicemen's associations in Leipzig in August 1933: "Many had obviously expected that now, with the National Government at the helm, there would be a whirl of colonial publicity to the accompaniment of tom-toms and martial music. But this is not what has happened. Instead, the National Government is very prudent, bearing in mind the situation we are faced with, for the world around us has remained as hostile to us as ever . . . Consequently, the Reich Government is necessarily cautious in its approach to the colonial question . . . However, the free political associations are not bound to treat the colonial question with equal restraint." He added that it was the task of the "legitimate standard-bearers of the colonial movement . . . not to allow the impression to be created that the German people were about to renounce their colonies . . . We must follow this line until Germany is in a position to notify and assert her claims."[26]

The relationship between the colonial associations and the government was characterized by the kind of division of labour which Epp had explained in his speech. After a decree promulgated in June 1933 had made Goebbels' ministry responsible for all propaganda activities in Nazi Germany, including those aimed at the return of the former German colonies, the ministry issued specific directives for the treatment of the colonial question in November 1933. These stipulated that direct official propaganda should be avoided and that this matter should be left to the Reichskolonialbund. Furthermore, in line with the policy of giving priority to eastward expansion and settlement in the East, the directives said it was inadmissible to cite the need for settlement in support of colonial "claims" overseas; and described all colonial propaganda as a matter of no immediate relevance.[27] The leaders of the DKG, especially Schnee, regarded these directives as unsatisfactory, all the more so as the government had failed to make the statement underlining

[25] *W. W. Schmokel*, op. cit., pp. 20—21.

[26] *F. Ritter von Epp*, Ein Leben für Deutschland, ed. by Joseph H. Krumbach, Munich 1939, pp. 261—262.

[27] *K. Hildebrand*, op. cit., pp. 272—3 and 279.

the importance of the colonial question which Schnee had requested in a conversation with Hitler on 30 March 1933.[28]

One institution, however, was not unduly concerned about the Nazi government's restraint: the Deutsche Bank. Commenting on the directives, its co-director Dr Kurt Weigelt observed that "they are unlikely to be the last word on the colonial question in Germany."[29] Weigelt was regarded as an authority on colonial affairs and as "Foreign Minister" of the Bank, which acted as the economic focus of the colonial interests of German big business at the time. As early as 1916, when he was a deputy director, the Deutsche Bank had nominated him to serve on the executive of the Colonial Economic Committee (KWK).[30] From 1927 he was one of the directors and a board member of the bank as well as a member of the boards of 35 companies.[31] Under the Nazi regime he became the undisputed representative of monopolist big business in the field of colonial economic planning.

Weigelt naturally made use of his connections to influence the treatment of colonial issues. He carried on a lengthy argument on the future tasks of the Witzenhausen Colonial School with Walther Darré, "Reich Peasant Leader" and head of the "Race and Settlement Affairs Office" of the Nazi party, who was opposed to regaining colonies in Africa because he saw no possibility of settling Germans there on any major scale. Darré demanded that the Colonial School should no longer train colonial personnel for Africa but future "settlers in the East". On 10 October 1933 the Minister of the Interior, Wilhelm Frick, decided the matter in Weigelt's favour. After he had carried his point regarding the school, Weigelt, in a "programme" for Hitler dated 23 October 1933, emphasized that it was imperative to establish new Lebensraum not only in the East but also in "other areas", by which he meant overseas colonies, of course.[32]

---

[28] ZStA, DKG, no, 571, p. 76, Confidential report delivered by Schnee at the Korag session of 3 April 1933.

[29] ZStA, Deutsche Bank, no. 21696, p. 184, Weigelt to Arning, 2 Jan. 1934.

[30] *Verhandlungen des Vorstandes* des Kolonial-Wirtschaftlichen Komitees e.V., 1 April 1916, p. 4.

[31] *R. Lakowski*, op. cit., pp. 7—8. Although Weigelt was on the list of the 42 industrialists put on trial as war criminals, he regained a leading position in the economy of the Federal Republic and was awarded one of its highest decorations in 1954. He died at an advanced age in 1968.

[32] Source: *H. Radandt*, Zu den Beziehungen zwischen dem Konzern der Deutschen Bank und dem Staatsapparat bei der Vorbereitung und Durchführung des zweiten Weltkrieges, in: Der deutsche Imperialismus und der zweite Weltkrieg, vol. II, Berlin 1960, p. 20.

On 14 March 1934 Weigelt addressed a memorandum to Hitler's deputy, Rudolf Hess, through the agency of Dr Jung of the Colonial Policy Sector of the Nazi party's Reich Executive. As in his "programme" submitted in October, he demanded that existing economic positions in Africa should be safeguarded and that measures be taken to assist colonial firms, above all in East Africa and Cameroon, in preparation for the day when Germany would be a colonial power once again. In this connection he stressed the political significance of the DOAG, the financially strongest of all German colonial firms, which had close links with the Deutsche Bank.[33]

Apparently it was because of Weigelt's initiatives that Hess on 5 May 1934 ordered the Colonial Policy Sector to be upgraded to the Colonial Policy Department (Kolonialpolitisches Amt). The new department, with Epp as its head, was put in charge of all matters of colonial policy within the Nazi organizations and their press.[34] An official Nazi party institution had thereby been created which was "responsible" for the politics of colonial expansion. Outwardly, however, these matters continued to fall within the competence of the Foreign Office.

Weigelt was made head of the Economic Branch of the new Colonial Policy Department, which meant that the Deutsche Bank could exert a decisive influence on all economic aspects of colonial policy. An opportunity to increase that influence still further presented itself soon afterwards when, as part of a reorganization of the employers' organizations, the Afrika-Verein, e.V., an interest group of Hamburg colonial firms and shipowners, was founded in late August and early September 1934. Understandably, Weigelt showed a keen interest in the new organization and became a member of its executive committee.

The Nazi regime, just like the Weimar Republic, was willing to fulfil Weigelt's demands for financial aid to German firms operating in Africa. It was mainly a question of subsidizing plantation companies and farms and of marketing coffee produced by German companies and farmers in Tanganyika. During a meeting with Legation Counsellor Gunzert in January 1935, for example, Weigelt secured an undertaking on the part of the Foreign Office to support the German planters in the vicinity of the Kibwele tea packing plant, which belonged to the DOAG. Weigelt said that "by no stretch of the imagination" could the loans granted

[33] ZStA, Deutsche Bank, no. A 26/23, Memorandum of the Deutsche Bank, handed to Dr Jung on 14 March 1934 for transmission to Rudolf Hess.

[34] The directive is to be found in: *F. Ritter von Epp*, op. cit., p. 264.

"be described as commercial" as their real purpose was to keep the German planters going.[35]

A similar case was the financial restoration by the Foreign Office of the enterprises run by the Brandis family who owned 11 per cent of German property in Tanganyika. In the first half of 1935 these enterprises, for the most part engaged in sisal cultivation, were on the verge of bankruptcy. The aim of the rescue operation was to prevent the bulk of Tanganyika's sisal production passing into British hands.[36]

Thus the fascist government lent financial aid in order to safeguard existing economic positions in Africa in compliance with the demands of the Deutsche Bank while, in its official policy, it continued to tread warily out of regard for the overall interests of German imperialism. That this official attitude was accepted by the Deutsche Bank may be inferred from a note of 8 November 1934 in which Weigelt recommended that colonial matters should not be discussed in public "pending a definitive statement of the Führer on the colonial questions and prior to the settlement of the Saar question."[37]

By playing on the anticommunism and anti-Sovietism of the Western powers and by feigning a genuine concern for peace, the Hitler regime succeeded in undercutting one provision of the Versailles Treaty after another and thereby increasing its power step by step. The reintroduction of compulsory military service in March 1935 and the conclusion of the Anglo-German naval agreement in June of that year marked a decisive breakthrough in this respect. When German troops entered the demilitarized Rhineland in March 1936, this signalled an evident change in the relation of forces in favour of Hitler's Germany. Thus began the transition to a policy of overt aggression which ultimately led to war.

2. Colonial Demands and Preparations 1935/36—1937

Once it had consolidated its position, the Nazi regime gradually changed its tactics in the colonial issue in 1935—36. Italy's invasion of Ethiopia and the annexation in May 1936 of this African state, a move condoned by the Western powers, may well have encouraged it to do so. The first time Hitler broached the subject of the return of the one-time German

---

[35] ZStA, Deutsche Bank, no. 21782, p. 286, Weigelt to Urbig, 19 Jan. 1935.

[36] R. Lakowski, op. cit., pp. 20—1.

[37] ZStA, Deutsche Bank, no, A 26/23, Memo by Weigelt, 8 Nov. 1934.

colonies was during talks with British Foreign Secretary John Simon and Lord Privy Seal Anthony Eden in March 1935. And one year later, at the time of the occupation of the Rhineland, the Hitler government formulated the demand for "colonial equality" for the first time in an official document, i.e. a memorandum addressed to the signatories of the Locarno Treaty. From then on Hitler, seconded by Goebbels and Göring, raised the colonial question at every opportunity that presented itself. But invariably, their demands were confined to the return of Germany's one-time overseas possessions. Their interest focussed on Africa whereas the former German colonies in eastern Asia and the Pacific receded into the background as the relations between Nazi Germany and Japan grew closer, for the Japanese considered these territories to be part of their own sphere of interest.

The new approach to the colonial question also found its expression in an upsurge of colonial propaganda during the summer and autumn of 1935 and in the reorganization of the Reichskolonialbund, begun in the autumn of 1935. The purpose was to turn this association into a mass organization affiliated to the Nazi party, not only in order to make more use of it in the realm of foreign policy, but primarily, to utilize it as a vehicle for ideological war preparation of the German people in general.[38] The man in charge of the reorganization was Hitler's special envoy, Joachim von Ribbentrop, who by order of Hitler's deputy Hess had been given overall responsibility for the Colonial Policy Department and the Nazi party organization abroad in February 1935.[39] After the DKG and the other colonial associations had been dissolved, Ribbentrop completed his task in June 1936. Epp was placed in charge of the Reichskolonialbund while continuing as head of the Colonial Policy Department.

But colonial propaganda was still subordinated to the requirements of foreign policy. In November 1935, for example, State Secretary Lammers intervened on Hitler's instructions because a newspaper report about the intended reorganization of the Reichskolonialbund had "caused disquiet in British public opinion over the aims of German foreign and colonial policy." Lammers informed Epp that Hitler deplored this fact and asked him to "make every effort to ensure that the dimensions of the propaganda conducted for our colonial aims by all concerned

---

[38] The Reichskolonialbund had a membership of one million in 1938 and of 2.1 million by the time it was dissolved in 1941. *W. W. Schmokel*, op. cit., pp. 31—32.

[39] ZStA, RKolA, no. 7543, pp. 23 ff, Order by Hitler's deputy of 21 Feb. 1935.

will always conform with the current state and direction of our foreign policy as determined by the Führer."[40]

The reorganization of the Reichskolonialbund was nonetheless, in 1936, accompanied by a considerable increase in colonial propaganda. Leading the way was the press, now thoroughly Nazified, which published large numbers of articles, commentaries and news reports for a readership running into many millions. The press campaigns for the return of the erstwhile German colonies, invariably adjusted to the international situation of the moment, were also calculated in large measure to influence foreign opinion or to support foreign policy manoeuvres.

The following years up to the beginning of the war witnessed a veritable flood of colonial propaganda inundating the German book market. These publications ranged from penny dreadfuls, pseudo-romantic and sentimental colonial novels and memoirs, to pseudo-scientific propaganda writings, articles in journals and "correspondence lessons" for Nazi party members. There was no instrument of mass persuasion that was not used systematically to popularize the demand for colonies. Exhibitions, radio broadcasts, films and plays were devoted to this theme.

As in Imperial Germany and under the Weimar Republic, it was considered especially important to educate schoolboys and -girls in a colonialist spirit. Not only did the officially prescribed curricula require teachers to deal with "German colonial demands" during history and geography lessons; teachers were, in fact, expected to use every part of school education for this purpose. The short stories of Hans Grimm were to be read during German lessons, colonial propaganda posters painted during art lessons, and fictitious colonial statistics used in arithmetic lessons. Teachers were to make a special point of refuting the "myth of Germany's colonial guilt" and to glorify German "colonial pioneers" such as the notorious Carl Peters.[41]

The colonial propaganda of the Nazi regime was one of the chief methods of preparing the German people for war. It constituted an effective ideological vehicle for preparing armed aggression since it afforded ample opportunity to extol the conquest of other countries and the oppression of other peoples without restraint. Sentimental

---

[40] Ibid., no. 4618, pp. 19—20, Lammers to Epp. 25 Nov. 1935.

[41] H. Kühne, Faschistische Kolonialideologie und zweiter Weltkrieg, Berlin 1962, pp. 107ff., 47 and 76; H. Behrend (i.e. Albert Norden), Von Rohrbach zu Rohrbach. Unser Kampf gegen Hitlers Kolonialpolitik, in: Die Internationale, 1936, no. 2—3, p. 35.

romances in a colonial setting and stories exalting the freebooter mentality of the "colonial pioneers" could be used to whet the appetite for annexations. This propaganda was not only "agitation for colonies as such, but a broadly conceived attempt to stir up feeling in favour of territorial conquest generally," as Albert Norden noted in 1936.[42] Then, too, the demands for colonies offered the advantage that they could be presented as "legitimate claims" of the German people to their "stolen colonies" in connection with the struggle against the Treaty of Versailles. As it was directed against the western powers, colonial propaganda was also a suitable instrument for fomenting anti-British sentiments, an aspect which became important during the immediate war preparations from late 1938 onwards.

It was not necessary, however, to advocate war as a necessary means of recovering the lost colonies. Hitler stressed on more than one occasion that Germany's colonial claims constituted no ground for military conflicts. It was quite sufficient to demand a negotiated "solution of the colonial question" so that if the western powers refused to yield on all points, the general feeling would be one day that only an armed confrontation could offer a way out of the supposed impasse. Addressing representatives of the Nazi press on 10 November 1938, Hitler admitted that he had been compelled to keep talking about peace in order to be able to rearm without hindrance. It had been necessary, therefore, "to present certain foreign policy developments to the German people in such a light that their own inner voice slowly began to cry out for the use of force."[43] Colonial propaganda played no small part in these psychological preparations for armed aggression.

To demonstrate the "need" for the return of the former German colonies, the Nazi propagandists not only invoked "national honour" and sought to dispel the "myth of Germany's colonial guilt" but, even more important, referred to what they claimed were economic necessities. Citing the thesis of insufficient "living space" for the German people, they described colonies as indispensable sources of raw materials for the "domestic economy" while stressing that the space required for large-scale settlement would have to be acquired through eastward expansion. By ascribing Germany's economic difficulties, especially her lack of foreign exchange, largely to the fact that she had been "robbed" of her colonies the Nazi regime was able to cover up the true causes of

---

[42] Source: *H. Kühne*, op. cit., p. 40.

[43] Source: Vierteljahreshefte für Zeitgeschichte, no. 2, 1958, p. 182. Hitler's speech to the German press.

these difficulties, viz. its relentless military build-up, and to depict the solution of the colonial question as a "vital necessity" for Germany.[44] Proclaiming the Four-Year Plan at the Nazi party congress in September 1936, Hitler asserted: "1. The 136 inhabitants per square kilometre in Germany cannot . . . find enough food at home . . . To make up for this deficiency through imports is all the more difficult as Germany also lacks a number of important raw materials . . . 2. The German economy is therefore compelled to close the food and raw materials gap by exporting industrial goods . . . If the German people and the German Reich had not been bled white for 15 years and deprived of all its [sic] international savings, if it had not lost all its capital invested abroad and, most important, if it still had its colonies, we could certainly accomplish these tasks more easily."[45]

Another crucial element of the Nazis' colonial ideology, beside the "living space" theory, was the fascist "racial theory", the most reactionary brand of racism ever devised. This theory denies the importance of the class struggle for human development and substitutes the "struggle between the races" for it. As the Nazi "race theorist" Alfred Rosenberg put it, "history and the tasks of the future no longer mean a struggle between one class and another, but a struggle between blood and blood, race and race, people and people."[46] He contended that history had been shaped by "leading races" called upon by their "natural superiority" to impose their "right of the stronger" on others. In this way the imperialist oppression and exploitation of other peoples, and finally even genocide, were portrayed as necessary for the advance of human civilization, which constitutes an outright perversion of the concept of progress.

According to this theory, the Europeans and especially the "Nordic peoples" represent a "superior race" and by virtue of their "hereditary disposition" have "a fundamental right" to be "ruling peoples".[47] In "Mein Kampf" Hitler distinguished between "founders", "preservers" and "destroyers" of civilization. The only "founders of civilization" in his eyes were the so-called Aryans "who laid the foundations and erect-

[44] M. Warnack, Koloniale Ergänzungswirtschaft, Zahlen und Tatsachen, Berlin 1939, p. 15.

[45] Schulthess' Europäischer Geschichtskalender 1936, Munich 1937, pp. 119—20.

[46] A. Rosenberg, Der Mythus des 20. Jahrhunderts, Munich 1934, pp. 1—2. Cf. also A. Hitler, Mein Kampf, vol. 1, pp. 319—324.

[47] G. Hecht, Die Bedeutung des Rassegedankens in der Kolonialpolitik, in: Deutscher Kolonial-Dienst, 15 Nov. 1937, p. 5. On the whole subject cf. H. Kühne, op. cit., pp. 55ff.

ed the walls of every great structure in human culture".[48] By contrast, the peoples of Africa were said to have no potential for development at all. Accordingly, the Nazi ideologists depicted the oppression and exploitation of the Africans as a natural phenomenon founded on alleged biological differences. Even the well-known German ethnographer Richard Thurnwald stated that "colonial expansion is . . . deeply rooted in the life processes of tribes, peoples and states. It becomes understandable only from this biological point of view."[49]

As to the status intended for Africans in the new German colonial empire, Paul Rohrbach, who had been a leading advocate of colonialism in imperial Germany and under the Weimar Republic, declared bluntly in 1935: "The black man will not live in such houses as the German settlers. He will read no books and write no letters. He will not eat the way Europeans do, and he will have less need of domestic utensils, tools and daily necessities. He will not travel, spend no money on the education of his children and require no expensive machines."[50]

An important reason for stressing racist aspects was a desire to discredit the western powers and their colonial policies. The Nazi propagandists accused these powers of undermining "white supremacy" by failing to adopt a clear stand on the "racial question". They claimed that disturbances and uprisings and the spread of "Bolshevism" in the colonies (the term "colonial Bolshevism" was invented in this context) were — in the words of the Deutscher Kolonial-Dienst — attributable to a "waning of the true master instincts of the white race".[51] The conclusion was that only Nazi Germany was capable of ensuring a correct "racial policy". These allegations were variously used to attack the western powers or to lend emphasis to the demand for colonies by claiming that a correct "racial policy" could protect the whole imperialist colonial system from the storms sweeping across Asia and Africa.[52]

The year 1936 saw not only a change in the way the colonial question was treated in the domain of foreign policy and propaganda, but also the beginning of direct preparations (largely hidden from the public) for the takeover of colonies at a later date. These preparations initially

---

[48] *A. Hitler*, op. cit., vol 1, p. 318.

[49] *R. Thurnwald*, Koloniale Gestaltung. Methoden und Probleme kolonialer Ausdehnung, Hamburg 1939, pp. 16—7.

[50] *P. Rohrbach*, Deutschlands koloniale Forderung, Hamburg 1935, p. 140.

[51] *H. Nachrodt*, Die Weltanschauung in der Kolonialpolitik, in: Deutscher Kolonial-Dienst, 15 Jan. 1939, p. 4.

[52] *H. Kühne*, op. cit., pp. 65 and 73..

dealt with economic questions and included the planning of economic ventures in Africa. In February 1936 Weigelt informed the Hamburg Chamber of Commerce and the executive of the Afrika-Verein confidentially that the Colonial Policy Department of the Nazi party had been instructed to observe economic developments in the colonial territories. The aim was to establish criteria for "defining colonial production in terms of domestic needs, stability and future trends and for determining the relative contribution of the various territories and thus their value, for future negotiations." Weigelt added that the Colonial Policy Department had to be prepared for the start of the colonial forward movement as regards "the programme and the personnel needed". He said that the preparations should be advanced so far "that we can then not only take over the administration at once, but also begin to carry out a programme suited to our domestic economy."[53]

As can be seen from an article written in 1937, Weigelt believed that the former German colonies could meet only a small portion of the German demand for raw materials. Yet he added that the annual contribution of these colonies "if they had remained in our hands would doubtless have amounted to over 400 million marks" and that it was "not irrelevant whether, given a trade turnover of roughly 4,000 million, about one-tenth of this sum accrues from colonies of our own or not." According to Weigelt, such a proportion was soon attainable provided production in these territories could be developed with German capital. The products he had in mind were minerals, raw materials for the textile industry, cocoa and coffee, bananas, skins, hides, tans, timber, oil seeds and rubber. It all depended, he said, on whether "we are allowed to organize production under our own flag and finance it with our own currency."[54]

Weigelt's efforts to prepare the ground for this eventuality were raised to a new level on 28 July 1936 with the founding of the Group of German Colonial Business Enterprises (Deko Group) by order of the Reich Minister of Economics. This association, modelled on similar organizations in other branches of the economy, was to comprise all German firms operating in the former German colonies.[55] In accordance with Weigelt's request, the directive establishing the group was not published

[53] ZStA, Deutsche Bank, no. A 26/45, Lecture by Weigelt, 26 Feb. 1936, pp. 13 and 9.
[54] *K. Weigelt*, Koloniale Rohstoffversorgung im Rahmen der heimischen Volkswirtschaft, in: Veröffentlichungen des Deutschen Instituts für Außenpolitische Forschung, vol. I, Beiträge zur deutschen Kolonialfrage, ed. by Diedrich Westermann, Berlin, Essen and Leipzig 1937, pp. 84, 81 and 89.
[55] ZStA, Deutsche Bank, no. 21914, p. 44, Charter of the Deko Group.

in the official gazette in order to "avoid foreign policy repercussions".[56] Weigelt was placed in charge of the Deko Group after having played a decisive part in its foundation. Thus the prominent banker strengthened his key position in the systematic preparations for colonial expansion in Africa still further.

According to Weigelt it was the task of the Deko Group to watch the colonial sphere at home and abroad critically and to make the conclusions thus gained available to its members. It was also "to assist existing enterprises capable of producing part of their output in former German colonies on the basis of German currency."[57] Furthermore the Deko Group was to undertake "all manner of practical preparations in anticipation of the recovery of Germany's colonial possessions". The organization was supposed to "gather about itself the business circles which will later be capable of carrying out a programme aimed at maximum output within their own spheres of activity or, if these do not yet exist, of increasing their economic involvement in the countries eligible for our colonial development . . ."[58]

In September 1936 Weigelt declared in connection with the founding of the Deko Group: "I have now been given a mandate to go ahead with the preparations for the development of colonies at some later date."[59] In February 1937, if not earlier, the Colonial Policy Department also began administrative preparations in cooperation with various Reich ministries, and in late 1937 the Wehrmacht started to work out military measures to be taken in case of a colonial transfer.[60]

The inauguration of "preparatory colonial planning" in 1936—37 must be seen in the context of the general intensification of war preparations at that time. September 1936 saw the proclamation of the Four-Year Plan, a measure designed to conclude the economic and military preparations for a new war. The rationale behind the Four-Year Plan makes it clear that the Nazi regime was heading for war not only against the Soviet Union, but also against the western powers, the possessors of the bulk of the African colonies.

While the Four-Year Plan stressed the need to achieve as much self-sufficiency as possible in strategic raw materials, it also provided for the promotion of exports as a source of foreign exchange needed for the con-

---

[56] Ibid., p. 67, Note by Weigelt, 19 June 1936.

[57] Ibid., p. 193, Weigelt to the Reich Chamber of Economics, 15 Sept. 1937.

[58] Ibid., p. 180, Notes by Weigelt, 9 Aug. 1937.

[59] Ibid., p. 75, Weigelt to Loeb, 29 Sept. 1936.

[60] R. Lakowski, op. cit., pp. 58—9.

tinuation of the armaments drive.[61] It was thought that colonies could be of some use for the fulfilment of the Four-Year Plan by saving foreign exchange needed to import raw materials. So it was no accident that the Deko Group pursued its economic activities in Africa in close touch with the most important branch of the Four-Year Plan Authority placed under Göring's command, the Office for German Raw Materials.[62]

The office evinced special interest in those projects of the Deko Group which could help improve the raw materials situation even before the colonies had been recovered. The colonial firms affiliated to the Deko Group were entrusted with "special tasks"[63] within the framework of the Four-Year Plan as can be seen from the draft for a letter by Weigelt dating from July 1937. The draft said that the Deko Group, "in agreement with the Foreign Office, the Reich Ministry of Economics and the Office for German Raw Materials . . . initiated several projects and conducted negotiations on these on a private, and partly international, basis." These projects, which were chiefly designed to "supply Germany with more colonial raw materials from West Africa", provided for systematic preparations to procure timber, extract minerals, increase deliveries of fat and similar measures. According to the draft letter, the Raw Materials Office was setting great store by the centralization of the projects and was prepared to grant financial support "with each project being considered on its merits and without this being brought to public notice."[64]

In August of that year Weigelt informed the Reich Ministry of Economics that plans had been drawn up, at the instance of the Raw Materials Office, to establish — apart from a timber syndicate — a syndicate for the exploration of mineral deposits in Togo, Dahomey and Cameroon and that cooperation with French business circles and government departments had been initiated for this purpose. The four major Berlin banks were to participate in the syndicate as were the "two shipping lines operating services to Africa", the "metal trading business", the Otavi-Gesellschaft, the Metall-Gesellschaft and the AEG. Also mentioned in this

---

[61] Cf. *G. Thomas*, Geschichte der deutschen Wehr- und Rüstungswirtschaft, ed. by Wolfgang Birkenfeld, Boppard 1966, p. 122.

[62] As early as September 1936 Weigelt got in touch with Lieutenant-Colonel Loeb, of the Raw Materials and Foreign Exchange Task Force, which was soon to become the German Raw Material Office. ZStA, Deutsche Bank, no. 21914, p. 75, Weigelt to Loeb, 29 Oct. 1936.

[63] Ibid., Weigelt to the Board of Directors of the Reichsbank, 6 March 1937.

[64] Ibid., pp. 147—148, Draft of a letter by Weigelt to the Werberat, July 1937.

context were the Otto Wolff corporation, the Stahl-Union,[65] Siemens, Mansfeld, IG-Farben and others. The Raw Materials Office was also scheduled to take part.[66]

In early 1937 negotiations had already taken place on the founding of a Franco-German "society for the development of commercial relations between Germany and overseas France", in which Weigelt participated. The plan met with lively interest among German industrialists.[67] Concurrently, Weigelt was pursuing a scheme for the exploration and mining of ore deposits in Liberia, in which Krupp, among other companies, took an interest.[68]

The names of the firms mentioned make it clear who was drawn to the colonial business sphere. Apart from major banks and shipping companies and iron and steel interests, the new industries — especially the chemical and electrical industries — were in evidence.[69] The increased interest of German big business circles in colonies, as reflected in the projects of the Deko Group, was closely related to the more vigorous pursuit of colonial aims by the Nazi state from 1936 onwards.

While the colonial ambitions of the monopolist business groups and the preparations set in motion remained largely hidden from view, the colonial demands persistently raised by the Hitler government from 1936 and the place henceforth accorded to the colonial issue in diplomatic

---

[65] The Vereinigte Stahlwerke AG is probably meant here.

[66] Ibid., pp. 188—9, Weigelt to the Reich Ministry of Economics, 4 Sept. 1937. The mining syndicate failed to materialize because the French government considered a "German presence" in Franch colonial territories in opportune" at the present moment". Ibid., pp. 204—5, conversation between Weigelt and Colonial Minister Moutet in Paris, 29 Oct. 1937. A later project aimed at setting up a consortium of the coal and steel firms interested in colonies, including the Gutehoffnungshütte and Krupp. (Ibid., p. 258, Note of 28 Oct. 1938).

[67] Ibid., no A 26/24, n.p. The attitude of the French side prevented the foundation of the society. In early 1939 Weigelt conducted further negotiations in Paris on economic collaboration with France in the former German colonies. K. Hildebrand, op. cit., pp. 602—3.

[68] Ibid., no. A 26/24, n.p.

[69] The IG Farben demonstrably gave financial support to the colonial movement from the early thirties. From 1932 it maintained a "retraining centre for settlers and emigrants" which trained specialists for various vocations in the former colonies. R. Lakowski, op. cit., pp. 10ff.; O. Groehler, Kolonialforderungen als Teil der faschistischen Kriegszielplanungen, in: Zeitschrift für Militärgeschichte, 5/1965, p. 550.

relations with Britain were attracting much attention. Both contemporary observers and historians of our day have repeatedly expressed doubts as to whether the diplomatic moves made by the Hitler government on the colonial question were really designed to extract concessions from the western powers, and have assessed the colonial demands as little more than foreign policy manoeuvres within the context of European politics.[70]

Such a use of the colonial problem can indeed be observed on more than one occassion. During his talks with Simon and Eden in March 1935 Hitler already demanded "colonial equality" as a prerequisite for Germany's return to the League of Nations. His apparent intention was to obviate any such demand on the part of his guests.[71] In actual fact, the Nazi government did not wish to re-enter the League of Nations under any circumstances, concerned as it was to maintain its full freedom of action. For Hitler the demand for a revision of the colonial system was on this occasion merely an expedient for disguising his real intentions and for countering the demands of the other side and keeping them waiting.

When the Rhineland was occupied and the Locarno Pact denounced in 1936, Hitler made similar use of the demand for colonies. In order to placate the western powers, he submitted to the signatories of the pact proposals for "new agreements on establishing a European system of of safeguarding peace"[72], including Germany's return to the League of Nations, a step which, however, as in the year before, was made conditional on "colonial equality". When the western powers took up Hitler's proposals for a "peace settlement" and asked for precise details, the Nazi government repeated its colonial demands but remained evasive on the questions posed.

From then on the colonial demands cropped up almost regularly when the western powers, in an effort to secure their own positions, approached Nazi Germany with proposals for an agreement. As the British position was initially one of outright rejection and even Chamberlain was only prepared to make limited concessions in this matter later on, the colonial issue could well be used to pursue deceptive and delaying tactics, to stave off demands by the other side, to sabotage one's own peace proposals and, at the same time, to exert pressure with a view to

[70] Cf. for example D. Aigner, op. cit., p. 43; K. Hildebrand, op. cit., pp. 449ff.

[71] This is documented by the records of the Anglo-German talks, March 1935, ZStA, A.A., no. 60960, p. 2017.

[72] Schulthess' Europäischer Geschichtskalender 1936, pp. 50ff.

exacting concessions. This explains why the colonial question could play a disproportionate role in German-British relations almost up to the beginning of World War II, at times even appearing to be the crux of a German-British understanding. German colonial demands were debated in the British Parliament 75 times between January 1935 and January 1939.[73]

But the Hitler government used the demand for the return of the former German colonies not only as a device for tactical manoeuvres on the diplomatic front. From mid-1936 to early 1937 it obviously intended to wring concessions in the colonial sphere from the western powers if possible. In a conversation with the US Ambassador in Paris on 18 May 1936, the German Foreign Minister von Neurath said "that there were certain colonies which might be useful" and that Germany would "attempt to obtain Cameroon . . ."[74] In late August 1936, the Reich Minister of Economics and Governor of the Reichsbank, Hjalmar Schacht, went to Paris with Hitler's approval to conduct talks with Premier Léon Blum on the possibilities for a revision of the colonial system. He met with understanding and the French government agreed to discuss the problem. Schacht was given assurances that the French would take the matter up with the British.[75]

The West German historian Klaus Hildebrandt believes that this initiative was merely a concession on Hitler's part to his "financial dictator" Schacht, who was especially interested in colonies but whose career was nearing "the beginning of the end" in 1936.[76]

Schacht is known to have been a political exponent of the colonial interests of German financial circles even before the First World War. During the twenties he had campaigned for the recovery of German colonial possessions, and in the early years of the Nazi dictatorship he had again taken up the colonial cause. His interest in this matter can be seen from a large number of speeches and publications. In 1934 he began, together with Weigelt, to try and secure economic positions for Germany in the Portuguese colonies.[77]

---

[73] *B. M. Wood*, Peaceful Change and the Colonial Problem, New York 1940, p. 125.

[74] *Nazi Conspiracy and Aggression*, vol. 7, Washington 1946, p. 892.

[75] *H. Schacht*, 76 Jahre meines Lebens, Bad Wörishofen 1953, pp. 477ff.

[76] *K. Hildebrand*, op. cit., pp. 210—1.

[77] Weigelt resumed these efforts in Lisbon in 1935, and in late 1936 and early 1937 other persons close to Schacht and the Rhenish iron and steel industry followed suit in Portugal. *K. Hildebrand*, op. cit., pp. 209, 501, 891.

From the spring of 1936 onward, Schacht found himself increasingly at odds with Göring on matters of economic and foreign policy, and after the proclamation of the Four-Year Plan he saw his influence wane more and more. But it was not until November 1937 that he was replaced as Minister of Economics.

Schacht is to be regarded as a foremost representative of the group of monopoly capitalists that included the Dresdner Bank and the section of the coal and steel industry (notably Thyssen) cooperating with American financial groups. He deemed it necessary to rearm at a slower pace and on a more solid basis, and he wanted, if at all possible, to keep the United States as well as Great Britain out of a future war.[78] Obviously, the demand for colonies figured rather high on his list of priorities, but in view of the agreement he was seeking with the United States and Britain it was to remain limited in scope and to be settled by negotiations.[79]

Göring, for his part, was then the political exponent of the other group, which was dominated by IG Farben. The monopoly capitalists of this group were pressing for rearmament at as fast a pace as possible and for a large measure of economic self-sufficiency in raw materials which would enable Germany to withstand a blockade for a certain space of time. They looked not only on the Soviet Union but also on Britain and the United States as major targets of expansion.[80] The prevalent feeling among this group was that colonies and spheres of interest overseas would have to pass into German hands on a major scale following a military conflict with the western powers.

For the time being, however, the differences of opinion within the monopolist bourgeoisie seem to have had little, if any, influence on the practical handling of the colonial question. The critical foreign exchange and foreign trade situation which Germany was facing from the summer of 1936 must have made the rapid acquisition of some colonies by diplomatic means before a war appear desirable, not least in order to support the Four-Year Plan initiated by the Göring-IG Farben group. The Raw Materials Office, the key institution of the Four-Year Plan Authority headed by Göring, at any rate took an active interest in obtain-

---

[78] D. Eichholtz, Geschichte der deutschen Kriegswirtschaft 1939—1945, vol. 1: 1939—1941, Berlin 1984, pp. 42—3, 49, 151.

[79] Cf. W. W. Schmokel, op. cit., pp. 97—8. Schacht was a close friend of Paul Rohrbach, a very active advocate of German colonial expansion in Africa from the beginning of the century.

[80] D. Eichholtz, op. cit., pp. 50, 152.

ing raw materials in African colonies and supported negotiations to this effect.

Göring himself, during talks with Mussolini in Rome in January 1937, inter alia mentioned his government's interest in colonies. He said that Germany had not yet been able to achieve any results in this respect because she had to rearm first. It was still too early to say when a German move would become possible, Germany was upholding her demand and would not allow herself to be put off with Togo or Cameroon alone. The conversation makes it clear that the Nazi regime had an interest in the immediate acquisition of colonies and that it may have set its sights on overseas territories even before the country was ready, three or four years' later, as Göring assured Mussolini, "to take on the English shoulder to shoulder with Italy".[81]

So it was by no means Schacht alone who displayed a keen interest in the revision of the colonial system at this time. The US Ambassador in Berlin, William E. Dodd, concluded in October 1936: "The German government seems willing to risk everything in order to compel England to restore her pre-war colonies. There is much discussion here of a proposed Locarno conference as a means of restoring the colonies."[82] Concurrently with Schacht's efforts[83], Hitler and other Nazi leaders officially raised the demand for colonies in late 1936 and in 1937. Hitler did so at the Reich Party Rally on 9 September 1936 and during a speech delivered in the Reichstag on 30 January of the following year.

When Ribbentrop was made Ambassador in London, he, too, took up the colonial question. During a reception given by the Anglo-German-Fellowship on 16 December 1936 he said that a reasonable solution of the colonial problem was "extremely desirable" and "in the interest of all of us".[84] At the end of 1936 Ribbentrop broached the issue in talks with the Foreign Secretary Eden, and during a meeting with Lord Halifax, Lord President of the Council with special responsibility for foreign affairs, on 13 February 1937 he demanded the return of all one-time Ger-

[81] ZStA, A.A., no. 60960, Summary of the Meeting of Minister-President Göring and the Duce, 14 Jan. 1937, p. 47, 49.

[82] *W. E. Dodd*, Ambassador Dodd's Diary 1933—1938, New York 1941, pp. 355—6.

[83] In January 1937 Schacht published an article on "Germany's colonial problem" in the American journal Foreign Affairs, and early that year he also conducted negotiations with the chief financial adviser of the British government, Frederick Leith-Ross, on the same subject. *I. Colvin*, The Chamberlain Cabinet, London 1971, p. 39.

[84] Völkischer Beobachter, 17 Dec. 1936, p. 9.

man colonies. Ribbentrop expressly refused to link the colonial problem to other issues and told Halifax that he hoped "England would solve the colonial question in direct negotiations with us without connecting it with any other question". The Nazi Ambassador suggested that "England should for once make a voluntary and generous gesture. This would be of crucial importance for the entire development of our relations and would have an entirely different psychological effect on the solution of other problems from England's practice in recent years of making concessions only when compelled to do so by the force of circumstances."[85] Concessions on the colonial issue were here demanded as a necessary "goodwill gesture" on Britain's part to bring about an Anglo-German *rapprochement* along the lines envisaged by Nazi Germany.

So in 1936—37 the fascist Hitler regime clearly attempted to make some headway in the colonial field. It should be borne in mind, however, that the issue could also be used as a lever for securing concessions as regards territorial expansion in Europe.

While the French government was quite willing to enter into negotiations on the question of colonies,[86] the British government was rather reluctant at the time, and the *démarches* undertaken by Schacht and Ribbentrop came to nothing. On 2 March 1937 Eden told the House of Commons that the British government had no intention of transferring colonies to Germany.[87] He confirmed this attitude during a meeting with Ribbentrop in early May.[88]

Nazi Germany's demand for the return of the mandated territories affected Britain directly: concessions on this matter could hardly be made at the expense of other powers. The dangers inherent in the German claim for the British were stressed at a meeting of 200 members of parliament of all political parties in early 1937. Speakers at the meeting were of the opinion that the abandonment of territories where the Union Jack had been hoisted would endanger the strategic security of the British Empire and undermine its cohesion.[89] There were fears that if Tanga-

---

[85] Note by Ribbentrop, 14 Feb. 1937, in: *K. Hildebrand*, op. cit., pp. 898ff.

[86] Cf. *W. W. Schmoekl*, op. cit., pp. 100—101; *E. N. Peterson*, Hjalmar Schacht for and against Hitler, Boston 1954, p. 168.

[87] *Parliamentary Debates*, House of Commons, vol. V, Session 1936—37, London 1937, p. 211.

[88] *Foreign Relations of the United States*, Diplomatic Papers 1937, vol. I, Washington 1954, p. 59.

[89] *W. W. Schmokel*, The Hard Death of Imperialism: British and German Colonial Attitudes, 1919—1939, in: Britain and Germany in Africa, ed. by P. Gifford and W. R. Louis, New Haven/London 1967, p. 320.

nyika reverted to Germany British possessions in West Africa and Rhodesia might be threatened from Dar es Salaam with the aid of Italy, which was occupying Ethiopia. Similar considerations applied to South West Africa which, moreover, the Union of South Africa regarded as an integral part of its territory (in contravention of the terms of its League of Nations mandate). Especially with public opinion in mind, there could be no question of concessions being made without a quid pro quo.

During a cabinet meeting on 4 November 1936, Eden had already declared that no further debate on this matter was possible "until the European settlement, which I have already referred to, has been reached. In the meanwhile, so far as we are concerned, the colonial issue is not even discussible."[90] As part of its policy of appeasement the British government was at this time striving for a new agreement with the Hitler regime to replace the Locarno Pact, for Germany's return to the League of Nations and arrangements on the limitation of certain types of armaments. In this way it was hoped to meet the danger of German expansionist moves in Western Europe and, at the same time, pave the way for a general Anglo-German settlement allowing for German expansion in an eastward direction.

Hitler's government, for its part, was also interested in an understanding. At the time in question it seems to have been, at least for the time being, still willing to renounce the idea of gaining any colonies other than the former German possessions. Yet the British were supposed to pay a high price: to turn a blind eye to German expansion on the continent. Hitler had hinted at such an offer as early as 1935 in conversation with Simon and Eden.[91] But Simon had told Hitler in no uncertain terms that Britain did not want to "replace one friend by another".[92] Ribbentrop, too, who during a meeting with Halifax on 13 February 1937 invoked the "mandate which the Führer had given him to promote Anglo-German friendship", spoke of the need for a "clear definition of the vital interests" of the two countries and warned the Lord President:

---

[90] Public Record Office, London, Cabinet Meetings, 62, 4 Nov. 1936.

[91] Hitler had declared that Germany was perfectly aware of her inability to defend on her own the colonial possessions she might obtain. But there was also the possibility of Britain needing outside support to defend her possessions. If a formula for such an eventuality could be found, this would lead not only to cooperation in Europe, but to an especially close friendship between Britain and Germany. ZStA, A.A., no. 60968, p. 39.

[92] Ibid.,

"The two nations must guard against being drawn into another war in which they would confront each other as enemies, standing up for interests which are of no vital importance to them."[93] Ribbentrop obviously meant that questions of continental Europe did not affect Britain's vital interests. But the Nazi leaders prudently refrained from disclosing to their imperialist rivals the full extent of their expansionist ambitions and their terms for a settlement. As it turned out, the British were prepared to make concessions, even very substantial ones if this should prove necessary. But they did not wish to see Germany reign supreme over the European continent and were especially concerned not to be isolated from France. Any other attitude would have run counter to Britain's traditional policy of safeguarding her leading position in Europe and overseas.

Far from corresponding to each other, the understanding envisaged by the Hitler government and the "general settlement" sought by the British side were in fact irreconcilable. They reflected the conflicting interests of German and British imperialism.

In May 1937 Schacht undertook another journey to Paris. However, his talks on the colonial issue did not yield any tangible results.[94] In June of that year Foreign Minister von Neurath was due in London to discuss this matter, among other things, but the visit was cancelled at short notice and the British government was informed that while Germany needed colonies of her own, this question was not urgent. The colonial issue was dismissed as an *idée fixe* of Schacht's. Instead, the British government's attention was drawn to Austria, the Sudetenland, Danzig, the Polish Corridor and Memel.[95]

Clearly the Nazi regime was already preparing the annexation of Austria[96], and the policy of annexations in Central Europe, which enjoyed priority in the Nazi programme for expansion, assumed more and more importance. Consequently, the return of Germany's erstwhile colonial possessions was no longer a matter of immediate interest to the Hitler government. After it had failed in its bid to secure colonial concessions by diplomatic means, but without offering something in return, it could hardly expect to fare better while pursuing an annexationist course in Central Europe. Outlining his foreign policy to Rausch-

[93] Note by Ribbentrop, in: *K. Hildebrand*, op. cit., pp. 898ff.

[94] *H. Schacht*, op. cit., p. 478.

[95] *K. Feiling*, The Life of Neville Chamberlain, London 1947, p. 329.

[96] Cf. *Geschichte der Internationalen Beziehungen*, ed. W. G. Truchanowski, vol. I, Berlin 1963, p. 399.

ning, Hitler had stated unequivocally: "I shall take one step after the other, never two at a time."[97]

None the less the German fascists continued to clamour for colonies, the propaganda drive reaching a peak in October and November 1937.

The Hitler regime's policy of colonial expansion included the establishment of a network of bases and agents in Africa, which relied in large measure on German settlers and plantation owners in South West Africa and Tanganyika.[98] In these two former German colonies, German farmers and employees of German firms together with their families accounted for a considerable part of the "white" population. In South West Africa the Germans numbered 9,632 in 1937, amounting to one third of the white population.[99] In Tanganyika their total number was much lower, but they constituted an equally high proportion of the white inhabitants. Especially in South West Africa, many of them were members of local German associations and church congregations and sent their children to schools reserved for Germans. German missionary societies were active in both colonies.

An intensive and initially noisy campaign was begun among these Germans in 1933 to win them over to the fascist cause, with the result that in the following year the Nazi party and the Hitler youth were banned in South West Africa by the South African authorities. (In Tanganyika, political organizations based in the German Reich were not permitted to engage in public activities since Britain took over.) As it turned out, these and other restrictions and bans imposed by South African and British colonial administrations were much less of an obstacle to the "Gleichschaltung" of the Germans in both colonies than the fact that many settlers preferred life in a mandated territory to life under a fascist regime which, economically speaking, seemed to offer nothing but disadvantages. Only gradually did Nazi agents in the guise of consular officials or employees of German firms succeed in bringing German organizations and institutions (professional associations, sports clubs, musical and other cultural societies, schools, newspapers, etc.) under their control and inducing the majority of German settlers, through

---

[97] H. Rauschning, op. cit., p. 33.

[98] On this subject, which cannot be dealt with in detail, see H. Kühne, Faschistische Kolonialideologie und zweiter Weltkrieg, Berlin 1962, pp. 125—145, 189, 192; B. Bennett, Hitler over Africa, London 1939, especially the documentary annex pp. 157—179; L. Smythe Barron (ed.). The Nazis in Africa (Lost Documents on the Third Reich, vol. III.), Salisbury, N.C., 1978.

[99] Lord Hailey, An African Survey, London 1957, p. 268.

relentless propaganda and threats, to join the Deutscher Bund für Süd-westafrika or the Deutscher Bund für Ostafrika (German Leagues for South West Africa and East Africa respectively).

The two organizations had been set up during the twenties to represent the interests of the settlers vis-à-vis the authorities of the two mandated territories. In early July 1935, two weeks after the signing of the Anglo-German Naval Agreement, Ribbentrop instructed the Nazi party's foreign branch to make sure all Germans in the former German colonies joined the respective Bund.[100] Ribbentrop wrote that it was the prime task of the two organizations "to foster the idea of Deutschtum and of a single national community in the spirit of the Third Reich." The leader of each Bund and his deputies would have to enjoy "the confidence of the party". The directive added that "in so far as the Deutsche Bund receives instructions and guidelines from Germany, these will be trans-mitted, after my approval has been obtained by the foreign branch, through the channels of the Foreign Office to the representative of the German Reich in the colony concerned . . ." In the following year the Germans living in the former German colonies were expressly made liable to conscription into the Labour Service and the Wehrmacht in Germany.

Germans who refused to join the Bund or to identify themselves with the Hitler regime were subjected to threats and a social and economic boycott until they gave in or left the territory to live elsewhere. In many cases the representatives of the foreign branch pointed out the dire con-sequences which a refusal would have for those concerned once the colony reverted to Germany, which they said was certain. (As the reports of the authorities in the mandated territories revealed, a fair number of those converted under pressure strongly opposed the idea of the colony in which they lived being surrendered to fascist-ruled Germany.) By employing the methods set out here, Nazi agents managed by 1937 to set up a fifth column in South West Africa and Tanganyika, with the Nazi party's foreign branch and the German consulates as its backbone.

From 1937 the Nazi Germans in both colonies became something of a state within a state. The local Nazi party leaders often behaved among the German settlers as though they were back home in Hitler's Reich. Germans in both colonies (with the exception of Jewish exiles in Tanganyika) withdrew from all organizations of which they had been members together with the British, Afrikaners and others of European stock and henceforth formed a self-contained community. Lawsuits

---

[100] Directive of 3 July 1935. Source: *H. Kühne*, op. cit., pp. 189—90.

involving only Germans were no longer handled by South African or British courts but by unofficial German "courts of arbitration". Even so the authorities continued to record signs of dislike for Hitler's fascism among not a few German settlers, which stemmed from an awareness that its policies posed a direct threat to their existence. In Tanganyika many German farmers even made secret donations to the Tanganyika League founded by British settlers with the aim of preventing the colony from passing into German hands.[101]

This well-organized fifth column would have greatly facilitated the take-over of the two colonies by Wehrmacht units put ashore even though the Hitler government did not dare to arm these organizations. A decree issued by the South African Administrator in South West Africa in 1937, whereby Nazi agents brought in from Germany were no longer allowed to be members of the Bund, changed little. Both the South African authorities in South West Africa and the British administration in Tanganyika took some further defensive steps after 1937 but refrained from any drastic measures. After all, they were dealing with whites, not with organizations of "subversive" Africans. It was not until just before the beginning of the Second World War that the South African government reinforced its police force in South West Africa and armed it with automatic weapons so that an attempted Nazi coup could be crushed at once.

3. The Colonial Issue in Anglo-German Relations and "Preparatory Colonial Planning" 1937—1939

At a Nazi party rally in early September 1937, Hitler made another official pronouncement on the colonial question. He said: "Without colonies Germany's living space is too small for our people to feed themselves without difficulty ... The demand for colonial possessions, therefore, is dictated by economic necessity, and the attitude of the other powers to this demand is simply incomprehensible."[102]

.While the colonial propaganda campaign in the Nazi press was in full swing, Hitler on 5 November 1937 held a secret conclave with the commanders of the Wehrmacht and Foreign Minister von Neurath,

---

[101] Report by the US Consul in Nairobi, 8 Feb. 1939, in: *L. Smythe Barron*, op. cit., p. 143.

[102] *Schulthess' Europäischer Geschichtskalender* 1937, p. 133.

during which he outlined his real short-term objectives. Hitler set forth the several stages of the policy of annexations to be practised shortly, and singled out Austria and Czechoslovakia as the immediate targets. He said he believed that "almost certainly, England, and probably France, have already tacitly written off the Czechs." At the same time, he envisaged a military confrontation not only with France, but also with Britain at some later date because a "German colossus in the midst of Europe would be a thorn in their side."[103] This approach indicated that the views of the Göring/IG Farben group had prevailed.[104]

Regarding the colonial question, Hitler gave the following assessment (according to the notes of an adjutant): "Owing to the objections of the dominions Britain was unable to cede any of her colonial possessions to Germany. After the loss of British prestige caused by Abyssinia's passing into Italian hands, the restitution of East Africa is not to be counted upon. At best, England will leave it to our discretion to satisfy our colonial wishes by taking away colonies which are not at present in British hands, e.g. Angola. Any French concessions will be along the same lines. A serious discussion over the return of colonies to Germany would be conceivable only at a time when England is in difficulties and the German Reich is strong and well-armed." Hitler did not believe "that the British Empire is unshakable".[105]

Since a military conflict with Britain was expected in the course of European expansion, the prospect of a far-reaching redistribution of colonies and spheres of interest in Germany's favour now seemed less remote. Therefore partial solutions were no longer thought desirable. As far as Africa was concerned, it would no longer be merely a question of regaining the former German colonies. Hitler himself intimated as much during his meeting with Halifax in November 1937. Asked what would happen if there were a "free play of forces" in this matter, he said: "What Germany would take for herself in such a case is impossible to say."[106]

While Nazi Germany was preparing to annex neighbouring countries and was contemplating a future military confrontation with Britain, the new British government formed in May 1937 with Neville Chamberlain as Prime Minister proceeded to make even larger concessions to

[103] *ADAP*, Series D, vol. I, Baden—Baden 1950, p. 27.

[104] *D. Eichholtz*, op. cit., p. 50.

[105] *ADAP*, op. cit., p. 28.

[106] *Dokumente und Materialien* aus der Vorgeschichte des zweiten Weltkrieges, vol. I. Moscow 1948, p. 21, Conversation between Hitler and Halifax.

the Hitler regime. The idea behind this policy was to induce the German side, on the basis of anticommunist and anti-Soviet positions held in common, to agree to a settlement of the kind sought by Britain and to direct its expansionist urge eastward, especially against the Soviet Union. In this context the British government now took the initiative on the colonial issue.[107]

On 19 November 1937 Halifax, while on an official visit to Germany, had a conversation with Hitler. The British minister praised Germany "as a bulwark of the West against Bolshevism" and stressed his country's interest in an understanding which would also include Italy and France. In so doing, he recognized that changes in the European system concerning "Danzig, Austria and Czechoslovakia" would have to take place, merely attaching the condition that "these changes be brought about by way of peaceful evolution".

Hitler, however, was unsympathetic and showed no particular interest in further negotiations. He asserted that the question of colonies was the sole bone of contention between Germany and Britain, and added that it was not of much consequence for Anglo-German cooperation. Asked how he felt this problem could be solved, the Nazi leader referred to Germany's "claim" to her former colonial holdings, but allowed for the possibility of a substitute "if for some reason or other the return of a particular colony should be deemed impossible."[108] Then Hitler invited Britain and France to make up their minds "whether and in what way" they intended to satisfy German colonial demands. While the matter was not represented as being urgent, it was clearly his aim to keep the British government occupied with the colonial question without committing himself in any way.

In the months that followed, the British government discussed possible colonial concessions to Germany. In January 1938 the foreign policy committee of the British cabinet considered the possibility of ceding Togo, Cameroon and parts of northern Nigeria to Germany, with France receiving part of the Gold Coast from Britain as compensation. Belgium was to be persuaded to give up part of the Congo and Portugal was supposed to relinquish Angola. All colonial possessions in the area were to be placed under a new joint regime of the major powers so that the

---

[107] Even before assuming office in April 1937 Chamberlain had advocated concessions on the colonial issue under certain conditions and set out his views on the matter in a memorandum. *I. Colvin*, op. cit., pp. 39 ff.

[108] *Dokumente und Materialien . . .*, vol. I. pp. 34—35, 40 and 42, Conversation between Hitler and Halifax.

new arrangement could have been presented to the public not as a surrender of colonies to Germany, but as a reform motivated by "lofty
ideals".[109] Camouflage appeared necessary because of the widespread
opposition such moves were bound to provoke in Britain. And there
were also the protests of the Africans directly affected to reckon with.

The betrayal of Ethiopia by Britain and France, as a result of which
the country was occupied by the Italian aggressors, had given rise to
fears among the people of a number of African colonies that they might
be left to the mercy of Hitler's Germany. The growing uneasiness discernible in West and East Africa from 1936 onwards was increased by
the treatment of German colonial demands in the British and French
press. Nationally minded circles in the Gold Coast colony and in Nigeria raised the question of whether Africans could be simply passed
on from one colonial power to another without even being consulted.
Most important, the barbaric racist ideology and policy of the Nazi
regime provoked fierce African opposition to a possible return of former
German colonies to Germany.

In late 1937 and throughout 1938 Africans in all four British colonies
in West Africa objected against the transfer of West African colonies
to Germany.[110] In the course of a heated argument with Governor
Bourdillon on 29 October 1938 a delegation of the Nigerian Youth Movement demanded assurances that in the event of negotiations with Germany on her colonial demands the British government "would not do
anything affecting the welfare or the interests of the people of Nigeria
without first consulting their views." Subsequently, O. Alakija, a member of the movement and of the Legislative Council, called on the government to state unequivocally that there was no danger of Nigeria (which
he probably meant to include West Cameroon, a mandated territory
administered as part of Nigeria) passing into German hands. When
the Governor described these fears as "quite fantastic" the representatives of the movement demanded that his statement be reaffirmed by
the Colonial Secretary.[111]

The newspaper West African Pilot on 20 January 1939 carried an
article by the leading Nigerian politician N. Azikiwe in which he denounced the German government's attitude towards Africans. He quot-

---

[109] P. Wilby, How we nearly let the Nazis into Africa, in: Observer, 5 Jan. 1969. Cf.
I. Colvin, op. cit., pp. 89—90.

[110] S. K. P. Asante, Pan-African Protest: West Africa and the Italo-Ethiopian Crisis,
1934, 1941, London 1977, p. 210, note 71.

[111] Ibid., p. 187.

ed at length from the Koloniales Jahrbuch of 1939 (featuring articles by Wilhelm von Alwurden and Rudolf Karlowa) which reviled British and French policy in Africa as being guided by a blind liberalism and as extremely harmful. The publication quoted from had described Africans identifying themselves with British or French democracy as Bolsheviks who would have to be eliminated. Azikiwe called on the Africans to resist this challenge together with the colonial power.[112] Owing to the racist policy of the Nazi dictatorship, not only the paramount chiefs and Muslim rulers installed by the British, but all politically aware Nigerians immediately sided with the colonial power at the beginning of the Second World War.[113]

In the former German colony of Cameroon, administered as a French mandate, the country's first political organization with the support of the colonial administration vigorously took up the demand that the restoration of German rule should be rejected. The organization, founded in 1938 and known as Jeunesse Camerounaise Française (Jeucafra), evolved into an important catalyst for national aspirations, like the Nigerian Youth Movement.[114] A group of anticolonial exiles in Paris, the Comité de Défense des Intérêts du Cameroun, declared that there could be no question of collaborating with a regime whose leaders described Africans as "half-apes" and deplored the "Negroization" of France.[115]

In respect of Tanganyika, the British journalist B. Bennett wrote at the end of 1938: "Beneath the smoke of Hitler's verbal battle over Africa, the natives in the Mandated Territory become restive, suspicious that their future is being decided without reference to their wishes or needs. Largely inarticulate, their small band of leaders urge Britain not to abandon them again to German sovereignty or 'protection'."[116]

While the British cabinet was discussing colonial "appeasement", there were major changes in the Wehrmacht leadership and in the German government at the turn of 1937—38 in accordance with the foreign

---

[112] *G. O. Olusanya*, The Second World War and Politics in Nigeria 1939—1953, Lagos 1973, pp. 41—2.

[113] Ibid., pp. 42ff.

[114] *R. A. Joseph*, Radical Nationalism in Cameroun. Social Origins of the U.P.C. Rebellion, Oxford 1977, pp. 40—44.

[115] *R. A. Joseph*, The German Question in French Cameroon, 1919—1939, in: Comparative Studies in Society and History. An international quarterly, vol. 17 (1975), no. 1, p. 87.

[116] *B. Bennett*, Hitler over Africa, London 1939, pp. 151—2.

policy formulated by Hitler on 5 November. As mentioned above, Schacht was replaced as Minister of Economics, and in February 1938 Neurath was succeeded as Foreign Minister by Ribbentrop. One month before, in a memorandum intended for Hitler, the latter had recommended keeping up the pretence of seeking an understanding with Britain and added: "It is necessary for us to continue confirming England in her belief that an accommodation and an understanding between Germany and England are possible in the long run. This prospect might act as a brake on any intentions the English government may have to intervene in the event of a local conflict involving Germany in Central Europe but not affecting England's vital interests."[117] This meant that the Nazi government wanted to exploit the policy of appeasement for its expansionist strategy as long as possible.

This approach was reflected in Hitler's address to the Reichstag on 20 February 1938 in which he expressed his resolve to act in the matter of Austria but, at the same time, pretended hypocritically that as far as Europe was concerned Germany had "no more territorial demands to make on France" and "no quarrels whatever" with Britain, "apart from our colonial wishes."[118] Hitler asserted his readiness to cooperate with the western powers, but once again described the colonial issue as the only matter under dispute in order to divert attention from the questions that were really exercising the minds of their leaders, to temporize and, at the same time, to deceive world opinion about the real objectives pursued.

Nine days before German troops entered Austria, on 3 March 1938, the British Ambassador in Berlin, Neville Henderson, had a conversation with Hitler during which he submitted "an attempt at a solution by the British government". He stressed that what his government had in mind was "an attempt to lay the foundations for a genuine and cordial friendship with Germany". This meant that after Eden's resignation as Foreign Secretary the British side was prepared to make colonial concessions regardless of an overall settlement. As to what Britain would expect in return the ambassador merely cited a peaceful settlement of Nazi Germany's claims to Austria and Czechoslovakia and negotiations on arms limitation.

---

[117] *Was wirklich geschah.* Die diplomatischen Hintergründe der deutschen Kriegspolitik, Darstellung und Dokumente, ed. by Heinz Holldack, Munich 1949, pp. 293—297. "Note for the Führer" of 2 Jan. 1938.

[118] *Schulthess' Europäischer Geschichtskalender* 1938, pp. 40—1.

The proposal provided for a redistribution of colonies in an area roughly corresponding to the Congo Basin and extending from 5° latitude in the north to the Zambezi in the south "on the basis of a new regime of colonial administration". What the British government had in mind was a system similar to the regime envisaged in the Act of the Berlin Conference of 1885. "Germany would be given her share in such a redistribution and thus gain colonial territory placed under her sovereignty. All powers with colonies in this Central African territory would however have to assume certain obligations regarding demilitarization, freedom of trade and treatment of the natives."

Hitler's response to the questions raised by the British side was negative. Commenting on the proposed colonial formula, he asked why "the colonial question could not be solved by giving back the former German colonies ... rather than by establishing a complicated new system." He said that Paris and London had "committed themselves too firmly against their return". He therefore did not wish to press the case but was quite prepared to "wait another four, six, eight or ten years ... Germany did not want the colonial settlement to cause difficulties for other states that were not involved." Given the "importance of the question", Hitler added that he would give a written reply, but this never came.[119]

Not only was the proposed system, with its provisions on the freedom of trade, far from acceptable to the German imperialists, but, as we have seen, all interest in the rapid acquisition of some colonies by diplomatic means had evaporated. Such acquisitions would have been politically inopportune for the implementation of the programme for step-by-step expansion, especially in the light of widespread opposition among British public opinion. Also, any short-term economic interest in a partial "solution of the colonial question" was bound to pale into insignificance beside the much greater prospects offered by Austria's economic potential after that country's annexation. It was easy to shelve the matter for the time being by referring to the British government's insufficiently accommodating attitude. But the demand for colonies was kept up after the annexation of Austria, in diplomacy and propaganda, to serve in case of need for foreign policy manoeuvres.

Chamberlain, for his part, remained willing to make colonial concessions as part of his policy of appeasement. After the "Anschluss", however, the British government found it impossible, because of domestic opinion, to take any action in this matter. When the British Ambassador

---

[119] *Dokumente und Materialien* ..., vol. I. pp. 52 ff.; conversation between Hitler and Henderson.

called on Ribbentrop on 2 April 1938 to hand over the note in which his government recognized the annexation in principle, the colonial issue was also raised. Henderson remarked in this context that "there was, of course, public opinion in Britain to contend with. Some time would have to elapse before further discussions became possible."[120]

In the spring and summer of 1938 the "Sudeten crisis" provoked by the Nazis was in the centre of public attention. Exploiting the British government's anti-Soviet policy of appeasement, the Hitler regime secured the annexation of parts of Czechoslovakia as a first step towards the total dismemberment of that state. At the same time the British side was strengthened in the belief that, as Ribbentrop told Halifax in August 1938, "after a solution of the Sudeten German problem and a reasonable settlement of the colonial issue, the way would be open — in the absence of any divergent interests — to cooperation in a climate of trust."[121] Then, on 23 September, when Chamberlain conferred with Hitler at Bad Godesberg for the second time, the Nazi leader asserted that "the Czech problem" was the "last territorial demand which he had to make in Europe. Over and above this, Germany . . . would, of course, raise the colonial question. But this was no warlike demand which had anything to do with mobilization."[122] This statement was obviously meant to keep alive the hopes of British politicians for an accommodation with Nazi Germany that would meet the interests of British imperialism. Invariably, the colonial issue was mentioned as the last — but small — obstacle.

After the Munich Agreement the British government tried, in accordance with the Anglo-German declaration of 30 September 1938, to commence negotiations with Germany in order to settle matters in dispute. Despite the rhetorical broadsides which Hitler fired at Britain at Saarbrücken on 9 October, Chamberlain and other British politicians invited Germany directly or indirectly, as can be seen from a note of Ambassador Dirksen, "to indicate her demands so that talks can be opened; the subjects mentioned included . . . colonies, raw materials and disarmament.[123] The delimitation of economic spheres of interest

---

[120] *ADAP*, Series D, vol, I. op. cit., p. 501, Note by Ribbentrop, 2 April 1938.

[121] Ibid., vol, II. p. 478, Ribbentrop to Halifax, 21 Aug. 1938.

[122] Ibid., p. 724.

[123] Obviously, the British side called for statements on the limitation of armaments to allay misgivings in Britain over Chamberlain's policy of appeasement. Cf. ibid., vol. IV, Baden—Baden 1951, p. 267, Note by Dr Fritz Hesse, London, 11 Oct. 1938.

was named as a topic in private conversations."[124] The German side, however, set no store by the British efforts. Nazi official statements and press reports were adverse.[125]

At the same time, the Chamberlain government was facing a rising tide of public discontent with its policy of appeasement. The anti-Semitic pogrom staged by the Nazis on 10 November 1938 marked a critical juncture in this respect. Chamberlain now deemed it necessary to declare during a cabinet meeting on 16 November that the colonial question could be discussed only "as part of a general settlement. Such a settlement was clearly impossible in present circumstances, and it followed that there could be no question of a return of colonies to Germany."[126]

Subsequently, the British government was no longer in a position to make any official move on the colonial issue.[127]

During a conversation with Hitler on 24 November 1938 the pro-fascist South African Minister of Defence, Oswald Pirow, tried to act as a mediator with regard to an Anglo-German *rapprochement*. This was the last time the subject of changes in the distribution of colonies was discussed at the diplomatic level in full view of the international public. But the meeting shed no fresh light on the issue and failed to produce any results.[128]

At this time Hitler was already planning the annexation of what remained of Czechoslovakia, and the attack on Poland. Colonies were no immediate objective of the Nazi policy of aggression. For propaganda purposes, however, the colonial issue was kept in the forefront of Nazi rhetoric. In speeches delivered on 8 November 1938 and on 30 January 1939, Hitler once again insisted that the colonial question was the sole point of contention between Germany and Britain.

While the Nazi leadership no longer expected to acquire colonies through diplomatic efforts (all they could hope for was in any case the return of the former German colonies), the preparations for a colonial take-over — in the context of the general preparations for war — showed

---

[124] *Dokumente und Materialien* . . ., vol. II, p. 164, Zusammenfassende Aufzeichnungen Dirksens. Cf. also *ADAP*, Series D, vol. IV, pp. 277ff, Dirksen to the German Foreign Office, 31 Oct. 1938, and *B.-J. Wendt*, The Economic Appeasement, Düsseldorf 1971, pp. 26ff.

[125] *Dokumente und Materialien* . . ., vol II, p. 165, Cf. also *ADAP*, Series D. vol. IV, p. 271, Weizsäcker to Dirksen, 17 Sept. 1938.

[126] Public Record Office, London, Cabinet Meetings, 55, 16 Nov. 1938.

[127] Cf. also *ADAP*. Series D, vol. IV, p. 290, Dirksen to the German Foreign Office, 17 Nov. 1938.

[128] Ibid., p. 291, Conversation between Hitler and Pirow, 24 Dec. 1938.

how seriously the Hitler regime was pursuing the aim of colonial expansion in Africa, as the outcome of military victories in Europe.

Ever since the Deko Group had been founded and the Colonial Policy Office of the Nazi party had begun, in early 1937, to go ahead with "preparatory colonial planning" in the administrative sphere, such preparations had advanced considerably. Specific problems such as postal services and communications were being dealt with by the appropriate ministries.[129] The Reich Office for Cartography had begun preparing detailed maps in late 1937. The task of drafting legal codes for the future Nazi colonial empire had been entrusted to the Committee for Colonial Law, a body attached to the so-called Academy for German Law and headed by State Councillor Professor Baron von Freytag-Loringhofen. The comittee commenced work at the beginning of 1937.

Weigelt wished to see colonial legislation completed in outline by the time the first officials entered colonial territory.[130] Three subcommittees and seven working groups drawn from the Academy, the Nazi party and various government agencies were set up for this purpose. Here again, Weigelt secured a key role for himself by assuming the chairmanship of the subcommittee for "legal matters concerning the white and native population" and of the working group for "native law". By the summer of 1938 the first drafts were ready: those of the budget law for the "protectorates" and of the laws relating to colonial officials and the colonial police force.

The selection and training of personnel for the administration and the police force had also begun. In December 1937 the Reich Ministry of Justice instructed the chief judges of the provincial high courts to identify and register all former colonial officials in the judicial service. Soon after, all ministries began to select prospective colonial administrators. The Reich School for Colonial Administration at Ladeburg near Berlin, which had been set up in mid-1938, provided training courses for them. From late 1937 onwards preparations were also under way for the establishment of colonial police forces, for which 380 officers and 2,000 policemen volunteered by June 1939. The Ministry of the Interior arranged for police officers to undergo practical training in the Italian colonies.

A large number of university teachers supporting the Nazi regime's colonial policy helped with the "colonial preparations" in a variety

---

[129] Cf. R. Lakowski, op. cit., pp. 58ff.

[130] ZStA, Reichsjustizministerium, no. 10832, p. 9, Weigelt's address to the meeting of the Colonial Law Committee on 8 April 1937.

of ways. Already in the winter term of 1935—36 no less than 31 universities, colleges and commercial schools offered lectures and training in different fields of "colonial science"[131], and such activities increased in the following years. "Colonial science" comprised not only colonial history, the geography and ethnography of Africa and Asia, "colonial economics" and "colonial jurisprudence", but also "colonial linguistics", tropical medicine, tropical agricultural science and engineering, geology, hydrology and, last but not least, the notorious fascist "racial studies". Those engaged in "colonial science" did not confine themselves to furnishing a pseudoscientific rationale for the "German colonial claims", but helped to pave the way for colonial domination and exploitation in every conceivable field of activity.

In addition to specialized journals featuring articles on "colonial science", there existed the Koloniale Rundschau, edited by Professor Carl Troll[132], as a kind of official mouthpiece for "colonial scholars". The years after 1936 also saw the publication of countless theses and treatises dealing with colonial subjects. In 1939 the Deutscher Kolonialdienst announced that thanks to the indefatigable efforts made "in every branch of German colonial science [the scholars concerned] can report to the Führer: We are ready."[133]

Military preparations for the take-over of colonies had begun in late 1937.[134] The Navy was naturally especially active. By the end of 1938 it had trained two companies of marines at Cuxhaven and Swinemünde for service under tropical conditions, and in January 1939 it started equipping them for this purpose. These two companies were set up on the assumption that the colonies would merely have to be occupied: the military conflict over Germany's future colonial possessions was to take place in Europe, not Africa. Under the terms of a peace settlement imposed by the German fascists the future colonial empire would be simply surrendered by the vanquished western powers. The mission assigned to the marines was to occupy strategic points along the coast while army units were to take possession of the interior.

On 20 December 1938 the head of the Colonial Policy Office, von Epp, Vice-Admiral Canaris and Captain (naval) Bürkner, representing the Armed Forces Supreme Command (OKW), met in Munich to discuss

---

[131] Cf. H. Kühne, op. cit., pp. 109 ff.

[132] The geographer Troll, later a prominent defender of neocolonialism in the Federal Republic, became rector of Bonn University in 1960.

[133] Deutscher Kolonial-Dienst, 1939, no. 6, p. 162.

[134] R. Lakowski, op. cit., pp. 58 ff.

the state of colonial preparations. They resolved to work closely together in all colonial matters and to begin immediately with preparations for the setting up of colonial forces. As can be seen from a report on colonial preparations of February 1939, ten officers attached to the OKW and the Army, Navy and Air Force High Commands had colonial assignments at the time. The OKW, which was responsible for mustering colonial forces, first adopted measures to register all officers considered suitable for service in such units and to lay down the "structure of the protective forces" down to the last detail.[135] Since officers who had served in the colonies before 1918 were, with few exceptions, held to be too old, the OKW negotiated with the three Wehrmacht branches on the transfer of younger officers. At the outbreak of war the Wehrmacht was fully prepared to land in and take over colonies within a short space of time.

After Epp had given Hitler a report on the state of colonial preparations on 13 February 1939, the latter officially charged the Colonial Policy Office with directing the activities in progress. On 9 March Epp received a written directive to this effect from Lammers, the head of the Reich Chancellery, confirming that Hitler had noted the plans of the Office with interest and expressed his approval. The directive stressed that "the moment the colonies are recovered the future colonial administration must be prepared and ready to commence its activities instantaneously." Although Hitler did not endorse Epp's proposal to create a ministry of colonies, probably for reasons of foreign policy, he instructed Epp "vigorously to go ahead with the preparatory work for the future colonial administration and to make the necessary arrangements for the establishment of a Reich Colonial Office [i.e. ministry]."[136] The treatment of the colonial issue in foreign affairs was to remain the prerogative of the Foreign Office.

The systematic preparations outlined here and Hitler's instructions show that Nazi Germany was pursuing colonial expansion in earnest. Hitler was obviously looking ahead to the moment when "England is in difficulties", as he had put it in November 1937. Territorial aims far exceeded the former German colonies as is shown by a statement made in early December 1938 by Colonel von Geldern-Crispendorf, the OKW officer in charge of "colonial preparations". He said that it was necessary "to analyse not only the capacity of the former German colonial territories as regards war economy, but also the capacity of adjoining African

---

[135] Ibid., pp. 61—2.
[136] Lammers to Epp. 9 March 1939, in *K. Hildebrand*, op. cit., pp. 904—5.

territories such as Angola, Mozambique, the Belgian Congo and French Equatorial Africa."[137] Fleet commander Admiral Carls outlined the tasks of the Navy as follows in September 1938: "If Germany is to acquire secure world power status, as is the Führer's will, she needs — apart from sufficient colonial territory — secure sea communications and guaranteed access to the high seas."[138]

During a secret meeting with military leaders on 23 May 1939 Hitler expressed his determination to attack Poland and emphasized the prospect of a military conflict with Britain which, in his words, saw in Germany's development the establishment of a hegemony "which would weaken England".[139] Referring to the blockade which almost certainly would be imposed on Germany, he rejected the idea that the cession of colonies before the war could solve the problem of food supplies after hostilities had begun.

Nevertheless, the colonial issue was to appear once again during the secret Anglo-German negotiations of July and August 1939. Although the British government had, together with France, begun negotiations with the Soviet Union to explore the prospects of an alliance against the fascist aggressors, an understanding with Germany, as Dirksen aptly observed, "remained the most desirable, paramount goal for Britain"[140] even after the dismemberment of Czechoslovakia. But the secret negotiations aiming at such an understanding soon showed that Chamberlain's efforts at further appeasement were far from enough for the Hitler regime: the imperialist antagonism between the two powers had become too deep to be bridged by the concessions Chamberlain was able to offer.

When Chamberlain's chief adviser, Horace Wilson, conferred with State Councillor Wohltat[141] in July 1939, he submitted not only proposals for a non-intervention treaty, arms limitations and the demarcation of economic spheres of influence, but also a proposal for "solving the colonial question", which again centred on the idea of Africa being

---

[137] Memo on a meeting held on 6 Dec. 1938 to discuss th state of colonial preparations in the Wehrmacht and in the Reich generally. Source: *R. Lakowski*, op. cit., p. 90.

[138] Trial of the Major War Criminals before the International Military Tribunal, vol. 34, Nuremberg 1949, p. 190, Doc. No. 023—C.

[139] *ADAP*, Series D, vol. VI, Baden—Baden 1956, p. 479.

[140] *Dokumente und Materialien . . .*, vol. II, p. 75, Report by Dirksen to the German Foreign Office, 24, July 1939.

[141] *ADAP*, Series D, vol. VI, pp. 826 ff.

jointly developed by the European colonial powers. Wilson intimated that other practical formulas might also be considered.[142] Wohltat's reply was that any general settlement would have to be preceded by a solution of the colonial question. However, the Hitler regime had no intention whatsoever of committing itself by a formal agreement with the western powers. Göring dismissed Wilson's offers as "totally absurd" and was not prepared to take them seriously.[143] But in August the regime continued to put forward in public the demand for "colonial revision" — as in a declaration Hitler made on the 25th of that month — as part of its tactics of pretending to seek a peaceful arrangement with Britain.[144] The only result of this mendacious rhetoric was to deceive many millions of Germans.

The attempts of the western powers, notably Great Britain, to negotiate a compromise with Nazi Germany and to restrict the expansionist drive of German imperialism to eastern Europe, with the Soviet Union as the main target, failed not because Britain refused to meet German demands for a cession of colonies in Africa but because the overall conflict of interests between these two imperialist powers proved insuperable. The rulers of fascist Germany were not prepared to reduce their programme of expansion. Not content with their expansionist drive eastward, they were seeking undisputed hegemony on the European continent as a stepping-stone to world power, which would of course include colonies in Africa and overseas spheres of influence on a major scale.

---

[142] Ambassador Dirksen later reported that the British cabinet had decided in late February 1939 to return Germany's former colonies (*Dokumente und Materialien . . .*, vol. II, p. 171). The minutes of the British cabinet meetings do not contain any evidence confirming this. Chamberlain pointed out on 3 May 1939, according to the minutes, that "in his view it was quite impossible to discuss with Germany any question of the return of the Colonies at the present time, and that nothing should be said which would imply that we were prepared to do so." Public Record Office, London, Cabinet Meetings. 26, 3 May 1939.

[143] *Documents on British Foreign Policy* 1919—1939, Series 3, vol. VI, London 1953, p. 749, conversation between Dahlerus and Göring, 24 July 1939.

[144] *ADAP*, Series D, vol. VII. Baden—Baden 1956,   p. 233 ff.

XII. The Second World War

1. The Territorial Aims

(a) The Colonial War Aims of the Deutsche Bank and IG Farben

In September 1939 German imperialism unleashed the Second World War in an attempt to repartition the globe and, ultimately, achieve world domination. The primary object was to destroy the Soviet Union and establish a "New Order" in Europe, but the ruling alliance of bankers, industrialists, generals and Nazi leaders was also determined to acquire a vast colonial empire in sub-Saharan Africa.

These colonial ambitions formed part of the expansionist and world power designs of German imperialism. Some historians citing divergent views on the extent and sequence of the expansionist goals and other disparities, especially conflicting statements by Hitler, contend that the colonial war aims were not pursued in earnest. West German historians have occasionally even dismissed the preparations made in this connection as mere sand-box exercises. Yet in actual fact, there never were any basic differences of opinion on the alleged necessity of acquiring a colonial empire in Africa. There was disagreement only on timing, methods and scope. This reflected the different interests of the various monopoly capitalist groups involved and the variety of political and military tasks of the government departments and other state institutions concerned with colonial policy and preparations.

The attempts of German big business to bring about a repartition of the world resulted from its perpetual struggle for raw material markets and investment outlets which required the creation of new political and strategic realities. This intrinsic feature of the imperialist, monopoly capitalist system, demonstrated by Lenin during the First World War in his work 'Imperialism, the Highest Stage of Capitalism', was also very much apparent during the Second World War. The colonial war aims of German fascism bear witness to the continuity of imperialist German policy: the makers of that policy stressed the need to build up an enormous

379

colonial empire in Central Africa as a pillar of German world power from the beginning of the century right until defeat in the Second World War, although the chances of erecting such an empire became less and less.

Poland and colonies in Africa: those were the two areas for which concrete programmes were drawn up from September 1939 onwards. Representatives of many influential groups were involved in working out these programmes and in other preparations for the empire to come: the Nazi state and party, the industrial monopolies and banks, the economic umbrella organizations, the OKW and the high commands of the three armed services, and various scientific institutions. Their relatively large number underlines the importance attached to this work, but at the same time contributed to differences in the proposals made. The differences were, however, less numerous than the points of agreement. All plans and programmes showed a clear affinity to ideas put forward by the Pan-German League before the First World War and the aims of the German monopoly bourgeoisie during that war. They concerned the establishment of an economically united Europe dominated by Germany, to which would be attached an extensive colonial empire in sub-Saharan Africa.

The first, and most comprehensive, programme for colonial expansion was written by Kurt Weigelt, leading financier and colonial affairs specialist of the Deutsche Bank. Immediately after the outbreak of the war, on 20 September 1939, with Poland's fate sealed, he received green light for his plan to draft a memorandum on colonial policy from the head of the Colonial Policy Office, General (ret.) von Epp.[1] Only three days later Weigelt submitted a general outline of the projected document. His task had been greatly facilitated by the "preparatory colonial planning" which had long been under way to provide material for precisely this purpose. In particular, he was able to draw on a compilation from his own pen concerning the production of raw materials in the former German colonies and the adjoining countries.[2] For the rest he drew heavily on the memoranda prepared during the First World War, primarily by the Imperial Colonial Office.

---

[1] Archives of the DWI, Bestand Deutsche Bank, Koloniale Denkschrift, no. A 26/43, Note of Weigelt dated 4 Oct. 1939. (The files examined by the author are now in the ZStA.)

[2] Cf. K. Weigelt, Koloniale Rohstoffversorgung im Rahmen der heimischen Volkswirtschaft, in: Beiträge zur deutschen Kolonialfrage, ed. by Diedrich Westermann, Essen 1937.

In presenting this memorandum, the Deutsche Bank was the first to raise colonial demands in connection with the war.[3] The paper consisted of two parts. The second part, which was not confidential, gave a description of the different colonies and was meant to assist the Colonial Policy Office and the Deko Group in their work.

But the first, confidential part was far more important. Featuring diagrams and maps of Central Africa, it was intended for consideration "at the top level". In fact, Weigelt wrote to Epp in August 1940: "In the event of deliberations with the Führer I would humbly request being chosen to present the economic subject matter."[4] The banker prepared a decision "at the top level" by systematically sending his memorandum to influential persons who might further his ends.[5] As far as territorial claims were concerned, he laid the main emphasis on the countries of West Africa, Cameroon, and the French and Belgian Congo.

Weigelt's ideas were chiefly designed to strengthen Nazi Germany rapidly in military and economic terms, especially by taking possession of the rich, densely populated and conveniently located colonies bordering the West African seaboard and situated in the Congo Basin. His memorandum, which was endorsed by Epp, is the most remarkable and most elaborate statement of German colonial war aims in the Second World War. Apparently the earliest such document, it was submitted to key figures in the government, the Nazi party and the business world. The extent of the territories claimed in the memorandum reflected the aspirations of the most important sections of the monopolist bourgeoisie. The Deutsche Bank, in its capacity as the nerve centre of the German economy, pursued not only its own financial interests but those of the ruling class as a whole. This was shown, for example, by a report prepared by the director of the Deutsche Bank, Gaettens, who was also a member

---

[3] Unfortunately, this important document has not been found, but references in the files of the Deutsche Bank shed much light on its content. By 25 July 1940 50 copies had been printed and were being distributed by Weigelt. Cf. *D. Eichholtz*, Die Kriegszieldenkschrift des Kolonialpolitischen Amtes der NSDAP von 1940. Steckbrief eines Dokuments. In: Zeitschrift für Geschichtswissenschaft, 1974, pp. 308—324.

[4] Archive of the DWI, op. cit., Weigelt to Epp, 12 Aug. 1940.

[5] Recipients of the memorandum included Bethke (Ministry of Economics), Puhl (Vice-President of the Reichsbahn), Körner and Backe (Secretaries of State), Bielfeld and Ruppel (Foreign Office), Funk (Minister of Economics), Keppler (Secretary of State), Bouhler (top Nazi party official), Schwerin von Krosigk (Minister of Finance), von Lindequist (former Secretary of State for Colonies), Ernst von Weizsäcker (Secretary of State in the Foreign Office), Hinrich and Hewel (diplomats), and Lammers (head of the Reich Chancellery).

of the board of the DOAG and deputy chairman of the Deutsche Holzgesellschaft on behalf of the Deko Group in 1940.[6] Gaettens thought
that the rising demand for timber by various industries could best be
met by acquiring a vast stretch of suitable territory in Africa including
French Equatorial Africa, Cameroon and Nigeria.

Even though the countries of West Africa were at the centre of Weigelt's demands, he was by no means unsympathetic to more far-reaching
demands. His files contain a note dated 30 July 1940 listing beside West
African colonies the following territories as forming part of Germany's
sphere of interest in Africa: Tanganyika, Ruanda-Urundi, Cameroon,
the Belgian Congo, French Equatorial Africa, Kenya, Uganda, and
Northern Rhodesia.[7]

His list anticipated, at least in part, demands from a powerful quarter:
Secretary of State Wilhelm Keppler, Hitler's administrator of economic
affairs, in a letter to Epp of 24 September 1940[8] considered it essential
to acquire areas with raw materials that could not be produced industrial-
ly in Germany, first and foremost, metals and minerals such as phosphates
and sulphur. He stressed that neither the former German colonies nor
the West African territories mentioned in the memorandum (from the
Gold Coast to Cameroon) were producing these raw materials in large
quantities and that West Africa was of no importance in this respect.
Keppler therefore drew Epp's attention to the copper deposits and cobalt
resources in Northern Rhodesia and the high-grade chromium found
in Southern Rhodesia.

The immense IG Farben group was also committed to the establishment of a large colonial empire in sub-Saharan Africa, as some documents
from its archives show. Under the Acetylsalicylic Acid Convention
concluded with a US corporation on 20 July 1940, IG Farben was expressly given the right to deliver its products to German "protectorates
and any German colonies that might be established".[9] On 14 August
1940 the chemical giant served notice to its foreign agents (both German
and non-German firms) that the agreements on colonial territories in
force since 1930—31 were to be abrogated. According to incomplete
data, this applied to French West Africa, British West Africa, Cameroon

---

[6] ZStA, Deutsche Bank, no. 21918, pp. 1—2.
[7] Archive of the DWI, Koloniale Vorbereitungen, no. A 26/44, Note of 30 July 1940.
[8] Ibid., Keppler to Epp. 24 Sept. 1940.
[9] Cf. *J. Schmelzer*, IG-Farben stoßen nach Afrika. Zur Kolonialgeschichte und kolonialen Tradition der IG-Farben-Nachfolgegesellschaften, Bitterfeld/Wolfen 1965,
p. 31.

and Spanish Guinea. This step was taken in order to have a free hand in the expected "new colonial order".[10]

The views of IG Farben were stated more precisely in a survey prepared by its Special Export Group on 22 November 1940.[11] This divided Africa into political spheres of interest dominated by Germany, Italy, France, Spain and Portugal, and then analysed each sphere from an economic viewpoint. The regions allotted to Germany were subdivided into two categories, the first comprising the colonies proper and the second the countries singled out for indirect control. The future German colonial empire was to include the Gold Coast, Togo, Dahomey, Nigeria, Cameroon, Spanish Guinea with Fernando Po and Sao Tomé, French Equatorial Africa, the Belgian Congo, Ruanda-Urundi, Tanganyika, Zanzibar and Pemba, Mauritius, Réunion, the Seychelles, and Madagascar. The second category was to include South West Africa, the Union of South Africa, Basutoland, Bechuanaland, Swaziland, Southern and Northern Rhodesia, and Mozambique. While Tunisia, Libya, Egypt, the Anglo-Egyptian Sudan, Eritrea, Ethiopia, Somaliland, Uganda and Kenya were assigned to allied Italy, the remaining parts of North and West Africa were divided among France, Spain and Portugal.[12]

The IG Farben scheme revealed to what extent the plans of the big companies were motivated by their profitmaking interests. The reason why the economically more important part of West Africa, with its dense population, was singled out for the future colonial empire was that it would constitute a large market for the company's products, chiefly dyes and medicines.

The similarity between these plans and those of the Deutsche Bank as advocated by Weigelt was no coincidence. The ties linking that bank with the colonial trading and plantation companies, for which West Africa was the most important region because of its manpower resources and natural conditions, gave rise to similar territorial demands.

(b) The memoranda of the Foreign Office and the Navy Command

Soon after Weigelt, the Foreign Office and the Navy began to formulate concrete demands. As early as 14 October 1939 the Navy Command Office (Marinekommandoamt) produced a document entitled "First

---

[10] Ibid., pp. 33—4.
[11] ZStA, IG Farben, no. B. 6549/44, pp. 25—6, Note of 22 Nov. 1940 (G./Ausfuhr-Sondergruppe).
[12] Ibid., pp. 143 and 201.

considerations concerning the Recovery of German Colonies". Colonial planning was then stepped up considerably in the spring of 1940 and especially after the French surrender on 22 June of that year.

   The course of the war in the first half of 1940 had created the impression that the wildest dreams of the Nazis were about to come true. Even before the French surrender, Foreign Minister Joachim von Ribbentrop instructed the deputy head of the Foreign Office's Economic Policy Department, Carl Clodius, and the ambassador Karl Ritter to work out proposals for a "New Order in Europe".[13] In addition to a redrawing of European frontiers in favour of German imperialism, both Clodius and Ritter suggested a redistribution of the colonies in Africa. But unlike Weigelt, they sketched the colonial objectives only in general terms. Both assumed that a compromise peace with Britain would be possible after the defeat of France. The British were to acknowledge German supremacy in Europe and return the former German colonies, but British possessions in Africa were to remain largely untouched whereas the German colonial empire was to be enlarged at the expense of Belgium and France. According to Ritter's proposal the German empire should comprise the former colonies, the Belgian Congo, French Equatorial Africa and, possibly, Nigeria. The function assigned to these overseas territories "after a prolonged period of intensive development" was to meet the entire demand of Nazi-dominated continental Europe for tropical and sub-tropical vegetable products and a large proportion of its copper requirements. Development was to be facilitated by inviting Germans from Latin American and other foreign countries to settle in Africa.[14]

   Clodius, who also based his considerations on a "New Order in Europe", dealt with "Economic Aspects of Peace" in a study dated 30 May 1940 in which he advocated a colonial empire including all former German possessions as well as the Belgian Congo.[15]

   More projects were to follow soon. Within days of Clodius and Ritter having submitted their proposals, on 3 June, the Naval War Staff (Seekriegsleitung), always to the fore in matters of overseas expansion, put forward a memorandum dealing with territorial expansion and military

---

[13] Note by Carl Clodius dated 30 May 1940 and note by Karl Ritter dated 1 June 1940, in: *Anatomie der Aggression*. Neue Dokumente zu den Kriegszielen des faschistischen deutschen Imperialismus im zweiten Weltkrieg, ed. and with an introduction by G. Hass and W. Schumann, Berlin 1972, pp. 42—54.

[14] Ibid.

[15] *ADAP*, vol. 9, Doc. no. 345, pp. 390—1.

bases. Besides demanding a reshaping of Europe to bring "the peoples hitherto inhabiting this region into a state of complete political, economic and military dependence on Germany", the naval chiefs called for a contiguous stretch of territory in Central Africa. This was supposed to include the French possessions south of the estuary of the Senegal River, the erstwhile German colonies of Togo and Cameroon plus the Belgian Congo. South West Africa was to be exchanged for other territories in order to round off the Central African empire. They also wished to see bases established on islands in the Atlantic and the Indian Ocean. The memorandum deliberately left open whether more far-reaching demands would be raised if the outcome of the war with Britain made this possible.[16]

The Naval High Command (Oberkommando der Kriegsmarine), sharing the assumption that only the French and Belgian possessions were so far available, submitted a memorandum entitled "Military Bases to Defend the Colonial Empire" on 27 July 1940. In presenting this document, the naval command drew the attention of the Foreign Office and the government and party hierarchy to their specific interests in the establishment of a colonial empire. They urged that the four former German colonies in Africa, together with parts of French West Africa, French Equatorial Africa and the Belgian Congo should be transformed into a "territorially contiguous German colonial empire in Central Africa". In this context they submitted a list of bases which ought to be set up along the continent's west and east coast and on various islands.[17] They also pressed for the establishment of bases in the Azores and the Canary Islands. Claims to British possessions (such as Nigeria, Kenya and Northern Rhodesia) were made conditional on "future political developments".[18]

The location and number of the bases envisaged demonstrate the Navy's desire not only to safeguard Nazi Germany's sea links with Africa but also to create favourable conditions for a future conflict with the United States.

---

[16] International Military Tribunal. The Trial of the Major War Criminals, vol. 34, Nuremberg 1949, Document no. 041—C.

[17] These included the seaports of Dakar, Conakry, Freetown, Douala, Pointe Noire, Boma, Zanzibar, Dar es Salaam, Mombasa, Diego Suarez, the islands of Fernando Po, Sao Tomé, St Helena, Ascension, Pemba, the Comoros, the Seychelles, Mauritius, etc.

[18] ZStA, A.A., no. 61120, pp. 1ff., Naval High Command to the Foreign Office, 27 July 1940.

While the plans of the Deutsche Bank reflected economic interests, the proposals of the Foreign Office and the Navy were strongly influenced by considerations of strategy and foreign policy. There is every likelihood that the views of the Deutsche Bank did not remain without influence on the authors of other memoranda dealing with colonial war aims. Ritter is known to have had ties with the Deutsche Bank. He was to assume the chairmanship of the DOAG in the spring of 1939 at the instigation of Weigelt who described him not only as an "old colonial" but also as a "close friend of our firm".[19]

The preparations for the invasion of the USSR from June 1940 and the fact that no understanding or compromise with Britain was reached had their effect on activities in the colonial sphere, and after the invasion in June 1941 interest in the programmes and scenarios for a colonial empire in Africa clearly declined. Colonial aims were modified in that Britian's possessions were no longer spared or relegated to second place because it had become evident that a fascist colonial empire could only be founded after overwhelming the Soviet Union and then defeating Britain and breaking up the British Empire.

(c) The Colonial Aims after the Decision to Invade the Soviet Union
During the preparations for the attack on the Soviet Union, Hitler's government reconsidered the question of a repartition of Africa in the late summer of 1940 with the need to win allies in mind. Two of Germany's potential allies in a war of aggression against the USSR — Italy and Spain — wished to see their colonial holdings in Africa enlarged, while the Vichy regime was anxious to retain the French dominions. In several talks with representatives of these powers, some of them conducted by Hitler himself, the Nazi government tried to reconcile the conflicting interests of its potential allies without committing itself, hoping to settle the issue as it saw fit after a final victory.

As mentioned above, the shift in policy affected the place accorded to Britain's possessions in the fascist plans for territorial expansion. In contrast to the plans submitted in the early summer of 1940, the British colonies were no longer excluded in the memoranda prepared. The first indication of this was given in a note of 4 September 1940[20] prepared by the Foreign Office representative at the Army High Command, Hasso von Etzdorf, which provided for an alternative course of action if no

[19] ZStA, Deutsche Bank, no. 21 762, p. 29, Weigelt to Urbig, 29 Nov. 1939.
[20] *ADAP*, vol. 11, Doc. no. 16, pp. 18—9. After the Second World War Hasso von Etzdorf served as Bonn's Ambassador in London.

agreement with Britain was reached. This document suggested that in the event of a "peaceful partition arrangement with England", i.e. a compromise between the British imperialists and their German rivals, the former German colonies, the French and Belgian Congo, the Lake Chad area and French Equatorial Africa should be allotted to Germany. If the British Empire fell apart, Etzdorf wrote, Uganda, Zanzibar, the southern part of Kenya (including Nairobi), Nigeria, the Gold Coast, and Dahomey should also be brought under the sway of Nazi Germany.

In November 1940 the objectives of German imperialism were summarized in a detailed memorandum of the Foreign Office.[21] Its author, Ernst Bielfeld, was the leading colonial expert of the Political Department of the Foreign Office and scheduled to become undersecretary and head of Department I (police, personnel, administration, colonial policy)[22] in the projected Ministry of Colonial Affairs. The memorandum sums up the views of the Deutsche Bank and IG Farben, taking into account Hitler's general foreign policy at the time. Its point of departure was the demand "on principle" for the return of the former German colonies by France, Belgium, Britain, Australia, and New Zealand. The "claims" upon Japan regarding one-time German possessions in the Pacific and upon Portugal concerning the Kionga Triangle were to be made the object of barter deals. Bielfeld left aside the issue of South West Africa because this was to be part of "the settlement of our future relationship with the Union of South Africa".

The "final aim", according to Bielfeld, was the regular supply of colonial products to a German-dominated "Greater European economic zone" with a population of approximately 150 million. The memorandum stressed that the German-ruled regions in Africa should be of such a size that they would make it possible to dominate the rest of the continent. The former German colonies of Cameroon, Togo and East Africa would form the nucleus "with the new German colonial possessions grouped around them". In the opinion of the Foreign Office expert, it was absolutely essential to secure control of the Belgian Congo because of its enormous natural wealth.

"Its rich mineral resources", he wrote in the memorandum, "would go a long way towards satisfying German needs. Germany's demand for copper amounts to about 300,000 [metric] tons annually: Katanga has a current output of 200,000 [metric] tons, which could be raised to 300,000. The Belgian Congo has the world's largest deposits of industrial

[21] Published in: *Anatomie der Aggression* (cf. note 13), pp. 115—123.
[22] *ADAP*, vol. 11, Doc. no. 16, p. 18.

diamonds. Germany has so far been unable to use diamonds in the treatment of hard steel for lack of foreign exchange. Our tin requirements amount to about 12,000 [metric] tons per annum. The tin deposits so far discovered in the Belgian Congo (including Ruanda-Urundi) add up to 300,000 [metric] tons. Germany has an urgent need for cobalt as a catalyst for oil synthesis in the Fischer-Tropsch process and for the manufacture of powerful, i.e. light, magnets. Forty per cent of the world output of this metal come from the Belgian Congo, which supplies about 1,700 [metric] tons. In addition, there are deposits of iron ore, high-grade manganese ore, rich radium ore and gold in the Belgian Congo." Moreover, the acquisition of this colony would give the Navy the seaport of Boma which it wished to have.[23]

According to Bielfeld, French Equatorial Africa, which formed part of the Congo Basin, was Cameroon's natural hinterland. It was chiefly because of its valuable timber resources that he wished to see this territory ceded to Germany. He also advocated acquiring at least part of Nigeria, "an economically well-developed and hence especially valuable British colony". Furthermore, the French parts of Togo and Dahomey were to be incorporated into Germany's colonial empire whereas the Gold Coast and western Nigeria were to be allotted to France in recompense for the territories ceded. As far as East and southern Central Africa was concerned, Bielfeld demanded Uganda, Kenya, Zanzibar and Pemba, and possibly Northern Rhodesia as well as northern Niassaland while the question of control over Southern Rhodesia, especially important because of its strategically important minerals (copper), was left open. He largely echoed the Navy's demands for bases, supporting the idea that Dakar or Bathurst, as well as Conakry and Freetown, should be seized. Finally, Bielfeld called for the acquisition of Madagascar "to settle the Jews there" and for the establishment of a naval base on the island, and on Réunion and the Comoro Islands, on strategic grounds.

The French colony Madagascar was chosen as the site of a ghetto settlement in connection with the Nazi plans for the "final solution of the Jewish question". The Nazi leaders and their accomplices were considering the possibility of setting up a Jewish state under German "protection" there. Details of this project can be found in a memorandum written by Franz Rademacher, legation counsellor at the Foreign Office, who later played a prominent part in organizing the extermination of French Jews. After their property had been confiscated, Jews from all

---

[23] *Anatomie der Aggression*, pp. 117—8.

over Europe were to be deported to Madagascar, which was also to become the site of naval and air force bases.[24]

The strategic planning of the Foreign Office under Ribbentrop served the ultimate aim of world domination. Seen in this light, the plan for a future fascist colonial empire was also directed against Germany's most powerful imperialist rival, the United States. At the same time, Bielfeld was at pains not to harm the interests of the Vichy regime more than the rapacity of German imperialism required, and in so doing acted in accordance with Hitler's intention of first destroying the Soviet Union and then turning against the British Empire.[25]

In January 1942 the Undersecretary at the Foreign Office, Ernst Woermann (a nephew of Adolf Woermann), on Ribbentrop's instructions prepared a study in which he not only set out Nazi Germany's objectives in Africa but also discussed various formulas for a compromise between Germany, the Vichy regime and Spain.[26] Woermann made use of Bielfeld's memorandum, taking up his colleague's proposals. He outlined a "Central African colonial empire" comprising "the eastern part of Nigeria, Cameroon, French Equatorial Africa, Uganda, Kenya, German East Africa and possibly Northern Rhodesia". The Belgian Congo was to be attached to this entity "in some way or other". The Undersecretary felt that France should be compensated for colonial possessions ceded to Germany by others equal in size, but that Spain should be rewarded for entering the war by being given British and French colonies. Although Britain was to lose all her African possessions, Woermann was unable to reconcile Spain's claims with the efforts of the Vichy government to save France's overseas territories without reducing Germany's imperial ambitions. He concluded "that the territories available are insufficient to give France full compensation for the losses sustained while at the same time offering Spain a full equivalent for her claims to French Morocco, etc." The search for compromise formulas, a conspicuous

---

[24] *ADAP*, vol. 1, Doc. no. 101, p. 92, Note of Legation Counsellor Rademacher dated 3 July 1940.

[25] Two days before Bielfeld prepared the memorandum, on 4 Nov. 1940, Hitler told Gen. Franz Halder, the Army Chief of Staff: "North West Africa, together with Equatorial Africa, may become the starting point of a major confrontation between the European and the Anglo-Saxon powers." *F. Halder*, Kriegstagebuch, ed. by H.-A. Jacobsen, vol. 2, Stuttgart 1963, p. 163.

[26] Published in: *W. Schumann* and *L. Nestler* (eds.), Weltherrschaft im Visier, Berlin 1975, pp. 317—319.

feature of Woermann's study, must be seen in the context of Nazi Germany's new difficulties after the failure of the Blitzkrieg against the Soviet Union.

2. The Climax and Conclusion of "Preparatory Colonial Planning"

(a) The Colonial Activities of the Business World

In the firm belief that the fulfilment of their colonial ambitions was close at hand, the representatives of the big companies and various institutions of the Nazi state continued their "preparatory colonial planning" after the beginning of the war. The reaction of the stock exchange reflected these hopes. The prices of colonial shares, which had not been traded for years, began to rise. They reached a first peak in 1940, and a second one in October 1941[27] when Hitler's troops were advancing on Moscow.

A number of firms began to show a keen interest in future business in or with the colonies. Negotiations on the sale of government-owned shares in the Deutsche Afrika-Linien to a group led by State Councillor J. T. Essberger were concluded at the end of 1940.[28] Other firms applied for concessions in Africa and for the takeover of business enterprises already existing there.[29] Legation counsellor Gunzert of the Foreign Office had to reject as "premature" the application of a Bremen tobacco factory, referring it to Weigelt, who was responsible for such matters.[30] Colonial firms established before the First World War such as the Gesellschaft Südkamerun asked the Foreign Office and the Colonial Policy Office for the return of all their former African properties. The company submitted plans to be put into effect after Cameroon had been regained and requested that British plantations be allotted to it.[31]

[27] ZStA, Dresdner Bank, no. 817, Berliner Börsenberichte, 6 Oct. 1941.

[28] ZStA, Deutsche Bank, no. 19606, pp. 9ff, Report of the Woermann-Linie for 1940, dated 16 May 1941. The management of the Afrika-Linien tried to make sure at once, through arrangements with the Wehrmacht, that their company would undertake the expected troop transports and carry single passengers as well. Koloniale Unterrichtung des Amtes Ausland Abwehr des OKW, no. 6 of 5 Oct. 1941. MA, W 63.30—125.

[29] ZStA, RKolA, no. 683, p. 236, Letter by Messrs Kannegiesser to Legation Counsellor Gunzert of the Foreign Office, 21 Nov. 1940.

[30] Ibid., p. 238, draft for Gunzert's reply to Messrs Kannegiesser, 27 Nov. 1940.

[31] Ibid., no. 3460, pp. 177—8. Confidential interim report of the Gesellschaft Süd Kamerun on the financial year 1940, 31 Dec. 1940.

Large manufacturing concerns also began to take steps for a greater business activity in Africa. The Telefunken-Gesellschaft mbH developed radio equipment for use under tropical conditions. The installations intended for export were constructed in such a way that only minor readjustments were necessary for them to be employed in the African colonies.[32] Of especial significance was the fact that the IG Farben group now began to lay claim to African territories in earnest. On 28 and 29 June 1940 the Commerce Committee of IG Farben decided to set up an "African Committee" which was to represent the company's interests in dealings with the government and the Nazi party.[33] At the same time, the group raised its financial outlay for purposes of colonial expansion, the Colonial Economic Committee henceforth receiving 10,000 instead of 5,000 marks.[34] In response to an application made in September 1940, the Control Office for the Chemical Industry gave the company permission for "unhindered trade in all chemical products in all African countries".[35] This move was all the more important because IG Farben operations in Africa before the war were, by its own account, more or less limited to Egypt. In South Africa, sales had made a promising start, only to fall sharply after a boycott imposed by Jewish businessmen there. "The overall business situation is such," the company's economic policy department stated in a report, "that we shall have to rebuild our sales organization on a new basis after the end of the war, taking into account the ensuing political and territorial changes in that continent."[36] The directors decided in 1941 to spend 50,000 marks on IG Farben's own colonial school, twice as much as before, and to engage two additional teachers.[37]

The Business Committee observed the activities of the Afrika-Verein, an association formed by companies intending to do business in the continent, and took note of the plans being pursued by other firms in Africa.[38] By 10 May 1941, the Mannesmann-Röhren- und Eisenhandel

---

[32] Ibid., no. 7190, pp. 39—40. Record of a conversation with the head of the international department of Telefunken, 6 Nov. 1940.

[33] J. Schmelzer, op. cit., p. 31.

[34] Ibid.

[35] ZStA, IG Farben, no. B 6549/43, p. 39, The Reich Commissioner of the Control Office for the Chemical Industry, 18 Sept. 1940.

[36] Ibid., no. B 4371, p. 1, Letter of the Economic Policy Department to the Chemicals Department, 16 May 1941.

[37] Cf. J. Schmelzer, op. cit., p. 37.

[38] ZStA, IG Farben, no. B 6549/43, p. 189, Note attached to the record of the general meeting of the Afrikaverein held in Hamburg at the end of March 1941.

GmbH, the Siemens and Halske AG, the Siemens-Schuckert-Werke AG and the Schering AG had joined the Afrika-Verein along with IG-Farben.[39] In September, State Councillor Hermann Bücher of the AEG, who in the words of Weigelt "often furnishes us with valuable aid by proffering advice"[40], asked the latter for a copy of his memorandum.

The Dresdner Bank also attempted to stake out a claim. Its director A. Meyer tried to secure a share in the "development" of Africa during negotiations with the Colonial Department of the Foreign Office, arguing that a "task of this magnitude" could not be mastered by the Deutsche Bank alone.[41] But the position of the Deutsche Bank was practically unassailable. Through its director, Kurt Weigelt, it continued to play a key role in shaping the policy of colonial expansion. Weigelt regarded his position as so important that he flatly rejected the proposal to enter the projected Colonial Ministry[42] and, in February 1941, resigned as head of the Economic Division of the Colonial Policy Office.[43] Through the agency of Weigelt, the Deutsche Bank exerted decisive influence on the firms united in the Afrika-Verein and the Deko Group.

Both organizations now considered it their task to act as a link with the various government departments and the Nazi party on all economic matters concerning the prospective African colonies.[44] The Deko Group was especially active in this regard, formulating demands addressed by colonial interest groups to the government. In January 1940 it compiled a catalogue listing measures which were to be completed by the autumn at the latest. These included the drafting of economic plans for East, West and South West Africa, preparations for the growing of specific crops, and the establishment of an information service.[45] Representatives

---

[39] Ibid., pp. 181—2, Circular addressed by the Afrikaverein to all its members, 13 May 1941.

[40] Archive of the DWI, Kolonialdenkschrift, no. A 26/43, Note of Weigelt, 27 Sept. 1941.

[41] ZStA, RKolA, no. 6409, p. 8, Note of 28 Aug. 1940.

[42] ZStA, Deutsche Bank, Handakten Weigelts, no. 21 054, p. 127, Letter by Weigelt of 7 Aug. 1940, and ibid., no. 21 914, pp. 329 ff., Weigelt to Epp. 25 July 1940.

[43] MA, W 63.30—125, Koloniale Unterrichtung no. 11, 12 Feb. 1941.

[44] ZStA, Deutsche Bank, no. 21 921, pp. 37 ff, Minutes of the extraordinary general meeting of the Afrikaverein on 24 June 1940.

[45] Ibid., no. 21 914, pp. 310 ff, Copy of a secret directive of the Deko Group dated 2 Jan. 1940. A "crash programme" for East Africa had been completed in October 1941. MA, W 63.30/126, the Minister of Economics to the War Economy Office, 31 Oct. 1941.

of the Deko Group and of industry jointly ascertained the demand for machinery, equipment and tools to be expected in the colonies.[46]

A very comprehensive report which was concrete in its demands was prepared by the bank director Gaettens on behalf of the Deko Group, concerning the interests of the timber industry.[47] As well as stating specific territorial aims in Africa, the report set out in detail what was to be done when the areas in Central Africa richest in timber had come under German control. Foreign firms, concessions and all means of transport were to be confiscated. In order to ensure that the foreign-held assets could be taken over without a hitch, Gaettens suggested that German timber specialists should be sent into English and French firms in good time. Then, too, the economic situation of the firms to be expropriated would have to be carefully examined, and all timber works united in a central umbrella organization. On behalf of the timber industry Gaettens demanded from the Reich, as long-term measures, the solution of the manpower problem, the improvement of the communications network in the colonies and the construction of power generating plants. A propaganda drive was to be mounted in Germany to stimulate the use of timber from the colonies. The companies in question were to reap higher profits through low railway tariffs and sea freight rates and through concessions in easily accessible areas whereas the state was expected to defray the additional costs incurred.

All in all, the formulation of colonial economic policy was in the hands of a few very influential monopolies so that the economic potential of the state and private enterprises could be used in the interests of just these monopolies.

(b) Administrative Preparations

In the field of general policy, too, "preparatory colonial planning" was brought to a conclusion in 1940. In February of that year the Foreign Office described it as essential to the war effort and expressly called for more intensive efforts in the colonial sphere.[48] A month before, Hitler's deputy Rudolf Hess had once again defined the respective spheres of

---

[46] ZStA, Deutsche Bank, no. 21918, pp. 11—2, Circular addressed by the Deko Group to its members, dated 3 Jan. 1941.

[47] Ibid., no. 21918, pp. 1 ff, Report prepared by Gaettens on behalf of German colonial firms, Berlin 1940.

[48] ZStA, RMdI, no. 27190, p. 207, Foreign Office to Department VI of the Interior Ministry, 21 Feb. 1940.

competence of the key political bodies involved in colonial expansion. The Foreign Office was instructed to deal with "questions relating to the recovery of the German colonies" while the Colonial Policy Office of the Nazi party was charged with the preparations for their administration.[49] In March 1940 Hitler gave orders "to press ahead with the work for the future colonial administration and to make preparations for the establishment of a Reich Colonial Office [i.e. Ministry]." These tasks had been "almost completed" by Epp in mid-June in conjunction with all relevant authorities of the state and the Nazi party, and other institutions.[50] At this stage the chief of the Reich Chancellery, Hans Heinrich Lammers, demanded a "speedy conclusion". This explains why Epp was anxious to see all necessary law drafts and other preparations completed by early August[51], in which he appears to have been largely successful.[52]

The Colonial Policy Office of the Nazi party, which was designed to become the Colonial Ministry (for the time being a change of status was postponed for reasons of foreign policy), had since the outbreak of war increased its staff considerably. The number of persons entrusted with preparing a colonial administration was remarkable by wartime standards.[53] With its seven departments, numerous sub-departments, its branch offices in Brussels, Paris and Hamburg, its press office in Munich, and the Reich Colonial Institute in Berlin-Grunewald[54], the Colonial Policy Office was a ministry in everything but name. It had its own substantial "interim" budget[55] and a building of its own, constructed

[49]   ZStA, Fall XI, no. 279, p. 92, Directive of the Führer's deputy, dated 23 Jan. 1940.
[50]   ZStA, RMdI, no. 27190, p. 173, Lammers, head of the Reich Chancellery, to the supreme authorities of the Reich, 15 June 1940.
[51]   Ibid., p. 171, Dep. VI, Ministry of the Interior to Secretary of State, 19 June 1940.
[52]   Drafts of the following laws and regulations were being prepared or had been completed by early September: the Reich Colonial Act, aliens ordinance, laws relating to colonial officials and pay questions, the Colonial Budget Act, codes of justice applicable to Germans and to "natives", ordinances relating to real estate, mining, animal epidemics, registration of births, marriages and deaths, and the police force. MA W 63.30/125, Koloniale Unterrichtung no. 5, 6 Sept. 1940.
[53]   ZStA, RMdI, no. 27191, Tätigkeitsbericht des Kolonialpolitischen Amtes abgeschlossen am 1. 7. 1941, p. 12. Working for the Colonial Policy Office were 36 senior civil servants, 44 medium-level officials, and 129 employees and workers.
[54]   ZStA, RDR, no. 7200, pp. 49—50, Structure of the Colonial Policy Office as of late July 1941.
[55]   A sum of 6,222,250 marks had been made available to the Colonial Policy Office for the financial year 1940. Ibid., p. 516, Lammers, head of the Reich Chancellery, to the Auditor-General of the German Reich, 7 Dec. 1940. The budget was described

together with a residence for its chief, General Franz Xaver von Epp.[56]

The Colonial Policy Office had set up several task forces in preparation for the takeover of the colonies. The group responsible for West Africa, codenamed "Banana", was headed by an SS officer named Ruhberg who had served as head of the Nazi party branch in Cameroon for several years and was scheduled to become governor of that territory. Similar arrangements had been made for East Africa (under the codename "Sisal") and for the other colonies.[57]

Compared with the Colonial Policy Office, the Colonial Department of the Foreign Office with its four officials was positively modest in size. The work of these civil servants was intimately bound up with the activities of the Colonial Policy Office. Acting "in a voluntary capacity" they worked out staffing proposals for the general colonial administration. Epp praised the results of this collaboration.[58]

The important tasks of Department III, the former Economic Branch of the Colonial Policy Office, had been accomplished in much the same way, i.e. by drawing on volunteers from the Reich Economics Ministry, the Reich Forestry Office and other government agencies. After the French surrender, in June 1940, the Colonial Policy Office was given branch offices in Brussels and Paris, their function being to search the archives of the French and Belgian colonial ministries for documents that might be of use. On behalf of the Colonial Policy Office, Weigelt instructed working groups of the Deko Group to design, with the help of some of the captured documents, plans for the economic sector of the future colonial administration, which was done.[59]

Of special interest to Weigelt were the activities of the institutions which were charged with the infrastructural development required to bring Central Africa under German control and incorporating it into the economic system of the Reich. The construction of roads, railways and

as "provisional" by the Colonial Policy Office because it had been prepared without the extent of the future colonies being known. Ibid., p. 12, Wenig, Stabsleiter of the Colonial Policy Office, to the Auditor-General of the German Reich, 9 May 1941.

[56] The Marstall (the former Royal Horse Stables) had been chosen as the site of the future Colonial Ministry, which was to have between 850 and 1,000 rooms there. The cost of the alterations undertaken was almost one million marks. Staatsarchiv Potsdam, Bausachen (ungeordnet), Rep. 42.

[57] ZStA, RMdI, no. 27191, pp. 79—80, Tätigkeitsbericht des Kolonialpolitischen Amtes, abgeschlossen am 1. 7. 1941.

[58] Ibid., Report p. 13.

[59] Ibid., Report pp. 40 and 22.

aerodromes was regarded as an important prerequisite for effective rule over the future colonies. From 1937 onwards a committee for colonial transport questions in the Reich Ministry of Transport, headed by Minister Julius-Heinrich Dorpmüller, was working on the solution of transport problems together with the Colonial Policy Office.[60] A number of firms received government contracts and soon began delivering the necessary materials. Simultaneously, the postal authorities set to work on their "colonial tasks". Providing substantial funds for this purpose[61], the Ministry of Posts made preparations for the establishment of a telecommunications network in Africa, installed transmitters for radio communication between Germany and Africa, and laid the foundations for postal services and payments transactions in the colonies.

Road construction planning was in the hands of the Todt Organization whose head, Fritz Todt, agreed in June 1940 to submit detailed proposals for road building schemes in the colonies at short notice.[62] A working group for "colonial road construction" attached to the Road Research Association was to create the theoretical basis for practical work in Africa.[63]

Another task was entrusted to the working group for colonial cartography attached to the Reich Cartographic Survey. Set up in December 1937, the group saw its staff increase from 27 to 45 by 1940. Using material captured from the French and the Belgians[64], they did a thorough job mapping anew the whole of Africa. The results of their efforts were to serve as a basis for the repartition of Africa in future negotiations and as aids for the administration in the colonies.

Further preparations included those for the establishment of a health service [65] and increased efforts to select and instruct suitable members of the police force. SS chief Heinrich Himmler, who was commander of all German police forces, ordered the preparations begun before the war to be continued. The years 1940 and 1941 saw another series of courses

[60] Ibid., Report p. 29.

[61] Archiv des Ministeriums für das Post- und Fernmeldewesen, no. 15. Letter of the Minister to the Central Post Office, dated 5 Sept. 1940. 3.5 million marks was put at the disposal of the Office for the purchase and stockpiling of technical equipment.

[62] ZStA, GdS, no. 1119, p. 5, Letter of Todt to Epp, 22 June 1940.

[63] Ibid., pp. 14—5, Minutes of a session of the Working Group for Colonial Road Construction, 3 Dec. 1940.

[64] ZStA, RKolA, no. 3390, p. 71, Letter of the Paris office of the Foreign Office dated 20 Nov. 1940.

[65] Ibid., p. 170. Memo dated 31 May 1940.

held at Oranienburg near Berlin for police officers earmarked for colonial service.[66] A second colonial police college was set up in Vienna towards the end of 1941,[67] and courses arranged by the Nazi security service (Sicherheitsdienst) for the same purpose took place in Italy during 1940.[68] Political training was the principal method employed to prepare police officers and civil servants for colonial service. The pre-war system of instruction was largely retained, but intensified and expanded. By July 1941 the following courses had been held: eight for officials of the postal services (attendance 1,110), three for members of the Reich Main Security Office (369), two for bank clerks (101), and three for prospective members of the colonial police force (280).[69] In addition to all this, the Reich Colonial League and the Nazi party used the close-knit system of political indoctrination to spread colonialist ideas on an increased scale. Colonial trades instruction centres such as the one at Rendsburg, which catered exclusively for women, also stepped up their activities.[70]

(c) The Preparations of the Nazi Wehrmacht at their Height
The Wehrmacht was not only concerned with the military aspects of colonial expansion but was also interested in the economic side of colonial planning. In particular the War Economy and Armaments Office of the Armed Forces High Command (OKW) cooperated closely with the Colonial Policy Office on this matter. The latter's branches in Paris and Brussels were under instructions to afford the War Economy Office an insight into the captured material at their disposal. In order to ensure a stable connection, the War Economy Office appointed the head of the group charged with economic preparations for the colonies, Major Rentsch, to act as liaison officer with the Colonial Policy Office.[71]

In the summer of 1940 the military preparations reached their climax. Early in July 1940 the Commander-in-Chief of the Army gave orders to set up a colonial regiment at the Bergen military training-ground. The

---

[66] Staatsarchiv Potsdam, Pro. Br. Rep. 2 A Reg. I, Pol. nos 665—667.
[67] MA, W 63.30./125, Koloniale Unterrichtung no. 17, 18 Dec. 1941. For further details on the training of police officers see *A. Kum'a Ndumbe*, Hitler voulait l'Afrique, Paris 1980, pp. 218—9.
[68] ZStA, RMdI, no. 27191, Tätigkeitsbericht des Kolonialpolitischen Amtes, abgeschlossen am 1. 7. 1941, p. 33.
[69] Ibid., p. 36.
[70] ZStA, RMdI, no. 27215, p. 2, Letter sent by the head of the Rendsburg Colonial School for Women to Ministerialrat Dr Wagner, 10 Oct. 1940.
[71] MA, W 63.30./126, Wenig (Colonial Policy Office) to the War Economy Office, 13 June 1941.

necessary troops were to be drawn from army divisions about to be disbanded and from the new levies. A staff for colonial matters was formed within the General Department of the Army High Command.[72]

Contrary to what some Wehrmacht circles appear to have believed, these steps were not taken in order to conquer African colonies by armed force. The official view was that colonies would not be taken over from their former owners until a peace settlement had been reached and a "plan for occupation" worked out in negotiations.[73] Colonel Joachim von Geldern-Crispendorf, colonial specialist of the OKW, noted in January 1941 that "the OKW, having reconsidered its policy, has no intention of intervening militarily in the colonies while the war lasts or to conquer colonies by force of arms. Nor are any preparations being made along these lines."[74]

The Wehrmacht body responsible for colonial preparations was a section of the Foreign Countries Department of the OKW.[75] Operating in close touch with the three services and the Colonial Policy Office, this section directed the preparatory work performed by the various branches of the Wehrmacht. Not only were the colonial staffs of the Navy, the Air Force and the Army expanded, clothing and equipment procured for the colonial troops, and courses for Wehrmacht officials arranged, but additional armed contingents were soon available for possible deployment in the colonies. By the end of December 1940, for example, a fully-trained 350-strong "Forestry Defence Unit" had been formed under Göring's authority.[76]

The colonial activities of the Wehrmacht did not have an adverse effect on the fascist war effort because they did not bind any major military forces. They even turned out to be useful: the tropical uniforms and quipment manufactured in 1940 enabled the OKW to set up the Afrikakorps at short notice and to intervene in the fighting between Italy and Britain in North Africa in February 1941. The equipment designed for the colonial forces could thus be tested under war conditions in a subtropical region.

In the late autumn of 1940, when practical preparations for the invasion of the Soviet Union began, the colonial plans of the Wehrmacht receded into the background for a while, leading to certain reductions in the

[72] Franz Halder, op. cit., vol. II, p. 10, entry dated 5 July 1940.

[73] MA, W 63.30./125, Koloniale Unterrichtung no. 1, 8 July 1940.

[74] ZStA, GdS, no. 1119, p. 12, Note of 6 Jan. 1941.

[75] MA, W. 63.30./125, Koloniale Unterrichtung no. 2, 27 July 1940.

[76] Ibid., Koloniale Unterrichtung no. 9, 30 Dec. 1940.

staffs and the material resources designated for this purpose.[77] But activities continued to some extent. The draft of a "Colonial Code" of the Wehrmacht was completed in January 1941.[78] Colonel von Geldern-Crispendorf undertook several trips to the Wehrmacht formations fighting in North Africa in order to gather experience.[79] Throughout 1941 he strove, with the support of the Colonial Policy Office and the relevant government agencies, to improve material preparations[80] and to select and train men for the future colonial force. Various departments of the OKW continued dealing with organizational matters relating to the colonies, with general, military and economic aspects of colonial policy, and much else besides.[81]

(d) The Role of Science

The preparations for colonial expansion were actively supported by scientists who had already made a name for themselves in this field such as two university professors from Hamburg, Vageler and Heske. The former, a geologist, was praised by Weigelt in October 1939 for his contribution to "the German colonial economy", both official and private.[82] Heske, a forestry specialist, had likewise done a good deal to "recommend" him. In his memorandum of 22 April 1941 entitled "The Decisive Significance of Colonial Preparations for the Outcome of the War"[83] he alleged an urgent need for colonial annexations. They were imperative, he claimed, because of the enmity of the United States which could become highly dangerous in the event of an economic war against fascist-ruled Europe. To forestall such a development, he argued, Africa

---

[77] *Kriegstagebuch des Oberkommandos der Wehrmacht* (Wehrmachtsführungsstab), vol. 1, 1940/41, ed. by H. A. Jacobsen, Frankfurt am Main, p. 87.

[78] MA, W 63.30./125, Koloniale Unterrichtung no. 12, 25 July 1941, and no. 13, 4 Aug. 1941.

[79] Ibid.

[80] Same as note 61, no. 15/1, Letter by Sattelberg (Official of the Central Post Office) to the Minister, 5 June 1941.

[81] MA, W 63.30./125, Koloniale Unterrichtung no. 3, 31 July 1940, no. 15, 23 Sept. 1941, no. 16, 20 Nov. 1941, and no. 17, 18 Dec. 1941.

[82] ZStA, Deutsche Bank, no. 21917, pp. 211 ff, Letter by Weigelt to F. Bethke (Ministry of Economics), 21 Oct. 1939.

[83] Published in: *W. Schumann* and *L. Nestler* (eds.), op. cit., pp. 296—298; Similar views are expressed in *K. Krüger*, Kolonialanspruch und kontinentale Wirtschaftsplanung, ed. by Gesellschaft für europäische Wirtschaftsplanung und Großraumwirtschaft e.V., Dresden 1940, p. 28.

should be occupied at once and a vast European-African zone created.

Heske's memorandum contained proposals which were carried out not in Africa, but chiefly in the East European territories occupied by the Nazis. By ruthlessly exploiting the population there, they hoped to gain economic advantages which would enable them to alter the military constellation of forces in their favour and win the war.

In order to use the potential of German science to the best advantage, a Colonial Scientific Department headed by a Dr Günter Wolff was formed under the auspices of the Reich Research Council in October 1940. Wolff set up 27 specialist groups, which were able to draw on the advice of the foremost authorities in each field of learning. This guaranteed that all questions raised were dealt with by the 500 or so scientists in touch with the Department.[84] Cooperation with the Colonial Policy Office was ensured by the fact that Wolff was a member of the latter's staff. "The scientific problems of the Colonial Policy Office of the NSDAP are their problems (the reference is to the Colonial Scientific Department), their scientific work is the work of the Colonial Policy Office of the NSDAP, and the success of their work will at the same time be the success of the Colonial Policy Office or the future Colonial Ministry," wrote Wolff.[85]

The activities of the Colonial Scientific Department were by no means confined to arranging meetings and awarding scholarships.[86] The Department organized scientific research on problems of the projected colonial economy, e.g. the best methods of exploiting the African population, Africa's role as a producer of raw materials and foodstuffs and as a market for capital goods and manufactured goods, as well as medical and technical problems.[87]

Centres of research at a number of colleges were engaged in the systematic investigation of specific problems. In collaboration with the Reich Centre for Soil Research, the Colonial Mining Research Centre of the

[84] ZStA, Reichsministerium für Wissenschaft, Erziehung und Volksbildung, no. 3101, pp. 3—4, Report of the Colonial Scientific Department of the Reich Research Council, dated 16 Aug. 1941. Up to that date the Department had awarded 180 research assignments at a cost of 950,000 marks.

[85] Ibid., p. 14.

[86] Up to April 1942 the Colonial Scientific Department organized 23 working sessions. Aufgaben der deutschen Kolonialforschung, ed. by Kolonialwissenschaftliche Abteilung des Reichsforschungsrates, Stuttgart and Berlin 1942, p. 8 (minutes of the experts' session of 17—18 Sept. 1941, marked "for official use only").

[87] Same as Note 84, Report by Wolff on the work of the Colonial Scientific Department, n.d., pp. 32—3.

Freiberg School of Mining, for example, surveyed "German colonial space" in Africa from a geological perspective with a view to "discovering and developing the mineral resources it contains".[88] According to a proposal by Professor Schumacher from Freiberg, the head of the specialist group responsible for "Colonial Mining", geological branch offices were to be set up in the colonies. In order to secure the effective exploitation of Africa's mineral deposits as soon as possible, Schumacher suggested establishing "research centres adjacent to deposits". He demanded that the state limit its role to "reducing the risks involved and providing systematic guidance" in exploring and mining deposits while leaving the rest to private enterprise.[89]

Not only scientists directly concerned with the practical aspects of colonial planning such as Schumacher, the geographers Obst and Dietzel, or the geopolitician Schmitthenner[90] worked for a Nazi "New Order" in Europe and the ensuing redistribution of African colonies in favour of German inperialism. There were others less directly involved who also supported the Nazi policy of colonial expansion, e.g. the Africanist Diedrich Westermann as head of the specialist group charged with linguistic research, the Arabic scholar Richard Hartmann as head of the group for religious studies, as well as the ethnographer Bernhard Struck and the historian Egmont Zechlin, each leading the group dealing with his field of study.[91] At the beginning of September 1940, 166 lecturers at German universities and other institutions of higher learning announced no less than 278 lectures and seminars in the field of African studies.[92]

The German Society for Tropical Medicine, too, mobilized its members for the "new challenges arising from the impending recovery of our colonies", as its chairman, Professor P. Mühlens, declared at the society's 11th Session in October 1940. The session was devoted to the theme "Colonial Health Management in Africa". The opening event was attend-

---

[88] ZStA, GdS, no. 11/9, p. 36, The Rector of the Freiberg School of Mining to Todt, 11 Mar. 1941.

[89] Archives of the DWI, Koloniale Vorbereitung, no. A 26/44, Report by Prof. Schumacher on geological prospecting in the German colonial territories, 1 Nov. 1940.

[90] For example in: *Lebensraumfragen europäischer Völker*, vol. II, Europas koloniale Ergänzungsräume, Leipzig 1941, ed. by Prof. K. H. Dietzel, Prof. O. Schmieder, Prof. H. Schmitthenner et al.

[91] *G. Wolff*, Der Aufbau der deutschen Kolonialforschung, in: Deutscher Kolonialdienst, no. 10, 1941, pp. 147 and 152.

[92] Leading the way was the University of Hamburg with 35 lectures and 48 courses, followed by Berlin with 29 lectures and 77 courses. *G. Wolff*, Über die Aufgaben der deutschen Kolonialforschung, Berlin 1940, p. 2.

ed by Dr Leonardo Conti, the "Reich Health Leader", and by Karl Otto Kaufmann, the Gauleiter (regional Nazi leader) of Hamburg. Those present promised Hitler that they would "devote all their skill and knowledge to the establishment of a healthy German colonial empire" and then went on to listen to 42 scientific papers, many of them referring to experiences gained in the German colonies prior to 1914.[93]

Colonial preparations, which covered a great number of areas, had reached such an advanced stage in June 1941 that the Colonial Policy Office was able to sum up the situation as follows: "At any rate it can safely be said today that with the means at our command all tasks that it was possible to formulate or construe here in Germany are well in hand and, in part, have already been accomplished. When the Führer, the architect of Germany's destiny, gives orders to go ahead in the colonial sphere, he will find the Colonial Policy Office well-equipped to carry out these orders to the best of its abilities."[94]

3. The Blueprint for a Fascist Colonial Empire in Africa

(a) The Structure of the Projected Empire

That the Hitler government was pursuing its colonial plans in earnest can be seen from the political, military and economic preparations that were being made. The basic assumption was that what appeared to work in Europe was likely to work even better in Africa. Therefore, the Nazi officials felt that the best way of laying the foundations for a colonial administration was to apply Nazi methods of government to the future empire in a modified form.

Consul-General Karlowa from the Ribbentrop Bureau submitted a proposal for the administration of future German colonies as early as April 1937, but without going into details.[95] He suggested that the colonies should become a kind of appendage (Nebenland) of Germany to be administered by the Minister for the Colonies, the Governor and an

---

[93] *Koloniale Gesundheitsführung in Africa.* Verhandlungen der XI. Tagung der Deutschen Tropenmedizinischen Gesellschaft vom 3.—5. Oktober 1940 in Hamburg, Leipzig 1941, passim.

[94] ZStA, RMdI, no. 27191, Tätigkeitsbericht des Kolonialpolitischen Amtes, abgeschlossen 1. 7. 1941, p. 46.

[95] ZStA, Reichsjustizministerium, no. 10832, pp. 9—10, Confidential minutes of the meeting of the Colonial Law Committee of the Academy of German Law, 8 April 1937.

advisory council in each colony assisting the latter. The Nazi party was to enjoy the same rights as in metropolitan Germany.

Karlowa's views at the time were still influenced by the institutions of imperial colonial rule. This goes especially for the advisory councils he proposed. But on the other hand his thinking revealed fascist elements. With the Four-Year Plan of the Nazi regime in mind, Karlowa spoke of a "planned economy" designed to help meet the mother country's demand for raw materials. At a meeting of the working group studying the role of "The State in the Colony", held in December 1938, he described the "leadership principle" and "state control of the economy" as the decisive criteria of the future colonial administration.[96]

The colonial planners, guided partly by past colonial practice and partly by the requirements of the Nazi state, summed up their ideas in a draft for a Reich Colonial Act. In June 1940, the head of the Berlin branch of the Colonial Policy Office, Asmis, acting on behalf of the Office, invited Hitler's deputy, Rudolf Hess, and representatives of the Foreign Office and the Ministries of the Interior, of Justice and Finance for a discussion of the draft[97], and by 30 July 1940 the Minister of the Interior, Wilhelm Frick, had the ninth draft of the Act circulating in the departments of his Ministry, asking for comments.[98]

The ninth draft of the Reich Colonial Act conformed with Karlowa's intentions. It stipulated that both economically and politically, the colonies should be part of the Reich. The "leadership principle", race laws and the government regulation of the economy typical of state monopoly capitalism were to be the basic concepts of fascist colonial rule. Using the draft as a basis, the Colonial Policy Office went on to draw up a number of supplementary pieces of legislation, including laws relating to mining, hunting and banking.[99] In the opinion of the Interior Ministry, however, the draft was not entirely satisfactory because it failed to lay sufficient stress on the colonies' status as "administrative districts". The Ministry wished to see the overseas territories transformed into

---

[96] ZStA, Reichsjustizministerium, no. 10833, pp. 33—4, The administrative structure in the protectorate. Guidelines for future German colonial legislation, based on the meetings held on 7 Aug. and 9 Dec. 1938.

[97] ZStA, RMdI, no. 27190, p. 172, Memo of the Secretary of State, 21 June 1940.

[98] Ibid., p. 223, The Minister to the Departments Z, II to VI, 30 July 1940. The ninth draft has been published in a French translation by *A. Kum'a Ndumbe*, op. cit., pp. 361—364.

[99] Ibid., no. 27191, Tätigkeitsbericht des Kolonialpolitischen Amtes vom 1. 7. 1941, pp. 25 and 28.

"genuine colonies". It urged legislative measures to preclude any tendency for them to evolve into autonomous entities or into mere "protectorates". The political and economic life of the colonies would have to be intimately bound up with that of the "mother country".[100]

Since the Nazi regime, like imperial Germany, depended on armed force to establish and uphold its rule over an overseas empire, the Wehrmacht prepared for colonial operations. The head of the OKW, Field Marshal Wilhelm Keitel, had appointed Colonel von Geldern-Crispendorf, the OKW officer responsible for this task, to serve as liaison officer with the Colonial Policy Office. Acting in an analogous position were Maj. Eymael for the Army, Lt-Cdr. Peucer, Lt-Cdr. Wenig and Lt. Hasslauer for the Navy, and Maj. Rother for the Air Force.[101] The military counterpart of civilian legislation in the colonial sphere was the "Colonial Code" of the Wehrmacht. It had been drawn up within the OKW (the first draft was submitted in January 1941) and was well known in the top echelons of the three services. The Code was not only meant as a set of regulations for military service, but was to provide "guidelines for the fulfilment of military tasks in the colonies".

The reasons cited in the Code for the possession of colonies were no different from those given by other fascist institutions. If anything, they were stated in more forthright terms and with military precision. The aims, according to the Code, were to secure "sources of raw materials and sales outlets" and to enhance the "world power status" of Hitler's Germany. The function of the Wehrmacht in the colonies was to establish strategic positions outside Europe, to safeguard the empire and to "educate the natives".[102] Except for the erection of strategic bases, the decisive task of the projected German forces in Africa was to hold down the indigenous population. In other words, the character of these forces was largely dictated by fear of African resistance to alien rule. In addition, the colonies were to serve as a huge training camp for German units temporarily stationed there even in times of peace in Europe. The "educational function" of colonial service for Nazi cadres was regarded as very important even outside the Wehrmacht.

In the autumn of 1940 Hitler laid down where the future colonial forces should come from. He intended simply to transfer contingents of

---

[100] Ibid., Letter of the Ministry of the Interior to the Colonial Policy Office, dated 21 Aug. 1940, pp. 14—15.

[101] Ibid., Tätigkeitsbericht des Kolonialpolitischen Amtes vom 1. 7. 1941, p. 34,

[102] MA, W 63.30./126, Kolonialordnung der Wehrmacht, erster Vorbereitungsentwurf vom 1. 1. 1941, pp. 1—2.

the three Wehrmacht services for certain periods of time to the colonies. Hitler rejected the idea of African mercenary units — in marked contrast to Epp and the OKW who advocated a combination of special Wehrmacht units and "native troops".[103]

The Colonial Code provided for mobilization of the colonial forces either to deal with a foreign enemy or with "native tribes", and it stipulated that the military commander in every colonial territory would be responsible for ensuring "the participation of the Wehrmacht in suppressing internal unrest", with the Wehrmacht units, the police and the Waffen SS working closely together.[104]

The OKW not only demanded military command in the colonies, but also wanted a voice in all fundamental decisions relating to administrative matters. One of the instruments used for this purpose was the War Economy Office, which was charged with ensuring local supplies for the colonial troops, procuring raw materials for the armaments industry in Germany, and similar tasks. Its projected participation in oil drilling, ore mining, plantation schemes and the manufacture of war materials in the colonies was an indication of the role state institutions intended to play there.[105] Within the War Economy Office a special group for "Africa and African Colonies" was set up in late 1940. Its responsibilities included the collection of information on Africa's potential as a source of supplies, the opening up of mineral resources, the extraction of raw materials, "native" and labour matters, capital investment, transport questions and numerous other economic problems.[106] The OKW thus added many economic tasks to the functions of the armed forces as an (intended) instrument of oppression and aggression in Africa as it had already done in the occupied areas of Eastern and Western Europe.

Without regard for the rights and vital interests of the people inhabiting that continent, Africa was declared to be a natural and perennial "appendage" of German-dominated Europe. Colonies in tropical Africa were meant to supply raw materials, provide markets and spheres of investment and at the same time be a springboard for world supremacy.

---

[103] Ibid., p. 4. Plans to this effect had already been worked out. As regards the attitude of the OKW on this matter, see Microfilm 99 De4F2331, Comments on the value of coloured and white troops in tropical colonies, n.d.

[104] Ibid., Kolonialordnung der Wehrmacht, p. 24.

[105] Ibid., pp. 5 and 14.

[106] Ibid., Order by Gen. Thomas of 3 Dec. 1940; Tasks and structure of the group for "Africa and the African colonies", 7 Jan. 1941.

The Reich authorities and the Nazi party institutions planned the establishment of the colonial empire in such a way as to give maximum influence to the big business interests. As a Nazi legal expert wrote in 1939, the "colonial economy" was to be subject to state planning but "allow private initiative sufficient latitude".[107] Special emphasis was laid on the planning aspect, i.e. state monopolist regulation in the exploitation of the colonies.[108] The Colonial Policy Office stressed that "strict state control" was essential "to accomplish the comprehensive tasks of the German colonial economy".[109] It drew up organization charts featuring economic departments of the colonial authorities at both central and regional level.

The Colonial Policy Office entrusted the Reich Groups for Trade and Industry with drawing up lists of firms eligible for trade in Africa and with assessing customs, wages and price questions.[110] Thus, right from the start, the big corporations dominating the Reich Groups had every opportunity to assert their own interests on these matters. It was also in their interest that a decision was taken, during a meeting at the Reich Ministry of Economics, to "settle customs and currency questions once and for all through the Reich Colonial Act".[111] Under this arrangement the traffic of goods between Germany and her colonial empire would be exempted from customs duties even if government subsidies were needed to finance the ambitious goals of colonial exploitation.

In the autumn of 1938 the Reich Agency for Economic Expansion had suggested that a state-owned bank (the institution they had in mind was the Bank für Industrieobligationen) should cater for the needs of the colonial firms.[112] The purpose of this scheme was to strengthen existing companies and to set up a fund for financing the future German colonial economy.[113] The idea did not go down well with the Deutsche

[107] *W. Günther*, Die verfassungsrechtlichen Verhältnisse der deutschen Schutzgebiete und ihre künftige Neugestaltung (thesis), Jena 1939, p. 69.

[108] See for example *K. H. Dietzel*, Vom Wesen der Kolonisation, in: Afrika, Beiträge zu einer praktischen Kolonialkunde, ed. by Paul Rohrbach, Berlin 1943, p. 104.

[109] ZStA, RMdI, no. 27191, p. 79, Tätigkeitsbericht des Kolonialpolitischen Amtes, abgeschlossen am 1. 7. 1941, p. 22.

[110] Ibid., p. 25.

[111] Archives of the DWI, Koloniale Vorbereitung, no. A 26/42 Note concerning a meeting on colonial customs and currency questions held on 8 July 1940.

[112] ZStA, RKolA, no. 6402, p. 58, Invitation by the Reich Agency for Economic Expansion to a meeting on 5 Oct. 1938.

[113] Ibid., pp. 61—2, Abridged minutes of the meeting held by the Reich Agency for Economic Expansion on 5 Oct. 1938.

Bank which had conducted most financial transactions for the colonial firms so far. In accordance with its wishes, the Reich Minister of Economics rejected the suggestion.[114] By contrast, when the Deutsche Bank in mid-1940 intended to found a "German Bank for Africa" which would finance colonial business operations on a large scale, this proposal was welcomed by the Ministry, although shelved as premature.[115]

At this time, too, some Germans who had been taken in by the fraudulent rhetoric of the Nazis insisted that the lower middle classes should be given a share in the expected colonial windfall. A one-time farmer from South West Africa demanded that a large number of German settlers should be installed in the future German colonial empire extending from Mozambique to Ethiopia, from the Transvaal to the Sudan and from the Orange River to Dakar, and that a credit policy should be instituted which would favour financially weak farmers.[116] Such ideas did not, however, find, any place in the planning of the Nazi state. German settlement in Africa on a major scale was not in the interest of the corporations. Quite apart from their economic interests in that continent, the big companies were afraid that a mass exodus of Germans would weaken their economic and political position in Europe. Emigration was tantamount to decentralization, which might endanger plans for aggression yet to come. Furthermore, a large-scale settlement of Germans in Africa might have entailed the emergence of a white working class in the colonies which was to be avoided at all costs. As early as 1938 an official of the Racial Policy Office of the Nazi party, F. Zumpt, had pointed out that "it will never be a question of mass settlement but of selecting particularly suitable and affluent farmers who in themselves provide a guarantee that they will not descend to the level of a fickle and politically dangerous 'white proletariat'."[117] Paul Rohrbach advocated what he termed "quality settlement" reserved for people with a capital of between 25,000 and 30,000 marks at their command.[118] This would ensure the "superior status" of the German colonizers[119] and produce a stratum of "white masters" to safeguard the colonial system.

---

[114] Ibid., p. 81, Note of 3 Dec. 1938.

[115] Ibid., p. 84, Letter of the Economics Ministry, dated 22 July 1940.

[116] ZStA, RKolA, no. 6267/1, pp. 22—3, Memorandum by A. Meyer to the Foreign Office, dated 2 Jan. 1941.

[117] F. Zumpt, Deutschlands Ringen um kolonialen Raum. Kolonialfrage und nationalsozialistischer Rassenstandpunkt, Hamburg 1938, p. 23.

[118] P. Rohrbach, Deutschlands koloniale Forderungen, Hamburg 1940, p. 50.

[119] P. Rohrbach, Afrika als Siedlungsgebiet, in: Kolonialprobleme der Gegenwart, Berlin 1939, p. 58.

Another matter to be settled was the treatment of the non-African people residing in the future colonies. This was a question of economic significance because Indians, Greeks and Syrians formed the bulk of petty tradesmen in wide parts of "German Central Africa". Together with the fate of British and French colonials, the method of expropriating their property had to be decided on.

A member of the Deko Group's advisory council, Julius Ruppel, who was very close to Weigelt, had completed the draft of a memorandum on the treatment of Europeans in 1940 and sent it to the banker, asking for comments he might then take into account in the final version.[120] Ruppel confined himself to Cameroon, but at the same time expressed ideas of general relevance. He urged that Europeans and Asians should be expelled because initially there would be no other way of securing land for German entrepreneurs. He also recommended abstaining from the "purchase" of African land for the time being and leaving the "no man's land" untouched in order not to provoke the indigenous population. To prevent foreign-owned assets from falling into the "wrong hands", in other words to ensure that they were transferred to the German corporations, Ruppel suggested that the colonial authorities should be responsible for the proper distribution of the property becoming "available".

Later the Reich Group for Trade took up similar problems in a letter to the Ministry of Economics.[121] Referring to the future status of Indians, Greeks and Syrians in Africa and their replacement by German firms, the Reich Group called for a diversified approach so as not to cripple retail trade. Given the importance which these nationalities had in the commercial sector, the Group suggested that measures be taken which would make them "superfluous" after a certain period so that they could be got rid of one after the other.

The Reich Group for Trade also outlined the problems which according to the firms affiliated to the Group needed to be tackled first. Not only would Africa's trade conditions have to be subjected to close scrutiny, but concrete proposals worked out. These were to include the treatment of "enemy" assets, the most effective organization of trade, the number of firms and the spheres of operations assigned to them, and the availability of manpower in the trading sector. What the views of

---

[120] Archives of the DWI, Koloniale Vorbereitung, no. A 26/44, Letter by Ruppel to Weigelt, 4 April 1940.

[121] ZStA, RKolA, no. 6816, pp. 22ff, Comments by the Reich Group for Trade on the preparations for trading operations in Africa, 23 July 1941.

the Reich Group amounted to was the allotment of "adequate fields of activity in both territorial and material terms" to the German trading companies once the non-German firms operating in Africa had been eliminated.[122] The Group wanted to see British and French companies placed under the trusteeship of German firms who would at the same time take over the sphere of operations of those companies.[123] This would have enabled German trading firms to add British and French assets to their property and, at the same time, to profit from the business links of their predecessors.

Price and wages policy was also to reflect the interests of the big industrial and commercial enterprises. For political reasons they did not deem it advisable to change price and wages levels in the colonies during the initial stages of Nazi domination even though German goods would have to replace cheaper British products. As the Reich Group for Trade was convinced that with the existing price levels the sale of German manufactured goods in the colonies would not be profitable, it demanded government subsidies. The big companies did not wish to see any decline in the living standards of the African population, which were at any rate extremely low, because this would have brought about not only "political repercussions" but also a reduction of their purchasing power and a drop in productivity, i.e. a loss of profits. The same vested interests were behind the proposed system of customs tariffs for trade between Germany and her future colonies. In order to "render the ties between the mother country and the colonies as close as possible", tariffs were to be kept at a minimum or abolished altogether. On the other hand, high tariffs were to be levied on goods from other countries, especially India and Japan, in order to raise their prices.[124]

The design for Nazi Germany's colonial empire reflected the extent to which the state and big business had become intertwined in Hitler's "Third Reich". The projected colonial policy of the Nazi regime bore the stamp of the Deutsche Bank and other economic giants with close ties to the fascist state. Its central feature was the elimination of all competitors to give the German monopoly associations free access to the raw materials and markets of an extensive colonial domain. The role of the colonial administration was to be that of a subordinate executive organ.

---

[122] Ibid., pp. 37 and 1.
[123] Ibid., pp. 31—2.
[124] Ibid., pp. 34—5.

(b) The Status of the Africans in the Projected Colonial Empire

The policy to be pursued towards the "natives" occupied a central position in the colonial planning of the Hitler regime. The reason why the Nazi experts devoted special attention to the African population was that they regarded it as the chief source of profits in the colonies.

Ideologically, the racist policy adopted was reminiscent of the time before the First World War when Germany was a colonial power, but it was now propagated with much greater brazenness. In putting forward their racist doctrine to justify imperial ambitions, the Nazi colonialists drew on the writings of scholars and racial theorists and missed no opportunity to learn from rivals more experienced in colonial matters. In order to utilize the experiences of other countries, the Racial Policy Office of the Nazi party in 1938 commissioned one of its officials to study racial legislation in South Africa and the status of the various ethnic groups in Brazil and Mexico.

The purpose of the fascist racial doctrine was to convince the Germans that the exploitation of other peoples was legitimate and to divert attention from the real motives behind Germany's policy of colonial expansion. According to this theory the Germans belonged to the "master race" and it was the natural function of other peoples such as the Africans to do their bidding.

In a treatise published in 1938,[125] Günter Hecht, an official at the Racial Policy Office, advanced the view that it was not merely the right but actually the duty of Germans, as members of the "master race", to take part in the colonization of Africa. His semi-official paper provided a broad outline of Nazi racial policy. Hecht stressed that German colonial rule would have to be based on strict racial segregation and that no African should be allowed to acquire German citizenship. Intermarriage between whites and blacks and any other close contacts were to be prohibited. Africans would be barred from theatres, cinemas, and any places of entertainment and recreation frequented by whites, for the author rejected the idea of cultural assimilation. Needless to say, he ruled out any advanced education for Africans going beyond the training needed to fill posts in the lower grades of the administration. Hecht's treatise makes it clear that the Nazi directives for colonial racism bore the imprint not only of the racist practices in the colonies of imperial Germany, but also of the "Nuremberg Laws" of September 1935 in which the Nazis sought to codify their "Aryan" creed.

---

[125] G. Hecht, Kolonialfrage und Rassegedanke, no. 16 of the Schriftenreihe des Rassenpolitischen Amtes der NSDAP, Berlin 1938.

In 1940 the Racial Policy Office issued guidelines[126] summarizing the principal measures to be adopted in this field in the future colonial empire. These guidelines were based on the racist postulate that men are intrinsically unequal. They emphasized that the aim of colonial policy, namely the "expansion and safeguarding of the economic foundations of our life", could be achieved only "with the aid of the natives". Therefore "psychologically and practically effective leadership" was of great significance. According to the document it was the foremost task of the whites to play the role of lord and master and to organize their lives accordingly.

A strict colour bar was to be enforced. In order to ensure complete segregation the Racial Policy Office set down rules which barred unmarried whites from entering the colonies, limited colonial service for unmarried soldiers to one year, etc. Contact between white and African communities was to be prevented by absolute separation of areas of residence, with all communication between European and African quarters subject to special permission. Anyone entering into an intimate relationship with someone from the other population group would face heavy penalties, even death in the case of African men. By this extreme and barbaric racist policy the Nazis intended, so they alleged, to guide the Africans towards a "distinctive, legally protected way of life and an order suited to their own race", which meant that the indigenous population was to learn only what was necessary for them to do unskilled work for their German "masters". To ensure the guidelines were put into practice, the Office demanded that "specialists in racial policy" be assigned to the administration in each colony.

The various official documents on policy towards the "natives" illustrate better than anything else what Nazi colonial rule would have been like. The legal basis was provided by a number of laws which presupposed the African peoples to be inferior, immature and unfit to govern themselves. Most important was Article 3 of the draft Reich Colonial Act, which said: "Natives are members of the indigenous population of the German colonies. They are persons under the protection of the Reich."[127] These "persons under protection" were to be subject to a special code of justice not applying to Germans. The Colonial Act also provided for the preservation of African "customs and traditions"

---

[126] *Rassenpolitische Leitsätze* zur deutschen Kolonialpolitik. Sonderdruck des Rassenpolitischen Amtes der NSDAP, n.p., 1940.

[127] ZStA, RMdI, no. 27190, 9. Entwurf des Reichskolonialgesetzes vom 30. 7. 1940, pp. 224—5.

provided they did not "run counter to the interests of German colonial policy".[128]

The rules for the treatment of Africans, which the draft of the Colonial Act stated in very general terms, were set forth in detail in the drafts of several specific laws. One of these was the "Colonial Race Protection Act" framed by the Colonial Policy Office in conjunction with the Reich Ministry of Justice in October 1940. This represented a tightened version of the "Law for the Protection of German Blood and German Honour" of 15 September 1935, the first of the Nuremberg Laws.[129] Article 2 of the draft barred marriages between Germans and other whites with Africans or persons of mixed race. Article 4 read as follows: "In the German colonies extramarital sexual intercourse between persons who may not contract marriage with each other under Article 2 is prohibited." And Article 6 stipulated that "members of the African and mixed-race communities as stated in Article 2 . . . who have sexual intercourse with a white woman in the German colonies shall be punished by death. In case of mitigating circumstances, punishment may take the form of penal servitude or imprisonment with hard labour."

The approach to the "manpower question" in the future colonies conveys a vivid impression of the fate intended for the African peoples.

Proposals concerning the treatment of workers in East Africa had been submitted by the ethnographer Professor Richard Thurnwald as early as July 1938.[130] He began by emphasizing the role of the "planned economy" in exploiting the raw materials of the colonies and in settling the manpower question as well as the need to apply Nazi racial policies to Africans. He went on to propose dividing the colonial territories into a "black" area for Africans and a "white" area only for Europeans. The only link between the two areas would consist in the employment of Africans in firms located within the "white area". In order to prevent the emergence of a proletarian consciousness, Thurnwald suggested the systematic preservation or revival of old traditions in the villages and the establishment of village-type worker colonies in the proximity of white firms.

---

[128] Ibid., Art. 9.

[129] Source: *A. Kum'a Ndumbe*, Pläne zu einer nationalsozialistischen Kolonialherr-schaft in Afrika, in: Wolfgang Benz and Hermann Graml (eds.), Aspekte deutscher Außenpolitik im 20. Jahrhundert. Aufsätze. Sondernr. d. Schriftenreihe d. Viertel-jahreshefte für Zeitgeschichte, Stuttgart 1976, p. 179.

[130] ZStA, RKolA, no. 6287, pp. 48ff, Report on the organization of native labour in East Africa and ways of developing it along national socialist lines, 11 July 1938.

The experience gained by pre-1914 Germany and by the other colonial powers indicated that, since the payment of very low wages was taken for granted, only effective coercive measures by the State could assure the German firms and the administration of a sufficient number of workers. All deliberations of the Colonial Department and the Colonial Policy Office, therefore, culminated in the introduction of a forced labour system. A Reich Labour Ministry official named Karstedt proposed that the colonial authorities should exercise control in certain matters of importance. He demanded that the colonial administration be empowered to define the areas in which workers may be "recruited" and to fix their number in relation to the total population of these areas. No worker was to be permitted, under threat of prosecution, to go on strike, leave his place of work or refuse to carry out a job assigned to him. To settle all the manpower problems involved, Karstedt provided for the establishment of a "labour commissariat" in the administration of each colony.[131]

In June 1941 the diplomat Ernst Bielfeld transmitted to Weigelt the draft of a manpower deployment ordinance applying to Africans and aliens of equal status[132] which he had prepared by order of the Colonial Policy Office. This draft, evidently inspired by directives issued under Wilhelm II, also stressed the Governor's responsibility for the regulation of manpower resources. He was to be assisted by an official for labour matters and by labour commissioners in the various parts of the colony. The regulations stipulated that in the event of a shortage of voluntary workers any male African or alien of equal status could be forced to perform paid labour for a period of up to three months. Under special circumstances the authorities would be able to order the performance of unpaid labour.

In the previous year, Monteton, a member of the Deko Group's advisory council, had put forward more radical demands. He called for the registration of all male Africans on the basis of existing tax records.[133]

---

[131] Ibid, The Minister of Labour to the Foreign Office, c/o Dr Bielfeld, 3 Jan. 1940, pp. 93 ff. Karstedt, like Gunzert and Ruppel, had served in colonial administrations in Africa before 1914.

[132] Archives of the DWI, Koloniale Vorbereitung, no. A 26/44, Bielfeld to Weigelt, 25 June 1941. The term "aliens of equal status" was used to denote ethnic groups which were neither of European nor of African origin such as Indians and Syrians.

[133] ZStA, RKolA, no. 6287, pp. 75–6, Monteton (Deko Group) to Gunzert (Foreign Office), 4 Oct. 1940. Monteton's views bear a striking resemblance to current practices in South Africa.

Following registration each worker was to be issued with a work card that he would have to carry with him in a metal case at all times. Monteton demanded that every able-bodied male African should be compelled, if required, to perform labour for two to four months annually.

The views of the Deko Group betrayed a concern, similar to Thurnwald's, to prevent the complete proletarianization of the Africans at all costs. Hence the call for the preservation of the "native smallholding system in the tribal area".[134] This meant that the transfer of entire tribes to less populated districts would have to take place in such a way that new villages rather than worker settlements came into being. Monteton's proposal to issue work cards to all workers indicates the ways in which they would be coerced. A card covered 30 work days, and its holder was to be punished by the authorities if he failed to perform the stated amount of labour within a period of 40 days. Legation councillor Gunzert, in a reply to Monteton, advised moderation in labour matters out of regard for the overall interests of the colonial economy.[135] He rejected a compulsory labour service in the initial years of renewed German rule on security grounds.

We can see here part of the inextricable dilemma in which the Nazi colonial planners found themselves. On the one hand, the colonial economy they longed for was inconceivable without forced labour, but on the other hand, any forcibly imposed system of labour was bound to provoke resistance that might shake the very foundations of colonial rule. There was general agreement that any sign of resistance would have to be nipped in the bud by resorting to the harshest methods of repression. Not surprisingly, therefore, the proposed code of justice for Africans provided for the reintroduction of an apparently indispensable instrument of German colonialism: corporal punishment. The only point of controversy between the Ministry of Justice and the Colonial Policy Office was the question of how this type of punishment could be legally endorsed without attracting much attention.

The status of the Africans as perceived by the Nazis was determined by the profit-making interests of the big companies. The fate reserved for the African peoples was that of helots without rights of any kind, cut off from the rest of the world and ruthlessly exploited for the benefit of a doomed social system.

[134] Ibid., p. 78.
[135] Ibid., pp. 81—2, Gunzert to Monteton, 9 Nov. 1940.

4. Defeat

As has been described here in detail, the upper echelons of the Nazi state and party strove, in collaboration with the Deutsche Bank and the colonial associations, to set up a colonial empire in tropical Africa. In the eyes of Hitler and other leading fascists, the colonial objectives were neither "final targets of conquest"[136] nor were his policies "inconsistent"[137] or "exclusively continental"[138] in outlook. Rather, the strategic designs and "plans for a New Order", of which the colonial war aims formed an integral part, served the aspirations of German imperialism for world-wide hegemony. Hitler's ultimate goal was to gain world supremacy, an ambition he pursued step by step, heedful of the lessons of the First World War. The sequence of the various stages was not determined beforehand, but resulted from the given political situation, with the "New Order" in Europe providing the basis for overseas expansion.

The territorial objectives in sub-Saharan Africa formulated in 1940 were not only reminiscent of First World War plans[139], but largely identical with them — a fact which clearly underlines the continuity of German imperialism's policy of colonial expansion. During both world wars the colonial war aims focussed on a vast African empire stretching from coast to coast and designed to serve economic and strategic purposes. But this is not to say that ends and means in the Second World War were exactly the same as in the First World War.

From the First World War onwards monopoly capitalism in Germany evolved into state monopoly capitalism, a process which was intensified after 1933 under a fascist regime and at a time of heightened rivalries among the imperialist powers. Because of this fact and the defeat suffered in the First World War, the German imperialist policy of colonial expansion in Africa during the Second World War was marked by some distinctive characteristics. One was the increased direct influence which corporations and economic groups, notably the Deutsche Bank, exerted. Bearing in mind the experience of the First World War, the Nazi

---

[136] R. von Albertini, Dekolonisation. Zur Diskussion über die Verwaltung und Zukunft der Kolonien 1919—1960, Cologne and Opladen 1968, p. 31.

[137] G. Moltmann, Weltherrschaftsideen Hitlers, in: Europa und Übersee, Festschrift für Egmont Zechlin, ed. by Otto Brunner and D. Gerhard, Hamburg 1961, p. 214.

[138] W. Malanowski, Der Widerstreit von Tradition und Doktrin in der deutschen Außenpolitik. Von der Revisionspolitik zur einseitigen Liquidation des Vertrages von Versailles 1932—1936, Thesis, University of Hamburg 1955, p. 15.

[139] Thus A. Hillgruber, Hitlers Strategie, Politik und Kriegsführung 1940—1941, Frankfurt am Main 1965, p. 72.

leaders made carefully planned and detailed preparations for the take-over of colonies. (These elaborate and costly "colonial preparations" prompted the American historian W. W. Schmokel to ask whether ever before in human history a non-existent empire had been administered so thoroughly). Organs of the fascist state and the Nazi party were so closely intertwined with semi-private and private business organizations and interests that in this sphere, too, it is perfectly correct to speak of a merger of state and monopoly power.

At the same time, the Nazi dictatorship left its own imprint on the policy of overseas expansion. This policy was marked by extreme rapacity, unrestrained aggressiveness and virulent racism. Its fascist character determined the basic features of the prearranged system of colonial domination, a complex set of harsh repressive and exploitative rules, regulations, and measures serving the profit-making and power interests of the most reactionary elements of the monopolist bourgeoisie.

When Hitler saw himself at the zenith of his power, he left no room for doubt that after a sweeping fascist victory in Europe tropical Central Africa would become the colony of the "Greater German Reich" presiding over the "New Order" in Europe.[140] His later pronouncements to the contrary[141], e.g. his remark that colonies would be questionable possessions, must be attributed to the deteriorating war situation. Weigelt, for his part, began to contemplate the possibility of rather modest colonial acquisitions shortly after the failure of the Blitzkrieg strategy in the winter of 1941—42.[142] Yet although "final victory" became an increasingly elusive goal in the course of 1942, there were no signs during that year (or later on for that matter), that the colonial aims had been abandoned. Preparatory activities were continued in several areas, especially in the scientific field, in 1942 and 1943 even though developments on the eastern front prompted Hitler on 13 January 1943 to issue instructions to the effect that the activities of the Colonial Policy Office "to lay the foundations of the future colonial administration [be suspended] for the duration of the war."[143]

[140] F. Halder, Kriegstagebuch. Tägliche Aufzeichnungen des Chefs des Generalstabes des Heeres 1939—1942, ed. by Arbeitskreis für Wehrforschung, vol. II., Stuttgart 1963, p. 29, entry dated 30 June 1941.

[141] Cf. for example H. Picker, Hitlers Tischgespräche im Führerhauptquartier, Stuttgart 1965, pp. 144 et al.

[142] ZStA, Deutsche Bank, no. 21915, pp. 111 ff, Weigelt to Erdmann (Reich Economic Chamber), 27 Jan. 1942.

[143] ZStA, RDR, no. 7200, p. 131, Circular by Epp, dated 16 March 1943.

With Germany's situation worsening after the severe defeat at Stalingrad in early 1943, there emerged a tendency to depict the future exploitation of Africa more as a "European cooperative effort". This line of reasoning is discernible in the proposals which Hans Frohwein, an economic expert serving on the armistice delegation in Wiesbaden, submitted on 7 June 1943. He wrote: "The political and military organization of Africa as a dominion of the community of European nations will be laid down in specific treaties. The foremost task will be to redraw the colonial map of Africa or, where it is to remain unchanged, to confirm it as well as to settle fundamental questions relating to the natives."[144] Similar views were set forth in the guidelines issued by the "European Committee" of the Foreign Office on 9 September, which contain this passage: "Through systematic work in the economic sphere all the manpower and other resources of Europe and her ancillary territories in Africa can be developed to a maximum degree . . ."[145]

In March of that year the Colonial Policy Office produced a study dealing with white personnel in the Congo.[146] Rudolf Asmis, the author of this paper, intended to furnish an example of "cooperation between the European colonies". Whereas proposals worked out in 1940 and 1941 had stressed the need to remove the entire non-German stratum of colonials step by step from the future German colonial empire, Asmis offered different ideas. It was quite sufficient, he argued, for the leading political positions in the colonies to be occupied by Germans while other, less important posts could be left to non-German Europeans to fill. As a successful example of such practices he cited the Congo State of Leopold II, subsequently the Belgian Congo, in which he had served as German consul prior to 1914. What had been possible there, he concluded, "may well be feasible later in the colonization of Africa by the European nations under German leadership." The "cooperation between all civilized European nations in Africa" rediscoverd by Asmis was, of course, largely a retreat to plans for a collective colonialism such as Weigelt had considered shortly after the end of the First World War and Chamberlain had proposed in 1938. The only difference was the insistence on "German leadership".

The tendency to "Europeanize" the colonial plans, apparent since the tide of war turned in 1942—1943, must be seen in the context of the

---

[144] *Anatomie der Aggression*, op. cit., p. 187.

[145] Ibid., p. 217.

[146] ZStA, RMdI, no. 27191, pp. 109—10, Asmis to the Ministry of the Interior, 26 March 1943.

Hitler government's propaganda slogans about the "common destiny of Europe". These were designed to keep allies and collaborators from deserting the Axis and to prevent neutrals from drawing closer to the Allies. In the final stages of the war, the increased emphasis on "European bonds" also served to prepare the ground for the post-war development of a "united Europe" or "Occident" dominated by anti-Sovietism and anticommunism. Such a "united Europe" would leave room for the chiefs of German finance and industry and Hitler's generals to operate within its framework.

But even the appeal to "Europe" did not save the Nazi regime from utter defeat. The outcome of the war thwarted all plans to create a Germanruled tropical Africa and gave rise to a new international constellation of forces which enabled the peoples of Africa to cast off the fetters of colonialism once and for all.

Select Bibliography

1. Bibliographies

Historische Forschungen in der DDR. Analysen und Berichte. Zeitschrift f. Geschichtswissenschaft, Sonderhefte (Special issues) 1960, 1970, 1980.

Die deutsche Kolonialliteratur. Published by the Deutsche Kolonialgesellschaft, ed. Maximilian Brose. For 1897—1914 annually one vol., Berlin 1898—1916.

Die deutsche Kolonialliteratur von 1884—1895. ed. Maximilian Brose. Annual special issue of: Beiträge zur Kolonialpolitik und Kolonialwirtschaft, Berlin 1899/1900 to 1907

Bridgman, Jon and Clarke, David E. German Africa. A select annotated bibliography. Stanford University, Calif. 1965.

Bibliographie zur Außen- und Kolonialpolitik des Deutschen Reiches 1871—1914. Ed. Max Gunzenhäuser, Stuttgart 1943.

Köhler, Jochen, Deutsche Dissertationen über Afrika. Ein Verzeichnis für die Jahre 1918—1959, Bonn 1962.

Gann, Lewis H. and Duignan, Peter (eds.), Colorialism in Africa. Vol. 5: A Bibliographical Guide to Colonialism in Sub-Saharan Africa. Cambridge, Mass. 1973, pp. 380—410: German Africa.

2. Official publications, journals etc.

Jahresbericht über die Entwicklung der Deutschen Schutzgebiete im Jahre 1898/99 bis 1907/8. Beiträge z. Deutschen Kolonialblatt, Berlin 1900—1909. (These annual reports were published since 1892 in the Anlagen zu den Reichstagsverhandlungen as: Denkschrift betreffend die Entwicklung des Schutzgebietes . . .)

Die deutschen Schutzgebiete in Afrika und der Südsee, Amtliche Jahresberichte. Edited by the Reichskolonialamt. Vol. 1 (1909/10)—4 (1912/13), Berlin 1911—1914.

Deutsches Kolonialblatt. Amtsblatt für die Schutzgebiete des Deutschen Reichs. Published by the Kolonialabteilung des Auswärtigen Amtes, later the Reichskolonialamt. Vols. 1—32, Berlin 1890—1921.

Die deutsche Kolonial-Gesetzgebung. Sammlung der auf die deutschen Schutzgebiete bezüglichen Gesetze . . . Ed. Assessor Riebow, Alfred Zimmermann and others. 13 vols., Berlin 1893—1910.

Deutsche Kolonialgesetzgebung, Textausgabe. Ed. Philipp Zorn. 2nd edition revised by Franz Josef Sassen, Berlin 1913.

Medizinalberichte über die deutschen Schutzgebiete. Published by the Kolonialabteilung des Auswärtigen Amts, later the Reichskolonialamt, Berlin 1903—4 (1905)—1911—12 (1913—15).

Stenographische Berichte über die Verhandlungen des Deutschen Reichstages, Berlin 1871 ff.

Deutscher Kolonialkongreß, Berlin. Verhandlungen des Deutschen Kolonialkongresses 1902 zu Berlin am 10. und 11. Oktober 1902, Berlin 1903.

Verhandlungen des Deutschen Kolonialkongresses 1905 zu Berlin am 5., 6. und 7. Oktober 1905, Berlin 1906.

Deutscher Kolonialkongreß, Berlin. Verhandlungen des Deutschen Kolonialkongresses 1910 zu Berlin am 6., 7. und 8. Oktober 1910.

Deutsche Kolonialzeitung. Published by the Deutsche Kolonialverein, later the Deutsche Kolonialgesellschaft. Vols. 1—39, Frankfurt/M., later Berlin 1884—1922.

Beiträge zur Kolonialpolitik und Kolonialwirtschaft. Published by the Deutsche Kolonialgesellschaft. Berlin 1899, since 1904: Zeitschrift für Kolonialpolitik, Kolonialrecht und Kolonialwirtschaft, 1913—1914: Koloniale Monatsblätter.

Koloniale Rundschau, Monatsschrift für die Interessen unserer Schutzgebiete und ihrer Bewohner. Ed. Diedrich Westermann. Vols. 1—34, Berlin 1909—1943.

3. German imperialism

Lenin, Vladimir I., Imperialism, the highest stage of Capitalism. In: Selected Works, Moscow 1977, or: Works, vol. 22, Moscow.

Jerussalimski, Arkadi S., Die Außenpolitik und die Diplomatie des deutschen Imperialismus Ende des 19. Jahrhunderts, Berlin 1954.

Klein, Fritz, Deutschland von 1897/98 bis 1917. Deutschland in der Periode des Imperialismus bis zur Großen Sozialistischen Oktoberrevolution, 4th edn, Berlin 1977.

Engelberg, Ernst, Deutschland von 1871 bis 1897. Deutschland in der Übergangsperiode zum Imperialismus, Berlin 1965.

Kuczynski, Jürgen, Studien zur Geschichte des deutschen Imperialismus. Vol. II. Propagandaorganisationen des Monopolkapitals, Berlin 1950.

Hallgarten, George W., Imperialismus vor 1914. Die soziologischen Grundlagen der Außenpolitik europäischer Großmächte vor dem Ersten Weltkrieg, 2nd edn, 2 vols., Munich 1963.

4. The annexation of colonies in Africa and early colonial policy

Jerussalimski, Arkadi S., Bismarck. Diplomatie und Militarismus, Berlin 1970.

Carnyj, Israil S., Nacalo kolonial'noj ekspansii Germanii v Afrika (1879—1885), Moscow 1970.

Nussbaum, Manfred, Vom "Kolonialenthusiasmus" zur Kolonialpolitik der Monopole. Zur deutschen Kolonialpolitik unter Bismarck, Caprivi, Hohenlohe, Berlin 1962.

Müller, Fritz Ferdinand, Deutschland-Zanzibar-Ostafrika. Geschichte einer deutschen Kolonialeroberung 1884—1890, Berlin 1959.

Jaeck, Hans-Peter, Die deutsche Annexion. In: Kamerun unter deutscher Kolonialherrschaft. Studien, ed. H. Stoecker, vol. 1, Berlin 1960.

Klauß, Klaus, Die Deutsche Kolonialgesellschaft und die deutsche Kolonialpolitik von den Anfängen bis 1895. Ph. D. Thesis, Humboldt University, Berlin 1966.

Wehler, Hans-Ulrich, Bismarck und der Imperialismus, Cologne/(W)Berlin 1969.

Pogge v. Strandmann, Hartmut, Domestic Origins of Germany's Colonial Expansion under Bismarck. In: Past & Present. A Journal of Historical Studies. No. 42, Feb. 1969.

Bade, Klaus J., Friedrich Fabri und der Imperialismus in der Bismarckzeit. Revolution-Depression-Expansion. Freiburg 1975.

Stern, Fritz, Gold and Iron. Bismarck, Bleichröder, and the Building of the German Empire. New York 1977.

Washausen, Helmut, Hamburg und die Kolonialpolitik des Deutschen Reiches 1880—90, Hamburg 1928.

Windelband, Wolfgang, Bismarck und die europäischen Großmächte 1879—1885, Essen 1940.

Aydelotte, William O., Bismarck and British Colonial Policy. The Problem of South West Africa 1883—1885. 2nd revised edition, New York 1970.

Meritt, H. P., Bismarck and the German Interest in East Africa, 1884—1885. In: The Historical Journal, Vol. 21 (1978).

Krone, Dagmar, Die Rolle der 'Afrikanischen Gesellschaft' in der kaiserlich-deutschen Kolonialpolitik Ende des 19. Jahrhunderts. In: Asien—Afrika—Lateinamerika, vol. 11 (1983), no. 3.

5. Colonial policy and rule

Müller, Fritz Ferdinand, Kolonien unter der Peitsche. Eine Dokumentation, Berlin 1962.

Müller, Helmut and Fieber, Hans-Joachim, Die Deutsche Kolonialgesellschaft (DKG) 1882(1887)—1933. In: Die bürgerlichen Parteien in Deutschland. Handbuch der Geschichte der bürgerlichen Parteien und anderer bürgerlicher Interessenorganisationen vom Vormärz bis zum Jahre 1945. Ed. D. Fricke. Vol. 1, Leipzig 1968.

Kolonial'naja politika kapitalisticeskich derzav (1870—1914). Ed. E. E. Yurovskaya, Moscow 1967. (A collection of sources.)

Zimmermann, Alfred, Geschichte der deutschen Kolonialpolitik, Berlin 1914.

Darmstädter, Paul, Geschichte der Aufteilung und Kolonisation Afrikas. Vol. 2, Berlin/Leipzig 1920.

Spellmeyer, Hans, Deutsche Kolonialpolitik im Reichstag, Stuttgart 1931.

Schnee, Heinrich (ed.), Deutsches Koloniallexikon. 3 vols., Leipzig 1920.

Gifford, Prosser und Louis, William Roger (eds), Britain and Germany in Africa. Imperial Rivalry and Colonial Rule, New Haven/London 1967.

Gann, Lewis, H. and Duignan, Peter, The Rulers of German Africa 1884—1914.
Stanford 1977.

Smith, Woodruff D., The German Colonial Empire, Chapel Hill 1978.

Winckelmann, Ingeborg, Die bürgerliche Ethnographie im Dienste der Kolonialpolitik des Deutschen Reiches (1870—1918). Ph. D. Thesis, Humboldt University,
Berlin 1966.

6. *Colonial economy*

Weinberger, Gerda, Die Auseinandersetzung zwischen den „Gewaltpolitikern" und
den Anhängern „ökonomischer" Methoden kolonialer Ausbeutung in Deutschland. In her book: An den Quellen der Apartheid. Berlin 1975.

Ballhaus, Jolanda, Wesen und Charakter der kolonialen Landgesellschaften Ende
des 19. Jahrhunderts. In: Jahrbuch für Wirtschaftsgeschichte, Berlin, 1972/I.

Schulte, Dieter, Die Monopolpolitik des Reichskolonialamts in der „Ära Dernburg"
1906—1910. Zu frühen Formen des Funktionsmechanismus zwischen Monopolkapital und Staat. In: Jahrbuch für Geschichte, vol. 24, Berlin 1981.

Henderson, William Otto, Studies in German Colonial History, Chicago 1962.

Mayer, Otto, Die Entwicklung der Handelsbeziehungen Deutschlands zu seinen
Kolonien, Thesis, University of Tübingen 1913.

Warnack, Max (ed.), Unsere Kolonialwirtschaft in ihrer Bedeutung für Industrie,
Handel und Landwirtschaft. Kolonialwirtschaftliches Komitee e. V., Berlin (1914).

Decharme, Pierre, Compagnies et sociétés coloniales allemandes. Paris 1903.

Diouritch, Georges, L'Expansion des Banques allemandes à l'Étranger, Paris/Berlin
1909.

Anon, Die Arbeit des Kolonial-Wirtschaftlichen Komitees 1896—1914, Berlin 1914.

Jöhlinger, Otto, Die koloniale Handelspolitik der Weltmächte, Berlin 1914.

Hauth, Dieter, Die Reedereiunternehmungen im Dienste der deutschen Kolonialpolitik. Thesis, TH Munich 1943.

Brackmann, K., 50 Jahre deutscher Afrikaschiffahrt, Berlin 1935.

Kucklentz, Karl, Das Zollwesen der deutschen Schutzgebiete in Afrika und der Südsee,
Berlin 1914.

7. *Colonial education*

Schlunk, Martin, Die Schulen für Eingeborene in den deutschen Schutzgebieten am
1. 6. 1911 auf Grund einer statistischen Erhebung der Zentralstelle des Hamburger
Kolonialinstituts, Hamburg 1914.

Mehnert, Wolfgang, Schulpolitik im Dienste der Kolonialherrschaft des deutschen
Imperialismus in Afrika (1884—1914), Ph. D. Thesis, University of Leipzig 1965.

Mehnert, Wolfgang, Zur Genesis und Funktion der „Regierungsschulen" in den
Afrika-Kolonien des deutschen Imperialismus (1884—1914). In: Études Afri-
caines/African Studies/Afrika-Studien. Ed. W. Markov. Karl Marx University,
Leipzig 1967.

Mehnert, Wolfgang, The language question in the colonial policy of German imperialism. In: African Studies — Africa-Studien. Dedicated to the 3rd International Congress of Africanists in Addis Ababa. Ed. Th. Büttner and G. Brehme, Berlin 1973.

Bade, Klaus J. (ed.), Imperialism und Kolonialmission. Kaiserliches Deutschland und koloniales Imperium. Wiesbaden 1982.

8. South Africa

Jerussalimski, Arkadi S., Die Außenpolitik und die Diplomatie des deutschen Imperialismus Ende des 19. Jahrhunderts, Berlin 1954.

Hallgarten, George W. F., Imperialismus vor 1914. 2nd edn, vol. 1, Munich 1963.

Helfferich, Karl, Georg von Siemens, vol. 2, Berlin 1923.

Wüd, J. Andreas, Die Rolle der Burenrepubliken in der auswärtigen und kolonialen Politik des Deutschen Reiches in den Jahren 1883—1900. Ph. D. Thesis, University of Munich 1927.

Thimme, Friedrich, Die Krüger-Depesche. In: Europäische Gespräche, vol. 2, 1924, No. 3.

Bixler, Raymond W., Anglo-German Imperialism in South Africa 1880—1900. Baltimore 1932.

Lovell, Reginald I., The Struggle for South Africa 1885—1899. A Study in Economic Imperialism, New York 1934.

Butler, Jeffrey, The German Factor in Anglo-Transvaal Relations. In: Britain and Germany in Africa. Imperial Rivalry and Colonial Rule. Ed. P. Gifford and Wm. R. Louis, New Haven/London 1967.

Backeberg, H. E. W., Die Betrekkinge tussen die Suid Afrikaanse Republiek en Duitsland tot na die Jameson Inval (1852—1896). In: Archives Year Book for South African History, Pretoria 1949.

Van-Helten, J. J., German Capital, the Netherlands Railway Company and the Political Economy of the Transvaal 1886—1900. In: The Journal of African History, vol. XIX (1978).

Weinberger, Gerda, Das Victoria-Falls-Power-Project der AEG und die deutsche Kapitaloffensive in Südafrika vor dem ersten Weltkrieg. In: Jahrbuch für Wirtschaftsgeschichte 1971/IV.

Kubicek, Robert V., Economic Imperialism in Theory and Practice. The Case of South African Gold Mining Finance 1886—1914. Durham N. C. 1979. (Chap. 7 on German investments.)

9. South West Africa

Drechsler, Horst, Let Us Die Fighting. The Struggle of the Herero and Nama against German Imperialism (1884—1915). London, 1980 (extensive bibliography on pp. 256—275).

Drechsler, Horst, Jakob Morenga: A new kind of South West African leader, in: Afrika-Studien, ed. W. Markov, Leipzig 1967.

Weinberger, Gerda, An den Quellen der Apartheid, Studien über Koloniale Aus-
beutungs- und Herrschaftsmethoden in Südafrika und die Zusammenarbeit des
deutschen Imperialismus mit dem englischen Imperialismus und den burischen
Nationalisten (1902—1914). Berlin 1975.

Bley, Helmut, South West Africa under German Rule, 1894—1914, London 1968.

Bridgman, Jon, The Revolt of the Hereros, Berkeley 1981.

Loth, Heinrich, Die christliche Mission in Südwestafrika. Zur destruktiven Rolle der
Rheinischen Missionsgesellschaft beim Prozess der Staatsbildung in Südwestafrika
(1842—1893), Berlin 1963.

De Vries, Johannes Lukas, Mission and Colonialism in Namibia, Johannesburg 1978.

Witbooi, Hendrik, Afrika den Afrikanern! Aufzeichnungen eines Namahäuptlings aus
der Zeit der deutschen Eroberung Südwestafrikas 1884 bis 1894. Ed. W. Reinhard,
(W)Berlin/Bonn 1982.

(German General Staff) Die Kämpfe der deutschen Truppen in Südwestafrika auf
Grund amtlichen Materials bearbeitet von der Kriegsgeschichtlichen Abteilung I
des großen Generalstabs. 2 vols. Berlin 1906—07.

François, Curt von, Deutsch-Südwestafrika. Geschichte der Kolonisation bis zum
Ausbruch des Krieges mit Witbooi, April 1893, Berlin 1899.

Leutwein, Theodor, Elf Jahre Gouverneur in Deutsch-Südwestafrika, Berlin 1906.

Erzberger, Matthias, Millionengeschenke. Die Privilegienwirtschaft in Südwestafrika,
Berlin 1910.

Wege, Friedrich, Die Anfänge der Herausbildung einer Arbeiterklasse in Südwestafrika unter der deutschen Kolonialherrschaft. In: Jahrbuch für Wirtschaftsgeschichte 1969/I.

Wege, Friedrich, Zur sozialen Lage der Arbeiter Namibias unter der deutschen
Kolonialherrschaft in den Jahren vor dem ersten Weltkrieg. In: Jahrbuch für Wirtschaftsgeschichte 1971/III.

10. German East Africa

Müller, Fritz Ferdinand, Deutschland—Zanzibar—Ostafrika. Geschichte einer deutschen Kolonialeroberung 1884—1890, Berlin 1959.

Büttner, Kurt, Die Anfänge der deutschen Kolonialpolitik in Ostafrika. Eine kritische
Untersuchung an Hand unveröffentlichter Quellen, Berlin 1959.

Kimambo, I. N. and Temu, A. J. (eds.), A History of Tanzania, Nairobi 1969.

Kaniki, M. H. Y. (ed.), Tanzania under Colonial Rule. Historical Association of
Tanzania 1980.

Iliffe, John, Tanganyika under German Rule 1905—1912, Cambridge 1969.

Iliffe, John, A modern history of Tanganyika, Cambridge 1979.

Kieran, J. A., Abushiri and the Germans. In: Hadidth no. 2, Nairobi 1975.

Jackson, Robert D., Resistance to the German Invasion of the Tanganyikan Coast,
1888—1891. In: Protest and Power in Black Africa, ed. R. I. Rotberg and A. A.
Mazrui, New York 1970.

Kjekshus, H., Ecology Control and Economic Development in East African History.
The Case of Tanganyika 1850—1950, London 1977.

Meritt, H. P., Bismarck and the partition of East Africa. In: English Historical Review, vol. 91 (1976).

Büttner, Kurt and Loth, Heinrich (eds.), Philosophie der Eroberer und koloniale Wirklichkeit. Ostafrika 1884—1918, Berlin 1981.

Loth, Heinrich, Griff nach Ostafrika. Politik des deutschen Imperialismus und anti-kolonialer Kampf. Legende und Wirklichkeit, Berlin 1968.

Tetzlaff, Rainer, Koloniale Entwicklung und Ausbeutung. Wirtschafts- und Sozial-geschichte Deutsch-Ostafrikas 1885—1914, (W)Berlin 1970.

Bald, Detlef, Deutsch-Ostafrika 1900—1914. Eine Studie über Verwaltung, Interessen-gruppen und wirtschaftliche Erschließung, Munich 1970.

Götzen, Adolf Graf v., Deutsch-Ostafrika im Aufstand 1905/06, Berlin 1909.

Gottberg, Achim, Unyamwesi. Quellensammlung und Geschichte. Studien zur Ge-schichte Asiens, Afrikas und Lateinamerikas, ed. W. Markov. vol. 21, Berlin 1971.

Austen, Ralph A., Northwest Tanzania under German and British Rule. Colonial Policy and Tribal Politics 1889—1939, New Haven/London 1968.

Louis, William Roger, Ruanda-Urundi 1884—1919, Oxford 1963.

Launicke, Gerhard, Zur Geschichte und Sozialstruktur der Staaten Rwanda und Burundi bis zum Ende der deutschen Okkupation. Ph. D. Thesis, Karl Marx Uni-versity, Leipzig 1968.

Niesel, Hans-Joachim, Kolonialverwaltung und Missionen in Deutsch-Ostafrika 1890—1914. Thesis (W)Berlin 1971.

Wright, Marcia, German Missions in Tanganyika 1891—1941: Lutherans and Mora-vians in the Southern Highlands, Oxford 1971.

11. Cameroon

Mveng, Engelbert, Histoire du Cameroun, Paris 1963.

Ardener, Shirley G., Eye-Witnesses to the Annexation of Cameroon 1883—1887, Buea 1968.

Stoecker, Helmuth (ed.), Kamerun unter deutscher Kolonialherrschaft, Studien vol. 1, Berlin 1960; vol. 2, Berlin 1968.

Rudin, Harry R., Germans in the Cameroons 1884—1914. A Case Study in Modern Imperialism, New Haven 1938.

Hausen, Karin, Deutsche Kolonialherrschaft in Afrika. Wirtschaftsinteressen und Kolonialverwaltung in Kamerun vor 1914, Zürich/Freiburg 1970.

Wirz, Albert, Vom Sklavenhandel zum kolonialen Handel. Wirtschaftsräume und Wirtschaftsformen in Kamerun vor 1914, Zürich/Freiburg 1972.

Schömann, Hartmut, Der Eisenbahnbau in Kamerun ünter deutscher Kolonialherr-schaft. Ph. D. Thesis, Humboldt University, Berlin 1965.

Rüger, Adolf, Die Widerstandsbewegung des Rudolf Manga Bell in Kamerun. In: Études africaines/Afrika-Studien. Ed. W. Markov. Karl Marx University, Leipzig 1967.

Kuczynski, Robert René, The Cameroons and Togoland. A Demographic Study, London 1939.

Rüger, Adolf, Zur Rolle des außerökonomischen Zwanges im Prozeß der Herausbildung der Arbeiterklasse in Kamerun. In: Zeitschrift f. Geschichtswissenschaft,
vol. IX, 1961, special no.

Mandeng, Patrice, Auswirkungen der deutschen Kolonialherrschaft in Kamerun.
Die Arbeitskräftebeschaffung in den Südbezirken Kameruns während der deutschen
Kolonialherrschaft 1884—1914, Hamburg 1973.

Chilver, Elizabeth M., Paramountcy and Protection in the Cameroons: The Bali and
the Germans, 1889—1913. In: Britain and Germany in Africa. Imperial Rivalry
and Colonial Rule, eds. P. Gifford and W. R. Louis, New Haven/London 1967.

Ruppel, Julius (ed.), Die Landesgesetzgebung für das Schutzgebiet Kamerun, Sammlung der in Kamerun zur Zeit geltenden völkerrechtlichen Verträge, Gesetze, Ver-
ordnungen und Dienstvorschriften . . ., Berlin 1912.

Walz, Gotthilf, Die Entwicklung der Strafrechtspflege in Kamerun unter deutscher
Herrschaft 1884—1914, Freiburg 1981.

Gomsu, Joseph, Colonisation et Organisation Sociale. Les chefs traditionels du Sud-
Cameroun pendant la période coloniale allemande (1884—1914), Thesis, Saarland
University, Saarbrücken 1982.

12. Togo

Nussbaum, Manfred, Togo — eine Musterkolonie? Berlin 1962.

Kuczynski, Robert R., The Cameroons and Togoland. A Demographic Study, London
1939.

Newbury, Colin, W., The Western Slave Coast and its Rulers. European Trade and
Administration among the Yoruba and Adja-speaking peoples of South-Western
Nigeria, Southern Dahomey and Togo, Oxford 1961.

Cornevin, Robert, Histoire du Togo, Paris 1969.

Sebald, Peter, Togo — die deutsche „Musterkolonie", Berlin (Monographic study,
forthcoming).

Sebald, Peter, Malam Musa — Gottlob Adolf Krause (1850—1938). Forscher — Wis-
senschaftler — Humanist. Leben und Lebenswerk eines antikolonial gesinnten
Afrika-Wissenschaftlers unter den Bedingungen des Kolonialismus, Berlin 1972.

Akakpo, Amouzouvi, La naissance du Togo, In: Afrika zumani (Yaoundé), vol. 8—9
(1978).

Amenumey, D. E. K., German Administration in Southern Togo. In: The Journal
of African History, vol. X, no. 4 (1969).

Knoll, Arthur J., Togo under Imperial Germany, 1884—1914: A Case Study in
Colonial Rule, Stanford 1978.

Debrunner, H. W., A Church between Colonial Powers. A Study of the Church in
Togo, London 1965.

13. Morocco

Nimschowski, Helmut, Die Expansion des deutschen Imperialismus nach Marokko
vom Ausgang des 19. Jahrhunderts bis zur 1. Marokkokrise, Ph. D. Thesis, Karl
Marx University, Leipzig 1964.

Nimschowski, Helmut, Marokko als Expansionssphäre der deutschen Großbourgeoisie. In: Kolonialismus und Neokolonialismus in Nordafrika und Nahost, Berlin
1964. (Studien zur Kolonialgeschichte, vol. 10/11.)

Guillen, Pierre, L'Allemagne et le Maroc de 1870 à 1905, Paris 1967.

Parsons, Fed V. The origins of the Morocco question, 1880—1900, London 1967.

Williamson, Francis Torrance, Germany and Morocco before 1905, Baltimore 1937.

Miège, G. L., Les débuts de la politique allemande au Maroc, 1870—1877. In: Révue
historique, vol. 234 (1965).

Hallgarten, G. W., Imperialismus vor 1914. Die soziologischen Grundlagen der
Außenpolitik europäischer Großmächte vor dem ersten Weltkrieg. vol. 2, Munich
1963.

Fischer, Fritz, Krieg der Illusionen. Die deutsche Politik von 1911 bis 1914, Düsseldorf 1969.

Heidorn, Günther, Monopole — Presse — Krieg. Studien zur deutschen Außenpolitik in der Periode von 1902 bis 1912, Berlin 1960.

Pogge v. Strandmann, Hartmut, Rathenau, die Gebrüder Mannesmann und die Vorgeschichte der Zweiten Marokkokrise. In: Deutschland in der Weltpolitik des 19.
und 20. Jahrhunderts. Fritz Fischer z. 65. Geburtstag. Ed. Imanuel Geiss and
Bernd Jürgen Wendt, Düsseldorf 1973.

Gutsche, Willibald, Zu den Hintergründen und Zielen des „Panthersprungs" nach
Marokko von 1911. In: Zeitschrift für Geschichtswissenschaft, vol. 28 (1980), no. 2.

Guenane, Djamal, Les rélations franco-allemandes et les affaires marocaines de 1901
à 1911. Algiers 1975.

Allain, Jean-Claude, Agadir 1911. Une crise impérialiste en Europe pour la conquête
du Maroc, Paris 1976.

Oncken, Emily, Panthersprung nach Agadir. Die deutsche Politik während der Zweiten
Marokkokrise 1911, Düsseldorf 1981.

14. "German Central Africa"

Jerussalimski, A. S., Die Außenpolitik und die Diplomatie des deutschen Imperialismus Ende des 19. Jahrhunderts, Berlin 1954.

Drechsler, Horst, Deutsche Versuche, das deutsch-englische Abkommen von 1898
über die portugiesischen Kolonien zu realisieren. In: Zeitschrift für Geschichtswissenschaft, vol. IX (1961).

Drechsler, Horst, Germany and South Angola, 1898—1903. Présence Africaine
XIV/XV, no. 42/43 (1962).

Willequet, Jacques, Le Congo belge et la Weltpolitik (1894—1914), Brussels 1962.

Fischer, Fritz, Krieg der Illusionen. Die deutsche Politik von 1911 bis 1914, Düsseldorf 1969.

Vagts, Alfred, M. M. Warburg & Co. Ein Bankhaus in der deutschen Weltpolitik
1905—1933. In: Vierteljahrschrift für Sozial- und Wirtschaftsgeschichte, vol. 45
(1958).

Cookey, S. J. S., Britain and the Congo Question 1885—1913, London 1968.

Hatton, P. H. S., Harcourt and Solf: the Search for an Ango-German Understanding through Africa, 1912—14. In: European Studies Review, vol. I (1971), no. 2.

15. The First World War

(a) Military operations

Moberly, Frederick James, Military Operations, Togoland and the Cameroons 1914—16, London 1931. (History of the Great War, based on official documents.)

Gorges, Edmund Howard, The Great War in West Africa, London 1930.

Aymerich, Joseph G., La conquête du Cameroun (Ier Août 1914—20 Fév. 1916), Paris 1933.

Mentzel, Heinrich, Die Kämpfe in Kamerun 1914—16. Vorbereitung und Verlauf, Berlin 1936.

Oelhafen, Hans v., Der Feldzug in Südwest 1914/15, Berlin 1923.

Hordern, Charles and Stacke, H. F., Military Operations, East Africa. Vol. I, August 1914—September 1916, London 1941. (History of the Great War, based on official documents.)

Boell, Ludwig, Die Operationen in Ostafrika, Weltkrieg 1914—18, Hamburg (1952).

Helbig, Klaus, Legende und Wahrheit. Der erste Weltkrieg in Ostafrika und die Rolle des Generals Lettow-Vorbeck. Ph. D. Thesis, Karl Marx University, Leipzig 1968.

Gardner, Brian, German East. The story of the First World War in East Africa. London 1963.

Forster, Kent, The quest for East African neutrality in 1915. In: The African Studies Review, Waltham, Mass., vol. XXII, no. I (April 1979).

Loth, Heinrich, Schwarzafrika im ersten Weltkrieg. Die Ausnutzung antikolonialer Tendenzen durch die kriegführenden Mächte. In: Zeitschrift für Militärgeschichte 1971.

(b) War aims

Klein, Fritz; Gutsche, Willibald and others, Deutschland im ersten Weltkrieg. 3 vols, Berlin 1968—69.

Fischer, Fritz, Germany's Aims in the First World War, London 1967.

Stoecker, Helmuth, The expansionist policy of imperialist Germany in Africa south of the Sahara 1908—1918. In: Etudes Africaines/African Studies/Afrika-Studien. Ed. W. Markov, Leipzig 1967.

Maschkin, M. N., Zur Geschichte der Kolonialziele des kaiserlichen Deutschlands im Jahre 1918. In: Jahrbuch für Wirtschaftsgeschichte 1965/III.

Sebald, Peter, Die Kriegsziele der deutschen Togo-Interessenten im ersten Weltkrieg. In: Wissenschaftliche Zeitschrift der Humboldt-Universität Berlin, vol. XIII (1964).

Kersten, Dietrich, Die Kriegsziele der Hamburger Kaufmannschaft im Ersten Weltkrieg. Ph. D. Thesis, University of Hamburg 1963.

16. The policy of colonial expansion 1919—1945

Jerussalimski, Arkadi S., Der deutsche Imperialismus, Geschichte und Gegenwart, Berlin 1968.

Rüger, Adolf, Die kolonialen Bestrebungen des deutschen Imperialismus vom Waffen-stillstand von Compiègne bis zur Unterzeichnung des Versailler Vertrages, in: Wissenschaftliche Zeitschrift der Humboldt-Universität zu Berlin, vol. XIII (1964).

Rüger, Adolf, Die kolonialen Bestrebungen der imperialistischen deutschen Bourgeoi-sie und ihre Reaktion auf Forderungen nach Freiheit für Afrika 1917—1933. In: Jahrbuch für Geschichte, vol. 24 (1981).

Fieber, Hans-Joachim, Die Kolonialgesellschaften — ein Instrument der deutschen Kolonialpolitik in Afrika während der Weimarer Republik, in: Zeitschrift für Geschichtswissenschaft, vol. IX, special issue 1961.

Krebs, Siegfried, „Neue" Kolonialpolitik und Koloniale Siedlung in Tanganyika. Ein Beitrag gegen die neokolonialistische Verfälschung der Geschichte der deutschen Kolonialpolitik in der Zeit der Weimarer Republik, Ph. D. Thesis, Karl Marx University, Leipzig 1964.

Hinnenberg, Wolfgang, Die deutschen Bestrebungen zur wirtschaftlichen Durch-dringung Tanganyikas 1925 bis 1933. Ein Beitrag zur Geschichte der deutschen Kolonialpolitik in der Weimarer Republik. Thesis, University of Hamburg 1973.

Burckhardt, Richard, Deutsche Kolonialunternehmungen. Ihr Schicksal in und nach dem Weltkrieg. Econ. Thesis, University of Berlin 1940.

Fünfzig Jahre Deutsche Kolonialgesellschaft 1882—1932, Berlin 1932.

Mammach, Klaus, Zur Unterstützung des Kolonialismus durch die rechten Sozial-demokraten in Weimar und heute. In: Beiträge zur Geschichte der deutschen Ar-beiterbewegung 1961—62.

Schmokel, Wolfe W., Dream of Empire: German Colonialism 1919—1945, New Haven/London 1964.

Logan, Rayford, W., The African Mandates in World Politics, Washington 1948.

Kühne, Horst, Faschistische Kolonialideologie und 2. Weltkrieg, Berlin 1962.

Sagindykov, N., Neotloznaja programma germanskogo imperializma dlja Afriki. O kolonialnych planach germanskogo imperializma v Afrika do i posle vtoroj mirovoj vojny, Alma-Ata 1964.

Hildebrand, Klaus, Vom Reich zum Weltreich. Hitler, NSDAP und koloniale Frage 1919—1945, Munich 1969.

Weinberg, Gerhard L., German Colonial Plans and Policies 1938—1942. In: Ge-schichte und Gegenwartsbewußtsein. Festschrift f. Hans Rothfels z. 70. Geburts-tag. Ed. W. Besson/F. Frhr. Hiller v. Gaertringen, Göttingen 1963.

Lakowski, Richard, Die Kriegsziele des faschistischen Deutschland im transsahari-schen Afrika. Ph. D. Thesis, Humboldt-Universität Berlin 1970.

Groehler, Olaf, Kolonialforderungen als Teil der faschistischen Kriegszielplanung. In: Zeitschrift für Militärgeschichte, vol. 4 (1965), no. 5.

Eichholtz, Dietrich, Die Kriegszieldenkschrift des Kolonialpolitischen Amtes der NSDAP von 1940. Steckbrief eines Dokumentes, in: Zeitschrift für Geschichts-wissenschaft 1974, no. 3.

Schumann, Wolfgang and Nestler, Ludwig (eds.), Weltherrschaft im Visier. Doku-mente zu den Europa- und Weltherrschaftsplänen des deutschen Imperialismus von der Jahrhundertwende bis Mai 1945, Berlin 1975.

Hass, Gerhard and Schumann, Wolfgang (eds.), Anatomie der Aggression. Neue Dokumente zu den Kriegszielen des faschistischen deutschen Imperialismus im zweiten Weltkrieg, Berlin 1972.

Kum'a N'Dumbe, Alexandre, Hitler voulait l'Afrique. Le project du 3^e Reich sur le continent africain, Paris 1980.

Timm, Klaus and Richard Thurnwald: „Koliniale Gestaltung" — ein „Apartheid-Projekt" für die koliniale Expansion des deutschen Faschismus in Afrika. In: Ethnographisch-archäologische Zeitschrift 1977 no. 4.

Index